SELECTED LETTERS OF
ROBERT LOUIS STEVENSON

Stevenson in 1887. (Photo Notman of Boston, Stevenson House, Monterey)

SELECTED LETTERS
OF
ROBERT LOUIS
STEVENSON

edited by

ERNEST MEHEW

YALE UNIVERSITY PRESS
NEW HAVEN AND LONDON

THIS SELECTION
IS DEDICATED
WITH LOVE AND GRATITUDE
TO MY WIFE, JOYCE

Set in Bembo by Best-set Typesetter Ltd., Hong Kong
Printed and bound in Great Britain by St Edmundsbury Press

Library of Congress Cataloging-in-Publication Data
Stevenson, Robert Louis, 1850–1894.
   [Correspondence, Selections]
   Selected letters of Robert Louis Stevenson/edited by Ernest Mehew.
   Includes bibliographical references and index.
   ISBN 0–300–07376–3 (cl.)
   1. Stevenson, Robert Louis, 1850–1894 – Correspondence.
2. Authors, Scottish – 19th century – Correspondence. I. Mehew, Ernest. II. Title.
PR5493.A3 1997
828'.809 – dc21
   [B]   97–18029
                                                             CIP

A catalogue record for this book is available from the British Library.

CONTENTS

INTRODUCTION

In a letter written in 1883 Robert Louis Stevenson exclaimed: 'O if I knew how to omit, I would ask no other knowledge. A man who knew how to omit would make an *Iliad* of a daily paper.' This dictum may well be true of the art of writing but it does not help in the task of making a one-volume selection from the riches to be found in the Yale Edition of *The Letters of Robert Louis Stevenson*, published in eight volumes in 1994–5. In that edition I brought together over 2800 letters, of which more than 2400 were taken from the original manuscripts. As well as printing a great many letters for the first time, the edition provided full and accurate texts of those letters which had appeared in incomplete and expurgated versions in the editions of Stevenson's letters edited by his close friend and literary mentor, Sir Sidney Colvin, the latest of which appeared as long ago as 1924.[1]

This selection prints, in whole or in part, 317 letters by Stevenson plus one by his wife, Fanny. I have chosen a representative group of letters from each period of Stevenson's mature life, giving preference to those that seemed the most characteristic and amusing, those of literary interest and those that throw light on his life, work and personality. The aim has been to provide readers who do not wish to read the eight volumes of the complete edition with a generous sample which conveys the flavour of Stevenson as a letter-writer. In attempting to put a gallon into a pint-pot I have necessarily had to omit a great deal. I have left out all the letters written in childhood and begun the selection with RLS's student days. At the other end of his life I have omitted the long letters he wrote to *The Times* about the complex political situation in Samoa, castigating the incompetence of the white officials.

Approximately one-third of the letters in the complete collection are addressed to four close friends: Sidney Colvin, Frances Sitwell, W.E. Henley and Charles Baxter; when we add the letters to his parents (by far the largest single group) we account for half the known letters. These correspondents are well represented in the selection along with such other friends as Bob Stevenson, Edmund Gosse, William Archer and Henry James. A number of correspondents have had to be excluded. From 1888

---

[1] The only volume of letters published since Colvin's edition has been *R.L.S. Stevenson's Letters to Charles Baxter*, ed. DeLancey Ferguson and Marshall Waingrow (1956). I was able to add a few more letters to Baxter and to make some corrections to this scholarly edition.

onwards RLS wrote regularly to Edward L. Burlingame of his American publishers, Charles Scribner's Sons. The letters contain reports of work in progress, serialisation arrangements with *Scribner's Magazine*, business details and requests for books. They do not lend themselves to selection and the information in them is more interestingly and characteristically conveyed in parallel letters to Colvin, Baxter or other friends; I have therefore omitted them.

The long journal letters that RLS wrote to Colvin every month from Samoa for the last four years of his life present a special problem; when Colvin first published them, in expurgated form, as *Vailima Letters* in 1895 they constituted a volume in themselves. I have made a selection from them but in most cases I have had to abridge them, sometimes severely, to save space. I have also abridged some other long letters from the Samoan period. In a few cases elsewhere in the volume I have been able to save space by omitting one or two non-essential postscripts and abridging letters. No conclusions should be drawn from the fact that there is often a gap in letters to a particular correspondent. It does not mean that RLS was not writing to him or her; merely that they have had to be omitted to provide space for more interesting letters. At one period RLS was writing almost every day to Henley with his many ideas for literary projects; he wrote regularly to his parents; and only a sample can be given of the long letters he wrote to Mrs Sitwell in the mid-1870s.

Even with these limitations I hope enough remains to show what a good letter-writer Stevenson was. Henry James, reviewing Colvin's truncated edition of the letters in 1899, wrote: 'The shelf of our library that contains our best letter-writers is considerably furnished, but not over-crowded; and its glory is not too great to keep Stevenson from finding there a place with the very first.' Reviewers of the complete edition have echoed James's judgement and written of the wit and wisdom and exhilaration they found in the letters. In the published prose we find Stevenson, the literary stylist and craftsman dedicated to his art, who has redrafted and polished his work in order to convey his ideas in the most effective way. In some of his early letters, for example in the set pieces of descriptive writing to Mrs Sitwell, we can catch a glimpse of the prentice writer still learning his trade, but in most of them (in Colvin's words) 'Stevenson the deliberate artist is scarcely forthcoming at all'. In his own edition of the *Letters* Colvin gives a good summary of their qualities which applies even more strongly to the uncut texts:

He does not care a fig for order or logical sequence or congruity, or for striking a key of expression and keeping it, but becomes simply the most spontaneous and unstudied of human beings. He has at his command the whole vocabularies of the English and Scottish languages, classical and slang, – the slang both of general use and of a kind of private code current among his intimates, – with good stores of the French, and tosses and tumbles them about irresponsibly to convey the impression or affection, the mood or freak of the moment; pouring himself out in all manner of rhapsodical confessions and speculations, grave or gay, notes of observation and criticism, snatches of remembrance and autobiography, moralisings on matters uppermost for the hour in his mind, comments on his own work or other people's, or mere idle fun and foolery.

Many foolish books have been (and, alas, are still being) written about Stevenson. He has been sentimentalised by extreme admirers, 'debunked' by his detractors and patronised by the literary critics. Despite the efforts of J.C. Furnas in his major biography *Voyage to Windward*, some biographers continue to put forward theories unsupported by the facts and the old legends and biographical fantasies still linger; the level of accuracy in some recent academic studies has been appallingly low. One of my objects in editing the complete edition was to allow Stevenson to speak for himself. In his letters we can see him as a real human being, highly emotional and given to quick outbursts of anger, more irreverent and ribald than he appears in Colvin's expurgated edition, and more critical and forthright in his comments on people and events. We watch him responding to the concerns of everyday life, protective of his wife and family and coping with the special problems that face an author. What comes across strongly is his sense of fun and the shared jokes with his family and friends, his great zest for life under conditions that would daunt most people, and his many enthusiasms. In almost every letter in the last fourteen years of his life there is some reference to his own health: there is little or no bitterness in these comments and no self-pity, but certainly nothing of the cheerful optimist of legend. Underlying it all is a more serious, even solemn, attitude which leads him to drop without warning into passages of moralising or wry reflection on the ironies and absurdities of life. Overriding everything else is Stevenson's dedication from his early days to what he called 'my trade of words'. He sums it up in a letter to Meredith in September 1893:

For fourteen years I have not had a day's real health; I have wakened sick and gone to bed weary; and I have done my work unflinchingly. I have written in bed, and written out of it, written in hemorrhages, written in sickness, written torn by coughing, written when my head swam for weakness; and for so long, it seems to me I have won my wager and recovered my glove.

I have set the letters in a biographical framework (derived from that in the complete edition, which established the fullest and most accurate chronology of Stevenson's life) and provided detailed annotation enabling them to be read in their context. The letters give us a vivid self-portrait. We can follow Stevenson from his troubled youth, through his slow growth to maturity and his struggles to achieve success as an author, to the world-wide fame he had attained by the time of his sudden death.

Henry James deplored the fact that interest in Stevenson as a personality and picturesque character had effectively killed serious consideration of him as a literary artist. Although his letters feed that interest, I hope that the many comments he makes in them on his own work and the picture they reveal of his devotion to his art will lead to greater regard for him as a serious writer. But there is surely no reason why in reading Stevenson's letters we should not combine both interests: his superb qualities as a letter-writer are now an important part of his literary fame. We can continue to indulge our fascination in Stevenson as a person by reading about him in his own words in his letters. I hope that this selection will enable even more readers to do this.

★   ★   ★

In the Introduction to the complete edition I set out the various problems facing the editor of Stevenson's letters. A major one is his handwriting. This is never easy to read and gets worse in the Samoan period when he suffered from writer's cramp. At times one despairs of ever being able to decipher what he actually wrote and it is often only the context or familiarity with RLS's turn of phrase that enables one to guess at the right word. Colvin, a close friend, made many mistakes and others have done no better. As I said in the full edition, it is too much to hope that I have made no misreadings of Stevenson's handwriting but I have done my best not to make him write nonsense.

Another problem is dating. Until he reached Samoa, when mail was collected only on set sailing dates each month, Stevenson rarely dated his letters: at best he gives the day of the week, and even that is sometimes wrong. Very few postmarked envelopes survive and one cannot always be sure that they relate to the correct letters. Fortunately some recipients, notably Mrs Stevenson and Charles Baxter, took the trouble to record postmarks or to guess at approximate dates. A great deal of literary detective work was necessary to establish the dates and the correct sequence of the letters. I relied on a wide variety of factors ranging from the handwriting and paper to internal evidence, for example, of work in progress or events mentioned in other letters as well as references to external events recorded in the wonderfully detailed newspapers of the time. But the greatest source of information both for dating and annotation has been the wealth of contemporary documentation (much of it in Yale University Library) by Stevenson's relatives and friends. It includes a vast collection of letters *to* Stevenson, the many letters that Fanny Stevenson wrote to her mother-in-law, Colvin and other friends, and above all the series of pocket diaries kept by Mrs Stevenson in which she recorded her son's movements. In this selection I have not thought it necessary to repeat the detail provided in the complete edition to substantiate the dating.

I should record that some of the manuscripts have been subjected to censorship. As well as expurgating the texts of the letters he published, Colvin deleted material from the letters to himself and Mrs Sitwell which he considered too personal for outsiders to read. This ranged from the obliteration of a single word or phrase to the cutting away or masking of an offending passage. The authorities at Harvard University Library (where the Vailima Letters to Colvin are held) managed to remove the pasted strips and such passages have been restored: a good example is the letter of April 1893 (p. 531), describing Fanny Stevenson's mental illness. The letters to Henley went through the hands of RLS's old friend Lord Guthrie, who was easily shocked. He resolutely rubbed out swear-words and other improprieties and destroyed a few letters. Stevenson's mother destroyed some letters and censored a few others by cutting away the manuscript or obliterating words. I have noted cases where this has happened.

The manuscripts of Stevenson's letters are to be found in major libraries throughout the world. Over half of them are in the great treasure-house of Stevenson material bequeathed to Yale University Library by Edwin J. Beinecke; and that library accounts for about a third of the letters in the present selection. Next in importance come the National Library of Scotland and Harvard University Library. Other important sources are the British Library; the Huntington Library; the Silverado Museum, St Helena; the Writers' Museum, Edinburgh; the Berg Collection in the New York Public Library; and Princeton University Library. Many other libraries in both England and America, as well as private owners, have contributed.

In the complete edition I gave details of the provenance of each letter, including the location of the manuscript; where it was not possible to trace the manuscript I relied on a variety of printed sources and copies. In this edition I have not thought it necessary to repeat all this information. An asterisk in front of the heading to the letter indicates that the text is *not* taken from the manuscript. In this selection twenty-six letters come from printed sources, mainly from Colvin's edition of the *Letters* and his galley-proofs; all the rest have been taken from the manuscript or from a facsimile. In the full edition I also provided (where relevant) information about earlier publication, in whole or part; there seems no point in repeating this. All the texts in this selection come from the complete edition; I have taken the opportunity to make minor corrections to the text of a letter to his father (p. 296), previously printed from a sale catalogue, the original manuscript of which has since been acquired by Yale University Library.

Stevenson's letters were often hurriedly and carelessly written and include notes on scraps of paper scribbled in pencil from his sick-bed. Any attempt to reproduce the layout of these in type on a different page-size would result in an unreadable text without conveying the flavour of the original. The editorial principles adopted in the full edition and also used in this selection are summarised here. The address and date are given in italics at the head of the letter, regardless of where they appear in the manuscript. The address is printed on the right, abbreviated to the essential minimum, and no distinction is made between printed or written addresses. The date is given in standardised form on the left. Dates or locations supplied editorially are enclosed in square brackets and queried when doubtful. To save space, the beginning and ending of each letter have been run into the body of the letter, and punctuation and capitalisation provided where necessary. Superior letters have been lowered and contractions and abbreviations have been expanded save in such standard cases as 'Mr', 'Dr', and so on; ampersands have been expanded except where they are used in the names of firms. I have retained a few favourite contractions such as 'vol.' and 'Mag.'. Contractions and abbreviations used for comic effect have been retained. Figures of small numbers are usually written out in words. It is not possible to reproduce all the manual flourishes, doodles, variations in the size of writing and signatures of which Stevenson was so fond, although some of his comic drawings are reproduced in facsimile where they add to the gaiety of the letter.

Stevenson set great store by his own idiosyncratic punctuation (cf. his angry rebuke to a publisher's reader on p. 349). I have tried to be as faithful as possible to his punctuation, but since we are dealing with hurriedly written letters, I have not scrupled to add or delete an occasional punctuation mark for ease of reading. I have regularised his use of initial capital letters where his practice seems to have no significance. The printing of titles has been standardised: those of books, plays and periodicals are in italics; those of poems, stories and articles in quotation marks.

All his life RLS had trouble with the spelling of certain words. He was uncertain of the spelling of 'ei' words such as neighbour, leisure, seize and weigh; he often wrote 'excercise', 'carreer' and 'adition'. To perpetuate such misspellings would merely distract the reader's attention and I have silently corrected them. Misspellings used for comic effect have been retained, as have a few deliberate archaic spellings and words adapted from the French.

The annotation has been adapted from that in the full edition. My aim has been to explain RLS's references to his family, his work, books read and contemporary events, and to identify people mentioned (except where they are major literary or historical figures). Quotations have been identified so far as possible, except where they seem too obvious. From his upbringing, Stevenson's mind was full of biblical phrases and his letters are larded with them, sometimes for humorous effect. I have thought it useful to identify these references. As these are selected letters, many details of Stevenson's life and work have had to be omitted; I have tried to give some of the missing links in the notes. The source of any material quoted in the notes can be found in the complete edition. The references to 'Colvin' are to material in his edition of Stevenson's *Letters* (1924); those to 'Balfour' are to Graham Balfour's authorised biography (1901).

★   ★   ★

I should like to renew my thanks to everyone listed in the Acknowledgements in Volume I of the full edition, including the institutions and private owners who made their original letters available. By helping with that edition they have also made an indispensable contribution to this selection. Special thanks are due to those who helped me with this volume. Richard Garnett, who read the proofs of the eight volumes of the collected edition to that edition's great benefit, has kindly read the proofs of this one. Douglas Matthews, whose indexes for the original edition have been of immense help in the editing of this volume, has again provided the index. Candida Brazil of Yale University Press has dealt with the arrangements for publication (including the copy-editing of my manuscript) with great care and patience. In the original edition I paid tribute to the devoted support and encouragement I had received from my wife Joyce; I can only echo what I said then, that no words can adequately express my gratitude to such an ideal collaborator.

ERNEST MEHEW

Abbreviations of Names

Belle	Isobel (Belle) Osbourne, later Strong, RLS's stepdaughter.
Bob	Robert Alan Mowbray Stevenson, RLS's cousin.
Fanny	Fanny Van de Grift Osbourne, later RLS's wife.
Lloyd	Samuel Lloyd Osbourne, RLS's stepson.
MIS	Margaret Isabella Stevenson, RLS's mother.
TS	Thomas Stevenson, RLS's father.

I. STUDENT DAYS IN EDINBURGH: ENGINEERING AND LAW 1868–1873

Thomas Stevenson and Margaret Isabella Balfour were married on 24 August 1848. Their only child, Robert Louis Stevenson (or Robert Lewis Balfour, as he was baptised)[1] was born on 13 November 1850 at 8 Howard Place, Edinburgh.

Thomas Stevenson (1818–87) was the youngest of the five children who survived infancy of Robert Stevenson (1772–1850), the famous lighthouse engineer, and his wife Jean (or Jane) Smith (1779–1846).[2] Robert Stevenson was Engineer to the Northern Lighthouse Board for nearly half a century, during which time he was mainly responsible for the inauguration of the Scottish lighthouse system, his greatest achievement being the building, under hazardous conditions, of the Bell Rock lighthouse, 1807–11. Three of his four sons, Alan, David and Thomas, joined him in the family firm of civil engineers and became in their turn Engineers to the Northern Lighthouse Board. Thomas was made a junior partner in 1846 after his father's retirement, and from 1853, following their brother Alan's retirement because of ill-health, David and Thomas ran the firm of D. and T. Stevenson. In addition to their major work as lighthouse engineers, the Stevensons were engaged in the construction of harbours and docks and the improvement of rivers and estuaries. Thomas's great achievement as an inventor was in the field of optics as applied to lighthouse illumination, which earned him from his son (in the dedication of *Familiar Studies of Men and Books*) the tribute '. . . by whose devices the great sea lights in every quarter of the world now shine more brightly'.

Margaret Isabella Balfour (1829–97) was the youngest of the nine surviving children of the Revd Lewis Balfour (1777–1860), who had been the minister at Colinton, four miles from Edinburgh, since 1823, and his wife Henrietta Scott Smith (1787–1844). She was known as Maggie by

---

[1] The change of name from Lewis to Louis was made when RLS was about eighteen. The third name was dropped in 1873, as RLS explained to Charles Baxter: 'After several years of feeble and ineffectual endeavour with regard to my third initial (a thing I loathe) I have been led to put myself out of the reach of such accidents in the future by taking my first two names in full.'

[2] Robert Stevenson was the apprentice and then the partner of his stepfather, Thomas Smith (1753–1815), a pioneer in lighthouse illumination and the first Engineer to the Northern Lighthouse Board. Smith had married (as his third wife) Robert's widowed mother; Robert's wife was also his stepsister, being Thomas Smith's eldest daughter by his first wife.

her family; later, RLS's stepchildren and the family at Vailima (their Samoan home) called her 'Aunt Maggie'. Her Balfour ancestors were mainly ministers, advocates and merchants. Lewis Balfour was the third son of the third Laird of Pilrig – a house and estate halfway between Edinburgh and Leith.

RLS gives us a vivid pen-picture of his father in the essay he wrote immediately after his death:

> He was a man of a somewhat antique strain: with a blended sternness and softness that was wholly Scottish and at first somewhat bewildering; with a profound essential melancholy of disposition and . . . the most humorous geniality in company; shrewd and childish; passionately attached, passionately prejudiced; a man of many extremes, many faults of temper, and no very stable foothold for himself among life's troubles.

Thomas Stevenson was a deeply religious man and his adherence to the harsh and gloomy doctrines of Scottish Calvinistic Christianity dominated his whole attitude to life. RLS described his father's 'sense of the fleetingness of life and his concern for death' as 'morbid': 'He had never accepted the conditions of man's life or his own character; and his inmost thoughts were ever tinged with the Celtic melancholy.'

In some brief notes he wrote about his mother RLS said that in temperament she was 'sanguine, cheerful, very fond of amusement, [and] very easily amused'; she was 'fond of literature of a smiling order'. Sidney Colvin complements this description by calling her 'a determined looker at the bright side of things, and hence better skilled, perhaps, to shut her eyes to troubles or differences among those she loved than to understand, compose or heal them'. As a minister's daughter she was a devout Christian, but in a gentler way than her husband: an organiser of church bazaars and a member of women's committees.

The marriage was a very happy one and both parents were devoted to the care of their much-loved son. In January 1853 the family moved from Howard Place to the nearby 1 Inverleith Terrace, but following the doctor's advice that the house (at the end of the Terrace) was too cold for the delicate child, they moved in May 1857 to the familiar address, 17 Heriot Row.

Stevenson remembered his childhood as 'a golden age' but it was, as he later admitted to William Archer (p. 283), 'in reality a very mixed experience, full of fever, nightmare, insomnia, painful days and interminable nights'. He recalled three main impressions – ill-health, nightmares and other nocturnal terrors inspired by morbid religious fears, and the delights of convalescence at his grandfather's manse at Colinton.

> My ill-health principally chronicles itself by the terrible long nights that I lay awake, troubled continually with a hacking, exhausting cough,

and praying for sleep or morning from the bottom of my shaken little body. . . . [I] cannot mention [these nights] without a grateful testimony to the unwearied sympathy and long-suffering displayed to me on a hundred such occasions by my good nurse . . . How well I remember her lifting me out of bed, carrying me to the window and showing me one or two lit windows, up in Queen Street across the dark belt of gardens; where also, we told each other, there might be sick little boys and their nurses, waiting, like us, for the morning.

The 'good nurse' to whom tribute is paid in these reminiscences was Alison Cunningham (1822–1913) daughter of a weaver of Torryburn, Fife, who joined the Stevenson household when RLS was eighteen months old. Her devoted care is celebrated in the Dedication to *A Child's Garden of Verses* and in the many loving letters RLS wrote to her throughout his life. There was, unfortunately, a darker side to Cummy's influence: she was much stricter and narrower in her religious views than Stevenson's parents, and it was to her influence that he owed 'the high-strung religious ecstasies and terrors' that disfigured his early years.

The deeply religious atmosphere in which RLS was brought up was not one of unrelieved piety. Thomas Stevenson (in spite of his moods of religious melancholy) had a great sense of fun and romance, and Cummy, for all her strictness, was full of life and merriment. She read to the boy from the Bible, the Shorter Catechism, *Pilgrim's Progress* and from her favourite religious books, but these were not his sole diet. At an early age he was introduced to the pleasures of *Robinson Crusoe*, the adventure stories of R.M. Ballantyne and Captain Mayne Reid and the volumes of *Punch* in his father's library. All his life he remembered the serial stories Cummy read to him in *Cassell's Illustrated Family Paper*, and it was because he was anxious to find out what the pictures were about in two bound volumes of the paper that he finally learned to read when he was eight, while recovering from an attack of gastric fever.

Both parents came from large families, and his mother's diaries show a constant flow of visits between relatives in Edinburgh and at holiday resorts. On the Stevenson side there were the children of his father's brother David and his sister Jane Warden. A very special cousin and the closest friend of Stevenson's youth was Bob Stevenson, the only son of Alan Stevenson (see p. 10). There were even more cousins on the Balfour side. Chief among them were Willie and Henrietta Traquair, the children of Margaret Stevenson's sister Henrietta (see p. 236). Together with other cousins, the children of Mrs Stevenson's brothers who worked in India, they were often to be found at their grandfather's manse at Colinton, where they were looked after by his unmarried daughter Jane Whyte Balfour (1816–1907), celebrated in *A Child's Garden* as 'Chief of our Aunts': 'The children of the family came home to her to be nursed, to be educated, to be mothered, from the infanticidal climate of India. There must sometimes have been half a score of us children about the Manse; and all were born a second time from Aunt Jane's tenderness.'

Throughout Stevenson's childhood his mother suffered from a 'weak chest' and it was on her account as much as his that the family spent a good deal of time away from Edinburgh. In the summer months they would usually take a furnished house at one of a number of Scottish health resorts: two favourite places were Bridge of Allan and North Berwick, and in 1864 and 1865 they were at Peebles. In July 1862 RLS had his first experience of foreign travel when he accompanied his parents to Homburg, whither his father had been ordered by his doctor to take the waters. In January 1863, because of his mother's illness, there was a visit to Nice and Mentone which lasted three months. It was followed by a 'Grand Tour' of Italy, taking in Genoa, Naples, Rome, Florence and Venice; they crossed the Alps by the Brenner Pass and came home via Munich and Nuremberg and down the Rhine. Mrs Stevenson had to go back to Mentone in November 1863, and RLS joined her there from school at the end of the year; they remained in the South of France until May 1864. Cummy accompanied the family on both occasions. RLS was to recall these visits when he himself passed the winter of 1873–4 in Mentone and spent two years living in the South of France at Marseilles and Nice in 1882–4. In the spring of 1865 and 1866, again because of Mrs Stevenson's health, they stayed on the south coast of England at Torquay. In 1867 Thomas Stevenson took a lease of Swanston Cottage, just outside Edinburgh, at the foot of the Pentland Hills. It was a much-loved country home – and a favourite haunt of RLS, in both summer and winter – until 1880.

Stevenson went to school for the first time on 30 September 1857, to Mr Henderson's preparatory school in India Street, Edinburgh. He did not stay for more than a few weeks and was not well enough to return until October 1859. During his many absences he was taught by private tutors. On 1 October 1861 he went to Edinburgh Academy and stayed there (with interruptions) for about fifteen months. In the autumn of 1863 (when his mother was at Mentone) he spent one term at an English boarding school at Isleworth, Middlesex. By this time his health had shown considerable improvement and in October 1864 he resumed his regular education in Edinburgh at Robert Thomson's private school in Frederick Street; he continued there until he went to university.

Even before he could write RLS was dictating stories and accounts of his doings to two willing amanuenses, his mother and his nurse. He won a prize, given by his uncle, David Stevenson, for his 'History of Moses' dictated to his mother when he was six: 'from that time forward it was' (in her words) 'the desire of his heart to be an author'. A number of manuscript magazines and other childish efforts still survive; when he was in his teens he moved on to more ambitious works. As a child he had been introduced by Cummy to the writings about the Covenanters by Patrick Walker, Robert Wodrow and others (see p. 569).[3] Their influence remained with him all his life; it was thanks to her, as he later wrote, that he had a 'Covenanting childhood'. A long novel about the Pentland Rising was converted into an historical essay and published anonymously in 1866 at his father's expense, in pamphlet form, as *The Pentland Rising: A Page of History, 1666.*

A number of childish letters survive, beginning with one to his father, dictated to his mother when he was three years old. They show a lively, imaginative and much-loved child on close and happy terms with his parents. Many of them were written to his father, who was frequently away from home on business. A number were written when he was unhappy at boarding school: 'My dear Papa you told me to tell you whenever I was miserable. I do not feel well and I wish to get home.' The clumsy handwriting and bad spelling reflect the lack of formal education. There is little in them to indicate the future author and they give a very imperfect record of his childhood. To save space I have omitted them all.

Stevenson was enrolled as a student at Edinburgh University in November 1867 and for the next three and a half years began dutifully, if half-heartedly, to prepare himself for the family profession. During the summer months an attempt was made to teach him something of the practical side of the engineering business. The first two letters in this section (a sample of the many written to his parents) concern his stay in Wick in 1868, where the firm was carrying out harbour works, and his visit to the Isle of Earraid in 1870, when the Dhu Heartach lighthouse was being built.

RLS regarded his formal education as 'a mangle through which I was being slowly and unwillingly dragged' and he acted (as he was later to write in 'Some College Memories') 'upon an extensive and highly rational system of truantry, which cost me a good deal of trouble to put in

---

[3] The Covenanters were the adherents of the two Covenants of 1638 and 1643 setting out and defending the Protestant faith and the Presbyterian organisation of the Scottish Church, which formed the background to the religious disputes in seventeenth-century Scotland. The Covenanters in whom RLS was interested (and to whom the name is now usually applied) were the extremists, mainly in the south-west of the country, who resisted the religious settlement made by Charles II at the Restoration. Nearly 300 ministers, who refused to accept the authority of the bishops or to renounce the Covenants, were ejected from their parishes. Secret outdoor meetings, often attended by hundreds of people, were held by these 'outed' ministers and the authorities took harsh measures to suppress them and to punish the participants. Growing discontent led to the ill-fated Pentland Rising. The Covenanters endured many years of brutal persecution, culminating in the notorious 'Killing Time' (1685) when they were hunted down by troops. RLS's unfinished novel *Heathercat* (begun in 1893) is set in this period. Great cruelty and intolerance were shown on both sides.

exercise . . . and sent me forth into the world and the profession of letters with the merest shadow of an education'. But while he was neglecting with such ingenuity his formal education he was reading widely and setting about the task of learning to write.

On 27 March 1871, at a meeting of the Royal Scottish Society of Arts, Stevenson read his paper 'On a New Form of Intermittent Light for Lighthouses', for which he was later awarded a silver medal. This effectively ended his brief career as an engineer. A week later, after the university session had ended, RLS plucked up the courage to tell his father how he felt. On what he was later to describe (see p. 348) as 'a dreadful evening walk' with his father, it came out that he was learning nothing: 'On being tightly cross-questioned . . . I owned I cared for nothing but literature. My father said that was no profession; but I might be called to the bar if I chose; so at the age of 21, I began to study law.' Margaret Stevenson recorded in her diary that her husband was 'wonderfully resigned' but he was bitterly disappointed, feeling as she later told Colvin, 'that it was a cutting short of his own life, as he had looked forward to its being continued in his son's career'.

In 1871 Bob Stevenson returned to Edinburgh after taking his degree at Cambridge. RLS (in his fragment of autobiography) described this as having changed the course of his life. Bob was an ideal confidant: 'The miserable isolation in which I had languished was no more in season; and I began to be happy . . . I was done with the sullens for good; there was an end of greensickness for my life as soon as I had got a friend to laugh with.' To this period belong the elaborate practical jokes called 'Jink' (p. 70, n. 1), and 'Libbelism' (p. 224, n. 8). Soon RLS gathered round him (in addition to Bob) the group of special friends who were to play an important part in his life: Charles Baxter, who became a lawyer, a close friend and lifelong correspondent (see p. 18); James Walter Ferrier (p. 26) and Sir Walter Simpson (see p. 22). All three were fellow-members of the Speculative Society at the university.

This famous literary and debating society was founded in 1764 and still flourishes. RLS became a member on 2 March 1869, and took an active part in its weekly meetings held every Tuesday from November to March. Proceedings included the reading of an essay by a member and a debate. Baxter records that RLS was never 'anything as a speaker. He was nervous and ineffective . . . but his papers were successful.' RLS's continuing interest in the society is shown in his description in 'A College Magazine' and his references in the dedicatory letter to *Kidnapped* and in *Weir of Hermiston*. Another link between this group of friends was the mysterious society the L.J.R. (see p. 21, n. 7).

In his later correspondence with Baxter RLS often remembered the fun they had together in the pubs in the Lothian Road when they were hard put to find the few pennies needed to pay for their drinks. This 'low life', inevitably, finds no expression in his early letters. In his auto-biography Stevenson tells us:

> I was always kept poor in my youth, to my great indignation at the time, but since then with my complete approval. Twelve pounds a year was my allowance up to twenty-three . . . and though I amplified it by a very consistent embezzlement from my mother, I never had enough to be lavish. . . . Hence my acquaintance was of what would be called a very low order; looking back upon it, I am surprised at the courage with which I first ventured alone into the societies in which I moved; I was the companion of seamen, chimney sweeps and thieves; my circle was being continually changed by the action of the police magistrate; I see now the little sanded kitchen, where 'velvet-coat', for such was the name I went by, has spent days together, generally in silence and making sonnets in a penny version book; and rough as the material may appear, I do not believe these days were among the least happy I have spent.

Looking back from Vailima at this period of his life RLS told Balfour:

> You know I very easily might have gone to the devil: I don't under-stand why I didn't. Even when I was almost grown up I was kept so short of money that I had to make the most of every penny. The result was that I had my dissipation all the same but I had it in the worst possible surroundings. At the time I used to have my headquarters in an old public house frequented by the lowest order of prostitutes – threepenny whores – where there was a room in which I used to go and write. I saw a good deal of the girls – they were really singularly decent creatures, not a bit worse than anybody else. But it wasn't a good beginning for a young man.

RLS scorned the polite Edinburgh society in which his parents moved and was contemptuous of its conventional entertainments. He preferred to go his own way, with his own small circle of friends, 'scraping acquaint-ance [as he later described himself in 'Lay Morals'] with all classes of man- and womankind'. In return, many of those in that society looked askance at the strange young man in his disreputable clothes and, failing to see the genius beneath the eccentricities, pitied the Stevensons for having such a wayward son.

In guarded phrases, Colvin sums up the inner conflicts at this period of RLS's life:

> The ferment of youth was more acute and more prolonged in him than in most men even of genius. There met in him many various strains

and elements, which were in these days pulling one against another in his half-formed being at a great expense of spirit and body. Add the storms, which from time to time attacked him, of shivering repulsion from the climate and conditions of life in the city which he yet deeply and imaginatively loved; the moods of spiritual revolt against the harsh doctrines of the creed in which he had been brought up, and to which his parents were deeply, his father even passionately, attached; the seasons of temptation, most strongly besetting the ardent and poetic temperament, to seek solace among the crude allurements of the city streets.

To his Mother

Saturday [5 September 1868]   *[Wick]*[1]

My dear Mother, To go on with my description: – Wick lies at the end or elbow of an open triangular bay, hemmed on either side by shores, either cliff or steep earth-bank, of no great height. The grey houses of Pulteney extend along the southerly shore almost to the cape; and it is about half-way down this shore – no six-sevenths way down that the new breakwater extends athwart the bay. A in the plan[2] represents my present domicile.

Certainly Wick, in itself, possesses no beauty: bare, grey shores, grim grey houses, grim grey sea: not even the gleam of red tile: not even the greenness of a tree.[3] The southerly heights when I came here, were black with people, fishers waiting on wind and night. Now all the SYs[4] (Stornaway boats) have beaten out of the bay and the Wick men stay indoors or wrangle on the quays with dissatisfied fish-curers, knee-high in brine, mud and herring refuse. The day when the boats put out to go home to the Hebrides, the girl here told me there was 'a black wind'; and

[1] Herring fishing port and county town of Caithness in the extreme north of Scotland. Pulteneytown, the commercial and fisheries area, was built by the British Fisheries Society. The Society had ambitious plans for building a breakwater as part of a new harbour and employed the Stevenson firm as engineers. Construction began in 1863 but in December 1868 a considerable portion was swept away in a great storm; further gales in 1871 and 1872 continued the damage and the work was abandoned in 1874. RLS wrote in his essay on his father: 'The harbour of Wick, the chief disaster of my father's life, was a failure; the sea proved too strong for man's arts; and after expedients hitherto unthought of, and on a scale hyper-cyclopean, the work must be deserted and now stands a ruin in that bleak, God forsaken bay.' TS, accompanied by RLS, arrived in Wick on 27 August for his yearly inspection of the harbour works. He left the next day. RLS stayed on throughout September and left on 6 October.

[2] A crude sketch by RLS.

[3] In 'The Education of an Engineer' RLS calls Wick 'one of the meanest of man's towns, and situate certainly on the baldest of God's bays'.

[4] SY is the identification code for ships from Stornaway.

on going out, I found the epithet as justifiable as it was picturesque. A cold, *black* southerly wind, with occasional rising showers of rain: it was a fine sight to see the boats beat out a-teeth of it.

In Wick I have never heard anyone greet his neighbour with the usual 'fine day' or 'Good morning'. Both come shaking their heads and both say: 'Breezy, breezy!'[5] And such is the atrocious quality of the climate, that the remark is almost invariably justified by the fact.

The streets are full of the Highland fishers, lubberly, stupid, inconceivably lazy and heavy to move. You bruise against them, tumble over them, elbow them against the wall – all to no purpose: they will not budge; and you are forced to leave the pavement every step.

To the south however is as fine a piece of coast scenery as I ever saw. Great black chasms, huge black cliffs, rugged and over-hung gullies, natural arches and deep green pools below them, almost too deep to let you see the gleam of sand among the darker weed: there are deep caves too. In one of these lives a tribe of gypsies. The men are *always* drunk, simply and truthfully always. From morning to evening, the great villainous looking fellows are either sleeping off the last debauch, or hulking about the cove 'in the horrors'. The cave is deep, high and airy and might be made comfortable enough. But they just live among heaped boulders, damp with continual droppings from above, with no more furniture than two or three tin pans, a truss of rotten straw and a few ragged cloaks. In winter, the surf bursts into the mouth and often forces them to abandon it.

An *émeute* of disappointed fishers was feared; and two ships of war are in the bay to render assistance to the municipal authorities.[6] This is the ides; and to all intents and purposes, said ides have passed. Still there is a good deal of disturbance, many drunk men and a double supply of police. I saw them sent for by some people and enter an inn in a pretty good hurry: what it was for I do not know.

You would see by Papa's letter about the carpenter who fell off the staging: I don't think I was ever so much excited in my life. The man was back at his work and I asked him how he was; but he was a Highlander, and – need I add it? – dickens a word could I understand of his answer. What is still worse I find the people here about – that is to say the Highlanders, not the northmen – don't understand *me*.

Have you seen or heard any more of the American?

---

[5] This anecdote is repeated in 'On the Enjoyment of Unpleasant Places', where RLS (without naming it) gives a description of the bleak scenery and unpleasant climate of Wick.
[6] Because of the failure of the fishing season many of the Highland fishermen could not be paid. There were fears of a riot and the gunboat *Lizard* joined the gunboat *Netley* off Wick on Saturday 5 September. It left on the Monday.

I have lost a shilling's worth of postage stamps, which has damped my ardour for buying big lots of 'em: I'll buy them one at a time as I want 'em for the future.

The Free Church minister and I got quite thick.[7] He left last night about two in the morning. When I went to turn in, he gave me the enclosed. I remain, Your affectionate son   R.L. Stevenson

To Bob Stevenson[1]

Tuesday 29 March 1870   *17 Heriot Row, Edinburgh*

My dear Bob, During almost the whole of this winter, I have been free from my usual attacks of morbid melancholy; to which circumstance you may attribute the small number and the small size of my letters to you; but today I was in the depths again. To what I should attribute this, I cannot

---

[7] In an earlier letter RLS had described his meeting with a Free Church minister: 'Ah fie! What a creed! He told me point blank that all Roman Catholics would be damned.' RLS deplored 'this harsh, judging, self-righteous form of faith'.

[1] Robert Alan Mowbray (Bob) Stevenson (1847–1900) was the only son of TS's brother Alan (1807–65) and his wife Margaret Scott Jones, known as Aunt Alan (1812–95). In the winter of 1856–7 Bob stayed with the Stevensons at Inverleith Terrace and the two highly imaginative boys formed a close bond. Bob was educated at Windermere College and went up to Sidney Sussex College, Cambridge in 1866, taking his B.A. degree in 1871. RLS wrote to Bob regularly when he was at Cambridge and Bob's return to Edinburgh to study painting at the School of Art (as already related – see p. 6) changed the course of RLS's life by providing him with a close friend and confidant. In a fragment of autobiography RLS described Bob as

> the man likest and most unlike to me that I have ever met. Our likeness was one of tastes and patterns, and, for many years at least, it amounted in these particulars to an identity. He had the most indefatigable, feverish mind I have ever known; he had acquired a smattering of almost every knowledge and art; he would surprise you by his playing, his painting, his writing, his criticism, his knowledge of philosophy, and above all, by a sort of vague, disconnected and totally inexplicable erudition.

As subsequent letters show, Bob went on to study art, first in Antwerp and then in Paris. He and RLS became constant companions in the art-colonies at Barbizon and Grez. Their life is reflected in *The Wrecker*, where they figure as Stennis *aîné* and Stennis *frère*, 'a pair of hare-brained Scots'. Bob married Louisa Purland in 1881 (see p. 206. n. 1). To the despair of his friends Bob seemed to lack ambition and drive. He had no success as a painter and a desperate need for money forced him into writing for a living (see p. 279). His success as an art critic led to his appointment as Professor of Fine Arts at University College, Liverpool 1889–93 (see p. 394, n. 3). From 1893 until 1899 he was art critic for the *Pall Mall Gazette*. He crowned his reputation as a critic with his study of *Velasquez* (1895).

All his friends agreed that Bob's true gift was as a talker. RLS put him into 'Talk and Talkers' as 'Spring-Heel'd Jack'; H.G. Wells tried to give 'a faint impression of his style of imaginative talking' in Ewart in *Tono-Bungay*; and W.B. Yeats declared that he was a better talker than Wilde. As RLS later recalled (p. 206) the stories in 'New Arabian Nights' had their origin in the cousins' talks together; Bob was the original of the Young Man with the Cream Tarts in the first story and of Paul Somerset in *The Dynamiter*. RLS's letters to Bob, with their exuberant use of slang and private jokes give some impression of what their talks together must have been like.

think. Yesterday, I was in high spirits writing 'Deacon Thin';[2] and today
even, my health is perfect. But from the morning I was gone, tried to find
out where I could get Haschish, half-determined to get drunk and ended
(as usual) by going to a graveyard. I stayed about two hours in Greyfriars
Churchyard in the depths of wretchedness.[3] If I had travelled a year, I
could not have found a better place. The castle, the old town, the spire of
the Tolbooth Church, loomed indistinctly through the cold grey mist.
The grass was wet. A sexton was at work upon a grave; and two wretched,
filthy women, one of them with a child were walking up and down there,
with occasional harsh strident laughters. As I walked towards the university, I looked down College Wynd, with its clothes poles and harridan
faces craning from the windows and its steep narrow roadway clotted with
fish barrows and loafing prostitutes. Near the top, two small boys held
a skipping rope. A haggard sickly little girl was performing on it, with
bouts of laughter that reminded one fantastically of the old women in
the graveyard, and blaspheming with the most horrible and filthy oaths.
Watching and listening to this, was almost the only thing that interested
me that morning. – At the College I met a commonplace friend, who
wished me to walk with him. I told him I was not fit to walk with the
devil; but he got me away. He is a very nice fellow; but I must have rather
astonished him. To begin with, I scarcely spoke to him for about ten
minutes. But the grand finale was when I was getting better. I saw some
children playing at marbles in a stable lane; and I don't know why, the
idea of playing pleased me. So I insisted on going away and buying a halfpenny worthy of marbles and setting to work with my companion. By
good luck, the shop I tried did not possess the article; and my better angel
(generally my worst) laziness, prevented me from doing anything more.
You should have seen my friend's face!

I am better now; but it leaves me in a state of intellectual prostration,
fit for nothing but smoking, and reading Charles Baudelaire. By the bye,
I hope your sisters don't read him: he would have corrupted St Paul.

In literary work, I have two essays on 'The Right Conduct of the
Imagination' simmering in my brain. One of them is in draught. When
you come, you must bring me *Monmouth*.[4] I have improved a little in

[2] Posthumously published as 'The Builder's Doom' in the Edinburgh Edition (1898) and
previously thought to have been written as one of the Moral Tales during the Davos period
1881–2. This seems to be an earlier version called 'The Deacon's Crescent'.

[3] RLS often visited churchyards when he felt unhappy (see 'Old Mortality'). His description of
Greyfriars Churchyard is in *Picturesque Notes*, V. On 30 March MIS records: 'Lou still complaining and in very low spirits.'

[4] RLS tells us that in this play, written in verse, he 'reclined on the bosom of Mr Swinburne'. The
original plan was for the play to be written in collaboration with Bob, and RLS set out his ideas
in several letters to him in 1868. RLS finally wrote it on his own but dedicated it to Bob. The
MS came to light in 1922 and was privately printed in 1928. The theme (which was still in

dramatic diction – less of the buskin. So I must have a shot at that subject again. I see the possibilities of a first rate acting piece in it. Believe me, Ever your affectionate friend and cousin   R.L. Stevenson

Tell me what you think of 'Deacon Thin,' and write something interesting.

To his Parents

Thursday 5 [actually 4] August 1870   *Earraid*[1]

My dear Mother, I have so much to say, that needs must I take a large sheet; for the notepaper brings with it a chilling brevity of style. Indeed, I think, pleasant writing is proportional to the size of the material you write withal.

From Edinburgh to Greenock, I had the ex-secretary of the E.U. Conservative C[lub], Murdoch.[2] At Greenock I spent a dismal evening, though I found a pretty walk. The Tontine is a dirty uncomfortable house, and there was no one in the smoking room. Next day on board the *Iona*,[3] I had Maggie Thomson to Tarbert: Craig, a well-read, pleasant medical to Ardrishaig; and Prof., Mrs, and all the little Fleeming Jenkinseses.[4] Their

RLS's mind ten years later – see p. 138) is completely unhistorical. James, Duke of Monmouth (1649–85), illegitimate son of Charles II, led an unsuccessful rebellion in the west of England against his uncle James II and was beheaded.

[1] The islet off the Isle of Mull near Iona was being used as a base for the construction of the Dhu Heartach lighthouse by the family firm. RLS describes this visit in 'Memoirs of an Islet'. As Aros it became the setting for 'The Merry Men' and under its own name the scene of David Balfour's misadventures in ch. 14 of *Kidnapped*. MIS records that RLS left Swanston on Monday 1 August.

[2] Patrick Alexander Murdoch (1847–1912), practised as a surgeon in Fulham 1874–89, but later inherited the estate of Mount Annan, Dumfriesshire and changed his name to Pasley-Dirom. RLS was treasurer of the Edinburgh University Conservative Club in 1870, and made his first public speech there on 6 February 1871.

[3] Summer tours by steamer from Glasgow to Oban and the west coast and islands were very popular with Victorian tourists. The *Iona* was a luxuriously fitted paddle-steamer that took passengers from Glasgow and Greenock to Ardrishaig. Here they boarded a small steamer for the passage through the Crinan Canal and then went by another boat northwards to Oban. From Oban steamers made the round trip through the Sound of Mull and down the west coast of Mull to the island of Staffa (famous for Fingal's Cave) to the island of Iona and back to Oban. RLS disembarked at Iona and then went on to Earraid.

[4] Henry Charles Fleeming Jenkin (1833–85), a distinguished electrical engineer whose major work was in the manufacture, testing and laying of submarine telegraph cables. He became Professor of Engineering at Edinburgh University in 1868 where RLS was one of his students. He married (1859) Anne Austin (died 1921). She was a gifted amateur actress and the Jenkin theatrical productions were a feature of the Edinburgh social scene. The Jenkins warmly befriended RLS at a difficult period of his life. RLS wrote a 'Memoir' of Jenkin in 1887 and put him into his essay 'Talk and Talkers' as Cockshot. The Jenkins had three sons: Austin Fleeming (1861–1910) became a barrister; Charles Frewen (1865–1940) was the first Professor of Engineering Science at Oxford University 1908–29; Bernard Maxwell (1867–1951) was a Consulting Engineer.

oldest boy is a disgusting, priggish, envious, diabolically clever little specimen. For example, I asked what was the second one's *specialité*. 'Gardening,' quoth his father, 'I think his is the best garden.' 'My garden,' answers my young friend, 'is very good too.' 'Yes,' says the Professor; 'but Junior[5] is the best gardener.' 'Yes,' replies the young imp, with an inimitable sneer, 'I suppose Mr Brown *is* the best gardener.' 'At least, my son,' answered his father severely, 'whoever may be the best gardener, I don't like to see you the best runner-down of the family.' The little beggar knows geology; and apropos of Austin, Mrs F.J. told [me][6] a good story. 'I like your children very much,' said a friend to her: 'at least I like the two younger; and *respect* Osy.' Mrs Jenkin [is] very jolly. They went on to Corran Ferry, near which they have taken a farm, to which I stand invited.

At Oban, that night, it was delicious. Mr Stephenson's[7] yacht lay in the bay, and a splendid band on board played delightfully. The waters of the bay were as smooth as a millpond; and, in the dusk, the black shadows of the hills stretched across to our very feet and the lights were reflected in long lines. At intervals, blue lights were burned on the water; and rockets were sent up. Sometimes great stars of clear fire fell from them, until the bay received and quenched them. I hired a boat and sculled round the yacht in the dark. When I came in, a very pleasant Englishman on the steps fell into talk with me, till it was time to go to bed.

Next morning I slept on or I should have gone to Glencoe. As it was, it was blazing hot; so I hired a boat, pulled all forenoon along the coast and had a delicious bathe on a beautiful white beach. Coming home, I *cotoyai'd*[8] my Englishman, lunched alongside of him and his sister and took a walk with him in the afternoon, during which I find that he was travelling with a servant, kept horses *et caetera*. At dinner, he wished me to sit beside him and his sister; but there was no room. When we came out he told me why he was so *empressé* on this point. He had found out my name, and that I was connected with lighthouses, and his sister wished to know if I were any relative of the Stevenson in Ballantyne's *Lighthouse*.[9] All evening, he, his sister, I and Mr Hargrove, of Hargrove and Fowler, sate in front of the hotel. I asked Mr H. if he knew who my friend was.

[5] I am not certain of this word.
[6] The word is obscured by a large blot.
[7] George Robert Stephenson (1819–1905) of Glen Caladh Castle, Kyles of Bute, nephew of the famous railway engineer, was himself an engineer and proprietor of locomotive works at Newcastle upon Tyne.
[8] RLS must have been thinking of the French *côtoyer*.
[9] R.M. Ballantyne's *The Lighthouse* (1865), an account of the building of the Bell Rock lighthouse by RLS's grandfather. In a fragment of autobiography dictated at Vailima (posthumously published as part of 'Memoirs of Himself'), RLS describes his tongue-tied meeting with Ballantyne while he was writing the book.

'Yes,' he said, 'I never met him before; but my partner knows him. He is a man of old family; and the solicitor of highest standing about Sheffield.' At night, he said, 'Now if you're down in my neighbourhood, you must pay me a visit. I am very fond of young men about me; and I should like a visit from you very much. I can take you through any factory in Sheffield; and I'll drive you all about the *Dookeries*.' He then wrote me down his address; and we parted huge friends, he still keeping me up to visit him. Here is his address:

> Henry Go Watson,[10] Shirecliffe Hall, Sheffield,
> or, The Park Cottage, Worksop.

Saul also among the prophets, Mrs S.[11]

Hitherto, I had enjoyed myself amazingly; but today has been the crown. In the morning I met Bough[12] on board, with whom I am both surprised and delighted. He and I have read the same books, and discuss Chaucer, Shakespeare, Marlowe, Fletcher, Webster, and all the old authors. He can quote verses by the page, and has really a very pretty literary taste. Altogether, with all his coarseness and buffoonery a more pleasant, clever fellow you may seldom see. I was very much surprised with him; and he with me. 'Where the devil did you read all these books?' says he; and in my heart, I echo the question. One amusing thing I must say. We were talking about travelling; and I said I was so fond of travelling alone, from the people one met and grew friendly with. 'Ah,' says he, 'but you've such a pleasant manner you know – quite captivated my old woman, you did – she couldn't talk of anything else.'[13] Here was a compliment, even in Sam Bough's sneering tones, that rather tickled my vanity; and really my social successes of the last few days, the best of which is yet to come, are enough to turn anybody's head. To continue, after a little go in with Samuel, he going up on the bridge, I looked about me to see who there was; and mine eye lighted on two girls, one of whom was sweet and pretty, talking to an old gentleman. '*Eh bien*,' says I to myself,

---

[10] Henry Edmund Watson (1815–1901), knighted 1886, Sheffield solicitor and company director. RLS seems to have written his second name as 'Go'.

[11] I Samuel 10:11.

[12] Sam Bough (1822–78), born in Carlisle, worked as a boy with his father as a cobbler and then briefly as a lawyer's clerk before abandoning this in favour of a Bohemian life wandering about the country, associating with gypsies while making water-colour sketches and working as a scene-painter in the theatre. Eventually he won recognition as a landscape painter of distinction and became a member of the Royal Scottish Academy, 1875. RLS wrote an affectionate obituary notice in the *Academy*, 30 November 1878, recording that Bough's rough and sarcastic manner 'was no more than a husk, an outer man, partly of habit, partly of affectation; and inside the burr there was a man of warm feelings, notable powers of mind, and much culture'.

[13] MIS records: 'In June while attending Prof. Jenkin's summer session and levelling on the Braid Hills, he ran a levelling rod into his leg and with some difficulty got as far as the house of Sam Bough, the artist. His wife is very kind and takes a great fancy to Lou.'

'that seems the best investment on board.' So I sidled up to the old gentleman, got into conversation with him and so with the damsel; and thereupon, having used the patriarch as a ladder, I kicked him down behind me. Who should my damsel prove, but Amy Sinclair, daughter of Sir John George?[14] She certainly was the simplest, most naïve specimen of girlhood I ever saw. By getting brandy and biscuit and generally coaching up her cousin who was sick, I ingratiated myself; and so kept by her the whole way to Iona, taking her into the cave at Staffa and generally making myself as gallant as possible. I never was so much pleased with anything in my life, as her amusing absence of *mauvaise honte*: she was so sorry I wasn't going on to Oban again: didn't know how she could have enjoyed herself if I hadn't been there: and was so sorry we hadn't met on the Crinan. When we came back from Staffa, she and her aunt went down to have lunch; and a minute after up comes Miss Amy to ask me if I wouldn't think better of it, and take some lunch with them. I could not resist that of course; so down I went; and there she displayed the full extent of her innocence. I must be sure to come to Thurso Castle the next time I was in Caithness, or The Mount, Upper Norwood (whence she would take me all over the Crystal Palace) when I was near London; and (most complete of all) she offered to call on us in Edinburgh! Imagine if Sir J.G. had been there and that beholding! Of course, I had to say we should be delighted and give our address, though I could scarce keep [from] laughing, and blushed, I must say, at her aunt's satyrical face and sharp ears on the other side. Wasn't it delicious? She is a girl of sixteen or seventeen, too, and the latter, I think.

In the meantime, Miss Amy has run away with my pen; and I must turn back to get into chronology. Coming off Staffa, Sam Bough (who had been in huge force the whole time, drawing in Miss Amy's sketch-book and making himself agreeable or otherwise to everybody) pointed me out to a parson and said, 'That's him!' This was Alick Ross and his wife. Ross seems very nice, but his wife is a horrid woman, so forward, pushing and brazen.

The last stage of the steamer now approached, Miss Amy and I lamenting pathetically that Iona was so near. 'People meet in this way,' quoth she, 'and then lose sight of one another so soon.' We all landed together, Bough and I and the Rosses with our baggage; and went together over the ruins. I was here left with the cousin and the aunt (a Mrs Malcolm) during which I learned that said cousin sees me *every* Sunday in St Stephens.[15] Oho! thought I, at the 'every'. Mrs Malcolm was very

---

[14] Amy Camilla Sinclair (died 1925), elder daughter of Sir John George Tollemache Sinclair, Bt (1824–1912). She married John Henry Fullarton Udny of Udny Castle, Aberdeen, in 1874.
[15] Where the Stevensons regularly worshipped from 1869.

anxious to know who that strange, wild man was? (didn't I wish Samuel
in Tophet!) Of course in reply, I drew it strong about eccentric genius and
my never having known him before, and a good deal that was perhaps
'strained to the extremest limit of the fact'. But Act Vth was yet to come,
alas!

The steamer left, and Miss Amy and her cousin waved their handker-
chiefs, until my arm in answering them was nearly broken. I believe
women's arms must be better made for this exercise: mine ache still; and
I regretted at the time that the handkerchief had seen service. Altogether,
however, I was left in a pleasant frame of mind; but the disclosure of the
Act Vth, above referred to, fell as a wet blanket on my hopes. Mrs
Malcolm had thanked Bough for his attention; and what said the wild man
of Jordan Lane to her, but this? 'I can only say in the words of Hamlet,
"Fair maid, in thy orisons be all my sins remembered."'

Before I go to bed (for it is now near midnight) I shall epilogize on
Miss Amy Sinclair. As a psychological study she was quite a discovery to
me. I never yet saw a girl so perfectly innocent and fresh, so perfectly
modest without the least trace of prudery. *Demain, Madame, j'espère de vous
raconter ce qui reste (et ce n'est pas rien, ma foi) de nos aventures d'aujourdhui.*

Friday morning [5 August]

Being thus left alone, Bough, I, the Rosses, Professor Blackie,[16] and an
English parson, called Malin. These people were going to remain the
night, except the Professor who is resident there at present. They were
going to dine *en compagnie* and wished us to join the party; but we had
already committed ourselves by mistake to the wrong hotel and besides we
wished to be off soon as wind and tide were against us to Earraid. We
went up, Bough selected a place for sketching and blocked in the sketch
for Mrs Ross; and we all talked together. Bough told us his family history
and a lot of strange things about old Cumberland life; among others, how
he had known 'John Peel', of pleasant memory in song and of how that
worthy hunted. At five, down we go to the Argyll Hotel, and wait dinner.
Broth, 'nice broth', fresh herrings, and fowl had been promised. At 5.50,
I get the shovel and tongs and drum them at the stair-head till a response
comes from below that the nice broth is at hand. I boast of my
engineering and Bough compares me to the Abbot of Arbroath who
originated the Inchcape Bell.[17] At last, in comes the tureen and the

---

[16] John Stuart Blackie (1809–95), Professor of Greek at Edinburgh University 1852–82, was a
much loved Edinburgh figure, famous for his eccentricities. RLS was a consistent truant from
his classes.

[17] There is a tradition, commemorated by Southey in his ballad, that a bell was hung on the
Inchcape or Bell Rock – the dangerous reef on which the lighthouse was built – by an Abbot
of Arbroath, and that the pirate who removed it was himself wrecked on the rock.

handmaid lifts the cover. 'Rice Soup!' I yell, 'O no! none o' that for me!' – 'Yes,' says Bough, savagely, 'But Miss Amy didn't take me downstairs to eat salmon.' Accordingly he is helped. How his face fell. 'I imagine myself in the accident ward of the infirmary,' quoth he. It was, purely and simply, rice and water. After this, we have another weary pause, and then herrings in a state of mash and potatoes like iron. 'Send the potatoes out to Prussia for grape-shot,' was the suggestion.[18] I dined off broken herrings and dry bread. At last 'the supreme moment comes', and the fowl in a lordly dish, is carried in. On the cover being raised, there is something so forlorn and miserable about the aspect of the animal that we both roar with laughter. Then Bough, taking up knife and fork, turns the 'swarry'[19] over and over, shaking doubtfully his head. 'There's an aspect of quiet resistance about the beggar,' says he, 'that looks bad.' However, to work he falls until the sweat stands on his brow and a dismembered leg falls, dull and leadenlike, onto my dish. To eat it was simply impossible. Toughness was here at its farthest. I did not know before that flesh could be so tough. 'The strongest jaws in England,' says Bough piteously harpooning his dry morsel, 'couldn't eat this leg in less than twelve hours.' Nothing for it now; but to order boat and bill. 'That fowl,' says Bough to the landlady, 'is of a breed I know. I know the cut of its jib whenever it was put down. That was the grandmother of the cock that frightened Peter.' – 'I thought it was an historical animal,' says I, 'What a shame to kill it. It's as bad as eating Whittington's cat or the Dog of Montargis.'[20] – 'Na – na it's no old,' says the landlady, 'but it eats hard.' – 'Eats!' I cry, 'where do you find that? Very little of that verb with us.' So with more raillery, we pay six shillings for our festival and run over to Earraid, shaking the dust of the Argyll Hotel from off our feet.

I can write no more, just now and I hope you will be able to decipher so much; for it contains matter. Really the whole of yesterday's work would do in a novel without one little bit of embellishment; and, indeed, few novels are so amusing. Bough, Miss Amy, Mrs Ross, Blackie, Malin the parson, all these were such distinct characters, the incidents were so entertaining, and the scenery so fine, that the whole would have made a novelist's fortune. Believe me, Your very affectionate son

R.L. Stevenson

---

[18] The Franco-Prussian war began in July 1870 and continued until January 1871.

[19] A humorous spelling of *soirée* in the sense of a social evening (cf. 'a friendly swarry', *Pickwick Papers*, ch. 37); here by extension the evening meal itself.

[20] *The Forest of Bondy, or the Dog of the Montargis* was one of the juvenile dramas celebrated by RLS in 'A Penny Plain and Twopence Coloured'. Aubrey de Montdidier was murdered in the Forest of Bondy by Richard de Macaire. Aubrey's dog excited suspicion by always snarling at Macaire. The King ordered a judicial combat between dog and man; Macaire was overcome by the dog, confessed his guilt and died.

My dear Father, No landing today, as the sea runs high on the rock. They
are at the second course of the first story on the rock. I have as yet had
no time here; so this is α and ω of my business news. Your affectionate
son   R.L. Stevenson[21]

To Charles Baxter[1]

Friday 5 March [actually April] 1872   *Dunblane[2]*

My dear Baxter, By the date you may perhaps understand the purport of
my letter without any words wasted about the matter. I cannot walk with
you tomorrow and you must not expect me. I came yesterday afternoon
to Bridge of Allan, and have been very happy ever since, as every place is
sanctified by the eighth sense, Memory.[3] I walked up here this morning
(three miles, *tudieu!* a good stretch for me) and passed one of my favourite
places in the world, and one that I very much affect in spirit, when the
body is tied down and brought immovably to anchor in a sick-bed. It is
a meadow and bank at a corner on the river, and is connected in my mind
inseparably with Virgil's *Eclogues*. '*Hic corulis mistas inter consedimus ulmos*',
or something like that the passage begins (only I know my short-winded
Latinity must have come to grief over even thus much of quotation); and
here, to a wish, is just such a cavern as Menalcas might shelter himself
withal from the bright noon, and, with his lips curled backward, pipe
himself blue in the face, while *Messieurs les Arcadiens* ('*Arcades ambo*') would

---

[21] In 'Memoirs of an Islet' RLS remembered his visit as mainly a holiday 'of sea-bathing and sun-
burning'. His parents arrived at Earraid on 19 August on board the lighthouse ship, the *Pharos*.
They all left the next day.

[1] Charles Baxter (1848–1919), was the son of Edmund Baxter (1813–94), a well-known Edinburgh lawyer, Writer to the Signet (W.S.) – the elite of Scottish solicitors – and Auditor of the
Court of Session 1866–94. Baxter became a W.S. in 1871 and in due course joined his father's
law firm of Mitchell and Baxter. Underneath the façade of the serious lawyer lurked a very
different person who could hold his own with RLS in witty conversation and comic foolery
– a side of him portrayed in Michael Finsbury (for which Baxter was the original) in *The Wrong
Box*. A friendship that began against a background of youthful dissipation, when they were
boon companions in the pubs of the Lothian Road, developed into a close and lasting
relationship, with Baxter acting as RLS's legal, business and financial adviser. Baxter's sympathy,
loyalty and common-sense never failed RLS. Baxter married Grace Stewart in 1877 (see p. 127)
and had two sons and a daughter. After her death in 1893, he married in 1895 Marie Louise
Gaukroger; they had one daughter. Baxter retired from his law firm and the family lived first
in Paris and then in Siena in Italy.

[2] After his law classes finished in March, RLS was in poor health. So he went to Dunblane
and Bridge of Allan, coming home every few days to take part in rehearsals for the
amateur theatricals organised by Professor Jenkin. RLS had a minor part in *The Taming of the
Shrew*.

[3] The Stevensons regularly stayed at Bridge of Allan during RLS's childhood. He recalled the
walk along the river and the cave in a letter to Bob in November 1868.

roll out these cloying hexameters, that sing themselves in one's mouth to such a curious lilting chaunt.[4]

In such weather, one has the bird's need to whistle; and I, who am specially incompetent in this art, must content myself by chattering away to you on this bit of paper. All the way along I was thanking God that he had made me and the birds and everything just as they are and not otherwise; for although there was no sun, the air was so thrilled with robins and blackbirds that it made the heart tremble with joy, and the leaves are far enough forward on the underwood to give a fine promise for the future. Even myself, as I say, I would not have had changed in one *iota* this forenoon, in spite of all my idleness and Guthrie's[5] lost paper, which is ever present with me – a horrible phantom; except perhaps in that one direction, in which I have so sorely over-ridden and disenchanted my poor mind and body.

No one can be alone at home or in a quite new place. Memory and you must go hand in hand with (at least) decent weather, if you wish to cook up a proper dish of Solitude. It is in these little flights of mine that I get more pleasure than in anything else; and yet I am not really happy. Happiness is a matter of bottled stout and roast beef – by the way, how memory loves to dwell over that rare joy, a really good roast of beef. Now, at present, I am supremely uneasy and restless – almost to the extent of pain; but O! how I enjoy it and how I *shall* enjoy it afterwards (please God) if I get years enough allotted to me for the thing to ripen in. When I am a very old and very respectable citizen, with white hair and bland manners and a gold watch and an unquestioned *entrée* to the Sacrament, I shall hear these crows cawing in my heart, as I heard them this morning. I vote for old age and eighty years of retrospect. Yet, after all, I daresay a short shrift and a nice, green grave are about as desirable.

Poor devil! how I am wearying you! Cheer up. Two pages more and my letter reaches its term, for I have no more paper. What delightful things inns and waiters and bagmen are! If we didn't travel now and then, we should forget what the feeling of life is. The very cushion of a railway carriage – 'The things restorative to the touch.'[6] I can't write, confound

---

[4] At the beginning of the Fifth Eclogue, Menalcas invites Mopsus to sit with him 'among these elms interspersed with hazels' (*Hic corylis mixtas inter consedimus ulmos*). Instead they chose to shelter in a small cave, where they sing and play on reed pipes. *Arcades ambo* (Both Arcadians) is in *Eclogues* VII.

[5] Charles John Guthrie (1849–1920), son of Thomas Guthrie, one of the leaders of the Free Church, was a fellow member of the Speculative Society. He had a distinguished legal career, becoming a Q.C. in 1899 and a judge (as Lord Guthrie) in 1907. His *Robert Louis Stevenson: Some Personal Recollections* appeared in 1920.

[6] 'The Thing's restorative, / I' the touch and sight' – Browning, *The Ring and the Book* (1868), I, 89.

it.[7] That's because I'm so tired with my walk. I wish I could think of
something else to say, for when this letter is done, I shall be handed over
to my own restlessness for several hours, and then not all my weariness
will be able to keep me still, and walking is the devil and all for my health.
Such a nice little girl went past the window just now, in black and as
mignonne as your warmest mood could fancy, that I felt inclined to run out
and kiss her for her mother. I know exactly the sort of warm, brown,
melting hand the little darling would and *must* have; but the gloomy
waiter 'held me with his eye'.[8] He seemed to have all the beadle-staves
and constable-batons of united respectability under his arm, instead of one
poor napkin. Believe me, Ever your affectionate friend

R.L. Stevenson

To Charles Baxter

Tuesday 9 April 1872   *Dunblane*

My dear Baxter, I don't know what you mean. I know nothing about the
Standing Committee of the *Spec.*,[1] did not know that such a body existed
and even if it doth exist, must sadly repudiate all association with such
'goodly fellowship'. I am a 'Rural Voluptooary', at present. *That* is what
is the matter with me. The Spec. may go whistle, may go be——. As for 'C.
Baxter Secy', who is he? I know one Charles Baxter (or Bagster), Jinkster,
Jokester, ——ster, ——ster; but I know nought of this '*Secy*'. 'One Baxter, or
Bagster, a secretary,' I say to mine acquaintance, 'is at present disquieting
my leisure with certain illegal, uncharitable, unchristian and unconstit-
utional documents called *Business letters: the affair is in the hands of the
POLICE.*' Do you hear *that*, you evil-doer? Sending business letters is
surely a far more hateful and slimy degree of wickedness than sending
threatening letters: the man who throws grenades and torpedoes is less
malicious: the Devil in red-hot hell, rubs his hands with glee as he reckons
up the number, that go forth spreading pain and anxiety with each
delivery of the Post.

I have been walking today by a colonnade of beeches, along the

---

[7] RLS crossed out and re-wrote two words in the preceding sentence.
[8] 'He holds him with his glittering eye . . .' – Coleridge, 'The Ancient Mariner', I, l. 13. RLS has
deleted 'glassy' before 'eye'.
[1] On 11 March 1872, RLS was elected one of the five Presidents of the Speculative Society for
the following session, and Baxter was elected Secretary. The five Presidents and the Secretary
made up the Standing Committee. The Minutes (in Baxter's hand) in the Society's records show
that RLS did in fact attend a meeting of the Standing Committee on 15 April.

brawling Allan.[2] My character for sanity is quite gone, seeing that I cheered my lonely way, with the following, in a triumphant chaunt: 'Thank God for the grass, and the fir-trees, and the crows, and the sheep, and the sunshine and the shadows of the fir-trees.' I hold that he is a poor mean devil who can walk alone, in such a place and in such weather, and doesn't set up his lungs and cry back to the birds and the river. Follow, follow, follow me. Come hither, come hither, come hither – here shall you see – No enemy – except a very slight remnant of winter and its rough weather.[3] My bedroom, when I awoke this morning, was full of bird-songs; which is the greatest pleasure in life. Come hither, come hither, come hither, and when you come bring the third Part of the *Earthly Paradise*:[4] you can get it for me in Elliots[5] for two and tenpence (2s/10d) (*business habits*). Also bring an ounce of Honey Dew from Wilsons.[6]

The whole of the latter part of this letter was written to a chaunt; and may be read in a similar style by the judicious reader, if he be as light-hearted.

Do come. I think you will find me nice, but know not, as I speak very little.

I send here competition sonnet to the *L.J.R.*:[7] you will soon get one from Bob, and will please consider yourself as Judge and lawgiver over us in this matter.

---

[2] A notebook carried by RLS on this visit contains law notes and rough drafts of a number of poems. One begins:

> Calm runs my blood. By this high colonnade
> Of secular beeches that in order fair
> Follow the brawling river, I repair . . .

[3] Cf. *As You Like It*, II.v.5–8.

[4] Volume three of William Morris's poem had appeared in 1870. The notebook contains a page listing RLS's expenses connected with this visit. It includes 3/6d for *The Earthly Paradise*.

[5] Andrew Elliot, bookseller, 17 Princes Street, had published *The Pentland Rising* by RLS in 1866.

[6] A tobacconist's shop in Leith Street, which RLS used as his 'headquarters'. He told Balfour at Vailima: 'The tobacconists' shops in Edinburgh used to be a curious institution. Young men who couldn't afford a club used to use them for the same sort of purposes. You used to have letters sent there, or meet friends whom you didn't want to bring to your father's house. You weren't expected to buy anything as long as the people knew you'.

[7] A mysterious society (commemorated in the dedication to *Kidnapped*), comprising RLS, Baxter, Bob, Ferrier and two others, which met at a pub in Advocates' Close. The initials signified Liberty, Justice and Reverence. Its tenets set out in the constitution (drafted by Baxter) included the abolition of the House of Lords and that its members were not to be bound by the doctrines of the Established Church. In correspondence in 1891, RLS and Baxter recalled the painful scene between father and son when TS discovered the document (see p. 476).

To the Members of the L.J.R.[8]

As Daniel, bird-alone in that far land,
Kneeling in fervid prayer, with heart-sick eyes,
Turned thro' the casement toward the westering skies;
Or as untamed Elijah, that red brand
Among the starry prophets; or that band
And company of faithful sanctities
Who, in all times, when persecutions rise
Cherish forgotten creeds with fostering hand;
Such do ye seem to me, light-hearted crew,[9]
O turned to friendly arts with all your skill,
That keep a little chapel sacred still,
One rood of Holy-ground in this bleak earth
Sequestered still (an homage surely due!)
To the twin Gods of mirthful wine and mirth.

R.L. Stevenson

To his Mother[1]

28 July 1872   *Hotel Landsberg, Frankfurt*

My dear Mamma, I enclose some cuttings from a newspaper, very smartly written they are, which will give you an idea of the heat if Monsieur can remember his formula for reducing Centigrade to Fahrenheit. I think the highest we have had is somewhere about 93 in the shade; but the calculation is Simpson's, not mine.

On Thursday afternoon,[2] under a burning sun and refreshed by a wind that seemed to blow out of a furnace, we went all about the town on the outside of a tramway; and in the evening accompanied Simpson's friends to a concert in the zoological gardens. Next day, Simpson went to

---

[8] A rough draft of this poem is in the notebook referred to in n. 2. Another MS showing minor variations is dated 'Above Dunblane, by the riverside 1872'. 'Bird-alone' or 'burd-alane' in l. 1 is a Scots phrase for the only child left in a family, hence 'all alone'.

[9] 'That follow joy with all your store of skill,' deleted.

[1] In May RLS's scheme of going to Germany for the summer had to be abandoned when MIS had a fit of hysterics at the thought that she might never see him again. Eventually it was agreed that he could go for a few weeks, and he left for London with Sir Walter Simpson on his way to Germany on 20 July. RLS's letter was written on their arrival in Frankfurt. Sir Walter Grindlay Simpson (1843–98) succeeded his father, Sir James Young Simpson (the physician who pioneered the use of chloroform as an anaesthetic), as second Baronet in 1870. He was one of RLS's special friends at this period and figures as Athelred in 'Talk and Talkers'. He was a fellow-member of the Speculative Society and was also studying law, becoming an advocate in 1873.

[2] In Brussels.

Antwerp and I spent the day in the swimming bath and at Café doors, drinking coffee and iced drinks under an awning. In the evening I went to a Garden Theatre and heard rather an amusing French farce; it was quite like an English one, and tho' it turned on ticklish matters, was more moral than can be imagined.

That night, Friday, we left at half-past ten for Cologne. Up to the last moment we were undecided whether to go or stay and it was at last only my shame to own our indecision that decided us. I wonder how much of your boasted firmness comes from the same cause. In the carriage with us was a youth with a hundred horse power of somnolence, a handsome young Greek, his sister, his little boy and HIS WIFE. Simpson and I talked about her in whispers for near an hour, as she lay with her head on her husband's shoulder and her small white hand lying like a bird in the middle of his. She was one of the most perfectly pretty little women I ever saw; and with one accord we compared her to Dora in *David Copperfield* for both her prettiness and her stupidity. It was too much to suppose that she had any mind — one might as well expect cerebration in a violet. At Liège we got in a siphon of *eau de seltz*; and I gave some of this to our Greeks and got back some champagne in exchange. Madame looked at me with a sort of motherly interest all the time I was drinking it. '*Pas bon?*' she said when I had done; but I wish you could have heard the tone. It was the first time that I had profited by my youthful appearance. She was not a bit older than I, but she evidently looked upon me as *in loco filii*. All the next stage we dozed and looked at her; but at Verviers our twenty minutes' stoppage wakened us all up and we got fairly into conversation. I did the most of the talk on our side; for Simpson, with his charming characteristic prudence, had inwardly determined to have as little to do with her as possible, so as to guarantee peace of mind in the future. They had been the grand tour; and in talking over this place and that, we soon saw that we had underestimated her mind. At last, when I was making very very heavy weather of something, she said '*Parlez en anglais — je vous comprendrai.*' And then it turned out that she never travelled without some 'British Authors'[3] in her portmanteau, that she had read all Shakespeare twice and almost every novel we named, and (*enfin*) that her favourite novel was *David Copperfield* and one of her favourite characters was that very *Dora* to whom we had been profanely comparing her an hour or two before. She never read French novels unless she knew about them — '*il y a tant de mauvais auteurs en Français.*' Like you, Madame, she hated books that end badly. She has a sister who reads even more English than she — who *devours* 'British Authors'. I wish I could meet that sister. At last, the

---

[3] Collections issued by continental publishers such as Tauchnitz.

day breaking white and silent, here comes hateful Aachen. We shoot into the empty station. '*Et voilà l'oncle Fritz.*' *L'oncle Fritz*, in a big burly German voice, demands jocularly who is this that arrives '*à trois heures de matin*'. Much kissing on the platform. '*Bon voyage, messieurs*' from madame. '*Serviteur, messieurs. Charmer d'avoir fait votre connaissance*' from monsieur. Tra-la-la on the ineffectual trumpet of the German railways; and

> 'Maid of Athens, ere we part
> Give, oh give me back my heart.'[4]

Simpson and I were left in a state of glorious excitement, I can tell you, and kept debating what sort of an impression we had made, until we arrived at a comfortable decision that she would tell her friends (*l'oncle Fritz*, I suppose – happy uncle Fritz) that she had met '*deux bons écossais*' – compatriots of Valter Scott. I am sure anyone who told us that she was laughing at us would have had a warm reception.

And there is really all that I have to say about one of the most charming people that I have ever seen. Three pages of small foreign letter paper and even those written large, not to say written badly; and yet that night journey will surely hold a place until the hour I die, among the most beautiful of my remembrances. And so – these are the plain facts and an epilogue in my best style.

For a long while we sat and talked of her, but at last we dropped over and slept to Cologne, where we got up, dead with sleep and more filthy than words can express. I shall never forget the sort of inane smile with which Simpson staggered against the door post as we left the Station. Just outside a commissionaire nailed us and took us to a pot house, close by the Cathedral, where in a couple of rooms, which as Simpson said must have been originally a balcony, we went incontinently into a pretty sleep. I was dimly conscious through my slumber of a bell (as I then guessed it) about the size of St George's Church being rung at my ear; but I clung hard to Morpheus, got through its terrible brâm-brâm and did not waken till eleven o'clock in the forenoon. We then had breakfast, saw the Cathedral, had a swim in the Rhine and sat under a trellis in front of a hotel in Deutz,[5] for about three hours, drinking a sharp, red German wine (not unpleasant) and iced water. At last we found strength to move, and spent the afternoon trying to find different objects of interest and finding none, except indeed shady seats which, in this weather, are objects of more interest than anything else. Simpson spent about fifteen minutes, on one of these seats, trying to understand German money, a process by which he reduced himself to the beasts of the field in intellect. He

[4] Byron, 'Maid of Athens'.
[5] A suburb of Cologne on the right bank of the Rhine.

communicated to me the *fact* that while *one* Groschen equalled twopence, *two* Groschen only equalled twopence farthing. '*What*??' 'Yes' he replied, with the greatest *sérieux*. 'It's very disheartening; but so it is.' I don't think I have laughed more for a month; but as I did not want to bring him home in a strait waistcoat, I recommended him to give over his financial studies; and he did. We dined at a Restaurant and then went to the Tivoli Gardens where, in a Summer Theatre we had the pleasure of hearing a Five Act play in German called *Mutter und Sohn*.[6] In the first act, the son of a countess is discovered to have stolen (so far as we could make out) a red, silk pocket handkerchief, whereupon his mother and a fair percentage of the other relatives faint and the curtain falls on a grand tableau. During the next four acts, this peculative scion of the aristocracy makes himself a public nuisance by hanging about his mother's house, in a white hat and a most wicked and harrowing necktie and performing so far as I could see the most heroic and unnecessary acts of self-sacrifice. Thro' these, or thro' the white hat, or thro' the restitution of the pocket handkerchief or thro' something or other, he is at last reconciled to his mother; whereat the audience testified lively pleasure. For my part, I was only very tranquilly happy at this *dénouement*, as the hero by his unjustifiable choice of clothing had long alienated all my sympathies.

That night, Saturday, I left Cologne at twelve, midnight, leaving Simpson to follow in the steamer and join me, I don't quite know when, at this hotel. I *did* the Rhine in grand style, seeing I never woke till I got to Bingen, except when a brutal guard made me change carriages in a state of somnambulism, I staggering in front with one eye open and the guard walking behind to pick up my parcels as, one after another, I let them fall. From Bingen to Mainz, I travelled with rather a nice Englishman, and from Mainz to Frankfurt slept like a child. You can understand that in weather like what we have been having, night travelling is almost the only possible method of getting over the ground.

I enjoy the heat and agree with it very well. I have not heard from [you] since London and I cannot get out my letters here till Simpson comes with my letter of credit as a voucher.

Today it has thundered and rained much, and is a good deal cooler. Sunday is observed in Frankfurt, just as it is in London – all the shops shut except Cafés and Tobacconists. I saw a very exciting scene in the streets, a man who had stabbed another being run down, captured, held until the arrival of the police and then led away among a chorus of groans and hisses. Believe me, Ever your affectionate son   R.L. Stevenson

---

[6] *Mutter und Sohn* (1843) by the prolific but now forgotten German actress and dramatist Charlotte Birch-Pfeiffer (1800–68) was a free adaptation of *Grannarna* (*The Neighbours*) by the Swedish author Fredrika Bremer (1801–65). In the play Bruno, the favourite son, takes some money

To James Walter Ferrier[1]

Saturday 23 November 1872[2]   *17 Heriot Row*

My dear Ferrier, Our intentions must have been set close to each other in the infernal mosaic, for the removal of yours so loosened mine that it has only taken me a fortnight's labour to get the great big block dislodged and set before me. It looks very rough and shapeless; but I hope to carve it into a very comely epistle before I have made an end.

You did not come to Edinburgh? or, did you? It is conceivable to me that you may be lying *perdu* in some of these new and undiscoverable suburbs that are being wedged into all manner of odd corners about the town; on one of which, by the way, Bob and I stumbled the other afternoon. It lay between Leith Walk and the London Road; and, though split new in all its members, was already of a goodly size and possessed the necessary organs of life – a tobacconist's, the London Journal and a Public House.

And now, old man, how are you getting on? You are already so clouded over with myths and legends, that we rationalists of Edinburgh have begun to question your existence. By common repute, there is scarcely a crime that you have not committed. Simony, arson, fraud, adultery,

> 'Wi' mair o' horrible and awful',
> Which ev'n to name wad be unlawfu','[3]

are already identified with your memory. If you go on at this rate, you will become a very famous man – a 'bug to frighten babes withal.'[4] If all this be true you seem to have run the race which is set before you,[5] with laudable industry and swiftness of foot.

Seriously, however, you have left a very motley reputation behind you; and godly people, when your name is mentioned, draw closer round the fire and look fearfully over their shoulders.

from his mother's money-box in order to prevent the disgrace of his half-brother, who has embezzled money from his office. The half-brother, whose wedding-day it is, promises to replace the money in a few days from his wife's dowry. Before he can do so, the 'theft' is discovered and Bruno identified as the thief on the circumstantial evidence of a torn fragment of his handkerchief jammed in the money-box; Bruno is disowned by the mother and disappears. Fifteen years later he reappears as a mysterious stranger and is eventually reconciled with his mother after a death-bed confession by the half-brother.
[1] James Walter Ferrier (1850–83), one of the small group of RLS's close Edinburgh friends, was a fellow-member of the Speculative Society and the L.J.R. His early death grieved RLS deeply and he paid tribute to his memory in 'Old Mortality'.
[2] RLS must have begun the letter on 20 November (see n. 15).
[3] Burns, 'Tam o'Shanter', ll. 141–2.
[4] 'As bugs to fearen babes withall' – Spenser, *Faerie Queene*, II.xii.25.
[5] Hebrews 12:1.

As for me, I suppose you knew that I *was* going away to Germany with
Simpson; so I may now tell you that the plan was carried out; and a very
good time we had of it – what with sunshine, idleness and amourettes. Sir
W. however was telegraphed home, because the chinee-God was thought
to be dying; so I left Frankfurt where we had been staying and proceeded
onward to Leipzig and Dresden; then to B. Baden Esq., where I met my
family; and thence home with them thro' France.[6] This latter part was
somewhat spoilt by the most inconceivable insubordination on the part of
my liver – a lewd liver, indeed – who exhibited every form of misconduct
that malice could suggest. I was not however quite clear in my own
conscience; for I dined twice in the forenoon, a liberty always resented by
the human organism.

I am now, *working hard (credite posteri!).*[7] I am at Political Economy,
which I love; and Scots Law, which is a burthen greater than I can bear.
The large white head of the professor[8] relieved, in the pale gaslight, against
the black board, is the one *'taedii dulce lenimen'*[9] that we poor students
have. He is called 'The Bum-Faced', by those who know him.

I have served myself universal heir to you; but the assets consist of five
Speculative keys, sent me in an envelope by your mother, and one
eighteen-penny book on Spiritualism; while the liabilities, as far as yet
disclosed, are a very fair, good, honest, downright pound or two and half
a hundred weight of library books. I shall probably abscond.

And now for yourself.

Jowett is good and Malvern also is good.[10] Both of these are 'good
holts' for you, my lad. But they are not what you want. What you want
is to *publish that Heine manuscript of yours.*[11] There can be comparatively
little difficulty about it for you, because you are your father's son, your
grandfather's grandson, and the brother-in-law of him that married your
sister.[12] Don't say who you are, but give a brief genealogy – give in an

---

[6] Walter Simpson was summoned home because of the serious illness of his artist brother William
Simpson (1850–1911). RLS left Frankfurt on 11 August and joined his parents in Baden-Baden
on 23 August. They travelled home via Strasbourg, Paris and Boulogne, reaching Edinburgh on
11 September.

[7] Believe it, future generations – Horace, *Odes*, II.xix.2.

[8] Norman Macpherson (1825–1914), Professor of Scots Law 1865–88.

[9] Pleasant balm for tedium adapted from 'O laborum dulci lenimen' (O sweet balm of troubles),
Horace, *Odes*, I.xxxii.15.

[10] Apparently essays by Ferrier.

[11] Ferrier read essays on Heine to the Speculative Society on 24 January 1871 and 16 January
1872.

[12] Ferrier's father, James Frederick Ferrier (1808–64), Professor of Moral Philosophy and Political
Economy at St Andrews, was a nephew of the novelist Susan Ferrier. He married (1837) his
cousin Margaret Anne Wilson (1813–78), eldest daughter of John Wilson (1785–1854), the
'Christopher North' of *Blackwood's Magazine* and author of *Noctes Ambrosianae*. Their daughter
Susan married Sir Alexander Grant (1826–84), classical scholar, Principal of Edinburgh University 1868–84.

extract register of birth instead of a visiting card. Go to Grant's publisher, or your father's publisher – or, go to the devil if you like, but *publish that Heine*. Write a damned good witty critical thing for the beginning; but look sharp. I happen to know that the Comptist club are at work on a complete edition of Heine; so you must get before them.

Now, old man, all this *is wrote* powerful serious. I know what you want, and I know what would do you more good than all the Malverns in the world in a brown paper parcel, or a luncheon box of concentrated essence of Jowett. You want to get your name up a bit – that's what's the matter with you, and that also is what is the matter with ever-yours-faithfully-R.L. Stevenson.

All which is good sense and very good sense, In Witness Whereof . . .

I am reading Herbert Spencer[13] just now very hard. I got over the fingers at the Spec., the other night. I proposed 'Have we any authority for the inspiration of the New Testament?' as a subject of debate; when I was not seconded and Colin Macrae[14] protested. The liberty of free speech is the greatest boon of this happy and glorious – happy and glorious – ever victorious – country of Pharisees and whiskey.

We have a sight of new men in that august Society; and black balled one named (with cheerful anachronism) Daniel Macbeth[15] no longer gone than last night; on which occasion it will interest you to hear that Omond[16] was inarticulate and foolish, and subsided gradually into an infantile slumber.

Write again and (if you please) let me hear something definite about Heine. Ever yours truly   Louis Stevenson

P.S. As so long has elapsed, I think I shan't try the hotel but send this to Bonchurch.

---

[13] 'Close upon my discovery of Whitman, I came under the influence of Herbert Spencer. No more persuasive rabbi exists, and few better. . . . His words, if dry, are always manly and honest . . . I should be much of a hound if I lost my gratitude to Herbert Spencer' – RLS, 'Books Which Have Influenced Me' (1887).

[14] Colin George Macrae (1844–1925), W.S. 1871; Chairman of Edinburgh School Board 1890–1900; knighted 1900. He was present at a Spec. meeting on 5 November. On 12 November RLS read an essay: 'Two Questions on the Relation between Christ's Teaching and Modern Christianity'.

[15] Daniel Macbeth (1851–1928) became an advocate. He was blackballed at the Spec. on 19 November.

[16] George William Thomson Omond (1846–1929), one of the founders, with RLS, Ferrier and Robert Glasgow Brown of the shortlived *Edinburgh University Magazine* (January–April 1871), to which RLS contributed some essays. He became an advocate and author. He was one of the few people RLS strongly disliked and was the original of Frank Innes in *Weir of Hermiston*. Omond read an essay on 19 November on 'Church Tendencies in Scotland at the Present Time' and also put a question about library books.

To Charles Baxter

Sunday 2 February 1873   *17 Heriot Row*

My dear Baxter, The thunderbolt has fallen with a vengeance now. You know the aspect of a house in which somebody is still waiting burial – the quiet step – the hushed voices and rare conversation – the religious literature that holds a temporary monopoly – the grim, wretched faces; all is here reproduced in this family circle in honour of my (what is it?) atheism or blasphemy. On Friday night after leaving you, in the course of conversation, my father put me one or two questions as to beliefs, which I candidly answered. I really hate all lying so much now – a new-found honesty that has somehow come out of my late illness – that I could not so much as hesitate at the time; but if I had foreseen the real Hell of everything since, I think I should have lied as I have done so often before. I so far thought of my father, but I had forgotten my mother. And now! they are both ill, both silent, both as down in the mouth as if – I can find no simile. You may fancy how happy it is for me. If it were not too late, I think I could almost find it in my heart to retract; but it is too late; and again, am I to live my whole life as one falsehood? Of course, it is rougher than Hell upon my father; but can I help it? They don't see either that my game is not the light-hearted scoffer; that I am not (as they call me) a careless infidel: I believe as much as they do, only generally in the inverse ratio: I am, I think, as honest as they can be in what I hold. I have not come hastily to my views. I reserve (as I told them) many points until I acquire fuller information. I do not think I am thus justly to be called a 'horrible atheist'; and I confess I cannot exactly swallow my father's purpose of praying down continuous afflictions on my head.

Now, what is to take place? What a damned curse I am to my parents! As my father said, 'You have rendered my whole life a failure.' As my mother said, 'This is the heaviest affliction that has ever befallen me.' And, O Lord, what a pleasant thing it is to have just *damned* the happiness of (probably) the only two people who care a damn about you in the world. You see when I get incoherent, I always relapse a little into the Porter in *Macbeth*.[1]

---

[1] In a letter to Baxter in December 1872 RLS had written: 'Do you remember the knocking in *Macbeth*? That is some pumpkins. There is not much knocking about the world that can come up to that. The porter is a man I have a great respect for. He had a great command of language. All that he says, curiously enough, my mother left out when she read *Macbeth* to me – I suppose it was too affecting. By jingo! I remember the day my mother read *Macbeth* to me. A terrible, black, stormy day, when neither of us could go out of the house; and so we both sat over the fire and she read and I had snakes and newts and others to crawl up and down my spine.'

I should like to − blast!

I think if Cambridge could be managed, it would be the best thing. A little absence is the only chance.

Imagine, Charles, my father sitting in the arm chair, gravely reading up Butler's *Analogy*[2] in order to bring the wanderer back. Don't suppose I mean this jocularly − damn you. I think it's about the most pathetic thing I ever heard of − except one; and *that* I could not tell, but I can write it. My mother (dear heart) immediately asked me to join Nicholson's[3] young men's class: O what a remedy for me! I don't know whether I feel more inclined to laugh or cry over these naivetés; but I know how sick at heart they make me.

What is my life to be, at this rate? What, you rascal? Answer − I have a pistol at your throat. If all that I hold true and most desire to spread, is to be such death and worse than death, in the eyes of my father and mother, what the *devil* am I to do? Here is a good heavy cross with a vengeance, and all rough with rusty nails that tear your fingers: only it is not I that have to carry it alone: I hold the light end, but the heavy burthen falls on these two.

Charles Baxter, if you think it likely that you will ever beget a child, follow Origen's specific;[4] it is painful, but there are worse pains in this world.

If PEOPLE ONLY WOULD admit in practice (what they are so ready to assert in theory) that a man has a right to judge for himself; and is culpable if he do not exercise that right − why, it would have been better for a number of people − better for Wycliffe and Servetus and even Whitefield,[5] nay and even me. Better on the other hand, for many a doubting Torquemada, and for my father and mother at the present date.

Don't − I don't know what I was going to say. I am an abject idiot; which all things considered is not remarkable. Ever your affectionate and horrible Atheist.   R.L. Stevenson, C.I., H.A., S.B., Etc.[6]

---

[2] Joseph Butler (1692–1752), Bishop of Durham; *The Analogy of Religion* (1736) is his famous defence of Christianity and divine revelation.

[3] Maxwell Nicholson (1818–74), minister of St Stephen's Church, Edinburgh 1867–74.

[4] To avoid the temptations of the flesh Origen, the famous third-century Church Father, endured castration, thus obeying the injunction in Matthew 19:12 to make oneself a eunuch 'for the kingdom of heaven's sake'. In a cynical footnote, Gibbon commented: 'As it was his general practice to allegorize Scripture, it seems unfortunate, that in this instance only, he should have adopted the literal sense.'

[5] All religious reformers.

[6] Careless Infidel, Horrible Atheist, Son of Belial(?).

To Elizabeth Crosby[1]

July 1873   *Speculative Society Hall. University Edinburgh*

My dear Miss Crosby, I was very glad to get your letter; and very sorry to read it. I cannot say I was surprised. When you were here, you were just escaping into a new world, and thought that all the dulness was owing to the restrictions you were going to throw aside; now, you have learned that the world at large is as wearisome as woman's world, and that the arts and manufactures are as unsatisfying as embroidery and making jam. So be it. I sympathise with you on the disillusion; but there is no cure for it. Any one has always the crew of the blue devils at his right hand, with MM. Werther, Obermann, René and company[2] ready to sicken him with insipid condolences. There is no door of escape from this ennui. I try to evade it by constant change; by science, law, literature, perfect sunshine idleness when the weather permits, science again, law again, literature again, and perhaps a little, at the end of the cycle, of what has been mendaciously called 'life'. But leap as I may from one to the other, disgust is always at my back.

It is a most hateful mood; and can only be cleaned out by a little wholesome laughter or still wholesomer sympathy. There is something too much in the notion of people in good health and not hungry, muling over life; life *is* a bad thing, and that's the end of it; but we are not the people who have to bear the worst. Things are so settled for us by an omniscient tradition, that the worst of life cannot be mentioned even in a letter; but you will believe me, at least, when I say that something I saw, a week ago, is enough to make any Werther ashamed of his sham sorrows.

I beg your pardon for preaching. I am not in the humour for much else, and your letter was sad enough to justify me perhaps. Of course, they are not satisfying; nothing is; those are the terms on which we have to make the best of a very bad bargain.

I shall be down in England, most likely, in July or August, and I should much like to see you.

---

[1] Elizabeth Russel Crosby (1845–1931), a London solicitor's daughter, was a friend of RLS's cousin Mary Warden (daughter of TS's sister Jane). She stayed with the Stevensons 25 February–1 March 1871. This is RLS's second letter to her; he was to write three more, the last in 1874. She married (1878) Dr Hugo Müller, F.R.S. (1834–1915), a German-born chemist who was ultimately a partner in De la Rue & Co., and head of their stamp department.

[2] The melancholy and introspective heroes of Goethe's *Sorrows of Young Werther* (1774), Etienne Pivert de Senancour's *Obermann* (1804), and Chateaubriand's *René* (1802). The first page of an unpublished essay by RLS on Obermann written in 1870 is at Yale, and in 'Old Mortality' (1884) he speaks of having 'fed upon the cheerless fields of Obermann'. In his essay on Whitman RLS refers to 'this *Maladie de René* . . . the blue devils dance on all our literary wires'.

The Physician has so utterly failed to cure himself that I have not the heart to go on. I must wait for a better humour before I finish, and not come to visit you metaphorically speaking, in a hearse. –

[3]Do you know I find it very difficult to write to you. It is so long since we have met, and now I am not the same person, and no more, I am sure, are you. I may be committing gaucheries at every word – you know what I mean? Correspondence is impossible by fits and starts; you cannot write to a person whom you have neither seen nor written to, for a year; and so I am afraid I simply cannot write to you.

I can only say that I am in good health, that I rise at half past six in the morning and walk into town alone before nine – the walk is very pleasant often – that I go to classes, or oftener stay away from them and sit smoking in the Public Princes Street Gardens, where one sees a great deal of easy life in shirt-sleeves, shop girls and shopmen during their interval, tract distributors, vague wandering old men with all the Ancient Mariner's desire to tell their story and no story after all to tell. I must begin a new sentence for breath's sake; though I don't think the last is finished. Then I am driven out to Swanston again, eat a very good dinner, smoke very placidly in the garden, read or write, and go early to bed. A life of beautiful regularity, is it not? and kept interesting by the daily contrast of town and country. It is especially pleasant to arrive in the outskirts of the town at that hour, before the day's dust has risen. I meet pleasant little circumstances, tramps, troops of German musicians and the like, going out for a day's round in the country; that sort of thing always makes you feel cool about the heart I think. I like especially to think over the German band, going out into the plain, every step new to them, playing in shadowy courts behind old country houses or creating a small stir in a village street. I remember having a fancy once for a sort of Hawthorne sketch; how some spoony, sentimental yokel in the country gets a small legacy from a distant relative and, his heart being very full and his head very empty, imagines the life of an organ grinder the most pleasant on earth – imagines him going about and visiting place after place like a sunbeam – a wandering providence to children. You can finish the story for yourself; after he has spent all his money and bought his organ, you can imagine how cruel a first day one might give him in the streets of a town.

I am very sorry, Miss Crosby, that I can do nothing but maunder today; and even that, so sicklily. I hope this letter will not find you in too rational a state, or in extra good spirits, as in either case, it will go hard with it.

Bob is well and doing – well, a little. I think he has been too long here, there is nothing here to spur him on the side of art; I am only a colossal

---

[3] The beginning of a new page in different ink; the letter was apparently continued after an interval.

distraction. He will go to Antwerp, I hope, this spring, and thence to London. It is very good of me to say *hope*, as with him I shall lose about a fifth of my waking life; and this town of ours will be duller than ever.

My mother bids me say that – I forget what – something about not being able to answer your letter. She has not been very well; but is getting all right again.

Do you know, by the way, that I have never been right round the Queen's Drive, since the day we played truant together.

I hope you will forgive this dreary letter and give me an answer in mercy, as family worship has it. Believe me, Yours very sincerely

Robert Louis Stevenson

What formidable paper to envelope!

To Alison Cunningham

[? 1873][1]   [*Edinburgh*]

My dear Cummy, I was greatly pleased by your letter in many ways. Of course, I was glad to hear from you; you know, you and I have so many old stories between us, that even if there was nothing else, even if there was not a very sincere respect and affection, we should always be glad to pass a nod. I say 'even if there was not.' But you know right well there is. Do not suppose that I shall ever forget those long, bitter nights, when I coughed and coughed and was so unhappy, and you were so patient and loving with a poor, sick child. Indeed, Cummy, I wish I might become a man worth talking of: if it were only that you should not have thrown away your pains.

Happily, it is not the result of our acts that makes them brave and noble; but the acts themselves and the unselfish love that moved us to do them. 'Inasmuch as you have done it unto one of the least of these.'[2] My dear old nurse, and you know there is nothing a man can say nearer his heart except his mother or his wife – my dear old nurse, God will make good to you all the good that you have done, and mercifully forgive you all the evil. And next time when the spring comes round, and everything is beginning once again – if you should happen to think that you might have had a child of your own, and that it was hard you should have spent so many years taking care of some one else's prodigal: just you think this: you have been for a great deal in my life; you have made much that there

---

[1] It is impossible to date this letter with certainty. MIS records that Cummy left the Stevensons on 14 November 1871 'to keep her brother's house at Swanston'.

[2] Matthew 25:40.

is in me, just as surely as if you had conceived me; and there are sons who are more ungrateful to their own mothers than I am to you. For I am not ungrateful, my dear Cummy, and it is with a very sincere emotion that I write myself Your little boy   Louis

II. COCKFIELD RECTORY AND NEW FRIENDS July–October 1873

On 26 July 1873, Stevenson paid what he was later to call 'a very fortunate visit' to Cockfield Rectory in Suffolk, the home of his cousin Maud and her husband, Professor Churchill Babington.[1] It was a turning point in his life: at a critical time he gained the friendship of Frances Sitwell and Sidney Colvin.

Frances Jane Fetherstonhaugh (1839–1924), was a member of a long-established Anglo-Irish family which had fallen on hard times. She married in 1869 the Revd Albert Hurt Sitwell (1834–94) and lived with him briefly in Calcutta and then in the East End of London, where he was first a curate and then a vicar in Stepney. Albert Sitwell was described as 'a man of unfortunate temperament and uncongenial habits' and we are told that the couple were 'not well matched'. Whatever the problem (it may have been drink), the marriage fell under greater strain when in 1869 Sitwell was given the living of Minster, a village in the Isle of Thanet near Ramsgate; Frances seems to have decided to break away from her husband following the death of the elder of their two sons, Frederick (aged twelve) in April 1873.

It was at this sad and difficult time in her own life that Mrs Sitwell, accompanied by her surviving son Francis Albert ('Bertie'), a boy of ten, came to Cockfield to stay with her close friend Maud Babington. They had become friends because Maud's sister, Sidney Wilson was married to Isla Sitwell, one of Albert Sitwell's brothers. Frances Sitwell was clearly a remarkable woman; she is described by her friends as having 'a sibylline beauty over which time had no power' and an 'irradiating charm'. The impression is of a person not only of wit and intelligence but also of great tenderness, warmth and vitality, with a sympathetic understanding of other people's problems. All these qualities were to be shown to the full in her relationship with RLS.

Many years later, Lady Colvin (as she had become) recalled the arrival of 'a slim youth in a black velvet jacket and straw hat, with a knapsack on his back' who had walked out from Bury St Edmunds in the heat. RLS soon captivated the entire household, and between himself and Mrs

---

[1] Matilda (Maud) Whytt Wilson (1844–1919), was one of the daughters of MIS's sister Marion Wilson. She married (1869) Professor Churchill Babington (1821–89), Disney Professor of Archaeology at Cambridge 1865–80, and Rector of Cockfield 1866–89. She later married Colonel William Henry Wright and figures in Graham Greene's *A Sort of Life* (1971).

Sitwell there sprang up what Colvin described as 'an instantaneous under-standing'. Later biographers, on the evidence of the letters that followed that meeting, have said more simply that during the happy five weeks at Cockfield RLS fell in love. Mrs Sitwell wrote to her friend Sidney Colvin begging him not to delay his promised visit to the Rectory if he wanted to meet a 'fine young spirit'.

Sidney Colvin (1845–1927), was the youngest son of Bazett David Colvin, a partner in a leading London firm of East India merchants, and his wife Mary Steuart. Both sides of the family had been connected with India, either as merchants or as administrators in the old East India Company. He went up to Trinity College, Cambridge in 1863 and was third in the first class of the Classical Tripos of 1867; he was made a Fellow of Trinity in 1868. On leaving Cambridge, Colvin settled in London and soon established a reputation as a critic of the fine arts. He wrote regularly for the *Pall Mall Gazette*, the *Fortnightly Review*, the *Portfolio* and other magazines. At some time in these years he met and fell in love with Frances Sitwell, but he was unable to marry her until over thirty years later.[2] A few months before the first meeting with RLS Colvin had been elected Slade Professor of Fine Art at Cambridge; he was re-elected four times and from 1876 to 1884 he was also Director of the Fitzwilliam Museum in Cambridge. In 1884 he took up an appointment as Keeper of the Department of Prints and Drawings at the British Museum, a position he held until his retirement in 1912; he was knighted in 1911.

Stevenson's new friends recognised his potential as a writer and saw their task as 'to strengthen, encourage and steady him'. The long diary-letters that RLS wrote to Mrs Sitwell over the next two years constitute a remarkable and touching record of the young man's slow growth to maturity. To her he poured out his feelings of unhappiness and near-despair over the religious conflict with his father and what he saw as his parents' lack of understanding; he confided his ambitions and disappoint-ments in his literary work, and received encouragement in return. Although there can be no doubt of his love and emotional dependence on Mrs Sitwell, as she progressed from being his 'Claire' to his 'madonna', there was something unreal about the relationship: one feels that he treats her with the reverence accorded a goddess rather than in the way a lover behaves to a flesh-and-blood woman.

With characteristic generosity and kindness Colvin helped and encour-aged RLS in his literary aspirations by introducing him to publishers and editors and tirelessly promoting his interests. At first, as he later admitted,

---

[2] Although Albert Sitwell died in 1894, Colvin and Mrs Sitwell did not marry until 1903, when he was fifty-eight and she was sixty-four. Apparently Colvin, because of financial problems, did not feel able to support a wife as well as his mother and delayed his marriage until his mother's death. The clue to these financial troubles is to be found on pp. 135 and 405.

Stevenson was somewhat in awe of this austere and rather reserved man, but for the rest of his life he regarded Colvin as his literary mentor and closest friend. Colvin's own loyalty and unselfish devotion both to Stevenson himself and later to his memory never faltered.

In a fragment of autobiography dictated to his stepdaughter at Vailima (probably in 1892), Stevenson wrote:

> It is very hard for me, even if I were merely addressing the unborn, to say what I owe to and what I think of this most trusty and noble-minded man. If I am what I am and where I am, if I have done anything at all or done anything well, his is the credit. It was he who paved my way in letters; it was he who set before me, and still, as I write, keeps before me, a difficult standard of achievement; and it was to him and to Fleeming Jenkin that I owed my safety at the most difficult periods of my life.[3]

To his Mother

Tuesday 28 [actually 29] July 1873

Cockfield Rectory,
Sudbury, Suffolk

My dear Mother, I am too happy to be much of a correspondent. Mrs Sitwell is most delightful; so is the small boy; so is the Professor; so is the weather; and the place.

On Sunday, we had two diets, two sermons from the Professor which would have been counted in Scotland as poor, but quite orthodox. Yesterday we were away to Melford and Lavenham; both exceptionally placid, beautiful old English towns; Melford scattered all round a big green, with an Elizabethan Hall and Park, great screens of trees that seem twice as high as trees should seem, and everything else like what ought to be in a novel, and what one never expects to see in reality, made me cry out how good we were to live in Scotland, for the manyhundredth time. I cannot get over my astonishment – indeed it increases every day, at the hopeless gulph that there is between England and Scotland, and English and Scotch. Nothing is the same; and I feel as strange and outlandish here, as I do in France or Germany. Everything by the wayside, in the houses,

---

[3] The years immediately after Stevenson's death were occupied by Colvin in the completion of the Edinburgh Edition of Stevenson's Works, seeing through the press works left uncompleted such as *Weir of Hermiston* and *St Ives*, and in editing the letters; all this in addition to his official duties at the British Museum and in spite of poor health. After acrimonious rows with Fanny and Lloyd (Fanny's son from her first marriage) over the delay Colvin abandoned his cherished plan of writing the official biography. In 1921 he published *Memories and Notes*, a volume of reminiscences which contains a chapter on RLS.

or about the people, strikes me with an unexpected unfamiliarity; I walk among surprises, for just where you think you have them, something wrong turns up.[1]

I got a little Law read yesterday and some German this morning, but on the whole, there are too many amusements going for much work; as for correspondence I have neither heart nor time for it today. I enclose a *pièce justificative*, which was deposited in my room yesterday.   R.L.S.

To Frances Sitwell

Monday 1 September [1873][1]   *17 Heriot Row*

I have arrived, as you see, without accident; but I never had a more wretched journey in my life. We were packed very tightly all the way and I was haunted by a face that I saw looking out of a window in London and that made me very sad. I could not settle to read anything; I bought Darwin's last book[2] in despair, for I knew I could generally read Darwin, but it was a failure. However, the book served me in good stead, for when a couple of children got in at Newcastle, I struck up a great friendship with them, on the strength of the illustrations. These two children (a girl of nine and a boy of six) had never before travelled in a railway; so that everything was a glory to them and they were never tired of watching the telegraph posts and trees and hedges go racing past us to the tail of the train; and the girl I found quite entered into the most daring personifications that I could make. A little way on, about Alnmouth, they had their first sight of the sea; and it was wonderful how loath they were to believe that what they saw was water: indeed it was very still, and grey and solid-looking under a sky to match. It was worth the fare, yet a little farther on, to see the delight of the girl when she passed into 'another country', with the black Tweed under our feet crossed by the lamps of the passenger bridge; I remembered the first time I had gone into 'another country', over the same river from the other side.

Bob was not at the station when I arrived; but a friend of his brought me a letter and he is to be in the first thing tomorrow. I am very tired, dear, and somewhat depressed after all that has happened. Do you know, I think yesterday and the day before were the two happiest days of my life. It seems strange that I should prefer them to what has gone before; and yet

---

[1] RLS developed these ideas further in his essay 'The Foreigner at Home': 'A week or two in such a place as Suffolk leaves the Scotchman gasping.'
[1] RLS spent a few days in London before returning home. He stayed with Colvin at his cottage in Norwood in South London, and apparently with the Sitwells.
[2] *The Expression of the Emotions in Man and Animals* (1872).

after all, perhaps not. O God, I feel very hollow and strange just now. I had to go out to get supper and the streets were wonderfully cool and dark, with all sorts of curious illuminations at odd corners from the lamps; and I could not help fancying as I went along all sorts of foolish things – *chansons* – about showing all these places to you, Claire,[3] some other night; which is not to be. Dear, I would not have missed last month for eternity.

I trust you were well all today and that le chapelain[4] did not trouble you. Give all sorts of good messages to the sole-lessee (B. Sitwell) and say what is necessary, if you like, or if you think anything necessary, to the Curate of Cumberworth and the Vicar of Roost.[5] Good-bye, my dear. Ever yours   R.L.S.

It is very hard to stop talking to you tonight; for I can't do anything else. Sleep well; and be strong. I *will* try to be worthy of you and of *him*.[6]

To Frances Sitwell

Tuesday 9 September 1873   [*17 Heriot Row*]
11.40 P.M.

I was sitting up here, working away at John Knox, when the door opened and Bob came in. At first I thought he was drunk; he came in with his hands over his face and sank down on a chair and began to sob. He was scarcely able to speak at first, but he found voice at last and I then found that he had come to see me, had met my father in the way and had just brought to an end an interview with him. There is now, at least, one person in the world who knows what I have had to face – damn me for facing it, as I sometimes think, in weak moments – and what a tempest of emotions my father can raise when he is really excited. It seems that this poor cousin of mine has hated Bob and me all through his life, that our words have been a sharp poison to him, and our opinions horrible, and our presence an intolerable burthen: he always met us as friends; he was too weak it seemed to show what he disliked and what shocked him, and he led us on, unconsciously I daresay, to play with him cards-down, and

---

[3] In the 1920s G.S. Hellman and J.A. Steuart built up an elaborate story of a love affair of great importance between RLS and an Edinburgh prostitute (a blacksmith's daughter in some versions) called 'Claire'. This reference helped J.C. Furnas in *Voyage to Windward* to demolish the foolish story and to show that 'Claire' was in fact an 'emotion-charged pseudonym' for Mrs Sitwell.

[4] Her husband, the Revd Albert Hurt Sitwell, Vicar of Minster, was also honorary chaplain to the Archbishop of Canterbury.

[5] The titles of two moral tales by the Revd Francis Edward Paget published anonymously in 1859. The first story concerns a self-opinionated clergyman and the second, a worldly vicar.

[6] I.e. Colvin.

keep nothing secret.[1] A little before death, he relieved his feelings to my
father; Bob, he said, was a 'blight', a 'mildew'; it was matter of wonder to
him 'how God should have made such a man'; I was the one depraved
and hideous one who could endure Bob's presence; *und so weiter, in
infinitum*. My father's interview with Bob has been long coming; and has
now come. I am so tired at heart and tired in body that I can only tell you
the result tonight. They shook hands; my father said that he wished him
all happiness, but prayed him as the one favour that could be done him,
that he should never see him between the eyes again. And so parted my
father and my friend. Tomorrow I shall give more details.

Wednesday

The war began with my father accusing Bob of having ruined his house
and his son. Bob answered that he didn't know where I had found out
that the Christian religion was not true, but that *he* hadn't told me. And,
I think from that point, the conversation went off into emotion and never
touched shore again. There was not much said about me – my views
according to my father, are a childish imitation of Bob, to cease the
moment the *mildew* is removed; all that was said was that I had ceased to
care for my father, and that my father confessed he was ceasing, or had
greatly ceased, to care for me. Indeed, the object of the interview is not
very easy to make out; it had no practical issue except the ludicrous one
that Bob has promised never to talk to me about Religion any more. It
was awfully rough on him, you know; he had no idea that there was that
sort of thing in the world, although I had told him often enough – my
father on his knees, and that kind of thing. O dear, dear, I just hold on to
your hand very tight, and shut my eyes. I wonder why God made *me*, to
be this curse to my father and mother. If it had not been for the thoughts
of you, I should have been twice as cut up; somehow it all seems to
simplify when I think of you; tell me again that I am not such cold poison
to everybody as I am to some. What my poor cousin said of me, what
dying testimony he left against me and all my works, I shall now never
learn; even if my father attempts to begin, I must stop him. I am going up
on another hunt for a letter from you; if I find one, and you are well and
happy, the sky will be all blue once more.

3 P.M.

No letter. I hope you are well. To continue the story, I have seen Bob
again, and he has had a private letter from my father, apologising for

[1] RLS's cousin Lewis ('Noona') Balfour (1842–73), eldest son of MIS's brother Lewis, had died
in Edinburgh on 6 August 1873.

anything he may have said; but adhering to the substance of the interview. There was more in this letter (which Bob, perhaps by rather a breach of confidence, allowed me at my earnest desire to see) of his wailings over a ruined life and hopes overthrown which are intolerable to think about. Moreover I learn that my mother had hysterics privately last night, over it all. If I had not a very light heart and a great faculty of interest in what is under hand, I really think I should go mad under this wretched state of matters. Even the calm of our daily life is all glossing; there is a sort of tremor through it all and a whole world of repressed bitterness. I do not think of it, because it is one of those inevitable Fates that no thinking can mend. As Luther said *'Ich kann nicht anders – hier stehe ich – Gott helfe mir'*.[2] And yet, my dearest, I did not wish to harm anyone; and don't, and I *would* do what I could, if I could do anything.

Now, don't get bothered about this. It has been as bad before any time this last year, and then I had no one to take the bitterness to. I have just had this cry on your shoulder (so to speak) and I feel better again. Only let need be the excuse for my bothering you with yet another letter. And, at any rate as long as you are away from home I did want to write to you often; for after that I must write very seldom, must I not? Do you think once a fortnight would be too often?

I am afraid this letter is again incoherent a little; but this and yesterday have been rather bad days with me. My dear, how poor all my troubles are after all compared with yours; I am such a scaly alligator and go through things on the whole so toughly and cheerily. I hope you will not misunderstand this letter and think I am *Werthering* all over the place. I am quite happy and never think about these bothers and I am sure if you were to ask my father and mother, they would tell you that I was as unconcerned as any Heathen deity; but 'heartless levity' was always one of my complaints. And a good thing too. 'Werena my heart licht, I wad die.'[3] And now, my darling, I may say just a word about *you* before I end, may I not. I have dreamed about you the last nights often, only I never see you properly. It is worth while to dream of you though, even unhappily, because you come up before me when I waken sometimes very vividly. This is Wednesday the 10th of September; three weeks ago I was not alone in my room here. I take it kind in Nature, having a day of broad sunshine and a great west wind among the garden trees, on this time of all others; the sound of wind and leaves comes in to me through the windows, and if I shut my eyes I might fancy myself some hundred miles away under a certain tree. And that is a consolation, too; these things *have been*.

[2] 'Here stand I. I can do no other. God help me' – Martin Luther's speech before the Diet of Worms, 18 April 1521.
[3] The best-known song by Lady Grizel Baillie (1665–1746).

'Tomorrow, let it shine or rain,
Yet cannot this the past make vain;
Nor uncreate and render void
That which was yesterday enjoyed'[4]

I have the proof of it at my heart, my darling; it never felt so light and so happily stirred in the old days. Just now when the whole world looks to me as if it were lit with gas, and life a sort of metropolitan railway, it is a great thing to have clear memory of sunny places and of love. How my mind rings the changes upon sun and sunny! Farewell, my dearest friend

R.L.S.

To Frances Sitwell[1]

Monday 22 September [1873]   *Edinburgh*

My dear friend, how could you have fancied any slight; or rather, for I know you did not do so, how could you fail to see the true rationale of what took place. Another of my melancholy little periods of wretchedness having come upon me, I began to write to S.C. (as I had to do) with a heart so full of bitterness that it flowed slaveringly over upon my beard; for which I have since suffered intense shame.[2] I have just had another disagreeable tonight. It is difficult indeed to steer steady among the breakers; I am always touching ground; generally it is my own blame, for I cannot help getting friendly with my father (whom I *do* like) and so speaking foolishly with my mouth. I have yet to learn in ordinary conversation that reserve, and silence that I must try to unlearn in the matter of the feelings. We have both (as you say) a main unpleasant road to travel and we must hold hands firmly and mutually keep up our hearts.

I am more vexed than I can say at having broken out to S.C.; but he has taken it very kindly. One may fall in the mire in the company of gentlemen without much uproarious laughter, thank God. But that is a side to my self – an imbecile, decrepid side – that I hate to think about; and every new illustration of it costs me much pain.

---

[4] Sir Richard Fanshawe's translation of Horace, *Odes*, III.xxix.43f. in his *Selected Parts of Horace*, 1652.
[1] This letter was begun on the same day that RLS finished a long letter to Mrs Sitwell (begun a week earlier) about his rows with his father over religion: 'It was really pathetic to hear my father praying pointedly for me today at family worship, and to think that the poor man's supplications were addressed to nothing better able to hear and answer than the chandelier.'
[2] RLS had begun his letter to Colvin on 16 September: 'I have just been having a long talk with my father; and you may cry to the deaf sea or the devil or anything, and hope as soon for something respondent. Always the gulf over which no man can go, always a great hell between people.'

Colvin has taken the trouble to write me six sides of advice about my little paper. I do not know how I shall find words to thank him. In fact I cannot, even to you, say how much obliged I am. The news that 'Roads' would do reached me in good season; I had begun utterly to despair of doing anything.[3] Certainly I do not think I should be in a hurry to commit myself about the Covenanters; the whole subject turns round about me and so branches out to this side and that that I grow bewildered; and one cannot write discreetly about any one little corner of an historical period, until one has an organic view of the whole. I have however, given life and health, great hope of my Covenanters; indeed there is a lot of precious dust to be beaten out of that stack even by a very infirm hand.

What a fool I was to write to Bertie about the book – it is out of print; and he must just have patience; I shall find ultimately something else as good.

I am just going to buckle to, to remodel 'Roads' according to S.C.'s prescriptions.

Much later

I can scarcely see to write just now; so please excuse. We have had an awful scene. All that my father had to say has been put forth – not that it was anything new; only it is the devil to hear. O dear God, I don't know what to do – the world goes hopelessly round about me – there is no more possibility of doing, living, being anything but a *beast* and there's the end of it.

It is eleven, I think; for a clock struck. O Lord there has been a deal of time through our hands since I went down to supper. All this has come from my own folly; I somehow could not think the gulph so impassable and I read him some notes on the Duke of Argyll[4] – I thought he would agree so far and that we might have rational discussion on the rest. And now – after some hours – he has told me that he is a weak man and that I am driving him too far, and that I know not what I am doing. O dear God, this is bad work.

I have lit a pipe and feel calmer. I say, my dear friend, I am killing my father – he told me tonight (by the way) that I alienated utterly my mother – and this is the result of my attempt to start fresh and fair and to do my best for all of them.

I am a beast to bother you, with all your troubles, over this; but tonight has been really very bad – worse than ordinary. If I could only cease to

[3] This essay, planned during walks at Cockfield, was ultimately published in the *Portfolio* and was RLS's first paid contribution to a periodical.
[4] An essay, read to the Spec. on 11 February on 'Law and Free Will – Notes on the Duke of Argyll' – an attack on *The Reign of Law* (1866) by the 8th Duke of Argyll (1823–1900).

like him, I could pull through with a good heart; but it is really insupportable to see his emotion – an impotent emotion rather, to make things worse – his sort of half threats of turning me out and O God bless the whole thing.

I have a ringing headache so please excuse this scrawl of nonsense. I should not send it off I know and yet I do wish a little consolation. You don't know what a difference it makes; especially now that Bob is very difficult to get at. I *did* mean to make him nearly happy all this time my mother was away; and see the result! O dear God, I wish I could think *he* was happy. It has been a terrible blow to him. He said tonight, 'He wished he had never married', and I could only echo what he said. 'A poor end,' he said, 'for all my tenderness.' And what was there to answer? 'I have made all my life to suit you – I have worked for you and gone out of my way for you – and the end of it is that I find you in opposition to the Lord Jesus Christ – I find everything gone – I would ten times sooner have seen you lying in your grave than that you should be shaking the faith of other young men and bringing such ruin on other houses, as you have brought already upon this' – that is a sort of abstract of one speech. There is a jolly son for you – there is the staff I have been to his declining years. 'I thought,' he said, 'to have had someone to help me, when I was old.' Much help he has had.

I must wait till tomorrow ere I finish. I am tonight too excited.

Tuesday [23 September]

I shall not read over the foregoing as I know I shall suppress it and I don't want to suppress it. The sun is shining today which is a great matter and altogether the gale having blown off again, I live in a precarious lull. On the whole I am not displeased with last night; I kept my eyes open through it all, and I think, not only avoided saying anything that could make matters worse in the future, but said something that *may* do good. But a little better or a little worse is a trifle. I lay in bed this morning awake, for I was tired and cold and in no special hurry to rise, and heard my father go out for the papers; and then I lay and wished – O if he would only *whistle* when he comes in again! But of course he did not. I have stopped that pipe.

I am going to push on and finish the patching up of 'Roads' according to S.C.'s receipt. I can not amplify as he proposes I should; but I'll do all the suppressing he wants and have it all written over today sometime and ready to send off. I am very glad I have that to busy myself with and be a little hopeful over.

Now please don't think this has been much worse than usual. It is only a second, third, fourth, fifth performance of a piece that can never be stale.

I shall always be a good deal interested when that organ is ground, of course, because my own fingers are in among the works.

Now you see I have written to you this time and sent it off, for both of which God forgive me. Ever your faithful friend   R.L.S.

My father and I together can put about a year through in half an hour. Look here, you mustn't take this too much to heart. I shall be all right in a few hours. It's impossible to depress me. And of course, where you can't do anything, there's no need of being depressed. It's all waste tissue.   L.

To Frances Sitwell

Monday 6 October [1873]   [*17 Heriot Row*]

My dear, it is a magnificent glimmering moonlight night, with a wild, great west wind abroad, flapping above one like an immense banner and every now and again swooping furiously against my windows. The wind is too strong perhaps, and the trees are certainly too leafless for much of that wide rustle that we both remember; there is only a sharp angry sibilant hiss, like breath drawn with the strength of the elements, through shut teeth, that one hears between the gusts only. I am in excellent humour with myself for I have worked hard and not altogether fruitlessly; and I wished before I turned in just to tell you that things were so. My dear friend, I feel so happy all over when I think that you remember me kindly. Life is doubled for me. I have been up tonight lecturing to a friend on life and duties and what a man could do; a coal off the altar had been laid on my lips,[1] and I talked quite above my average and I hope I spread, what you would wish to see spread, into one person's heart; and with a new light upon it.

I shall tell you a story. Last Friday, I went down to Portobello, in the heavy rain, with an uneasy wind blowing *par rafales* off the sea (or '*en rafales*' should it be? or what?). As I got down near the beach a poor woman, oldish and seemingly lately, at least, respectable, followed me and made signs. She was drenched to the skin, and looked wretched below wretchedness. You know I did not like to look back at her; it seemed as if she might misunderstand and be terribly hurt and slighted; so I stood at the end of the street – there was no one else within sight in the wet – and lifted up my hand very high with some money in it. I heard her steps draw heavily near behind me and, when she was near enough to see, I let the money fall in the mud and went off at my best walk without ever turning

---

[1] Cf. Isaiah 6:6–7.

round. There is nothing in the story; and yet you will understand how much there is, if one chose to set it forth. You see, she was so ugly; and you know there is something terribly, miserably pathetic in a certain smile, a certain sodden aspect of invitation on such faces. It is so terrible, that it is in a way sacred; it means the outside of degradation and (what is worst of all in life) false position. I hope you understand me rightly.

Tuesday [*7 October*]

I wish just to salute you, my dearest friend. I have not done so much today, I am sorry to think; somehow work would not come through my hands. I have received a rather interesting letter from the Miss Crosby I called on when I was staying with you; which I purpose sending along with this as it may interest you.

Tonight it has rained fearfully, and thundered. One peal came loud and sharp, like a single stroke upon some immense drum; it would have been a good piece of 'effect' for some scene in a novel. I do trust you are better, my dear. My heart is as full of you as it can be.

By the way, what a nice person Maud is; her letter to you made me think much per cent more of her even than I had thought before. Good Maud!

Dear if I could but put you up before the world – you don't know what I mean, because no woman could; but I know. I want to make you appear to everyone what you are – do you know? I cannot say it, but I feel it.

9.20

I have finished the first draught of 'Walt Whitman'![2] *Gloria in excelsis!*

Wednesday [*8 October*]

My mother took hysterics today at lunch – she had been bothered about some family troubles of which you have heard, and the advertisement of the marriage in today's Scotch papers finally knocked her up[3] – so my father has taken her away with him to Ireland, where he is called

---

[2] An essay on Whitman, later abandoned.

[3] The *Scotsman* of 8 October recorded the marriage at Galle, Ceylon of 'Mackintosh Balfour to Caroline Louisa, daughter of the late Colonel Sissmore, Bengal Army, and widow of the late Lewis Balfour.' These were MIS's brothers. Lewis Balfour (1817–70) was a merchant in Calcutta; Mackintosh Balfour (1825–84) was a bank manager in India. Caroline Sissmore (died 1924) was the second wife of both brothers. Because of this marriage the Stevensons were estranged from Mackintosh and his wife, and were not reconciled until Mackintosh was on his deathbed. Marriage to a deceased brother's wife was forbidden by Church and State, and such marriages usually took place abroad.

on business. I am alone in the house, and so I allowed myself, at dinner, the first light reading I have indulged in since my return in the shape of some Montaigne. And I *have* enjoyed it.

My little triumphant flourish of last night was sadly impertinent. I have looked over the said boasted first draught and it is so bad that I very nearly despaired ultimately. If I could only *write* like Colvin! I have lots to say. However I shall persevere. This 'first draught' let me mention means only the first stringing together of laborious fragments.

I have been all day in the house for I smashed my little toe against the leg of a table while I was *en costume de bain* this morning, and am as lame as Vulcan in consequence.

Do you know, I have been thinking a little of my wretchedness when your letters did not come; and the whole business is knocked most unpleasantly at my conscience. I too left letters unanswered until they ceased to come, from a person to whom the postage even must have been a matter of parsimony; left them unanswered, on purpose that they might cease. O God! a thing comes back to me that hurts the heart very much. For the first letter, she had bought a piece of paper with a sort of coarse flower-arabesque at the top of it. I wish you would write cruelly about this – I wish you would by God! I want something to make me take up arms in my own defence – no I don't. Only I could not help writing this to you because it is in my mind – or my heart; and I hope you won't hate me for it. Only one thing gives me any little pleasure, and it is a very, very faint one. I never showed the letters to anyone, and some months ago they became insupportable to me and I burnt them. Don't I deserve the gallows?

Thursday [9 October]

I found one of these letters that I had somehow missed in destroying them, and it has not helped to put me into a better humour with myself. If I were a remorseful person, I should be very useless and mournful, shut up here in the house alone, with a lame foot and the rain and cold. However I am not so; only by God, this is not to happen again. On that I think my mind is made up very resolvedly.

Last night, a friend dropped in about supper time and strangely enough he was in much the same humour as myself and full of regrets for past hard-heartedness, utter, stark inhumanity of the cheerful butterfly order, surely the most abhorrent thing in this shameful world. If there is a 'moral governor of the universe', he must feel heartily ashamed of having ever made me. My friend and I sat up till twelve and mutually confessed each other and strengthened our sense of shame I think much. Montaigne has been a tremendous comfort to me since my people have left; he is the most charming of table-companions. I have not yet heard from you that you are better; but I intend to believe that you are ever improving until I hear the contrary. There is no word of 'Roads'; I suspect the *S.R.* must have looked darkly upon it, in spite of all S.C.'s kind revision and correction.[4] Amen – so be it; we must just try to do something better. 'Walt Whitman' in the meantime is in a pitiable bad way. The style sticks in my throat like badly made toffy.

I hope the V.[5] does not bother you now you are ill. Believe me, my dear friend (and this comes, considering my present mood, from a very unimpeachable witness) you *must* be hard-hearted and firm and, at all prices, take your health out of the shadow of that incubus.

My own health, *à propos*, is I think almost re-established.

I have got your letter, and I do not care now about anything; I am all as full of happiness as I can hold – I feel a perfect ocean of it in my breast, sunlit and living. You know that isn't nonsense, although it looks like it. I have not got my breathing quiet yet, after reading it and so you must excuse what is written. Don't be afraid for me, what I say above is true. I think I am *quite* well again; though of course I am still a little played out.

I shall take your advice about my work, although one feels they can do so little for an exam. in this short time. I have been working about three hours a day for it. I shall try now to work more.

I am sorry to hear S.C. is not so well. I shall write to him soon.

After Dinner

You cannot think how pleasant it is for me to live alone here. I have learned the lost art of solitary life – that of not gulping one's meals and feel myself far on in the apprenticeship for a Hermitage.

A little while ago there was a very distant organ in the streets and, as organs are things rather more rare in Edinburgh than they are with you, the sound of an organ about dinner time when the evening has fallen, carries a great many reminiscences into the market-place of my memory from all sorts of odd corners where they had long lain hid. I sat a long while and brooded on dead and disaffected relatives, and my own childhood; and a whole decameron of little stories came back upon me. It would be impossible to bring before you, what went before me; you would not understand the little symbols that pass current in my memory, any more than I could understand the similar currency in yours. Broadly, however, you can understand that I lived a long while very far back, before people whom I really loved were estranged from me, and a long while before I came suddenly, in my thoughtless journey, upon a corner

---

[4] On 18 October RLS learned that the *Saturday Review* had indeed rejected 'Roads'.
[5] The Vicar, i.e. Albert Sitwell.

and, turning it, saw the sun. – There are little local sentiments, little abstruse connexions among things, that no one can ever impart. There is a pervading impression left of life in every place in one's memory, that one can best parallel out of things physical, by calling it a *perfume*. Well, this perfume of Edinburgh, of my early life there, and thoughts, and friends – went tonight suddenly to my head, at the mere roll of an organ three streets away. And it went off newly, to leave in my heart the strange impression of two pages of a letter I had received this afternoon, which had about them a colour, a perfume, a long thrill of sensation – which brought a rush of sunsets, and moonlight, and primroses, and a little fresh sentiment of springtime into my heart, that I shall not readily forget. It is by writing such letters to harassed people that one harmonises the universe in their ears; recalling beautiful things, and a beautiful spirit; lovely things, and love.

What I hear out of the utterances of a certain V. is not to me unfamiliar. The saying has been said to me so often, in all enthusiastic earnestness, that it has lost much of its significance for me. However, it is always respectable here; there, it should be repressed with stern contempt. There will be plenty of trouble there in the future; but the 'sweet, passionate, old idea' will triumph: I believe in the good cause; the good cause fought for by worthy Christ and (in some ways) unworthy Voltaire, and so many others. It shall not die; thrown even on the wayside it shall flourish and fructify.

Friday [10 October]

Last night, the fire was let out in my room, so I went down to Portobello, missed the last train and had to walk home, lame foot and all, between twelve and one. A violent west wind blew against me; the whole sky was lit up with the diffused glimmer of the moon, although the moon herself was invisible: the wide wet road returned this light after a fashion ghostly enough. About half-way, I found a man serenading a house by the roadside with a cornet – something almost incredible. He was sent away shortly, I suppose, for he was behind me all the rest of the way up to town and little snatches of music followed me at every lull in the wind. There was something uncanny about the whole walk; I was glad enough when I came near the outskirts and saw the double line of lamps come running out of the town to meet me, as it were servants with flambeaux. In the streets too there was this unpleasant pallid glimmer; it had a sort of resemblance to dawn – a still-born dawn – a dawn with something wrong with it.

I do feel inclined to suppress some sheets of this letter, but I won't. I don't want you to be the friend of any imaginary character, but the friend of R.L.S. So you had better know him for the brute he is.

Sunday [*12 October*]

I have destroyed some of this letter; but I want to preserve out of it, a quotation: −

> *Les yeux par la lune pâlis*
> *Me semblent pleins de violettes.*

To which, I had added: *Bien Sonnent.*

I expect to come to town about the twenty-fifth. The Exam is on the thirtieth, and I require to have made certain preliminary arrangements before the 28th. I shall be plucked, I am sure.[6]

This is the day that is of all days most lovely in Edinburgh. It is raining pitilessly. There is no sound but the fire talking to itself, and the dull patter of the rain; and I have the sense of isolation, of intervals of space, very strongly upon me; this little room is an ark upon the illimitable deluge, or a star in the empty heavens; you know what I mean, don't you? These times make one feel a great hunger and yearning, and I know not what wonderful rehabilitation of the past. Large tracts of one's memory seem lit up with a sudden burst of sunshine. I have been living in Cockfield garden all morning; coming and going in the shrubberies; and leaning a long while over the gate. Every place is sacred; reminiscences gather about my feet like bramble-sprays: I feel if I were there, really, I should not know where to go first.

And this person of fine sentiments is the hero of what has been referred to already; I can't write any more when I think of that; everything sounds like a mockery. And yet, it *is* I: and that wasn't: be not afraid. I had not opened my eyes; but I have opened them now, and I see with blinding clearness. I hope you won't feel hatred for me; and yet I think you ought. I don't know if I can reconcile you again with yourself, if you do not hate me; I think I was a madman for telling you.

Do you see the strange way in which I regard anything I have written, as having reached you already? What I have written, I have written. I have an odd sort of reverence for it; and it requires very strong motives of prudence to make me lay sacrilegious hand (as I have done today already) upon any word.

3 P.M.

I have done my quantum of History; and have just stopped to make my first addition to Claire. I have added some few sentences out of this letter, making the meaning clearer of course and trying to better the loose

---

[6] RLS was planning to take the preliminary exam for one of the Inns of Court with a view to being called to the English Bar.

expression one uses in *really* writing letters to dear friends[7] – those sentences about the organ recalling the 'perfume' of my past life here, and how the thought of your letter came in upon me so strongly.

I have determined to wait till I come to town and let Bert choose for himself.

What a curious impersonal thing writing a letter is. I don't know that it is so egotistical, after all, to be egotistical as I am, when I write to you. It really seems now to be quite the reverse: I say things about myself, out of a desire that you should hear them. As Montaigne says, talking of something quite different: '*Pour se laisser tomber à plomb, et de si haut, il faut que ce soit entre les bras d'une affection solide, vigoureuse et fortunée.*'[8] It argues a whole faith in the sympathy at the other end of the wire; and an awful want to say these things.

Monday [*13 October*]

I must tell you the bad news I heard last night. Our doctor thinks my father very far from well. You may imagine what this news is to me; and I cannot say it. I am very much better; quite well in health, only below *par* a little. Plainly, 'Roads' is refused, which is a sell: however I am going ultimately, when I am done with my Exam, to make something good out of 'Walt Whitman': I am not depressed about that.

Keep well, my dearest friend. That is the great thing after all. Let me think of you, as you said yourself, still ready to grasp at every corner of happiness, still your own beautiful self. And do not be sad about me: it is enough to know that you still live and have not forgotten me. Ever your faithful friend   R.L.S.

[7] RLS had written to Mrs Sitwell on 26 September: 'Of course, I have not been going on with Claire: I have been out of heart for that; and besides it is difficult to act before the reality. Footlights will not do with the sun; the stage moon and the real, lucid moon of one's dark life, look strangely on each other.' RLS, as these passages show, was trying to work extracts from his letters to Mrs Sitwell into a novel, presumably an epistolary one in the same form as *The Edifying Letters of the Rutherford Family* (posthumously published, 1982), a thinly fictionalised account of events in his own life at this time.

[8] Montaigne, 'De la Physionomie': 'To let oneself fall plump down, and from so great a height, it ought to be in the arms of a solid, vigorous, and fortunate friendship' – Charles Cotton's translation, revised by W.C. Hazlitt.

III. ORDERED SOUTH: MENTONE
October 1873–April 1874

Stevenson came to London on 25 October to take the preliminary law examination in order to enter one of the Inns of Court. Colvin and Mrs Sitwell were worried by his ill-health and in particular by the nervous exhaustion largely brought about by the bitter disagreements with his father. At their prompting he saw Dr Andrew Clark[1] who forbade him to take the examination or to return home. The next day, in a written opinion, Clark recommended that to hasten his recovery he should go to the South of France. As soon as they heard the news RLS's parents hurried down to London to consult Clark themselves. They saw him on 4 November. He was quite firm that RLS should go to the South of France, and equally firm that his mother should not accompany him. RLS wrote triumphantly to Mrs Sitwell: 'Clark is a trump. He said I must go abroad and that I was better alone – "Mothers", he said, "just put fancies into people's heads and make them fancy themselves worse than they are." My mother (with some justice) denied this soft impeachment. However they are evidently bent on my return in six weeks at longest; I hope they may find resignation for methinks I shall manage to disappoint them.'

By 6 November RLS was in Paris and travelling south via Sens, Lyons, Orange and Avignon, he reached Mentone on the 12th. His essay 'Ordered South' (published in *Macmillan's Magazine*, May 1874) describes his feelings at this time. It is (as Colvin points out) 'the only one of his writings in which he took the invalid point of view or allowed his health troubles in any degree to colour his work'.

Mentone had become part of France as recently as 1860. Like many of his contemporaries, RLS usually spelled it in the Italian manner as Mentone but sometimes he used the more correct French spelling of Menton. I have followed Colvin in standardizing the spelling as Mentone.

To Frances Sitwell

[*10 November 1873*]   *Avignon*

I have just read your letter up on the top of the hill beside the church and castle. The whole air was filled with sunset and the sound of bells; and

---

[1] Andrew Clark (1826–93) was a fashionable London physician who specialised in the treatment of lung diseases; President of the Royal College of Physicians 1888; created a baronet 1883.

I wish I could give you the least notion of the *southernness* and *Provençality* of all that I saw. I thought (as I had often thought before though I do not know that I ever put it into words) that I should like to read nothing but letters from you. So you *had* it out with my father; I thought you must have played some strong card; he seemed to think so much more of you than he had done before he left and in the cab (he drove with me to the station) he was continually bringing round the conversation upon you.

I cannot write while I am travelling; *c'est un défaut*; but so it is; I must have a certain feeling of being at home and my head must have time to settle. The new images oppress me, and I have a fever of restlessness on me. You must not be disappointed at such shabby letters; and besides, remember my poor head and the fanciful crawling in the spine.

Your letter has done me so much good. It was just like getting a long breath again. – So it is all true.

I am so glad the lectures are going on all right.[1]

I don't know the day of the month; nor (what is my climax of happiness) the day of the week. I knew the day of the month yesterday or this morning; the other has been gone a good while.

It is wonderful how seldom I consciously think of you; only whenever I try to express anything to myself, it is a letter to you; and whenever I make to myself any scheme for the future, it is always subject to you; and in fact, though it rarely boils over, my mind is in a constant quiet simmer of you and all your belongings.

I am back again in the stage of thinking there is nothing the matter with me, which is a good sign; but I am wretchedly nervous. Anything like rudeness, I am simply babyishly afraid of; and noises, and especially the sounds of certain voices, are the devil to me. A blind poet who I found selling his immortal works in the streets of Sens, captivated me with the remarkable, equable strength and sweetness of his voice; and I listened a long while and bought some of the poems; and now this voice, after I had thus got it thoroughly into my head, proved false metal and a really bad and horrible voice at bottom. It haunted me some time; but I think I am done with it now.

I hope you don't dislike reading bad style like this, as much as I do writing it; it hurts me when neither words nor clauses fall into their places, much as it would hurt you to sing when you had a bad cold and your voice deceived you and missed every other note. I do feel so inclined to break the pen and write no more; and here *à propos* begins my back.

---

[1] Colvin was giving the Slade lectures at Cambridge during November and December.

After dinner

It blows tonight from the north down the valley of the Rhone and
everything is so cold that I have been obliged to indulge in a fire. There
is a fine crackle and roar of burning wood in the chimney which is very
homely and companionable, though it does seem to postulate a town all
white with snow outside.

I have bought Sainte-Beuve's *Chateaubriand* and am immensely delighted with the critic.[2] What a miraculous ideal of literary demerit
Chateaubriand is. Of course, he is clever to the last degree; but he is such
a — liar, that I cannot away with him. He is more antipathetic to me than
anyone else in the world.

I begin to wish myself arrived tonight. Travelling, when one is not
quite well, has a good deal of unpleasantness. One is easily upset by cross
incidents, and wants that *belle-humeur* and spirit of adventure that make a
pleasure out of what is unpleasant.

What a character you have given me. I should have liked to have heard
the interview [with] my poor father; he was in the hands of one that was
too strong for him!

Tuesday 11 November

There! There's a date for you. I shall be in Mentone for my birthday
with plenty of nice letters to read. I went away across the Rhone and up
the hill on the other side that I might see the town from a distance.
Avignon followed me with its bells and drums and bugles; for the old city
has no equal for multitude of such noises. Crossing the bridge and seeing
the brown turbid water foam and eddy about the piers, one could scarce
believe one's eyes when one looked down the stream and saw the smooth
blue mirroring tree and hill. Over on the other side, the sun beat down
so furiously on the white road that I was glad to keep in the shadow and,
when the occasion offered, to turn aside among the olive yards. It was
nine years and six months since I had been in an olive yard; I found myself
much changed, not so gay, but wiser and more happy. I read your letter
a fourth time and sat a while looking down over the tawny plain and at
the fantastic outline of the city. The hills seemed just fainting into the sky;
even the great peak above Carpentras (Lord knows how many mètres
above the sea) seemed unsubstantial and thin in the breadth and potency
of the sunshine.

I should like to stay longer here; but I can't. I am driven forward by
restlessness, and leave this afternoon – about two. I am just going out now
to visit again the church, castle and hill, for the sake of the magnificent

---

[2] *Chateaubriand et son Groupe Littéraire Sous l'Empire* (1861).

panorama, and besides because it is the friendliest spot in all Avignon to me.

Marseilles

You cannot picture to yourself anything more steeped in hard bright sunshine than the view from the hill. The immovable inky shadow of the old bridge on the fleeting surface of the yellow river seemed more solid than the bridge itself. Just in the place where I sat yesterday evening, a shaven man in a velvet cap was studying music – evidently one of the singers for *La Muette de Portici*[3] at the Theatre tonight. I turned back as I went away; the white Christ stood out in strong relief on his brown cross against the blue sky, and the four kneeling angels and four lanterns grouped themselves about the foot with a symmetry that was almost laughable; the musician read on at his music and counted time with his hand on the stone step.

12 November   *Mentone*

One letter only! S.C. is the only person worth anything; and even he is not worth much, seeing he writes as if he might not come. If there is not one from you tomorrow, I shall swear horribly which, considering the holy occasion, would be very wrong.

My first enthusiasm was on rising at Orange and throwing open the shutters. Such a great living flood of sunshine poured in upon me, that I confess to having danced and expressed my satisfaction aloud; in the middle of which the boots came to the door with hot water, to my great confusion.

Today has been one long delight, coming to a magnificent climax on my arrival here. I gave up my baggage to an hotel porter and set off to walk at once; I was somewhat confused as yet as to my directions, for the station of course was new to me and the hills had not sufficiently opened out to let me recognise the peaks. Suddenly, as I was going forward slowly in this confusion of mind, I was met by a great volley of odours out of the lemon and orange gardens, and the past linked on to the present and, in a moment, in the twinkling of an eye, the whole scene fell before me into order and I was at home. I nearly danced again.

I suppose I must send off this tonight to notify my arrival in safety and good humour and I think good health, before relapsing into the old weekly vein. I hope this time to send you a weekly dose of sunshine from the south, instead of the jet of *snell* Edinburgh east wind that used to was.

---

[3] Daniel Auber's opera (1829).

By 'holy occasion' I mean my birthday – the festival of St R.L.
Stevenson – and not the Lord's day, which – the Lord be praised – I got
over without knowing.

I am very curious to hear about you and the Vicar. By the way, I have
been exercised in mind about Bert. Keep him out of the way of little
French boys. One little French boy – and not a bad little French boy –
may do him a lot of harm; he is much safer with little English boys. Good-
bye. Ever your faithful friend   R.L.S.

To his Mother

[15 November 1873]   [Mentone]

I just jot down a word or two as the beginning of a note I shall try to
finish for you tomorrow.

I have received from Colvin a card to certain Andrews's[1] who live in
the Villa d'Adhémar and so are quite close. The Dewars[2] also are quite
close; and I met Mrs Dewar and the boy today and was asked very kindly
to call. There's a very nice man here called Dowson, with a pretty wife
and son;[3] he talks literature heavily with me. I am afraid although not
much inclined that I shall have to look out for society a little; for I cannot
read much and so sometimes lack for occupation. Little Barber[4] is here;
Dowson told him I was here and he recollected me and said he would
look me up. I have not yet found courage enough to go into Nice; but
must do so shortly I suppose and unbosom myself to Bennett.[5] Many
thanks for your letters; and the pamphlets. Tell my father I was very thick
with some commercial travellers at Orange; and that one of them, comparing France with England said I should never get so much cheated in

---

[1] James Bruyn Andrews (1842–1909), American lawyer who gave up his practice in New York
in 1871 because of ill-health and spent the rest of his life in Europe, mainly in Mentone. A
student of ethnology, archaeology and folklore, he published many articles on these subjects and
compiled a grammar and dictionary of the Mentonese dialect. He married (1869) Fanny,
daughter of the American financier Cyrus W. Field; she died 1905.

[2] At their London hotel the Stevensons had met Lt-Col. Alexander Cumming Dewar (1803–80)
of Vogrie, Midlothian and his wife. They were taking their son James Cumming Dewar (1857–
1908) out to Mentone because of his ill-health. RLS was to meet the son again in the Marquesas
in 1888, when Dewar's yacht *Nyanza* was on its round-the-world voyage.

[3] Alfred C. Dowson (died 1894), London businessman, his wife Annie and their son Ernest
(1867–1900) who became the poet of the Nineties. Alfred Dowson spent much time in the
South of France and translated *Bordighera and the Western Riviera* (1883), by Frederick Fitzroy
Hamilton.

[4] The Revd William Barber (died 1878), Vicar of Teynham, Sittingbourne 1872–8 and Chaplain
of the English Church, West Bay, Mentone.

[5] John Hughes Bennett (1812–75), an Edinburgh physician and physiologist who spent his winters
at Nice; Professor of Institutes of Medicine, Edinburgh University 1848–74.

France. I demurred. 'Well,' he said, 'just look at this – you never get cheated by a cabman in France, or overcharged at a Railway Station, as you do in England.' Perhaps after this remarkable inversion of his favourite statement, he will begin to prepare to commence to believe that no man can judge a foreign nation.

Next day [16 November]

Today it is cloudy a little and cold so I have had to light my fire and resign myself to the house for the afternoon. I forgot to thank you for Hill Burton yesterday;[6] *bien obligé.*

There are hereby, on the gate pillars of a villa, two inimitable plaster lions which are evidently the work of a humorist of the first water. One of them lies with his jowl on his spread paws, his eyes sleepily half-opened, a greasy smile on his wide mouth and bathed (so to speak) all over in an atmosphere of brutal repletion; the other, stretching his neck upward uneasily and showing his big teeth in the act of dolorous snarling, has plainly carried his dinner just a degree farther and is now undergoing the pains and penalties of speedy indigestion. I am sure my father would be delighted with this pair (*hac in re scilicet una gemelli*)[7] of jolly gormandisers.

Dowson has lent me Clough, which I like a good deal, and I am reading Miss Edgeworth's *Popular Tales for the Young*[8] with thorough gusto. They are often clumsy and transparent; but it is fine milk diet for the mind.

A Catholic (Mrs Devinish Walsh) lady, who goes in for being a swell and whose talk runs much on Princesses and Barons, Lords and Ladies and people of high degree, has told me of a book which will interest you (*Mrs Gerald's Niece* by Lady G. Fullerton).[9] It is about Roman Catholic controversies; but the scene is laid in Mentone and I hear that the descriptions are really charming; you had better see for yourself. Mrs Walsh is a good-natured person. She sits at the head of the table; then, Mr and Mrs Dowson (and at lunch, their little son); then (at dinner only) a certain Mr and Miss Moon, who do not much interest me. He, poor fellow, is evidently very ill however; quite the feeble one of the party; all the rest of us indeed look most happily robust. Dowson and I expressed mutual incredulity in each other's bad health; and Mrs Walsh is a jolly, fat, healthy, active, hustling woman of forty-five maybe, who looks as if she

---

[6] RLS's copy of John Hill Burton's *History of Scotland, from the Revolution to the Extinction of the Last Jacobite Insurrection* (2 vols, 1853) is at Yale.

[7] In this one point alike. Cf. '. . . *hac in re scilicet una multam dissimiles*' (quite different), Horace, *Epistles*, I.x.2.

[8] Maria Edgeworth's *Moral Tales for Young People* (1801) or her *Popular Tales* (1804).

[9] Lady Georgiana Charlotte Fullerton (1812–85) novelist, philanthropist and Roman Catholic convert. *Mrs Gerald's Niece* appeared in 1869.

had never been ill in her life. (Happy Thought Mrs Devilish Walsh) – a
person with a cold in his head, you see![10]

Next day [17 November]

I was down at the Dowsons' room last night, smoking a pipe. Dowson
is really a very pleasant man. This morning there is a nasty cold air about;
so I went up the Gorbio a good way, thinking a good deal of poor Jessie[11]
as you may imagine; and when I came down again presented my card at
the Villa d'Adhémar. Andrews seems very pleasant and we had a fierce
forenoon of it over meteorology. He has Bookan[12] (as he calls him) and a
vol. of the Magazine with him; and he remembered my name from some
of my father's papers in the latter.[13] I think tomorrow I must go to Nice;
but I shall not go until the wind is warmer. I got a little cold but it is gone
again; I do not wish another. I send home one of the letters you
forwarded to me (of course I knew that there were stages in depravity –
the moral horror that you allude to is, I quite feel, a lower stage than any
guilt in which you have hitherto imbrued your hands) as I think somebody might pay for me and intimate that I retire with the greatest relief
and thankfulness from the said Edinburgh University Boat Club. Will you
kindly ask the person who told you that about Simpson to close their
mouths in which case they will probably catch no flies. I wish you would
take any opportunity you find to contradict a lie that, I know, will be
offensive to him and that cannot fail to be unpleasant for the other
person.[14] Ever your affectionate son   R.L. Stevenson

To Charles Baxter

Private
[15 November 1873]   *Hôtel du Pavillon, Mentone*

My dear Charles, I feel that I ought to write to you; though after all you
never write to me; and yet I [am] not in good enough spirits to be tonight
a very pleasant correspondent. I am only gradually finding out how nearly

---

[10] *Happy Thoughts* (1866), and its sequels were a highly popular series of humorous books by
Francis Cowley Burnand, originally published in *Punch*.

[11] RLS's much-loved cousin Jessie Warden (1831–67), a daughter of TS's sister Jane, was often
with him in his boyhood; she had been with the Stevensons at Mentone in the winter of
1863–4.

[12] Alexander Buchan (1829–1907), meteorologist, Secretary of the Scottish Meteorological Society 1860 (of which TS was a member), Librarian of the Royal Society of Edinburgh. Famous
for his weather-forecasting, particularly for his discovery of Buchan's 'cold spells'.

[13] TS was a frequent contributor to *Nature*.

[14] Apparently a reference to Sir Walter Simpson's irregular marriage. See p. 125, n. 2.

done for I have been; I am awfully weary and nervous; I cannot read or write almost at all and I am not able to walk much; all which put together leaves me a good deal of time in which I have no great pleasure or satisfaction. However you must not suppose me discontented. I am away in my own beautiful Riviera and I am free now from the horrible worry and misery that was playing the devil with me at home. A friend in London[1] I must tell you, had a conversation with my father (this is in the strictest confidence – I am not supposed to know of it myself) and explained to him a little that I was not the extremely cheerful destroyer of home-quiet that he had pictured to himself, and that I really was bothered about this wretched business and I hope some good out of that if I can only pull my health round. I hope you will write to me and write something amusing. I shall write shortly to J.W.F. and Simpson, and you will oblige if you will announce this my intention (should you have an opportunity) in order that I may enjoy some gratitude *avant le coup* if either of them has any gratitude in him.

If you have any cheerfulness in you, write cheerfully; for all my correspondents I am sorry to say, are in a somewhat chilblained humour. Bob writes sadly from Antwerp where he feels lonely as yet[2] and there are other troubles besides my own that make the pack a little heavy just at present; I wish I could get it off my aching shoulders for half an hour. If I were pious I should pray for a night's sleep; for I slept badly yesterday and that plays one out when one is seedy.

I do not know how I am to apologise to you for this Jeremiad, which is not like the usual run of my correspondence with you at all; but the truth is, I am out of heart at this knock-down blow just when I was beginning to get a possibility of good work and a livelihood. It is beastly to have a bad head like this; and to have to pay for half an hour's thinking with a bad night or an hour or two of miserable nervousness. However, we keep our weather eye open, and still hope greatly. I cannot be a heretic to my own favourite gospel of cheerfulness altogether; and I have my jolly hours too, I can promise you, when the sun shines and the lemon gardens perfume everything about them more sweetly than the most delicate 'air oil.

---

[1] Mrs Sitwell.

[2] Bob had gone to Antwerp to continue his art studies. Soon after his arrival he wrote to RLS:

'I have been so accustomed to live entirely with you and see and do everything with, or with reference to you, that the being unable to tell you everything day by day, to hear what you say, and to have you for public audience world and everything that I am now quite stumped. Talking, I find was talking with you. Talking with other people I must have always thought, this I will tell Louis, this I won't, so that it was merely collecting material for my real talk with you. . . . Success means you, life means you, friendship means you, everything means you.

Next night [*16 November*]

I am placidly ignorant of the day of the week, but I think it is the sixteenth of the month. I had a good night, without specially committing myself to the Powers that be, and woke in time to see a magnificent dawn. I am in somewhat cheerier humour than before. Bob gave me the messages about the *Portfolio*. You will like it, I think; Simpson had better go without his number as he will contemn and loathe the article.[3] It is to be signed L.S. Stoneven; which makes not a bad name. O! what about the Spec.! Do for the Lord's sake, clear me of responsibility, and write and tell me how you get on this Session. I do think that the Spec. is about the only good thing in Edinburgh.[4] I should like to be present at a meeting tonight – O awfully. I would open a debate about the game-laws, or defend the Christian religion, or make the coffee outside with Clues,[5] or support the secretary in his tyranny, or do anything mean, sordid, and disreputable for that inestimable favour. Shouldn't I have a nice pipe in the lobby – no, up at the far end of the library sitting on the steps. Tell me how many of you are drunk at Barclay's dinner.[6]

I have just put another billet on the fire and it is most cheerful and companionable and gossips and chirps away to me like an old friend. The sea is quieter tonight; but it always wails among the shingle uneasily. It is a quiet, dark night outside with stars. I wonder strangely what everyone is about tonight – friends in London, Antwerp, Edinburgh; and me alone here up at the top of the house, with my two little windows shining, two little lighted beacons over the peaceful Mediterranean.

Talking of which, old man, take care of yourself, like a good chap, won't you? And believe me, Ever your affectionate friend

R.L. Stevenson

When you get *Leaves of Grass*, you'll send the two books off, won't you?[7]

---

[3] The essay 'Roads' in the November number of the *Portfolio*.

[4] Before he left for Mentone RLS wrote to Baxter, 'The Lord help you in that damned town, whose name even makes me shudder!'

[5] '"Clues" our worthy old soldier servitor' (Guthrie, *Robert Louis Stevenson*, 1920).

[6] Thomas Barclay (1851–1940) President of the Spec. 1873–5, advocate 1874, barrister Inner Temple 1876. Baxter explains that it was the habit to dine together in small parties before the meeting and that Barclay dispensed 'some splendid hospitality'.

[7] RLS had asked Baxter to send him Whitman's *Leaves of Grass* and to redeem *Democratic Vistas* from Wilson, the tobacconist in Leith Street.

To Frances Sitwell

Sunday [*16 November 1873*]   [*Mentone*]

I sat a long while up among the olive yards today, at a favourite corner where one has fair view down the valley and onto the blue floor of the sea; I had a Horace with me and read a little; but Horace, when you try to read him fairly under the open Heaven, sounds urban and you find something of the escaped townsman in his descriptions of the country, just as somebody said that Morris's[1] sea-pieces were all taken from the coast. I tried for long to hit upon some language that might catch ever so faintly the indefinable shifting colour of olive leaves; and above all, the changes and little silverings that pass over them, like blushes over a face, when the wind tosses great branches to and fro; but the Muse was not favourable. A few birds, scattered here and there at wide intervals on either side of the valley, sang the little broken songs of late autumn; and there was a great stir of insect life in the grass at my feet. The path up to this 'coign of vantage'[2] where I think I shall make it a habit to ensconce myself awhile of a morning, is for a little while common to the peasant and a little clear brooklet. It is pleasant, in the tempered gray daylight of the olive shadows, to see the people picking their way among the stones and the water and the brambles; the women especially, with the weights poised on their heads and walking all from the hips with a certain graceful deliberation.[3]

This thin paper utterly baffles and disconcerts me; it is like trying to write upon vapour. O that I had a pen of iron![4] The good prophet was probably in some similar strait.

Monday [*17 November*]

Today there was a coldish wind and I took refuge up a valley. Great bunches of reeds and a good many cypresses give somewhat of an oriental look to this valley. In the path, winding up by something between steps and a paved incline, between old walls tufted with green and discoloured with rain, I met a curious little group coming down. On the back of one of the great Mentonese asses (more like mules) were slung two kegs and between the kegs, sitting royally, upright and well back and with her feet thrust straight before her almost on to the ass's head, a girl. As the whole

[1] Philip Richard Morris (1836–1902) made an early reputation with his sea pictures but later painted religious subjects.
[2] *Macbeth*, I.vi.7.
[3] Cf. 'Ordered South': 'To some . . . their recollection may be most vivid of the stately gait of women carrying burthens on their heads.'
[4] Job 19:24.

pile swayed with every step of the ass there was something very strange about the look of it all.

Tuesday [18 November]

I must write a little to you; and yet I do not know what to write. In this suspense as to how things stand with you everything seems equally impertinent. I have written *des riens* − and very little of them − for two days; but today I must say something more. I have been to Nice today to see Dr Bennett; he agrees with Clark that there is no disease; but I finished up my day with a lamentable exhibition of weakness. I could not remember French, or at least I was afraid to go into any place lest I should not be able to remember it, and so could not tell when the train went. I walked about the streets; in such a rage with every person who came near me, that I felt inclined to break out upon them with all sorts of injurious language; and only didn't, I think, because I knew if I gave way at all, that I should give way altogether, and cry, or have a fit, or something. At last, I crawled up to the Station and sat down on the steps and just steeped myself there in the sunshine, until the evening began to fall and the air to grow chilly. This long rest put me all right; and I came home here triumphantly and ate dinner well. There is the full, true and particular account of the worst day I have had since I left Chepstow Place. I shall not go to Nice again for some time to come.

I have felt lonely sometimes, dear, but generally very happy; and I have been doing all I can not to think about you for some days back or to think of you only in the past. I am so much afraid for your health; I have some experience now of the results of such misery as you must be suffering. You have many friends at least, dear, who will be true to you whatever turns up; and some who think your friendship the greatest boast of their life, and the greatest pleasure. Whatever happens, you will not want for eager sympathy; very eager and warm sympathy, as you know well. The other morning at breakfast, my weak tea had a familiar taste in my mouth; and in a moment, Mentone had passed away and I was breakfasting in C.P. and you were there in the mob cap and the maroon dressing gown. I was very happy.

Ça! There is a little of my say out; and I feel happier.

Wednesday [19 November]

I have been very tired all day; lying outside my bed and crying in that feeble way that you recollect at C.P. Nevertheless your letter was a great comfort to me as it seems to show that some of the gale has gone over. O I do trust all will go well. I am so glad to hear that S.C. will come; so glad and yet so sorry; for you will be very lonely and miserable.

Thursday [20 November]

I am today quite recovered and got into Mentone today for a book which is quite a creditable walk. As an intellectual being I have not yet begun to re-exist; my immortal soul is still very nearly extinct; but we must hope the best. It was good of you to write to me at all, when you were in such distress; please remember in future not to write me a long wearying letter (I mean wearying to the writer, you know) but just drop a courtesy to me and say good morning. How you could have supposed that I was angry, God only knows; I must be even more feeble in the brain that I had thought myself, if I communicated that impression to you in my letter. You must excuse me if my letters are not interesting – I am so stupid. Now do take warning by me. I am set up by a beneficent providence at the corner of the road, to warn you to flee from the *hébétude* that is to follow. Being sent to the South is not much good unless you take your soul with you, you see; and my soul is rarely with me here. I don't see much beauty. I have lost the key; I can only be placid and inert, and see the bright days go past uselessly one after another. Therefore don't talk foolishly with your mouth any more about getting liberty by being ill and going south via the sick-bed. It is not the old free-born bird that gets thus to freedom; but I know not what manacled and hide-bound spirit, incapable of pleasure, the clay of a man. Go south! Why I saw more beauty with my eyes healthfully alert to see in two wet windy February afternoons in Scotland, than I can see in my beautiful olive gardens and grey hills in a whole week in my low and lost estate, as the Shorter Catechism puts it somewhere. It is a pitiable blindness, this blindness of the soul; I hope it may not be long with me. – So remember to keep well; and remember rather any thing than not to keep well; and again I say, *anything* rather than not to keep well.

Not that I am unhappy, mind you; I have found the words already; placid and inert; that is what I am; I sit in the sun and enjoy the tingle all over me, and I am cheerfully ready to concur with anyone who says that this is a beautiful place, and I have a sneaking partiality for the newspapers, which would be all very well, if one had not fallen from Heaven and were not troubled with some reminiscence of the 'ineffable aurore'.[5] I cannot be quite a beast; and I am fit for nothing else. I have such longings after the clear air and the lights of Eden; but the world is all before me where to choose,[6] I suppose, but I will not be content with any lower sphere.

---

[5] Cf. 'O *l'ineffable aurore où volaient les colombes!*' Victor Hugo, *L'Année Terrible* (1872), '*Janvier 1871*', VI line 46. Colvin quoted this passage in his review of the poem in *Macmillan's Magazine*, August 1872 (partly reprinted in *Memories and Notes*).

[6] *Paradise Lost*, XII. 646–7, describing Adam and Eve leaving Eden.

To sit by the sea and to be conscious of nothing but the sound of the waves and the sunshine over all your body, is not unpleasant; but I was an Archangel once.

Friday [21 November]

If you knew how old I felt. I am sure this is what age brings with it, this carelessness, this disenchantment, this continual bodily weariness; I am a man of seventy; O Medea, kill me, or make me young again![7]

Today has been cloudy and mild; and I have lain a great while on a bench outside the garden wall (my usual place now) and looked at the dove-coloured sea and the broken roof of cloud, but there was no seeing in my eye; so once again I have no little flower gathered out of Italian sunshine to put between the leaves for you! Let us hope tomorrow will be more profitable.

Saturday [22 November]

There is my dearest friend a fatality upon me; I did so wish to write to you a letter that would give you some pleasure and I cannot. I have an ignoble cold in my head today, which confines me to the house and shuts the last door upon my hope of amusing you. I can only return to my hopes about you and trust faithfully that the way has become once more plain and sunny before you.

I think a good deal of my future as you may fancy; and one thing I shall change (and one only I think) if I am restored to health and work and pleasure. I shall give my books away as far as I can without loss. That is the one thoroughly selfish taste that I find I have strong within me; a taste irreconcilable with all I hope for the world; and so go it shall. It has always made me recoil with a little shiver of selfishness from what I should otherwise have embraced; and so we must do with it what Christ recommended for right hands and eyes.[8] *Dieu Merci*, there are libraries, and friends are ready to lend. That is the only news I have to give you; what little life I have left, seems to have entered into its closet and shut door and windows, and to live now among colourless moral things.

I do wish a little scrap you know, now and then, to tell me how things go; but do not give yourself any unnecessary fatigue; be very frugal of your strength, cherish the flame with both hands – O God, if it were to go out and leave us in the dark.

I hope my letter will neither weary nor frighten you and that you will remember, now I have written to you in all the deformity of my

[7] Cf. in 'Ordered South' the paragraph describing the state of mind of the invalid doubtful of recovery: 'He will pray for Medea; when she comes, let her either rejuvenate or slay'.

[8] Cf. Matthew 5:29–30.

hypochondriasis and with all the sickly vanities – bed-side flowers after all that amuse and divert the mind – of a person who does not think himself well – remember that I come of a gloomy family, always ready to be frightened about their precious health; and so treat my narrative of today with abatement.

Good-bye, dear friend, do take care of yourself and don't make ship-wreck of your health and cheerfulness and vitality as I have done. Yours (I may say without exaggeration) in the hope of a blessed resurrection; and always your faithful friend   R.L.S.

To Charles Baxter

4 December [1873]   *[Mentone]*

My dear Baxter, At last, I must write. I began a letter to you before, but it broke miserably down and when I looked it over it seemed so con-temptible a fragment that I have put it in the fire. I must say straight out that I am not recovering as I could wish. I am no stronger than I was when I came here and I pay for every walk beyond say a quarter of a mile in length by one, or two, or even three days of more or less prostration. Therefore let nobody be down upon me for not writing. I was very thankful to you for answering my letter; and for the princely action of Simpson, in writing to me – I mean before I had written to him, I was ditto to an almost higher degree; I hope one or other of you will write again soon and, remember, I still live in hope of a reading of Graham Murray's address.[1] I do so much want somebody to be rude to me! The *Leaves of Grass* has not, I suppose, turned up. Damn. Not that it matters really as I could do no work to it, even if it were here. Of course, you must keep my cheerful auguries about my health to yourself or any of trustworthy ear who may be interested therein; but I do somewhat portend that I may not recover at all, or at best that I shall be long about it. My system does seem extraordinarily played out.

Yes, I am as moral as ever; more moral.[2] A man with a smashed-up constitution and 'on a diet' can be moral at the lowest possible figure; and

[1] Andrew Graham Murray (1849–1942), later Viscount Dunedin, had a very distinguished legal career, eventually becoming Lord Justice-General and Lord President of the Court of Session 1905–13. In a letter of 16 November Baxter wrote: 'Graham Murray's opening address was very successful, being not much of a discourse such as we have usually had, but rather a smart satirical attack upon the leading members of the Society, among whom were specially distinguished yourself and your humble friend.'

[2] In the same letter Baxter wrote: 'Are you still suffering from the paroxysm of virtue which characterised your last days here? Write me thereof, and of Mentone: is the sky blue? and does the sun shine?'

then I always was a bit of a Joseph, as you know. My whole game is morality now; and I am very serious about it. Indeed I am very serious about everything, and go to the boghouse with as much solemnity as another man would go to church with. I can't laugh at a mosquito, and I have not made a joke, upon my living soul, since I left London. O! except one, a very small one, that I had made before, and that I timidly repeated in a half-exhilarated state towards the close of dinner, like one of those dead-alive flies that we see pretending to be quite light and full of the frivolity of youth in the first sunshiny days. It was about Mothers' Meetings, and it was damned small, and it was my ewe lamb − the Lord knows I couldn't have made another to save my life −; and a clergyman quarrelled with me and there was as nearly an explosion as could be. This has not fostered my leaning towards pleasantry. I felt that it was a very cold, hard world that night.

My dear Charles, is the sky blue at Mentone? Was that your question? Well, it depends upon what you call blue, it's a question of taste I suppose − it's only about as blue as Hell, that's all, or bluer. Is the sky blue? You poor critter, you never saw blue sky worth being called blue in the same day with it. And I should rather fancy that the sun did shine, I should. And the moon doesn't shine neither. O no! (This last is sarcastic.)

Mentone is one of the most beautiful places in the world and has always had a very warm corner in my heart, since first I knew it eleven years ago. I went back certainly not

11 December

Let us, dearly beloved brethren, start fresh. I got a most charming letter from Simpson today at dinner which has braced up my nerves considerable; and I shall try now to finish mine epistle.

I know here the comicalest of cusses; one in appearance somewhat like an educated goat, with a negro's wig on, called Argyll-Bates, or (in the orthography of the *Courrier de Menton*) Arpel-Batts.[3] Argyll-Bates and I became acquainted while he stayed at this hotel; and both Dowson and I knew he would turn out eccentric. He asked me to go a drive with him to Bordighera; and I expected all sorts of strange manoeuvres; I thought he would bring out a long flute, or fife, in joints, out of different places of concealment about his person (having previously turned up his cuffs so as to convince me that there was no deception, spring or false bottom) and that having put them together, he would pass his fingers through his hair,

---

[3] Samuel Argyll-Bates (born 1827), son of a Leicestershire landowner, matriculated at Magdalen College, Oxford in 1851.

knock his hat in, hastily black his face and hands with a burnt cork and, standing up in the open carriage, begin to play wild music; or, I thought he would play the banjo; or, that he would bring out globes of water with gold fish in 'em. But he didn't. He only brought out a black bottle and drank Marsala from the neck. He herded much with gipsies when he was young; and he sang me gipsy songs. The other evening, I went along to his rooms and he read aloud to me a burlesque of his own composition. (O Lord! how our sins do find us out, how of our pleasant vices are fashioned the scourges wherewithal our buttocks tingle![4] But I never read anybody *a burlesque*.) He plays very well on the piano and that is about the best of him.

So you read an essay to the Spec.? And they didn't know very much more about J.P. after it than they had known before?[5] And that was damned little, you bet? Well, well, there have been other great works coldly looked upon; and verily, I say unto you, you –, you have your reward. I think I see J.P. rubbing his shadowy palms together in Hell and thanking God that he has been understood at last. When I say I think I see him, I don't mean anything very definite, for I shouldn't know him from Job if I were to see him. He didn't wear a collar, if I remember rightly? That was his best holt, wasn't it? It was very good – ha, ha! He didn't wear a collar! O Lord, that's rich! What a humorist! And the exquisite sense of fitness, too, that kept him from overdoing the pleasantry and not wearing trousers either!

– I wish he hadn't worn trousers, though. I could then have capped the jest so well by kicking his bottom.

– I hope I don't hurt your feelings. That *chef-d'oeuvre* about not wearing a collar is all I know about J.P.; but, as I said before, I think that capital.

This is the 26th consecutive day without rain or cloud. (That's not English, but that don't matter much.) You see the Mentonese is rather on the spot about weather, isn't he? His wife, about whom you asked with a spasm of ill-concealed Satyriasis,[6] is pretty for a short time, and then goes in for *tempus edax* what'shisname[7] without further scruple. I don't know whether she is faithful to him or not, but I should fancy she had few temptations after a certain age.

---

[4] Cf. *King Lear*, V.iii.170–71.

[5] Baxter read an essay on Jean Paul Richter to the Spec. on 2 December.

[6] Baxter: 'Is it better to be a Mentonian (I'm blessed if I know where the place is) than a Scotchman? are his wives prettier? his daughters more virtuous? his life purer, and his end happier?'

[7] '*Tempus edax rerum*' (Time the devourer of all things) – Ovid, *Metamorphoses*, 15.234.

I live in the same hotel with Lord Salisbury.[8] Ahem. He has black whiskers and looks not unlike Crum Brown;[9] only rather more of Crum B. than there is in the Edinburgh edition. He has been successful (or his wife has) in making some kids; rather a melancholy success; they are weedy looking kids, in highland clo'. They have a tutor with them who respires Piety and that kind of humble your-lordship's-most-obedient sort of gentlemanliness that noblemen's tutors have generally. They all get livings, these men, and silvery hair, and a gold watch from their attached pupil; and they sit in the porch and make the watch repeat for their little grandchildren, and tell them long stories beginning 'when I was a private tutor in the family of etc.'; and the grandchildren cock snooks at them behind their backs, and go away whenever they can, to get the groom to teach them bad words. – My friends, let us all kneel down and thank God that he has never made us tutors in a nobleman's family: there are some fates too pitiable for tears. I would sooner be a Macer. (Talking of whom, is there anything new about Johnny Adam?[10] Dear man! how my heart would melt within me and the tears of patriotism spring to my eyes, if I could but see him reel towards me, in his dress clo' like a moon at midday and smiling his vulgar, Scotch grin from ear to ear!) Can I do anything for you with Lord Salisbury? Ahem.

Foot-note in small print – Is he a dook, marquis, earl, or paper Lord?[11]

I see with pain that you are still as dissipated as the devil. Upon my word, Charles, I do not think you ought to leave the parent nest. I speak very seriously. I doubt if you would not be much the worse for it. Remember what is the invariable result of their absence, and perpend my man, perpend. Seriously, if it can be managed, stay where you are. It seems a rude thing to say; but I do think the terrors of the law are not unnecessary for you.

I question if anybody ever had such cold hands as I have just now; however, wonderful to state, I have no blood to the head, and so can go on writing.

I am reading Michelet's *French Revolution*; having somewhat surfeited myself on George Sand.[12] Even the most wholesome food palleth after

---

[8] Robert Arthur Talbot Gascoyne-Cecil (1830–1903), third Marquess of Salisbury; later three times Conservative Prime Minister. There were six children, ranging in age at this time from four to fifteen.

[9] Alexander Crum Brown (1838–1922), Professor of Chemistry, Edinburgh University, 1869–1908, half-brother of the author of *Rab and His Friends*.

[10] The drunken Clerk of Court celebrated in RLS's posthumously published poem 'To Charles Baxter, On the death of their common friend, Mr John Adam, Clerk of Court'.

[11] A judge whose title was not hereditary.

[12] RLS wrote to Mrs Sitwell on 30 November: 'I have found here a new friend, to whom I grow daily more devoted – George Sand. I go on from one novel to another and think the last I have read the most sympathetic and friendly in tone, until I have read another. It is a life in

many days banqueting; and History's little dish-full of herbs seemed at last preferable to the stalled ox of pampered fiction.[13]

Sidney Colvin will arrive here on Saturday or Sunday; so I shall have someone to jaw with. And seriously this is a great want. I have not been all these weeks in idleness, as you may fancy, without much thinking as to my future; and I have a great deal in view that may or may not be possible (that I do not yet know) but that is at least an object and a hope before me. I cannot help recurring to seriousness a moment, before I stop, for I must say that living here a good deal alone and having had ample time to look back upon my past, I have become very serious all over: not in religion, as you may fancy, but morally. If I can only get back my health, by God! I shall not be as useless as I have been. By God, or by Satan, or by the Unknowable, or by the Universum, or by Myself (because there is none greater alas!) or however we shall have to swear nowadays, when we have laid aside your religion, my gentle communicant, Ever yours, *mon vieux*   Robert Louis Stevenson

(Soon to Simpson.) Health really on *the improve*.

To Bob Stevenson

[*17 December 1873*]   [*Monaco*]

My dear Bob, I am at Monaco with Colvin, sitting outside in the sun on a seat behind the Casino. The band (one of the best in Europe) is just tuning up, putting me in mind of the tuning before Orosy's concert. Appropriately enough there is a piece of Chopin's in the programme – a *Marche Funèbre* from which I expect great things if I can only manage to listen to it, which is doubtful; the last time I went to the band, I had to come out straight – the brass made me quite mad and all my nerves got tense and stiff like whipcord. There is the hour, I am going in to try – a sell. This is not the classical afternoon, nothing but Adam, Auber, Hervé, Strauss and that lot. M. Eusèbe Lucas, the director, pleases me awfully, he has jolly shoulders and a good moustache. Directing a good band is very proud work and gives opportunity for much grace, if you can be graceful.

---

dreamland. Have you read *Mademoiselle Merquem*? I have just finished it and I am full of happiness.' He told Bob on 2 December: 'To begin with, I read George Sand from morning to night in great measure to keep myself from working, and I am more and more delighted with her. If you ever get within reach of *Consuelo*, don't fail to read it; you will find it extremely interesting as a novel, full of the most interesting things about music and with some of the best passages in the way of literary workmanship in the world.' Other novels praised were *La Petite Fadette* and *François le Champi*.

[13] Cf. Proverbs 15:17.

I feel as if I could be damned graceful at it, but perhaps the more solid requirements of the metier might go to blazes. Do you remember an old proposition of the *Messiah*, with me to conduct and you for tenor, M. Hart soprano etc? The recollection fills me with laughter. Has the sun of Jink[1] then set? God forbid, as St Paul would say, but rather it is risen again and this mortal has put on immortality.[2] Shine sweet sun forever upon the dusty ways of life. Thee often shall the wayfarer, or at the peep of morning or at noon, in devious error sunken, pause to hail etc. *À propos* of the music I have been hearing, a purely lyrical idea very sweet and pretty in itself has just been crushed out of existence by the whole weight of the orchestra. I am beginning to wonder a little that no letter comes for me from you; have you been expelled the Academy and sent forth an egregious exile?[3] I suppose not, or I should have heard of it: I hope you are getting on really well. Do you find any real difference in the way of teaching and does it seem to you better. Tell me about this like a good soul.

Colvin being here makes things very jolly for me. Yesterday I dined with Sir Charles Dilke and his wife;[4] Sir C. is a joke, awfully *bon garçon* and in such funny clothes – republican clo' I suppose. You know, he is the man who proposed to suppress the monarchy and got so much chaffed a few years ago. He is about thirty; and just Hell on laughing at jokes – his joke, your joke, my joke, anybody's joke.

Sunday 4 January [1874]

I have been a long while – nearly a fortnight since I wrote this last scrap. In the interval, I got your letter which amused me much.

Colvin and I are back again at *Mentone. Hotel Mirabeau*. A man shot himself at the gaming tables, when Colvin was in the room: He was a Pole, and had played everything; this gave us a distaste to the place, so we left.

I did hear Chopin's *Marche Funèbre* and Mendelssohn's *Hebrides Overture*; I enjoyed them awfully, but I was ill for three days after. So you see what it is to have played out your nerves.

[1] The special word used by Bob and RLS for their elaborate jokes. 'As a rule of conduct, Jink consisted in doing the most absurd acts for the sake of their absurdity and the consequent laughter' (RLS, 'Memoirs of Himself', Book III).
[2] Cf. I Corinthians 6:15 and 15:54
[3] '*egregius properaret exsul*' (he hastened away, an honourable exile) – Horace, *Odes*, III.v. 48.
[4] Sir Charles Wentworth Dilke, 2nd Baronet (1843–1911), Radical politician; MP for Chelsea 1868–86; President of the Local Government Board 1882–5. His notoriety at this time was due to his strong expression of republican views. Greater notoriety and the wrecking of his political career came with the Crawford divorce case in 1886. In 1872 he married Katherine Sheil, who died in childbirth in 1874.

Colvin and I get on awfully well; it is very jolly his being here, but he goes shortly and I shall feel very lonely.

There is a French artist here called Robinet,[5] a very decent fellow, a realist rather, perhaps a bit of a praeraphaelite; but as yet we only know him by his talk. He told me some good stories of Courbet, who is (as perhaps you know) *the* realist *par excellence*. He said he had done something that Ingres had never done. What is that? asked Robinet. 'Eh bien,' he said, '*j'ai peint deux cent cinquante fois mon vase de nuit.*' Several more of his stories would amuse you, but they are long. Colvin tells me that Courbet's grand climax of realism was a picture called *La Baigneuse* of a great, fat, obese *bourgeoise* clambering out of a bath with her big bum turned to you. It was the ugliest thing on record. The Empress had been looking at a picture of Rosa Bonheur's of a lot of percheron horses – those great, white draught horses with immense quarters; and when she saw Courbet's *Baigneuse*, she said: '*Est'ce aussi une percheronne?*'[6]

It is strange how long it takes one to recover, if you have once broken down. I am much better but horridly weak and not able for any work – I have not written above a few pages all these two months and these are not fit for fodder – *à propos*, I am afraid you did not get the *Portfolio*; at least mine was not sent and Colvin ordered the two at the same time: I am afraid it is too bulky for the post.

I have nothing to say, so you must be content with a mere scrap I am afraid. You must have had great sport these days. You do not say how you get on with your work.

How strange it is that you should go back to Mathilde Brand after so long. I certainly would see her if I had a chance; it will either cure you unpleasantly; or will ensure you a great pleasure for the time; and one may be too curious in looking forward and insisting on permanence in what gives our nerves a pleasant shock. No one would refuse to look at a sunset because a sunset cannot last. And besides, old man, the devil is not yet dead; there is life and hope in both of us; and the 'who knows?' may be answered some day with an affirmative.

Colvin thinks rather well of my Covenanting stories[7] and thinks if I string two or three of them out, it looks like coin; so that is a consolation.

[5] Paul Robinet (1845–1932): 'A bush-bearded French landscape painter, sometimes known as "*le Raphael des Cailloux*" from the more than pre-Raphaelite minuteness of his treatment of the foregound detail of pebbled shores; a devout Catholic and reactionary, and withal the best of genial good fellows' (Colvin).

[6] Courbet's painting, *Les Baigneuses* (now at the Musée Fabre, Montpellier) caused a scandal at the 1853 Salon. The anecdote about the Empress seems to be well-authenticated.

[7] RLS projected a series of Covenanting stories. A list of ten stories in an early geometry notebook is annotated *A Covenanting Story-Book*. It includes 'The Curate of Anstruther's Bottle', 'Strange Adventures of the Reverend Mr Solway', 'The Devil of Cramond' and 'The Story of Thrawn Janet'. A notebook of 1873/4 lists six stories under the heading *Covenanting Story Book*.

Please address Poste Restante, Mentone; it is always better. Ever your affectionate friend   Robert Louis Stevenson

To Frances Sitwell

Tuesday 13th [*January 1874*]   [*Mentone*]

I lost a Philippine[1] to little May Johnson[2] last night; so today I sent her a rubbishing doll's toilet and a little note with it, with some verses telling how happy children made every one near them happy also, and advising her to keep the lines and some day when she was 'grown a stately demoiselle' it would make her 'glad to know, She gave pleasure long ago'; all in a very lame fashion; with just a note of prose at the end telling her to mind her doll and the dog and not trouble her little head just now to understand the bad verses; for, some time when she was ill, as I am now, they would be plain to her and make her happy. She has just been here to thank me, and has left me very happy. Children are certainly too good to be true.

I got Bert's nice letter and yours this morning.

Yesterday, I walked too far and spent all the afternoon on the outside of my bed; went finally to rest at nine and slept nearly twelve hours on the stretch. Bennet (the doctor)[3] when told of it this morning augured well for my recovery; he said youth must be putting in strong; of course I ought not to have slept at all. As it was, I dreamed *horridly*; but not my usual dreams of social miseries and misunderstandings and all sorts of crucifixions of the spirit; but of good, cheery, physical things – of long successions of vaulted, dimly lit cellars full of black water, in which I went swimming among toads and unutterable, cold, blind fishes; now and then these cellars opened up into sort of domed music-hall places, where one could land for a little on the slope of the orchestra, but a sort of horror prevented one from staying long and made one plunge back again into the dead waters. Then my dream changed and I was a sort of Siamese pirate, on a very high deck with several others. The ship was almost captured and we were fighting desperately. The hideous engines we used and the perfectly

---

[1] A game in which a person finding a nut with two kernels eats one and gives the other to a person of the opposite sex. When the two next meet, the one who first says 'Good morning, Philippine', is entitled to a present from the other.

[2] RLS's letters at this period are full of his 'immensity of delight' in the antics of the three children at the hotel, among them May (or Marie) Johnson (or Johnstone), the eight-year-old daughter of an American couple.

[3] James Henry Bennet (1816–91), London physician and specialist in gynaecology, whose recovery from consumption through residence at Mentone made him an advocate of the Riviera for sufferers from lung disease. He is regarded as the discoverer of Mentone as a health resort and it became his permanent winter home.

incredible carnage that we effected by means of them, kept me cheery as you may imagine; especially as I felt all the time my sympathy with the boarders and knew that I was only a prisoner with these horrid Malays. Then I saw a signal being given and knew they were going to blow up the ship. I leaped right off and heard my captors splash in the water after me as thick as pebbles when a bit of river bank has given way beneath the foot. I never heard the ship blow up; but I spent the rest of the night swimming about among some piles with the whole sea full of Malays searching for me with knives in their mouths. They could swim any distance under water, and every now and again, just as I was beginning to reckon myself safe, a cold hand would be laid on my ankle – ugh!

However, my long sleep troubled as it was put me all right again and I was able to work acceptably this morning and be very jolly all day; though as usual after an overfatigue, rather creepy in the back, my hand toward the end of the last paragraph showing pretty definite traces thereof. This evening I have had a great deal of talk with both the Russian ladies; they talk very nicely and are bright likeable women both. They come from Georgia.[4]

Wednesday [14 January]

What a sell this morning's fat letter was; not however unwelcome. I was very glad to think that was so.

I have been out nearly all day, latterly in the front of the hotel with my adorable little child,[5] her nurse and her mother, who is (I think I can spell it now) the Princess Zasetsky. Rather a hard name to call a fellow creature? isn't it? I am very well today; and that little look into a month ago has let me see how much progress I have made and put me in good heart. A somewhat amusing thing reached me this afternoon. The nurse

[4] Mme Sophie Garschine and her elder sister Mme Nadia Zassetsky. It was some time before RLS learned how to spell their names correctly. Colvin says that they were fifteen or more years older than RLS and both he and Furnas make the point that Russian character and temperament were not then as familiar in the West as they have since become through translated plays and novels. In *Memories and Notes*, Colvin writes: 'Both were brilliantly accomplished and cultivated women, one [Madame Z.] having all the unblushing outspokenness of her race; its unchecked vehemence and mutability in mirth and anger, in scorn, attachment, or aversion; the other much of an invalid, consistently gentle and sympathetic, and withal an exquisite musician.' For their part they were puzzled by RLS and in the early days Mme Garschine embarrassed him by her flirtatious manner; he thought they were trying to make a fool of him. He told Mrs Sitwell: 'They are both of them the frankest of mortals; and have explained to me, in one way or other, that I am to them as some undiscovered animal. They do not seem to cultivate R.L.S.'s in Muscovy. It has been rather a curious episode.' Mme Zassetsky was the original of the Countess von Rosen in *Prince Otto*.
[5] Nelitchka, a child of two and a half, described in other letters as 'a little polyglot button' and 'a hell of a jolly kid'.

(who is English) lugged in, after so head-and-shoulders a fashion that I
suspected she had been told to do so, an assurance to the effect that Mme
la Princesse had not been offended by my leaving the room on the
occasion of her *fête* but had been quite pleased by the freedom. I confess
to having had a difficulty to keep from grinning; at the time, I did not
know she was a Princess or anything else and of course never thought
twice of going away whenever the music was introduced and never
made any apology except to Robinet because he had paid for the
hautboys.

Miss Ward[6] leaves on Saturday for San Remo for a fortnight at least. I
am afraid she does not improve; tho' she is very plucky about it.

An organ came into the garden this afternoon and played for some
time, Nelitchka dancing up and down in front of the hotel, with solemn
delight.

10.30

We have all been to tea tonight at the Russians' villa;[7] tea was made out
of a samovar, which is something like a small steam engine, and whose
principal advantage is that it burns the fingers of all who lay their profane
touch upon it. The tea was, I believe all that black tea can be; it costs ten
francs to fourteen a pound; the same brand green (if so I translate rightly
fleur de thé) costs seventy francs a pound. We had also caviar, which is not
very good on the whole. After tea Madame Zasetsky played Russian airs,
very plaintive and pretty; so the evening was Muscovite from beginning to
end. Madame Garschin's daughter[8] danced a tarantella, which was very
pretty. Please tell S.C. that the Prince (according to the excellent testimony of his wife) resembles Bonfils[9] to a hair. There, I think that's all very
instructive.

I am keeping as cheery as can be, you see; either this hotel is immensely
nicer than the Pavillon, or I am much better; I think there is something
of both in it.[10]

I blame myself sometimes, when I find that I can always write to you,
whereas when I set myself down to write to my people I always plead ill
health; but I can't help it: it is so. I want to write to you, and I don't want
to write to them; I suppose that's the plain English of it all.

---

[6] Agnes and Maria Ward were sisters of the journalist and author, Humphry Ward.

[7] The Russians lived at the Villa Marina, but took their meals at the hotel.

[8] The eight-year-old Pella (Bella) whose full name was Pelagie.

[9] Stanislas Bonfils (1822–1909), archaeologist; founder and curator of the museum at Mentone.

[10] RLS told his mother: 'The population of the hotel is all jolly: I like it infinitely better than the
Pavillon lot of horrid English. This is such a jolly mixture from the mildest milk and water
English clergyman's washed-out daughters to the somewhat roystering yankeedom of Johnson
or the jolly fine graceful manners of the Mesdames Russes.'

Thursday [15 January]

A jolly letter today from S.C. Tell him he is a bird of paradise, and that his letter made me very cheery in every way. It gave good news of you, and good news to me in many ways.

I have some journals sent me about the Edinburgh *revival* and I have made myself nearly sick over them.[11] It is disheartening beyond expression. I wish I had been there that I might have seen the movement near at hand; but I am afraid I should have taken up a testimony and made everybody at home very much out of it.

Nelitchka brings me a flower generally in the morning which I wear. I do wear flowers when they are given me by certain persons, as you know or ought to know.

I am awfully stupid today; as indeed I have been for some time back; but it is a cheery stupidity. I don't suppose you will mind a gibbering letter, so long as the gibber is in good spirits.

I may remark that I don't understand the Russians at all; not at all; not in the very least. I was simply regaled this afternoon with a family secret; and a very curious story it is. Certainly Madame Zasetsky was a great deal moved immediately before; but at the time she told the story she was as cool as a cucumber. I shall immediately prove how worthy of confidence I am by telling it to you. Bella is not Mme Garschin's daughter; but Madame Zasetsky's. Madame Garschin had no family and was cut up; Madame Z. agreed with her husband that the next should be given to Mme G. It was done, and the child is the curse of the poor adoptive mother's existence. She loves her devotedly and has spoiled her without limit, and Bella repays her with disobedience and drives her into hysterics every day or two. Today, this took place and the scene, that I saw between the mother and daughter – supposed aunt and niece – was very strange. Madame Zasetsky became perfectly resplendent with anger – I did not think she had so much energy in her, tho' I knew she had plenty – and broke forth over the child in the plainest, bitterest language; told her she was killing her mother; imitated her praying for her mother's recovery – '*Vous avez beau prier. C'est trop tard, Mademoiselle, je vous dis que c'est trop tard.*' She almost screamed as she said this, and the girl ran away to complain to her mother (as she supposed) that is her aunt; and Madame turned round to Mr Johnson and me with the sublimest nonchalance – '*Vous ne savez pas – Bella est ma fille, à moi.*' I have intolerably muddled the story; but if you can follow it, it does not want for interest. Mme Garschin

[11] The revival meetings conducted in Edinburgh November 1873 to January 1874 by the American evangelists Dwight L. Moody and Ira D. Sankey aroused immense enthusiasm and MIS went to several of the services. RLS wrote to Baxter: 'They sent me magazines about it; the obscenest rubbish I was ever acquainted with.'

lives upon the imposture; cannot bear any one to know. Mme Zasetsky is inconsolable that she should have had anything to do with such a miserable bargain. I do think the child is (what her mother called her) a devil.

7.30

The more I think of it that scene on the beach seems the more striking to me. It is one of the most dramatic situations one can conceive – the mother giving up a child, dedicating it before it was conceived, to complete the happiness of her sister. This child hating her mother, whom she takes for a cross grained aunt, scarcely refraining from putting out her tongue at her today, when she broke out into this righteous indignation. The sister having set the whole worth of her life upon this child, whom she destroys, on the condition of this fiction, which cannot be long supported. God knows what a tragedy lies before the family.

It is difficult to believe that this nasty girl is the sister of the quite adorable Nelitchka; of whom an anecdote by the way. Whenever she cries, and she never cries except from pain, all that one has to do is to start 'Malbrook s'en va-t-en guerre', she cannot resist the attraction, she is drawn through her sobs into the air; and in a moment there is Nellie singing, with the glad look that comes into her face always when she sings, and all the tears and pain forgotten.

I have written a great deal to you these past three days, and on the whole (considering the writer) with very little egotism. I am afraid the hand is horrid. I shall write to my people for some photographs, and send one to Bert when they come. I have received a *carte* from Mary Johnson, *voire aussi celle de la poupée*.

The weather has been superb.

I cannot get that story out of my head. I keep trying to figure to myself the evolution of the imbroglio; and, turn it how I may, the future does not look promising for either Mme Garschin or Bella.

10

I cannot keep from writing to you although I have nothing to say. I can just hear the sea on the beach, and I daresay you can hear from where you are 'The same voice of woods and seas' (or however it goes) in the living tides of Paris. We have been playing again at *la Salette* (or *Sallette*)[12]: I am pronounced not at all *drôle*, which is cheery: I must have changed oddly: I thought I was rather given that way. Johnson (Bourbon Whiskey) tells a story better, I think, than almost any man I have ever heard. His anecdotes are full of close observation; the pantomime thoroughly just and

[12] I.e. *la sellette*, the culprit's stool, the stool of repentance.

significant in conception and admirably brought before one in language. His story of a dog that was lost, has left a series of pictures in my mind, as vivid and characteristic as any I ever got from a book. Why does not a man with so good a faculty, try writing? he would be very successful surely.

S.C.'s note was awfully nice. Good-bye, my dear friend. Ever your faithful friend   Robert Louis Stevenson

It is wonderful, before I shut this up, how that child remains ever interesting to me. Nothing can stale her infinite variety; and yet it is not very various. You see her thinking what she is to do or to say next, with a funny grave air of reserve; and then the face breaks up into a smile, and it is probably 'Berechino!',[13] said with that sudden little jump of the voice that one knows in children, as the escape of a jack in the box; and – somehow – I am quite happy after that!   R.L.S.

To Sidney Colvin

[c. *20 January 1874*]   [*Mentone*]

My dear Colvin, The bird of paradise has arrived duly. I shall have it framed. The Ruskies were much amused; I explained the circumstance to them in my best French. I am thought to have vastly improved in my French, by the way. I have spent the last three evenings with them; they are awfully kind and jolly. I have bought a hat. Please send me a cake and some money to buy a cricket bat.

I have worked today at 'Ordered South'. I think 'Ordered South' will have to be ordered to Jericho. I don't mean that, only I am a fool, a cheery, gibberous fool. I am really a little more hopeful about it; I have now got all the stuff together; and perhaps another transcription will get it sort of right.

How was you tomorrow? I feel very humorous and inclined to stand up and wink at myself in the mirror. There is no extry charge. It is odd although I feel so funny, the jokes don't seem to come. If I attempt it with an English quill will you take, O reader, for the deed, the will?[1] Laugh, will you. Why the devil, don't you laugh?

---

[13] RLS's misspelling of the Italian *birichino* – little rascal. Nelitchka usually called him by this name.
[1] Longfellow prefaced 'The Blind Girl of Castèl-Cuillè', a translation 'from the Gascon of Jasmin', with the following:

> Only the Lowland tongue of Scotland might
> Rehearse this little tragedy aright;
> Let me attempt it with an English quill;
> And take, O Reader, for the deed the will.

I have felt serious once and twice but at the present moment, I can scarcely say that I do. I don't care a bit about suffering humanity. I am a bird of paradise. It's awful humbug having to go to bed. As jolly old Sir Thomas Browne said, 'The huntsmen are already up in Persia';[2] and here at my ear, a cock is crowing for the morning with no apparent sense of incongruity. I have the desire to sit up all night and it contraries me sorely to have to thwart it. But we must be good. May God bless you and keep you and lift up the light of his rubicund countenance upon you, and send his angels to look arter you lest by any chance you should stumble and go a mucker.[3] Amen. Amen. Amen. Amen. Ever yours

Robert Louis Stevenson

Postscriptum. I am not mad, most noble Festus,[4] only gibberous – a malady incident to R.L.S.

To Frances Sitwell

Wednesday [4 February 1874]   [*Mentone*]

My dear friend, It has snowed today, and blown and been the very devil in the way of weather. Andrews lunched with me and in the afternoon we both had tea at the Villa Marina. I am so sleepy that I see I can write no sense; so I must shut up.

Thursday [5 February]

It is still so cold, I cannot tell you how miserable the weather is. I fear S.C. will feel the change badly. I have begun my 'Walt Whitman' again seriously; many winds have blown since I last laid it down, when sickness took me in Edinburgh. It seems almost like an ill considered jest to take up these old sentences, written by so different a person under circumstances so different, and try to string them together and organise them into something anyway whole and comely; it is like continuing another man's book. Almost every word is a little out of tune to me now, but I shall pull it through for all that and make something that will interest you yet on this subject that I had proposed to myself and partly planned already before I left for Cockfield last July.

I am very anxious to hear from you how you are. My own health is quite very good; I am a healthy octogenarian; very old, I thank you, and

---

[2] 'The Huntsmen are up in America, and they are already past their first sleep in Persia.' From the last paragraph of Browne's *The Garden of Cyrus* (1658).
[3] Echoing Numbers 6: 24–6 and Psalm 91: 11–12.
[4] Acts 26:25.

of course not so active as a young man, but hale withal: a lusty December. This is so; such is R.L.S.

I am a little bothered about Bob, a little afraid that he is living too poorly. The fellow he chums with spends only 2 francs a day on food, with a little excess every day or two to keep body and soul together; and though he is not so austere, I am afraid he draws it rather too fine himself.[1]

Friday [6 February]

We have all got our photographs; it is pretty fair, they say, of me, and as they are particular in the matter of photographs, and besides partial judges, I suppose I may take that for proven. Of Nellie there is one quite adorable; I shall be so proud to show it to you. The weather is still cold. My 'Walt Whitman', at last, looks really well: I think it is going to get into shape in spite of the long gestation.

You have not yet heard of my book? O yes you will have heard of it perhaps from S.C. *Four Great Scotchmen* – John Knox, David Hume, Robert Burns, Walter Scott. These, their lives, their work, the social media in which they lived and worked, with, if I can so make it, the strong current of the race making itself felt underneath and throughout – this is my idea. You must tell me what you think of it. The Knox will really be new matter, as his life hitherto has been disgracefully written, and the events are romantic and rapid; the character very strong, salient and worthy; much interest as to the future of Scotland and as to that part of him which was truly modern under his Hebrew disguise. Hume, of course, the urbane, cheerful, gentlemanly, letter-writing eighteenth century, full of niceness, and much that I don't yet know as to his work. Burns, the sentimental side that there is in most Scotchmen, his poor troubled existence, how far his poems were his personally, and how far national, the question of the framework of Society in Scotland and its fatal effect upon the finest natures. Scott again, the ever delightful man, sane, courageous, admirable; the birth of Romance, in a dawn that was a sunset; snobbery, conservatism, the wrong thread in History and notably in that of his own land. *Voilà, madame, le menu. Comment trouvez vous? Il y a de bon viande, si on parvient à la cuire convenablement.*

Sunday [8 February]

Still cold; gray and a high imperious wind off the sea. I see nothing particularly *couleur de rose* this morning: but I am trying to be faithful to my

[1] Bob had just moved from Antwerp to Paris. He enrolled in the studio of the portrait painter Carolus-Duran. Before Colvin met him that month, RLS wrote to him: 'You know *me* now. Well, Bob is just such another mutton, only somewhat farther wandered and with perhaps a little more mire on his wool.'

creed, and hope. O yes, one can do something to make things happier and
better; and to lighten the old intolerable burthens; and to give a good
example before men and show them how goodness and fortitude and faith
remain undiminished, after they have been stripped bare of all that is
formal and outside. We must do that my friend; you have done it already;
and I shall follow and do something nice. I shall make a worthy life, and
you must live to approve me.

Evening

Your letter has come. Thank you, my dear friend. We see the thing
with the same eyes, thank God; it has made me very happy. You see I
have journalised after all, but you are to think of that now, as a chance.
You do not say much of your health; I want truth about it. Mine I assure
you, is as well as if this had not happened. The cold winds are rough upon
me but that is all.

By the way, much that S.C. will tell you about Mme Garschine is true
indeed, but not quite true. She told me the story of her life, herself, at
some length, yesterday and today, although I rather fled the confidence;
but she said she knew her sister had told me a lot already and she wished
me to respect her on just grounds. What astonishes me is the excellent
way in which everybody tells stories; Madame G.'s autobiography was a
masterpiece of clear, vivid, interesting narration; I feel with shame that I
could not write so well.

Do not fear, dear friend. I will trust you in everything, and wholly.
You are my faith, as you know. Ever your faithful friend

Robert Louis Stevenson

To his Mother

Friday [13 February 1874]   *[Mentone]*

The wine has arrived and a dozen of it has been transferred to me; it
is much better than Folleté's[1] stuff. We had a masquerade last night at the
Villa Marina: Nellie in a little red satin cap, in a red satin suit of boy's
clothes, with a funny little black tail that stuck out behind her, and
wagged as she danced about the room, and gave her a look of Puss in
Boots; Pella as a contadina; M. Robinet as an old woman; Mademoiselle
as an old lady, with blue spectacles; and to see all these incongruous,
impossible people go flitting about the room, leaping, and turning and
dancing hand in hand to the music – above all if you keep in view the

---

[1] The proprietor of the Hôtel Mirabeau.

disproportion of size between Nellie, diminished to the smallest of cats in her tight costume, on the one hand, and Robinet on the other, exaggerated into a giant by his long white drapery – it was as good as a dream, or better. (If you think I have got creditably out of that sentence, I am sure *I* am quite pleased.)

Yesterday, we had a visit from one of whom I had often heard from Mrs Sellar[2] – Andrew Lang. He is good-looking, delicate, boyish, Oxfordish etc. He did not impress me unfavourably; nor deeply in any way.[3]

My cloak is the most admirable of all garments.[4] For warmth, unequalled; for a sort of pensive, Roman stateliness, sometimes warming into Romantic guitarism, it is simply without concurrent: it starts alone. If you could see me in my cloak, it would impress you. I am hugely better, I think: I stood the cold, these last few days without trouble, instead of taking to bed as I did at Monte Carlo. I hope you are going to send the Scotch music.

I am stupid at letter writing again. I don't know why. I hope it may not be permanent; in the meantime you must take what you get and be hopeful. The Russian ladies are as kind and nice as ever. Ever your affectionate son   Robert Louis Stevenson

★ *To Frances Sitwell*

Monday [30 March 1874]   *[Mentone]*

My last night at Mentone. I cannot tell how strange and sad I feel. I leave behind me a dear friend whom I have but little hope of seeing again between the eyes.

---

[2] Eleanor Mary Dennistoun (1829–1918), who was MIS's bridesmaid, married (1852) William Young Sellar (1825–90), Professor of Humanity at Edinburgh 1863–90. He was Andrew Lang's uncle.

[3] Andrew Lang (1844–1912), scholar, folklorist, poet and man of letters, was at this time a Fellow of Merton College, Oxford. He, too, had developed lung trouble and was wintering at Mentone. He described the meeting in *Adventures Among Books* (1905): 'He looked . . . more like a lass than a lad, with a rather long, smooth oval face, brown hair worn at greater length than is common, large lucid eyes. . . . I shall not deny that my first impression was not wholly favourable. "Here," I thought, "is one of your aesthetic young men, though a very clever one."' Lang remembered, too, RLS's 'big blue cloak' and Tyrolese hat. Lang and RLS soon became warm friends.

[4] 'It had been a very cold Christmas at Monaco and Monte Carlo, and Stevenson had no adequate overcoat, so it was agreed that when I went to Paris I should try and find him a warm cloak or wrap. I amused myself looking for one suited to his taste for the picturesque and piratical in apparel, and found one in the style of 1830–40, dark blue and flowing and fastening with a snake buckle' (Colvin).

★ As explained in the Introduction (p. xiii), the texts of this letter and others marked with an asterisk are not taken from the manuscript.

Today, I hadn't arranged all my plans till five o'clock: I hired a poor old cabman, whose uncomfortable vehicle and sorry horse make everyone despise him, and set off to get money and say farewells. It was a dark misty evening; the mist was down over all the hills; the peach-trees in beautiful pink bloom. Arranged my plans; that merits a word by the way if I can be bothered. I have half arranged to go to Göttingen in summer to a course of lectures. Galitzin is responsible for this. He tells me the professor is to Law what Darwin has been to Natural History, and I should like to understand Roman Law and a knowledge of law is so necessary for all I hope to do.[1]

My poor old cabman; his one horse made me three-quarters of an hour too late for dinner, but I had not the heart to discharge him and take another. Poor soul, he was so pleased with his pourboire, I have made Madame Zassetsky promise to employ him often; so he will be something the better for me, little as he will know it.

I have read 'Ordered South'; it is pretty decent I think, but poor, stiff, limping stuff at best – not half so well straightened up as 'Roads'. However the stuff is good.

God help us all, this is a rough world: address Hotel St Romain, rue St Roch, Paris. I draw the line: a chapter finished: Ever your faithful friend
                                                      Robert Louis Stevenson

The line.

_____

That bit of childishness has made me laugh, do you blame me?

To Frances Sitwell

[? 11 April 1874]   [Paris]

My dear friend, I am up again in an arm chair by the open window, the air very warm and soft and full of pleasant noise of streets. I have had a very violent cold; the chirruppy French-English doctor who attended me, said I might compliment myself on what I had, as I might just as well have had small-pox or typhoid fever or what you will. Now, look here, with

---

[1] Prince Lev Sergeevich Golitsyn (Leon Galitzine) (1845–1915), a cousin of the two Russian ladies and a member of one of the most famous Russian families, arrived in Mentone in the last two weeks of RLS's time there. A man of wide interests and many enthusiasms, he had been a law student at Göttingen University and was a friend and devoted disciple of Rudolf von Jhering (1818–92). Later Galitzine took up archaeology but he is now remembered as a pioneer of the modern Russian wine industry and was appointed winemaker to the Czar in the 1890s.

all this violent cold my chest remains unaffected: I am bronchial a bit and cough, and I have my mucus membrane raw over the best part of me and my eyes are the laughablest deformed loopholes you ever saw; and withal my lungs are all right. So you see that's good.

I have not had a letter from home since I left Mentone. You know, I was doing what they didn't want; but I put myself out of my own way to make it less unpleasant for them; and surely when one is nearly twenty-four years of age one should be allowed to do a bit of what one wants without their quarrelling with me. I would explain the whole thing to you, but believe me I am too weary. Also, please show Colvin this letter and explain to him that whenever I can, I will write to him; and that in the meantime, if it will not bore him, a note from him will always be most agreeable.

Nothing can be done to assist me: if I get permission, I shall probably go straight away to Germany without delay: by permission, I mean money.

I cannot pretend that I have been very happy this while back; but this morning, I was relieved from a great part of my physical sufferings and at the same time heard you speak more determinedly about your troubles. For God's sake carry these through; if you do, I'll promise to get better and do my work in spite of all.

Monday [? 12 April]

Last night I set to work and Bob wrote to my dictation three or four pages of 'V. Hugo's Romances'[1]: it is d—d nonsense, but to have a *brouillon* is already a great thing. If I had the health of a (simile wanting) I could still rake it together in time.

Yesterday afternoon, I got quite a nice note from my father (after a fortnight's silence), with scarcely a word of anger or vexation or anything: I don't quite know what to make of that. But it does not matter; as I see clearly enough that I must give up the game for the present: this morning I am so ill that I can see nothing else for it than to crawl very cautiously home; the fact is, the doctor *would* give me medicine, and I think that has just put the copestone on my weakness. I just simply perspire without ceasing in big drops that I can hear falling in the bed, and I have a fine generous tic that makes my forehead into that sort of hideous damned-soul mask of bitterness and pain with which the public are already acquainted – I mean such of the public as know *me*. I am going to cut the doctor and sort myself; and the first warm day, I shall fly: a change of air is the only thing that will pull me through. But the north is such an error; cold I am

---

[1] 'Victor Hugo's Romances' became RLS's first contribution to the *Cornhill Magazine* in August 1874; it was reprinted in *Familiar Studies*.

unfit for, I cannot come cold at all. My spirits are not at all bad, I thank you; but my temper is a little embittered, and I have employed more French oaths this morning, in order to try to awaken the placid imperturbable *garçon de chambre* to the fact that I was angry, than I thought that I had in me.

It is curious how in some ways real pain, is better than simple prostration and uneasiness. I seem to have wakened up to meet this tic, it has put me on the alert, I come on smiling. It is so odd; a day ago, I did not care at all for life and would just as soon have died; pain comes, and – I beg pardon, sir, you have made a mistake, I shall pull through in spite of you and be d—d to you – that is my sentiment; I also want to make it a fact.

Tell S.C. that the instant my health is anyway together again, I shall prefer to take to plays than to anything else. I have already a good subject in Gibbon; or rather it was suggested long ago by the *Corpus Juris*;[2] and has been recalled to me by Gibbon: a sort of domestic drama under the low empire; tax gatherers, slaves, cheatery, chicane, poverty; suddenly drums and sunlight and the pageantry of imperial violence: an admirable contrast, and one just suited for the stage. So you see, I shall just be in the humour to consider Diana of the Ephesians.[3] Ever your faithful friend

Robert Louis Stevenson

I shall be in London shortly, if I can; I shall seek rooms at the Paddington Hotel, where my people were, so that on the first opportunity I can come along and see you; if you can, I should like to see you alone, but of course that must be how it can. I shall see you, and S.C., and show Clark my carcase and lift coins from *Portfolio*, and then slowly north by easy stages. And O! if I could get into a sort of clean wide bed in an airy room, and sleep for months, and be wakened in mid July by birds and the shadows of leaves in the room, and rise and dress myself and be quite well and strong and find that dozens of things had been dreams and were gone away for ever!

R.L.S.

[2] *Corpus Juris Civilis*, the Emperor Justinian's great compilation of Roman law.
[3] 'Some of our talk at Mentone had run on the scheme of a spectacle play on the burning of the temple of Diana at Ephesus by Herostratus, the type of insane vanity *in excelsis*' (Colvin).

IV. LITERATURE, LAW AND
MRS SITWELL April 1874–July 1876

Stevenson arrived home on Sunday morning, 26 April 1874, 'looking' his mother thought 'wonderfully well'. Although there were still tensions at times, relations with his parents were greatly improved and (in Balfour's words) 'in the religious question a *modus vivendi* seems to have been established with his father.' He continued to pour out his day-to-day thoughts and feelings in long journal-letters to Mrs Sitwell, and to both her and Colvin he outlined his many literary projects. He was able, too, to obtain some escape from his Edinburgh 'cage' by periodic visits to them in London. It is clear that there was an emotional crisis that summer in his relations with Mrs Sitwell. The only evidence is in his letters, and biographers can do no more than speculate about the exact nature of it.

In November 1874 (in pursuance of his promise to his father), RLS resumed his legal studies at Edinburgh University. The following February came his first meeting with William Ernest Henley.

To Frances Sitwell

Wednesday [*29 April 1874*]   *17 Heriot Row*

Only a word ere I go to sleep, to show that I am not forgetful. The spring-time is delightful; the greenery and the lilac flower, and the daisies, and the songs of the birds are all good for the heart; though in truth the stealthy pulses of bitter air from the east are somewhat bad for the poor tabernacle. I am very fairly well, and quite peaceful and happy in all ways.[1]

Friday [*1 May*]

I have never been so well with my mother as I am now; she is really awfully nice, and I must tell you what I ought to have foreseen myself, that she knew and suspected a great deal more than anybody imagined. She says nothing, but, as her habit is, she implies much. She told me last night that what had hurt her most was that I should have gone to church

---

[1] RLS had visited Mrs Sitwell in London on his way home. He wrote to her on arrival in Edinburgh: 'I cannot pretend that I am glad to be back in Edinburgh. I find that I hate the place now to the backbone and only keep myself quiet by telling myself that it is not for ever.'

with you my last Sunday in England: she said to herself 'he is lost to me now for ever'. She suspected that Clark's opinion was a put-up thing, and that my object was to go away and never to return to them at all. As you see, we have been very intimate, and I know now how much she has concealed from my father of what she thought. She has been far nicer than I imagined.

Evening

I am alone in the house once more, and by the fire in my own room; I have written to you so often just thus, and this is the last time I shall have the chance to do so again for a long while anyway, as we go to the country tomorrow. So I must say my say. I have just been reading *Maud.* Do not fear, dear; it has not been unpleasant to me; I see and know and accept all the limitations without a grudge.[2] Only just tonight I cannot write any half words. I can think of nothing but of how much I love you and how happy it makes me that I do so. I would not give up my love of you for eternity: I would not go back for God.[3]

Monday [4 May]

We are now at Swanston Cottage, Lothianburn, Edinburgh. The garden is but little clothed yet, for you know, here we are six hundred feet above the sea. It is very cold, and has sleeted this morning. Everything wintry. I am very jolly however, having finished 'Victor Hugo' and just looking round to see what I should next take up. I have been reading Roman Law and Calvin this morning; my people are very nice to me indeed and I hope we shall go on well; I have had lots of talk with my mother and take much hope from what has passed between us.

Evening

I went up the hill a little this afternoon. The air was invigorating but it was so cold that my scalp was sore. With this high wintry wind, and the grey sky, and faint northern daylight, it was quite wonderful to hear such a clamour of blackbirds coming up to me out of the woods and the bleating of sheep being shorn in a field near the garden, and to see golden patches of blossom already on the furze, and delicate green shoots upright and beginning to frond out among last year's russet bracken. Flights of crows were passing continually between the wintry leaden sky and the

---

[2] In 'On Falling in Love' RLS mentions Tennyson's *Maud* along with *Adelaide* and Heine's songs as an 'absolute expression' of the 'hyperbolical frame of mind' of someone falling in love.
[3] This is the end of one page of a folded sheet. The other page seems to have been torn away and part of the text may have been lost.

wintry cold-looking hills. It was the oddest conflict of seasons. A wee rabbit – this year's making beyond question – ran out from under my feet and was in a pretty perturbation, until he hit upon a lucky juniper and blotted himself there promptly: evidently, this gentleman had not had much experience of life.

I have made an arrangement with my people: I am to have £84 a year – I only asked for 80 on mature reflexion – and as I should soon make a good bit by my pen, I shall be very comfortable. We are all as jolly as can be together, so that is a great thing gained. The letter that I wrote from Mentone repents me, as it seems to have knocked my father to pieces awfully.[4] The explanation they made of it was characteristic – they thought I was out of my mind. Perhaps, after all, it is just as well I did write so and they should have heard for once something like an authentic utterance of what I feel.

I got your letter today, dear friend; you will address now to what is at the top of the page; thank you, for finding time for a word to me in all your hurry.

You do not know the pleasure I have had out of my two photographs: I just thought today, Maud will see my two pictures! It is very egotistical, is it? or no? but, egotistical or no, so it is – I am as pleased, as proud, about my two photographs as I can be, and I hope you will like them if it were only to keep me from being foolish in this little vanity.

Wednesday [6 May]

It is colder than ever after a little respite yesterday. I am going into town tonight to dine with a friend and make some calls, business and dentist, tomorrow morning.

Yesterday I received a letter that gave me much pleasure from a poor fellow student of mine who has been all winter very ill, and seems to be but little better even now. He seems very much pleased with 'Ordered South'. 'A month ago,' he says, 'I could scarcely have ventured to read it – today I felt on reading it as I did on the first day that I was able to sun myself a little in the open air.' And much more to the like effect. It is very gratifying.

I wish I had sent you a *Macmillan*. I suppose it is too late now; after this I shall always send you every magazine that has anything of mine in it.

---

[4] RLS told Mrs Sitwell on 22 November 1873 that he had intended to make his letter to his father calm and rational but got 'carried away' and wrote 'at white-heat of emotion': 'I refused to promise because I said such promises were wrong; I said that nothing would make me return to the life we had been leading for half a year back and that I had determined, in the interest of all three of us, to take my life into my own guidance and implored him to have some confidence in me.' RLS's letter has not survived. MIS recorded laconically in her diary: 'Hear from Lou. He seems in low spirits.'

So, I have at last summoned up courage to leave the fire and write at table. I am working very hard and with satisfaction to myself. Good-bye, dear friend. Be well and happy. Ever your faithful friend

Robert Louis Stevenson

To his Mother[1]

Friday [? 3 July 1874]   *Hampstead*

My dear Mother, I must try to write you a better letter than I had time for yesterday.

I wish somebody would explain to me the climate of Hampstead. To be so near London, and yet to be in an atmosphere more that of like Peebles than any other I can think of, is surely a puzzle in meteorology. Hampstead is all my fancy painted it; it is so quiet, healthful and beautiful; and yet one can go in and dine at the Club[2] in three-quarters of an hour, or thereabout. I like my club very much; the *table d'hôte* dinner is very good: it costs three bob: Two soups, two fish, two entrées, two joints and two puddings; so it is not dear; and one meets agreeable people.

I have never told you about my health. I am very well, I have stopped my tonic now for a fortnight without harm, and I can walk a great deal more: I am better indeed not to go too much into London; for that is wearisome; but out here, I keep very jolly.

Appleton is editor of the *Academy*.[3]

Bertie Sitwell has measles very slightly and they are gone, or going, somewhere to the country.

There is rather a nice article of Colvin's in this *Macmillan*.[4] Wicked Leslie Stephen is not going to publish me for other two months, I fear.[5]

I am getting through a good deal of work.

I do not know what more to say; so the nice letter has again fallen through. Story – I'll tell you a story which a lady told me the other night. She and her brothers kept rabbits. Once they had no money and wanted

---

[1] RLS came south on 13 June and spent a month in London, meeting editors and spending much time with Mrs Sitwell. He and Colvin stayed in lodgings in Abernethy House, Hampstead at the corner of Mount Vernon and Holly Place.

[2] RLS was elected to the Savile Club on 3 June. Colvin proposed him and he was supported among others by Andrew Lang and Fleeming Jenkin.

[3] Charles Edward Cutts Birch Appleton (1841–79), founder and editor of (in Colvin's phrase) the 'severely cultured and scientific weekly journal, the *Academy*' 1869. Appleton lived at Netley Cottage, Hampstead. RLS contributed a number of book-reviews to the journal.

[4] 'The Shadow of Death', an account of Holman Hunt's picture in the July issue of *Macmillan's Magazine*.

[5] Leslie Stephen (1832–1904), man of letters, mountaineer and agnostic, father of Virginia Woolf; knighted 1902. He was editor of the *Cornhill Magazine*, 1871–82 and first editor of the *Dictionary of National Biography*, 1882–91.

some badly for food for the animals. What was their expedient? They formed themselves into a congregation, the eldest boy preached a charity sermon, and they sent a hat round. They were quite pained and disappointed when they found nothing in it. Ever your affectionate son

R.L.S.

The lady was a Mrs Holiday,[6] who lives up here.

To his Mother

[*July 1874*]   *Yacht Heron, Oban*[1]

My dear Mother, I shall try to write you a note at last, although I hope almost in irony that you may be able to read it, as the pen is bad and my hands are hard and stiff and I have forgotten how to write. That is scarcely a joke; but when I say that I have forgotten how to think, it is in bitter seriousness. I am so stupid, I never do think, I prattle and am very easily satisfied with my own and other people's jests, I eat, I drink, I bathe in the briny, I sleep; generally I live as a beast with the beasts of the field. It is so nice. It is also so healthful. It is very thick-headed, stolid, real satisfaction. Simpson and I sleep at one end of the cabin, Stout and Barclay at the other. In the middle we batten over food. It is dirty. We try to keep our own glasses, but occasionally Tom mixes them up in what he calls cleaning it. Simpson looking at his glass the other day suspiciously through half-shut eyes, opined that 'Tom had been *tampering* with it'; and the word was hailed with acclamation. However he doesn't tamper much with anything. We have the most of the mercies packed up in small tins, by a dear man in Aberdeen.[2] I don't think mercies are improved by packing up in tins. Apart from the dear man's preparations, we live principally on chops and steaks, with every now and again a leg of mutton: a leg of mutton is a very great thing. It is boiled and we have mutton broth. Real mutton broth is better than mutton broth out of the dear man's tins. You observe how I use the word *real* there; it is a common locution with us; things out of the Aberdonian tins are called *sham*. Ever yours

Robert Louis Stevenson

[6] Henry Holiday (1839–1927), painter and worker in stained glass, perhaps best-known as the illustrator of *The Hunting of the Snark*, married (1864) Catherine Raven (died 1924), a talented musician who helped popularise Wagner's work in England.

[1] RLS was on a yachting cruise with Walter Simpson and Thomas Barclay in the Inner Hebrides. Balfour says that the *Heron* was a fore and aft schooner of sixteen tons and had two Devon men as crew.

[2] 'I will go as far as most people on tinned meats; some of the brightest moments of my life were passed over tinned mulligatawny in the cabin of a sixteen-ton schooner, storm-stayed in Portree Bay' – RLS in *The Silverado Squatters*, 'With the Children of Israel'.

To Frances Sitwell

[August 1874]   *[Yacht Heron]*
[Beginning of letter missing. MS begins with sheet headed '2']

. . . to be unworthy of yourself.

Ten years ago, does it seem to you? To me it seems a whole long lifetime. I have crossed such a dizzy chasm that I do not yet dare to look back; so I look hopefully forward. And my health is better: I work like a common sailor when it is needful, in rain and wind, without hurt. And my heart is quite stout now. The storm is over. I believe in the future faithfully. I am not sad nor angry, nor regretful. I am fully content and fear nothing, not death, nor weakness, nor any falling away from my own standard and yours. I shall be a man yet, dear, and a good man; although day by day, I see more clearly by how much I still fall short of the mark of our high calling; in how much I am still selfish and peevish and a spoiled child.[1]

You will see that I am writing out of a great blackness. It is true, but it does not apall me. (I don't know how to spell that word.) And there is a good deal of it due to the tempest that is roaring over my head and filling the little cabin with draughts and shudderings of the air. We lie here in a good roadstead; and so do I, in my own constancy. Let the wind blow.

I am so glad you like my little girls:[2] you are the only one who will like them, or nearly so. May God bless you my dear. Ever your faithful friend
Robert Louis Stevenson

To Sidney Colvin

Tuesday [1 September 1874]   *Swanston*

My dear Colvin, What is new with you? There is nothing new with me: Knox and his females begin to get out of my restraint altogether; the

---

[1] Before leaving on his yacht cruise RLS wrote to Mrs Sitwell: 'I don't know what to write . . . that will be agreeable to you, except the one fact that I have been and am very content. I do think the passion is over; I would not be too sanguine or fancy there would never be any momentary relapse; but in the meantime, I am quite strong and satisfied.' These and a few other cryptic references in his letters to her at this time led Furnas and later biographers to speculate that during RLS's June visit to London there had been an emotional crisis in his relations with Mrs Sitwell and that he had been warned not to overstep the boundary between passionate friendship and a physical love affair, and perhaps reminded that her loyalties were to Colvin. From this time RLS attempted (not always successfully) to write in the role of a loving son rather than a lover.

[2] The sight of children playing with a skipping-rope underneath his window in Hampstead coupled with reminiscences of Nelitchka inspired RLS's essay 'Notes on the Movements of Young Children', published in the *Portfolio* for August 1874.

subject expands so damnably, I know not where to cut it off.[1] I have another paper for the *PTFL* on the stocks: a sequel to the two others; also, that is to say, a word in season as to aesthetic contentment and a hint to the careless to look around them for disregarded pleasures.[2] Seeley[3] wrote to me asking me to 'propose' something: I suppose he means – well I suppose I don't know what he means. But I shall write to him (if you think it wise) when I send him this paper, saying that my writing is more a matter of God's disposition than of man's proposal; that I had from 'Roads' upward ever intended to make a little budget of little papers all with this intention before them, call it ethical or aesthetic as you will; and thus I shall leave it to him (if he likes) to regard this little budget, as slowly they come forth, as an unity in its own small way. Twelve or twenty such Essays, some of them purely ethical and expository, put together in a little book with narrow print in each page, antique, vine leaves about, and the following title.

XII (or XX) ESSAYS ON THE
ENJOYMENT OF THE WORLD:
BY ROBERT LOUIS STEVENSON

(a motto in italics)

Publisher
Place and date.

Of course the page is here foreshortened but you know the class of old book I have in my head. I smack my lips; would it not be nice! I am going to launch on Scotch ecclesiastical affairs, in a tract addressed to the clergy; in which doctrinal matters being laid aside, I contend simply that they should be just and dignified men at a certain crisis: this for the honour of humanity. Its authorship must, of course, be secret; or the publication would be useless. You shall have a copy, of course, and may God help you to understand it.[4]

I have done no more to my fables.[5] I find I must let things take their time. I am constant to my schemes; but I must work at them fitfully as the humour moves.

---

[1] Ultimately published as 'John Knox and his Relations to Women' in *Macmillan's Magazine* in September and October 1875 and collected in *Familiar Studies*.

[2] 'On the Enjoyment of Unpleasant Places', published in the *Portfolio* for November 1874.

[3] Richmond Seeley, proprietor and publisher of the *Portfolio*.

[4] *An Appeal to the Clergy of the Church of Scotland* was set up in type early in September 1874 but not published until the following February. A copy of this anonymous pamphlet was given to every member of the General Assembly of that year. According to Colvin, it attracted 'no attention whatever'.

[5] The *Fables* were not published until after RLS's death but 'The House of Eld' and 'Yellow Paint' were probably (as Colvin suggests) written at this period.

– To return. I wonder, if I were to make a budget of such essays as I dream, whether Seeley would publish them; I should give them unity, you know, by the doctrinal essays; nor do I think these would be the least agreeable. You must give me your advice and tell me whether I should throw out this delicate feeler to R.S.; or, if not, what I am to say to this 'proposal' business.

Tell me about your work for the love of God. I shall go to England or Wales, with parents, shortly: after which, a dash to Poland before setting in for the dismal session at Edinburgh.

Spirits good, with a general sense of hollowness underneath: Wanity of Wanities etc. Ever yours   Robert Louis Stevenson

P.S. Parents capital; thanks principally to them; yours truly still rather bitter, but less so.

To Bob Stevenson

[*September 1874*]   *Llandudno*[1]

I want to hear about you, *mon vieux*, and I don't know your address because you have not told it to me; which is a good enough reason. I am still in better health, and work away fairly well as times go; though I am still rather bothered about what you know; I am always keeping myself from thinking of it and always wakening to the fact that there it is still, as if it were some sort of a pin [in] my cushion. It has busted me up a good deal, God knows, and haunts me at all odd moments with an ugly look.

You will be sorry to hear, for I am, that Colvin seems in a poor state of health. He is away to Siena with a bad back, and very much vexed not to meet with you when you were in London. He wants to know if *none* of the Stevenson family ever give intimation of their movements in good time.

I was the other day, at an old house in Merionethshire,[2] where there were some jolly pictures. One – a Caracci – gave me about as much pleasure as ever I had from a picture in my life. *Comme couleur*, it was everything heart could wish; and so *interesting* which pictures rarely are. There was a background of hills, blue and then olive-green – a wonderful blue and a wonderful olive green – and between the olive green hills and the foreground there stretched a green plain, touching the sky in one place, I think; in the foreground, were old-mastery sort of trees with

---

[1] RLS was on a tour with his parents, visiting Chester, Barmouth and Llandudno.
[2] The Stevensons visited Cors-y-Gedol, a mansion six miles north of Barmouth, on 16 September.

marshy pools below them, and a white woman reclining: not indecent in my eyes, but indecent enough in the eyes of others to have got the name of *A Magdalene* for the whole picture. The score was in these two lines of hills; I am enthusiastic about it, without any feigning, and begin to believe in old-mastery a bit. There were some Turners there; I wouldn't have spit over my shoulder to possess them.

How about your work? Stick in; we shall never be swells, but we can be cheesy sort of shits, with a push. Is Arthur[3] there? And, look here, your health. Will you try what has suited me so well? After one has done work for the evening, take a drop of liquor; then go a dark solitary walk – pretty smartly; then come home, put your backside in cold water, sponge your arms, and turn in. After this discipline, I have tasted of real refreshing genuine slumber (patent) such as any hinfant might be proud on.

I am away with my father and my mother. Terms, moderate – I mean (damn the quotation) I mean we are on good terms. I am in the middle of a paper called 'John Knox and the Controversy about Female Rule'. I have just had a very poor thing accepted by the *Portfolio* – I'm not drunk, though it looks like it, only sleepy.[4] Good night. I'll go on tomorrow.

Tomorrow truly

I am sure you should try that cold water at night; it is a good thing; you feel so fresh and quiet after it; there is none of the stuffy feeling of a bed; you feel as if you were sleeping in the open air with the stars looking at you.

I have made up my mind that whenever I can justly afford it, I shall buy a caravan; I can hire a horse whenever I'm in the humour for a cruise; I should have accommodation for two, or perhaps three, plenty tin soups and meats, a kettle, a stove for wet weather etc. Yachting on dry land. All the filth and fresh air and pigging of it; only trees and nice inland scenery, instead of sea-coast places, which I loathe. I *shall* start one; if I live ever to be in easy enough circumstances. And you'll come and cruise with me, won't you.

I have a fairish lot of irons in the fire. My *PTFL* (*Portfolio*) Essays mean to become a little collection some of these days, which a few people I think will like and the rest of the world leave on the other side of the way most carefully. Also, my stories; I am at another just now in spare moments; they, too, I mean to make a little book of, to which the same remark I fear, may apply. Then there is John Knox; and behind him the

[3] An American with whom Bob shared lodgings in Paris.
[4] There are a number of crossings out in this paragraph and RLS wrote and deleted *Academy* before writing *Portfolio*.

Reformation generally, which I mean to wake up as I have told you, I think. Ever your affectionate friend   Robert Louis Stevenson

Address Heriot Row.

To his Mother

[16 October 1874]   *Euston & Victoria Hotels, Euston Station*

My dear Mother, I am so sorry that I shall not be able to be home on Saturday night; I must wait other twelve hours; it would be nonsense just to miss Colvin, after so long; so it will be Sunday morning before I am back.[1]

I had a very nice time at Oxford[2] and in Buckinghamshire[3] – Bucks is, I believe, the knowing way to refer to it. And I say, you must not be vexed at my absences. You must understand (I want to say this in a letter) that I shall be a nomad, more or less, until my days be done. You don't know how much I used to long for it in old days; how I used to go and look at the trains leaving, and wish to go with them. And now, you know, that I have a little more that is solid under my feet, you must take my nomadic habits as a part of me. Just wait until I am in swing, and you will see I shall pass more of my life with you than elsewhere; only, take me as I am, and give me line. I *must* be a bit of a vagabond; it's your own fault after all, isn't it? You shouldn't have had a tramp for a son!

I was sucking up this evening at the Savile, to my present ideal of all that is good and great in humanity – one Markheim,[4] a Pole with an Irish mother; at the bar and an Oxford Don; and a man, as I say, whom I adore – for the immediate present. Masson[†5] was dining opposite, but he was with a party so I had no opportunity of introducing myself. Besides I was so down on my Pole! Ever your affectionate son Robert Louis Stevenson

[†] *Masson*, for your clearer intelligence.
À Dimanche

---

[1] At the end of his Welsh tour RLS paid another visit to London on 23 September. He arrived home on Sunday 18 October.

[2] This must have been when he stayed with Andrew Lang at Merton College.

[3] The walking tour in Buckinghamshire is the subject of 'An Autumn Effect' (*Portfolio*, April and May 1875).

[4] Henry William Gegg Markheim (1845–1906), son of a missionary at Smyrna; Fellow of Queen's College Oxford from 1871; Inspector of Schools 1876–90. An authority on Molière and French literature.

[5] David Masson (1822–1907), Scottish biographer and man of letters, Professor of Rhetoric and English Literature at Edinburgh University 1865–95. He was the first editor of *Macmillan's Magazine*. RLS wrote the name again in the postscript because he thought it was not clear.

To Bob Stevenson

[20 October 1874]   17 Heriot Row

My dear Bob, the notion I had of coming over for a couple of days was relinquished for considerations of coin and parents but I mean to turn up in the course of the winter for perhaps a week. Do you know, I am mad about art now, too; but not European art – Japanese. I went to see the Elgin Marbles by the way, and of course I do prefer them to anything; the three Fates are unspeakable; I have a big photograph of them for my room, which is wonderfully satisfactory, as indeed statuary is the only thing photography is fit to reproduce. But apart from the Elgin Marbles and a few consummate things, art, as you know, has always seemed to me a failure. Now just the other day I came across Japanese art, practically speaking for the first time, and it did seem to me as if here was something at last that fetched me. Of course, there is a good deal to be set down to the novelty of subjects, and the first effect of the bedevilled imaginative violence of the figures; but making all the allowance I can for this and that, the fact remains that this art is above all others in two points. First, in that it tells its story, not for the story's sake only, but so as to produce always a magnificent decorative design. I have here by me, for instance, a picture in which an army is crossing an arm of the sea by night; the background is cool and solemn; black night sky, and green water and gray coast of hills (the colour you know is never imitative, never what you call realistic, always quite imaginative); in the foreground, the army goes past; or rather not the army, but the army's banners; and if you could see the pattern, the splendid hurly burly of bright colours and strange forms that they have thus thrown out against the dark background, you would see what imaginative truth we sacrifice, to say nothing of decorative effect, by our limping, semi-scientific way of seeing things. Second. The colours are really fun. For themselves, you know; they are their own exceeding great reward; they're not a damned bit like nature, and don't pretend to be and they're twice as nice. I know I've mixed up these two reasons for my preference and must explain again; I mean, first, because they treat a story decoratively, instead of really, and second, because their decoration is good – better than anything else in the world – Rubens and Raphael were two pretty men; so were Vinci, and others; and M. Angelo could do a thing or two, but they're not such fun as the Japanese. I am quite the Japanee now-a-days: I love them better than anything on earth, I think, except Shakespeare and a few others who wrote and made music. I want you awfully to see some Japanee picters; I think they should shake you up; perhaps you had better not see them just yet, in case they disquiet you; but after a while and when once you've a dull fit on you, go in for the heathen J.'s – and they'll be new life to you.

Is it the third or the fifth book of Virgil you so much liked; I have taken to reading the third. I tried to read Tennyson's Ode on the Dook of Wellington (which is the finest lyrical poem in the language in case you don't know) aloud this morning, and I had a hand at my throat tightening steadily as I read, until I could articulate no more and had to throw the book away. That is one of the experiences in life worth having; so were the Elgin Marbles. Mrs Sitwell took me there, and I cried; I don't know why; I just cried: these three women are so hellish calm and can see so far away, can't they? and the whole group is so *coloured*, all green as of vine leaves and purple as of a sunset sky, for all that it's only white, and the white dirty. I can't speak of these women; but I'm damned glad to have seen them; and I think I'm glad they've lost their heads, I don't think any faces could be worthy of those beautiful, *meaning* bodies.

There's some gush about art for you; on which I am death at present like yourself.[1] It irks me horridly to have to write about John Knox in this humour; but John Knox is J.K., and money is money, and as my first article is in proof, I have to get the second ready soon. I am going to write two nice things as soon as I have time; one notes of a real tour, an autumn effect, called 'In the Beechwoods'; the other notes of a sham tour, sham people, sham legends etc. called 'The Seaboard of Bohemia' – *Winter's Tale*, you understand.

I shall send you *Democratic Vistas* soon, to 4 Rue Racine I suppose.

I am sorry to hear about Katharine.[2] I did not twig it myself and she said nothing; but then I did not see them much and was not thinking of it much. The thing she has written is quite childish in style; but it is all right, and shows power; she will be able to write well if she has patience. Of course, one always knew De Mattos had no nerves, and was rather a braying ass; I never should have liked to marry him myself; and I'm damned sorry Katharine has, since it's come to that. It's awful depressing, like most things. Write soon. Ever your affectionate friend

Robert Louis Stevenson

---

[1] In an undated letter from Hotel Siron, Barbizon, Bob says he is 'death on Art at present'. He asks for a copy of *Democratic Vistas* for a Frenchman who wanted to translate it. 'To be death on' is a slang phrase meaning to be very fond of.

[2] Bob writes: 'I suppose you have heard from Katharine about De Mattos. They do not get on together I am sorry to say. He is a fool.' Bob's sister Katharine Elizabeth Alan Stevenson (1851–1939), a favourite cousin of RLS's, had married on 25 June 1874 'to the great horror of the family' William Sydney de Mattos (1851–?) who took his B.A. at Trinity College, Cambridge. De Mattos (described by RLS as an atheist) became a member of the Fabian Society and after the failure of the marriage emigrated to Canada.

To Frances Sitwell

Wednesday [*21 October 1874*]   [*17 Heriot Row*]

I have been hard at work all yesterday, and besides had to write a long letter to Bob, so I found no time until quite late and then was sleepy. Last night, it blew a fearful gale; I was kept awake about a couple of hours, and could not get to sleep for the horror of the wind's noise; the whole house shook; and mind you our house *is* a house, a great castle of jointed stone that would weigh up a street of English houses; so that when it quakes, as it did last night, it means something. But the quaking was not what put me about; it was the horrible howl of the wind round the corner; the audible haunting of an incarnate anger about the house; the evil spirit that was abroad; and above all the shuddering silent pauses when the storm's heart stands dreadfully still for a moment. O how I hate a storm at night! They have been a great influence in my life I am sure; for I can remember them so far back – long before I was six at least, for we left the house in which I remember listening to them times without number, when I was six. And in those days, the storm had for me a perfect impersonation; as durable and unvarying as any heathen deity. I always heard it, as a horseman riding past with his cloak about his head, and somehow always carried away, and riding past again, and being baffled yet once more, *ad infinitum*, all night long. I think I wanted him to get past; but I am not sure; I know only that I had some interest either for or against, in the matter and I used to lie and hold my breath, not quite frightened but in a state of miserable exaltation.[1]

My first 'John Knox' is in proof, and my second is on the anvil. It is very good of me so to do; for I want so much to get to my real tour and my sham tour, the real tour first: it is always working in my head and if I can only turn on the right sort of style at the right moment, I am not much afraid of it. One thing bothers me; what with hammering at this J.K., and writing necessary letters, and taking necessary exercise (that even not enough, the weather is so repulsive to me, cold and windy), I find I have no time for reading except times of fatigue when I wish merely to relax myself. O – and I read over again for this purpose – Flaubert's *Tentation de St Antoine*:[2] it struck me a good deal at first, but this second time it has fetched me immensely; I am but just done with it, so you will know the large proportion of salt to take with my present statement that

---

[1] RLS refers to this childhood image of the storm as a galloping horseman in the early sketch 'Nuits Blanches'; in his 'Notes of Childhood' (dated 18 May 1873); in the posthumously published 'Stormy Nights'; and in 'Windy Nights' in *A Child's Garden*.
[2] Published 1874.

it's the finest thing I ever read! Of course, it isn't that, it's full of *longueurs*, and is not quite 'red up', as we say in Scotland, not quite articulate; but there are splendid things in it.

I say, do take your macaroni with oil, L.S.:[3] *do*, *please*. It's *beastly* with butter.

I think I'll send this off because I want to know how you are badly, and I don't fancy you'll write till you hear. Ever your faithful friend

Robert Louis Stevenson

To Frances Sitwell

Saturday [14 November 1874]   *[17 Heriot Row]*

I have found what should interest you dear. A paper in which I had sketched out my life, before I knew you. Here is the exact copy even to spelling; the incertitude of the date is characteristic:

'I think now, this 5th or 6th of April 1873, that I can see my future life. I think it will run stiller and stiller year by year; a very quiet, desultorilly studious existence. If God only gives me tolerable health, I think now I shall be very happy; work and science calm the mind and stop gnawing in the brain, and as I am glad to say that I do now recognise that I shall never be a great man, I may set myself peacefully on a smaller journey; not without hope of coming to the inn before nightfall.

O dass mein Leben
Nach diesem Ziel ein ewig Wandeln sey![1]
Desiderata
I. Good Health
II. 2 to 3 hundred a year
III. *O du lieber Gott, friends!*
AMEN
Robert Louis Stevenson.'

I can't quite say that I know what the 'inn' was, therein referred to, but I think I do. It was rather an interesting find, was it not?

I am all right now, having got hard to work at this story. I am not quite sure that it will do; it seems to me so much more talking about a story,

---

[3] Lady Superintendent. In 1874 Mrs Sitwell separated from her husband and in July became Secretary of the College for Working Women (later the New College for Men and Women), Queen Square, Bloomsbury; she moved to 2 Brunswick Row, Queen Square.

[1] 'That my life may be an eternal striving for this goal!' – Goethe, *Torquato Tasso*, I.iii.501–2.

than telling it. However, it amuses me in the meantime, and of course, I am no judge.

Monday [16 November]

Do you know, Madamina,[2] I think you will like my heroine, I feel almost as if she were going to be a success. The story, as a story, I repudiate and condemn without pity. It is no story. However, in time, I begin to think, I may be able to write a good long tale worth reading. I am pleased with the result of this attempt.

Madamina, I have newly come in from an orchestral concert[3] and I *must* tell you of that. I got a loan of two shillings returned to me today – very opportunely, was it not? – and immediately spent one of them in a ticket for this concert. There were three things – the three last numbers I stayed to hear – that were profoundly delightful to me. The first was a symphony of Mozart's – thoroughly Mozartian, and of the colour and scent of rose leaves. The second was Cherubini's overture to Anacreon; and that seemed to me the colour of green bronze. I know you will not laugh at these farfetched analogies of mine; but for the third, I can give you none. It was a 'Jota Aragonese' by one Glinka; and it was better than gold, yea than much fine gold.[4] If you have a chance for Christ's sake go to hear it. It is the breath of man's nostrils. I dared not stay any longer, lest (as Coleridge said so jollily) lest[5] aught more mean should stamp me mortal.[6] And I got out into the street in such a state of excitement, that I sang at the pitch of my voice and went away down streets with the echoes clamouring about me. About half way down, my improvisations were interrupted with the sound of a poor wretched fiddler. You know my humour when I am really happy; so I crossed the streets and made the fiddler very happy, and me 'poor indeed'.[7]

By heaven, I wish I had been Glinka. *À propos,* I wonder who he was? Do you know?

Good night, my slumber begins to wear off, I mean my excitement begins to wear off – and slumber to come on me as with a great cloud. Good night.

---

[2] This word, both here and in the next paragraph, was heavily scored out in the MS. It survives in Colvin's TS copy. RLS was doubtless remembering the 'Catalogue Aria' in Act I, Scene 2 of Mozart's *Don Giovanni*.

[3] This orchestral concert, the first of a series of eight given by the Edinburgh Choral Union in the winter of 1874/5, was held on 16 November. The cheapest seats cost a shilling. The programme included Mozart's Symphony in E flat, and what is described as 'a pleasing novelty, a *capriccio brillante* by the Russian composer Glinka'.

[4] Psalm 19:10.

[5] The rest of the MS is missing; the text is taken from the TS copy.

[6] 'To the Author of *The Robbers*.'

[7] *Othello*, III.iii.161.

You need not be afraid about your letters, by the bye, they never see my letters; because I have read them and am away with them in my pocket to College, before anyone else is downstairs.

I am going to send this off to you today; for the cause that you seem put about, and I should wish you to know that I was quite recovered.

O – Glinka's thing has never been played in London. They experimented with it here, as they do often you know; and as it was a success, you will likely have it in London soon. Do go to hear it; it is no end.

Good-bye, my dear. *Je t'aime*[8] . . . *revoir.* Ever your faithful friend

Robert Louis Stevenson

Madamina, I wish you quite to understand my illness. It was merely a cessation of mind; I became a cretin, placid and a little depressed. And the very cold weather we then had was I think at the bottom of it.

Is not this verse pretty?

> Thou wast that all to me, love,
> For which my soul did pine,
> A green isle in the sea, love,
> A fountain and a shrine.[9]

To Frances Sitwell

Monday [21 December 1874]   [*17 Heriot Row*]

I have come from a concert and the concert was rather a disappointment. Not so my afternoon skating – Duddingston, our big loch, is bearing; and I wish you could have seen it this afternoon, covered with people, in thin driving snow flurries, the big hill grim and white and alpine overhead in the thick air, and the road up the gorge, as it were into the heart of it, dotted black with traffic. Moreover, I *can* skate a little bit; and what one can do, is always pleasant to do. Do you know I have been thinking a great deal of you today; when I came home in the snow from Duddingston at dusk, and again at the concert. Madonna, you are a very sweet thought to me, and a long longing – it seems so hard we should not be together. But I am brave, and happy in the thought of what is. Good night, madonna.

[8] The TS copy is torn and a few words have been lost.

[9] Edgar Allan Poe's 'To One in Paradise', reprinted in his story, 'The Assignation'. RLS reviewed the first two volumes of J.H. Ingram's edition of Poe's Works containing *The Tales* (1874) in the *Academy*, 2 January 1875.

Tuesday [22 December]

Madonna, I got your letter today and was so glad thereof. It was of good omen to me also. I worked from ten to one (my classes are suspended now for Xmas holidays) and wrote four or five *Portfolio* pages of my Buckinghamshire affair[1] – very satisfactorily, too, I fancy. Then I went to Duddingston and skated all afternoon. If you had seen the moon rising, a perfect sphere of smoky gold, in the dark air above the trees, and the white loch thick with skaters, and the great hill, snow-sprinkled, overhead! It was a sight for a king. O my dear lady, you are dear to me indeed; and I feel as if you need never concern yourself any more about me – I feel so well, and so good, and so much, in every way, what you would wish me. Only, I have a tendency to get *giddy at the nape of the neck* (if that is comprehensible), when I work: that is my one thorn in the flesh.

Well, about my mother: she was a little dry; but I think it did good; besides I am sure she was frank with me, and that is a great thing.

Wednesday [23 December]

I stayed on Duddingston today till after nightfall. The little booths that hucksters set up round the edge, were marked, each one by its little lamp. There were some fires too; and the light, and the shadows of the people who stood round them to warm themselves, made a strange pattern all round on the snow-covered ice. A few people with torches began to travel up and down the ice, a lit circle travelling along with them over the snow. A gigantic moon rose, meanwhile, over the trees and the kirk on the promontory, among perturbed and vacillating clouds.

The walk home was very solemn and strange. Once, through a broken gorge, we had a glimpse of a little space of mackerel sky, moon-litten, on the other side of the hill; the broken ridges standing gray and spectral between; and the hill-top over all, snow-white and strangely magnified in size.

This must go to you, dear, tomorrow; so that you may read it on Christmas day, for company. I hope it may be good company to you: God knows it comes from a good heart. And now I think of you reading it in bed behind the little curtain, and no Bertie there, I do not know what longing comes to me to go to you for two hours, and tell you, you have another son. This letter will not speak to you plainly enough; and you must eke it out with what you know of me, madonna – and you do know that I love you dearly –; and think of what I would say to you if I were there; and what I should look like as I saw you again, out of the body with delight; and how childish I should be for very pleasure; and so, if you love

---

[1] 'An Autumn Effect' published in the *Portfolio*.

me, this letter shall be to you as a son's Christmas kiss. And I do think, madonna, that you love me; and, believing this, I am not out of hope that I may make this day something more joyful than it would have been without me: which is my best hope in this world, so help me God.

Thursday [24 December]

Outside, it snows thick and steadily. The gardens before our house are now a wonderful fairy forest. And O this whiteness of things, how I love it, how it sends the blood about my body! Maurice de Guérin hated snow;[2] what a fool he must have been. Somebody tried to put me out of conceit with it by saying that people were lost in it. As if people don't get lost in love, too, and die of devotion to art; as if everything worth were not an occasion to some people's end.

What a wintry letter this is! Only I think it is winter seen from the inside of a warm greatcoat. And there is, at least, a warm heart about it somewhere. Do you know what they say in Xmas stories is true, I think one loves their friends more dearly at this season.

I hesitate to close this letter. I want to say something to make you happy; something that will come as near to your heart, as if we shook hands. But you will see, dear madonna, that I am very happy as I write; and that will make you happy, as you read, will it not? You must be happy: I will not have a sad deity in my chapel, she must be all smiles, and peace must look eloquently out of her eyes. And she must not know what doubt is. Nor need she doubt just now, on my account; for I do feel all that she could wish, happy and good and industrious. So — there's a hymn to myself, by way of conclusion.

And now let us put out the taper for a while (for we must be thrifty in this chapel, and the priest needs some of them to study by, so that he may be a worthy priest); only the little red heart-shaped lamp, let us leave burning, just before the shrine: it has not been extinguished since it was first lighted, eighteen months ago among the summer trees; and it is the rule of my order that it shall be kept ever trimmed and bright; so that the priest himself may warm his hands at it when he is sad, and others perhaps, seeing it through the window, may have the better courage for life.

So, madonna, I give you a son's kiss this Christmas morning, and my heart is in my mouth, dear, as I write the words. Ever your faithful friend and son and priest   Robert Louis Stevenson

---

[2] Maurice de Guérin (1810–39), French poet and mystic who won recognition after his death with the publication of his *Journals* (1860). RLS is recalling de Guérin's references to snow and cold weather in his Journals of 8 and 9 March 1833: '*Oh! jette donc vite ta cape d'hiver et prends-moi ta mantille printanière, tissue de feuilles et de fleurs.*'

To Frances Sitwell

Monday [11 January 1875]   [*17 Heriot Row*]

Dearest Mother, This is E.A. Poe: −

> Because I feel that, in the Heavens above
>   The Angels, whispering to one another,
> Can find, among their terms of burning love,
>   None so devotional as that of 'Mother,'
> Therefore by that dear name I long have called you
>   You who are *more than mother unto me*
> *And fill my heart of hearts.*[1]

I do not know to whom it was that I wrote last spring, when I was at the bottom of sorrow at Mentone − but I think it was to Bob; if it was not to him, it was to you − calling for a mother; I felt so lonely just then; I cannot tell you what sense of desertion and loss I had in my heart; and I wrote, I remember, to some one, crying out for the want of a mother (my poor mother at home here, it was so hard to her to have written it − and to write it now) − nay, when I fainted one afternoon at the Villa Marina, and the first sound I heard was Madame Garschine saying 'Berechino' so softly, I was glad − O so glad! − to take her by the hand as a mother, and make a mother of her for the time, so far as it would go.

You do not know, perhaps − I do not think I knew perhaps myself, until I thought it out to-day − how dear a hope, how sorry a want, this has been for me. For my mother is my father's wife; to have a French mother there must be a French marriage; the children of lovers are orphans. O dear mother, I am so pleased, so content, so satisfied; I am very young at heart − or (God knows) very old − and what I want is a mother, and I have one now, have I not? Some one from whom I shall have no secrets; some one whom I shall love with a love as great as a lover's and yet more; with whom I shall have all a lover's tenderness and none of a lover's timidity; who shall be something fixed and certain and forever true. If I said, I thought myself *de trop* (dear, look back at the place) it was because I am so *exigeant*, because I seek so much and am so wearing and captious, that I thought your dear body and spirit had enough to care for without me; and I think I added that I would continue to love you, did I not? And so I shall, before God. You *have* adopted me, consolation of my soul, I *am* yours and you have a duty to me; you are bound to me, and I am bound to you, by something holier than an oath. And I will be *exigeant*, I will demand from you sympathy and comprehension and

---

[1] Poe's 'To my Mother' (addressed in fact to his mother-in-law).

forgiveness; I will not give you any time or quarter, mother; I will make you my mother to the full significance of the name.[2]

Tuesday [12 January]

I am so tired, I cannot write. I have nearly finished the story of which I wrote to you; it is not nearly so good as 'King Matthias'; that is to say it is not so simple, straightforward and uniform in colour; it has, however, many more elements, and is much longer.[3] I hope it is good; *si ce n'était que pour toi – O mère, tu es bien chère, tu est bien mère, tu es ma pensée la plus intime. Si seulement j'avais le don de chanter mon amour pour toi, tu l'entendrais bien, je crois – mais parler, mais écrire, O dieu que les lieux sont longues quand on parle ou quand on écrit.* I should like to know why I like sometimes to write to you in bad French, when I could do it, if I chose, in good enough English for all practical purposes. Can't you find out? O dear mother, I am badly in want of you; I shall try to be worthy of you: I can say no more.

Good night – O dear, if I were but with you.

Wednesday [13 January]

I want to send this off; and as I have determined to do no work today, I may manage it. I overworked shamefully yesterday, and was really played out in the afternoon. I wrote from nine to 12.30, and then from one to 2.45. It is such a temptation to get on while one is in the humour. The worst of this story, as a story, is perhaps the idyll at the beginning, continued and finished at the end, after the long *baroque*, wicked interlude of the story proper; but I don't know – that may be just the best of it: it is so difficult to judge when one is in the thick of it; and the two bits *are* nice I think, simple and really pleasant. You shall see.

Dear, I am wonderfully happy. Pleased with my work, not disquiet about you, I must never disquiet myself about you any more; you will have strength for all that comes, after you have found strength for what has come; and I believe you will never change to me any more; I believe it is safe. Henceforth there is laid up for me, the perpetual treasure of your

---

[2] A few days later (on 16 January) RLS wrote to her: 'I long to be with you most ardently, and I long to put my arms about your neck and kiss you, and then sit down with my head on your knees, and have a long talk, and feel you smoothing my hair: I long for all that, as one longs for – for nothing else that I can think of. And yet, that is all. It is not a bit like what I feel for my mother *here*. But I think it must be what one *ought* to feel for a mother.' He added a footnote: 'That's a lie; nobody loves a mere mother, so much as I love you, *madonna*. Before God.'

[3] 'When the Devil was Well', a story set in Renaissance Italy, was privately printed in 1921, and published in the Vailima Edition and later collected editions. The MS of the earlier story, 'King Matthias's Hunting Horn' has not survived.

heart; and I cannot be separated from your love, by height nor depth nor any creature.[4]

Then again, I have nice books to read. The new French poets. Sully Prudhomme is adorable – I shall have a lot of Sully Prudhomme to read when I come to you. Soulary[5] better perhaps – better certainly, *comme forme*, but so unsympathetic compared to Prudhomme in character and thought. Prudhomme is a *good* man. Fancy! And a modern French poet! Wonders after that will never cease.

I am so sick of the mechanical exercise of writing – you can't think! And my right thumb nail is quite flattened. I have written four and a half or five hours the last four days. And it is too much.

Good-bye, darling mother, your son   Robert Louis Stevenson

To Frances Sitwell

Sunday [31 January 1875]   *[? 17 Heriot Row]*

My dearest Mother, I have been busy and knocked about and found no time to write. How the weather changes. On Friday, I went to Bridge of Allan.[1] A beautiful clear sunny winter's day, all the Highland hills standing about the horizon in their white robes. It was not cold. I went up my favourite walk by the riverside among the pines and ash trees. There is a little cavern here, by the side of a wide meadow, which has been a part of me any time these last twelve years – or more. On Friday it was wonderful. A large broken branch hung down over the mouth of it, and it was all cased in perfect ice. Every dock-leaf and long grass, too, was bearded with a shining icicle. And all the icicles kept dropping and dropping, and had made another little forest of clear ice among the grasses and fallen branches and dockens below them. I picked up one of these branches and threw it on the ground; and all the crystal broke with a little tinkle; and behold! a damp stick. Yesterday, a thick fog, rain and then snow, and then rain; and all along the roads the snow lay melting, and the pools froze and thawed alternately. And now today, a big blustering west wind and splendid sunshine, darkened ever and again by clouds and angry squalls of rain.

I am all right again, I think, though still taking eleven to twelve hours sleep per night. And I am quite strong and virtuous again, and determined

---

[4] Cf. Matthew 6: 19–20 and Romans 8:39.

[5] René François Armand Sully-Prudhomme (1839–1907) and Joséphin Soulary (1815–91).

[1] RLS went to Bridge of Allan with his parents on Friday 29 January. He returned home alone on the Sunday. It seems likely that the letter was written on his return.

to take no more money from my parents. It's all nonsense, it should be enough and shall.

My father also is better and quite like himself again, of which I am very glad. Ever yours   Robert Louis Stevenson

To Frances Sitwell
(Extract)

Saturday [*13 February 1875*]

Yesterday, Leslie Stephen, who was down here to lecture, called on me and took me up to see a poor fellow, a bit of a poet who writes for him, and who has been eighteen months in our Infirmary and may be, for all I know, eighteen months more. It was very sad to see him there, in a little room with two beds, and a couple of sick children in the other bed; a girl came in to visit the children and played dominoes on the counterpane with them; the gas flared and crackled, the fire burned in a dull economical way; Stephen and I sat on a couple of chairs and the poor fellow sat up in his bed, with his hair and beard all tangled, and talked as cheerfully as if he had been in a King's Palace, or the great King's Palace of the blue air. He has taught himself two languages since he has been lying there. I shall try to be of use to him.[1]

---

[1] Leslie Stephen came to Edinburgh on 9 February to give two lectures on 'Alpine Travel'. He wrote home to his wife: 'I had an interesting visit to my poor contributor. He is a miserable cripple in the infirmary, who has lost one foot and is likely to lose another – or rather hopes just to save it, – and has a crippled hand besides. . . . He writes poems of the Swinburne kind, and reads such books as he can get hold of. I have taken one of his poems for the *Cornhill*. I went to see Stevenson this morning, Colvin's friend, and told him all about this poor creature, and am going to take him there this afternoon. He will be able to lend him books, and perhaps be able to read his MSS and be otherwise useful'. This was the first meeting between RLS and William Ernest Henley and the beginning of the close friendship which was to play an important part in both lives.

William Ernest Henley (1849–1903), poet, journalist and editor, was the eldest son of an unsuccessful bookseller in Gloucester. From the age of twelve he was never wholly free from pain and illness caused by a tuberculous disease. In 1868 his left leg was amputated a few inches below the knee and thereafter he had a wooden leg and walked painfully with the aid of crutches. A few years later, faced with the threat of the loss of his right foot, Henley sought treatment at the Royal Infirmary from Professor Joseph Lister (later Lord Lister), the great pioneer of antiseptic surgery. Lister saved his foot, but Henley had to spend nearly two years in bed receiving treatment. His schooling had been scrappy and the enforced leisure of the sick-bed enabled him to study. From these experiences came the remarkable sequence of 'In Hospital' poems which established his worth as a poet. Apart from the meeting with RLS, the important consequence of his stay in Edinburgh was his meeting with his future wife (see p. 142, n. 3).

Henley was drawn into the close circle of RLS's friends and with two of them – Bob and Baxter – formed lifelong friendships. The emotional warmth and rather adolescent character of the friendship between RLS and Henley evidently supplied for RLS some element missing from

To Bob Stevenson

[c. 10 March 1875]   17 Heriot Row

My dear old man, I shall be with you somewhere about the 20th or 22nd;
I don't yet quite know which, but shall write you from London; where I
shall go on Saturday 13th, and where my address is Savile Club, 15 Savile
Row. I shall require to go as far as possible on the cheap, so perhaps you
can rig up a mattress in your studio or otherwise dispense me from hotel
fees.

I have been working like Hell at stories and have, up to the present,
failed. I have never hitherto given enough attention to the buggers
speaking – my dialogue is as weak as soda water, and poor stuff at that.
However I *shall* pull through: that is my intention.

We shall have a good deal to say, shall we not?

I have a poet in stock here, a poor ass in the infirmary with one leg off
and the other more than shaky – scrofula you know – but *bougrement*
intelligent, and he writes straight enough verses, I think. He's learning,
you know. But he makes good songs and here and there has a good idea.
His hospital sonnets are very true and boldly real – not realistic, a word I
have now learned to hate. However, art theories shall be ventilated at
large, when we meet.

Art – art – art; that is the straight tip. Wine is not extry crooked either,
as tips go, but requires to be used in moderation. The 'cooling influences
of external nature'[1] are rayther on the spot also. And lovely wooman is on
a certain platform – only there are so few woomans lovely for any one

his other relationships but it contained the seeds of their later discord. Henley never reconciled
himself to the more mature person that Stevenson was to become; the Stevenson he loved and
remembered (as he wrote in his notorious *Pall Mall Magazine* article in 1901) was 'the unmarried
and irresponsible Lewis: the friend, the comrade, the *charmeur*'. This was the youthful Stevenson
he portrayed in his poem 'Apparition', beginning, 'Thin-legged, thin-chested, slight unspeak-
ably'. Stevenson's most famous partial portrait of Henley is in *Treasure Island*. In a letter of May
1883 he confessed: 'It was the sight of your maimed strength and masterfulness that begot John
Silver. . . . Of course, he is not in any other quality or feature the least like you; but the idea of
the maimed man, ruling and dreaded by the sound was entirely taken from you.'

After a short period working for the *Encyclopaedia Britannica* in Edinburgh Henley returned
to London and for the rest of his life earned a fairly precarious living as a journalist and editor.
He was a prolific contributor to the *Athenaeum*, *Saturday Review* and other journals. His first spell
as editor was on the magazine *London*, 1877–9 (see p. 126, n. 9); he went on to become editor
of the *Magazine of Art*, 1881–6; and showed himself to be an editor of genius on the *Scots
Observer* (later the *National Observer*), 1889–94, and the *New Review*, 1894–8. Recognition as a
poet came with the publication of his *A Book of Verses*, 1888, and later collections. In the 1890s
he did some editorial work of distinction, including (in collaboration with T.F. Henderson) a
major edition of Burns, 1896–7. He was touchy and quick to take offence, and at one time or
another quarrelled with most of his friends.

[1] RLS quotes the phrase in 'Some Aspects of Walt Whitman'. Whitman uses it (with 'material
nature' instead of 'external nature') in a footnote to *Democratic Vistas* (1871).

man; and I have dropped out of my service to the second rates. There –
that is a taste of yours truly, jest to keep your hand in. Ever yours

                                                        Robert Louis Stevenson

Write to me, and say how you can manage to get me economically
stowed. S. Club; 15 Savile Row London.[2]

To Frances Sitwell

Wednesday [5 May 1875]   [*17 Heriot Row*]

A moment, at last. These last few days have been as jolly as days could
be, and by good fortune I leave tomorrow for Swanston so that I shall not
feel the whole fall back to habitual self. The pride of life could scarce go
further. To live in splendid clothes, velvet and gold and fur, upon –
principally champagne and lobster salad, with a company of people nearly
all of whom are exceptionally good talkers; when your days began about
eleven and ended about four – I have lost that sentence; I give it up; it is
very admirable sport anyway.[1] Then both my afternoons have been so
pleasantly occupied – taking Henley drives. I had a business to carry him
down the long stair, and more of a business to get him up again; but while
he was in the carriage, it was splendid. It is now just the top of spring with
us. The whole country is mad with green. To see the cherry blossom
bitten out upon the black firs, and the black firs bitten out of the blue sky,
was a sight to set before a king. You may imagine what it was to a man
who has been eighteen months in a hospital ward. The look of his face
was a wine to me. He plainly has been little in the country before.
Imagine this: I always stopped him on the Bridges to let him enjoy the
great *cry* of green that goes up to Heaven out of the river beds, and he
asked (more than once) 'What noise is that?' – 'The water.' – 'O' almost
incredulously; and then quite a long while after: 'Do you know the noise

---

[2] RLS duly went to London as planned and then joined Bob in Paris. Under Bob's tutelage RLS
paid his first visit to the forest of Fontainebleau and the art-colony centred at Siron's inn at
Barbizon. He wrote to his mother, 'I am in love with the forest and the life at Barbizon.' His
impressions were the subject of his essay, 'Forest Notes' in *Cornhill* of May 1876. He returned
home on 23 April.

[1] RLS had been acting in *Twelfth Night* in the Jenkin theatricals. He wrote to Mrs Sitwell on 2
May:

> I play Orsino every day, in all the pomp of Solomon; splendid Francis the First clothes,
> heavy with gold and stage jewellery. I play it ill enough, I believe; but me and the clothes,
> and the wadding wherewith the clothes and me are reconciled, produce every night a thrill
> of admiration. Our cook told my mother (there is a servants' night, you know) that she and
> the housemaid were 'just prood to be able to say it was oor young gentleman'. To sup
> afterwards with these clothes on and a wonderful lot of gaiety and Shakespearian jokes about
> the table, is something to live for.

of the water astonished me very much.' I was much struck by his putting
the question *twice*; I have lost the sense of wonder of course; but there
must be something to wonder at; for Henley has eyes and ears and an
immortal soul of his own.[2]

I hope you too have been happy dear; I am afraid you are not with that
damned college and all; I say you must be happy mind you; it makes me
feel so wicked when I have been happy, and I think of you, madonna, and
fear you have been sad. O my dear, I have been seeing a lot of nice people
these last days, and it makes me see more and more what a nice person
you are.

I shall send this off today to let you know of my new address Swanston
Cottage, Lothianburn Edinburgh. Salute the faithful in my name. Salute
Priscilla, salute Barnabas, salute Ebenezer[3] – O no, he's too much, I
withdraw Ebenezer; enough of early Christians. Good-bye. *Je te serre la
main.* Ever your faithful   Robert Louis Stevenson

To Frances Sitwell

[*21 June 1875*][1]   [*Swanston*]

Simply a scratch. All right, jolly, well, and through with the difficulty.
My father a little grumbly but pleased about the Burns.[2] Never travel in
the same carriage with three able-bodied seamen and a fruiterer from
Kent; the a-b's speak all night, as though they were hailing vessels at sea,
and the fruiterer as if he were crying fruit in a noisy market place: such,
at least is my *funeste* experience. I wonder if a fruiterer from some place
else – say Worcestershire – would offer the same phenomena: insoluble
doubt. Madonna, *je me trouve à merveille. J'ai respiré, vois tu. Tout à toi*
                                                                    R.L.S.

Tuesday [*22 June*]

Forgive me, couldn't get it off. Awfully nice man here tonight. Public
servant – New Zealand.[3] Telling us all about the South Sea Islands till I

---

[2] John Connell (*W.E. Henley*, 1949) says that the memory of these drives remained with Henley
all his life and that years later, after he and RLS had quarrelled, he made a sentimental pilgrimage
with Charles Whibley and 'recalled the jokes he had made and the happiness he had felt'.

[3] Parodying St Paul's Epistles (cf. II Timothy 4.19).

[1] RLS visited London 17–21 June.

[2] A commission to write the article on Burns for the ninth edition of the *Encyclopaedia Britannica*.
The article was written but rejected.

[3] William Seed (1827–90), New Zealand civil servant who became Secretary and Inspector of
Customs and Marine 1882. He visited Samoa in 1870 to report on trade and made a tour of
British lighthouses in 1875. His daughter, Katherine Eleanor Seed, married in 1874 RLS's
cousin, Lewis Wilson.

was sick with desire to go there; beautiful places, green forever; perfect climate; perfect shapes of men and women, with red flowers in their hair; nothing to do but to study oratory and etiquette, sit in the sun, and pick up the fruits as they fall. Navigator's Islands is the place; absolute balm for the weary. Ever your faithful friend   R.L.S.

To Frances Sitwell

Thursday [*1 July 1875*]   [*Swanston*]

This day fortnight, I shall fall or conquer. Outside the rain still soaks; but now and again the hilltop looks through the mist vaguely. I am very comfortable, very sleepy and very much satisfied with the arrangements of providence.

Saturday – no Sunday [*4 July*] *12.45*

Just been – not grinding alas! – I couldn't – but doing a bit of 'Fontainebleau'.[1] I don't think I'll be plucked. I am not sure though. I am so busy, what with this d—d law, and this 'Fontainebleau' always at my elbow, and three plays (three, think of that!) and a story, all crying out to me, 'finish, finish, make an entire end, make us strong, shapely, viable creatures!' it's enough to put a man crazy. Moreover, I have my thesis[2] given out now, which is a fifth (is it fifth? I can't count) incumbrance. At least you see I'm keeping jolly ever since my London business, which is the great affair for me, is it not?

Sunday

Là, madonna, I've been to church and am not depressed – a great step. I was at that beautiful church my P.P.P. was about.[3] It is a little cruciform place, with heavy cornices and string course to match, and a steep slate

---

[1] 'Forest Notes'.

[2] RLS's formal thesis in Latin, on a title of the Pandects, Lib XLI, IX 'Pro Dote', is in the National Library of Scotland.

[3] In May and June RLS wrote at least fifteen *Petits Poèmes en Prose*. Six are known to have survived, among them 'Sunday Thoughts', dated 2 June 1875, which begins: 'A plague o' these Sundays! How the church bells ring up the sleeping past! I cannot go into sermon; memories ache too hard; and so I bide out under the blue heaven, beside the small kirk whelmed in leaves.' The reference is to Glencorse Church in the Pentlands, now a picturesque ruin. Alexander Torrence (1789–1877), ordained 1818, was assistant and successor to his father William Torrence (1746–1836) who was minister at Glencorse from 1788. The church and the clergyman reappear in ch. 6 of *Weir of Hermiston*. The gravestones are still there. The French prisoner was Charles Cotier, captured during the Napoleonic wars and killed in January 1807 when a sentry was ordered to fire at random into the prison; there was a public outcry and the officer responsible was sentenced to nine months' imprisonment.

roof. The small kirkyard is full of old gravestones; one of a Frenchman from Dunkerque, I suppose he died prisoner in the military prison hard by. And one, the most pathetic memorial I ever saw: a poor school-slate, in a wooden frame, with the inscription cut into it evidently by the father's own hand. In church old Mr Torrence preached, over eighty and a relic of times forgotten, with his black thread gloves and mild old foolish face. One of the nicest parts of it was to see John Inglis,[4] the greatest man in Scotland, our Justice General and the only born lawyer I ever heard, listening to the piping old body, as though it had all been a revelation, grave and respectful, though I don't suppose he believed a word of it.

Wednesday [*7 July*]

Madonna, I am all well in this baking hot weather, taking lots of exercise and working (a good deal) for my exam. I have got Burns all right. Cannot write. Ever your faithful   R.L.S.

To Frances Sitwell

[*14 July 1875*]

[Facsimile page 112]

To his Mother[1]

[*August 1875*]   *Chez Siron, Barbizon*

My dear Mother, I have been three days at a place called Grez, a pretty, and very melancholy village on the plain.[2] A low bridge of many arches choked with sedge; great fields of white and yellow water lilies; poplars and willows innumerable; and about it all such an atmosphere of sadness and slackness, one could do nothing but get into the boat and out of it again, and yawn for bed time.

Yesterday Bob and I walked home; it came on [a] very creditable thunderstorm; we were soon wet through; sometimes the rain was so

[4] John Inglis, Lord Glencorse (1810–91), Lord Justice-General of Scotland 1867–91. He lived at the nearby Glencorse House.

[1] Two days after he had passed his Final Examination for the Scottish Bar RLS was called to the Bar and appeared in his wig and gown. On 23 July his mother noted in her diary that he had received his first (complimentary) brief. The next day she recorded: 'Lou sails for London with Sir W. Simpson en route for France.' By early August he was at Barbizon.

[2] RLS describes this visit to Grez in 'Forest Notes'. Despite the unfavourable first impressions, RLS and his friends made Grez their headquarters from 1876 onwards.

Madonna,

Passed.

ever

your

R.

L.

heavy that one could only see by holding the hand over the eyes; and to crown all, we lost our way and wandered all over the place, and into the artillery range, among broken trees, with big shot lying about among the rocks. It was near dinner time when we got to Barbizon; and it is supposed that we walked from twenty-three to twenty-five miles: which is not bad for the advocate, who is not tired this morning. I was very glad to be back again in this dear place and smell the wet forest in the morning.

Simpson and the rest drove back in a carriage and got about as wet as we did.

Why don't you write. I have no more to say. Ever your affectionate son   Robert Louis Stevenson

To Sidney Colvin

[*November 1875*]   [*17 Heriot Row*]

My dear Colvin, Thanks for your letter and news. The Brittany game is simply 'on it'. There are no two ways of that.[1] Look here, my young and lovely friend, if you overwork like that, your numskull will cave in again. I wish to see your big lucubrations very much. No – my 'Burns' is not done yet, it has led me so far afield that I cannot finish it; every time I think I see my way to an end, some new game (or perhaps wild goose) starts up and away I go. And then again, to be plain, I shirk the work of the critical part, shirk it as a man shirks a long jump. It is awful to have to express and differentiate Burns, in a column or two. O golly, I say you know, it *can't* be done at the money. All the more as I'm a going to write a book about it. *Ramsay, Fergusson and Burns: an Essay*[2] (or *A Critical Essay*? but then I'm going to give lives of the three gentlemen, only the gist of the book is the criticism) 'by Robert Louis Stevenson, Advocate, M.S., P.P.C., etc.' How's that for cut and dry? And I *could* write that book. Unless I deceive myself in a superior style, I could even write it pretty adequately. I feel as if I was really in it, and knew the game thoroughly. You see what comes of trying to write an essay on Burns in ten columns.

Meantime, when I have done 'Burns', I shall finish 'Charles of Orleans'[3] (who is in a good way, about the fifth month, I should think,

---

[1] 'At the Land's End of France', an unsigned article by Colvin in the November *Cornhill*, celebrating his holiday in Brittany. It was reprinted in *Memories and Notes* in 1921.

[2] Allan Ramsay (1686–1758), author of the pastoral drama *The Gentle Shepherd* (1725), a pioneer editor and populariser of Scots vernacular poetry. Robert Fergusson (1750–74), the Edinburgh poet acknowledged by Burns as 'my elder brother in Misfortune, By far my elder brother in the Muse' whose life ended tragically in a madhouse. RLS always felt a strong sense of kinship with him.

[3] Charles of Orléans (1391–1465), whose court at Blois was a centre for poets, wrote many skilful and graceful ballades and rondeaux and inspired RLS's own interest in these forms.

and promises to be a fine healthy child, better than any of his elder
brothers for a while); and then perhaps a 'Villon', for Villon is a very
essential part of my *Ramsay Fergusson Burns*; I mean, is a note in it and will
recur again and again for comparison and illustration; then perhaps I may
try 'Fontainebleau', by the way. But so soon as Charles of O. is polished
off, and immortalized forever, he and his pipings, in a solid imperishable
shrine of R.L.S., my true aim and end will be this little book, booky,
booklet, bookkin, bookicky – yes, that's it – bookicky. Suppose I could
jerk you out 100 *Cornhill* pages; that would easy make 200 pages of decent
form; and then thickish paper – eh? would that do? I daresay it could be
made bigger; but I know what 100 pages of copy, bright consummate
copy, imply behind the scenes, of weary manuscribing: I think if I put
another nothing to it, I should not be outside the mark; and 1000 *Cornhill*
pages of 500 words, means I fancy (but I never was good at figures,
although an amateur of the female figure in all its branches) means
500,000 words. There's a prospect for an idle young gentleman who lives
at home at ease! The future is thick with inky fingers. And then perhaps
nobody would publish. *Ah nom de dieu!* What do you think of all this, will
it paddle think you?

I hope this pen will write; it is the third I have tried.

About coming up, no, that's impossible; for I am worse than a bank-
rupt. I have at the present six shillings and a penny; I have a sounding lot
of bills for Christmas; new dress suit for instance, the old one having gone
for Parliament House; and new white shirts to live up to my new
profession; I'm as gay and swell and gummy as can be; only all my boots
leak, one pair water, and the other two simple black mud; so that my rig
is more for the eye, than a very solid comfort to myself. Besides, I owe
about six quid to Simpson, about as much to my mother, and 40 francs to
you. That is my budget. Dismal enough; and no prospect of any coin
coming in; at least for months. So that here I am, I almost fear, for the
winter; certainly till after Xmas, and then it depends on how my bills 'turn
out', whether it shall not be till spring. So meantime, I must whistle in
my cage. My cage is better by one thing; I am an advocate now. If you
ask me why that makes it better, I would remind you that in the most
distressing circumstances a little consequence goes a long way, and even
bereaved relatives stand on precedence round the coffin. I idle finely. I
read Boswell's *Life of Johnson*, Martin's *History of France*,[4] Allan Ramsay,
Olivier Basselin,[5] all sorts of rubbish *à propos* of Burns, Comines,[6] Juvenal

---

[4] Henri Martin (1810–83), author – according to the *Oxford Companion to French Literature* – of a
'mediocre history of France'.
[5] Fifteenth-century author of drinking songs known as *Vaux-de-vire*. RLS's quotation comes from
'*À Son Nez*'.
[6] Philippe de Comines or Commines (*c*.1446–*c*.1511). RLS's copy of his *Mémoires* (edition of
1561) is at Yale.

des Ursins[7] etc.; I walk about the Parliament House five forenoons a week, in wig and gown;[8] I have either a five or six mile walk, or an hour or two hard skating on the rink, every afternoon, without fail; and – well, this is not so good perhaps but is a part of my system – I sit up late at night and sometimes wet my whistle.

> On dit qu'il nuit aux yeux; mais
> seront-ils les maistres?
> Le vin est guarison
> De mes maux: J'aime mieux perdre
> les deux fenestres
> Que toute la maison.

(That's O. Basselin; *c'est assez choite, n'est-ce pas?*) Which means for me that, in the meantime, I must *live*; because if I die just now, I shall have little profit of all my abstinence.

I have not written much; but (like the seaman's parrot in the tale) I have thought a deal.[9] You have never, by the way, returned me either 'Spring' or 'Béranger', which is certainly a d–d shame.[10] I always comforted myself with that, when my conscience pricked me about a letter to you. 'Thus conscience' –[11] O no, that's not appropriate in this connexion.
Ever yours   Robert Louis Stevenson

I say, is there any chance of your coming north this year. Mind you that promise is now more respectable for age than is becoming.

R.L.S.

---

[7] Jean Juvenal des Ursins (1388–1473), chronicler of the reign of Charles VI.

[8] After his return to Edinburgh in September, RLS made some slight effort over the next few months to practise as an advocate. A brass plate with his name was affixed to the door of 17 Heriot Row. His mother records that he had four briefs in all, and he told Balfour at Vailima that he earned less than £10 in fees. His mother described what happened:

> For a few months Louis went every day to the Parliament House [where advocates waited for business] and it was hoped that he might carry on his writing in the library but he soon found that it was impossible; the Parliament House was too pleasant a place to be idle in and he told his father that he would fall between two stools if he went on, so the pretence was given up and he stayed at home and worked busily and happily at his literary work.

[9] A man who noticed one silent parrot amongst a host of talkative ones for sale asked the bird the reason for its silence. He was delighted with its reply, 'I think the more'; but when, on the strength of this he had bought the parrot, he discovered that they were the only words it could say.

[10] In May 1875 RLS had written an essay 'On the Spirit of Springtime' which he described as 'a jolly mixture of sensuality and awful pretty sentimentality'. Colvin promptly lost the MS. 'Béranger' is RLS's article on Pierre-Jean de Béranger for the ninth edition of the *Encyclopaedia Britannica*; it was reprinted through successive editions until 1926.

[11] '. . . does make cowards of us all' – *Hamlet*, III.i.83.

To Frances Sitwell

[*9 July 1876*]   *Swanston*

Well, here I am at last; it's a Sunday, blowing hard, with a gray sky, with the leaves flying; and I've nothing to say. I ought to have, no doubt; since it's so long since last I wrote; but there are times when people's lives stand still. If you were to ask a squirrel in a mechanical cage, for his autobiography, it would not be very gay. Every spin may be amusing in itself, but is mighty like the last. You see I compare myself to a light hearted animal; and indeed I have been in a very good humour. For the weather has been passable; I've taken a deal of exercise, and done some work. But I'm just in the humour which makes letter writing most impossible; for I just value an experience at the moment, I do not look forward, and as soon as a thing's past, I forget it as much as I can. This is a floating way of life, not very serious, but diverting enough. Morality, virtue, love, and these kind of things are very hard and very painful even, but they string your life together; now mine's all in rags; and I can't say anything about it.

I have the strangest repugnance for writing; indeed I have nearly got myself persuaded into the notion, that letters don't arrive, in order to salve my conscience for never sending them off.

I'm reading a great deal of XVth Century: *Trial of Joan of Arc*,[1] *Paston Letters*,[2] *Basin*[3] etc. Also, Boswell daily, by way of a Bible; I mean to read Boswell now until the day I die. And now and again, a bit of *Pilgrim's Progress*. Is that all? Yes, I think that's all. I have a thing in proof for the *Cornhill* called 'Virginibus Puerisque', which I should not suppose you will like. 'Charles of Orleans' is again laid aside, but in a good state of furtherance this time. A paper called 'A Defence of Idlers' (which is really a defence of R.L.S.) is in a good way. Also, I'm writing scurrilities about City men, at £4 a scurrility.[4] Scurrilities are all my fancy painted them, they're easy and they pay. And what's more, only it wouldn't go into the adaptation, they are amusing to do. So you see I am busy in a tumultuous, knotless sort of fashion; and as I say, I take lots of exercise, and I'm as brown as a berry.

This is the first letter I've written for – O I don't know how long.

---

[1] Jules Quicherat (1814–82), *Procès de Condamnation et de Réhabilitation de Jeanne d'Arc* (5 vols, 1841–9).

[2] Letters of a fifteenth-century Norfolk family, later used by RLS as source material for *The Black Arrow*.

[3] Thomas Basin (1412–91), Bishop of Lisieux, *Histoire des Règnes de Charles VII et de Louis XI* (4 vols, 1855–9).

[4] Possibly in *Vanity Fair*, but they have not been identified.

I daresay you may fancy I had a curious time in London last spring; it was the only occasion (save three wet days with no money, a cold and only one pair of trousers, last October, when really the straits of the position kept me well occupied) – save this, it was the only occasion I have been in London since I knew you, on my own resources; and it was odd, you may believe. I was several times very near Queen's Square, but went away again. I once went down Southampton Row, and felt in a fine flutter in case you should come out of Cosmo Place. But you didn't. I daresay you know a great deal more about me now, as I know much more of you: and both of us must have learned something of the inscrutable ways of fate. How dark and foolish are the mazes in which people once walked, thinking them then lit up with eternal sunlight, and what we now see to be so much gauze and cardboard, imperishable masonry! O for Samson's heave of the shoulder! But at the end, after much wandering, the door appears; or rather two doors. And one person finds himself alone; possibly, in some cases, two; for a tiff, a twig, a theory. God help us all, amen. For I do cling a little to God, as I have lost all hold on right or wrong. You can't think things both right and wrong you know; the human mind cannot do it, although I daresay it would be devilish clever, if you could; and when you come to a stone wall in morals, you give them up, and be d—d to them. I beg your pardon, but that's the only English idiom which explains my meaning. So I say I cling to God; to a nice immoral old gentleman who knows a bit more about it all than I do, and may, some time or other, in the course of the ages, explain matters to his creature over a pipe of tobacco; nay, and he may be something more than this and give one that sense of finish and perfection that can only be had one way in the world: I daresay, it's all a lie; but if it pleases me to imagine it –

God bless you. I am going to bed.

My dear, I don't know when this is going off. Maud and the Professor are here;[5] and I've been seedy, sore throat and toothache; but I'm all right now.

30 July

This is I suppose three weeks after I began. Do please forgive me. For all I am pretty stationary to outward view, the billows have gone over my head since then; and I have need[ed] all my courage, and I have lots of it, to bear up in good spirits against it all.[6] And letter writing, especially when

---

[5] The Babingtons visited the Stevensons 11–17 July. MIS records that from 17–24 July RLS stayed at the Hawes Inn, Queensferry, 'for quiet' as there were so many visitors at Swanston.
[6] In an undated letter to his future wife, Henley refers to meeting RLS in the Inn at Queensferry: 'He was in trouble (a secret), and before his affliction I suppressed my own. We had a long talk.'

it is of a sort to take one very vividly into the past, is an intolerable pain under certain circumstances, and knocks all the pluck out of you. I say just so much, not by way of excuse, but lest you should ever come to hear of it (which I pray God you never may) when you will have it under my hand that I could not bring my mind to write to you at the moment. However, for all the world is such rough water, I thank God he has given me so good a pluck. And I am glad I am off on my holidays. To the Highlands, first, to the Jenkins, then to Antwerp; thence, by canoe with Simpson, to Paris and Grez (on the Loing and an old acquaintance of mine on the skirts of Fontainebleau) to complete our cruise next spring (if we're all alive and jolly) by Loing and Loire, Saone and Rhone, to the Mediter-ranean. It should make a jolly book of gossip, I imagine. God bless you.

Robert Louis Stevenson

P.S. 'Virginibus Puerisque' is in August *Cornhill*. 'Charles of Orleans' is finished and sent to Stephen; 'Idlers' ditto and sent to Grove;[7] but I've no word of either. So I've not been idle.   R.L.S.

Address: Attadale, Strathcarron, Scotland for a week. Then P. Restante Liège.

---

[7] George Grove (1820–1900) knighted 1883, was editor of *Macmillan's Magazine* 1868–83; his enduring fame rests on his *Dictionary of Music and Musicians* (1878–89). 'Charles of Orleans' was published in *Cornhill* for December 1876 and 'An Apology for Idlers' in the same magazine in July 1877.

V. FRANCE AND FANNY OSBOURNE: PROGRESS AS AN AUTHOR
August 1876–July 1879

Stevenson went south with Walter Simpson in August 1876. After a brief stay in London, they set off for Belgium to begin the canoe journey which was to form the subject of RLS's first book, *An Inland Voyage*. The voyage began in Antwerp on 25 August and ended at Pontoise on 13 or 14 September.

In the last paragraph of *An Inland Voyage*, RLS wrote the much-quoted words: 'You may paddle all day long; but it is when you come back at nightfall, and look in at the familiar room, that you find Love or Death awaiting you beside the stove; and the most beautiful adventures are not those we go to seek.' He was to find Love awaiting him in the person of his future wife, Fanny Van de Grift Osbourne, when he arrived at Grez some time in September 1876.

Fanny had already lived for half of her life and had many and varied experiences before this first meeting with the man who was to become her second husband. Frances Matilda Vandegrift (1840–1914) was born in Indianapolis, the capital of Indiana, the eldest of six surviving children (five girls and one boy) of Jacob Vandegrift (1816–76), a lumber merchant and dealer in real-estate, and his wife Esther Thomas Keen (1811–94). She always called herself 'Fanny' and later adopted the earlier and more aristocratic-looking spelling of her surname 'Van de Grift'. In 1857 Fanny married Samuel Osbourne, a handsome twenty-year-old from Kentucky, who was at that time private secretary to the Governor of Indiana. He was remembered by his children as a man of great kindness and charm but he proved unsatisfactory as a husband and over the years the marriage fell under increasing strain because of his infidelities. After brief service in the Civil War, Sam's restlessness led him to travel out to California, and then, attracted by the lure of silver-mining, to move on to the mining-camp of Austin in Nevada. Fanny, with her young daughter, Isobel (Belle), born in 1858, joined him there in 1864, after a difficult and hazardous journey. At Austin and later at Virginia City, under the most primitive conditions, Fanny performed wonders of housekeeping, creating a comfortable home in these rough, lawless mining-towns. She learned, too, to roll and smoke cigarettes – thereafter a lifelong habit – and to fire a revolver.

Sam failed to make his fortune in silver mining, and after further vicissitudes – including a period when he disappeared on a prospecting trip in Montana, and was falsely reported to have been killed by Indians – the Osbournes came to San Francisco and their son, Samuel Lloyd Osbourne (later known as Lloyd) was born there in 1868. Soon afterwards Fanny caught Sam out in fresh philanderings and returned for a year to her father's farm in Clayton, Hendricks County, Indiana. There was another reconciliation and married life was re-established in their cottage at East Oakland (across the Bay from San Francisco). Sam secured a position as an official shorthand reporter in the District Court. Fanny was able to enjoy a wide range of interests and activities. Her greatest joy was in her garden, but she also dabbled in photography, practised at a rifle-range, made clothes on her sewing-machine, and when the servant was away did the cooking. She became friendly with a group of people (who were also Sam's friends) prominent in the cultural life of San Francisco; they included the artist Virgil Williams and his artist wife Dora Norton (with whom she corresponded for the rest of her life), and Timothy Rearden, a lawyer who was librarian of the Mercantile Library and teased her and flirted with her.[1] With Rearden's encouragement she tried (not very successfully) to write stories. A more important step was to join her daughter Belle in studying art at Virgil Williams's School. Belle was to show the greater talent but Fanny did sufficiently well to gain a silver medal for drawing.

A second son, Hervey, had been born in June 1871 but the marriage continued to deteriorate and in 1875 Fanny made the decision not only to leave her husband again but to travel with her three children to Europe, where she and Belle could continue their art studies. No doubt the advantage for Belle of art instruction in Europe played some part in what seems a puzzling decision. After a brief visit to Indianapolis to see her parents, Fanny travelled from New York to Antwerp, arriving there in August 1875. After three months in Antwerp she moved on to Paris, where she and Belle enrolled as art students in the Atelier Julian. Sam seems to have paid her an allowance throughout her stay in France but they were often desperately poor. In April 1876 the beautiful but delicate Hervey died after a long and painful illness; Sam joined his wife in Paris and was with her when their son died but he returned to America almost immediately.

Fanny, in a state of shock after Hervey's death, was worried about the health of her other son, Lloyd. She took him to Grez for three weeks and

[1] Virgil Williams (1830–86), an American artist who studied in Rome was Director of the School of Design in San Francisco, 1874–86. His second wife, Dora Norton (1829–1915), was described by Belle as 'a slim, straight-backed, decisive Yankee woman who prided herself on a frankness that was sometimes rather appalling'. The Williamses befriended RLS in San Francisco and Dora was a witness at the wedding. Timothy Rearden (1839–92) was appointed Judge of the Superior Court in 1883.

he soon recovered. At that time the artists who made the place their summer headquarters had not arrived. When she made her second visit in June or July the artists were there and made a great fuss of her. They painted her, took her for walks and treated her as a very special person. She began to lose her 'tragic look' and to take part in the boating games. The only contemporary record of Fanny's life at this period is to be found in the long, coquettish letters she wrote to her San Francisco friend Timothy Rearden. To him she wrote: 'The garden of our house runs down to the river, and we have a canoe apiece as well as other boats. I can manage a canoe perfectly just as I would ride a horse, and am sunburned and blackened and bruised until you would hardly know me.' The ringleader in all these activities was Bob Stevenson, to whom both Fanny and Belle were attracted (and who fell in love with Belle).

Clearly several weeks passed before RLS arrived. The traditional family account is told by Fanny's sister, Nellie Sanchez, in her biography:

> One evening in the summer of 1876 the little party of guests at the old inn sat at dinner about the long table in the centre of the *salle-à-manger* . . . it was a soft, sweet evening, and the doors and windows were open; dusk drew near, and the lamps had just been lit. Suddenly a young man approached from the outside. It was Robert Louis Stevenson, who afterwards admitted that he had fallen in love with his wife at first sight when he saw her in the lamplight through the open window.

Belle and Lloyd have basically the same story in their reminiscences. They add the detail that RLS vaulted through the open window and was greeted with cries of delight by the whole company. It is impossible now to disentangle fact from fiction, but there is no reason to disbelieve that something like this happened. Stevenson himself lends support to it when writing to Fanny from Manasquan in May 1888 to celebrate their eighth wedding anniversary by wishing that he knew some other more important dates, including 'the day when I looked through the window'.

We are back on firmer ground in a letter written by Belle to a friend in September 1876:

> Stevenson's [i.e. Bob's] cousin has turned out a charming fellow and he is perfectly charmed with Mamma; they can't get him to go off boating or canoeing or anything, he just sits by the stove and smokes cigarettes and talks to her. I never heard such a good talker. He has quite a reputation as a conversationalist and I never heard anything like his stories . . . He's a very good actor and I'd rather hear him talk than read the most charming novel. He's an ugly man only twenty-five.

Letters show that RLS was back in Paris by 10 October and home in Edinburgh on the 16th. He can have had therefore little more than three weeks at Grez with Fanny, but stray references in the letters written that winter show that he was already in love.

For RLS, writing to Fanny in May 1888, another important unknown date was 'the day when I came to see you in Paris after the first absence'. This must have been in early January 1877. Fanny (mindful no doubt that her letters might be seen by her husband) gives no indication to Rearden of any special feelings for Stevenson. She says she likes him very much and that he is 'the wittiest man I ever met', but her main comments concern his hysterical behaviour: 'When he begins to laugh, if he is not stopped in time, he goes into hysterics, and has to have his fingers bent back to bring him to himself again; and when his feelings are touched he throws himself headlong on the floor and bursts into tears.'

As late as April 1877 she sends a wonderfully misleading account of the lives of both Bob and RLS (based no doubt on gossip picked up in Grez and Paris) and concludes: 'You are quite right. I shall miss my Bohemian friends when I get home . . . the two mad Stevensons who with all their sufferings are men . . . so filled with the joyousness of mere living that their presence is exhilarating, I shall never see again.'

Before Fanny had written these words, RLS's own essay 'On Falling in Love' had appeared in the February 1877 *Cornhill*. Written in November 1876, it describes falling in love as 'the one illogical adventure, the one thing of which we are tempted to think as supernatural, in our trite and reasonable world'.

To his Mother

[*9 September 1876*]   *Compiègne*

My dear Mother, I have at last overtaken all your letters from August 23rd down to September 4th. Do not imagine I am such an ass as to leave letters 'rotting' in Post Restantes; I always change my address; and keep them all floating about from place to place until, after an infinity of calculation and seamanship, I can manage to make my own line of movement and theirs converge upon the same point. Do not suppose any more that it is particularly easy to give addresses; on the contrary it is very difficult. Places often disappoint us by being far too far; some of them off the river altogether. However, I won't scold or explain, which I take to be neither more nor less than a very unkind and underhand form of scolding; for I think you have behaved very well on the whole and borne your cross like an Angel; and the proof is that I am trying to write you a long letter.

As for the questions about shopping in your Antwerp letter, I wrote you about that already.

We have had deplorable weather quite steady ever since the start; not one day without heavy showers; and generally much wind, and cold wind forby. From Antwerp to Brussels we canoed; from Brussels to Maubeuge by rail; from Maubeuge hither, with the exception of seven or eight miles on a cart between Étreux and Vadencourt, small places you will scarcely find upon the map, all by canoe. I must say, it has sometimes required a stout heart; and sometimes one could not help inwardly sympathizing with the French folk who hold up their hands in astonishment over our pleasure journey. Indeed, I do not know that I would have stuck to it as I have done, if it had not been for professional purposes; for an easy book may be written and sold, with mighty little brains about it, where the journey is of a certain seriousness and can be named. I mean a book about a journey from York to London must be clever; a book about the Caucasus may be what you will. Now, I mean to make this journey at least a curious one; it won't be finished these vacations.

Hitherto a curious one it has been; and above all in its influence on S. and me. I wake at six every morning; and we are generally in bed and asleep before half past nine. Last night, I found my way to my room, with a dark cloud of sleep over my shoulders, so thick that the candle burnt red, at about the hour of 8.40. If that isn't healthy, egad, I wonder what is.

We were very near giving up yesterday forenoon coming here from Noyon, it was so wet and cold. We stopped from one to two in a little public house, and commiserated ourselves over a fire of brushwood.[1] But the afternoon cleared up finely, though still cold; and the river rapidly widening, for the canal was emptied into it at Jarville (beg pardon, that could have no effect, Mr Stevenson; you are perfectly richt there, sir) and shortly after the Aisne joined it, and a fine ripple in the wind keeping the boats alive, put us into a good humour, which was confirmed by the appearance of Compiègne rather sooner than we had hoped. We found a pretty girl at the window of a floating house beside the bridge who gave us leave to pull the boats in by the water door of her establishment, which proved to be a washing establishment. My mind is already giving way. Address. 4 Rue Racine. Paris.[2]

---

[1] They had lunch in a 'little inn at Pimprez and were so sadly drenched that the landlady lit a few sticks in the chimney for our comfort'. Later, after listening to their conversation: ' "These gentlemen travel for their pleasure?" asked the landlady, with unconscious irony' (*An Inland Voyage*, 'Down the Oise: to Compiègne').

[2] As explained in the introduction to this section, RLS went on to Paris and thence to his first meeting with Fanny Osbourne at Grez. He was back in Edinburgh on 16 October and spent the rest of the year there, writing essays, and telling Baxter in November that he was 'damnably in love'.

To his Mother

[*January 1877*]   [*Paris*][1]

My dear Mother, *Major Adair* seems to me in the author's happiest vein;[2] there is a lyrical note which I have not before observed in his works. I was out last night at a party in a fellow's studio over in the Rue Notre Dame des Champs. It was patronised by a person who had been an Austrian Countess; but by nineteen years of America, had been turned into a yankee. Some of the people were in costume. One girl was so pretty and looked so happy that it did your heart good to see her. One of the matrons was a very beautiful woman indeed; I played old fogy and had a deal of talk with her, which pleased me. She turned out to be the mother of the *pretty girl*.[3]

The studio looked very strange lit with Chinese lanterns and a couple of strange lamps. The floor had been rubbed with candles, and was very slippery. O'Meara[4] in his character of Young Donnybrook, tumbled about like a pair of old boots; and Bloomer,[5] for all he is so little, managed to fall into the arms of every girl he danced with as he went round in the last figure of the quadrille. There was nothing to eat but sweet biscuits, and nothing to drink but sirup and water. It was a rum event.

Yes – please refuse all invitations. I am at work again – after a fashion. I'm so sorry to hear of my father's gums. Tell him to live it down, Peter. Ever your affectionate son   R.L. Stevenson

---

[1] RLS joined Fanny in Paris in early January 1877, their first meeting since their time in Grez the previous autumn. He returned to Edinburgh on 19 February.

[2] Possibly a serial story in one of the weekly newspapers.

[3] RLS wrote a detailed description of the party in an essay in *London* (see p. 126 n. 9) for 10 February 1877: 'In the Latin Quarter. No 1. A Ball at Mr Elsinare's' (reprinted in *The Lantern Bearers and Other Essays*, 1988). In the essay RLS introduced many of those present under thinly-disguised names. The pretty girl and her mother are, of course, Fanny Osbourne and her daughter Belle (Belle Bird in the article). In a letter to Balfour when he was writing the biography, Fanny commented on this reference: 'That is nonsense. I don't know why Louis should have written it. I knew him quite well then. I suppose that he could not refrain from mentioning me, and yet did not want Aunt Maggie's fussy questioning, so pretended he was speaking of a stranger.'

[4] Frank O'Meara (1853–88), Irish painter of great promise, who studied in Paris under Carolus-Duran and spent much of the rest of his life at Grez. He and Belle Osbourne fell in love, and when they parted he gave her his portrait by Sargent. There has been a revival of interest in his work and an exhibition of his paintings was held in Dublin in 1989.

[5] Hiram Reynolds Bloomer (1845–1908), American landscape painter. In the same letter to Balfour, Fanny described him as 'a gentle, proud, sweet simple creature that everybody loved, and whose feelings no-one would hurt for the world . . . it was he that Louis asked what was the matter and received the answer as Bloomer raised his head (his face had been buried in his hands) "I am old, and I am poor, and I am bald." '

To Charles Baxter

[*? March or April 1877*]   [*Edinburgh*]

My dear Charles, I am ashamed of my silence. But what the devil! we all know what a nasty thing letter writing is. This may reach you while you are lying a bleeding corse under the southern palms; or you may be engaged in performing that feat at present. Well, God help us, such is life. My *Obus* is in an irritable condition, but has not yet exploded.[1] The man with the linstock is expected in May; it makes me sick to write it. But I'm quite insane; and when the mountain does not come to Mahomet, Mahomet will to the mountain. The Simp is also close hauled with all manner of troubles and trials;[2] love (the course of true) never did run smooth. The little bow-boy plays such almighty Hell in these neighbourhoods, and everybody has been thumped under the left pap to such an egregious degree,[3] that nothing, by your leave, will satisfy any of us but marriage. Dear God, where are the old days – but where are the snows of yesteryear?[4]

Give my love to your Americans and French; as also, to the Dey of Algiers; and tell the latter that my heart is in the Highlands wherever I go.[5] Also, my mother bids me bind my hair[6] in the old manner, but I have promised to my *obusière* to wear it after a patent of hers; also, whene'er I take my walks abroad, how many poor I see,[7] but I am reluctantly obliged to pass them by with averted countenance as I am engaged in economising for another and, I trust, speedy course of *obusery*.[8]

---

[1] A howitzer shell – the potentially explosive situation of a love-affair with Fanny Osbourne (the *obusière* i.e. a female howitzer) whose husband, Sam Osbourne (the 'man with the linstock'), was expected in May. Osbourne paid a brief visit to France at this time. He was in Paris by 28 May 1877 and after a week at Grez cut short his visit because of bad reports about the San Francisco stock market. He left on 9 June and was in London on 12 June *en route* for America.

[2] Simpson had contracted an irregular Scottish marriage with Anne Fitzgerald Mackay, whom he formally married on 13 January 1881.

[3] Proceed, sweet Cupid: thou hast thumped him with thy bird-bolt under the left pap' – *Love's Labour's Lost*, IV.ii.25. RLS uses the phrase 'the blind bow-boy' (from *Romeo and Juliet*, II.iv.15) in 'On Falling in Love'.

[4] Rossetti's translation (1870) of Villon's '*Où sont les neiges d'antan*'.

[5] Burns, 'My Heart's in the Highlands'.

[6] The well-known Scots song by Mrs Anne Hunter (1742–1821) that RLS never tired of quoting or parodying:

> My mother bids me bind my hair
> With bands of rosy hue,
> Tie up my sleeves with ribbons rare,
> And lace my bodice blue!

[7] Isaac Watts, 'Praise for Mercies' (*Divine Songs for Children*).

[8] I.e. a return to France and Fanny.

You will observe that my once powerful genius is in a state of pitiable decline. It is true. *London* is rapidly hustling me into the abhorrèd tomb; I do write such damned rubbish in it,[9] that's a fac'; and I hate doing it so inconceivably. I declare I would ten times rather break stones, or – or in short do anything that didn't involve an office. As for offices, the abhorrèd tomb aforesaid seems to me welcome in comparison. At least, you have only to go *once* to that office. And then, you know, according to some writers of repute, its business exterior is no more than a trap for the Ingenuous Public; and after having passed through a few benches and ledgers and Gaelic clerks in the front apartment, you escape into a large back garden, covered with daisies and umbrageous trees, where there are swings and croquet sets for giddy youth, while austere age is supplied with rocking chairs, tobacco, summer beverages of an eminently intoxicating character, and the light and vicious literature of France. Hence, Charles, we should never presume to pass a judgment on the arrangements of providence. His little games are so dark and wily that, for anything we know, they may be intended for the best; and the Mind that created Johnny Adam and Eben Scott,[10] and placed them in the same town, is surely far beyond the reach of our feeble comprehension.

I suppose you are going to turn upon me like a wild beast and say you wanted news. Well, it's a pity. All our news is so damned compromising that I prefer not writing it. And at any rate, I hate news. Love to the Dey. To Hell with the Pope. A man's a man for a' that. And three merry men are we; I on the Land (that's to say high and dry – no coin) – Thou on the Sand (Afric's golden sand, down which the sunny fountains pour) – And Simp on the Gallows Tree![11] (or at least he ought to be – so should you for that matter – but you and I have chosen the better part, and each sits merrily on a little *obus* of his own, awaiting the moment when – paff! – no more *obus* and no more man of good fortunes!). Yours ever

R.L. Stevenson *Duc et pair*

---

[9] The weekly magazine *London* was founded and originally edited by Robert Glasgow Caldwell Brown (died 1878), the mysterious and charming adventurer commemorated by RLS in 'A College Magazine'. Henley was closely involved and later became editor. In its early days (the first number was dated 3 February 1877) RLS contributed anonymous book reviews and other journalism as well as a serial story 'An Old Song' (first identified and published in 1982).

[10] Ebenezer Erskine Scott (1816–1902), Public Accountant, who published widely used tables of logarithms used in insurance offices. Presumably a staid character contrasted with the drunken Clerk of Court (see p. 68, n. 10).

[11]
> For three wild lads were we, brave boys,
> And three wild lads were we;
> Thou on the land, and I on the sand,
> And Jack on the gallows-tree.

– Scott, *Guy Mannering* ch. 34, plus an echo of Bishop Heber's hymn 'From Greenland's Icy Mountains'.

Tommy make room for your uncle.[12]
Tell me shepherds have you seen my Flo-ora pass this way.[13]
Tol de rol de rol de rol de rol. Singing Rule Britannia, Britannia rules
the waves.

To Charles Baxter

[*June or July 1877*]   [*? Paris or Grez*]

My dear Chawles, I shall make my arrangements. The convoy shall be
followed; and sincerely, it will give me a very hearty pleasure to be chief
mourner.[1] I do not know whether I am quite following out your jest in
a jesting spirit, or with a modicum of whimper. But the fact is that I have
felt a great pleasure in your request; and damn it all. I am not eloquent.
I'll hold the bottles. And I wish you a rare good time, and plenty of
children. If you have as good a time in the future as you had in the past,
you will do well. For making all allowance for little rubs and hitches, the
past looks very delightful to me; the past when you were not going to be
married, and I was not trying to write a novel; the past when you went
through to B. of Allan to contemplate Mrs Chawles in the house of God
and I went home trembling every day lest Heaven should open and the
thunderbolt of parental anger light upon my head; the past where we have
been drunk and sober, and sat outside of grocers' shops on fine dark
nights, and wrangled in the Speculative, and heard mysterious whistling in
Waterloo Place, and met missionaries from Aberdeen:[2] generally, the past.
But the future is a fine thing also, in its way; and what's more, it's all we
have to come and go upon. So, let us strike up the Wedding March,
and bedeck ourselves with the loose and graceful folds of the frockcoat,
and crown ourselves with Sunday hats as with laurel; and go, leaping, and
singing, and praising God,[3] and under the influence of champagne and all

---

[12] The popular music-hall song by T.S. Lonsdale (1876) which makes another appearance in *The Wrong Box*.

[13] The glee 'Ye Shepherds, tell me' (or 'The Wreath') by Joseph Mazzinghi (1765–1844). Mr Crisparkle sings it in ch. 2 of *Edwin Drood*.

[1] Charles Baxter married on 24 July 1877 Grace Roberta Louisa, youngest daughter of Major-General Robert Stewart, of the Bengal Native Infantry. RLS was best man.

[2] RLS dictated this anecdote to Belle at Vailima in November 1892 for her MS *Grouse in the Gun-room*: 'Baxter and I were at the Public Room at the Granton Hotel when three serious-looking youngish men came in and sat down to dinner. The dish was taken off and they were beginning to help it when I strode across the room took my position at the empty side of their table and remarking firmly that I would allow nobody to eat like heathen in my presence, inflicted upon them a prodigiously long grace. The man who was opposite to me looked at me severely – "Perhaps you are not aware, Sir, that I am a missionary from Aberdeen," said he. Charles leaped at him – "All my life I have been longing to meet a missionary from Aberdeen," he cried in an ecstasy. Needless to say that we brought our glasses over and made a merry afternoon of it all five.'

[3] Acts 3:17.

the finer feelings of humanity, towards that sacred edifice, or secular drawing room, from whence you, issuing forth, shall startle mankind with the first splendours of the wedded Chawles. Proudest moment of my life, C.B. Ever your old friend   Louis Stevenson

Commend me to the Object, as Lang used to call his one.

I'll likely come home for it: awful expense, you'll say, but I really should like to do the part, for auld lang syne.[4]

To Frances Sitwell

[*10 August 1877*]   [*Penzance*][1]

You will do well to stick to your burn; that is a delightful life you sketch, and a very fountain of health. I wish I could live like that; but alas, it is just as well I got my 'Idlers' written and done with, for I have quite lost all power of resting. I have a goad in my flesh continually, pushing me to work, work, work. I have an essay pretty well through for Stephen; a story 'The Sire de Malétroit's Mousetrap', with which I shall try *Temple Bar*,[2] another story, in the clouds, 'The Stepfather's Story',[3] most pathetic work of a high morality or immorality, according to point of view; and lastly, also in the clouds, or perhaps a little further away, an essay on the 'Two St Michael's Mounts', historical and picturesque; perhaps, if it didn't come too long, I might throw in the Bass Rock, and call it 'Three Sea Fortalices', or something of that kind. You see how work keeps bubbling in my mind. Then I shall do another XVth century paper this autumn. 'La Sale and *Petit Jehan de Saintré*'; a kind of XVth century *Sandford and Merton*,[4] ending in filthy immoral cynicism, as if the author had got tired of being didactic and just had a good wallow in the mire to wind up with and indemnify himself for so much restraint.

Cornwall is not much to my taste, being as bleak as the bleakest parts of Scotland and nothing like so pointed and characteristic. It has a flavour of its own, though, which I may try and catch, if I find the space, in the proposed article.

[4] RLS, who had gone to France on 19 June, returned home on 19 July.

[1] RLS was on a tour of Cornwall with his parents. They reached Penzance on 7 August and visited St Michael's Mount on 9 August; the following day they went to Land's End. RLS left for Grez on 16 August.

[2] Published in *Temple Bar*, January 1878 as 'The Sire de Malétroit's Door' and reprinted in *New Arabian Nights*.

[3] Included as 'The Story of a Stepfather' in a list of thirteen *Fables and Stories* in the *Inland Voyage* notebook, but nothing more is heard of it.

[4] Antoine de La Sale (1383–?1469), author of the prose romance *Histoire du Petit Jehan de Saintré*. *Sandford and Merton* (1783–9) is a didactic children's tale by Thomas Day.

'Will o' the Mill', I suspect, is bosh.[5] But I sent it, red hot, to Stephen, in a fit of haste; and have not yet had an answer. I am quite prepared for a refusal. But I begin to have more hope, in the story line, and that should improve my income anyway. I am glad you liked Villon; some of it was not as good as it ought to be, but on the whole it seems pretty vivid and the features strongly marked. Vividness and not style, is now my line; style is all very well, but vividness is the real line of country; if a thing is meant to be read, it seems just as well to try and make it readable.

I am such a dull person now, I cannot keep off my own blarsted immortal works. Indeed they are scarcely ever out of my head. And yet I value them less and less every day. But occupation is the great thing; so that a man should have his life in his own pocket, and never be thrown out of work by anything.

I am glad to hear you are better. Please ask S.C. to write to me again; I will try to write to him. Love to all. I must stop – going to Land's End. Always your faithful friend   Robert Louis Stevenson

To W.E. Henley[1]

[December 1877]   17 Heriot Row

My dear Henley, Your kind letter did me all the good in the world. I am in the house; so can't get the watch. I must work, though it's bad for the eyes; above all as the weather is so dark that I have to light the gas all day long; but then life's not possible, for a *positively*, not negatively, lonely man, without it. I am at 'Walt Whitman';[2] and a pretty good rattle-trap I am making of him in my opinion. The Edinburgh articles[3] are a sure drain, and a sharp strain; they won't come right, and be damned to them; and it is important that they should come right: as if I and the pictureists can hit it off well enough, we shall sail into book form in due time, with more coins and honour.

I don't know that I'm unhappy; I'm cast down about my eyes; and I'm a miserable widower; but as long as I work, I keep cheerful; and I find I have no tendency to reproach God, or disown the highly respectable solar

---

[5] Published in *Cornhill*, January 1878, and reprinted in *The Merry Men*.

[1] From August to October RLS had been in Grez and then in Paris with Fanny and her children. At the beginning of November Fanny, worried by RLS's persistent eye infection, took him to London for treatment. While there she had an operation on her foot, fell very ill herself and had to stay in bed for three weeks. Colvin and Mrs Sitwell (whom she had not previously met) made a great fuss of her and she also met Henley and Leslie Stephen. This letter, written after RLS's return home is quoted by Furnas as evidence that RLS and Fanny had become lovers.

[2] 'The Gospel According to Walt Whitman', *New Quarterly Magazine*, October 1878 (reprinted in *Familiar Studies*).

[3] *Picturesque Notes on Edinburgh*, *Portfolio*, June to December 1878.

system on account of my little irritations. This over-personality seems to have fallen away from me; I'm in rare fettle for W. Whitman and his ranting optimism (a good phrase, by God – I think I'll use it); so you see, I'm not so black at heart as under the circumstances I might be. Indeed, should I not be an ungrateful dog, if after my great deliverance not yet a month old, I could see nothing but ill in our mixed world? And do I not love? and am I not loved? and have I not friends who are the pride of my heart? O no, I'll have none of your blues; I'll be lonely, dead lonely, for I can't help it; and I'll hate to go to bed, where there is no dear head upon the pillow, for I can't help that either, God help me; but I'll make no mountain of my little molehill, and pull no damnable faces at the derisive stars, as I think I had the honour of calling them somewhere; at least I know I called something derisive, and I daresay I was perfectly right.

The news from Paris is only so-so, which leads my heels a bit; but the devil's in it, we can't have all, and we can have hope and pluck. I think I have taken a leaf out of your hospital volume for good and all.

The Omadhaun[4] was very funny by the Lord; I saw Constable who said both Payn[5] and Kegan Paul[6] had very highly lauded you. Write. Yours ever   R.L.S.

To Sidney Colvin

[*December 1877*]   *17 Heriot Row*

My book would have been done by this time if I had not fallen seedy. As it is, I have upwards of 150 pages of it done; taking 220 words to the page, which is more than I should like to see.

An Inland Voyage
'– Thus sang they in the English Boat'
Marvell[1]

---

[4] '*The Omadhaun* at the Queen's', Henley's amusing account in *London* (1 December 1877) of the absurdities and complexities of the Irish melodrama by H.P. Grattan, which opened on 24 November 1877.

[5] James Payn (1830–98), author of *Lost Sir Massingberd* and a great many other once popular novels; editor of *Chambers' Journal* 1859–74 and *Cornhill* 1882–96; reader for Smith Elder & Co. from 1874.

[6] Charles Kegan Paul (1828–1902), author and publisher. He edited the *New Quarterly Magazine* 1879–80. After over twenty years as a clergyman in the Church of England he resigned his living in 1874 and subsequently progressed through Positivism to Roman Catholicism. He published *An Inland Voyage*, *Travels with a Donkey* and *Virginibus Puerisque*.

[1] This quotation from Andrew Marvell's 'Bermudas' is used on the title page of *An Inland Voyage*.

Instead of trying to finish, I shall go back on the beginning, which wants some licking, and let you have all that's done in a day or two: probably by Tuesday.

About Macmillan. Of course I leave everything to you, with the last of gratitude. But of course it wouldn't be possible to get Macmillan to make it a pretty book: his books are so foul to look upon. A small book like this should be in a small form, like the little old sixteenth and eighteenth century books, with catchwords, and the preface in italics.[2] Now Macmillan would try to make it a big book, and give me a page so ugly that shame would seize upon my heart whenever I looked at it. But of course that's a secondary consideration.

Molloy was not a canoeist; he went in a four oar gig. Moreover his book was not a book; it was only illustrated.[3] Now my work is a true *Reisebild;*[4] good or bad, well done or ill, it is the history of a man's life during some weeks of travel.

If you would like the title thus:

An Inland Voyage:
Flanders, Picardy, Isle de France

— why, it'll be true; and I will do anything to gratify you. I am in both Bentley and the *Cornhill* for January,[5] and have just received another proof from the latter. Quite right, my lord. Hüffer's the boy.[6] I hope he'll take it. There are good bits and bad in the paper, I fancy; but I could never have written it so well before.

I prefer not to speak of anything but business. You may see from my hand, that I'm not in my best estate; no more I am; and I cannot talk of what vexes me, or I get worse. But for one thing, the last accounts of F.'s little boy make me think he is going the way of the other.[7] And for

[2] The first edition was printed in an eighteenth-century style with proper names and various other words in italics.

[3] Colvin must have asked whether the work would not duplicate James Lynam Molloy's *Our Autumn Holiday on French Rivers* (1874), illustrated by Linley Sambourne. RLS later acknowledged that the success of Molloy's book had encouraged him to re-write and prepare for press the journal of his canoe journey.

[4] The *Pall Mall Gazette* of 24 June 1878 began its review: 'We cannot pay Mr Stevenson a greater compliment than by saying that while reading his *Inland Voyage* we were continually reminded of that most delightful of travellers' books, the early volumes of Heine's *Reisebilder.*'

[5] George Bentley (1828–95), publisher and author, was editor of *Temple Bar* (1866–95), in which 'The Sire de Maletroit's Door' appeared in January 1878. 'Will o' the Mill' was in *Cornhill.*

[6] Francis Hueffer (Hüffer)(1845–89), German-born journalist and music critic, son-in-law of Ford Madox Brown and father of the novelist Ford Madox Ford. He had recently purchased the *New Quarterly Magazine,* which he edited for a short time in 1878. Colvin must have suggested that he might publish the essay on Whitman.

[7] Fears that Fanny's surviving son, Lloyd, would suffer the fate of Hervey who had died in April 1876.

another, did you ever hear of spring? As a season, I believe it follows immediately on winter. Well, spring is my ——————————— term day.   R.L.S.

To his Father[1]

Friday 15 February 1878

Café de la Source, Boulevard St Michel [Paris]

My dear Father, A thought has come into my head which I think would interest you. Christianity is, among other things, a very wise, noble and strange doctrine of life. Nothing is so difficult to specify as the position it occupies with regard to asceticism. It is not ascetic. Christ was of all doctors (if you will let me use the word) one of the least ascetic. And yet there is a theory of living in the Gospels which is curiously indefinable; and leans toward asceticism on one side, although it leans away from it on the other. In fact, asceticism is used therein as a means, not as an end. This wisdom of this world consists in making oneself very little in order to avoid many knocks; in preferring others, in order that even when we lose, we shall find some pleasure in the event; in putting our desires outside of ourselves, in another ship, so to speak, so that, when the worst happens, there will be something left. You see, I speak of it as a doctrine of life, and as a wisdom for this world. People must be themselves, I suppose. I feel every day as if religion had a greater interest for me; but that interest is still centred on the little rough-and-tumble world in which our fortunes are cast for the moment. I cannot transfer my interests, not even my religious interests, to any different sphere. If I am to be a fellow worker with God, I still feel as if it must be here. How, with all the disabilities he has charged me with, I do not see; nor do I require to see it after all. From time to time, he gives me a broad hint, and I recognise a duty. That must suffice, and between whiles, we must go on as best we can.

In all this, I am afraid there will be a great deal that is disagreeable to you; but indeed, with a little good will, you may find something else which ought to please you in these lines. I have had some sharp lessons and some very acute sufferings in these last seven and twenty years, more than even you would guess; I begin to grow an old man; a little sharp, I

---

[1] RLS left Edinburgh on 22 December 1877 and after a brief stay in London joined Fanny in Dieppe. He was back in London in early January, involved in arrangements for the publication of *An Inland Voyage*, and then rejoined Fanny in Paris. Early in February TS visited Paris at his son's request. Colvin says that RLS took his father into his confidence 'about the new complications of his life'. RLS later told Mrs Sitwell: 'That all went off admirably, and is a great thing for F. and me.'

fear, and a little close and unfriendly; but still I have a good heart and believe in myself and my fellow men and the God who made us all. It is not for a few anonymous letters that I would give up mankind;[2] nor for a few cancers that I would lose my trust in him who made me. The truth is great, and it prevails within me. There are not many sadder people in the world, perhaps, than I; I have my eye on a sickbed; I have written letters today that it hurt me to write and I fear it will hurt others to receive; I am lonely, and sick and out of heart. Well, I still hope; I still believe; I still see the good in the web,[3] and cling to it. It is not much perhaps, but it is always something. Take what you can get, my dear father.

I find I have wandered a thousand miles from what I meant. It was this: of all passages bearing on Christianity in that form of a worldly wisdom, the most Christian, and so to speak, the key to the whole position, is the Christian doctrine of revenge. And it appears that this came to the world through Paul! There is a fact for you! It was to speak of this that I began this letter; but I have got into deeper seas, and must go on –

There is a fine text in the Bible, I don't know where, to the effect that all things work together for good to those who love the Lord.[4] Indeed, if this be a test, I must count myself one of those. Two years ago, I think I was as bad a man as was consistent with my character. And of all that has happened to me since then, strange as it may seem to you, everything has been, in one way or another, bringing me a little nearer to what I think you would like me to be. 'Tis a strange world, indeed, but there is a manifest God for those who care to look for him.

This is a very solemn letter for my surroundings in this busy café; but I had it on my heart to write it; and indeed I was out of the humour for anything lighter. Ever your affectionate son

Robert Louis Stevenson

P.S. While I am writing gravely, let me say one word more. I hope I have taken a step towards more friendly – no, not that (that could scarcely be) – but more intimate, relations with you. But don't expect too much of me. I am a narrow and a sad person. Try to take me as I am. This is a rare moment, and I have profited by it; but take it as a rare moment. Usually I hate to speak of what I really feel, to that extent that when I find myself *cornered*, I have a tendency to say the reverse.   R.L.S.

---

[2] In a letter to Henley at this time RLS wrote: 'Only yesterday, the anonymous letter writer made his welcome appearance in my life; I think I was positively pleased; I had been expecting him so long.'

[3] A guess at a puzzling word.

[4] Romans 8:28.

If this letter should give you pain, you have my authority to show it to MacGregor of St Cuthberts,[5] and ask him; to no one else in the clergy, but to him. I believe he will tell you there is some good in it.

★ *To Walter Crane*[1]

Burford Bridge Inn, Box Hill,
[c. *16 March 1878*]   *Dorking, Surrey*[2]

Mr Crane,
Dear Sir, I hope that is the orthodox beginning. Mr Kegan Paul has asked me to call on you; and I have tried to do so. Owing to time and tide, that could not be, so I take the other liberty of writing.

You have written to him promising a frontispiece for a fortnight hence for a little book of mine – *An Inland Voyage* – shortly to appear. Mr Paul is in dismay. It appears that there is a tide in the affairs of publishers which has the narrowest moment of flood conceivable: a week here, a week there, and a book is made or lost; and now, as I write to you, is the very nick of time, the publisher's high noon.

I should deceive you if I were to pretend I had no more than a generous interest in this appeal. For, should the public prove gullible to a proper degree, and one thousand copies net, counting thirteen to the dozen, disappear into its capacious circulating libraries, I should begin to perceive a royalty which visibly affects me as I write.[3]

I fear you will think me rude, and I do mean to be importunate. The sooner you can get the frontispiece for us, the better the book will swim, if swim it does. Believe me yours very hopefully

Robert Louis Stevenson

My mother (a good judge) says this is obscure and affected. What I mean is, couldn't you get that frontispiece sooner?   R.L.S.

My mother says the last is impolite: couldn't you as *a favour* get the frontispiece sooner?   R.L.S.

---

[5] James MacGregor (1832–1910), minister of St Cuthbert's 1873–1910, enjoyed the reputation of being one of the most eloquent preachers in the Church of Scotland.

[1] Walter Crane (1845–1915), artist, and book-illustrator, particularly of picture-books for children. He provided frontispieces for both *An Inland Voyage* and *Travels with a Donkey*.

[2] RLS, who had arrived from France a few days earlier, and his mother stayed at Burford Bridge Hotel 15–19 March and RLS had his first meeting with George Meredith. Crane's original pencil drawing for the frontispiece is annotated 'March 19 '78'.

[3] RLS was paid £20 for *An Inland Voyage*; royalties of 1/- a copy to begin after 1000 copies had been sold. The book was published on 28 April.

To Charles Baxter

[c. 27 May 1878][1]   *Albemarle Club, London*

My dear Charles, Herewith sheets of the prints (£1500's worth) stolen from Colvin on Saturday morning.[2] C. is answerable for value. Will you kindly hand one in at Hill's and other print gents, as we fear the thieves may try Edinburgh. Full details when I arrive. The Police are humbug. Yours ever   Robert Louis Stevenson

To his Parents

[? Summer 1878][1]   [France]

My dear Father and Mother, I wish to do no more today than tell you how much you are in my thoughts, and how much I love you. I am very sorry you don't like my ways; but I am conscious of not being so good a son to you as I should like to be, not in the matter you mention, although in many others. I am now twenty-seven years old; and perhaps a little entitled to follow my own way for a month or so. But please never imagine that you will lose me, or I lose you, until death interferes. I know I am not all you could wish; but do believe that I love you with all my heart – that I think my father the dearest and most honourable of men – and my mother the cleverest and most loving of women – and that I would indeed and most gladly give up almost anything earthly for your sakes.

I am afraid this sounds like phrases; perhaps this is a little my fault; but do take the sense of it – that I do indeed love you, my dear and good parents, and believe me, Yours most lovingly

Robert Louis Stevenson

---

[1] RLS was in London 22–9 May.
[2] Colvin had borrowed a quantity of engravings on approval from a London print-dealer in order to select some for purchase by the Fitzwilliam Museum. When Colvin was leaving the Savile Club on 26 May the porter put the portfolio of engravings into a cab and the driver made off with them. Although the thief was caught and sentenced, the prints were never recovered and Colvin had to bear the loss of £1537. This heavy financial commitment explains Colvin's straitened financial circumstances in later years. Baxter's records show that RLS lent Colvin £400 on 27 October 1878; Colvin was still repaying this at the end of 1884 when the account breaks off.
[1] Annotated by MIS: 'This must have been written in 1878 when we were vexed by his staying so much away from home.'

*   *   *

On 7 June 1878 RLS travelled to Paris as secretary to Fleeming Jenkin, who was a juror in the International Exhibition, but he evidently did little work in that capacity. Most of his time was spent with Fanny who had decided to go back to California. They were in Grez together in July. Later in the month Fanny and her children came to London and were taken by Bob to cheap lodgings in Radnor Street, Chelsea. Lloyd remembered RLS seeing them off at Euston Station on 12 August. Three days later the Osbournes sailed from Liverpool for New York on the Royal Mail steamer *City of Richmond.* We do not know what was agreed between RLS and Fanny about their future. Balfour (writing under Fanny's eye) says:

All was dark before them. She was not free to follow her inclination, and though the step of seeking a divorce was open to her, yet the interests and feelings of others had to be considered, and for the present all idea of a union was impossible. Stevenson, on his side, was still far from earning his own livelihood, and could not expect his parents to give their assistance or even their consent to the marriage.

On 19 August, Mrs Stevenson recorded in her diary: 'Hear that Louis has to go back to France for a time.' RLS, feeling 'pretty ill and pretty sad', was off on the walking tour through the Cevennes that became famous as *Travels with a Donkey.*

*   *   *

★To Charles Baxter

[? 8 September 1878]   *Chez Morel,*[1] *Le Monastier*

My dear Charles, I shall soon go off on a voyage, for which I think I shall buy a donkey, and out of which, if I do not make a book, may my right hand forget its cunning.[2] I am busy all day long, writing, sketching,[3] shooting with a revolver, dining with excisemen and *Ponts et Chaussées*

---

[1] Madame Irma Morel (1853–1931), described by RLS in 'A Mountain Town in France' (the posthumously published introductory essay to *Travels with a Donkey*) as 'pretty and young, [who] dressed like a lady and avoided *patois* like a weakness, [but] commonly addressed her child in the language of a drunken bully.'

[2] Psalm 137:5.

[3] An album containing twenty-three pencil sketches made by RLS in the Cevennes is at Yale. There is a selection (eight drawings) in *The Cevennes Journal* (1978).

people; for the first time for near a year I feel something like peace; it is like gold — yea, much fine ditto; it is like the dew of Hermon, or the pomade on Aaron's whiskers.[4]

In view of the journey I think forty quid would be a good thing; you might send it in a cheque on the Compagnie Générale at Le Puy: with that I shall not fear to go on my travels. Ever yours

Robert Louis Stevenson

Do write a word some of these days, and let me hear the news.[5]

To Charles Baxter

God knows what date, *vide* postmark
[*Postmark 19 September 1878*]   *Morel's*

My dear Charles, Yours (with inclosures) of the 16th to hand. All work done. I go to Le Puy tomorrow to dispatch baggage, get cash, stand lunch to engineer who has been very jolly and useful to me;[1] and hope by five o'clock on Saturday morning, to be driving Modestine towards the Gévaudan. Modestine is my *ânesse*; a darling; mouse colour; about the size of a Newfoundland dog (bigger between you and me); the colour of a mouse; costing 65 francs and a glass of brandy. Glad you sent on all the coin; I never know when I may have to send off coins to other gents, you know; and was half afraid I might come to a stick in the mountains, donkey and all, which would have been the devil. Have finished *Arabian Nights* and Edinburgh book;[2] and am a free man. Next address, Poste Restante, Alais, Gard. Give my servilities to the family. Health bad; spirits, I think, looking up. Ever yours   R.L.S.

---

[4] Psalms 19:10 and 133:2–3.

[5] Baxter's wife was awaiting the birth of their first child. Edmund Baxter was born on 9 September 1878.

[1] In one of the MSS of 'A Mountain Town in France', RLS describes him as 'a kind agreeable man with a high taste in eating, whom I used to accompany on his professional rounds'. In his notebook RLS recorded his name as Goguelat. He later gave the name to the locksmith in 'The Treasure of Franchard' and to the French prisoner killed by St Ives in the duel with scissor-blades in ch. 3 of *St Ives*.

[2] RLS had been writing the last stories in 'The Rajah's Diamond', part of the series of *Latter-Day Arabian Nights* which ran in *London* from 8 June to 26 October 1878; they were reprinted in *New Arabian Nights* (1882). He had also been sending to Henley the last articles on Edinburgh for publication in the *Portfolio*.

To W.E. Henley

[4 October 1878][1]   [Alais]

My dear Henley, I am in a considerable doubt about the Deacon;[2] Act III, putting aside the scenes which are to constitute Act IV according to your numeration, troubles me. (By the way, it would seem you have not received my last letter, wherein I spoke out my heart in admiration of your 'Mother Clarke's', wherein I told you I had a capital flat to go between the 'Excise' and the 'Parlour', and wherein I spoke to you of my two new plans. The King's Heart and The Dead Man's Shoes – alias, Monmouth; tell me of this at Lyons.) If we are to make Act III end with the Excise, upon my honour, I am half short of a situation for the actor. I am hellishly tempted by more than one wildfire; but all of them burn the piece. I wish we were at speaking distance. Par exemple, I find you a hell of a fine fellow to complain of my idleness with this cursed Deacon. Idleness! parbleu! I have just finished the Arabians and Edinburgh; I go on a tour on my two feet, goading a she ass before my face, pass most of the Cevennes, traverse a good distance, write about 24,000 words of Journal; and on my arrival, I find you complaining of my idleness! O Thunder of the firmament, O white bolt flashing in the hands of Jove, O horrid and prolonged uproar of the charging heavens! And O ye rills and fountains, wherein oft I have washed my countenance and dipped my humble culinary can – can (excuse repetition) can this be? It would seem as if it could. W.E.H.: you are unreasonable. Besides, I am going to get my proofs through before I do else. To do what has to be done to the Deacon on my part, even after the huge steps you have given it, needs squared elbows my son, and a clear outlook. Act II, Tableau I, is not up to so much as I had hoped; but we'll get in the guts in time; the scene with the two rogues somehow drags; it wants a pointing thunderbolt at the right moment.

My news, dear lad, is all cursed. Accurst and in a cursed hour, my letters hie to me. I have need of all my fresh air, and all my courage. I wish God would give me rest a little, before I go hence to be with the

---

[1] RLS arrived at St Jean du Gard after a journey of 'upwards of 120 miles' on the evening of 3 October. He sold Modestine on the morning of 4 October and travelled by stage-coach to Alais (present-day Alès) that afternoon.

[2] Since he was a boy RLS had been fascinated by the story of Deacon William Brodie (1741–88), who led a double life as a respectable Edinburgh cabinet maker and city councillor by day and gambler and burglar by night. In an interview in New York September 1887 he said: 'When I was about nineteen years of age I wrote a sort of hugger-mugger melodrama, which lay by in my coffer until it was fished out by my friend W.E. Henley. He thought he saw something in it, and we started to work together.' RLS had been sending Henley ideas for their play Deacon Brodie and also suggestions for other plays.

dead; but, *stolzes Herz, du hast es ja gewollt*,[3] or in humbler language, *Tu l'as voulu, George Dandin*.[4] The last I can spell at least. Such, dear lad, is my outlook on this weltering world. Long since, long since, it seems, when I was ready to run barefoot on the meadows of life, and turn somersaults with the best. Alas, the meadows are all set with gins, which catch, not the heels, but the unfortunate, throbbing heart of man. Mine is well caught; and the mills of God are a-grinding it exceeding small.[5] But I cling to my text. All things work together for good to those that love the Lord. 'Tis true they work roundabout; but with courage, my man, we may attain to see the end. And I thank whatever Gods there be for my unconquerable soul.[6] I have spoiled the quotation; but even thus mangled, an author will recognise his offspring. When I read that, my dear Henley, I thought myself a butterfly, I never dreamed to have occasion to repeat the thanksgiving on my own account. And yet so it is. I am a brave man, I believe, and I know very well that I am, Your friend   R.L.S.[7]

To Sidney Colvin

[? *Late March 1879*]   *Edinburgh*

My dear Colvin, My mother claims her book of extracts;[1] indeed she showed signs of the melting mood about its absence; for it's a fetish with her; *that's* her son, I hope, since the other is such a failure in practice.

I have not much news to give you. I've been sick and in pain, not much but enough to clew me up for I am no lover of pain. But I am weak and languid from lying, and cannot work, hence perhaps, O happy Colvin, happy, happy Colvin! – you stand the chance of a real letter from me, the denizen, and no mere mechanical note from one of the clerks in my clay bureaux. It's so long since I have written a letter that I scarce

---

[3] You, proud heart, you have what you desired. RLS quotes this line from Heine's 'Ich unglücksel'ger Atlas' in ch. 3 of *The Ebb-Tide*, calling the poem 'one of the most perfect of the most perfect of poets'.

[4] '*Vous l'avez voulu, Georges Dandin*', the rueful self-rebuke of the hero of Molière's comedy.

[5] Longfellow, 'Retribution'.

[6] Henley's 'Invictus'.

[7] In October RLS stayed with Henley in London and he was briefly in Cambridge in November. He was busy seeing *Edinburgh: Picturesque Notes* through the press (it was published in December), and working with Henley on their play *Deacon Brodie*. He finally returned home on 21 December after more than six months away. In January Henley joined him at Swanston Cottage and they completed work on the first version of *Deacon Brodie*.

[1] Colvin had borrowed MIS's scrapbook, in which she was collecting reviews of her son's work.

know how. For to F. I never write letters.[2] To begin with there's no good. All that people want by letters has been done between us. We are acquainted; why go on with more introductions? I cannot change so much, but she would still have the clue and recognise every thought. But between friends it is not so. Friendship is incomplete, and lives by conversation – on bits of knowledge not on faith. And I want to write to you for this reason, that I find I am losing my voice and can no longer declare myself in talk.

I want you to understand that with all my troubles, I am a happy man and happier than often of yore. I have mastered my troubles; they are under my hand; they are now a part of me and under where I sit and rule. And one thing I proclaim, that the mere act of living is the healthiest exercise, and gives the greatest strength that a man wants. I have bitter moments, I suppose, like my neighbours, but the tenor of my life is easy to me. I know it now; and I know what I ought to do for the most part and that's the important knowledge.

Only I draw into my shell a little; I like solitude and silence; to have been a whole day, and not said twenty words, refreshes me. I know it's not nice of me; I know it's an unkindly, anti-social way; but the other is worse. I am a little weary, for surely I have had a long, sore battle? The body is tired, and so is the mind. And I take my rest in silence. Above all, I must be silent a great deal more than I used, about what really concerns me. I can talk of books or the weather, or cut capers in words with the indifferent, better than talk straight out of my heart as I used to do. Perhaps I have more in my heart; perhaps I have been spoiled by a very perfect relation; and my heart, having been coddled in a home, has grown delicate and bashful and will not cross the door. At least, so it is. And I do not want you to think it cold or judge my friendship by my confidence. If the oyster shuts up, never fear, it is because there's still an oyster.

Indeed you do not know what a dozen of reasons make me hold my tongue. Just now I have a perplexity, and do you know I can tell it to none of my friends. There is a reason why none can hear it, except Baxter. To breathe it to another would be a mean thing. This is a sort of rigour on the part of Fortune, against which I am moved to protest. But so it is. I cannot even tell it to you, nor to Henley, nor to Bob, nor to Ferrier, nor

---

[2] In spite of this comment, RLS was evidently in touch with Fanny, anxious about her health and uncertain about their future. Colvin wrote to Henley on 26 February:

> Louis had been to pieces, and was together, or nearly together, again, when he went away yesterday week. He had got a quite sane letter from an intelligible address in Spanish California, where, after wild storms, intercepted flights, and the Lord knows what more, she was for the present quiet among old friends of her own, away from the enemy, but with access to the children. What next, who shall tell? Louis had eased his mind with a telegram, without, however, committing himself to anything. He won't go suddenly or without telling people. – Which is as much as we can hope at present.

to F., nor to Madame. As for my good father, he would not understand me, and would cut the knot in a way that would draw it the tighter on my conscience. I fear you will think I am at my usual games. Forgive me; I am trying to speak out as much as I can; you will say it is not much; but it does me good.

I can, as I say, do no work; but that's a trifle. My work on morals 'Man and Money' will be finished ere a month. It will be about half as long as *An Inland Voyage*. Hence quite useless, as too long for a magazine and too short for a book, but then I thought it true. In about the same time, the sensation novel that F. and I began should be finished.[3] I have changed the *dénouement* and it becomes a good, almost a kindly story.

[4]... that was not a secret, you will know it soon, but not just now.
Yours   R.L.S.

To W.E. Henley

[*Early April 1879*]   *17 Heriot Row*

My dear Henley, Heavens! have I done the like?[1] 'Clarify and strain', indeed? 'Make it like Marvell', no less. I'll tell you what – you may go to the devil; that's what I think. 'Be eloquent' is another of your pregnant suggestions. I cannot sufficiently thank you for that one. Portrait of a person about to be eloquent at the request of a literary friend. You seem to forget, sir, that rhyme is rhyme, sir, and – go to the devil.

I'll try to improve it, but I shan't be able to – O go to the devil.

Seriously you're a cool hand. And then you have the brass to ask me *why* 'my steps went one by one'? Why? Powers of man! to rhyme with *sun*, to be sure. Why else could it be? And you yourself have been a poet! Grrrr! I'll never be a poet any more. Men are so d—d ungrateful and captious, I declare I could weep.

> O Henley, in my hours of ease
> You may say anything you please;
> But when I join the muse's revel,
> Begad, I *wish* you at the devil!
> In vain my verse I plane and bevel,
> Like Banville's rhyming devotees;
> In vain by many an artful swivel

[3] *What was on the Slate.*
[4] About eight words deleted, evidently by RLS himself.
[1] RLS had sent Henley for comment his poem 'Our Lady of the Snows'. Henley pencilled his ideas 'pretty free on the margin' and replied: 'No, my dear Louis, the verses are not in the least like doggerel. They seem to me, on the contrary, to be very genuine and pleasant stuff indeed. . . . The matter with it is, that it wants weight and dignity. Your verse is too lax and too light. If you cannot brace and straighten it up to the kind of Andrew Marvell standing this octosyllabic rhyme must not be used to moralise in.'

> Lug in my meaning by degrees;
> I'm sure to hear my Henley cavil;
> And grovelling prostrate on my knees
> Devote his body to the seas,
> His correspondence to the devil!

Impromptu poem.

I'm going to Shandon Hydropathic[2] *cum parentibus*. Write here. I heard from Lang. Ferrier prayeth to be remembered; he means to write, likes his Tourgenieff greatly. Also likes my *What was on the Slate*, which under a new title, yet unfound and with a new and, on the whole, kindly *dénouement*, is going to shoot up and become a star.

Will you say all sorts of kind things to the Lady of Château Loftus:[3] The Knight of the Sofa salutes her from afar; his pennoned spear may be perceived with the naked eye, thridding the enchanted forest towards the ranks of war; his good sword, hight Waverley, Owl or Pickwick, and so oft referred to by contemporary scalds as 'a boon and a blessing to men',[4] lies sheathed awhile and forgets the trade of blood; but look me in his eye, burns there not there prophetic ardour and a design to make two hundred a year by pure and wholesome literature for the masses? Ride on, O gallant cavalier! But for God's sake, ride gently; easy over the stones; for does not the leech, the bearded Cadell,[5] prescribe a prostrate attitude and great quiet? Alas, O Knight.   R.L.S.

Bard, Scald, Poet, Prophit, Seer, Pure and wholesome literator, here we are again and (a-word-which-I-cannot-bring-my-pen-to-indite) the expense!

To Bob Stevenson[1]

[? *April 1879*]   [? *Gareloch*]

. . . poems. Why? Because they want to so badly. Can you give a better reason? It does not follow, of course, that anybody ought to read them.

---

[2] On the Gareloch near Helensburgh.

[3] Henley married Anna J. Boyle (1854–1925) in Edinburgh on 22 January 1878, with Baxter and Mrs Jenkin as witnesses. They had met when she came to visit her brother, Captain Boyle, a fellow-patient with Henley in the Old Infirmary. The Henleys had just moved to 36 Loftus Road, Shepherds Bush.

[4] 'They come as a boon and a blessing to men,

The Pickwick, the Owl and the Waverley pen.'

The well-known advertisement issued by Macniven and Cameron of Edinburgh.

[5] Francis Cadell (1844–1909), an Edinburgh doctor.

[1] This fragment is written on the back of a letter from Bob. *Travels with a Donkey* was published on 2 June 1879. RLS was paid £30; royalties of 2/− a copy to begin after the first 700 copies.

My book is through the press. It has good passages. I can say no more.
A chapter called 'The Monks', another 'A Camp in the Dark', a third 'A
Night among the Pines'. Each of these has, I think, some stuff in it in the
way of writing. But lots of it is mere protestations to F., most of which I
think you will understand. That is to me the main thread of interest.
Whether the damned public – But that's all one; I've got thirty quid for
it, and should have had fifty. And I doubt not Paul will. . . .

To Edmund Gosse[1]

[Postmark 24 July 1879]   *Swanston, Lothianburn, Edinburgh*

My dear Gosse, I have greatly enjoyed your article[2] which seems to me
handsome in tone and written like a fine old English Gentleman. But
is there not a hitch in the sentence at foot of p. 155; I got lost in it; it
seems to me unworthy of W.E.G. more worthy of Wegg. Whenever you
displease me in future, I shall call you Wegg.[3] I am in full Adamism just
now; and S.G.C. Middlemore[4] shall be SaGaCity Middlemore to me from
henceforth *in saecula*;[5] it suits his type, his eye, his character; and God has
marvellously pointed to it in his initials. I am safe. Mine defy you; all
consonants. Chapters VIII and IX of Meredith's story[6] are very good I
think. But who wrote the review of my book? Hake,[7] think you? or the
Kegan? Whoever he was, he cannot write; he is humane but a duffer; I

[1] Edmund William Gosse (1849–1928), civil servant, critic, biographer and minor poet. Knighted
1925. He and RLS first met briefly on board ship in the Hebrides in 1870 and became close
friends in London in the mid-1870s as fellow-members of the Savile Club. Gosse worked in the
catalogue section of the British Museum 1867–75 and was Translator to the Board of Trade,
1875–1904. At this time he was making his way in the literary world through his poetry (his first
independent volume, *On Viol and Flute*, appeared in 1873), and through his articles and reviews
and his cultivation of friendship with great men such as Browning and Swinburne (whose
biographer he became). Later he was Librarian to the House of Lords, 1904–14, and an
influential man of letters famous for his friendship with Henry James, Hardy and many others.
He is now best remembered for his account of his childhood, *Father and Son* (1907). In his
recollections of RLS, published in *Critical Kit-Kats* (1896), he called RLS 'the most unselfish and
the most lovable of human beings'.
[2] 'The Poetic Phase in Modern English Art' in the *New Quarterly Magazine* for July 1879.
[3] Gosse replied on 26 July: 'You are the victim of a delusion. . . . My initials are not W.E.G.:
those are the initials of the infamous People's William. Mine are E.W.G.; as you ought to know,
Mr. L.R.S. And so, forsooth, nothing can be made of your initials! ReLigiouS? but that's not
true. Rogue of Lothianburn Swanston? true enough, but too ponderous'.
[4] Samuel George Chetwynd Middlemore (1848–90), a fellow-member of the Savile, was on the
staff of the *Saturday Review* for several years. He translated Burckhardt's *Civilization of the
Renaissance in Italy*, 1878.
[5] *In saecula saeculorum*, for ever and ever.
[6] 'The Tale of Chloe' in the same issue of the *New Quarterly*.
[7] The review of *Edinburgh: Picturesque Notes* in the *New Quarterly*. Alfred Egmont Hake, journalist,
fellow-member of the Savile and biographer of General Gordon, was the son of the poet and
physician Thomas Gordon Hake (1809–1905).

could weep when I think of him; for surely to be virtuous and incompetent is a hard lot. I should prefer to be a bold pirate, the gay sailor boy of immorality, or a publisher at once. My mind is extinct; my appetite is expiring; I have fallen altogether into a hollow-eyed, yawning way of life, like the parties in Burne-Jones's pictures. By the by, you may Burn him if you like for me. Talking of Burns (is this not sad, Wegg? I use the term of reproach not because I am angry with you this time, but because I am angry with myself and desire to give pain). Talking I say of Burns, Robert, the inspired P., is a very gay subject for study.[8] I made a kind of chronological table of his various loves and lusts, and have been comparatively speechless ever since. I am sorry to say it, but there was something in him of the vulgar, bagmanlike, professional seducer. I could kick his bottom for it: that I could (this for greater confirmation). Oblige me by taking down and reading, for the hundredth time I hope, his 'Twa Dogs' and his 'Address to the Unco' Guid'. I am only a Scotchman after all, you see, and when I have beaten Burns I am driven at once, by my parental feelings, to console him with a sugar plum. But hang me, if I know anything I like so well as the 'Twa Dogs'. Even a common Englishman may have a glimpse, as it were from Pisgah, of its extraordinary merits.

> '*English*, the, a dull people incapable of comprehending the Scottish tongue. Their history is so intimately connected with that of Scotland, that we must refer our readers to that heading. Their literature is principally the work of venal Scots.'
> Stevenson's *Handy Cyclopedia*; Glascow: Blaikie & Bannock.

Gosse, is it not possible to annoy you? Man, I would like fine to annoy you! The fact is that without being at all in a bad temper, I have been led into sin, and punned. In short, and in verity, I don't know what I am writing; but by the powers of man, if you don't answer me, death, sir, death, will be too little to assuage my fury – I'll – yes, I will – I'll promulgate the name of Wegg! Now I come to think of it, I have you by the neck; and being needy and unscrupulous, I shall blackmail you – I shall make you sing to extinction of voice; and to begin with if I don't receive half a crown or at least eighteen pence by return of post, I'll pillory you before the world as Wegg!

Remember me in suitable fashion to Mrs Gosse,[9] the offspring and the cat. And believe me, Ever yours   Robert Louis Stevenson

---

[8] RLS's essay 'Some Aspects of Robert Burns' was published in *Cornhill* for October 1879.
[9] Gosse married Ellen (Nellie) Epps (1850–1929), daughter of George Napoleon Epps, a homeopathic doctor, in 1875. Their first child, Emily Teresa (Tessa), was born in 1877. Gosse says that at this time RLS was a frequent visitor to their home at 29 Delamere Terrace.

To Edmund Gosse

[*28 July 1879*]   *17 Heriot Row*

My dear Gosse, Yours was delicious; you are a young person of wit; one of the last of them; wit being quite out of date and humour confined to the Scotch Church and the *Spectator* in unconscious survival. You will probably be glad to hear that I am up again in the world; my news is better, Gosse; I have breathed again and had a frolic on the strength of it. The frolic was yesterday, Sawbath; the scene the Royal Hotel, Bathgate; I went there with a humorous friend,[1] the hero of the German Governess, to lunch; the maid soon showed herself a lass of character. She was looking out of window; on being asked what she was after 'I'm lookin' for my lad' says she. – 'Is that him?' – 'Weel, I've been lookin' for him a' my life and I've never seen him yet,' was the response. I wrote her some verses in the vernacular; she read them; 'They're no' bad for a beginner,' said she. The landlord's daughter, Miss Stewart, was present in oil colour; so I wrote her a declaration in verse and sent it by the handmaid. She, (Miss S.) was present on the stair to witness our departure, in a warm, suffused condition. Damn it, Gosse, you needn't suppose you're the only poet in the world. The address on the last would, I think, have pleased you. It ran thus: 'To Miss Stewart, whose portrait adorns the upstairs sitting room of the Royal Hotel, Bathgate, from a poetical admirer.'

> Canny moment, lucky fit,
> Is the lady lighter yet?
> Be it lad or be it lass
> Sign wi' cross and sain wi' Mass –
> Another Gosse, another dear,
> Another sixty pounds a year!
> Another offspring born to Weg;
> How soon must that eminent literary person Beg?[2]

Your burlesque and I may say impudent statement about your initials, it will be seen, I pass over in contempt and silence. When once I have made up my mind, let me tell you, sir, there lives no pock-pudding[3] who can

---

[1] Charles Baxter. MIS records that RLS stayed the weekend with the Baxters at Lochcote House near Bathgate.

[2] The first four lines are from the song of Meg Merrilies in ch. 3 of *Guy Mannering*. Gosse had told RLS on 26 July that 'there'll be another offspring in about a fortnight'. Philip Henry George Gosse (13 August 1879–1959) became a physician and naturalist and was an authority on the history of piracy.

[3] A pudding made in a poke or bag. The word is used contemptuously or humorously in Scotland to describe an Englishman. Cf. Scott, *Old Mortality*, ch. 20, '. . . to be sure, the pock-puddings ken nae better'.

change it. Your anger, I defy. Your unmanly reference to a well known statesman, I puff from me, sir, like so much vapour. Weg, is your name; Weg. WEG.

My enthusiasm has kind of dropped from me. I envy you your wife, your home, your child – I was going to say your cat. There would be cats in my home, too, if I could but get it! not for me, but for the person who should share it with me. I may seem to you 'the impersonation of life', Weg; but my life is the impersonation of waiting, and that's a poor creature.[4] God help us all, and the deil be kind to the hindmost! Upon my word, we are a brave, cheery crew, we human beings, and my admiration increases daily – primarily for myself, but by a roundabout process for the whole crowd; for I daresay they have all their poor little secrets and anxieties. And here am I for instance, writing to you as if you were in the seventh heaven, and yet I know you are in a sad anxiety yourself. I hope earnestly it will soon be over, and a fine pink Gosse sprawling in a tub, and a mother in the best of health and spirits, glad and tired and with another interest in life. Man,[5] you are out of the trouble, when this is through. A first child is a rival; but the second is only a rival to the first; and the husband stands his ground and may keep married all his life: a consummation heartily to be desired for both you and me. Good-bye, Gosse; write me a witty letter with good news of the mistress.   R.L.S.

---

[4] Gosse had written: 'How is it thou art feeble? It is a paradox, that you, the General Exhilarator, should feel depressed. I take you for my emblem of life, and you talk of feeling lifeless.'
[5] RLS may have written 'Marry'.

VI. THE AMATEUR EMIGRANT: AMERICA AND MARRIAGE
August 1879–August 1880

On 30 July 1879 Stevenson's parents expected him to accompany them to Gilsland, a small spa in Cumberland. Instead (as his mother later recorded) he met them at the train and told them that he had been called away on business. They later learned that he had left for America. He travelled first to London, presumably to make the final arrangements for the journey and to tell his friends. They were bitterly opposed to what Gosse called 'the maddest of enterprises' and tried in vain to dissuade him. Colvin and Henley saw him off on the night train to Glasgow. Here he embarked on the *Devonia*, which sailed for New York on Thursday 7 August.

The *Devonia*, an iron single-screw steamship of 4200 tons, was one of the ships of the Anchor Line owned by Henderson Brothers of Glasgow which operated a regular service carrying mail and all types of passengers across the Atlantic. To save money and to collect material for a travel book, Stevenson planned to travel as an emigrant, but by paying two guineas more than the six-guineas steerage fare he was able to go as a second cabin passenger, thus securing better food and the use of a table on which to write 'The Story of a Lie'.

Stevenson's own account of his journey is given in *The Amateur Emigrant*, posthumously published in a shortened form in the Edinburgh Edition. The full version, with the previously published text supplemented from the manuscript, was first published by James D. Hart in *From Scotland to Silverado* (1966).[1]

Margaret Stevenson, usually so meticulous about preserving her son's letters, must have deliberately destroyed all those from this period of family dissension and distress, and the manuscripts of a number of the published letters to Colvin and Henley do not appear to have survived. In the full edition of the *Letters* it was possible to piece together much of what happened through Mrs Stevenson's diary entries, letters by Colvin and Henley and some surviving correspondence of RLS's parents.

[1] Roger G. Swearingen made available the complete unrevised manuscript text of *The Amateur Emigrant* in two privately printed volumes (Ashland, Lewis Osborne, 1976 and 1977). Swearingen's and Hart's texts (with much of their annotation) were reproduced in Andrew Noble's *From the Clyde to California* (Aberdeen, 1985). In these notes I have referred to Anne B. Fisher's *No More a Stranger* (Stanford, 1946), a fictionalised account of RLS in Monterey, but with full notes on sources.

In reading the letters in this section, it should be borne in mind that letters took nineteen to twenty days – sometimes longer – to travel from California to London and Edinburgh.

To Sidney Colvin

[*6 August 1879*]   [*Greenock*]

Dear Colvin, The enclosed is to go to my father. I have never been so much detached from life; I feel as if I cared for nobody, and as for myself I cannot believe fully in my own existence. I seem to have died last night; all I carry on from my past life is the blue pill, which is still well to the front. I have seen my berth, or at least others of the same sort. They are all right. The weather is threatening; I have a strange, rather horrible, sense of the sea before me, and can see no further into the future. I can say honestly I have at this moment neither a regret, a hope, a fear or an inclination; except a mild one for a bottle of good wine which I resist – O and one fear! a fear of getting wet. I never was in such a state. I have just made my will and am reading Aimard's novels![1] *Que le monde est bête!* God bless you all and keep you, is the prayer of the husk which once contained   R.L.S.[2]

To W.E. Henley

[*18 August 1879*]   [*New York*]

Dear lad, I have passed the salt sea with comparative impunity, having only lost a stone and got the itch. I could not eat, and I could not sh–hush! – the whole way; but I worked,[1] . . . I worked, and am now despatching a story as long as my arm to the vile Paul, all written in a slantindicular cabin with the table playing bob-cherry with the ink bottle.[2] The voyage was otherwise great fun; passengers singing and spewing lustily; and the stormy winds did blow.

---

[1] Gustave Aimard, pseudonym of Olivier Gloux (1818–83), French traveller and author of novels of adventure, the most popular being *Les Trappeurs de l'Arkansas* (1858).
[2] RLS also wrote to Baxter and Bob on the same day. He told Bob: 'F. seems to be very ill; at least I must try and get her to do one of two things. I hope to be back in a month or two; but indeed God alone knows what may happen; it is a wild world.'
[1] Two or three words heavily scored out – probably an expletive.
[2] RLS had sent Colvin 'The Story of a Lie' for publication in Kegan Paul's the *New Quarterly* where it appeared in October 1879.

My news is bad and I am wet to the skin. F. has inflammation of the brain, and I am across the continent tonight.

Address under cover to Joseph D. Strong, Monterey, Cal.[3]

I am ever your sincere and wet and scouted American, lodging in a shilling Irish boarding house with a flee in my lug and the itch – or at least an unparallelled skin irritation;[4] ... sometimes stings like a whiplash; and sleep is impossible to me. Last night I did not close an eye, but sat on the floor in my trousers and scratched myself from ten p.m. to seven, when I arose much the better for the exercise. A little Irish girl just bursting into figure but dirty is now reading my book aloud to her sister at my elbow; they chuckle, and I feel flattered.[5] Yours   R.L.S.

P.S. Now they yawn, and I am indifferent: such a wisely conceived thing is vanity!

★To W.E. Henley[1]

[*Saturday 23 August 1879*]   *Crossing Nebraska*

My dear Henley, I am sitting on the top of the cars with a mill party from Missouri going west for his health. Desolate flat prairie upon all hands. Here and there a herd of cattle, a yellow butterfly or two; a patch of wild sunflowers; a wooden house or two; then a wooden church alone in miles of waste; then a windmill to pump water. When we stop, which we do often, for emigrants and freight travel together, the kine first, the men after, the whole plain is heard singing with cicadae. This is a pause, as you may see from the writing. What happened to the old pedestrian emigrants,

---

[3] Joseph Dwight Strong (1852–99), a San Francisco artist, lived as a boy in Honolulu where his father was a minister. He studied in Munich for four years. He had married Belle Osbourne in Monterey on 9 August 1879 but RLS and Fanny were not aware of this. He and Belle lived in Honolulu from 1882 to 1889, and he is highly regarded as one of the leaders of the Hawaiian school of painting. For RLS and Fanny, as the later letters show, Joe was to become a great trial as a drunken, feckless and irresponsible son-in-law.

[4] About six words heavily scored out. The editors of the *Baxter Letters* read them as 'very similar to syphylis', but this does not seem to be correct.

[5] In *The Amateur Emigrant*. RLS describes how he stayed the night of 17 August at Reunion House, a cheap lodging-house at No. 10 West Street, and spent the next day in 'nightmare wanderings in New York' visiting in pouring rain 'banks, post-offices, railway-offices, restaurants, publishers, booksellers, money-changers'. On his return to the lodging-house to write letters the landlord's daughter saw books in his open knapsack and enquired if any of them were nice. He gave her *Travels with a Donkey*, which she read until it was time for him to leave.

[1] The rail journey across America began from New York on the evening of Monday 18 August and there were several changes of train as RLS travelled to California.

what was the tedium suffered by the Indians and trappers of our youth, the imagination trembles to conceive. This is now Saturday, 23rd, and I have been steadily travelling since I parted from you at St Pancras. It is a strange vicissitude from the Savile Club to this; I sleep with a man from Pennsylvania who has been in the States Navy, and mess with him and the Missouri bird already alluded to. We have a tin wash-bowl among four. I wear nothing but a shirt and a pair of trousers, and never button my shirt. When I land for a meal, I pass my coat and feel dressed. This life is to last till Friday, Saturday, or Sunday next. It is a strange affair to be an emigrant, as I hope you shall see in a future work. I wonder if this will be legible; my present station on the waggon roof, though airy compared to the cars, is both dirty and insecure. I can see the track straight before and straight behind me to either horizon. Peace of mind I enjoy with extreme serenity; I am doing right; I know no one will think so; and don't care. My body, however, is all to whistles; I don't eat; my blood has broken out into a kind of blister, blain, blight and itch business, which is far more distressing than you might fancy; but, man, I can sleep. The car in front of mine is chock full of Chinese.

Monday [25 August][2]

What it is to be ill in an emigrant train let those declare who know. I slept none till late in the morning, overcome with laudanum, of which I had luckily a little bottle. All today I have eaten nothing, and only drunk two cups of tea, for each of which, on the pretext that the one was breakfast, and the other dinner, I was charged fifty cents, and neither of them, I may add, stood by me for three full minutes. Our journey is through the ghostly deserts, sage brush and alkali, and rocks, without form or colour, a sad corner of the world. I confess I am not jolly, but mighty calm in my distresses. My illness is a subject of great mirth to some of my fellow travellers, and I smile rather sickly at their jests.

We are going along Bitter Creek[3] just now, a place infamous in the history of emigration, a place I shall remember myself among the blackest. I hope I may get this posted at Ogden, Utah. You might give my news to Sidney Colvin.

---

[2] RLS records that all Sunday and Monday they travelled through Wyoming and then across the Rockies. He was taken ill at Laramie.
[3] In south-west Wyoming near Rock Springs.

To Sidney Colvin[1]

[c. 24 September 1879]   [Carmel Valley]

Here is another curious start in my life. I am living at an angora goat ranche, in the Coast Line Mountains, eighteen miles from Monterey.[2] I was camping out, but got so sick that the two rancheros took me in and tended me. One is an old bear hunter, seventy-two years old, and a captain from the Mexican war; the other a pilgrim and one who was out with the bear flag and under Frémont[3] when California was taken by the States. They are both true frontiersmen, and most kind and pleasant. Cap' Smith, the bear hunter, is my physician and I obey him like an oracle.

The business of my life stands pretty nigh still. I am, I hope, cured of the itch which I got aboard ship; yet as I was in great part flayed I still suffer nearly as much distress as ever. I work at my notes of the voyage. It will not be very like a book of mine; but perhaps none the less successful for that. I will not deny that I feel lonely today; but I do not fear to go on, for I am doing right. If only others would be as persistent, things would soon be straight. I have not yet heard a word from England, partly I suppose because I have not yet written for my letters to New York; do not blame me for this neglect; if you knew all I have been through, you would wonder I had done so much as I have. I teach the ranche children reading in the morning, for the mother is from home sick.[4]

I should say to you, if you were a praying man, pray for me. I am obliged to lie down to write for reasons best known to my breech, so you need not augur too badly from the writing. Ever your affectionate friend

R.L.S.

I reckon a letter to you, S.C., as good as two at least.
No news about 'Burns' or the story?

[1] RLS arrived in Oakland, California 'before the dawn' on Saturday 30 August, crossed by the ferry to San Francisco and then travelled some 130 miles south by rail to Monterey where Fanny, her children and her sister Nellie were staying. He wrote to Colvin soon afterwards: 'I have little to say: all is in the wind; things might turn well, or might not.' To Baxter he wrote on 9 September: 'My news is nil. I know nothing, I go out camping, that is all I know; . . . and now say good-bye to you, having had the itch and a broken heart.'
[2] The ranch of Jonathan Wright and his partner 'Captain' Anson Smith on San Clemente Creek in Carmel Valley.
[3] John Charles Frémont (1813–90), American explorer and army officer. He was the leading spirit in the abortive Bear Flag Revolt (June to July 1846) in which American settlers captured the Mexican headquarters at Sonoma and proclaimed the Republic of California by hoisting a flag portraying a grizzly bear facing a red star. California was formally ceded to the USA after the Mexican War of 1846–8, in which Frémont took a prominent part.
[4] Identified by Mrs Fisher as Sarah and Dolly Wright. They were both still alive in 1950.

To W.E. Henley

R.L.S. Monterey,
Monterey Co., Cal.

[*Late October/early November 1879*]

My dear Henley, Many thanks for your good letter which is the best way to forgive you for your previous silence. I hope Colvin or somebody has sent me the *Cornhill* and the *New Quarterly*, though I am trying to get them in San Francisco. I think you might have sent me (1) some of your articles in the *P.M.G.*; (2) a paper with the announcement of second edition and (3) the announcement of the essays in *Athenaeum*.[1] This to prick you in the future. One thing I will have; and that is your *Athenaeum* Labiche.[2] Again, choose, in your head, the best volume of Labiche there is, and post it to Jules Simoneau, Monterey, Monterey Co. Cal.: do this at once, as he is my restaurant man, a most pleasant old boy with whom I discuss the universe and play chess daily.[3] He has been out of France for thirty-five years, and never heard of Labiche. I have 83 pp. written of a story, about as bad as Ouida and not so good, called *A Vendetta in the West*.[4] And about 60 pp. of the first draft of the *Amateur Emigrant*. They should each cover from 130 to 150 pp. when done. (If you have not coin for the Labiche, Colvin can advance you some of mine that I told him to take for such expenses.) That is all my literary news. Do keep me posted, won't you? Your letter and Bob's made the fifth and sixth I have had from Europe in three months.

At times I get terribly frightened about my work which seems to advance too slowly. I hope soon to have a greater burthen to support, and must make money a great deal quicker than I used. I may get nothing for the *Vendetta*. I may only get some forty quid for the *Emigrant*; I cannot hope to have them both done much before the end of November. That would make £40 in three months; or about 12£ a month; and I spend, as it is, nearly ten, and shall likely spend a little more in the future. By God, that looks grave. I must arrest my thoughts.

---

[1] The *Athenaeum* of 27 September announced that RLS intended to publish a volume of essays containing nine papers from *Cornhill* and three from *London*. On 7 February 1880 it said that the volume would be published by Kegan Paul. The book finally appeared as *Virginibus Puerisque* in 1881.

[2] Henley's review in the *Athenaeum* of 21 February 1880 of the first ten volumes of the *Théâtre Complet de Eugène Labiche*. Eugène Labiche (1815–86) wrote many comedies, among them *Un Chapeau de Paille d'Italie*.

[3] Jules Simoneau became a lifelong friend and correspondent. RLS described him to Colvin as 'the stranded fifty-eight year-old wreck of a good-hearted dissipated and once wealthy Nantais tradesman'.

[4] An earlier alternative title was *A Chapter in the Experience of Arizona Breckonridge*. This novel, partly set in Monterey and the adjacent country, was eventually abandoned and the MS apparently destroyed.

O and look here why did you not send me the *Spectator* which slanged me?[5] Rogues and rascals, is that all you are worth?

As I hint, I believe things will go rightly say by January. All will be stopped up to Xmas for family reasons.[6] Yesterday I set fire to the forest, for which, had I been caught, I should have been hung out of hand to the nearest tree; Judge Lynch being an active person hereaway. You should have seen my retreat (which was entirely for strategical purposes). I ran like hell. It was a fine sight. At night I went out again to see it; it was a good fire, though I say it that should not.[7] I had a near escape for my life with a revolver; I fired six charges; and the six bullets all remained in the barrel, which was choked from end to end, from muzzle to breach, with solid lead; it took a man three hours to drill them out. Another shot and I'd have gone to Kingdom Come.

This is a lovely place, which I am growing to love. The Pacific licks all other oceans out of hand; there is no place but the Pacific Coast to hear eternal roaring surf. When I get to the top of the woods behind Monterey, I can hear the seas breaking all round over ten or twelve miles of coast from near Carmel on my left, out to Point Pinos in front, and away to the right along the sands of Monterey to Castroville and the mouth of the Salinas. I was wishing yesterday that the world could get – no, what I mean was that you should be kept in suspense like Mahomet's coffin until the world had made half a revolution, then dropped here at the station as though you had stepped from the cars; you would then comfortably enter Wolter's waggon[8] (the sun has just gone down, the moon beginning to throw shadows, you hear the surf rolling, and smell the sea and the pines). That shall deposit you at Sanchez's saloon, where we take a drink; you are introduced to Bronson, the local editor ('I have no brain music,' he says; 'I'm a mechanic you see,' but he's a nice fellow);

[5] The review of *Travels with a Donkey* in the *Spectator* of 27 September: 'Seldom has any book of the kind been woven out of slighter materials. . . . Still by the help of a graceful style of writing, he has given us a very readable volume. . . . Throughout the volume we have felt that the charms of a solitary journey in the company of a donkey would have not been so attractive to the author, if he had not desired to write a book. It was a pardonable and in the main a successful ambition.'

[6] RLS wrote to Baxter on 15 October: 'In coming here, I did the right thing; I have not only got Fanny patched up again in health; but the effect of my arrival has straightened out everything. As now arranged there is to be a private divorce in January . . . and yours truly will himself be a married man as soon thereafter as the law and decency permit.'

[7] RLS described the incident in 'The Old Pacific Capital', his essay on Monterey. He was experimenting to see if it was the moss in the tree which caught fire first.

[8] Manuel Wolter was proprietor of the livery stables and a haulier in Alvarado Street. Most of the other people RLS mentions appear in the advertisements in the *Monterey Californian* and in Mrs Fisher's *No More a Stranger*. Dr J.R. Hadsell was a druggist and stationer. RLS writes affectionately of Crevole Bronson (who took over as proprietor and editor of the *Monterey Californian* on 23 September), Simoneau and the rest of the company in 'Simoneau's at Monterey', an incomplete essay first published by Hart in *From Scotland to Silverado*.

to Adolpho Sanchez, who is delightful although no brain-musician either;[9] meantime I go to the P.O. for my mail; thence we walk up Alvarado Street together, you now floundering in the sand, now merrily stumping on the wooden side walks; I call at Hadsell's for my paper; at length behold us installed in Simoneau's little white-washed back room, round a dirty tablecloth, with François the baker, perhaps an Italian fisherman, perhaps Augustin Dutra, and Simoneau himself. Simoneau, François, and I are the three sure cards; the others mere waifs. Then home to my great airy rooms with five windows opening on a balcony;[10] I sleep on the floor in my camp blankets, you install yourself abed; in the morning coffee with the little doctor[11] and his little wife; we hire a waggon and make a day of it; and by night, I should let you up again into the air to be returned to Mrs Henley in the forenoon following. By God you would enjoy yourself. So should I. I have tales enough to keep you going till five in the morning, and then they would not be at an end. I forget if you asked me any questions, and I sent your letter up to the city to one who will like to read it. I expect other letters now steadily. If I have to wait another two months, I shall begin to be huffy. Will you [remember me] most affectionately to your wife; the celebrated lady of the castle. Shake hands with Anthony from me;[12] and God bless your mother. How is Edward John Uriah Dillwater Strange?[13]

God bless Stephen! Does he not know that I am a man and cannot live by bread alone but must have guineas into the bargain. 'Burns', I believe, in my own mind, is one of my high water marks; I have rarely been so trenchant and solid; Meiklejohn[14] flames me a letter about it, which is so complimentary that I must keep it or get it published in the *Monterey Californian*. Some of these days I shall send an *exemplaire* of that paper; it is huge. Ever your affectionate friend   Robert Louis Stevenson

[9] Adulfo Sanchez (died 1891), proprietor with his brother of the Bohemia Saloon in Monterey, married in September 1880 Nellie Van de Grift (1855–1935), Fanny's youngest sister who was living with her when RLS arrived. She later wrote books on Californian history and place-names, as well as the official biography of Fanny.

[10] Mrs Fisher says that no adobe in Monterey had five windows in one room and that RLS told his friends in Monterey that he was drunk when he thought he saw them. But this hardly reads like a letter written under the influence of drink.

[11] Dr J.P.E. Heintz. It appears that RLS actually lodged at the 'French House', a rough rooming-house run by Manuela Girardin, Dr Heintz's mother-in-law. RLS took many meals at the doctor's house and when he became ill, Dr and Mrs Heintz took him in and nursed him. The 'French House', much restored, is now a museum known as 'Stevenson House': it contains a collection of Stevenson family furniture from Vailima, portraits and other memorabilia.

[12] Anthony Warton Henley (1851–1914), Henley's brother, was an artist.

[13] Mrs Henley was expecting a child in December; the baby was stillborn.

[14] John Miller Dow Meiklejohn (1836–1902), Professor of Education at St Andrews 1876 and writer of school books. Colvin says that RLS heard Meiklejohn's laughter at the Savile Club and insisted on meeting the owner of such a laugh.

My health keeps along fairly; I do think it improves all the time; it had need; for I was pretty low at one time.

'*Yo no tengo su sombrero feo de V.*'

Le Spanish tongue.

To W.E. Henley

[? *17 November 1879*]   *Monterey*

My dear Henley, Herewith 'The Pavilion on the Links';[1] grand carpentry story in nine chapters and I should hesitate to say how many tableaux. Where is it to go? God knows. Perhaps Paul, for his damned *N.Q.*; perhaps George Bentley (*Upton Park, Slough, Bucks*). The former pays well; the latter ill. It is the dibbs that are wanted. It is not bad at that, though I say it; carpentry, of course, but not bad at that; and who else can carpenter in England, now that Collins is f—d out?[2] It might be broken for magazine purposes at the end of Chapter IV. I send it to you, as I dare say Payn may help, if all else fails. Dibbs and speed are my mottoes.

I have had an awful time. I got a telegram to come home because my father was ill. This I will not do anyway. He would be better or dead ere I got there anyway; and I won't desert my wife.[3] That same night, F. nearly died; and I have the worst account of her health. All kinds of miseries here anyway. I telegraphed to my people 'Send Money. Letter Following.' The money was of course a trick, to let the letter reach. I could not refuse by telegram; it is so brutal.

Do acknowledge the 'Pavilion' by return. I shall be so nervous till I hear; as of course I have no copy except of one or two places where the vein would not run. God prosper it, poor 'Pavilion'! May it bring me money for myself and my sick one, who may need it, I do not know how soon.

Love to your wife, Anthony and all. I shall write to Colvin today or tomorrow. Yours ever   R.L.S.

---

[1] RLS had planned the story and begun to write it a year before.

[2] Wilkie Collins (1824–89), the prolific sensation novelist, who had made his name with *The Woman in White* (1860) and *The Moonstone* (which RLS had enjoyed in serial form in 1868), continued to write until his death but his later novels are of deteriorating quality.

[3] TS had reacted violently to what in a letter to Colvin on 10 November he called 'this sinful mad business'. He had exhausted all his powers of persuasion without success and he begged Colvin to use his influence to get RLS to return home. A week later he told Colvin that as a last resort the family doctor had telegraphed to RLS that the state of his father's health required his presence at home. Colvin, fearful of the effect of Edinburgh in midwinter on RLS's ill health also telegraphed RLS advising him to send a temporising reply; at the same time he made discreet enquiries of Baxter as to whether TS was really seriously ill.

To Sidney Colvin

26 December [1879]   *608 Bush Street, San Francisco*[1]

My dear Colvin, I am now writing to you in a café waiting for some music to begin. For four days I have spoken to no one but to my landlady or landlord or to Restaurant waiters. This is not a gay way to pass Christmas, is it? And I must own the guts are a little knocked out of me. If I could work, I could worry through better. But I have no style at command for the moment, with the second part of the *Emigrant*,[2] the last of the novel, the essay on Thoreau, and God knows all, waiting for me. But I trust something can be done with the first part, or by God, I'll starve here. You see I'm in a sort of hole; as thus: Fanny has divorced her Master;[3] he behaved well and was to support her till we married, and of course, we were to hurry nothing so as to avoid scandal for him; and now he has lost his government appointment, and as he never saved anything, is on his back.[4] I must keep her, and to keep her and me apart costs, I daresay, more than twice as much as if we were together; aye, nearer thrice. I have upwards of £40 in hand. Baxter must still have upwards of £50, counting on the 'Lie' and 'Burns', and making the most liberal allowance for expenses. Well, now I come to put it down that's not so bad. That gives us I believe nearly – well no, but say it gives us four months clear, which it must and amply. O, we'll do. Before that time, it's the devil if I can't have made another £50 more or if it could only be another £100! God, how that would float us. Lemme see. 'Pavilion'; well, surely, 20. Thoreau, well, surely, 15. If the *Emigrant* can't make up the balance, why, damn the *Emigrant*, say I.

O Colvin, you don't know how much good I have done myself. I feared to think this out by myself. I have made a base use of you, and it comes out so much better than I had dreamed. But I have to stick to work now; and here's December gone pretty near useless. But Lord love you, October and November saw a great harvest. It might have affected the

---

[1] RLS had been seriously ill at Monterey with pleurisy and malaria. He later told Colvin that he had been 'dying of starvation': 'I suppose if I ate two ounces of food a day for nearly two months, it must have been the extreme outside; the rest was coffee, wine and soup.' He moved to San Francisco in late December; Fanny had already returned to her home in East Oakland. He wrote to Henley in late January: 'It was time I was out of Monterey.... To live alone in such a hole, the one object of scandal, gossip, imaginative history – well, it was not good.'

[2] RLS had sent the first part of *The Amateur Emigrant* to Colvin in early December.

[3] Fanny obtained her divorce on 15 December in the Nineteenth Judicial District Court.

[4] Sam Osbourne is shown as 'official reporter Third District Court' in the 1879 San Francisco City Directory, but this appointment is omitted from the 1880 Directory.

price of paper on the Pacific Coast. As for ink, they haven't any, not what I call ink; only stuff to write cookery books with, or the works of Hayley,[5] or the pallid perambulations of the – I can find nobody to beat Hayley. I like good, knock-me-down blackstrap to write with; that makes a mark and done with it. – By the way, I have tried to read the *Spectator*, which they all say I imitate, and – its very wrong of me I know – but I can't. It's all very fine you know, and all that, but blame me, if it's about anything. It's vapid. They have just played the overture to *Norma*,[6] and I know it's a good one for I bitterly wanted the opera to go on, I had just got thoroughly interested – and then no curtain to rise.

I have written myself into a kind of spirits, bless your dear heart, by your leave. But this is wild work for me, nearly nine and me not back! What [will] Mrs Carson[7] think of me! Quite a night hawk, I do declare. You are the worst correspondent in the world – no, not that, Henley is that – well, I don't know, I leave the pair of you to him that made you – surely with small attention. But I was made to be generous, and good and an egoist, and a damned idler, and a very indifferent literary gemman, and so here's my service and I'll away home to my den O! much the better for this crack, Professor Colvin. R.L.S.

If practicable, proofs! If the piratical reprint of 'Burns' in *Appleton's Journal* is a fair test, you – were not – successful. Your 'Art and Criticism', likewise there; so you see, we collaborate even here.[8]

Address Robert Louis Stevenson, Post Office, San Francisco, Cal.

(Don't forget the State, otherwise by the new law you are a dead letter).[9]

---

[5] William Hayley (1745–1820), friend of Blake and Cowper. His poetry was ridiculed by Byron in *English Bards and Scotch Reviewers* as 'For ever feeble and for ever tame'.

[6] Bellini's opera (1821).

[7] Mary Carson, RLS's Irish landlady.

[8] *Appleton's Journal: A Magazine of General Literature* (New York), reprinted 'Burns' in its December issue and Colvin's 'Art and Criticism' from the August *Fortnightly Review* in October.

[9] On receipt of this letter Colvin wrote to Baxter on 12 January: 'I have news from him today (so probably have you) which puts a new aspect upon matters, and as it seems to me, leaves no course whatever open to his friends but to put as good a face as possible upon all this and persuade his people to do so too. . . . At any rate it is idle to hope, things having gone that far, that threats of displeasure, disapproval, or indeed anything that can be thought of, would dissuade L. from marrying her.' Colvin said he doubted the persistency of TS's indignation – 'at any rate I mean to do my best to try and soften him. And under the circumstances which we now have to face, I do not see how any of Louis's friends can take any other line: since it is clear that he will take his chance of starving with her and her boy rather than refrain from uniting himself with her.'

To Sidney Colvin

[*Postmark 18 January 1880*]   608 *Bush Street, San Francisco, Cal.*

My dear Colvin, This is a circular letter to tell my estate fully. You have no right to it, being the worst of correspondents; but I wish to efface the impression of my last, so to you it goes.

Any time between eight and half past nine in the morning, a slender gentleman in an ulster, with a volume buttoned into the breast of it, may be observed leaving No. 608 Bush and descending Powell with an active step. The gentleman is R.L.S.; the volume relates to Benjamin Franklin, on whom he meditates one of his charming essays.[1] He descends Powell, crosses Market, and descends in Sixth on a Branch of the original Pine Street Coffee House; no less; I believe he would be capable of going to the original itself, if he could only find it. In the Branch he seats himself at a table covered with waxcloth; and a pampered menial, of high Dutch extraction and indeed as yet only partially extracted, lays before him a cup of coffee, a roll and a pat of butter, all, to quote the deity, very good. A while ago, and R.L.S. used to find the supply of butter insufficient; but he has now learned the art to exactitude, and butter and roll expire at the same moment. For this refection, he pays 10 cents or five pence sterling. (£0.0.5.)

Half an hour later, the inhabitants of Bush Street observe the same slender gentleman armed, like George Washington, with his little hatchet, splitting kindling and breaking coal for his fire. He does this quasi publicly upon the window sill; but this is not to be attributed to any love of notoriety, though he is indeed vain of his prowess with the hatchet (which he persists in calling an axe) and daily surprised at the perpetuation of his fingers. The reason is this: that the sill is a strong, supporting beam, and that blows of the same emphasis in other parts of his room might knock the entire shanty into hell. Thenceforth, for from three to four hours, he is engaged darkly with an inkbottle. Yet he is not blacking his boots, for the only pair that he possesses are innocent of lustre and wear the natural hue of the material turned up with caked and venerable slush. The youngest child of his landlady remarks several times a day as this strange occupant enters or quits the house: 'Dere's de author.' Can it be that this bright-haired innocent has found the true clue to the mystery? The Being in question is, at least, poor enough to belong to that honourable craft.

His next appearance is at the restaurant of one Donnadieu,[2] on Bush Street, between Dupont and Kearney, where a copious meal, half a bottle

---

[1] 'Benjamin Franklin and the Art of Virtue' was never written.
[2] Louis Donnadieu, 425 Bush Street.

of wine, coffee and brandy may be procured for the sum of four bits, alias
50 cents, £0.2.2 sterling. The wine is put down in a whole bottleful, and
it is strange and painful to observe the greed with which the gentleman in
question seeks to secure the last drop of his allotted half, and the scrupu-
lousness with which he seeks to avoid taking the first drop of the other.
This is partly explained by the fact that if he were to go over the mark –
bang would go a tenpence. He is again armed with a book; but his best
friends will learn with pain that he seems at this hour to have deserted the
more serious studies of the morning. When last observed, he was studying
with apparent zest the exploits of one Rocambole by the late Viscount
Ponson of Terrail.[3] This work, originally of prodigious dimensions, he had
cut into liths or thicknesses apparently for convenience of carriage.

Then the being walks; where is not certain; at other times he remains
concealed beside the debarkadery of the Oakland Ferry, seemingly with
a view to a tryst.[4] But by about half past four, a light beams from the
windows of 608 Bush; and he may be observed sometimes engaged in
correspondence, sometimes once again plunged in the mysterious rites of
the forenoon. About six, he returns to the Branch Original, where he
once more imbrues himself to the worth of five pence in coffee and roll.
The evening is devoted to writing and reading, and by eleven or half past
darkness closes over this weird and truculent existence.

The mere contemplation of a life so vile is more than enough for a
professing Christian; comment could only force its loathsome details,
perhaps with hurtful results, upon the young and innocent. Such an one
can be led for about £8 a month, all told. But it is hoped that none will
be tempted to follow in the footprints of the Being Mysterious.

When he will be married is another story; it may be, not for quite a
long while; we wish if possible to have no more quarrels, and several
family affairs stand most curiously in the way at present.[5] As for coin, you
see I don't spend much; only you and Henley both seem to think my
work rather bosh nowadays; and I do want to make as much as I was
making; that is £200; if I can do that, I can swim; last year with my ill
health I touched only £109; that would not do; I could not fight it
through on that; but on £200, as I say, I am good for the world and can
even in this quiet way save a little, and that I must do. The worst is my

---

[3] Pierre-Alexis, Vicomte de Ponson du Terrail (1829–71), prolific *roman-feuilletoniste*. 'His stock
character Rocombole, went through countless adventures told, with a serene, often ludicrous,
disregard for plot and style, in twenty-two volumes of *Les Exploits de Rocombole* (1859) and many
sequels' (*Oxford Companion to French Literature*). RLS mentions it in *The Silverado Squatters*, 'The
Toll House'.
[4] RLS and Fanny met and dined together about twice a week.
[5] In later letters in January RLS explained that Fanny's family had not yet been told of the
divorce, mainly because Fanny's widowed sister Elizabeth Patterson was seriously ill and a
mental breakdown was feared.

health; it is suspected I had an ague chill yesterday, I shall know by tomorrow; and you know if I am to be laid down with ague, the game is pretty well lost. But I don't know, I managed to write a good deal down in Monterey, when I was pretty sickly most of the time; and by God, I'll try, ague and all. I have to ask you frankly when you write, to give me any good news you can, and chat a little, but *just in the meantime, give me no bad*. If I could get 'Thoreau', *Emigrant* and *Vendetta*, all finished and out of my hand, I should feel like a man who had made half a year's income in a half year; but until the two last are *finished*, you see, they don't fairly count.

I am afraid I bore you sadly with this perpetual talk about my affairs; I will try and stow it; but you see, it touches me nearly; I'm the miser in earnest now; last night when I felt so ill, the supposed ague chill, it seemed strange not to be able to afford a drink. I would have walked half a mile, tired as I felt, for a brandy and soda.

You talk about lending me coin; you don't understand; this is a test; I must support myself; at what rate I have still to see. I am half in hopes a part of my expense will be off my hands soon, for I think the Party is going to keep his word and help support her till the marriage. He gave her nothing, not even what she brought him, not even her own lots which, by a neglect, he holds *pro indiviso*; and of course, she did not ask.[6] That is one of the drawbacks of being a fool; and we are a pair, real bad ones.
Ever yours　　　　　　　　　　　　　　　　　　　　　　　　R.L.S.

F. much better, I think, but am afraid to hope too much.[7]

To Edmund Gosse

[*Postmark 23 January 1880*]　　　　　　　608 *Bush Street, San Francisco*

My dear and kind Wegg, It was a lesson in philosophy that would have moved a bear, to receive your letter in my present temper.[1] For I am now

---

[6] In fact Osbourne deeded the East Oakland property to her on 26 October 1881.

[7] The exact nature of Fanny's illness is unknown. In late January RLS wrote to Henley: 'Fanny is so much better, so almost quite well – in spite of another fit; I count these damned fits like coffin nails – that my heart is very light.'

[1] RLS, ill in bed with pleurisy, wrote a despondent letter to Gosse on 8 December. Gosse had immediately sent a warm and friendly reply dated 29 December 1879:

Why do you write such letters to wring my heart? Here am I, who though determined that nothing signified to such an old party as me, as nearly as possible disgracing myself with crying over your letter just received. . . . Come straight back to us from that Monterey . . . I cannot bear to think of you all alone in the midst of strangers, fretting and tiring yourself to pieces. . . . Are you really so bad, dear child? . . . How can you say that I am not to believe

well and well at my ease, both by comparison. First, my health has turned
a corner; it was not consumption this time, though consumption it has
to be sometime as all my kind friends sing to me, day in, day out –
Consumption! how I hate that word; yet it can sound innocent, as, e.g.,
consumption of military stores. What was wrong with me, apart from
colds and little pleuritic flea-bites, was a lingering malaria; and that is now
greatly overcome. I eat once more, which is a great amusement and,
they say, good for the health. Second, many of the thunder clouds that
were overhanging me when last I wrote, have silently stolen away like
Longfellow's Arabs;[2] and I am now engaged to be married to the woman
whom I have loved for four years and a half. I do not yet know when the
marriage can come off; for there are many reasons for delay. But as few
people before marriage have known each other so long or made more
trials of each other's tenderness and constancy, I permit myself to hope
some quiet at the end of all. At least I will boast myself so far; I do not
think many wives are better loved than mine will be. Third and last, in the
order of what has changed my feelings, my people have cast me off, and
so that thundercloud, as you may almost say, has overblown. You know
more than most people whether or not I loved my father; but he is now
a stranger to me, and writes about how he has remarked my growing
aversion for him all these years.[3] These things are sad; nor can any man
forgive himself for bringing them about; yet they are easier to meet in fact
than by anticipation. I almost trembled whether I was doing right, until I
was fairly summoned; then, when I found that I was not shaken one jot,
that I could grieve, that I could sharply blame myself, for the past, and yet
never hesitate one second as to my conduct in the future, I believed my
cause was just and I leave it with the Lord. I certainly look for no reward,

---

half the bad I hear of you? First place, I never do and never have heard anything bad of you,
and second, if I did, there is this to be remembered, that I admire, honour and love you right
through, and should be as ready to believe ill of you as of any one of the six best people in
my world. Whether you live or die, you will live for ever in our hearts and in the roll of
men of genius. Nothing that anyone can say or do can darken the bright name you have
made for yourself. . . . My wife is as sad as I am about you, and she and I and everybody says
nothing but Come home straight.

[2] In 'The Day is Done'.
[3] Colvin, meanwhile, had interceded with TS to good effect, and his attitude was about to
change. On 26 January TS wrote to his son: '. . . I am quite aware that what you say is true. If
the account given by Colvin is correct, I admit that the case is not what I supposed, and
providing my wish is carried out, I shall be prepared to do my best in the matter. The wish is
that there be as long a delay as possible. . . .' On 17 February he wrote: 'You know I must make
the best of the business, and it is preposterous of you to scrimp yourself. Let me know what
money you want. . . . You have already had my letters informing you that I had entirely
misunderstood the *present* state of matters, which if Colvin was correct gives of course a very
different aspect to it. The actors have apparently changed their positions from what I had
supposed, and certainly materially for the better . . .'

nor for any abiding city either here or hereafter, but I please myself with hoping that my father will not always think so hardly of my conduct nor so very slightingly of my affection as he does at present.

You may now understand that the quiet economical citizen of San Francisco who now addresses you, a *bon homme* given to cheap living, early to bed though scarce early to rise in proportion (*que diable!* let us have style, anyway)[4] busied with his little bits of books and essays and with a fair hope for the future, is no longer the same desponding, invalid son of a doubt and an apprehension who last wrote to you from Monterey. I am none the less warmly obliged to you and Mrs Gosse for your good words. I suppose I am the devil (hearing it so often), but I am not ungrateful. Only please, Weg, do not talk of genius about me; I do not think I want for a certain talent, but I am heartily persuaded I have none of the other commodity; so let that stick to the wall: you only shame me by such friendly exaggerations.

When shall I be married? When shall I be able to return to England? When shall I join the good and blessed, including Hepworth Dixon, in a forced march upon the New Jerusalem?[5] That is what I know not in any degree; some of them, let us hope, will come early, some after a judicious interval. I have three little strangers knocking at the door of Leslie Stephen: 'The Pavilion on the Links', a blood and thunder story, *accepted*; 'Yoshida-Torajiro', a paper on a Japanese hero who will warm your blood, *postulant*; and 'Henry David Thoreau; his Character and Opinions' – postulant also.[6] I give you these hints knowing you to love the best literature, that you may keep an eye at the masthead for these little tit-bits. Write again, and soon, and at greater length to, your friend   R.L.S.

To Sidney Colvin

[*Late February 1880*]   *608 Bush St S.F. Cal.*

My dear Colvin, I received a very nice letter from you with two inclosures: one from Warner,[1] which looks good. I am still unable to finish

---

[4] RLS deleted 'proportionately' before 'early to rise'.

[5] In a postscript Gosse had written: 'Hepworth Dixon is just dead: I take it as a good omen, they evidently want the bad writers, not the good ones up there.' William Hepworth Dixon (1821–79), journalist, historian and traveller, editor of the *Athenaeum* 1853–69 and prolific author.

[6] RLS wrote to Henley on the same day expressing his delight that the 'Dooke de Korneel' had accepted 'The Pavilion on the Links'. It was published in *Cornhill* in September and October 1880. 'Yoshida Torajiro' appeared in the March *Cornhill* and 'Henry David Thoreau: His Character and Opinions' in June.

[1] Charles Warner (1846–1909), a well-known actor in melodrama. Henley, enthusiastically aided and abetted by Colvin, was trying to interest actors and managers in *Deacon Brodie*. On 3 February Henley wrote to RLS that Warner had been 'wonderfully fetched' by the play.

the *Emigrant* although there are only some 15pp. to do. The *Vendetta* is, I am afraid, scarce *Fortnightly* form; though after the 'Pavilion' being taken by Stephen, I am truly at sea about all such matters. I daresay my *Prince of Grünwald*[2] – the name still uncertain, would be good enough for anything if I could but get it done; I believe that to be a really good story. The *Vendetta* is somewhat cheap in motive; very rum and unlike the present kind of novels both for good and evil, in writing; and on the whole, only remarkable for the heroine's character, and that I believe to be in it. She is my g—d d—d sister-in-law; not a bad sort of girl, as you will see, but highly embarrassing for a plain man; she is so conscientiously selfish.

About my unsatisfactory letters, I am afraid I may be unkind; but to tell you the truth, you would still be in the same darkness if things had not changed; and with regard to my chance of return and plans in a dozen ways, I do wish you and others would understand that, till I see plain day, in the dark you shall remain. There is a little superstition in this; a little pride, for I do not choose to be caught 'on the hop', dreaming and then disarsed from my expectation; and still more of other and better feelings which I think you should be able to imagine for yourselves. But if you cannot, please try and make up your mind to this fact; until I am sure of anything, you will not hear of it; and consequently if another long period of uncertainty should fall to me, you will, for that while, hear nothing.

I do not know that you people in the east distinguish yourself for showing a good example to back up your precept. I know nothing of your own doings; not one word; little, and nothing to the purpose, of madonna's; but little of Henley's (though of him I do not complain – he is so much better than you); nothing of my own *Emigrant*, except that Isbister[3] is doing something or is not – but what? – God knows; nothing of the essays; etc. The latter part is not to complain; it is only for memorandum; just to show that I am not alone in vagueness; and that where I have a reason for mine (and have shown so, where that reason ceased to exist) you are vague just from cheeriness.

I am not well at all. But hope to be better. You know I have been hawked to death these last months. And then I lived too low, I fear; and anyway I have got pretty low and out at elbows in health. I wish I could say better; but I cannot. With a constitution like mine, you never know

[2] An early version of what was to become *Prince Otto* first announced in a letter to Henley in January as *The Forest State* or *The Greenwood State: A Romance*. In the dedication of the novel to Fanny's sister Nellie, RLS recalls dictating a few pages to her at Oakland.

[3] Negotiations for the serialisation of *The Amateur Emigrant* in *Good Words* had been conducted by Henley's friend, James Runciman, with the publisher William Isbister. On 4 February Donald Macleod, the editor, wrote to Runciman, 'It is capital – full of force and character and fine feeling, and quite the kind of thing which will suit *Good Words*.' Since Isbister was already over-supplied with material for 1880, he wanted to hold the MS until 1881, but was unwilling to pay in advance. Colvin and Henley thereupon withdrew the MS and sent it to Kegan Paul.

– tomorrow I may be carrying top gallant sails again; but just at present I
am scraping along with a jury-mast and a kind of amateur rudder. Truly
I have some misery, as things go; but these things are mere detail.
However I do not want to *crever*, *claquer* and cave in, just when I have a
chance of some happiness; nor do I mean to. All the same, I am more and
more, in a difficulty how to move every day; and that by reason of a
round dozen of different people. I am accepted all round for the most
selfish man in the world; and yet I find in most serious choices of my life,
I am the only one who never has a chance to be considered. Parents on
all sides now sit on me like so many thousands of bricks; I remain,
squelched, but smiling, underneath. But what a day or an hour might
bring forth, God forbid that I should prophesy. – Certainly; do what you
like about the stories, 'Will o' the Mill', or not. It will be Caldecott's book
or nobody's.[4]   R.L.S.

I was glad you liked the 'Guitar': I always did: and I think C. – could
make lovely pikters to it: it almost seems as if I must have written it for
him express.

And now, bage[5] man, about that £100.[6] It was a dream I believe.
There never was no such money sent, I am persuaded. And now I dare
not go to the Post Office: I dare not visit my friends; I have to avoid eager
acquaintances on the streets. When I think of the Ned I have raised, or as
they say here the 'partic'lar Harry', and how the post offices have groaned,
and the American citizen has had his mouth closed before my feverish
denunciations – and all about what? – a letter that was never sent, money
that was never in existence – why, damme, Colvin, I'm ashamed of you
– in the words of George S.[7]

I have already been a visitor at the Club[8] for a fortnight; but that's over,
and I don't much care to renew the period. Drink is more the order of the
day than wit. I want to be married, not to belong to all the damned clubs
in Christendie – I half think of writing up the Sand-lot agitation for
Morley;[9] it is a curious business; were I stronger, I should try to sugar in

---

[4] Randolph Caldecott (1846–86), artist and book illustrator, is remembered for his series of
illustrated children's books. Henley had already suggested that Caldecott should illustrate 'Will
o' the Mill'. On 11 December RLS proposed to Colvin that Caldecott should be asked to
illustrate a volume of RLS's short stories. Nothing came of this idea.

[5] Cf. Sairey Gamp's 'You bage [i.e. base] creatur' *Martin Chuzzlewit*, ch. 49.

[6] Colvin, misunderstanding some information from Baxter, had sent RLS a telegram wrongly
informing him that £100 was being sent to him.

[7] George Smith, the cracksman in *Deacon Brodie*. The remark is in III, ii of the 1880 version.

[8] The Bohemian Club in San Francisco. Sam Osbourne and Joe Strong were members.

[9] Denis Kearney (1847–1907) organised and led the Workingmen's Party of California and
harangued his followers almost nightly on the vacant 'sand lots' in San Francisco, protesting
against dishonest banking, unjust taxation, the monopoly position of the local railroads and

with some of the leaders: a chield amang them tak'in' notes.[10] One, Mrs Smith, who kept a brothel, I reckon, before she started socialist, particularly interests me. If I am right as to her early industry, you know she would be sure to adore me. I have been all my days a dead hand at a harridan; I never saw the one yet that could resist me; to the proprietor (retired but not retiring) of a bawdy house, I represent the ideal of manly accomplishment – *moi, chétive personne,* as the Kings of China used to say to Confucius. When I die of consumption, you can put that upon my tomb. Sketch of my tomb follows:

> Robert Louis Stevenson.
> born 1850, of a family of Engineers
> died - - - - - - - - - - - - - - - -
>
> '*Nitor Aquis*'
> —
> Home is the sailor, home from sea,
> And the hunter home from the hill.
> —

You, who pass this grave, put aside hatred; love kindness; be all services remembered in your heart and all offences pardoned; and as you go down again among the living, let this be your question: Can I make some one happier this day before I lie down to sleep? Thus the dead man speaks to you from the dust: you will hear no more from him.

Who knows, Colvin, but I may thus be of more use when I am buried than ever while I was alive? The more I think of it, the more earnestly do I desire this. I may perhaps try to write it better some day; but that is what I want in sense. The verses are from a beayootiful poem by me.[11]

R.L.S.

---

landowners and especially the competition from cheap Chinese labour. 'Originally an Irish drayman, he rose, by his command of bad language, to almost dictatorial authority in the State; throned it there for six months or so, his mouth full of oaths, gallowses and conflagrations' (RLS in 'Monterey').

John Morley (1838–1923), journalist and man of letters, was editor of the *Fortnightly* 1867–82, and of the *Pall Mall Gazette* 1881–3. He also edited the 'English Men of Letters' series of short biographies. He later became a Liberal Cabinet Minister, and the author of many books, including a biography of Gladstone. Created Viscount 1908.

[10] 'A chield's amang you takin notes,/And faith he'll prent it' – Burns, 'On Captain Grose's Peregrinations'.

[11] The first draft of 'Requiem' is dated 'Train August 79'; the final version, with an additional verse not in *Underwoods*, is dated '1880 Jan S.F.'. The verses are to be found on RLS's tomb.

To Lloyd Osbourne[1]

[? February 1880]   *[San Francisco]*

Mr Sam, Dear Sir, If the enclosed should be found suitable for the pages
of your esteemed periodical, you will oblige me by giving it an early
insertion.[2] My usual charges are at the rate of the price of half a doughnut
per column; but to a gentleman of your singular penetration, and for the
pleasure of appearing in a magazine which is, if I may so express myself,
the cynosure of literary circles, I am content to offer you an abatement of
68.005 per cent upon the terms above stated. I expect the fraction to be
remitted, being poor although honest and my mother having recommended me to bind my hair and lace my bodice blue.

I am, respected sir, Yours to hand

Robert Louis Stevenson

Perpetual assistant backdoor keeper of the Indigent Author's
Soup Kitchen; author of *The Night Mare Skeleton or Blue Fire
to Burn*, and other classical works of an improving tendency.

Not I!

1

Some like drink
In a pint pot.
Some like to think;
Some not.
Strong Dutch Cheese,
Old Kentucky Rye,
Some like these;
Not I.

2

Some like Poe
And others like Scott.
Some like Mrs Stowe;
Some not.

---

[1] Fanny's son Samuel Lloyd Osbourne (later called Lloyd), nearly twelve years old, was at
boarding school at Locust Grove near Sonoma but came home for the holidays.
[2] Lloyd had been given a printing press (later to win immortality through the productions of the
Davos Press) and had begun to print, in a very crude fashion, a small newspaper, *The Daily
Surprise*, of which three issues survive. This gave way to *The Surprise*, 'A Journel published Semi-
monthly by S.L. Osbourne & Co. at Locust Grove, Sonoma', three issues of which also survive.
The first verse of RLS's 'Not I' was published in the first issue of 'Saterday, March 6th'. The
poem later appeared in a shortened, revised form in the Davos Press booklet, *Not I, and Other
Poems*, 1881.

Some like to fight,
Some like to cry.
Sam likes to write;
Not I.

3

Now, there's enough,
Clear without a blot.
Some may like the stuff;
Some not.
Some will say 'Encore!'
And Some 'O fie!'
Some would do some more;
Not I!   R.L.S.

To Edmund Gosse[1]

16 April [1880]   *Post Office, San Francisco, Cal.*

My Dear Gosse, You have not answered my last; and I know you will
repent when you hear how near I have been to another world. For about
six weeks I have been in utter doubt; it was a toss up for life or death all
that time; but I won the toss, sir, and Hades went off once more
discomfited. This is not the first time, nor will it be the last, that I have
a friendly game with that gentleman; I know he will end by cleaning me
out; but the rogue is insidious, and the habit of that sort of gambling seems
to be a part of my nature; it was, I suspect, too much indulged in youth;
break your children of this tendency, my dear Wegg, from the first. It is,
when once formed, a habit more fatal than opium. – I speak, as St Paul
says, like a fool.[2] I have been very, very sick; on the verge of a galloping
consumption, cold sweats, prostrating attacks of cough, sinking fits in
which I lost the power of speech, fever, and all the ugliest circumstances
of the disease; and I have cause to bless God, my wife that is to be, and
one Dr Bamford[3] (a name the Muse repels) that I have come out of all
this, and got my feet once more upon a little hill-top, with a fair prospect

---

[1] Some time in March RLS's illness became worse and by mid-March he had moved to the
Tubbs Hotel in East Oakland. It was apparently here that he had a relapse, the first hemorrhage
occurred and he became dangerously ill. Fanny moved him into her own house and nursed him
herself.

[2] 2 Corinthians 11:23.

[3] Dr William Bamford (died 1881), an English physician, educated in Canada, who had worked
in East Oakland since 1867. RLS gave him a copy of *Travels with a Donkey* with a grateful
inscription and RLS's parents sent him copies of *An Inland Voyage* and *Picturesque Notes on
Edinburgh*.

of life and some new desire of living. Yet I did not wish to die, neither; only I felt unable to go on farther with that rough horseplay of human life; a man must be pretty well to take the business in good part. Yet I felt all the time that I had done nothing to entitle me to an honourable discharge, that I had taken up many obligations and begun many friendships which I had no right to put away from me; and that for me to die was to play the cur and slinking sybarite, and desert the colours on the eve of the decisive fight.

My father and mother have made all up, given me £250 a year for a marriage present (they do not so name it), and merely treat their earlier letters as *non scripta*.[4] I wish they had taken that view at once, as it would have spared me some misery; but all's well, that ends well. Of course I have done no work for I do not know how long; and here you can triumph! I have been reduced to writing verses for amusement. A fact. The whirligig of time brings in its revenges,[5] after all. But I'll have them buried with me, I think; for I have not the heart to burn them while I live. Do write, Wegg; and if you are angry with me, bury that damned hatchet right straight away and be hanged to you. I shall go to the mountains as soon as the weather clears; on the way thither, I marry myself; then I set up my family altar among the pinewoods, 3000 feet, sir, from the disputatious sea. I am, dear Wegg, most truly yours   R.L.S.

To Sidney Colvin

[May 1880]   [East Oakland]

My dear Colvin, It is a long while since I have heard from you; nearly a month, I believe; and I begin to grow very uneasy. At first I was tempted to suppose that I had been myself to blame in some way; but now I have grown to fear lest some sickness or trouble among those whom you love may not be the impediment. I believe I shall soon hear; so I wait as best I can. I am, beyond doubt, greatly stronger, and yet still useless for any work and, I may say, for any pleasure. My teeth[1] and the bad weather still keep me here unmarried; but not, I earnestly hope, for long. When ever I get into the mountains, I trust I shall rapidly pick up. Until I get away

---

[4] RLS's parents had earlier begun to relent. They were sending money and MIS was writing affectionate letters. The news of the hemorrhage reached them on 31 March and they were kept in touch with RLS's progress by an exchange of telegrams. RLS told Colvin: 'My dear people telegraphed me in these words: "Count on 250 pounds annually." You may imagine what a blessed business this was.'

[5] *Twelfth Night*, V.i.384.

[1] RLS had told Baxter: 'I am waiting till I get in my new teeth – the old ones having been gently removed with a pair of pliers.'

from these sea fogs and my imprisonment in the house, I do not hope to
do much more than keep from active harm. My doctor took a desponding
fit about me, and scared Fanny into blue fits; but I have talked her over
again. It is the change I want, and the blessed sun, and a gentle air in
which I can sit out and see the trees and running water; these mere
defensive hygienics cannot advance one, though they may prevent evil. I
do nothing now; but try to possess my soul in peace, and continue to
possess my body on any terms.

[*Late May*][2]   *Calistoga, Napa County, Cala.*

All which is a fortnight old and not much to the point nowadays. Here
we are Fanny and I and a certain hound in a lovely valley under Mount
Saint Helena, looking round or rather wondering when we shall begin to
look around for a house of our own. I have received the first sheets;[3] not
yet the second bunch, as announced. It is a pretty heavy, emphatic piece
of pedantry; but I don't care; the public I verily believe will like it. I have
excised all you proposed and more on my own movement. But I have not
yet been able to rewrite the two special pieces which, as you said, so badly
wanted it; it is hard work to rewrite passages in proof; and the easiest work
is still hard to me. But I am certainly recovering fast: a married and
convalescent being. Received James's *Hawthorne*,[4] on which I meditate
a blast, Miss Bird,[5] Dixon's *Penn*, a *wrong Cornhill* (like my luck) and
Coquelin:[6] for all which, and especially the last, I tender my best thanks.
I have opened only James; it is very clever, very well written, and out of
sight the most snobbish and (in his own word) provincial – provincialism
inside out – thing in the world; I have dug up the hatchet; a scalp shall
flutter at my belt ere long. – I think my new book should be good; it will
contain our adventures for the summer, so far as these are worth narrating;
and I have already a few pages of diary which should make up bright.[7] I
am going to repeat my old experiment, after buckling to a while to write

[2] RLS and Fanny were married on 19 May by the Revd William Anderson Scott (1813–85), a
Scots Presbyterian minister, at his home in Post Street, San Francisco. Fanny described herself in
the register as 'widowed'. After staying three days at the Palace Hotel they left San Francisco on
22 May and travelled by ferry and rail northwards (with an overnight stop at South Vallejo) to
the small spa-town of Calistoga in the Napa Valley, an area now famous for wine production.
This part of the letter must have been written from the Springs Hotel, Calistoga.
[3] The surviving galley sheets of *The Amateur Emigrant* contain queries, comments and suggested
deletions by Colvin and Kegan Paul and revisions by RLS.
[4] The biography in the 'English Men of Letters' series (1879).
[5] Probably *A Lady's Life in the Rocky Mountains* (1879) by traveller and author, Isabella Lucy Bird
(1831–1904).
[6] *L'Art et le Comédien* (1880) by the French actor Benoît Constant Coquelin (1841–1909) is
praised by Colvin in a letter to Henley, written at this time.
[7] RLS's journal (which formed the basis for *The Silverado Squatters*) was first published in full by
John E. Jordan as *Robert Louis Stevenson's Silverado Journal* (Book Club of California, 1954).

more correctly, lie down and have a wallow. Whether I shall get any of my novels done this summer I do not know; I wish to finish the *Vendetta* first, for it really could not come after *Prince Otto*. – Lewis Campbell has made some noble work in that *Agamemnon*;[8] it surprised me. – We hope to get a house at Silverado, a deserted mining camp, eight miles up the mountain, now solely inhabited by a mighty hunter, answering to the name of Ruf' Hansome,[9] who slew last year a hundred and fifty deer. This is the motto I propose for the new volume. '*Vixerunt nonnulli in agris, delectati re sua familiari. His idem propositum fuit quod regibus, ut ne qua re egerent, ne cui parerent, libertate uterentur; cujus proprium est sic vivere ut velis.*'[10] I always have a terror lest the wish should have been father to the translation, when I come to quote; but that seems too plain sailing. I should put *regibus* in capitals for the pleasantry's sake. We are in the Coast Range; that being so much cheaper to reach. The family, I hope, will soon follow. I have asked Baxter to insert my marriage announcement in the *P.M.G.* for London friends.[11]

I enclose a letter to Morley, having lost his address: pray forward it, or tell him that you lost it, if you prefer. Love to all. Ever yours   R.L.S.

To his Parents[1]

[c. 23 June 1880]   *Calistoga, Napa Co., Cal.*

My dear Father and Mother, It is a great while since I have written, and then only a note: but I am not so much to blame as I appear. Both Fanny and Sam have been very sick with no less than diphtheria; and I was afraid to tell you. I wrote, for instance, a little answer to a delightful letter I had

---

[8] Lewis Campbell (1830–1908), classical scholar, Professor of Greek at St Andrews, 1863–92. He had translated into English verse *Scenes from the Agamemnon* (Edinburgh 1880) for performance that year by the Jenkin private theatricals.

[9] Silverado, the deserted mining camp on the slopes of Mount Saint Helena, was chosen on the advice of the Russian-Jewish storekeeper whom RLS called Kelmar. The journey with the Kelmars to visit the Hansons (or Hansens) is dated 30 May in RLS's journal.

[10] Cicero, *De Officiis*, I.20. 'Some of them, too, lived in the country and found their pleasure in the management of their private estates. Such men have had the same aim as kings – to suffer no want, to be subject to no authority, to enjoy their liberty, that is, in its essence, to live just as they please' (Loeb Classical Library translation). This duly appeared as the motto to *The Silverado Squatters.*

[11] It appeared in the *Pall Mall Gazette* of 19 June.

[1] The Stevensons heard on 15 June that the marriage had taken place. The next day they received photographs of RLS and Fanny, presumably with a letter from RLS. In a long and friendly letter of 29 June, in which she sent her love to Fanny, MIS wrote: 'I hope you both understand that I don't care for ancient history at all – know nothing about it – but want modern letters. Tell me about your life among the mountains.' To Frances Sitwell on 17 June RLS had written: 'My people are as good as gold, I am so glad we waited; that was Fanny's doing. I, I confess, would have given way if she had let me. But she said truly, every day was a gain.'

from Auntie, but I did not like to send it, fearing my news would disquiet you. We had to get down from Silverado double quick; had I not been so quick, we might all have been dead, for though Sam was not very bad, and Fanny had only a slight case, yet he was pretty weak, and she was nearly three days more or less out of her head and quite unable to take any nourishment, and you can imagine what that would have been for me in such a place, with all the cooking etc. to do as well as to take care of these sick folk.[2] I have drawn another hundred. It is disgusting how slowly I recover, yet I think I may declare that I *am* recovering. I am distinctly better in a good many ways; and that in spite of all these accidents. How to get home is my great trouble; I fear to go by Panama, I suspect it would be a sort of kill or cure; I fear to go right through by rail, for I am scarce strong enough yet; now I have it in my head to come slowly, from place to place; it will cost fifty or sixty dollars more a head for railway fare only, to say nothing of lodging and such; but if I can do it no other way, I will that way. I am very homesick for once; I suppose from perversity, because it is for once really rather a difficult thing to get home; and also because I want to see both of you after so long an absence – the longest we have ever had – and all the more because you have both been kinder to me this time than, as it seems to me, all the sum of your former kindnesses would amount to. I have a very big heart when I think of it all; and I will say this: if you can love my wife, it will, I believe, make me love both her and you the better. I have a half hope, I may get away in a month or maybe less from now. O I shall be so glad to see my dear old country and my dear old people once again. If I think I can't (I am far from thinking it now; it is because I am so far, that I can talk of it: I could not, while the thing was more doubtful) I shall let you know and we shall hit upon some plan. To my mother, [?] middens are not in themselves desirable; but you will find they are inseparable from big powers and undertakings. There is a good deal in common between the worst and the very best people, which is not at all shared in by the middling decent or even the remarkably respectable. That is my position. Twiggez. Apply the law to people whom you know intimately, and you will for the most part see it borne out. The exceptions are the people who have a special talent for *being good*, rather than general talents including that. I shall cut this sad disquisition. I am ever your loving son   R.L.S.[3]

---

[2] RLS, Fanny and Lloyd installed themselves in the abandoned mining cabin at Silverado on 9 June. Six days later both Fanny and Lloyd caught diphtheria. They were not able to return until 25 June.

[3] Although his journal ends on 30 June, RLS and Fanny apparently stayed on at Silverado well into July, being joined by Joe and Belle Strong and Nellie. In late July they returned to San Francisco. They left San Francisco on 29 July and travelled by rail to New York, *en route* for England.

VII. SUMMERS IN SCOTLAND AND WINTERS AT DAVOS
August 1880–September 1882

Stevenson, Fanny and the twelve-year-old Lloyd (still known as Sam) arrived in Liverpool on the *City of Chester* on 17 August 1880. Colvin travelled there specially and was the first to greet them 'on the quays of the grey Mersey'. They then joined RLS's parents, and Colvin had lunch with the 'united family'. He reported, rather cynically to Henley:

> I daresay it made things pleasanter my being there; and I'm bound to say the old folks put a most brave and most kind face on it indeed. . . . It was too soon to tell yet how he really was; in the face looking better than I expected, and improved by his new teeth; but weak and easily fluttered, and so small you never saw, you could put your thumb and finger round his thigh. On the whole he didn't seem to me a bit like a dying man in spite of everything. It would have done, and will do, your heart good to shake hands with him again. . . . When I had him alone talking in the smoking room it was quite exactly like old times; and it is clear enough that he likes his new estate so far all right, and is at peace in it; but whether you and I will ever get reconciled to the little determined brown face and white teeth and grizzling (for that's what it's up to) grizzling hair, which we are to see beside him in future – that is another matter.

Stevenson's parents, accompanied by RLS, Fanny and Lloyd reached Edinburgh the next day and stayed at the Palace Hotel before leaving for a holiday in the Highlands. In spite of the background of family distress against which the marriage had taken place, the Stevensons treated Fanny with great kindness and affection. She soon made a conquest of her father-in-law and was thereafter treated indulgently like a favourite daughter. Fanny's letters show how genuine was her own affection for them. Fanny did not make as good an impression on Stevenson's friends. At their first meeting in October 1880 in their London hotel *en route* for Davos, her main concern was to try to prevent them overtiring her husband. She was, as she wrote to her mother-in-law, 'all the time furtively watching the clock, and thirsting for their life's blood because they stay so late'.

The next two years were passed in a vain search for better health. Two winters were spent in the Swiss Alps at the health resort of Davos, and two summers with his parents in Scotland: in 1881 in Pitlochry and Braemar and in 1882 at Stobo and Kingussie. Despite chronic illness they were years of growing success as an author for Stevenson. He wrote some of his finest short stories, including 'Thrawn Janet' and 'The Merry Men'; he saw through the press two volumes of collected essays, *Virginibus Puerisque and Other Papers* and *Familiar Studies of Men and Books*, and his first volume of collected stories, *New Arabian Nights*. At Braemar in the autumn of 1881 he began to write his most famous and popular work, *Treasure Island*.

To Sidney Colvin

[*? 27 August 1880*]   *Ben Wyvis Hotel, Strathpeffer*[1]

My dear Colvin and others, One or two words. We are here; all goes exceeding well with the wife and with the parents. Near here is a valley; birch woods, heather, and a stream; I have lain down and died; no country, no place, was ever for a moment so delightful to my soul. And I have been a Scotchman all my life, and denied my native land! Away with your gardens of roses, indeed![2] Give me the cool breath of Rogie waterfall, henceforth and forever, world without end.[3]

I inclose two poems of, I think, a high order. One is my dedication for my essays;[4] it was occasioned by that delicious article in which the *Spectator* represented me as going about the Cevennes roaring for women, and only disquieted at the monastery because it was not a bawdy house; for which more congenial scene, I accordingly aspired.[5] The other requires no

---

[1] The Stevensons arrived at Strathpeffer Spa, a popular resort eighteen miles from Inverness, on 25 August. It is described in contemporary advertisements as 'The Harrogate of Scotland' with 'the *strongest* sulphur waters in Europe and a mild chalybeate spring'.

[2] 'Away, ye gay landscapes, ye gardens of roses!' the first line of Byron's 'Lachin y Gair' in praise of the Highlands.

[3] On 27 August MIS recorded: 'Drive to the falls of Rogie. Louis acknowledges that the Highlands are the most beautiful place in the world.'

[4] The posthumously published poem beginning 'To her, for I must still regard her' refers to the *Spectator* as 'grandmamma' and includes the lines:

> To the Right Reverend THE SPECTATOR,
> I here, a humble dedicator,
> Bring the last apples from my tree.

This Dedication was later prefixed to a set of fair copies of twenty-two poems in a notebook dismembered by G.S. Hellman. He wrongly dated it 1886 and described it as a projected Dedication to *Underwoods*. As a result it was added without authority at the end of Book I of *Underwoods* in the Vailima and later collected editions.

[5] The *Spectator* review of *Travels with a Donkey* (see p. 153, n. 5) mentioned what it called RLS's 'susceptibility towards the softer sex' and proceeded humorously to itemise his various references to the subject culminating in the fact that even in a Trappist monastery he disclosed his 'true worship' by remembering the lines of a French song '*Que t'as de belles filles*'.

explanation; *c'est tout bonnement un petit chef d'oeuvre, de grâce, de délicatesse et de bon sens humanitaire. Celui qui ne s'en sent pas touché jusqu'aux larmes – celui là n'a pas vécu.* I wish both poems back,[6] as I am copyless; but they might return, via Henley.

My father desired me still to withdraw the *Emigrant*, in the meantime, and I have written to Paul to break it to him gently. I fear there will be a storm; and I suppose that at any rate I shall remain under an obligation to him to produce the book again, in better form, for the same sum. But whatever may be the pecuniary loss, my father is willing to bear it; and the gain to my reputation will be considerable.

I am writing against time and the post runner. But you know what kind messages we both send to you both. May you have as good a time as possible so far from Rogie![7]   R.L.S.

To Charles Baxter[1]

[28 October 1880]   *Troyes*

Dear Charles, Herewith a cheque and the old divorce, I have been pretty seedy and am just creeping towards Davos in the midst of wind, rain, coughing and night sweats. This is a stunning place; it consists pretty considerably of churches, but not (strange to say for a French place) of soldiers. I eat main well; wherefore, I believe I shall continue to inhabit the spacious firmament yet a while. I have a picture for Simp's study, tell him, but it's astray just now, and he must wait. You had better add that it was made by me, or he may think I have bought him a vioo maistre, *ce qui n'est pas.* The dog has bogged more upon this hostile soil, with a preference for hostile carpets, than could be believed of a creature so inconsiderable in proportions. The cat bogged so free (not having a tail, neither, to conceal consequences) that she was left in England. I regret the dog was not left also, grudging so much manure to a foreign land. Yet we all adore that dog.[2] Yours ever   R.L.S.

---

[6] The other poem is probably another posthumously published poem, 'On Some Ghastly Companions at a Spa', a copy of which was sent to Baxter.

[7] Colvin was in Llanthony, South Wales working on his life of Landor.

[1] The Stevenson family travelled back to Edinburgh from Strathpeffer in mid-September, and on 7 October RLS, Fanny and Lloyd left for London. They spent nearly a fortnight at the expensive Grosvenor Hotel, where RLS met his friends and then left London on 19 October *en route* for Davos by easy stages.

[2] Walter Simpson presented Fanny with a black, thoroughbred Skye terrier and his sister Eve gave her a Manx cat. The dog seems originally to have been called Wattie, but this was soon corrupted to Wogg or Woggin and he ended up as Bogue. Eve Blantyre Simpson (1856–1920), was the youngest child and only surviving daughter of Sir James Simpson. Her reminiscences were published as *Robert Louis Stevenson's Edinburgh Days* (1898).

To his Parents

5 November [1880]   Hôtel Belvedere, Davos[1]

My far too good people, Your two letters and fifty quid are all duly received. You spoil us to that extent that positively you leave me no excuse to be unhappy; but having spent your best years in spoiling me, you are not new to the business. We got to Davos last evening; and I feel sure we shall like it greatly. I saw Symonds[2] this morning, and already like him: it is such sport to have a literary man around. My father can understand me, when he thinks what it would be to come up here for a winter and find TAIT.[3] Symonds is like a Tait to me; eternal interest in the same topics, eternal cross-cause-waying of special knowledge. That makes hours to fly. When I came to the first 'Don't corrugate your eyebrows' in my father's letter, I was corrugating 'em, and confessed a hit; but when I came to the first 'Don't worry your moustaches' and was worrying them, I lay down and died.[4]

The doctor has been here;[5] he seems a boss human being – which is quite a different thing from a boss eye, being laudatory. He comes tomorrow ere I am up to have a worry at my human frame. He is going to attack me in every tender spot and make my life a burthen to me – said so, straight out. Well, well, we shall see; it's lang or the deil die at a dykeside.[6] I also got Fraser for which I thank you:[7] rayther heavy, I fear, the works of R.L.S.; but up here in the Halps, I shall make the ink spin.

---

[1] Davos-Platz is situated over five thousand feet above sea level in a broad valley flanked by high mountains in the Graubünden (French Grisons), the most easterly canton of Switzerland. The virtues of its intense cold and bright winter sunshine for the treatment of pulmonary tuberculosis had been recognised in the mid-1860s and over the next fifteen years it had begun to be developed from a small mountain village into a health resort. Hotels had been built and other facilities provided but in Stevenson's day (when it was catering for about a thousand winter visitors) it was in many ways an unattractive, dirty and insanitary place.

[2] John Addington Symonds (1840–93), critic, translator, biographer and historian of the Italian Renaissance who is better remembered today for his tormented homosexuality. He first went to Davos in 1877 in search of a cure for his tuberculosis and had just established his permanent home there. RLS had brought a letter of introduction from Gosse.

[3] Peter Guthrie Tait (1831–1901), mathematician and physicist, was Professor of Natural History at Edinburgh University 1860–1901. He was a friend of TS.

[4] Throughout his letter of 31 October TS interposed admonitions: 'Don't twirl your moustaches' or 'Don't corrugate your eyebrows'. He also vainly asked: 'For my sake do take the trouble to date your letters.'

[5] 'Dr Karl Ruedi of Davos, the good genius of the English in his frosty mountains' – RLS in the Dedication to Underwoods. Ruedi (died 1901) emigrated to America as a young man and practised in Colorado. He was in Davos 1875–91, and then returned briefly to America.

[6] The Scottish proverb, 'Lang e'er the Dee'l lie dead by the dykeside' is said when one is told that a wicked person is likely to die.

[7] Fraser's Magazine for November 1880 contained RLS's essay on Monterey, 'The Old Pacific Capital' and his verses, 'The Scotsman's Return from Abroad'.

The doctor is to put me on hours for every mortal thing, though. My uncle had written to him, and I recognise in the result the interfering disposition of T. Stevenson and the culpable weakness of Geo. Wil. Balfour.[8] To blow the gaff on the cigarettes, and to order three pipes a day! Either my father is right, or else he is a sneak and a give away; possibly the first.   R.L.S.

To Charles Warren Stoddard[1]

[December 1880]   Hôtel Belvedere, Davos-Platz

Dear Charles Warren Stoddard, Many thanks to you for your letter and the photograph. Will you think it mean if I ask you to wait till there appears a promised cheap edition?[2] Possibly the canny Scot does feel pleasure in the superior cheapness; but the true reason is this, that I think to put a few words, by way of notes, to each book in its new form; hence that will be the Standard Edition Without Which no g's l will be complete:[3] the edition, briefly, *sine qua non*. Before that, I shall hope to send you my essays, which are in the printer's hands. I look to get yours soon. I am sorry to hear the Custom House has proved fallible, like all other human houses and customs. Life consists of that sort of business and I fear there is a class of man, of which you offer no inapt type, doomed to a kind of mild, general disappointment through life. I do not believe that a man is the more unhappy for that. Disappointment, except with oneself, is not a very capital affair; and the sham beatitude 'Blessed is he that expecteth little'[4] one of the truest and, in a sense, the most Christlike, things in literature.

Alongside of you, I have been all my days, a red cannon ball of dissipated effort; here I am by the heels in this Alpine valley, with just so

---

[8] MIS's brother, Dr George William Balfour (1823–1903) – 'that wise youth my uncle' – an authority on diseases of the heart; physician to Royal Infirmary Edinburgh 1867–82.

[1] Charles Warren Stoddard (1843–1909), San Francisco author and traveller, member of the Bohemian Club and close friend of the Strongs. RLS had met him at his picturesque studio on Rincon Hill, San Francisco, as described in ch. 8 of *The Wrecker*. Stoddard's travels to Hawaii and Tahiti were recorded in his *South Sea Idyls* (1873), and he fostered RLS's interest in the South Seas by lending him this book, along with Melville's *Typee* and *Omoo*. Stoddard lived in Hawaii (1881–4) and wrote of his visit to the leper colony in *The Lepers of Molokai* (1885). A convert to Roman Catholicism, he was Professor of English at the University of Notre Dame, Indiana (1885–6), and at the Catholic University of America, Washington, D.C. (1889–1902).

[2] Stoddard had written on 9 November enclosing a photograph of himself and other members of the Bohemian Club and asking for autographed English editions of RLS's work.

[3] Cf. 'all those volumes which "no gentleman's library should be without"', in Lamb's 'Detached Thoughts on Books and Reading'.

[4] 'Blessed is the man who expects nothing, for he shall never be disappointed.' Quoted by Pope in a letter of 23 September 1725 to Fortescue.

much a prospect of future restoration as shall make my present caged estate easily tolerable to me – *shall* or *should*, I would not swear to the word before the trial's done. I miss all my objects in the meantime; and – I thank God, I have enough of my old and maybe somewhat base philosophy, to keep me on a good understanding with myself and providence.

The mere extent of a man's travels has in it something consolatory. That he should have left friends or enemies in many different and distant quarters, gives a sort of earthly dignity to his existence. And I think the better of myself for the belief that I have left some in California interested in me and my successes. Let me assure you, you who have made friends already among such various and distant races, that there is a certain phthisical Scot who will always be pleased to hear good news of you, and would be better pleased by nothing than to learn that you had thrown off your present incubus, largely consisting of letters I believe, and had sailed into some square work by way of change.

And by way of change, in itself let me copy on the other page, some broad Scotch I wrote for you when I was ill last spring in Oakland. It is no muckle worth; but ye shouldna look a gien horse in the moo'. Yours ever   R.L. Stevenson

Remember me to Unger, Rix, Harasthy, and, last but not least, my brither Scot, Austin.[5] Tell him I have not yet been near Dumfries; and you can get him to help you to decipher the verses, which are not worth that degree of trouble.

To C.W. Stoddard[6]

Ne sutor ultra crepidam;[7]
An', since that I a Scotsman am,
The Lallan ait I weel may toot
As ye can blaw the English flute;
An' sae, without a wordie mair
The braidest Scots ma turn sall sair'.

---

[5] Frank L. Unger (died 1915), poet and musician, assistant secretary of the Pacific Stock Exchange and deputy superintendent of streets in San Francisco, and Julian Rix (1850–1903), artist, were friends of Joe Strong and popular members of the Bohemian Club. Arpad Haraszthy was a wine-grower; his father, a Hungarian nobleman, was the first to experiment with vine-growing in the Napa Valley. Joe Austin is described by Belle as 'a big Scotchman with a red face, white hair and eyes as blue as china plates'; Belle named her son Austin from her admiration for Mrs Austin.

[6] The main Scots words or phrases in the verses are: l. 3 *Lallan* (now usually *Lallans*) the language of the Lowlands as distinct from the Gaelic spoken in the Highlands; *ait* oat, i.e. a pipe made from oat straw; l. 6 *sall sair* shall serve; l. 10 *cuist* cast; l. 16 *Waesucks* Alas; l. 19 *muckle* a good deal; l. 20 *ferlie* a marvel, a wonder; l. 25 *wheen* a good few; l. 29 *trystit* met.

[7] 'Let the cobbler stick to his last'. Proverbial from Pliny, *Historia Naturalis*, XXXV, 85.

Of a' the lingo's ever prentit
The braidest Scot's the best inventit,
Since, Stoddard, by a straik o' God's,
The mason-billies cuist their hods,
And a' at ance began to gabble
Aboot the unfeenished wa's o' Babel

Shakespeare himsel' (in *Henry Fift*)
To clerk the Lallan made a shift;[8]
An' Homer's aft been heard to mane:
'Waesucks, could I but live again!
Had I the Scottish Language kennt,
I wad hae clerk't the *Iliad* in't!'

(Follows the Aria)

Far had I rode an' muckle seen
    An' witnessed mony a ferlie,
Afore that I had clappit e'en
    Upo' my billy, Chärlie.

Far had I rode an' muckle seen
    In lands accountit foreign,
An' had foregather'd wi' a wheen
    Or I fell in wi' Warren.

Far had I rode an' muckle seen,
    But ne'er was fairly doddered
Till I was trystit as a frien'
    Wi' Chärlie Warren Stoddard!

To his Father

12 December [1880]   *[Davos]*

My dear Father, Here is the scheme as well as I can foresee.[1] I begin the book immediately after the '15, as then began the attempt to suppress the Highlands.

---

[8] Captain Jamy in *Henry V*, III.ii.

[1] While at Strathpeffer RLS had planned a book to be called *Scotland and the Union*. At Davos he developed the idea further, writing to Henley in December: 'I am reading hard for my work on *The Transformation of the Scottish Highlands*, which has grown, like Eve, out of one rib in *Scotland and the Union. The Highlands* will be a noble work; I mean, if I could do it, it would be; splendid stuff; various, romantic, human, scientific, religious; touching the privates of the old mystery of race.' He sent his father long lists of books he wanted but the project was eventually abandoned; the research stood him in good stead when he came to write *Kidnapped*.

I. Thirty Years Interval.

(1) Rob Roy.
(2) The Independent Companies: The Watches.
(3) Story of Lady Grange.
(4) The Military Roads and Disarmament: Wade and
(5) Burt.

II. The Heroic Age.

(1) Duncan Forbes of Culloden.
(2) Flora Macdonald.
(3) The Forfeited Estates; including Hereditary Jurisdictions; and the admirable conduct of the tenants.

III. Literature Here Intervenes.

(1) The Ossianic Controversy.
(2) Boswell and Johnson.
(3) Mrs Grant of Laggan.

IV. Economy

Highland Economics
The Reinstatement of the Proprietors.
The Evictions
Emigration.
Present State.

V. Religion.

The Catholics, Episcopals, and Kirk, and Society Propagation Christian Knowledge.
The Men.
The Disruption.

All this of course will greatly change in form scope and order; this is just a bird's eye glance. Thank you for Burt[2] which came and for your Union notes. I have read one half (about 900 pages) of Wodrow's *Correspondence*,[3] with some improvement but great fatigue. The doctor

---

[2] Edward Burt, *Letters from a Gentleman in the North of Scotland* (1754). Burt was one of the engineers employed by General Wade in the building of roads and bridges in the Highlands. I have not thought it necessary to annotate the historical background.
[3] *The Correspondence of the Rev. Robert Wodrow*, edited from Manuscripts by T. MacCrie (Wodrow Society, Edinburgh, 3 vols, 1842–3).

thinks well of my recovery, which puts me in good hope for the future. I should certainly be able to make a fine history of this.

My *Essays* are going thro' the press and should be out in January or February.[4] Ever affectionate son   R.L.S.

To his Mother

26 December 1880   [*Davos*]

My dear Mother, I was very tired yesterday and could not write; I toboggined so furiously all morning; we had a delightful day, crowned by an incredible dinner – more courses than I have fingers on my hands. Your letter arrived duly at night, and I thank you for it as I should. You need not suppose I am at all insensible to my father's extraordinary kindness about this book; he is a brick; I vote for him freely. The assurance you speak of, is what we all ought to have, and might have, and should not consent to live without. That people do not have it more than they do, is, I believe, because parsons speak so much in long-drawn, theological similitudes, and won't say out what they mean about life, and man, and God, in fair and square human language. I wonder if you or my father ever thought of the obscurities that lie upon human duty from the negative form in which the ten commandments are stated; or of how Christ was so continually substituting affirmatives. 'Thou shalt not' is but an example; 'Thou shalt' is the law of God. It was this that seems meant in the phrase that 'not one jot nor tittle of the law should pass'.[1] But what led me to the remark is this: a kind of black, angry look goes with that statement of the law in negatives. 'To love one's neighbour as oneself'[2] is certainly much harder, but states life so much more actively, gladly and kindly, that you can begin to see some pleasure in it; and till you can see pleasure in these hard choices and bitter necessities, where is there any Good News to men? It is much more important to do right than not to do wrong; further, the one is possible, the other has always been and will ever be impossible; and the faithful *design to do right* is accepted by God: that seems to me to be the gospel, and that was how Christ delivered us from the law. After people are told that, surely they might hear more encouraging sermons; to blow the trumpet for good would seem the parson's business: and since it is not in our own strength, but by faith and perseverance (no account made of slips), that we are to run the race, I do not see where they get the material for their gloomy discourses. Faith is,

---

[4] *Virginibus Puerisque and Other Papers* finally appeared in early April 1881. RLS was paid £20 for the copyright.

[1] Matthew 5:18.

[2] Leviticus 19:18; Matthew 19:19, and elsewhere.

not to believe the Bible, but to believe in God; if you believe in God (or, for it's the same thing, have that assurance you speak about) where is there any more room for terror? There are only three possible attitudes: Optimism, which has gone to smash; Pessimism, which is on the rising hand and very popular among clergymen who seem to think they are Christians – Lilley,[3] I daresay, for instance; and this Faith, which is the gospel. Once you hold the last, it is your business (1) to find out what is right and (2) to try to do it; if you fail in the last, that is by commission, Christ tells you to hope; if you fail in the first, that is by omission, his picture of the last day gives you but a black lookout. The whole necessary morality is kindness; and it should spring, of itself, from the one fundamental doctrine, faith. If you are sure that God, in the long run, means kindness by you, you should be happy; and if happy, surely you should be kind.

I beg your pardon for this long discourse; it is not all right, of course, but I am sure there is something in it. One thing, I have not got clearly; that about the omission and the commission; but there is truth somewhere about it, and I have no time to try to clear it just now. Do you know, you have had about a *Cornhill* page of sermon? it is, however, true.

Sam heard with dismay Fanny was not going to give me a present; so F. and I had to go and buy things for ourselves and go through a representation of surprise when they were presented next morning. It gave us both quite a Santa Claus feeling on Xmas eve to see him so excited and hopeful; I enjoyed it hugely.

I believe I have been only twice away before on Xmas; once last year, over which I draw a veil; and once in '75[4] I think when I spent the day reading old magazines in a deserted Savile Club, and dined at night at Simpson's with a French novel; I had a heavy cold, I remember, and was not precisely merry. This time it was very different. I am glad it comforts you to know me to be with my wife. I cannot tell you what a change it is to me; may God bless her, and spare us long in love to each other. I send you both my most affectionate love, except what I keep for my wife, and remain, Your affectionate son   Robert Louis Stevenson

To Sidney Colvin

[c. *12 March 1881*]   [*Davos*]

My dear Colvin, My health is not just what it should be; I have lost weight, pulse, respiration etc., and gained nothing in the way of my old bellows. But these last few days, with tonic, cod-liver oil, better wine

---

[3] James Philip Lilley (1845–1931), Free Church minister at Knox's Church Arbroath, petitioned for divorce in December 1880. His wife countered with allegations of ill-treatment.
[4] MS: '65. But 1877 seems to have been the only occasion when RLS spent Christmas in London.

(there is some better now) and perpetual beef-tea, I think I have progressed. To say truth I have been here a little overlong. I was reckoning up; and since I have known you, already quite a while, I have not, I believe remained so long in any one place as here in Davos. That tells on my old gipsy nature; like a violin hung up, I begin to lose what music there was in me; and with the music, I do not know what besides, or do not know what to call it, but something radically part of life, a rhythm, perhaps, in one's old and so brutally overridden nerves, or perhaps a kind of variety of blood that the heart has come to look for.

I purposely knocked myself off first. As to Bertie, I believe I am no sound authority; I alternate between a stiff disregard, and a kind of horror; sometimes I am brutally cynical and indifferent, sometimes (as last night) I get waked up by whiffs of intolerable dismay and agony. In neither mood can a man judge at all. I know the thing to be terribly perilous; I fear it to be now altogether hopeless.[1] Luck has failed; the weather has not been favourable; and if I were you, Colvin, I would hope no more. In her true heart, the mother hopes no more. But − well, I feel a great deal, that I either cannot or will not say, as you well know. It has helped to make me more conscious of the wolverine on my own shoulders; and that also makes me a poor judge and poor adviser. Perhaps if we were all marched out in a row, and a piece of platoon firing to the drums performed, it would be well for us: although, I suppose − and yet I wonder! − so ill for the poor mother and dear wife. But you can see this makes me morbid. *Sufficit; explicit.*

You are in the right about that adorable book;[2] F. and I are in a world, not ours; but pardon me, as far as sending on goes, we take another view; the first vol. *à la bonne heure!* but not − never − the second. Two hours of hysterics can be no good matter for a sick nurse; and the strange, hard, old being in so lamentable and yet human a desolation − crying out like a burnt child, and yet always wisely and beautifully − how can that end, as a piece of reading, even to the strong − but on the brink of the most cruel kind of weeping? I observe, the old man's style is stronger on me than ever it was − and by rights too, since I have just laid down his most attaching book. God rest the baith o' them! But even if they do not meet again, how we should all be strengthened to be kind; and not only in act − in speech also − that so much more important part. See what this apostle of silence most regrets − not speaking out his heart.

[1] Mrs Sitwell came to Davos in January with her surviving son the eighteen-year-old Francis Albert (Bertie) who was dying from consumption. He lingered on for several months but died in April. RLS's privately printed memorial poem 'To F.J.S. Davos, April 3, 1881' was reprinted as 'In Memoriam F.A.S.' (*Underwoods* I, XXVII).

[2] Carlyle's *Reminiscences*, edited by J.A. Froude, had just been published, a few weeks after his death. The second volume contains Carlyle's memoir of his wife, the publication of which caused controversy. I assume Colvin had asked RLS to send the book on to Mrs Sitwell.

I was struck as you were by the admirable sudden, clear sunshine upon Southey – even on his works. Symonds to whom I reported it, remarked at once: a man who was respected by both Carlyle and Landor must have had more in him than we can trace. So I feel with true humility.

It was to save my brain that S. proposed reviewing. He and, it appears, Leslie Stephen fear a little some eclipse; I am not quite without sharing the fear. I know my own languor as no one else does; it is a dead down-draught; a heavy fardel. Yet if I could shake off the wolverine aforesaid – and his fangs are lighter, though perhaps I feel them more – I believe I could be myself again awhile. I have not written any letter for a great time; none saying what I feel, since you were here, I fancy. Be duly obliged for it; and take my most earnest thanks not only for the books but for your letter. I feel it is asking you too much to write to me. But send me half a page now and then. Your affectionate   R.L.S.

The effect of reading this on Fanny shows me I must tell you I am very happy, peaceful, and jolly; except for questions of work and the states of other people.

Woggin sends his love.[3]

To Lloyd Osbourne

[c. *6 May 1881*]   [*Paris*][1]

My dear Sam, We are still stuck up here in Paris, where it has become pretty cold again. Wogg thinks it a very interesting but in some ways inconvenient city, it seemed to him that there was more opening for a young Wogg of promise about the Forest of Fontainebleau than anywhere he had been; business seemed brisker there. He now eats bread and vegetables like a great, big, red commercial drummer; long ago, he thought maybe pirates liked milk, but when he found out that was a mistake, he dropped all dealings on that side. Yesterday he tried to bite his mamma, and had a very sad interview with both his parents in conse-quence; the talk and whatnot lasted about ten minutes, and then it was suggested to him on all sides that he had better go into a dark closet and think. He went in and thank for about twenty minutes consecutively, and when he was let out again, said he had rather liked it than otherwise. But hc has been pretty polite, above all to his papa with whom he had most talking – ever since. He now waxes his moustache, and turns up the ends,

---

[3] The dog had bitten Colvin during his visit to Davos.
[1] RLS and Fanny left Davos in the third week of April, stayed at Siron's inn at Barbizon and then came on to Paris.

which looks mighty fierce; but he has given up Bonapartery; he met with several dogs who did not agree with him on that point, and soon caved in. A little white wog shot out of a shop at him, like an arrow through the air, bit him, as near as we could make out, in the place that he sits down upon, and was back again into that shop, before Wogg had time to remember that he was a pirate.

The French have five or six divisions and a fleet out after the Kroumirs; a tribe something like the Utes; if they were in India, we should send 1500 men after them; but there's nothing like making sure, you know, and it's fine exercise for the boys. They don't seem to have met any Kroumirs except a country parson; and they have lost two men; so it has not been so bloody as some of our wars.[2]

I haven't seen much American news; but then you see I'm in the land of French newspapers; the last two or three have been entirely filled by a duel between two fencing masters, who seem both to have hated it and hung back for dear life; but they had to stand up and fought two hours till one of them got a scratch to excuse them stopping.[3] Imagine, the account of this was longer than the war news. What a funny people it is!

Good-bye my dear Sam. Remember me to Mr Carter.[4] Yours affectionately   Robert Louis Stevenson

To Sidney Colvin
(Slightly Abridged)

[c. 24 June 1881]   Kinnaird Cottage, Pitlochry[1]

My dear S.C. Great and glorious news. Your friend sincere goes forth to war; His blood red banner blows afar;[2] He Louis the bold unfearing chap

[2] Under the pretext of attacking the Kroumirs, the French sent a military expedition against Tunis which occupied Bizerta on 1 May. On 12 May the French made the Bey sign a treaty accepting a French protectorate. The Utes are a tribe of American Indians in Utah and Colorado.

[3] The duel between MM. Pons and San Malato finally took place on 4 May and was reported in Paris newspapers of 6 May.

[4] The Revd Charles Clement Carter (1850–81) of Malton, Yorkshire, a patient at Davos, was Lloyd's tutor there: RLS arranged for him to continue to tutor Lloyd and Lloyd went to England with him in March. In a letter at this time Fanny said he was 'poor, married, has several children' and was dying of kidney disease.

[1] RLS and Fanny travelled from Paris to London in mid-May and were in Edinburgh by the end of the month. RLS left almost at once and Mrs Stevenson and Fanny joined him at the hotel in Pitlochry on 3 June. After a few days looking for a suitable house, they moved into Kinnaird Cottage, Moulin, a village just north of Pitlochry, on 7 June. Pitlochry, on the north bank of the river Tummel and in the centre of most picturesque Highland scenery, was becoming increasingly popular with holiday-makers and was recommended as a healthy spot for invalids.

[2] A reminiscence of the first verse of Bishop Heber's hymn:

Aims at a professorial cap, And now besieges, do and dare, The Edinburgh History chair. Three months in summer only it Will bind him to that windy bit; The other nine to range abroad Untrammel'd in the eye of God. Mark in particular one thing: He means to work that cursed thing: And to the golden youth explain, Scotland and England, France and Spain: Their quaint beliefs, their various rites,[3] And why they are such b—— s——.

In short, sir, I mean to try for this chair. I do believe I can make something out of it. It will be a pulpit in a sense; for I am nothing if not moral, as you know. My works are unfortunately so light and trifling they may interfere. But if you think, as I think, I am fit to fight it, send me the best kind of testi-anti-monial (I had too much of the latter when a child)[4] stating all you can in favour of me and, with your best art, turning the difficulty of my never having done anything in history, strictly speaking. Second, is there anybody else, think you, from whom I could wring one – I mean, you could wring one for me. Any party in London or Cambridge who thinks well enough of my little books to back me up with a few heartfelt words? You will understand why I write so sillily and fast; for I have many to write to. Jenkin approves highly; but says, pile in *English* testimonials. Now I only know Stephen, Symonds, Lang, Gosse and you, and Meredith, to be sure, and would Paul be any good – anyway, I doubt if *he* would. The chair is in the gift of the Faculty of Advocates, where I believe I am more wondered at than loved.[5] I do not know the foundation: one or two hundred, I suppose. But it would be a good thing for me, out and out good. Help me to live, help me to *work*, for I am the better of pressure, and help me to say what I want about God man and life.   R.L.S.

Heart broken trying to write rightly to people.
History and Constitutional Law is the full style.[6]

> The Son of God goes forth to war,
> A Kingly crown to gain;
> His blood-red banner streams afar: –
> Who follows in His train?

[3] Written above 'rights'.

[4] Fanny in her prefatory note to *A Child's Garden* records: 'When the child . . . took cold after cold, antimonial wine [sherry containing tartarated antimony] was administered continuously for a period extending into months; "enough" said Dr George Balfour, "to ruin his constitution for life." '

[5] The nomination to the chair belonged to the Faculty of Advocates (the electors). The final choice was the responsibility of the University Patrons (the curators).

[6] I have omitted the postscript, listing the various people to whom RLS had written for testimonials. RLS was ultimately unsuccessful in his attempt to secure the History chair.

★*To W.E. Henley*

[c. *3 July 1881*]   *Kinnaird Cottage, Pitlochry*

My dear Henley, I hope, then, to have a visit from you. If before August, here; if later, at Braemar. *Tope!*[1]

And now, *mon bon*, I must babble about 'The Merry Men', my favourite work. It is a fantastic sonata about the sea and wrecks. Chapter I. 'Eilean Aros' – the island, the roost, the 'merry men', the three people there living – sea superstitions. Chapter II. 'What the Wreck had brought to Aros'. Eh, boy? what had it? Silver and clocks and brocades, and what a conscience, what a mad brain! Chapter III. 'Past and Present in Sandag Bay' – the new wreck and the old – so old – the Armada treasure-ship, *Santissima Trinidad*[2] – the grave in the heather – strangers there. Chapter IV. 'The Gale' – the doomed ship – the storm – the drunken madman on the head – cries in the night. Chapter V. 'A Man out of the Sea'. But I must not breathe to you my plot. It is, I fancy, my first real shoot at a story; an odd thing, sir, but, I believe, my own, though there is a little of Scott's *Pirate* in it, as how should there not? He had the root of romance in such places. Aros is Earraid, where I lived lang syne; the Ross of Grisapol is the Ross of Mull; Ben Kyaw, Ben More. I have written to the middle of Chapter IV. Like enough, when it is finished I shall discard all chapterings; for the thing is written straight through. It must, unhappily, be re-written – too well written not to be.

The chair is only three months in summer; that is why I try for it. If I get it, which I shall not, I should be independent at once. Sweet thought. I liked your Byron well; your Berlioz better. No one would remark these cuts; even I, who was looking for it, knew it not at all to be a *torso*.[3] The paper strengthens me in my recommendation to you to follow Colvin's hint. Give us an 1830: you will do it well, and the subject smiles widely on the world. –

1830: *A Chapter of Artistic History*, by William Ernest Henley (or *of Social and Artistic History*, as the thing might grow to you). Sir, you might be in the Athenaeum yet with that; and, believe me, you might and would be far better the author of a readable book. Glad you think F.'s story in it; I thought it was.[4] Yours ever   R.L.S.

---

[1] French: Done! Agreed!

[2] In the final version the treasure-ship is the *Espirito Santo*.

[3] An unsigned review of Matthew Arnold's edition of *The Poetry of Byron* in the *Athenaeum* of 25 June 1881, and 'Hector Berlioz: A Biography' in the July *Cornhill*. Henley had complained bitterly that Stephen or Payn had made cuts in the *Cornhill* article.

[4] A short story, set in Monterey, called 'The Shadow on the Bed'; it was eventually published as 'The Warlock's Shadow' in the monthly magazine *Belgravia* in March 1886.

The following names have been invented for Wogg by his dear papa:–
Grunty-pig (when he is scratched).
Rose-mouth (when he comes flying up with his rose-leaf tongue
    depending), and
Hoofen-boots (when he has had his foots wet).
How would *Tales for Winter Nights* do?

To W.E. Henley

[*Mid-July 1881*]   *PITLOCHRY*
                                                        if you please

[*Dictated to Fanny*]

Dear Henley, To answer a point or two.[1] First. The Spanish ship was
sloop rigged, and clumsy, because she was fitted out by some private
adventurers, not over wealthy, and glad to take what they could get. Is
that not right? Tell me if you think not. That, at least was how I meant
it. As for the boat cloaks I am afraid they are, as you say false imagination,
but I love the name, nature, and being of them so dearly, that I feel as if
I would almost rather ruin a story than omit the reference. The proudest
moments of my life have been passed in the stern sheets of a boat with that
romantic garment over my shoulders. This, without prejudice to one
glorious day when standing upon some water stairs at Lerwick I signalled
with my pocket handkerchief for a boat to come ashore for me. I was then
aged fifteen or sixteen; conceive my glory.[2] (As there seems no more
coming, I will write a line or two on my own account and thank you for
your kindness in marking my work; it was just what I wanted, and has
given me a great lift. The only thing I fear is that my work will not be
good enough to go into the same book with Louis's upon which he has
set his heart.[3] Mine alone would not be noticed much, but would be
brought into such prominence by appearing with Louis's that I feel
doubtful whether it is not foolish. I hope you are both well, and that the
play is progressing. Has anyone else seen it yet? I should like to know

[1] Henley had written praising 'The Merry Men' – 'You are right about it. 'Tis your finest story'
– but that part of the letter containing the detailed points to which RLS replies does not seem
to have survived.
[2] RLS related the incident in a letter to his mother of 20 June 1869 during a tour of inspection
with his father to the Orkney and Shetland islands: 'We returned again to the water-stair beside
the town hall and waved a handkerchief for the gig, a romantic action which made me
remember many old daydreams when it was my only wish to be a pirate or a smuggler.'
[3] Henley had offered to mark Fanny's story 'The Shadow on the Bed' suggesting where it could
be improved. The original plan was for Fanny's story to be included in a book of ghost stories,
including RLS's 'Thrawn Janet' and others.

what other people think, though nothing will change my opinion. I was sure about the 'Merry Men', but Louis turned cold to it before it was done; I am glad that you agreed with me. F.)

(Louis) Several of the phrases you object to are proper nautical, or long shore phrases, and therefore, I think not out of place in this long shore story. As for the two members which you thought at first so ill united; I confess they seem perfectly so to me. I have chosen to sacrifice a long projected story of adventure because the sentiment of that is identical with the sentiment of 'My Uncle'. My uncle himself is not the story as I see it; only the leading episode of that story. It's really a story of wrecks, as they appear to the dweller on the coast. It's a view of the sea. Goodness knows when I shall be able to re-write; I must first get over this copper headed cold.   R.L.S.

To W.E. Henley

[c. *29 July 1881*]   [*Pitlochry*]

[*Dictated to Fanny*]

My dear Henley, God bless you for writing so often (Amen. F.) I am lying here in bed (I always go to bed now between meals, and when I can't get out.) lying here literally grilling in my blood about cursed American complications. We have just been bled of twenty pounds which we can ill afford;[1] houses are falling, taxes are owing, and begging letters three parts insult are the only communications that reach us from that happy strand. I am feeling better already; nothing like blowing off steam; if I could blow like a whale, and the act were only blasphemous, I believe none of these little matters would affect me; between my illness and this kettle of fish the head of the amanuensis is quite gone, so if this letter require a great deal of editing you will know the reason why. I have written a letter to Colvin with my own fist; and another under the inspiration of hellish resentment to one of the originals of my distress. It's a very odd trait, that of the people who always insult you when they beg. I presume it comes from dignity of character.

I beg you to remark that you can reach Braemar by steam to Aberdeen at a very trifling figure. To do so will be a very kind action to my unsound mind inside of my diseased body. I shall send along with this, or immediately following it the proof of 'Thrawn Janet' which I must ask

---

[1] RLS had had to send £20 to Joe and Belle Strong, whose son Austin was born on 18 April 1881.

you to send on at once,[2] as I have to beg for the money on the nail for the purposes of my insulting beggar. I am again relieved; every rough word I can apply to them is like a plaster to my sores. I am of your way of thinking about *Landor*.[3] It's a very pleasant work. As you say his life of R.L.S. will be a joke. 'Chapter 2. Youth in Edinburgh' is like to be a masterpiece of the genteely evasive. The amanuensis suggests that his will be the work for a fond parent. I seriously suggest that you should write a blackguard supplement – also a Christian one, for he will be apt to leave that out too – and be involved from thenceforward in a public insulting controversy with him. The best name for your work and perhaps for me is the Christian blackguard.[4]

I have not yet told you, have I, that I am getting my studies printed at my Papa's expense.[5] Would you advise me to offer the sheets in America? Write soon.

On Monday we shall proceed to Braemar. Address, apparently, Castleton, Braemar.[6]

To Edmund Gosse

> The Cottage
> (late the late Miss McGregor's)[1]

[Postmark 10 August 1881]   Castleton of Braemar

My dear Gosse, Come on the 24th; there is a dear fellow. Everybody else wants to come later, and it will be a godsend for, sir,

> yours sincerely

You can stay as long as you behave decently and are not sick of, sir,

> your obedient humble servant

We have family worship in the home of, sir,

> yours respectfully

Braemar is a fine country but nothing to (what you will also see) the maps of, sir,   yours in the Lord

---

[2] 'Thrawn Janet', accepted by Leslie Stephen on 23 June was published in *Cornhill* for October 1881.

[3] Colvin's biography in the 'English Men of Letters' series.

[4] This passage was quoted by Furnas in his biography, *Voyage to Windward*: 'As per invoice, time brought both, the evasion and Henley's blackguard supplement.' Henley made a notorious attack on Balfour's authorised life of RLS in his article in the *Pall Mall Magazine*, December 1901.

[5] The collection published in February 1882 as *Familiar Studies of Men and Books*.

[6] As planned, the Stevensons left Pitlochry on 1 August, spent the night at the Spital of Glenshee and arrived at Braemar on Tuesday 2 August.

[1] The tombstone of Miss Mary McGregor (1813–80), eldest daughter of James McGregor, tenant of Auchalater, is in the graveyard at Braemar.

A carriage and two spanking hacks draw up daily at the hour of two
before the house of, sir,   yours truly
The rain rains and the winds do beat upon the cottage of the late Miss
McGregor and of, sir,   yours affectionately
It is to be trusted that the weather may improve ere you honour the halls
of, sir,   yours emphatically
All will be glad to welcome you, not excepting, sir,
                                                 yours ever
You will now have gathered the lamentable intellectual collapse of, sir,
                                                 yours indeed
And nothing remains for me but to sign myself, sir,
                                                 yours
                                                 Robert Louis Stevenson

N.B. Each of these clauses has to be read with extreme glibness coming
down whack upon the 'sir'. This is very important. The fine stylistic
inspiration will else be lost.

I commit the man who made, the man who sold, and the woman who
supplied me with my present excruciating gilt nib to that place where the
worm never dies.[2] A friend of mind planned a sermon on (damn the pen)
that text, in these heads,

> 1st. Who is the worm?
> 2nd. Why does he do it?
> 3rd. How does he like it?

The reference to a deceased Highland lady (tending as it does to foster
unavailing sorrow) may be with advantage omitted from the address,
which would therefore run The Cottage, Castleton of Braemar.

*Postcard to Edmund Gosse

[Postmark 19 August 1881]   The Cottage, Castleton of Braemar

If you had an uncle who was a sea-captain and went to the North Pole,
you had better bring his outfit. Verbum Sapientibus. I look towards you.
                                                 R.L. Stevenson[1]

[2] Mark 9:44, 46, 48, quoting Isaiah 66:24.
[1] Gosse was at Braemar from Friday 26 August until 5 September. He gave a vivid picture of what
he called 'a most entertaining household' in the letters he wrote to his wife: 'All the persons in
it are full of character and force: they use fearful language towards one another quite promiscu-
ously and no quarrel ensues.' He found RLS (who had been spitting blood) 'sadly weak,
incapable of exertion, easily tired, excitable and feeble'. He played chess with him in his
bedroom in the mornings when he was forbidden to speak; Gosse saw no more of him until the
evenings when he came down to dinner and then read to them the early chapters of Treasure
Island. He thought Fanny 'very sweet and kind' and reported 'The arrangement is undoubtedly
a success and is accepted charmingly by the father and mother'.

To W.E. Henley

[*24 August 1881*]   [*Braemar*]

My dear Henley, Of course I am a rogue; why Lord, it's known, man: but
you should remember I have had a horrid cold and have been in a rather
blasted state sinsyne. Now, I'm better, I think; and see here – nobody not
you, nor Lang, nor the devil, will hurry me with our crawlers. They are
coming. Four of them are as good as done, and the rest will come when
ripe; but I am now on another lay for the moment, purely owing to Sam,
this one; but I believe there's more coin in it than in any amount of
crawlers: now, see here.

The Sea Cook
or Treasure Island:
A Story for Boys.[1]

If this don't fetch the kids, why, they have gone rotten since my day. Will
you be surprised to learn that it is about Buccaneers, that it begins in the
Admiral Benbow public house on [the] Devon Coast, that it's all about a
map and a treasure and a mutiny and a derelict ship and a current and a
fine old Squire Trelawney (the real Tre,[2] purged of literature and sin, to
shuit the infant mind) and a doctor and another doctor, and a Sea Cook
with one leg, and a sea song with the chorus 'Yo-ho-ho and a bottle of
Rum' (at the third Ho, you heave at the capstan bars) – which is a real
Buccaneer's song, only known to the crew of the late Captain Flint (died
of rum at Key West, much regretted, friends will please accept this
intimation) – and lastly would you be surprised to hear, in this connection,
the name of *Routledge*?[3] That's the kind of man I am, blast your eyes. Two
chapters are written and have been tried on Sam with great success; the
trouble is to work it off without oaths. Buccaneers without oaths – bricks
without straw. But youth and the fond parient have to be consulted.

[*25 August*]

And now look here – this is next day – and three chapters are written
and read: (Chapter I. The Old Sea-dog at the Admiral Benbow. Chapter
II. Black Dog Appears and Disappears. Chapter III. The Black Spot.) All
now heard by Sam, F., and my father and mother, with high approval –

---

[1] Lloyd, on holiday from school, had joined the Stevensons just before they left Pitlochry. *Treasure Island* had its origin in the map of an island which RLS drew and embellished while playing with Lloyd. RLS tells the story in 'My First Book' (1894).

[2] Edward John Trelawney (1791–1881), the swashbuckling friend of Byron and Shelley, died on 13 August.

[3] George Routledge (1812–88), London publisher; his 'Railway Library' numbered over a thousand volumes at a shilling each.

it's quite silly and horrid fun, – and what I want is the *best* book about the Buccaneers that can be had[4] – the later B.'s above all, Blackbeard[5] and sich, and get Nutt or Bain[6] to send it skimming by the fastest post. And now I know you'll write to me, for *The Sea Cook's* sake.

Your Admiral Guinea[7] is curiously near my line, but of course I'm fooling; and your Admiral sounds like a shublime gent. Stick to him like wax. He'll do. My Trelawney is, as I indicate, several thousand sea-miles off the lie of the original or your Admiral Guinea; and besides I have no more about him yet, but one mention of his name, and I think it likely, he may turn yet farther from the model in the course of handling. A chapter a day, I mean to do; they are short; and perhaps in a month *The Sea Cook* may to Routledge go, yo-ho-ho and a bottle of Rum! My Trelawney has a strong dash of Landor, as I see him from here. No women in the story: Sam's orders; and who so blythe to obey? It's awful fun boy's stories; you just indulge the pleasure of your heart, that's all. No trouble. No strain. The only stiff thing is to get it ended; that I don't see, but I look to a volcano. O sweet, O generous, O human toils. You would like my blind beggar in Chapter III, I believe. No writing, just drive along as the words come and the pen will scratch!   R.L.S.

Author of Boys' Stories

To W.E. Henley

[*September 1881*]   [*Braemar*]

My dear Henley, Thanks for your last. The £100 fell through, or dwindled at least into somewhere about £30. However that I've taken as a mouthful so you may look out for

The Sea Cook
or
Treasure Island:
A Tale of the Buccaneers.

in

Young Folks

---

[4] Henley duly sent RLS Captain Charles Johnson's *A General History of the Robberies and Murders of the most Notorious Pyrates* (1724). RLS took a number of details (including the name Israel Hands) from this work.

[5] Edward Teach or Thatch, known as Blackbeard (died 1718), English pirate.

[6] Alfred Trubner Nutt (1856–1910), head of the foreign bookselling and publishing business founded by his father David Nutt; publisher of finely produced books including the Tudor Translations series and Henley's works; folklorist and Celtic scholar. James Bain (1829–94) or his brother Thomas (1835–1921), RLS's regular booksellers at No. 1 Haymarket, London.

[7] Henley had written about his ideas for the play which he and RLS finally wrote in collaboration in 1884.

The terms are £2.10 a page of 4500 words; that's not noble, is it? But Gibbons and Manville Fenn[1] and other great writers get the same; and I have my copyright safe. Cards offer to do that page for £1.!!! I don't get illustrated: a blessing; that's the price I have to pay for my copyright.

I'll make this boy's book business pay; but I have to make a beginning. When I'm done with—*Young Folks*, I'll try Routledge or some one.

How about the *Arabian Nights* for Chatto?[2]

I feel pretty sure *The Sea Cook* will do to reprint, and bring something decent at that.

Japp is quite a good soul.[3] The poet[4] was very gay and pleasant. He told me much; Matthews[5] was right: simply the most active young man in England, and one of the most intelligent forby. He shall o'er Europe, shall o'er earth extend.[6] He is now extending over adjacent parts of Scotland.

I propose to follow up *The Sea Cook* at proper intervals by

Jerry Abershaw:[7] *A Tale of Putney Heath* (which or its site I must visit).
The Leading Light: A Tale of the Coast.
The Squaw Men; or the Wild West.[8]

and other instructive and entertaining works. *Jerry Abershaw* should be good, eh? good, sir, by G—.

---

[1] Possibly Charles Gibbon (1843–90), author of some thirty popular novels. George Manville Fenn (1831–1909), prolific writer of boys' stories; editor of *Cassell's Magazine*, 1870–74.

[2] Andrew Chatto (1840–1913), who had been with the publisher John Camden Hotten since the age of fifteen, bought the business from Hotten's widow in 1873 and turned it into a highly successful and respected firm. Much of the success was due to Chatto's own good personal relations with his authors. His partner William Edward Windus (1838–1910), author of two books of verse, did not take a very active part in the firm's affairs.

[3] Alexander Hay Japp (1837–1905), Scottish author, journalist and publisher; literary adviser to Isbister & Co.; assisted in editing *Good Words*; editor and biographer of De Quincey. Under the pseudonym H.A. Page he published *Thoreau, His Life and Aims* (1877). He and RLS became acquainted because Japp criticised some of RLS's comments in his essay on Thoreau. Japp visited RLS at Braemar and acted as intermediary in securing the serialisation of *Treasure Island* in *Young Folks* (see p. 196, n. 1).

[4] Gosse.

[5] James Brander Matthews (1852–1929); American man of letters who was Professor of Literature and then of Dramatic Literature at Columbia University 1892–1924. He lived in England for some time, was friendly with Gosse and Lang, contributed to the *Saturday Review* and became a member of the Savile Club.

[6] 'They shall o'er Europe, shall o'er Earth extend.' From a cancelled passage in Landor's *Gebir*, quoted in Colvin's *Landor*.

[7] Louis Jeremiah Abershaw (1773?–95) was a notorious highwayman on the roads between London, Kingston and Wimbledon, who was hanged for murdering a constable. He became the subject of an unfinished story *The Adventures of John Delafield*; this in its turn was incorporated into the unfinished *The Shovels of Newton French* (1891).

[8] The six-page MS of ch. 1 and part of ch. 2 of *The Squaw Man* has survived. It appears to have been begun for Lloyd's amusement at Davos. No more is heard of the other story.

Gosse's papa seems to be a fine old Plymouth brothering pyrate.[9]

I love writing boy's books. This first is only an experiment: wait till you see what I can make 'em with my hand in.

I'll

be

the

Harrison

Ainsworth[10]

of

the

Future.

and a chalk better by St Christopher, or at least as good. You'll see that even by *The Sea Cook*. D—d sight gayer than Mudie-ing, you bet.[11]

Jerry Abershaw – O what a title! O bless you, it was you and Theo. Watts[12] that brought it to my mind. Jerry Abershaw: d—n it, sir, it's a poem. The two most lovely words in English: and what a sentiment. Hark you, how the hoofs ring! Is this a blacksmith's. No, it's a wayside inn. Jerry Abershaw.

'It was a clear, frosty evening, not 100 miles from Putney etc.' Jerry Abershaw.

J.W.F. knew my address; but did not choose to write to me.

Jerry Abershaw. Jerry Abershaw. Jerry Abershaw. *The Sea Cook* is now in its XVIth chapter, and bids for well up in the thirties. Each three chaps is worth £2.10. So we've £12.10 already.

Don't read 'noble old Fred's *Pirate* anyhow;[13] it is written in sand with a salt spoon: arid, feeble, vain, tottering production. But then we're not always all there. *He* was *all* somewhere else that trip. It's *damnable*, Henley. I don't go much on *The Sea-Cook*; but Lord its a little fruitier than the *Pirate* by Cap'n Mary-at.

Since this was written *The Cook* is in his XIXth chapter. Yo-heave ho!

---

[9] Philip Henry Gosse (1810–88), zoologist. Gosse described his father's rigid religious beliefs in *Father and Son* (1907). Gosse, who had morning walks with TS, described him as 'something like father' and a 'singularly charming and strange old man'.

[10] William Harrison Ainsworth (1805–82) who had been immensely successful in his heyday in the 1840s as an historical novelist was by now virtually destitute.

[11] Writing novels suitable for respectable middle-class subscribers to Mudie's Circulating Library, founded in 1842.

[12] Walter Theodore Watts (1834–1914), critic, novelist and poet who wrote regularly for the *Athenaeum*. He controlled Swinburne's life from 1879 and lived with him at Putney. He changed his name to Watts-Dunton in 1897.

[13] Frederick Marryat's *The Pirate and the Three Cutters* (1836).

To W.E. Henley

[c. *19 September 1881*][1]   [*Braemar*]

Dear Henley, with a pig's snout on
I am starting for Londòn,
Where I likely shall arrive,
On Saturday, if still alive:
Perhaps your pirate doctor[2] might
See me on Sunday? If all's right,
I should then lunch with you and with she
Who's dearer to you than you are to me.

I shall remain but little time
In London, as a wretched clime
But not so wretched (for none are)
As that of bloody old Braemar.
My doctor sends me skipping. I
Have many facts to meet your eye.
My pig's snout's now upon my face;
And I inhale with fishy grace,
My gills out-flapping right and left,
Ol. pin. sylvest. I am bereft
Of a great deal of charm by this –
Not quite the bull's eye for a kiss –
But like a gnome of olden time
Or boguey in a pantomime.
For ladies' love I once was fit;[3]
But now am rather out of it.
Where'er I go, revolted curs
Snap round my military spurs;
The children all retire in fits
And scream their bellowses to bits.
Little I care: the worst's been done:
Now let the cold impoverished sun
Drop frozen from his orbit; let
Fury and fire, cold, wind and wet,

---

[1] Dr George Balfour arrived at Braemar on 13 September and telegraphed for the respirator immediately. MIS records that on Monday 19 September he 'ordered Lou away from Braemar'.
[2] Dr Zebulon Mennell, M.R.C.S., L.S.A. (1851–1911), Henley's regular doctor who lived in Shepherd's Bush Road. RLS sometimes called him 'the Pirate'.
[3] Cf. Horace, *Odes*, III.xxvi.1–2 – '*Vixi Puellis nuper idoneus*'.

> And cataclysmal mad reverses
> Rage through the federate universes;
> Let Lawson triumph,[4] cakes and ale,
> Whisky and hock, and claret, fail; –
> Tobacco, love and letters perish,
> With all that any man could cherish:
> You it may touch, not me. I dwell
> Too deep already – deep in hell;
> And nothing can befall, O damn!
> To make me uglier than I am.　　　　　　　　　R.L.S.

This yer refers to an ori-nasal respirator for the inhalation of pine wood oil. *Oleum pini sylvestris.*

> I shall be, I forgot to say
> At Chelsea on the appointed day
> St Leonard's terrace six and ten,
> Where lives or lived the prince of men,
> Bobus, to wit: than whom, I swear
> No man than-whom-er breathes the air.

To James Henderson[1]

Saturday 24 September 1881　　　　　　　　*17 Heriot Row, Edinburgh*

James Henderson Esq.

Dear Sir, I agree that you shall publish my story *Treasure Island* in your paper *Young Folks*, I retaining the copyright, and you paying me at the rate of twelve shillings and sixpence per column. Yours truly

Robert Louis Stevenson[2]

---

[4] Sir Wilfrid Lawson (1829–1906), Liberal M.P. for Carlisle; well-known temperance advocate and President of the United Kingdom (Temperance) Alliance. On 14 June 1881 his Resolution for 'local option' on licensing of public houses was carried in the House of Commons.

[1] James Henderson, Scottish-born newspaper proprietor; founder of the *South London Press* 1856 and of the *Weekly Budget* 1861. In 1871 he founded *Our Young Folks' Weekly Budget* which continued under various titles until 1897: from 1879–84 it was called *Young Folks. Treasure Island or The Mutiny of the Hispaniola* by Captain George North was serialised in the issues dated 1 October 1881 to 28 January 1882. *Young Folks* was on sale a week before the issue date. In view of RLS's stated intention to be in London by Saturday, it is possible that this letter was written there and the Edinburgh address added as his permanent address.

[2] In London RLS, Fanny and Lloyd stayed with 'Aunt Alan' (Bob's 'mother') at 16 St Leonard's Terrace, Chelsea. RLS (as he records in 'My First Book') spent some time alone at the 'Hand and Spear', Weybridge, correcting the proofs of *Treasure Island* in *Young Folks* and walking on the heath 'on the dewy autumn mornings'. By the second week in October they had left for Paris *en route* for Davos.

For this second winter the Stevensons occupied a small chalet called 'Villa am Stein' owned by, and on the hillside just above, the Hôtel Buol.

To Edmund Gosse

[*Postmark 9 November 1881*][1]

Davos

PRINTING OFFICE.

Managed by

SAMUEL LLOYD OSBOURNE & Co.

The Chalet.

Dear Weg, If you are taking *Young Folks*, for God's Sake Twig the *editorial style*: it is incredible; we are all left PANTING IN THE REAR. Twig, O twig it. His name is Clinton; I should say the most melodious prose writer now alive; it's like buttermilk and blacking; it sings and hums away in that last sheet, like a great old kettle full of bilge water. You know: none of us could do it, boy. See No. 571, last page; an article, called *Sir Claude the Conqueror*, and read it *aloud* in your best rhythmic tones; *mon cher, c'est épatant.*[2]

The story in question, by the by, was a last chance given to its drunken author; not Villiers, – that was a *nom de plume* – but Viles, brother to my old boyhood's guide, philosopher and friend, Edward Viles, author of *Black Bess* and *Blueskin: a Romance*. There is a byway of literary history for you; and in its poor way, a tragedy also.[3]

Observe in the same number, how Will. J. Sharman girds at your poor friend; and how the rhythmic Clinton (he wears blue spectacles, and is Pale) steps chivalrously forth in his defence.[4] The fate of Viles looms near

---

[1] The crude address printed by Lloyd is on much of the writing paper used at this period. Lloyd had begun operations on his printing press during the first winter at Davos, but the activities of the Davos Press became more ambitious during the second winter. An early production was RLS's *Not I, and Other Poems* (cf. p. 166).

[2] RLS is discussing the issue of *Young Folks* dated 12 November which appeared a week earlier than the published date. The Editor's note on *Sir Claude the Conqueror* begins: 'It is with sincere regret that we have to inform our readers that the publication of this story is discontinued from this date. It is never an agreeable duty to withhold a promised pleasure, but our readers will readily believe that we should not have broken off the story thus suddenly if we had not been forced to do so by circumstances which we need not describe in detail.'

[3] The stated author of *Sir Claude the Conqueror* was Walter Villiers. *Black Bess; or the Knight of the Road* by Edward Viles appeared in 254 penny numbers 1863–8. RLS writes in 'Popular Authors' of his delighted discovery of it when a boy at Peebles in the summer of 1864.

[4] In 'Our Letter Box', the editor commented: 'We cannot at all agree with the opinion you express on one of our stories. That which you condemn is really the best story now appearing in our paper, and the impress of an able writer is stamped on every paragraph of *The Treasure Island*. You will probably share this opinion when you have read a little more of it.'

and nearer. First the Rev. Purcell;[5] then Will J. Sharman: thick fall the barbèd arrows.

I wish I could play a game of chess with you.

If I survive, I shall have Clinton to dinner: It is plain I must make hay while the sun shines; I shall not long keep a footing in the world of penny writers, or call them obolists.[6] It is a world full of surprises, a romantic world. Weg, I was known there; even I. The obolists, then, sometimes peruse our works. It is only fair; since I so much batten upon theirs. Talking of which, in Heaven's name, get *The Bondage of Brandon* (3 vols) by Bracebridge Hemming.[7] It's the devil and all for drollery. There is a Superior (*sic*) of the Jesuits, straight out of Skelt. Bracebridge has never been in a real house with servants – no, Weg, not even of an errand. This is clearly proved in his work.

And now look here, I had three points: Clinton – disposed of – (Second) Benjamin Franklin – do you want him?[8] (Third) A radiant notion begot this morning over an atlas: why not, you who know the lingo, give us a good legendary and historical book on Iceland? It would, or should, be as romantic as a novel of Scott's; as strange and stirring as a dream. Think on't. My wife screamed with joy at the idea; and the little Sam clapped his hands; so I offer you three readers on the spot.

Fanny and I have both been in bed, tended by the hired sick nurse; Sam has a broken finger (so he did not clap his hands literally); Wog has had an abscess in his ear; our servant is a devil; I am, Yours ever, with both of our best regards to Mrs Gosse   Robert Louis Stevenson
The Rejected Obolist.

Do you wish to meet the rhythmic Clinton? I don't promise. Go and see Harrison Ainsworth, and if you do, give him my homage: say I dote on his works; name your maker, like a man, and swear that I'm his fond adorer.

---

[5] The Revd Edward Purcell (1847–1927). After taking his degree he became a curate at Oxford 1871–3 but never proceeded to priest's orders; Lecturer at Queen's College 1880–81 and public examiner 1885–6. In an unfavourable review of *Virginibus Puerisque* in the *Academy* for 9 July 1881, he complained of the 'barrenness of matter' in spite of the 'clever conceits and ingenious sallies'. His essential criticism was the lack of any 'well-rounded philosophy' or 'solid opinion': 'Some of this is merely superior fustian, much of it has been read before, none of it would one desire to read again . . . Death is a fashionable subject, but, if one must write for the mere sake of writing, it were more seemly to write of Tar-water.' Purcell's later views were more favourable (see p. 308).

[6] Obol or obolus, a small coin of ancient Greece.

[7] Bracebridge Hemyng (1841–1901), prolific writer of boys' stories including the very popular series about Jack Harkaway which began in *The Boys of England* (1871). RLS refers disparagingly to *The Bondage of Brandon* in 'Popular Authors'. Hemyng's social background was, in fact, impeccable: he was educated at Eton and qualified as a barrister.

[8] The *Century Magazine* (Gosse was their English representative) rejected the idea of an article on Benjamin Franklin.

To James Payn

[*9 December 1881*]   [*Davos*]

Hip, hip, hurrah for Charles Edward![1] – One cheer more, and believe me,
my dear James Payn,

> Your sincere admirer
> Robert Louis Stevenson
> Given under my fist this 9th day of December
> in the year of Grace one thousand eight hundred
> and eighty one, at my castle in Davos.

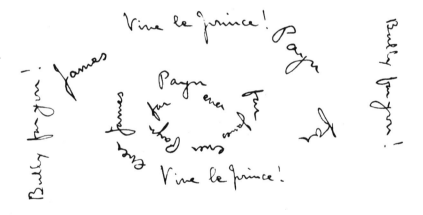

Do not let my childishness blind you to the serious nature of my admiration; Charles Edward is a really fine thing: the devil a man alive that could
have looked near it!

---

[1] Mr Charles Edward of Barton Castle, the eccentric recluse in Payn's *A Grape from a Thorn*
(1881), who considered himself the legitimate great-grandson of the Young Pretender and thus
heir to the English throne.

To Charles Baxter

15 December 1881   *Davos*

My dear Charles, That cheque to Ruedi has been lost; for God's sake stop
it and supply another. I lost it. I ought to have written about this before;
but we have been in miserable case here; my wife worse and worse; and
now sent away, with Sam for sick nurse, I not being allowed to go down.[1]
I do not know what is to become of us; and you may imagine how rotten
I have been feeling, and feel now, alone with my weasel-dog and my
German maid, on the top of a hill here, heavy mist and thin snow all
about me; and the devil to pay in general. I don't care so much for
solitude as I used to; results I suppose of marriage.

Pray write to me something cheery. A little Edinburgh gossip, in
heaven's name. Ah! what would I not give to steal this evening with you
through the big, echoing, college archway, and away south under the
street lamps, and to dear Brash's, now defunct![2] But the old time is dead
also; never, never, to revive. It was a sad time too, but so gay and so
hopeful, and we had such sport with all our low spirits, and all our
distresses, that it looks like a lamplit, vicious fairy land behind me. O for
ten Edinburgh minutes – sixpence between us, and the ever glorious
Lothian Road, or dear mysterious Leith Walk! But here, a sheer hulk, lies
poor Tom Bowling;[3] – here in this strange place, whose very strangeness
would have been heaven to him then; – and aspires – yes, C.B. with tears
– after the past.

See what comes of being left alone. Do you remember Brash? the
L.J.R.? the sheet of glass that we followed along George Street?[4] Granton?[5]
the night at Boroughmuirhead? the compass near the sign of the Twinkling Eye? the night I lay on the pavement in misery?

---

[1] Fanny, whose ill-health baffled the doctors, had been sent to Berne. RLS – who feared she had
cancer – brought her home on Christmas Day, after a difficult journey in the intense cold.

[2] Thomas Brash & Son, wine and spirit merchants of 44 Clerk Street, Edinburgh. Thomas Brash
died in 1873. His son (Thomas Brash Jr) carried on the business but the firm disappears from the
Edinburgh directories after 1878/9.

[3] The opening words of the song by Charles Dibdin (1745–1814), that RLS never tired of
quoting.

[4] J.D. of Colinton recorded the following anecdote (evidently told him by Baxter) in
'Stevensoniana', *T.P.'s Weekly*, 20 December 1907:

> One day the two friends were proceeding along George Street on their way to college when
> they met a party of six men carrying on their shoulders a large sheet of glass, rolled in a dark
> cloth or blanket. The men were moving with great care and gravity, and the effect of the
> whole was extremely like that of a funeral procession with pall, &c. This struck R.L.S. as
> irresistibly comic, so as soon as he and his friend had passed the group he wheeled his friend
> round, and the pair, lifting off their hats, and with downcast visage, fell into line as chief
> mourners.

[5] The missionaries from Aberdeen. See p. 127, n. 2.

> I swear it by the eternal sky
> Johnson – nor Thomson – ne'er shall die![6]
> Yet I fancy they are dead too; dead like Brash.   R.L.S.

To Charles Baxter

[*March 1882*]   *Hôtel & Pension Buol*

My dear Charles, This is intolerable, but we have been very unhappy, dog ill, wife ill and the rest; and you must try to excuse me. Anyway here is the receipt at last with best thanks. Fanny is I think going to be able to hold out here yet awhile, so the money was not as necessary as I feared it would be; but I'll keep it, for God knows it will be wanted ere we leave.

I am getting a steady, slow, sluggish stream of ink over paper, and shall do better this year than last.

Your remarks about your business forcibly recalled the early days of your connection, and the twopence that we once mustered between us in the ever radiant Lothian Road.

> O sweet Lothian Road ———
> O dear Lothian Road ———
>   Ever yours   R.L.S.

Ode by Ben Jonson, Edgar Allan Poe, and a bungler

> Long, long ago,
>   (It was in the Lothian Road)
> I saw two fellows wander long ago.
>   So merrily they strode
>   So high their spirits glowed,
> With twopence in their pockets long ago.
>
> Brash, Brash is dead,
>   That immortal Brash is gone
>   And the crowds go streaming on,
>   They go streaming, streaming forward, seeking Brash!
>   But he
>   I can see,
> On the great Olympus dwells, dispensing trash.
>   Gin, gin he sells,
>   Then as now;
> And with infuriate brow

---

[6] The names of the comic characters invented for themselves by RLS and Baxter.

Light-minded drinkers forth he drives, who bow
Not duly unto Brash.

Brash, Brash, Brash,
   How musical they clash
Words of pleasant savour, words endeared of yore!
   But Brash has gone before,
   Godlike Brash is gone.
   From earth's phantasmal shore
     In a flash
     Immortal Brash
   Burst, like Elijah, upward and was gone!

Yet fear not – we shall follow; for wherever
   Great Brash his way made plain, the common herd
   May follow that extraordinary turd
And with no unusual endeavour:
Brash was not wise, nor amiable nor clever;
   Brash was a beast as I have always heard;
   Fate could not act more palpably absurd
Than the dead Brash from other fools to sever.

Let us be fools, my friend, let us be drunken,
   Let us be angry and extremely silly;
     Then though divines and commentators clash,
We, when once dead and dry, dusty and shrunken,
   Buried and bundled hence, shall willy-nilly,
   Share the eternal destiny of Brash.[1]

To George Saintsbury[1]

[c. 20] March 1882   Chalet Buol, Davos

My dear Saintsbury, My father knew an old lady – excuse these old
personalities – who finding her stock of napery daily diminish, and having
no suspicion of the real culprit, adopted the following bold stratagem. She

---

[1] RLS went on to write a series of Brasheanna (or Brasheana) Sonnets (eleven in all) dedicated to
Baxter and a number of comic drawings about their 'hero'. They are all reproduced in the full
edition.

[1] George Edward Bateman Saintsbury (1845–1933), literary critic and historian with an encyclo-
paedic knowledge of English and French literature; Professor of Rhetoric and English Literature,
Edinburgh 1895–1915. He was a prolific journalist and reviewer on many journals at this period
including *Fortnightly Review, London*, the *Academy* and the *Saturday Review*, of which he was
assistant editor 1883–94.

placed in her napery closet, a large paper staringly written with these words:

'Thief, Thief, you are detected, and if you do not immediately replace the stolen articles you will certainly be comprehended.'

This merely to introduce this parody:

'George, George, you are detected, and if you do not immediately drink a bottle of Burgundy (to my health and Pepys's) you will certainly be damned.'[2]

I wish I could share it with you but I shall drink yours tonight at dinner in an extra *coup* of my draught Veltliner.[3] And I wish, I wish, I could introduce you to one old, dear, deceased vintage – a Sforzato, strong as port, elegant as chablis – that once illustrated this Alpine valley.

At least, and quite seriously, I thank you for your friendly silence in the past, and now for your friendly speech. Yours

An Author Definitely Young.[4]
Robert Louis Stevenson

To W.E. Henley

[*31 March 1882*]   [*Davos*]

My dear Henley,

Business

Herewith I will send all of *Silverado*, except four or five pages of introduction, which I reserve to alter, and they may take a day or so. If he thinks it will be too small, I send a plan of alternative combination book. It is this last that I propose to offer to the American Roberts Bros,[1] as soon as I get sheets of *Silverado*; so much I say frankly; but if Shatter your Windows do not dislike a very small book, I believe *Silverado* would

---

[2] Saintsbury had contributed an unsigned review of *Familiar Studies* to the *Pall Mall Gazette* of 18 March 1882. He found the essays very unequal in quality and reserved his praise for those on Thoreau, Burns and Pepys, especially the Pepys. He described it as 'almost perfect' and said that 'nothing much better has been published for years'.

[3] The German name for the wines produced in the valley of Valtellina in Lombardy. The valley was in Swiss possession for 300 years, until Napoleonic times, and the Swiss maintained the custom of importing these favourite wines. In *The Silverado Squatters* RLS writes of 'those notable Valtellines' and J.A. Symonds, who celebrates them in his essay 'Bacchus in Graubünden', describes Forzato or Sforzato as one of the strongest wines requiring several years to mature. The drinking of Valtelline wine was part of the recommended treatment for invalids at Davos.

[4] Saintsbury began his review, 'There is probably no author of the present day who may be definitely called young in regard to whom opinions are so much divided as is the case with regard to Mr Louis Stevenson.'

[1] Roberts Brothers, Boston, were RLS's first American publishers. They published *Travels with a Donkey, An Inland Voyage, Treasure Island, The Silverado Squatters* and *Prince Otto*.

look best alone. 'Tis, either way, the most transitional book. I never knew such a transitional book, I think. But all's one; there is some pretty stuff in it. Colvin, you know, *opt. max.*, passed the 'Emigrant Train';[2] so, if it is decided to have a bigger volume, there will be nothing absolutely disgraceful.

Pleasure

To you, death to me. Last night, we had a dinner party, consisting of the John Addington, curry, onions (lovely onions), and beefsteak. So unusual is any excitement, that F. and I feel this morning as if we had been to a coronation. However I must, I suppose, write.

I was sorry about your female contributor squabble.[3] 'Tis very comic, but really unpleasant; the Lindsays are leading people in the picture book business too. But what care I? Now that I illustrate my own books, I can always offer you a situation in our house – S.L. Osbourne & Co.; as an author gets a halfpenny a copy of verses and an artist a penny a cut, perhaps a proof reader might get several pounds a year.[4]

O that Coronation! What a shouting crowd there was! I obviously got a firework in each eye. The king looked very magnificent to be sure; and that great hall where we feasted on seven hundred delicate foods, and drank fifty royal wines – *quel coup d'oeil*! but was it not overdone, even for a coronation – almost a vulgar luxury? And eleven is certainly too late to begin dinner. (It was really 6.30 instead of 5.30.)

Your list of the books that Cassells have refused in these weeks is not quite complete; they also refused –

(1) Six undiscovered tragedies, one romantic comedy, a fragment of journal extending over six years, and an unfinished autobiography reaching up to the first performance of *King John*.

by William W. Shakespeare.

(2) The Holy Bible: a new edition, thoroughly revised and much extended

by the Holy Ghost.

(3) The Journals and Private Correspondence of David, King of Israel.

(4) Poetical Works of Arthur, Iron Dook of Wellington, including a Monody on Napoleon.

(5) VIII Books of an unfinished novel *Solomon Crabb*

by Henry H. Fielding.

(6) Stevenson's *Moral Emblems*.

---

[2] The second part of *The Amateur Emigrant*.

[3] In October 1881 Henley had been appointed editor of the monthly *Magazine of Art* (published by Cassell's); Colvin seems to have secured the appointment for him.

[4] RLS produced five woodcuts and accompanying verses which were printed by Lloyd in a little booklet called *Moral Emblems*. A second series, with five more woodcuts and verses followed.

You also neglected to mention, as *per contra*, that they had during the same time accepted and triumphantly published Brown's *Handbook to Cricket*, Jones's *First French Reader*, and Robinson's *Picturesque Cheshire*, uniform with the same author's *Stately Homes of Salop*.

O if that list could come true! How we would tear at *Solomon Crabb*! O what a bully, bully, bully business. Which would you read first – Shakespeare's autobiography, or his journals? What sport the monody on Napoleon would be – what wooden verse, what stucco ornament! That new Bible, too, would be very useful these days. I should read both the autobiography and the journals before I looked at one of the plays, beyond the names of them; which shows that Saintsbury was right, and I do care more for life than for poetry.[5] No – I take it back. Do you know one of the tragedies – a Bible tragedy too – *David* – was written in his third period – much about the same time as *Lear*? The comedy, *April Rain*, is also a late work. *Becket* is a fine ranting piece, like *Richard II*, but very fine for the stage. Irving is to play it this autumn when I'm in town; the part rather suits him – but who is to play Henry – a tremendous creation, sir. Betterton, in his private journal seems to have seen this piece: and he says distinctly that Henry is the best part in any play 'though,' he adds, 'how it be with the ancient plays I know not. But in this, I have ever feared to do ill, and indeed will not be persuaded to that undertaking.' So says Betterton. *Rufus* is not so good; I am not pleased with *Rufus*; plainly a *rifacimento* of some inferior work; but there are some damned fine lines. As for the purely satiric ill-minded *Abelard and Heloise*, another *Troilus*, – quoi! it is not pleasant, truly, but what strength, what verve, what knowledge of life, and the Canon! What a finished, humorous, rich picture is the Canon! Ah, there was nobody like William. But what I like is the David and Absalom business: Absalom is so well felt – you love him as David did; David's speech is one roll of royal music from the first act to the fifth.

I am enjoying *Solomon Crabb* extremely; Solomon's capital adventure with the two highwaymen and Squire Trecothick and Parson Vance; it is as good I think as anything in *Joseph Andrews*. I have just come to the part where the highwayman with the black patch over his eye has tricked poor Solomon into his place, and the Squire and the parson are hearing the evidence. Parson Vance is splendid. How good, too, is old Mrs Crabb and the coastguardsman in the third chapter, or her delightful quarrel with the sexton of Seaham; Lord Conybeare is surely a little overdone; but I don't know either; he's such damned fine sport. Do you like Sally Barnes? I'm in love with her. Constable Muddon is as good as Dogberry and Verges

---

[5] In his review of *Familiar Studies*, Saintsbury wrote: 'As a mere literary critic Mr Stevenson does not take a very high place. . . . It is, in fact, in the criticism of life, not of books, that Mr Stevenson is strong.'

put together; when he takes Solomon to the cage, and the highwayman gives him Solomon's own guinea for his pains, and kisses Mrs Muddon, and just then up drives Lord Conybeare, and instead of helping Solomon, calls him all the rascals in Christendom – O Henry Fielding, Henry Fielding! Yet perhaps the scenes at Seaham are the best. But I'm bewildered among all these excellences.

Stay, cried a voice that made the welkin crack –
This here's a dream, return and study BLACK![6] – Ever yours

R.L.S.

To Bob Stevenson

[16 April 1882]   [Davos]

My dear Bob, Yours received. I have received a communication by same mail from my mother, clamouring for news, which I must answer as soon as I've done this. Of course, I shall paint your game in lively colours.[1]

I hope to get away from here – let me not speak of it ungratefully – from here – by Thursday at latest. I am indeed much better; but a slip of the foot may still cast me back. I must walk circumspectly yet a while. But O to be able to go out and get wet, and not spit blood next day!

Yes, I remember the *enfantement* of the Arabian Nights: the first idea of all was the handsome cabs, which I communicated to you in St Leonard's Terrace drawing room. That same afternoon, the Prince de Galles and the Suicide Club were invented; and several more now forgotten. I must try to start 'em again.

Sam I believe is to be a printer – in the meantime he confines himself to being an expense. He is a first rate lad, for all that, one of the best boys I ever heard of; quite the man of the world, though oddly clerical. What he'll be, when he comes to the equinox, of course, God knows. He is now interrupting me about twice to the line, which does not condooce to clarity, I'm afraid.

Fanny is still far from well, quite far from well. My faith is in the Pirate.[2]

I inclose all my artistic works; they are wood cuts – I cut them with a knife out of blocks of wood; I am a wood-engraver; I aaaam a wooooood engraaaaver. Sam then prints 'em: are they not fun? I doat on them; in my

[6] William Black (1841–98), Scottish novelist who scored an early success with *A Daughter of Heth* (1871) and *The Strange Adventures of a Phaeton* (1872) and went on to write a great many popular sentimental novels.

[1] Bob married Harriet Louisa Purland (1856–1909) at the Marylebone Register Office on 27 August 1881, with Henley and Mary Ellen Purland as witnesses. She is described as the daughter of Theodosius Purland, Surgeon Dentist.

[2] Dr Zebulon Mennell.

next venture, I am going to have colour printing; it will be very laborious six blocks to cut for each picter, but the result should be pyramidal.

If I get through the summer, I settle in autumn in le pays de France; I believe in the Brittany and become a *SNOOZER*.[3] You will come and snooze awhile won't you; and try and get Louisa to jine?

Pepys was a decent fellow; singularly like Charles Baxter, by the way, in every character of mind and taste, and not unlike him in face. I did not mean I had been too just to him but not just enough to bigger swells. I would rather have *known* Pepys than the whole jing-bang; I doat on him as a card to know.

We shall be pretty poor at the start, of course, but I guess we can haul through. Only intending visitors to the Britannic Castle must not look for nightingale's tongues. When next you see the form of the *jeune et beau*,[4] pray give him my love. When I come to Weybridge, I'll hope to see him.

Ever yours affectionately   R.L. Stevenson *le roi de Béotie*

                                             R.L. Stevenson *1er Roi de Béotie*

                                             R.L. Stevenson *1er Roi de Béotie*

Pour copie conforme
Le Sécretaire Royale W.P. Bannatyne[5]

To W.E. Henley[1]

[*July 1882*]   *Hotel, Kingussie*

My dear Henley, The Garden Angel[2] refusing with many foul oaths to answer your letter, I am obliged to do so. The Garden (alias, the Affable

---

[3] RLS explains in his essay 'Fontainebleau' that 'Snoozers' was the slang term in the English colony at Barbizon for those resident painters who happily spent their time as students and apprentices but never progressed to become serious artists.

[4] Ferrier. '*Le jeune et beau Dunois*' is the hero of the famous French song, '*Partant pour la Syrie*' (1809).

[5] A recollection of the 'State Papers' for the rival Kingdoms of Nosingtonia and Encyclopaedia which RLS and Bob liked to concoct when they were children. Boetia was proverbial for the dullness and stupidity of its inhabitants. The signature 'W.P. Bannatyne' is in a very shaky hand. RLS credited one of the verses in *Travels with a Donkey* to him.

[1] RLS reached London at the end of April. His parents joined him and they all went to the Burford Bridge Hotel, Box Hill and RLS was able to renew his friendship with Meredith. In June he went with TS – on the last of his many journeys with him – to Lochearnhead, Ballachulish and Oban in search of local colour for his proposed article on the Appin Murder. At the end of the month RLS, Fanny and MIS went to Stobo Manse, near Peebles. The place did not suit them and they decided to move. RLS went to London to consult Dr Andrew Clark. On his recommendation RLS went to Kingussie on 22 July. In *Memories and Notes* Colvin records: 'While his wife remained with his parents in Edinburgh, I spent two or three weeks of radiant weather alone with him in the old hotel at Kingussie in Inverness-shire. He had little strength either for work or exercise but managed to draft the tale "The Treasure of Franchard", and rejoiced in lying out for hours at a time half-stripped in the sun.'

[2] The Guardian Angel, Fanny's name for Colvin 'The affable Archangel' is from *Paradise Lost*, VII.41.

Archangel) has quite surprised me by his rowdy conduct. He insists on raking out at night with a big stick and a white greatcoat, tally-ho-ing down the street of this long village and rattling with his cudgel on the doors. He is the Hero of the bar parlour; the young men and maidens follow him like a pipe. I sit in a rose garden in a bath chair, now making a little watercolour sketch, and from time to time laying my paints aside and waking the echoes of the mountains with my silvery flute. 'There's a Bow-er of Ros-es',[3] sings the slight reed, and all the happy valleys croon the air. Meanwhile up comes the uproarious Archangel, swinging his sprig of oak, and 'D—n you,' says he, 'what the d—l do you sit puking at there? Here's a set of jolly boys come in for a drink with us, by G–d; and d—mme, if you shall skulk – d—mme, if you shall!'

In consequence of this opposition of tastes, we see little of each other. I question if these excesses can ultimately benefit his health; but he seems decided on urging on his Wild Career. Yours ever   Henry Bishop

To his Wife

[?3 August 1882]   [Kingussie]

My dear Fanny, Good evening to your honour, likewise to the Sam, who is now I hope (I mean now, when you receive this) eating his dinner with a great appetite in Heriot Row, a far traveller, new alighted.[1]

If you are *at all* tired you must not come on Saturday or I shall be angry with you. But if you do come, tell my mother to send *some* Burgundy with you – any – as Colvin's stock, on which I have been living, runs low.

It will always cost more to get whisky from an hotel, will it not? But tell her anyway that the whisky here is good, but I think a trifle watered – O not much – O call it mild not watered!

I hate to think how I've spoiled you with all these letters, you'll be the death of me when next I go away; but I could not help it.

> With thoughts reverential and stilly
> This long correspondence I close;
> The union of you and your Billy
> Now pledges my pen to repose.
>
> On paper as white as a lily,
> In writing as sable as crows,

---

[3] Thomas Moore's popular song from *Lalla Rookh*, 'The Veiled Prophet of Khorassan', 2:247.
[1] MIS records that Lloyd arrived from school on Friday 4 August. The next day he and Fanny joined RLS at Kingussie in the house he had taken. MIS and the family servants followed on the 7th. They stayed at Kingussie until the beginning of September.

The thoughts of Uxorious Billy
Were daily sent forward in prose.

The postman, industrious gillie,
Has laboured, but now may repose;
For you and Uxorious Billy
On Saturday part from their woes.

But don't come if tired, dear. Your loving husband   Louis

DER MEETING
The fat and lean
Shall then convene.

I have no more to say. Madam, I have the honour to subscribe myself,
Your devoted Lord and Master   Robert Louis Stevenson
                                                      General Commanding
G. Angel
   Adjutant.

Where is my wife? where is my Wogg?
I am alone and life's a bog.
When my wife is far from me
The Undersined feels all at sea
                    R.L.S.

In this emblem, please to view
Uxorious Billy far from you.

I am as good as deaf
When separate from F.

I am far from gay
When separate from A.

I loath the ways of men
When separate from N.

Life is a murky den
When separate from N.

My sorrow rages high
When separate from Y.

And all seems uncanny
When separate from Fanny.

Though I should rise at morning
  And go to bed at night,
My person first adorning
  And then despoiling quite;
Though I should eat my dinner
  And then digest the same
Or drink, an arid sinner,
  Whatever vintage came —

post time

VIII. ORDERED SOUTH AGAIN: MARSEILLES AND HYÈRES
October 1882–June 1884

Stevenson left Edinburgh for London on 8 September 1882 and after consulting Dr Andrew Clark decided to set out for the South of France in search of a suitable place to stay for the winter. Fanny (still in Edinburgh) was too ill to accompany him so Bob went with him as far as Montpellier; then had to return to England because his wife was ill. RLS decided against Montpellier but moved on to Marseilles where Fanny joined him in mid-October. Here they found the Campagne Defli at St Marcel; RLS loved the house and garden but it was (in his words) 'as damp as a sponge, and poisonous with marshes'. After a short stay in Nice and various misadventures they at last discovered the Chalet La Solitude at the winter health resort of Hyères, eleven miles east of Toulon and three miles inland from the Mediterranean, and moved there in March 1883. Fanny described it twenty years later:

> A chalet was an incongruous object in Hyères, and it was made more conspicuous by its position, clinging to a low cliff almost at the entrance of the old town. From this cliff the ground rose with a gentle gradient and just outside our garden gate, where it became more rugged and steep, breaking out near the summit into rocky crags that were crowned with the ruins of an ancient Saracen castle. Our tiny chalet was the result of a visit of the owner to the Paris Exposition of 1878. There, amidst Chinese pagodas, Turkish mosques, and the like in miniature, stood a model Swiss chalet that so fascinated our landlord that he bought it outright and had it removed to be again erected on his property in Hyères. It was like a doll's house, with rooms so small that we could hardly turn round in them; but the view from the verandas was extensive, the garden was large and wild, with winding paths and old grey olive trees where nightingales nested and sang. Looking in one direction we could see the Îles d'Or, and in another, the hills beyond Toulon.[1]

As the letters show, RLS delighted in these surroundings and thoroughly enjoyed the pleasure of having a home of his own. It was a prolific time

---

[1] The house, much changed and modernised, is still there. Nicholas Rankin describes it in his *Dead Man's Chest* (1987). It bears a blue plaque placed there by the Stevenson Club of London in 1934 describing RLS as an 'English author.'

in the way of correspondence and as Colvin noted 'there is perhaps no period of his life when his letters reflect so fully the variety of his moods and the eagerness of his occupations'.

Looking back from Samoa in March 1891, RLS was to declare: 'I was only happy once: that was at Hyères.'

To Charles Baxter

17 October 1882   *Terminus Hôtel, Marseille*

Dear Charles, As üsual nae receipt; but I'll alloo 'at I hae gotten a cheque; I hope it'll be honoured. We have gotten a braw bit hoosie: nine rooms, twa dressin' rooms, and I dinnae ken hoo money presses; forbye, we hae gotten a big hash o' a weedy for a servant lass;[1] she says she can cook grand. Ma wife (Mrs Johnson) tells me to tell ye that it'll be a grand ploy for ye some o' thae days to get into the train and be hursled doon here to Marseilles and tak a bit keek at Campagne Defli, St Marcel, Banlieue de Marseille. We'll likely gang in there on the Sunday but I'll tell ye when ance we're fair settled.   Thamson

Doubts of the Poet Thamson

Campagne De – fli:
O me!
Campagne De – bug:
There comes the tug!
Campagne De – mosquito:
It's eneuch to gar me greet, O!
Campagne De – louse:
O God damn the house!

To William Dean Howells[1]

4 December 1882   *Campagne Defli, St Marcel*
W. D. Howells Esq.

Dear Sir, I have just finished reading your last book; it has enlightened (or darkened?) me as to your opinions; and as I have been sending, by all

---

[1] A big untidy widow. In a letter to TS Fanny described her as 'a most competent large middle-aged servant': 'Woggs promptly attacked her but when she spoke of her skill in cookery changed his mind.'

[1] William Dean Howells (1837–1920), American novelist and man of letters, editor of the *Atlantic Monthly* 1871–81.

possible intermediaries, invitations speeding after you, I find myself under the unpleasant necessity of obtruding on your knowledge a piece of my private life.[2]

My wife did me the honour to divorce her husband in order to marry me.

This, neither more nor less, it is at once my duty and my pleasure to communicate. According as your heart is, so will the meaning of this letter be.

But I will add this much: that after the kindness you showed me in your own country[3] and the sympathy with which many of your books have inspired me, it will be a sincere disappointment to find that you cannot be my guest. I shall bear up however; for I assure you I desire to know no one who considers himself holier than my wife.

With the best wishes, however it goes, believe me, Yours truly.

Robert Louis Stevenson

To his Mother

[5 January 1883]   [Grand Hôtel, Nice][1]

My dear Mother, Please continue to address me at St Marcel so that Fanny may have a sight of the letters; but here I am at Nice – Grand Hôtel – a little farther up the river than the old Chauvain – now Cosmopolitan. What a change from twenty years ago![2] The very river is now bridged over, and gardens and casinos and the like occupy its place. The old Chauvain, I looked into: gone was the gardened court, gone, of course, all the travelling carriages I used to play among with the little Italian girl and the little German boy. Only the Place Masséna still has its arcades and the identical café still remains where I remember seeing my father and Mr Abbott sitting in the moonlight, Abbott eating ices; and there is still the bastioned fort on the hill top over the old Mentone road, that I adored beyond anything in stone and lime I ever saw. Twenty years: dear

[2] In her biography of her father Mildred Howells comments: 'While Howells was in London, various mutual friends were anxious to have him meet Robert Louis Stevenson . . . It was arranged that they should see each other on the Continent, but before that could happen Stevenson read *A Modern Instance*, which he took for a general condemnation of divorce.' Howells made no reply to what he later called 'your inconceivable letter'. RLS finally wrote a friendly letter of apology in July 1893 and the two were reconciled.

[3] Howells had published one of RLS's poems in the *Atlantic Monthly* in October 1880.

[1] RLS had been seriously ill all the time they were at St Marcel. When an epidemic of fever broke out he thought it would be safer to move, although he was suffering from a hemorrhage. He travelled alone to Nice on 1 January, leaving Fanny to follow later.

[2] The Stevensons stayed at the Hôtel Chauvain in Nice in January 1863 when they visited the South of France. The Abbotts were American tourists met at the hotel.

me, I am an old man for all the good I've done. I think the change has
done me a great deal of good, however. This huge caravanserai is fearfully
dear, but I am still too weary to look for anything else; I stay mostly
in bed, eat and drink of the best I can find, and banish care with all
my might. Still it was a sell to have to leave home, when Sam was there
too.[3]

I am sorry my letter to my father went astray; it was engineering in
part, and so, let us hope, not valuable.

My best wishes to you both and my best love. Auld lang syne is very
close to me here.   R.L.S.

To his Mother

Saturday 6 January 1883   *Grand Hôtel, Nice*
EPIPHANY

My dear Mother, I never knew when Epiphany was before, but I believe
I know *what* it is now. The amount of epiphany we've been having is
beyond credence. Fanny got none of my letters; no one seems surprised
− ·· because it was new year; then she began to spring telegrams to the
police, and to assorted hotels; finally after an effusion of silver biscuits (five
franc pieces; it's Simpson's word) that cannot be believed, she arrived here
yesterday evening. Never, never has there been such a wretched job; such
misery and expense for nothing; the devil himself could have invented no
sillier imbroglio. Though I was supposed to be dead, she and Sam (my
widowed family) arrived with the silver box and a loaded revolver.[1] The
Wogg was left behind! I am better. Ever your affectionate son
                                              Robert Louis Stevenson

To Charles Baxter

[Postmark 12 January 1883]   *[Nice]*

Dear Charles, Thanks for your good letter. It is true, man, God's trüth,
what ye say about the body, Stevison. The deil himsel, it's my belief,

---

[3] Lloyd was at a small private school run by the Revd Henry John Storrs at his house in
Bournemouth. He was at St Marcel for the Christmas holidays.
[1] Telegrams and letters went astray and Fanny, having heard no news from RLS for four days,
feared he had died on the way to Nice. She arrived at Nice in a distraught state; after a few days
she returned to St Marcel. She later wrote exaggerated and over-dramatised accounts of both
journeys.

could nae get the soul harled oot o' the creature's wame, or he had seen the hinder end o' they proofs.[1] Ye crack o' Maecenas; he's naebody by you! He gied the lad, Horace, a rax forrit[2] by all accounts; but damn! he never gied him proofs like yon. Horace may hae been a better hand at the clink[3] than Stevison, – mind, I'm no sayin' 't – but onyway he was never sae weel prentit. Damned, but it's bony! Hoo mony pages will there be, think ye? Stevison maun hae sent ye the feck[4] o' twenty sangs – fifteen I'se warrant. Weel, that'll can make thretty pages, gin ye were to prent on ae side only, whilk wad be perhaps what a man o' your *great* idees would be ettlin' at, man Johnson. Then there wad be the Pre-face, an' prose ye ken prents oot langer than po'try at the hinder end, for ye hae to say things in't. An' then there'll be a title page and a dedication and a index wi' the first lines like, and the deil an' a'. Man, it'll be grand. Nae copies to be given to the Liberys!

I am alane mysel, in Nice, they ca't, but damned I think they micht as well ca't Nesty. The Pile-on,[5] 's they ca't, 's aboot as big as the river Tay at Perth; and it's rainin' maist like Greenock. Dod, I've seen's had mair o' what they ca' the I-talian at Muttonhole. I-talian! I havenae seen the sun for eicht and forty hours. Thomson's better, I believe. But the body's fair attenyated. He's doon to seeven stane eleeven, an' he sooks awa at cod liver ile till it's a fair disgrace. Ye see he tak's it in a drap brandy; and it's my belief, it's just an excuse for a dram. But the creature was aye drucken, that's weel ken't, an' sma' shame to'm. He an' Stevison gang aboot their lane, maistly; they're company to ither, like, an' whiles they'll speak o' Johnson. But *he's* far awa, losh me! Stevison's last book's in a third edeetion;[6] an' it's bein' translated (like the psalms o' David, nae less) into French; and a damned eediot they ca' Asher – a kind of a rival of Tauchnitz – is bringin' him oot in a paper book for the Frenchies an' the German folk in twa volumes.[7] Sae he's in luck, ye see. Yours

Thomson

[1] Baxter had sent RLS proofs of the first two Brasheanna Sonnets. Only one set (which had belonged to Baxter) survives and no more were set up in type.
[2] A push forward.
[3] Rhyme or jingle.
[4] Majority or bulk.
[5] The river Paillon.
[6] The one-volume *New Arabian Nights*. There was a French translation of 'The Rajah's Diamond' and 'The Suicide Club' in 1885.
[7] *New Arabian Nights* appeared as volumes 204–5 (1883) of 'Asher's Collection of English Authors' published by J.F. Richter of Hamburg. Tauchnitz, the Leipzig publisher, was the best-known producer of editions of British authors for circulation on the continent.

To his Parents

[1 February 1883]   *Hôtel du Petit Louvre, Marseille*

My dear people, How is my mother? Nothing, I observe, was said about her in the last. The trip might do her good.

> In eighteen hundred and eighty-three,
> America discovered me!

I am Columbus outside in. 'Tis a fine page for The Book.[1] I seem to be a kind of success nowadays; I have calculated that my six books have brought me in upwards of six hundred pounds, about four hundred of which came from the first publication of parts of them in magazines. I shall have a story in April and May, in *Longman's*.[2]

I keep decently well. I hope you have sent me money; as soon as it comes, I believe three days will get us out of this. You had better get the proper address of that Pension at Nice. Ever affectionate son   R.L.S.

To Sidney Colvin

15 February [1883]   *Hôtel du Petit Louvre, Marseille*

Dear Sir, This is to intimate to you that
> Mr and Mrs Robert Louis Stevenson
> were yesterday safely delivered
> of a
> Campagne.

The parents are both doing much better than could be expected; particularly the dear papa. I am, dear sir, Yours obstetrically   Jno. Brown
Midwife.

Professor Sidney J. Colvin
Trinitarian Professor of Theology.

There, Colving, I did it this time. Huge success. The proprietaires were scattered like chaff. If it had not been the agent, may Israel now say, if it had not been the agent who was on our side![1] But I made the agent march! I threatened law; I was IMMENSE – what do I say? – IMMEASURABLE.

---

[1] A very favourable review of *New Arabian Nights* in the February *Century Magazine* for MIS's scrapbook of reviews.
[2] 'The Treasure of Franchard' was rejected by James Payn for the *Cornhill*, RLS was to recall ten years later, 'as unfit for a family magazine'. It was published in *Longman's* for April and May 1883.
[1] 'Had not the Lord been on our side, may Israel now say' – Psalm 124:1 (Metrical Version).

The agent, however, behaved well, and is a fairly honest little one-eared, white-eyed, tom-cat of an opera-going gold-hunter. The proprietaire *non est inventa*; we countermarched her; got in valuators; and in place of 100 francs in her pocket, she got nothing, and I paid *one* silver biscuit! It *might* go farther, but I am convinced, will not, and anyway, I fear not the consequences. P.R. Hyères will now find us for a while.

The weather is incredible; my heart sings; my health satisfies even my wife. I did jolly well right to come after all; and she now admits it. For she broke down as I knew she would; and I, from here, without passing a night at the Defly, though with a cruel effusion of coach hires, took up the wondrous tale[2] and steered the ship through. I now sit crowned with laurel and literally exulting in kudos. The affair has been better managed than our two last winterings. I am yours   Brabazon Drum

To Alison Cunningham

16 February 1883   *Marseilles*

My dear Cummy, You must think and quite justly that I am one of the meanest rogues in creation. But though I do not write (which is a thing I hate) it by no means follows that people are out of my mind. It is natural that I should always think more or less about you; and still more natural that I should think of you when I went back to Nice.[1] But the real reason why you have been more in my mind than usual, is because of some little verses that I have been writing and that I mean to make a book of;[2] and the real reason of this letter (although I ought to have written to you anyway) is that I have just seen that the book in question must be dedicated to

Alison Cunningham,

the only person who will really understand it. I don't know when it may be ready, for it has to be illustrated; but I hope in the meantime you may like the idea of what is to be; and when the time comes, I shall try to make the dedication as pretty as I can make it.[3] Of course, this is only a

---

[2] 'The moon takes up the wondrous tale' from Addison's hymn beginning 'The spacious firmament on high'.

[1] Cummy accompanied the Stevensons on their 1863 visit.

[2] At Braemar in 1881 RLS had picked up his mother's copy of Kate Greenaway's newly published *Birthday Book for Children*, with verses by Mrs Sale Barker, and commented, 'These are very nice rhymes and I don't think they would be difficult to do' – Kate Greenaway (1864–1901) was the famous illustrator of children's picture books. From this time RLS began to write the poems which were to be collected as *A Child's Garden of Verses*.

[3] *A Child's Garden of Verses* is dedicated in verse 'To Alison Cunningham from her Boy'.

flourish, like taking off one's hat; but still a person who has taken the trouble to write things, does not dedicate them to any one without meaning it; and you must just try to take this dedication in place of a great many things that I might have said and that I ought to have done to prove that I am not altogether unconscious of the great debt of gratitude I owe you. This little book which is all about my childhood should indeed go to no other person but you, who did so much to make that childhood happy.

Do you know we came very near sending for you this winter? If we had not had news that you were ill too, I almost believe we should have done so, we were so much in trouble.

I am now very well; but my wife has had a very, very bad spell, through overwork and anxiety when I was *lost*! I suppose you heard of that. She sends you her love, and hopes you will write to her – though she – no more than I – deserves it. She would add a word herself, but she is too played out. I am, Ever your old boy   R.L.S.

To Will H. Low[1]

[*March 1883*]   *Chalet de la Solitude, Hyères*

My dear Low, *C'est d'un bon camarade*; and I am much obliged to you for your two letters and the inclosure. Times are a little changed with all of us, since the ever honourable days of Lavenue:[2] hallowed be his name! Hallowed his old Fleury – of which you did not see I think – as I did – the glorious apotheosis: advanced on a Tuesday to three francs, on the Thursday to six, and on Friday swept off, holus bolus, for the proprietor's private consumption. Well, we had the start of that proprietor. Many a good bottle came our way and was, I think, worthily made welcome.

I am pleased that Mr Gilder[3] should like my literature; and I ask you particularly to thank Mr Bunner (Have I the name right) for his notice,[4] which was of that friendly, headlong sort that really pleases an author like what the French call a 'shake-hands'. It pleased me the more coming from the States, where I have met not much recognition save from the buccaneers, and above all from pirates who misspell my name. I saw my book advertised in a number of the *Critic* as the work of one R.L.

---

[1] Will Hicok Low (1853–1932), American artist who studied in France 1872–7 and was a friend and contemporary of Bob Stevenson in the studio of Carolus-Duran. He became a lifelong friend of RLS and has left a sympathetic account of that friendship in *A Chronicle of Friendships* (1908). He later won success as a book-illustrator and with his mural decorations.
[2] The expensive Paris restaurant which RLS and his friends patronised when they were in funds.
[3] Richard Watson Gilder (1844–1909), American poet and editor of the *Century* (1881–1909).
[4] Henry Cuyler Bunner (1855–96), American author of light verse and short stories, editor of *Puck*, 1878–96. He had reviewed *New Arabian Nights* in the February *Century*.

Stephenson;[5] and I own I boiled. It is so easy to know the name of the
man whose book you have stolen; for there it is, at full length on the title
page of your booty. But no, damn him, not he! He calls me Stephenson.
These woes, I only refer to by the way, as they set a higher value on the
Century notice.

I am now a person with an established ill-health − a wife − a dog
possessed with an evil, a Gadarene spirit − a chalet on a hill, looking out
over the Mediterranean[6] − a certain reputation − and very obscure
finances. Otherwise, very much the same, I guess; and were a bottle of
Fleury a thing to be obtained, capable of developing theories along with
a fit spirit even as of yore. Yet I now draw near to the middle ages; nearly
three years ago, that fatal Thirty struck; and yet the great work is not yet
done − not yet even conceived. But so, as one goes on, the wood seems
to thicken, the footpath to narrow, and the House Beautiful on the hill's
summit to draw further and further away. We learn indeed to use our
means; but only to learn, along with it, the paralysing knowledge that
these means are only applicable to two or three poor, commonplace
motives. Eight years ago, if I could have slung ink as I can now, I should
have thought myself well on the road after Shakespeare; and now − I find
I have only got a pair of walking shoes and not yet begun to travel. And
Art is still away there on the mountain summit. But I need not continue;
for of course this is your story just as much as it is mine; and strange to
think, it was Shakespeare's too, and Beethoven's, and Phidias's. It is a
blessed thing that, in this forest of art, we can pursue our woodlice and
sparrows, *and not catch them*, with almost the same fervour of exhilaration
as that with which Sophocles hunted and brought down the Mastodon.

Tell me something of your work, and your wife − to whom I send the
warmest remembrances.[7] Our news here: Bob is married and ill; Bloomer
is married, and we have just had from him such a kind, wise, witty,
ungrammatical masterpiece of a letter as none but he could write;

[5] Henry Holt & Co. one of the American publishers of *New Arabian Nights* advertised the book
as 'Stephenson's' in the *Critic* of 16 December 1882.
[6] In a letter of 27 October RLS described La Solitude to Low:

> My address is still the same, and I live in a most sweet corner of the universe, sea and fine
> hills before me, and a rich variegated plain; and at my back a craggy hill, loaded with vast
> feudal ruins. I am very quiet; a person passing by my door half startles me; but I enjoy the
> most aromatic airs and at night the most wonderful view into a moonlit garden. By day, this
> garden fades into nothing, overpowered by its surroundings and the luminous distance; but
> at night and when the moon is out, that garden, the arbour, the flight of stairs that mount
> the artificial hillock, the plumed blue gum trees that hang trembling, become the very skirts
> of Paradise. Angels I know frequent it; and it thrills all night with the flutes of silence. Damn
> that garden; − and by day it is gone.

[7] Low married in 1875 Berthe Eugénie Marie Julienne (died 1908) whom Fanny described to
Balfour as 'a peasant girl from, I think Normandy (who) spoke *patois* and never thoroughly
mastered proper French'.

O'Meara, I know nothing of, except that I hear he is still the lady-killer; Naigly,[8] I don't know how to write his d—d name, I found snoozing at Barbizon some time ago; Lamé was there too. Do you remember Ernest, the bicycler at Nana's, Marlotte? The last I saw of him he was working and was said to have learned to paint. My dear fellow, I am yours ever

R.L. Stevenson

My wife begs to be remembered to both of you; I cannot say as much for my dog, who has never seen you, but he would like, on general principles, to bite you.

Tell me about the . . .[9] *worm?* is he alive or dead, married or single, famous or – hung?

To W.E. Henley

[*Early May 1883*]   [*Hyères*]

My dear lad, This is to announce to you the MS of *Nursery Verses*, now numbering XLVIII pieces or 599 verses, which of course one might augment *ad infinitum.*[1]

But here is my notion to make all clear.

I do not want a big ugly quarto; my soul sickens at the look of a quarto. I want a refined octavo, not large – not *larger* than the Donkey Book, at any price. I think the full page might hold four verses of four lines, that is to say counting their blanks at two, of twenty-two lines in height. The first page of each number would only hold two verses or ten lines, the title being low down. At this rate, we should have 78 or 80 pages of letterpress. The designs should not be in the text, but facing the poem; so that if the artist liked, he might give two pages of design to every poem that turned the leaf, i.e. longer than eight lines: i.e. to 28 out of the 46. I should say he would not use this privilege (?) above five times, and some he might scorn to illustrate at all, so we may say fifty drawings. I shall come to the drawings next.

But now you see my book of the thickness, since the drawings count two pages, of 180 pp. and since the paper will perhaps be thicker, of near

---

[8] Low later spells the name Nagely.

[9] One word has been obliterated. Later letters by Low show that the reference is to Walter Launt Palmer (1854–1932), American landscape painter, son of Erastus Dow Palmer, the sculptor, of Albany, New York. Low himself was born in Albany and had been helped by Erastus Palmer. Low and Walter Palmer were evidently close boyhood friends and fellow art-students in Paris (Palmer was a pupil of Carolus-Duran 1876–7). There was a serious quarrel in Paris, apparently in connection with Low's marriage, and RLS had strongly supported Low. In December 1893 Low told RLS that he and Palmer had had a reconciliation.

[1] The MS of the trial version of *A Child's Garden of Verses*, printed later in the year as *Penny Whistles*.

two hundred by bulk. It is bound in a quiet green with the words in thin gilt. Its shape is a slender, tall octavo. And it sells for the publisher's fancy; and it will be a darling to look at: in short, it would be like one of the original Heine books in type and spacing.

Now for the pictures. I take another sheet and begin to jot notes, for them, when my imagination serves: I will run through the book, writing when I have an idea.

There I have jotted enough to give the artis a notion. Of course I don't do more than contribute ideas, but I will be happy to help in any and every way. I may as well add another idea; when the hartis finds nothing much to illustrate, a good drawing of any *object* mentioned in the text, were it only a loaf of bread or a candlestick, is a most delightful thing to a young child. I remember this keenly.

Of course if the artis insists on a larger format, I must I suppose bow my head. But my idea I am convinced is the best, and would make the book truly, not fashionably, pretty.

I forgot to mention that I shall have a dedication; I am going to dedicate 'em to Cummy; it will please her, and lighten a little my burthen of ingratitude. A low affair is the Nurse business.

I will add no more to this lest you should want to communicate with the hartis, try another sheet. I wonder how many I'll keep wandering to.

O I forgot. As for the title, I think *Nursery Verses*, the best. Poetry is not the strong point of the text, and I shirk any title that might seem to claim that quality; otherwise we might have *Nursery Muses* or *New Songs of Innocence* (but that were a blasphemy), or *Rimes of Innocence*: the last not bad, or – an idea – *The Jews' Harp*, or Now I Have It:– *The Penny Whistle*.

THE PENNY WHISTLE:
NURSERY VERSES
BY
ROBERT LOUIS STEVENSON
ILLUSTRATED BY

And here we have an excellent frontispiece, of a party playing on a P.W. to a little ring of dancing children.

THE PENNY WHISTLE
is the name for me.

Fool! this is all wrong, here is the true name:–

PENNY WHISTLES
FOR SMALL WHISTLERS

The second title is queried, it is perhaps better, as simply
PENNY WHISTLES.

> Nor you, O Penny Whistler, grudge
> That I your instrument debase:
> By worse performers still we judge,
> And give that fife a second place!

Crossed penny whistles on the cover, or else a sheaf of 'em.

Suggestions[2]

IV. The procession – the child running behind it. The procession tailing off through the gates of a cloudy city.

IX. 'Foreign Lands'. This will I think want two plates: the child climbing, his first glimpse over the garden wall with what he sees – the tree shooting higher and higher like the beanstalk, and the view widening. The river slipping in. The road arriving in Fairyland.

X. 'Windy Nights'. The child in bed listening – the horseman galloping.

XII. The child helplessly watching his ship – then he gets smaller and the doll joyfully comes alive – the pair landing on the island – the ship's deck with the doll steering and the child firing the penny cannon. Query two Plates? The doll should never come properly alive.

XV. Building of the ship – Storing her – Navigation – Tom's accident, the other child paying no attention.

XXXI. 'The Wind'. I sent you my notion of already.

XXXVII. 'Foreign Children'. The foreign types dancing in a jing-a-ring, with the English child pushing in the middle. The foreign children looking at and showing each other marvels. The English child at the leeside of a roast of beef. The English child sitting thinking with his picture-books all round him, and the jing-a-ring of the foreign children, in miniature dancing over the picture-books.

XXXIX. Dear artist can you do me that?

XLII. The child being started off. The bed sailing, curtains and all, upon the sea. The child waking and finding himself at home, the corner of toilette might be worked in to look like the pier.

XLVII. The lighted part of the room, to be carefully distinguished from my child's dark hunting grounds. A shaded lamp.

Otto: *Otto* will be to the tune of 100 *Cornhill* pp. not less, nor much more.[3] Say from 95 to 115, as the extreme limits. It would thus run

---

[2] The poems without title are IV 'Young Night Thought'; XII 'My Ship and I'; XV 'A Good Play' – 'We built a ship upon the stairs'; XXXIX 'The Sun's Travels'; XLII 'My Bed is a Boat'; XLVII 'The Land of Story-Books'. Some of the numbering in *A Child's Garden* is different.

[3] RLS noted in his diary that he began *Prince Otto* on 10 April 1883. He wrote to Henley on 16 April: '*Prince Otto* is now in my head every moment . . . I have had the plan by me for three years, and all of a sudden chipped in and began it.' He had listed the main characters to Henley from San Francisco in January 1880 and told him that the Countess von Rosen was based on 'my old Russian friend, Nadia Zassetsky'.

through four or five numbers of a magazine. Through five, I fancy, most exactly. Bentley offered me a guinea for his small page, but I suspect at that figure, he would want the copyright. This I am determined to keep for Chatto, who (take him for all in all) is such an advance, such a heavenward soar, from the Paulinian swamp, that I cherish him near my heart. Still Bentley might be sounded. I can almost make myself bold to begin publishing it in autumn. Really, I ought to be able to begin by July; but caution is best, and I may have a back turn. The thing is to find a mag or paper who will take it *early*. J. Payn is full. Where do we turn? It had better be arranged as soon as possible.

To give you an idea: it is a semi-reasonable and sentimental Arabian Night: that is to say, the unreality is there and the classic pomp. But the people are of course more developed, though they all talk like books – none of your colloquial wash; and the action, if there ever had been such a State of Grünewald might have taken place. Otto is a sweet party, but as weak as paper; my wife thinks I rather have him. To be quite frank, there is a *risqué* character. The Countess von Rosen, a jolly, elderly – how shall I say? – fuckstress; whom I try to handle so as to please this rotten public, and damn myself the while for ruining good material. I could, an if I dared, make her jump.

Deacon. After all has not yet by any manner of means paid his way – which, note.[4] Sir, if I die for it, you shall have a romantic scenario ere long. But you are more captious than helpful.

Whisky letter. Excellent is Mr Fastidious Brisk.[5] Bunyan must have had me in his eye. I say, Bunyan could make names. You may add him to your list of men of genius; he has that surprising air of being commonplace and plain sailing and being quite master of himself and not in any alarm, that they all have. I would say Shakespeare, Molière, Chaucer (Molière's young first cousin), Fielding, Scott a little lower because of bad work and laziness; Balzac, a little lower by reason of an unsound temper – the lark was dead in his bosom. After these comes the geniusettes, the djinns: two will suffice: de Musset and Bunyan. And then we have to go to the Essayist sort of people for the next level of excellence: Montaigne, Wordsworth. Close behind the ranks of the geniuses, are one or two hangers on: a curious instance is Lesage, almost a man of genius, yet not a bit a djinn. The Djinns are always a little high, a little rank, a little spicy: as it were with originality. All the Essayist class are originals. But Lesage belongs wholly to the great tradition. Shakespeare is the only one of the

---

[4] An actor-manager called Haldane Crichton had bought the provincial rights for *Deacon Brodie* for one year. The play was produced at Bradford on 21 December 1882 and at Aberdeen on 16 April 1883. There was a later production in Glasgow on 25 June 1883.

[5] A name coined by Henley for RLS from the character in Jonson's *Every Man out of his Humour*. There is also a Mr Brisk in *The Pilgrim's Progress*.

men of genius who had any of that same originality, with which all the
djinns, and I, and Cotton, and Gongora, are more or less rotten. Byron,
if he had not been a dandy, promised to take to genius. If a djinn, or any
small card tries to take to genius, he is at once detected: he becomes dull.

I only owe you one cricket, which in my last I paid.[6] The April
number, as I told you, is to stand over till the volume is complete. Then
you'll hear why. Not till then. Ever yours   Fastidious Brisk[7]

pour copie
    john Libbel[8]

Who do you think of for the pictures? Greenaway? Crane? a new man?
Pray relieve my panting buzzum.

To his Parents

5 May [1883]   *Chalet Solitude*

My dearest people, I have had a great piece of news. There has been
offered for *Treasure Island* – how much do you suppose? I believe it would
be an excellent jest to keep the answer till my next letter. For two cents
I would do so. Shall I? Anyway I'll turn the page first. No – well – A
hundred pounds, all alive, oh! A hundred jingling, tingling, golden,
minted quid.[1] Is not this wonderful? Add that I have now finished, in
draft, the fifteenth chapter of my novel, and have only five before me; and
you will see what cause of gratitude I have.

The weather, to look at the per contra sheet, continues vomitable; and
Fanny is quite out of sorts. But really, with such cause of gladness, I have
not the heart to be dispirited by anything. My child's verse book is

[6] RLS was regularly sending Henley detailed criticisms of the complete contents of each month's
Magazine of Art (it has not been possible to include these in this selection).
[7] Written in a shaky hand.
[8] Also in a shaky hand. John Libbel was one of the joke names invented by Bob. Travelling back
home from Wales he needed half-a-crown for his train fare at Crewe. He dashed into the town
and pawned a pair of trousers, giving his name as 'John Libbel – two B's'. From this developed
'Libbelism', one of the pranks of which RLS and Bob were so fond in their youth. They went
to great lengths to build up evidence of this imaginary person's existence: handing out visiting
cards, sending parcels with nothing in them, making anxious enquiries at lodging-houses and so
on. RLS tells the story in 'Memoirs of Himself', Book III.
[1] It is often supposed (on the authority of this letter) that Cassell's bought *Treasure Island* outright
for £100. The agreement, signed on 2 June 1883, provided for the payment of £50 on
signature and a further £50 when the book was passed for press; thereafter RLS was to receive
a royalty of £20 per thousand copies sold after the first four thousand. Cassell's continued to pay
royalties until the book went out of copyright in 1944. The receipt for the first £50 was dated
Hyères 8 June 1883.

finished, dedication and all, and out of my hands – you may tell Cummy; *Silverado* is done, too, and cast upon the waters;[2] and this novel so near completion, it does look as if I should support myself without trouble in the future. If I have only health, I can, I thank God. It is dreadful to be a great, big man, and not be able to buy bread.

O that this may last!

I have today paid my rent for the half year, till the middle of September, and got my lease: why they have been so long, I know not.

I wish you all sorts of good things

When is our marriage day? Your loving and ecstatic son

Treesure Eilan

It has been, for me, a Treasure Island verily.

To W.E. Henley

[*June 1883*]   *La Solitude*

My dear lad, The books came some time since, but I have not had the pluck to answer: a shower of small troubles having fallen in, or troubles that may be very large.

I have had to incur a huge vague debt for cleaning sewers; our house was (of course) riddled with hidden cesspools, but that was infallible. I have the fever; Sam pines, I don't quite know why; it is uneasifying. I feel the duty to work very heavy on me at times, with the fever; yet go it must. I have had to leave 'Fontainebleau,'[1] when three hours would finish it and go full-tilt at tushery for awhile.[2] But it will come soon.

I think I can give you a good article on Hokusai;[3] but that is for afterwards; Fonty is first in hand.

---

[2] RLS was awaiting an offer from Chatto for *The Silverado Squatters*. Meanwhile, having been asked by Richard Watson Gilder of the *Century* for fiction, RLS had instead sent him *Silverado*. An incomplete version was published in the *Century* for November and December 1883.

[1] RLS sent his essay, 'Fontainebleau: Village Communities of Painters' to Henley at the end of the month. It appeared in the *Magazine of Art* for May and June 1884.

[2] James Henderson, the publisher of *Young Folks*, whose address was Red Lion Court, had asked RLS for a new story. RLS wrote to Henley in Late May: '[As] my good Red Lion Courter begged me for another Butcher's Boy, I turned me to – what thinkest-'ou? – to Tushery, by the mass! Ay, friend, a whole tale of tushery. And every tusher tushes me so free, that may I be tushed if the whole thing is worth a tush. *The Black Arrow: A Tale of Tunstall Forest* is his name: tush! a poor thing!' RLS began writing the story on 26 May. It was serialised in *Young Folks* from 30 June to 20 October under the pseudonym Captain George North.

[3] Cassell's advertisement leaflet for the eighth volume of the *Magazine of Art* beginning November 1883 listed a forthcoming article on Hokusai by RLS. This never materialised.

By the way, my view is to give the *Penny Whistles* to Crane or Greenaway. But Crane I think is likeliest; he is a fellow who at least, always does his best.

Cassell I suppose went back on 'em?

Shall I ever have money enough to write a play?

O dire necessity!

A word in your ear: I don't like trying to support myself. I hate the strain and the anxiety; and when unexpected expenses are foisted on me. I feel the world is playing with false dice.

Now I must Tush. Adoo   An aching, fevered, penny-journalist

'Tis odd, yet true. You have kind of gone up in the world, I kind of go down: I mean materially. My anxieties have come late, but they are not severe as anxieties go;

> So why should I complain?
> Let me the goblet drain, drain
> And fill it full again, again
> For trouble killed the cat.

But I must go tush![4]

---

[4] In the drawing RLS is referring to the sheets of characters and scenes published by Skelt for the toy theatre, which were one of the delights of his childhood, celebrated in his essay 'A Penny Plain and Twopence Coloured' published in the *Magazine of Art* in April 1884.

A lytle Jape of Tusherie
by A Tusher.

The pleasant river gushes
  Among the meadows green;
At home the author tushes;
  For him it flows unseen.

The Birds among the Bŭshes
  May wanton on the spray;
But vain for him who tushes,
  The brightness of the day!

The frog among the rushes
  Sits singing in the blue.
B'y'r la'kin! but these tushes
  Are wearisome to do!

The task entirely crushes
  The spirit of the bard:
God pity him who tushes –
  His task is very hard.

The filthy gutter slushes,
  The clouds are full of rain,
But doomed is he who tushes
  To tush and tush again.

At morn with his hair brushes,
  Still 'tush' he says, and weeps;
At night again he tushes
  And tushes till he sleeps.

And when at length he Pŭshes
  Beyond the river dark –
'Las to the man who tushes,
  'Tush' shall be God's remark!

To W.E. Henley

19 September [1883]   *La Solitude*

Dear Boy, Our letters vigorously cross: you will ere this have received a note to Coggie: God knows what was in it.[1]

---

[1] Walter Ferrier died on 9 September 1883. The death certificate gave the cause of death as 'chronic Bright's disease'. He had been an alcoholic for several years. His sister Elizabeth Anne Ferrier (1844–1917), known by the nickname 'Coggie', became a close friend of RLS.

It is strange, a little before the first word you sent me – so late – kindly late, I know and feel – I was thinking in my bed. When I knew you I had six friends. Bob I had by nature; then came the good James Walter – with all his failing – the *gentleman* of the lot, alas to sink so low, alas to do so little, but now thank God in his quiet rest; next I found Baxter – well do I remember telling Walter I had unearthed 'a W.S. that I thought would do' – it was in the Academy lane, and he questioned me as to the Signet's qualifications; fourth came Simpson; somewhere about the same time, I began to get intimate with the Jenk; last came Colvin. Then, one black winter afternoon, long Leslie Stephen in his velvet jacket met me in the Spec. by appointment, took me over to the infirmary and, in the crackling, blighting gaslight, showed me that old head whose excellent representation I see before me in the photograph. Now when a man has six friends, to introduce a seventh is usually hopeless. Yet when you were presented you took to them and they to you upon the nail. These eight, that now are but seven, stuck together near upon ten years; your own former friend Runciman has drifted off upon the billows of wrongheaded vanity;[2] but death has given the first dislocation to that party of eight. You must have been a fine fellow; but what a singular fortune I must have had in my six friends that you should take to all.

I wish to thank you particularly for your gentle warning. That was of a friend.

Lord, let us all stick together. I don't know if it is good Latin, most probably not; but this is enscrolled before my eyes for Walter: *Tandem e nubibus in apricum properat.*[3] Rest, I suppose, I know, was all that remained; but O to look back, to remember all the mirth, all the kindness, all the humorous limitations and loved defects of that character; to think that he was young with me, sharing that weatherbeaten, Fergussonian youth,[4] looking forward through the clouds to the sunburst; and now clean gone from my path, silent, – well, well. This has been a strange awakening. Last night, when I was alone in the house, with the window open on the lovely still night, I could have sworn he was in the room with me; I could show you the spot; and what was very curious, I heard his rich laughter, a thing I had not called to mind for I know not how long.

I see his coral waistcoat studs that he wore the first time he dined in my house; I see his attitude, leaning back a little, already with something of a

---

[2] James Runciman (1852–91), journalist and school teacher, brother of the first Lord Runciman. He was sub-editor of *Vanity Fair* in 1874 and later worked on *London*. He and Henley were close friends in the late 1870s, and Runciman apparently shared Henley's lodgings in Edinburgh; they were later estranged.

[3] At last he hastens from the clouds to a sunny place.

[4] RLS felt a strong sense of kinship with the Edinburgh poet, Robert Fergusson. See p. 113, n. 2 and p. 456, n. 9.

portly air, and laughing internally. How I admired him! And now in the West Kirk.

I am trying to write out this haunting bodily sense of absence, besides what else should I write of

Yes looking back, I think of him as one who was good, though sometimes clouded. He was the only gentleman of all my friends; the only gentle one, save perhaps the other Walter. And he was certainly the only modest man among the lot. He never gave himself away; he kept back his secret; there was always a gentle problem behind all. Dear, dear, what a wreck; and yet how pleasant is the retrospect! God doeth all things well, though by what strange, solemn and murderous contrivances!

It is strange: he was the only man I ever loved, who did not habitually interrupt. The fact draws my own portrait. And it is one of the many reasons why I count myself honoured by his friendship. A man like you had to like me; you could not help yourself; but Ferrier was above me, we were not equals; his true self humoured and smiled paternally upon my failings, even as I humoured and sorrowed over his.

Well first his mother, then himself, they are gone: 'in their resting graves.'[5]

When I come to think of it, I do not know what I said to his sister, and I fear to try again. Could you send her this? There is too much both about yourself and me in it; but that, if you do not mind, is but a mark of sincerity. It would let her know how entirely, in the mind of (I suppose) his oldest friend, the good true Ferrier, obliterates the memory of the other, who was only his 'lunatic brother'.

Judge of this for me and do as you please; anyway I will try to write to her again; my last was some kind of scrawl that I could not see for crying. This came upon me, remember, with terrible suddenness; I was surprised by this death; and it is fifteen or sixteen years since first I saw the handsome face in the Spec. I made sure, besides, to have died first.

Love to you, your wife and her sisters. Ever yours, dear boy

R.L.S.

I cannot express how much relieved I was to hear you had got over that start; be careful, be careful; we can't have any more of this.

I never knew any man so superior to himself as poor James Walter. The best of him only came as a vision, like Corsica from the Corniche.[6] He never gave his measure either morally or intellectually. The curse was on him. Even his friends did not know him but by fits. I have passed hours

---

[5] A favourite quotation from Patrick Walker (cf. *Edinburgh: Picturesque* Notes, V 'Greyfriars'). Mrs Ferrier died in June 1878.

[6] La Grande Corniche the great road – built by Napoleon in 1806 – running eastward from Nice towards Italy. It commands superb views and from it Corsica can be dimly seen.

with him when he was so wise, good, and sweet, that I never knew the like of it in any other. And for a beautiful good humour he had no match. I remember breaking in upon him once with a whole red hot story (in my worst manner) pouring words upon him by the hour about some trick not worth an egg that had befallen me; and suddenly, some half hour after, finding that the sweet fellow had some concern of his own of infinitely greater import, that he was patiently and smilingly waiting to consult me on. It sounds nothing; but the courtesy and the unselfishness were perfect. It makes me rage to think how few knew him; and how many had the chance to sneer at their better.

Well, he was not wasted; that we know; though if anything looked liker irony than this fitting of a man out with these rich qualities and faculties to be wrecked and aborted from the very stocks, I do not know the name of it. Yet we see that he has left an influence; the memory of his patient courtesy has often checked me in rudeness; has it not you?

You can form no idea of how handsome Walter was. At twenty, he was splendid to see; then, too, he had the sense of power in him, and great hopes; he looked forward, ever jesting of course, but he looked to see himself where he had the right to expect. He believed in himself profoundly; but *he never disbelieved in others*. To the roughest Highland student, he always had his fine, kind, open dignity of manner; and a good word behind his back.

Of all things the strangest to me was the ripening and softening that followed that awful smash and humiliation. A man of his pride felt it like a knife; but there was never a bitter word, although God knows what bitter feelings. The last time that I saw him before leaving for America – it was a sad blow to both of us – I waited hours for him, and at last he came. 'My God,' I said, 'you have had too much again.' He did not deny it, as he did in the old days. He said 'Yes,' with a terrible simplicity. The change that represents, to anyone who knows the disease and knew James Walter, is not to be exaggerated. This fresh humiliation, after all the brave words and projects, accepted so plainly and so humbly, it went to my heart like a knife.[7] When he heard I was leaving, and that might be the last time we might meet – it almost was so – he was terribly upset, and came round at once. We sat late, in Baxter's empty house where I was sleeping,

---

[7] In the fragmentary autobiography (written in America in 1880) RLS described Walter Ferrier as the 'most complete and gentle gentleman . . . I have known':

> but he was consumed and wrecked by a miserable craving for drink. Will he, I have still to ask myself as I write these words, will he outlive the tendency, and become a conscientious, and kind gentleman as we knew him in his sober hours? or will he go downward to the sot, the spunge and the buffoon? When last I parted from him, five months ago, he and I, for the first time in our intimacy, shed tears together over this alternative; he promised me, for my sake as well as for his own, to continue the good fight; and yet ever since I have feared to write to him.

and when we parted, for the only time, we parted with a kiss. My dear friend, Walter Ferrier: O if I had only written to him more! if only one of us in these last days had been well! But I ever cherished the honour of his friendship and now when he is gone, I know what I have lost still better. We live on meaning to meet; but when the life is gone, the pang comes.   R.L.S.

I don't know how he kept in these last years; but he had a great command over himself and fought a brave battle that last time we were together, and, I fancy, ever after. Even when he made a lapse at that time, it did not discourage him. He was very pious, brave and humble. And I think for a man of his pride after such a downfall, the fight was very noble.

It was essentially the gentleman in Walter that was the spring of his resistance. It was that which looked back with such distress upon the days of his obscuration. He rarely spoke of them to me, but when he did with equal constancy and delicacy. Thinking over this wrecked and still brave life, I grow to think of him more and more with honour. Few have made such a plunge; but few, having lost health, hope and pride, would have made so fine a stand. To me he was never thoroughly discouraged, even that last time in London. But that was but a visit, we had not time to renew the intimacy.   R.L.S.

Last night I went to sleep thinking of him, and this morning I wakened out of a dream in which he was talking with me. Is it not strange in this place, where he never was, his loss should be so sensible?

To W.E. Henley

[*Late September 1883*]   *La Solitude*

Dear lad, Decidedly Cassell's is a doomed mansion. They have never acknowledged the second map;[1] let a fortnight pass without a word in answer to a plea for money and to know if they have received the map. Today, in comes this stilted letter from Gell – addressed to Royat after all that has come and gone – containing no word of the map even yet – and, last of all, inclosing no draught![2]

[1] In 'My First Book' RLS explains that the original map which inspired the writing of *Treasure Island* was lost (Cassell's said it had never reached them), and it had to be reconstructed from the text. It was drawn again in his father's office and sent to Cassell's on 2 September.
[2] In a letter to RLS dated 24 September 1883, Cassell's said that they were enclosing a draft of £50, being the second instalment due for *Treasure Island*. RLS is complaining that they failed to enclose the money, and sent the letter to Royat, long after he had (as they knew) returned to Hyères. RLS and Fanny had stayed in Royat in July and August and his parents had joined

I have written to him gently describing the history of this correspondence. I also said I would write to you and try to clear up matters, adding
that I held myself bound by all you might decide.

Who is Havers? Who is she?

And generally, where are we.[3]

Mark me, Cassell's is doomed. A huge establishment, that cannot
answer letters, nor even acknowledge registered packets, is *doomed*. I give
it five years to bankruptcy. Not a year more. The bigger the ship, the
swifter will this disorganisation spread from circle to circle. I shall bury
that great house.

> Let us bury that great house
> With a nation's lamentation.[4]

The sight of so great an establishment so much below even poor myself
in common business decency has warmed my cockles. I feel good. My
bosom's lord[5] is literally swipey with elevation: my thin prophetic finger
indicates these spires, and while I point, the thunder rolls.

> When I am rich as Noddy Boffin[6]
> I shall ride on Cassell's coffin;
> And play and sing upon the Alpin'
> Tumulus of Petter and Galpin.[7]
> While all the sad cooperãtives
> Shall stand around and gape like natives.

I have written to Gell under the mark 'private' and expressed these views
in chaster but not less significant clothing.

Adoo Adoo   R.L.S.

---

them. Philip Lyttelton Gell (1852–1926) was head of Cassell's educational department. He was
Secretary to the Delegates of Oxford University Press 1883–97, and Director of the British
South Africa Company from 1899.

[3] In their letter Cassell's asked for RLS's personal wishes 'as to the publication of a little collection
of children's poems which Mr Henley had submitted to us some weeks back. We have been
perplexed by the somewhat vague and informal manner in which it came before us.' After
consideration they had 'discovered a suitable artist in the person of Alice Havers', but the MS
had been removed by Henley: 'Will you kindly let us know whether we are to regard your
poems as still under our consideration.' Alice Mary Havers (1850–90), watercolourist and
illustrator, later illustrated two of RLS's poems published in the *Magazine of Art*.

[4] Cf. the opening lines of Tennyson's 'Ode on the Death of the Duke of Wellington'.

[5] Cf. *Romeo and Juliet*, V.i.3. Colvin, commenting on the way in which RLS's letters conveyed
an impression of his talk, said that when he read this phrase he caught 'a far off but a genuine
note of that flood of mingled poetry and slang which used to pour from him in speech'.

[6] The 'golden dustman' in *Our Mutual Friend*.

[7] The printing firm of Petter and Galpin acquired Cassell's in 1853. Until 1883 they traded as
Cassell, Petter, Galpin & Company. George William Petter (1823–88) was Editorial Manager
and Thomas Dixon Galpin (1828–?) was Managing Director until he retired in 1888.

I said to Gell: 'These little rats, they say, will eat up great concerns; and a similar breed of my own still keeps my granary empty.' Neat and modest, hey? Dam my buttons!   George the Pieman[8]

To Bob Stevenson

[*? 30 September 1883*]   *La Solitude*

My dear Bob, Yes I got both your letters at Lyons,[1] but have been since then decading in several steps. Toothache; fever; Ferrier's death; swelled testicle; lung. Now it is decided I am to leave tomorrow, penniless, for Nice to see Dr Williams;[2] the only medical for me in these regions. I am now in the position of the ship's doctor in *Roderick Random* and may cry 'O my lungs and liver!'[3] The health is a putrid thing, to be sure.

About the Rhône, I know nothing as yet, but will let *you* know as soon as I do.[4]

If Louisa and the baby come,[5] we can get them a room alongside, and they can mess in the hut and enjoy our one luxury, the unrivalled garden.

The size of the hut precludes the acceptance of infants within its sacred walls; and the *bonne*, when sounded, threatened to go. But the Continental is our next neighbour and Weber has promised to give us rooms whenever we require them for guests. Four people and four only are to be admitted within the walls; yourself, Colvin, Henley and Baxter. No woman and no babe as well as I can understand Fanny; and no other men. Indeed it's not attractive as the spare room is about seven feet square and is the lumber room; it is now full of portmanteaus.

This churlish preface over, for God's sake, try and get money and come and see us: outside or in, you will both, as I am sure you know, be most heartily welcome to both of us. And we can get along pretty cheap. The average of the past month has been about 5.50 a day for household expenses. I have lots of money owing, lots of stuff out, but it won't come in, and I am dunned for my rent and have £5 in pocket to start to Nice

---

[8] A joke name used by George Smith, one of the robbers in *Deacon Brodie*.

[1] RLS stayed for a few days in Lyons on his way back from Royat.

[2] Both RLS and Fanny refer at this time to a Dr Williams of Nice but in 1884 the references are to Dr William Wakefield. On 4 February 1884 Fanny wrote to Baxter – 'As to Dr Williams, there is no such person in Nice'.

[3] In ch. 27 of *Roderick Random*, Mr Morgan, the surgeon's first mate, 'drank off a gill of brandy, sighed grievously three times, poured off an ejaculation of "Got pless my heart, liver, and lungs!" and then began to sing a Welsh song.'

[4] It had been suggested that RLS should make a journey up the Rhône for the *Century*, accompanied by Joseph Pennell who would make sketches.

[5] Bob's daughter, Margaret Mowbray, was born on 30 April 1883.

with. It must soon end; for really I have nearly £250 owing to me; but when and when, will it come? The d—d publishers delay; and my household removes[6] the money ere it comes. I can never get to the good, and, in my opinion, never will.

I was much struck by your last.[7] I have written a breathless note on Realism for Henley;[8] a fifth part of the subject hurriedly touched, which will show you how my thoughts are driving. You are now at last beginning to think upon the problems of executive, plastic art, for you are now for the first time attacking them. Hitherto you have spoken and thought of two things – technique and the *ars artium*, or common background of all arts. Studio work is the real touch. That is the genial error of the present French teaching. Realism, I regard, as a mere question of method. The 'brown foreground', 'old mastery', and the like, ranking with villanelles, as technical sports and pastimes. Real art, whether ideal or realistic, addresses precisely the same feeling, and seeks the same qualities: significance or charm. And the same – very same – inspiration is only methodically differentiated according as the artist is an arrant realist or an arrant idealist. Each, by his own method, seeks to save and perpetuate the same significance or charm: the one by suppressing, the other by forcing, detail. All other idealism is the brown foreground over again, and hence only art in the sense of a game, like cup and ball. All other realism is not art at all – but not at all. It is, then, an insincere and showy handicraft.

Were you to re-read some Balzac, as I have been doing, it would greatly help to clear your eyes. He was a man who never found his method. An inarticulate Shakespeare, smothered under forcible-feeble detail. It is astounding, to the riper mind, how bad he is, how feeble, how untrue, how tedious; and of course, when he surrendered to his temperament, how good and powerful. And yet never plain nor clear. He could not consent to be dull, and thus became so. He would leave nothing undeveloped, and thus drowned out of sight of land amid the multitude of crying and incongruous details. Jesus, there is but one art: to omit! O if I knew how to omit, I would ask no other knowledge. A man who knew how to omit would make an *Iliad* of a daily paper.

Your definition of seeing is quite right. It is the first part of omission to be partly blind. Artistic sight is judicious blindness. Sam Bough must have been a jolly blind old boy. He would turn a corner, look for one half or quarter minute, and then say: 'This'll do, lad.' Down he sat, there and then, with a whole artistic plan, scheme of colour, and the like, and begin by laying a foundation of powerful and seemingly incongruous colour on

---

[6] Possibly 'devours'.

[7] The concluding portion of Bob's letter survives. It discusses at length realism in art and uses the phrases RLS quotes in this paragraph.

[8] 'A Note on Realism' was published in the *Magazine of Art* for November 1883.

the block. He saw, not the scene, but the water colour sketch. Every artist by sixty should so behold nature. Where does he learn that? In the studio, I swear. He goes to nature for facts, relations, values – material; as a man, before writing a historical novel, reads up memoirs. But it is not by reading memoirs, that he has learned the selective criterion. He has learned that in the practice of his art; and he will never learn it well, but when disengaged from the ardent struggle of immediate representation, of realistic and *ex facto* art. He learns it in the crystallisation of day dreams; in changing not in copying fact; in the pursuit of the ideal, not in the study of nature. These temples of art are, as you say, inaccessible to the realistic climber. It is not by looking at the sea that you get
'The multitudinous seas incarnadine';[9]
nor by looking at Mont Blanc that you find
'Visited all night by troops of stars.'[10]
A kind of ardour of the blood is the mother of all this; and according as this ardour is swayed by knowledge and seconded by craft, the art expression flows clear, and significance and charm, like a moon rising, are born above the barren juggle of mere symbols.

The painter must study more from nature than the man of words. But why? Because literature deals with men's business and passions which, in the game of life, we are irresistibly obliged to study; but painting with relations of light and colour and significances and form which, from the immemorial habit of the race, we pass over with an unregardful eye. Hence this crouching upon campstools, and these crusts.[11] But neither one nor other is a part of art; only preliminary studies.

The reason why prating about art is so unprofitable is because the significance and charm which are its essence cannot be more than hinted at, and then only by subsidiary works of art. Hence the marrow of the business gets neglected; and we get grammar, signifying nothing.

I want you to help me to get people to understand that realism is a method, and only methodic in its consequences; when the realist is an artist, that is, and supposing the idealist, with whom you compare him, to be anything but a *farceur* and a *dilettante*. The two schools of working do, and should, lead to the choice of different subjects. But that is a consequence, not a cause. See my chaotic note, which will appear, I fancy, in November in Henley's sheet.

Poor Ferrier, it bust me horrid. He was, after you, the oldest of my friends.

[9] *Macbeth*, II.ii.62.
[10] Bob wrote that he had been reading Coleridge and quoted this and the preceding line from 'Hymn before Sunrise in the Vale of Chamouni', with the comment, 'It is a most daring work and to which our friend Realism will never lead.'
[11] *Crôutes*: crude studies from nature (Colvin).

I am now very tired and will go to bed, having prelected freely. Fanny will finish.

★ *To Henrietta Milne*[1]

[*? 23 October 1883*]   *La Solitude*

My dear Henrietta, Certainly; who else would they be?[2] More by token, on that particular occasion, you were sailing under the title of Princess Royal; I, after a furious contest, under that of Prince Alfred; and Willie, still a little sulky, as the Prince of Wales. We were all in a buck basket about halfway between the swing and the gate; and I can still see the Pirate Squadron heave in sight upon the weather bow.

I wrote a piece besides on Giant Bunker: but I was not happily inspired, and it is condemned.[3] Perhaps I'll try again; he was a horrid fellow, Giant Bunker! and some of my happiest hours were passed in pursuit of him. You were a capital fellow to play: how few there were who could! None better than yourself. I shall never forget some of the days at Bridge of Allan; they were one golden dream: see 'A Good Boy' in the *Penny Whistles*, much of the sentiment of which is taken direct from one evening at B. of A. when we had had a great play with the little Glasgow girl. Hallowed be that fat book of fairy tales! Do you remember acting the Fair One with Golden Locks? What a romantic drama! generally speaking, whenever I think of play, it is pretty certain that you will come into my head. I wrote a paper called 'Child's Play' once,[4] where, I believe, you or Willie would recognise things.

Yesterday I had toothache, and today I have a crick in my neck. These are details, but eloquent to me.

I wonder why Willie will be such an ass? he should be made to holiday – *Willie*-nilly. Tell him to write me a letter and I will answer it. I am taking my vacations at present, because of yesterday's toothache; my vacations generally last for twenty-four hours; but some day I mean to have a real [ ][5] in idleness. Now when the work is stopped, the letters begin.

---

[1] Henrietta Traquair (1850–1902) and her brother William (1851–1923) were the children of MIS's sister Henrietta (1828–55) and Ramsay Traquair, a farmer at Colinton; they were close childhood companions of RLS and are commemorated in one of the Envoys to *A Child's Garden*. Henrietta married James Milne in 1873.

[2] Henrietta had been reading *Penny Whistles*, the privately printed trial issue of *A Child's Garden*, a pamphlet of forty-eight poems. She recognised herself and her brother in 'A Pirate Story'.

[3] The MS of six lines of verse beginning 'The Giant Bunker, great and grim' is at Yale. It includes the line 'Will had a crossbow Puss a sword'. 'Puss' was a family nickname for Henrietta in childhood.

[4] Published in the *Cornhill Magazine* in September 1878 and reprinted in *Virginibus Puerisque*.

[5] Left blank in the printed text.

But what I want to know is, How about Mrs William Traquair? Surely Willie is just the man to marry; and if his wife wasn't a happy woman, I think I could tell her who was to blame. Is there no word of it?[6] Well, these things are beyond arrangement: and the wind bloweth where it listeth[7] – which, I observe, is generally toward the west in Scotland. Here it prefers a south-easterly course and is called the Mistral – usually with an adjective in front. But if you will remember my yesterday's toothache and this morning's crick, you will be in a position to choose an adjective for yourself. Not that the wind is unhealthy; only when it comes strong, it is both very high and very cold, which makes it the d-v-l. But as I am writing to a lady I had better avoid this topic; winds requiring a great scope of language.

Please remember me to all at home; give Ramsay[8] a pennyworth of acidulated drops for his good taste. And believe me, your affectionate cousin   Robert Louis Stevenson

To Mrs Milne, Colinton Road, Edinburgh.

★To Sidney Colvin

[*Early November 1883*]   *La Solitude*

Colvin, Colvin, Colvin, Yours received; also interesting copy of *P. Whistles*.[1] 'In the multitude of councillors the Bible declares there is wisdom,' said my great-uncle,[2] 'but I have always found in them distraction.' It is extraordinary how tastes vary; these proofs have been handed about it appears, and I have had several letters; and – distraction. *Aesop: the Miller and the Ass.*[3]

Notes on details:–[4]

---

[6] William Traquair married Cecilia Ross Munro on 11 June 1884. When the news of the engagement reached RLS in December 1883, Fanny wrote to MIS: 'He was much excited and pleased over the news, and wrote instantly to Willie Traquair'.

[7] John 3:8.

[8] Henrietta's son, Ramsay Traquair Milne (1879–1910).

[1] This copy of *Penny Whistles* contains marginal comments by Colvin and Henley.

[2] MIS's maternal uncle John Smith (1800–1880), a Glasgow merchant, and a devout Churchman. Cf. Proverbs 11:14.

[3] The miller and his son, taking their ass to the fair to sell it, get conflicting advice from passers-by and the ass is accidentally killed. The fable concludes with the miller's reflection 'that by endeavouring to please everybody he had pleased nobody, and lost his ass into the bargain.' RLS refers to the fable in *Travels with a Donkey*, 'Cheylard and Luc'.

[4] Colvin had commented on these five poems:
  (1) 'Looking Forward'. 'Jerky metre. I don't think the dropping of a first syllable suddenly at the beginning of a line is permissible in a set of poems like this.' Henley disagreed: 'Don't matter a bit.'

1. I love the occasional trochaic line; and so did many excellent writers before me.

2. If you don't like 'A Good Boy', I do.

3. In 'Escape at Bedtime', I found two suggestions. 'Shone' for 'above' is a correction of the press; it was so written. 'Twinkled' is just the error; to the child the stars appear to be there; any word that suggests illusion is a horror.

4. I don't care: I take a different view of the vocative.

5. Bewildering and childering are good enough for me. These are rhymes, jingles; I don't go for eternity and the three unities.

I will delete some of those condemned, but not all.[5] I don't care for the name *Penny Whistles*; I sent a sheaf to Henley when I sent 'em. But I've forgot the others. I would just as soon call 'em *Rimes for Children*, as anything else. I am not proud nor particular.

Your remarks on the *Black Arrow* are to the point. I am pleased you liked Crookback; he is a fellow whose hellish energy has always fixed my attention. I wish Shakespeare had written the play after he had learned some of the rudiments of literature and art rather than before. Some day, I will re-tickle the *Sable Missile*, and shoot it, *moyennant finance*, once more into the air; I can lighten it of much, and devote some more attention to Dick o' Gloucester. It's great sport to write tushery.

By this I reckon you will have heard of my proposed excursiolorum to the Isles of Greece, the Isles of Greece, and kindred sites. If the excursiolorum goes on, that is, if *moyennant finances* comes off, I shall write to beg you to collect introductiolorums for me. The introductiolorum being, I am led to believe, a bed-rock necessary in the Isles of Greece, the Isles of Greece.[6]

Distinguo: 1. *Silverado* was not written in America, but in Switzerland's icy mountains. 2. What you read is the bleeding and disembowelled

---

(2) 'A Good Boy'. Colvin called it 'priggish' and suggested deletion. Henley agreed.

(3) 'Escape at Bedtime'. In the second verse, Colvin amended the printed text from 'These above' to 'shone above'. RLS had written 'These shone'. In the next line of the poem Colvin suggested 'Twinkled half full' instead of 'would be half full'.

(4) 'The Wind'. Against the last line Colvin commented: 'It won't do: the vocative demands a second person in the verb: "singest"; or else the line must be differently turned.'

(5) 'Good and Bad Children'. Colvin called the rhyming of 'bewildering' with 'children' 'Cockney rhyme'. Henley added: 'Cf. Keats and Mrs Browning.'

[5] RLS dropped nine of the forty-eight poems in *Penny Whistles*. They were reprinted in the privately printed Widener Catalogue (1913) and first published in the limited edition of A *Child's Garden* produced by the Press in Tuscany Alley, San Francisco, 1978. Colvin suggested omission of 'System', 'The Lamplighter' – 'the lamplighter being an extinct animal to the modern child' – and described 'The Swing' as 'commonplace.'

[6] In October Lippincott's, the American publishers, had invited RLS to make a tour of the Greek Islands and to write a book about it. He was excited by the idea, but there was disagreement over the financial arrangements and he rejected their terms.

remains of what I wrote. 3. The good stuff is all to come – so I think. 'The Sea Fog', 'The Hunter's Family', 'Toils and Pleasures' – *belles pages.* Yours ever   Ramnugger

O! – Seeley is a man of hell's talent; I went insane over his book; he is too clever to live, and the book a gem.[7] But why has he read too much Arnold? Why will he avoid – obviously avoid – fine writing up to which he has led? This is a winking, curled-and-oiled, ultra-cultured, Oxford-don sort of an affectation, that infuriates my honest soul. 'You see' – they say – 'how unbombastic *we* are; we come right up to eloquence, and, when it's hanging on the pen, dammy, we scorn it!' It is literary Deronda-ism. If you don't want the woman, the image, or the phrase, mortify your vanity and avoid the appearance of wanting them.

To Charles Baxter[1]

Toddy Vale
[Postmark 7 December 1883]   *by Kilrummer*

Thomson, It's done. I'm a dissenter. I kenned fine frae the beginning hoo it would a' end; I saw there was nae justice for auld Johnstone. The last I tauld ye, they had begun a clash aboot the drink. O sic a disgrace! when, if onything, I rayther drink less nor mair since yon damned scandal aboot the blue ribbon. I took the scunner as faur back as that, Thomson; and O man, I wuss that I had just left the estayblishment that very day! But no; I was aye loyal like them that went afore me.

Weel, the ither day, up comes yon red-heedit, pishion-faced creeter – him a minister! 'Mr Johnstone,' says he, 'I think it my duty to tell 'ee that there's a most unpleisand fama[2] aboot you.' 'Sir,' says I, 'they take a pleesure to persecute me. What is't noo?'

What was't? Man, Thomson, I think shame to write it: *No Bony-Feed wi' the plate.*[3] Is'n that peetiful? The auld, auld story! The same weary, auld, havering claver[4] 'at they tauld aboot Sandie Sporran – him that was

---

[7] Colvin had sent RLS J.R. Seeley's recently published *The Expansion of England.*
[1] Sent under cover of a business letter beginning: 'Dear C.B., I inclose a further bulletin of the great crash of Johnstone.'
[2] In church law, a report of scandalous behaviour (Latin).
[3] Not *bona fide* with the plate. A joke that continued for several years in the Thomson/Johnson saga that one of them had stolen money from the plate used to collect contributions from members of the congregation. In March 1881 RLS wrote to Baxter: 'Man, yon was awfu' aboot the plate. I aye tell't ye, ye werenae fit to be an elder. I could see your elbow yeukin ower a fat collection; your moo wad be hingin' doon an' your e'e fair dazed; "Dod," says I, "yon's no a man to be sae near the plate." '
[4] Nonsensical chatter or gossip.

subsekently hanged, ye'll mind. And wi me – hoo improabable! But it a comes o' that silly hash aboot my brither Sandy's trust: a thankless office, the trustees!

Whatever, I saw that I was by wi't. Says I, 'I leave the Kirk.' 'Well,' says he, 'I think youre parfitly richt' and a wheen mair maist unjudeecial and unjudeecious observations. Noo, I'm a Morisonian,[5] an I like it fine. We're a sma' body, but unco tosh.[6] The prezentar's auld, tae; an' if ye'll meet in wi' our opeenions – some o' them damned hetrodox by my way o't, but a body cannae have a'thing – I mak nae mainner o' doobt but what ye micht succeed him. I'm a great light in the body; much sympathy was felt for me generally among the mair leeberal o' a' persuasions: a man at my time o' life and kent sae lang!   Aw. Johnstone

P.S. I'll hae to pay for the wean. In a so-ca'd Christian country! Mercy me!

To W.E. Henley

[Mid-December 1883]   [Hyères]

My dear lad, Yours to hand. Cricket gone a long while ago. I inclose a note written to Pollock under the sure belief, as you will see, that it was of his confection: a belief my wife shared. We fall from our height in hearing it is yours; but I am none the less pleased to be able to say that of all the reviews I ever had, it is the one that has given me the greatest pleasure; I have read it, I believe five times; and my wife thrice. It is a gem – for an author: to feel a critic accurately take his points.[1]

Of course my seamanship is jimmy; did I not beseech you I know not how often to find me an ancient mariner – and you whose own wife's own brother is one of the ancientest, did nothing for me?[2] As for my seamen, did Runciman ever know 18th Century Buccaneers? No? Well, no more did I. But I have known and sailed with seamen too, and lived and eaten with them; and I made my put-up shot in no great ignorance, but as a put-up thing has to be made; i.e. to be coherent and picturesque, and damn the expense. Are they fairly lively on the wires? Then, favour

[5] A member of the Evangelical Union founded (1843) by James Morison (1816–93).
[6] Very comfortable or happy.
[1] *Treasure Island* had been published on 14 November to a chorus of praise. Henley reviewed it anonymously in the *Saturday Review* of 8 December. RLS thought the review was by W.H. Pollock, who in a private letter had said that he thought *Treasure Island* was 'the best book that has appeared since *Robinson Crusoe*'. Walter Herries Pollock (1850–1926), journalist and author, was the editor of the *Saturday Review* 1883–94.
[2] Captain Boyle (see p. 142, n. 3).

me with your tongues.[3] Are they wooden, and dim, and no sport? Then it is I that am silent. Otherwise not. The work, strange as it may sound in the ear, is not a work of realism. The next thing I shall hear is that the etiquette is wrong in Otto's court! With a warrant, and I mean it to be so, and the whole matter never cost me half a thought. I make these paper people to please myself, and Skelt, and God Almighty, and with no ulterior purpose. Yet am I mortal myself; for as I remind you, I begged for a supervisory mariner. However my heart is in the right place. I have been to sea, but I never crossed the threshold of a court; and by God, the courts shall be the way I want 'em.

I'm devilish glad to think I owe you the review that pleased me best of all the reviews I ever had; the one I liked best before that was Pollock's on the *Arabians*.[4] These two are the flowers of the collection according to me. To live reading such reviews and die eating ortolans – sich is my aspiration.[5]

> 'Nor' West Passage: a Memory of Childhood'[6]
> or 'A Childish Memory', *comme vous voudrez*.

Whenever you come you will be equally welcome. I am trying to finish *Otto* ere you shall arrive, so as to take and be able to enjoy a well-earned, – O yes, a well-earned – holiday. Longman fetched by *Otto*:[7] is it a spoon or a spoilt horn? Momentous, if the latter: if the former, a spoon to dip much praise and pudding,[8] and to give, I do think, much pleasure. The last part, now in hand, much smiles upon me.

Railway fare, to come and go, need not I think exceed some £7. The friendly Cook will best equip you; as it is a great saving of trouble, and his second class tickets for such long distances entitle you to travel in the first class trains: a great boon and economy in one. If you come with C.B. you will sleep in the hotel hard by, and it will cost summat; if you come *solus*, we must try to rig you up the spare bedroom: a strange and noisome cupboard, with the one advantage of not costing anything.

How are your blame family? You never say anything: nothing about the Châtelaine, or Anthony or Edward John Trelawney,[9] or your Mother or any mortal being. Ever yours   R.L.S.

---

[3] I.e. keep silent. Cf. 'Favete linguis', Horace, *Odes*, III.i.2.

[4] A review of *New Arabian Nights* in the *Saturday Review* of 19 August 1882.

[5] Cf. 'Let me die eating ortolans to the sound of soft music!' – Disraeli, *The Young Duke* (1831), Book I, ch. 10.

[6] RLS had sent Henley some additional poems for *A Child's Garden*; one of them, 'North-West Passage' was published in the *Magazine of Art* for March 1884.

[7] Earlier in the month RLS had offered *Prince Otto* to Charles Longman for his magazine and sent him a portion of the MS. Charles James Longman (1852–1934) entered the family firm in 1874, became a partner in 1877, and continued as partner and later a director until his retirement in 1928. He edited *Longman's Magazine* 1882–1905.

[8] Cf. 'And solid pudding against empty praise' – Pope, *The Dunciad*, Book I, l. 52.

[9] Henley's actor brother Edward John (Teddy) Henley (1860–98).

Your grub either way will not cost you much: I have views on that point and when we can't dine at home, or C.B. doesn't entertain at his hostelry, I have unearthed a restaurant.

To his Father

20 December 1883   [*Hyères*]

My dear Father, I do not know which of us is to blame, I suspect it is you this time. The last accounts of you were pretty good, I was pleased to see; I am, on the whole, very well – suffering a little still from my fever and liver complications but better.

I have just finished reading a book which I counsel you above all things *not* to read; as it has made me very ill and would make you worse: Lockhart's *Scott*. It is worth reading, as all things are from time to time, that keep us nose to nose with fact, though I think such reading may be abused, and that a great deal of life is better spent in reading of a light and yet chivalrous strain. Thus no Waverley novel approaches in power, blackness, bitterness and moral elevation to the diary and Lockhart's narrative of the end; and yet the Waverley novels are better reading for every day than the life. You may take a tonic daily, but not phlebotomy.

The great double danger of taking life too easily, and taking it too lightly, how hard it is to balance that! But we are all too little inclined to faith; we are all, in our serious moments, too much inclined to forget that all are sinners and fall justly by their faults, and therefore that we have no more to do with that than with the thundercloud; only to trust, and do our best, and wear as smiling a face as may be for others and ourselves. But there is no royal road among this complicated business. Hegel, the German, got the best word of all philosophy with his antinomies: the contrary of everything is its postulate. That is, of course, grossly expressed, but gives a hint of the idea, which contains a great deal of the mysteries of religion, and a vast amount of the practical wisdom of life. For your part, there is no doubt as to your duty: to take things easy and be as happy as you can, for your sake, and my mother's, and that of many besides.

Excuse this sermon. Ever your loving son   R.L.S.[1]

---

[1] In his reply, of 23 December, TS wrote:

> As to Hegel and his 'secret' I really know nothing but the only prescription which I know for black views of life is the Gospel of Jesus Christ and when that doesn't light up the scene I fear Hegel is not likely to do so . . . I have reread your letter about Hegel and Lockhart. I have read the latter and have rather a pleasant recollection of it. But I admit *the end* is not a pleasant recollection – the fact is Sir W. did not cultivate religion. He did not pay much attention to it and did not consequently get much comfort from it in this world. He seemed to know nothing of St Paul's finality. 'Finally *rejoice* in the Lord.' [Philippians 3:1]

To his Mother

Last Sunday of 83 [30 December]   *[Hyères]*

My dear Mother, I give my father up. I give him a parable: that the
Waverley novels are better reading for every day, than the tragic life. And
he takes it backside foremost, and shakes his head, and is gloomier than
ever. Tell him that I give him up. I don't want no such a parent. This is
not the man for my money. I do not call that by the name of religion,
which fills a man with bile − and I may add stupidity. I write him a whole
letter, bidding him beware of extremes, and telling him that his gloom is
gallowsworthy; and I get back an answer − Perish the thought of it.

Here am I on the threshold of another year, when according to all
human foresight I should long ago have been resolved into my elements;
here am I, who you were persuaded was born to disgrace you and I will
do you the justice to add, on no such insufficient grounds, no such
burning discredit when all is done; here am I married against everybody's
wishes, and the marriage recognized to be a blessing of the first order, A.l.
at Lloyd's. There is he, at his not first youth, able to take more exercise
than I at thirty-three, and gaining a stone's weight, a thing of which I am
incapable. There are you: has the man no gratitude? There is Smeorock:[2]
is he blind? Tell him from me that all this

is

NOT THE TRUE BLUE

!

I will think more of his prayers, when I see in him a spirit of *praise*. Piety
is a more childlike and happy attitude than he admits. Martha, Martha, do
you hear the knocking at the door? But Mary was happy. Even the
Shorter Catechism, not the merriest epitome of religion, and a work
exactly as pious although not quite so true as the multiplication table, −
even that dryasdust epitome begins with a heroic note. What is man's
chief end?[1] Let him study that; and ask himself if to refuse to enjoy God's
kindest gifts, is in the spirit indicated. Up Dullard! It is better service to
enjoy a novel than to mump.

I have been most unjust to the Shorter Catechism, I perceive. I wish to
say that I keenly admire its merits as a performance; and that all that was
in my mind was its peculiarly unreligious and unmoral texture: from
which defect, it can never, of course, exercise the least influence on the

---

[1] Cf. RLS's comment in 'The Foreigner at Home', contrasting the English and Scottish rival
catechisms: '. . . the English tritely inquiring "What is your name?" the Scottish striking at the
very roots of life with, "What is the chief end of man?" and answering nobly, if obscurely, "To
glorify God and to enjoy Him for ever."'
[2] A favourite family dog.

mind of children. But they learn fine style and some austere thinking, unconsciously.

I have been spitting blood for a week and wrote no letters. It has now stopped. The efficient cause was Uncle George's Iodide: it is strange how that drug poisons me. But the chemist's wife here is equally susceptible to – what do you fancy? – to the mild, comfortable and domestic ginger. A happy new year to all, and may Mr Despondency cheer up. God bless you all. Ever your loving son   R.L.S.

Particularly thank the Samuel Boy for a charming letter.[3]

To David A. Stevenson

31 December 1883   *La Solitude*

My dear Davie, At the beginning of the end of this year, I had many thoughts of the past, many of yourself, and many of your mother,[1] who was the idol of my childhood. I had it in my mind to write to Uncle David, but I thought it might be merely an importunate intrusion, and decided to write rather to yourself.

The way in which life separates people is very painful. It is many a year since we had a New Year's walk; but I have not forgotten the past, and your mother I shall never forget. I am profoundly a Stevenson in the matter of not giving presents. Once only that I can remember did I, of my own motion, give a present: and that was before '57, when I 'asked leave' to give a present to Aunt Elizabeth. I do not suppose that a greater testimony could be given to her extraordinary charm and kindness. I never saw anybody like her: a look from Aunt Elizabeth was like sunshine.

Please excuse this very blundering scrawl; understand what is unsaid; and accept, for yourself and all in the family, my most sincere good wishes, Your affectionate cousin   Robert Louis Stevenson

★   ★   ★

Charles Baxter and W.E. Henley paid their long-promised visit to Hyères during the first week of January 1884. La Solitude was too small for the proper entertainment of these guests and (although far from well) RLS proposed that the four should go away together. On 12 January they travelled to Monaco and Monte Carlo and thence to Mentone; they returned by way of Nice. Here RLS caught what at first seemed to be a

---

[3] Lloyd was spending Christmas at 17 Heriot Row.
[1] Elizabeth Stevenson (*née* Mackay, 1816–71), wife of TS's brother David whom she married in 1840.

slight cold, but soon after Baxter and Henley had left the illness took a far more serious turn and at one point his life seemed to be in danger. Fanny bombarded Baxter with letters and telegrams begging for someone to come out to help her. Bob Stevenson accordingly went out to Nice in early February and as RLS slowly recovered, although still weak, managed to get him back to Hyères in mid-February.

★   ★   ★

To his Parents

[c. 6 *February 1884*]   [*Nice*]

My dear people, I inclose American reviews.[1] I keep improving, and hope soon to get back to Hyères where I much desire to be. I am reading St Augustine's *Confessions*; it is magnificent but I find the Latin very hard. I have a bad French crib to help me, but no dictionary.[2] I believe Uncle Alan swore by the work; it is certainly one of the most remarkable books I ever read.   R.L.S.

The news about Baker just in; of course it dooms Gordon, and the rest.[3] God will require these lives at the hand of that old man. I would rather be a louse this day than W.E. Gladstone. I give up this government. I think they should be ranged against a wall and shot.

---

[1] Of the *Silverado Squatters*. The book was published by Chatto on 8 January and later in the month in America by Roberts Brothers.

[2] RLS's marked copy of a French translation of St Augustine by Robert Arnauld d'Andilly (1589–1674) is at Yale. One of RLS's marginal notes reads: 'Arnauld is a common ass, he misses every merit of this author; I speak as a writer by trade.'

[3] The fanatical religious leader called the Mahdi had stirred up a nationalist revolt against Egyptian rule in the Soudan. The Liberal Government under Gladstone – effective rulers of Egypt since 1882 – decided not to involve British troops and after much indecision despatched General Charles Gordon (1833–85) to the Soudan with the near impossible task of evacuating the threatened Egyptian garrisons. Gordon reached Khartoum on 18 February; differences arose between him and the Government over the interpretation of his instructions and within a month he was besieged in Khartoum. Meanwhile on the Red Sea Coast near Suakin, the Mahdi's lieutenant, Osman Digna, had routed an ill-disciplined Egyptian force led by General Valentine Baker (1827–87) near El-Teb on 4 February. There was intense public feeling about the disaster. It was felt that if the Egyptians were unable to defeat the Soudanese under such favourable circumstances, they had no chance of holding the Soudan or even of evacuating their garrisons without support from British troops. Fears were also expressed about the personal safety of Gordon.

To his Mother

[*February 1884*]   [*Nice*]

My dear Mother, I see I must explain the whole affair to you. I have had
an acute illness, a fit of some hours of shuddering and vomiting, followed
by fever, delirium and congestion of lungs, kidneys and liver. I survived,
where a stronger man would not. There never were two opinions as to
my immediate danger; of course it was chuck farthing for my life. That
is over and I have only weakness to contend against. Wakefield[1] attended
me throughout with great kindness, and called in, of his own notion,
Drummond[2] to consult.

Neither one nor other can give any opinion as to my general health,
having only seen me in this illness. Only Vidal[3] when I get back to Hyères
will be able to tell what I have lost. I believe it will not be much. I very
nearly died of course; but I am making a good recovery. But if you have
a curiosity to know Drummond's opinion, he volunteered it; he told me
to leave off wine, to regard myself as 'an old man', and to 'sit by my fire'.
None of which I wish to do.

We have now made a kind of peace between Drummond and
Wakefield; each of whom swore that the other had promised him this
affair.

But now I hope you understand exactly. I had an *acute* illness, from
which I am now slowly but steadily recovering. And as for my general
health – as for my consumption – we can learn nothing till Vidal sees me,
but I believe the harm is little. My lungs are so tough. Ever your
affectionate son   R.L. Stevenson

To Sidney Colvin

9 March 1884   *La Solitude*

My dear S.C., You will already have received a not very sane note from
me; so your patience was rewarded – may I say, your patient silence?
However now comes a letter, which on receipt, I thus acknowledge.

I have already expressed myself as to the political aspect. About

---

[1] Dr William Wakefield (?1841–98), a former military surgeon, at this time spent the winter in
Nice and the summer in Aix-les-Bains. He was the author of *The Happy Valley: Sketches of
Kashmir and the Kashmiris* (1879) and *Our Life and Travels in India* (1878).
[2] James Drummond, Promenade des Anglais, Nice. M.D. St Andrews, 1852 and L.R.C.S.
Edinburgh, 1845.
[3] L.-Emp. Vidal, RLS's regular doctor at Hyères. Fanny called him 'a curious navy man; and I
think very clever'.

Graham, I feel happier; it does seem to have been really a good, neat, honest piece of work.[1] We do not seem to be so badly off for commanders: Wolseley and Roberts[2] (both perhaps a little hit-or-missy) and this pile of Woods, Stewarts, Alisons,[3] Grahams, and the like. Had we but ONE statesman on any side of the house. Parnell is an attorney: Forster a wooden moralist: Randy a journalist; Northcote a very honourable muff: Chamberlain a swindler; and Gladstone a man of fog,[4] evasions (to himself and others – not always alas! too clearly honest) and a general deliquescence of the spine. A sad tableau. 'And equally a want of books and men.'[5]

Two chapters of *Otto* do remain: one to rewrite, one to create; and I am not yet able to tackle them. For me, it is my chief o' works; hence probably not so for others: since it only means that I have here attacked the greatest difficulties. But some chapters towards the end: three in particular – I do think come off. I find them stirring, dramatic and not unpoetical. We shall see, however. As like as not, the effort will be more obvious than the success. For of course, I strung myself hard to carry it out. The next will come easier, and possibly be more popular. I believe in the covering of much paper: each time with a definite and not too difficult artistic purpose; and then from time to time, drawing oneself up and trying, in a superior effort, to combine the facilities thus acquired or improved. Thus one progresses. But mind, it is very likely that the big effort, instead of being the masterpiece, may be the blotted copy, the

---

[1] In February 1884 a British force commanded by Sir Gerald Graham (1831–99), was sent to Suakin in an attempt to retrieve the situation following Baker's defeat. Graham defeated Osman Digna at El Teb on 29 February and at Tamai on 13 March. The Soudanese fought with incredible bravery and disregard for their own lives.

[2] The two greatest British generals of the period. Sir Garnet Joseph Wolseley (1833–1913) crushed the rebellion of the Egyptian army at Tel-el-Kebir and occupied Cairo in 1882. He led the abortive Gordon relief expedition 1884–5. Sir Frederick Sleigh Roberts (1832–1914) was famous for his march from Kabul to Kandahar in the Afghan war in 1880. He succeeded Wolseley as Commander-in-Chief of the British army in 1900.

[3] British soldiers associated with Egypt. Sir Henry Evelyn Wood (1838–1919), first British Commander-in-Chief of the Egyptian army 1882–5; Sir Herbert Stewart (1843–85) took part in the Suakin expedition and was killed during the Gordon relief expedition; Sir Archibald Alison (1826–1907) fought at Tel-el-Kebir and commanded the army of occupation in Egypt 1882–3.

[4] Gladstone's second Liberal administration was in office 1880–85. Charles Stewart Parnell (1846–91) was the great Irish Nationalist leader whose party often held the balance of power in the House of Commons. William Edward Forster (1818–1916) was Chief Secretary for Ireland 1880–82, but resigned in disagreement with Government policy. Lord Randolph Churchill (1849–95), Sir Winston's father, a lively and pugnacious advocate of 'Tory Democracy', gained great popularity for his attacks both on Gladstone and the official leadership of his own party. Sir Stafford Northcote (1818–87), later Lord Iddesleigh, was leader of the Conservative opposition in the House of Commons 1880–85. Joseph Chamberlain (1836–1914), father of Neville, was President of the Board of Trade 1880–85; he left the Liberals on the Irish Home Rule issue in 1886.

[5] The last line of Wordsworth's sonnet, 'Great Men Have Been Among Us'. 'And' should be 'But'.

gymnastic exercise. This no man can tell; only the brutal and licentious public, snouting in Mudie's wash-trough, can return a dubious answer.

I am today, thanks to a pure heaven and a beneficent, loud-talking, antiseptic mistral, on the high places as to health and spirits. Money holds out wonderfully. Fanny has gone for a drive to certain meadows which are now one sheet of jonquils: sea-board meadows, the thought of which may freshen you in Bloomsbury. 'Ye have been fresh and fair. Ye have been filled with flowers' – I fear I misquote.[6] Why do people babble? Surely Herrick, in his true vein, is superior to Martial himself: though Martial is a very pretty poet.

Did you ever read St Augustine? The first chapters of the *Confessions* are marked by a commanding genius: Shakespearian in depth. I was struck dumb; but alas! when you begin to wander into controversy, the poet drops out. His description of infancy is most seizing. And how is this: '*Sed majorum nugae negotia vocantur; puerorum autem talia cum sint puniuntur a majoribus.*' Which is quite after the heart of R.L.S. See also his splendid passage about the '*luminosus limes amicitiae*' and the '*nebulae de limosa concupiscentia carnis*'; going on 'Utrumque *in confuso aestuabat et rapiebat inbecillam aetatem per abrupta cupiditatum.*' That is dam knowing for a Father of the Kirk. Altogether an interesting card. That '*Utrumque*' is a real contribution to life's science. Lust *alone* is but a pigmy; but it never or rarely attacks us single handed.[7]

Do you ever read (to go miles off indeed) the incredible Barbey d'Aurevilly?[8] A Psychological Poe – to be for a moment Henley. I own with pleasure I prefer him with all his folly, rot, sentiment and mixed metaphors, to the whole modern school in France. It makes me laugh, when it's nonsense; and when he gets an effect (though it's still nonsense and mere Poëry – not poesy) it wakens me. *Ce qui ne meurt pas* nearly killed me with laughing, and left me – well, it left me very nearly admiring the old ass. At least, it's the kind of thing, one feels one couldn't do. The dreadful moonlight, when they all three sit silent in the room – by George, sir, it's imagined, and the brief scene between the husband and wife is all there. *Quant au fond*, the whole thing of course is a fever dream and worthy of eternal laughter. Had the young man broken stones, and

---

[6] The opening lines of Herrick's 'To Meadows': 'fair' should be 'green'.
[7] Book I, ch. IX: 'But elder folk's idleness is called "business"; that of boys, being really the same is punished by those elders.' Book II, ch. II: 'And what was it that I delighted in, but to love and be beloved? but I kept not the measure of love, of mind to mind, *friendship's bright boundary;* but out of the *muddy concupiscence of the flesh,* and the bubblings of youth, mists fumed up which beclouded and overcast my heart, that I could not discern the clear brightness of love from the fog of lustfulness. *Both did confusedly boil in me, and hurried my unstayed youth over the precipice of unholy desires*' (Pusey's translation).
[8] Jules-Amédée Barbey d'Aurevilly (1808–89), French journalist, critic and dandy who wrote romantic and extravagant novels. *Ce qui ne meurt pas* had just appeared.

the two women been hard-working, honest prostitutes, there had been an end of the whole immoral and baseless business: you could at least have respected them in that case.

I also read Petronius Arbiter: which is a rum work, not so immoral as most modern works, but singularly silly. I tackled some Tacitus, too. (I got them with a dreadful French crib on the same page with the text, which helps me along and drives me mad. The French do not even try to translate. They try to be much more classical than the classics, with astounding results of barrenness and tedium): Tacitus, I fear, was too solid for me. I liked the war part; but the dreary intriguing at Rome was too much.   R.L.S.

To W.E. Henley

[c. 13 March 1884]   [Hyères]

Dear lad, I was delighted to hear the good news about Teddy:[1] Bravo, he goes uphill fast. Let him beware of vanity, and he will go higher: let him be still discontented, and let him (if it might be) see the merits and not the faults of his rivals, and he may swarm at last to the topgallant. There is no other way. Admiration is the only road to excellence; and the critical spirit kills, but envy and injustice are putrefaction on its feet.

Thus far the moralist. The eager author now begs to know whether you may have got the other Whistles, and whether a fresh proof is to be taken: also whether in that case the dedication should not be printed therewith; Bulk Delights Publishers (original aphorism: to be said sixteen times in succession as a test of sobriety).

Your wild and ravening commands were received; but cannot be obeyed. And anyway, I do assure you I am getting better every day; and if the weather would but turn, I should soon be observed to walk in hornpipes. Truly I am on the mend. I am still very careful. I have the new Bunctionary:[2] a joy, a thing of beauty, and – bulk. I shall be raked i' the mools[3] before it's finished: that is the only pity; but meanwhile I sing.

I beg to inform you that I – Robert Louis Stevenson, author of Brashiana and other works – am merely beginning to commence to prepare to make a first start at trying to understand my profession. O the

---

[1] E.J. Henley had appeared at the Globe Theatre in a successful revival of Henry Hamilton's farce, Our Regiment, followed by other plays. Henley wrote to Baxter on 3 February: 'Ted seems to be doing brilliantly at the Globe.'
[2] Part I (A-Ant) of A New English Dictionary (later called the Oxford English Dictionary) was published on 1 February 1884. The dictionary was completed in 1928.
[3] Buried in the grave. Burns, 'Address to the Toothache', l.21: 'Or worthy friends rak'd i' the mools.'

height and depth of novelty and worth in any art! and O that I am privileged to swim and shoulder through such Oceans! Could one get out of sight of land – all in the blue? Alas not, being anchored here in flesh, and the bonds of logic being still about us. But what a great space and a great air there is, in these small shallows where alone we venture! and how new each sight, squall, calm, or sunrise! An art is a fine fortune, a palace in a park, a band of music, health and physical beauty: all but love – to any worthy practiser. I sleep upon my art for a pillow; I waken in my art: I am unready for death, because I hate to leave it. I love my wife, I do not know how much, nor can, nor shall, unless I lost her; but while I can conceive my being widowed, I refuse the offering of life without my art. I *am* not but in my art: it is me; I am the body of it merely.

And yet I produce nothing, am the author of *Brashiana* and other works: tiddy-idity – as if the works one wrote were anything but prentice's experiments. Dear reader, I deceive you with husks, the real works and all the pleasure are still mine and incommunicable. After this break in my work, beginning to return to it, as from light sleep, I wax exclamatory as you see.

My love to the châtelaine:

Sursum Corda:
Heave ahead:
Here's luck.
Art and Blue Heaven,
April and God's Larks.
Green reeds and the sky-scattering river.
Wilins,[4] *un seul coup*.
A stately music.
Enter God!   R.L.S.

Ay, but you know, until a man can write that 'Enter God', he has made no Art! None!

Come, let us take counsel together and make some!

To Charles Baxter

[*Postmark 14 March 1884*][1]   *La Solitude*

Dear Thomson, I'm glad it's as muckle;[2] it micht be waur. Do ye ken, man Thomson, yon debatchery o' yours at the Coantinental's fair dis-

---

[4] I.e. violins.
[1] The envelope is addressed to 'R. Thomson Esq., c/o Charles Baxter Esq'. Baxter has numbered the letter I.
[2] Baxter noted: '£50 remitted'.

graced me wi' a'body here. I was kind o'respeckit, as it were, or you and Jaikson[3] cam; an noo! Losh, the very weans strone[4] upon the doorstep. They say, Mr Johnstone, ye may be a very decent-like kind of a man yersel but ye keep damd low company whatever – Folk says. An' what can I dae? Naething. Yon freend o' yours, folk says, he'll be a kind of a drouthy customer, I'm thinkin'. What can I say? It's üseless to deny ye were the waur o't. An accident, I says, I never sae muckle's smellt it off him, afore. Ay, they say, it's a kind of a cōmmon accident up your way.

To Charles Baxter[1]

[14 March 1884]   [Hyères]

Thomson, what did I tell ye? What did I hammer in the lugs of ye? Choky; that was what a said – and there ye are. Of coorse, it's a sair affliction to see a man that I hae been ower muckle mixed up wi – no to say, indentifeed – come to sic hōrrible example; but still and on, it's a consolation to ken that, whatever, I dinnae ken the disgrace o' a gaol, airns, an cōmmon malefactors. Be damd, you're in it noo! A bony exhibeetion. O Thomson, and me that has aye befreendit ye! But what did I say? No faurrer back nor Mononday, I said to a fine canty man, Thomson's in the wrang gait, I said, Thomson's fair lost. The warst 'at onybody could say o' me was jist maybe that I had been singl'erly oonfortinate in ma law cases, and had less nar justice frae weeg'd puggies[2] like Deas,[3] so ca'd Lord – a paper Lord! His language was actionable; and him on the bench – a man that should be an example. But even he said that he regretted he had nae poo'er to commit me. Aye the same impotent malice: Deas, and Ingles,[4] and a man they ca'd Hope:[5] Despair wad hae been a better name for him: aye the same story – lōngin' to persecute me and no able – gnashin' their auld stumps on Jōhnson, an' Johnson still defeein' them.

But you're on the justeeshiary side, my buckie. That's beyond a jest. They'll hang you – I tell ye – you'll see. You're by wi'it. And as for that miserable attemp' to get up releegion – Tht, think shame. Ye've been, since ever at I kent ye, a drunkard, a whoremonger, a blasphemer, and

---

[3] The name given to Henley in the Thomson-Johnson saga.
[4] Urinate.
[1] Probably enclosed with the previous letter. Baxter noted: 'II to Thomson in Gaol'.
[2] Monkeys.
[3] Sir George Deas (1804–87), Lord Ordinary of Session with judicial title (i.e. a paper Lord) of Lord Deas, 1853.
[4] John Inglis, Lord Glencorse (1810–91), Lord Justice-General of Scotland. 1867–91.
[5] There was no contemporary Lord of Session named Hope.

mair that I wouldnae like to name, you bein' whaur ye are and your letters likely opened. But ye need fear nae evidence frae me. The deil himsel couldnae harle me into a wutness boax. I've been there ower often, and never heard a ceevil word but frae my ain advocate, and the judges themsel, that should set the example, fair hōrrifyin' me wi their low, wauf expressions: 'Essentially fraudulent', 'ashamed of himsel', 'disgraceful exhibeetion', 'never had heard sic an exhibeetion', 'the defender's evident bād faith', 'the career o' seemin'ly random falsehood', (maist offensive), 'the cruel, heartless and unnatural behaviour of the defendant' (the defendant was aye me; catch me goin' to law if I could win oot of it). 'The defendant's statement' (this was Deas) 'may be dismissed, as not containing one word of truth.' 'The defendant may congrattilate himsel that he escapes a criminal persecution.' The defendant disn't appear for the first time (whae's fau't was that?) before this court; I would ca'tion him no' to appear again; he may not always be so fortinate.' Me that never gained a case. Onyway that's bad language and nae mair. I despise scurreelity – let-a-be frae the Bench. Yours   T. Johnson

To Charles Baxter
(Abridged)

[*15 March 1884*][1]   *La Solitude*

Jist what I said frae the first o't. Leave him alane, I said; nae fear o' Thamson; he'll wun through. Folk here werenae for believin' 't. I ken ye aye said sae, Mr John'son, says they; we ken ye were aye thriepin' 't[2] ower upon us; but wha (says they) wad hae believit? Yon man Thomson! (they says). A man wi physognomy fair brandit wi' drink an' gallows! Hooever, they says, we'll hae to allow that ye were right, Mr John'son, and telled us exac'ly hoo it wad lie.

Eh, man, what a triump! An ovawtion! An' yon Lord Bung[3] (what a bonny name be his!) – a ceevil, daycent Lord! Whaur d's hc sit? Damd, I'll bring an action! Yon's the man for me! But, man, whatten a clan ye got thegither! Jaikson, by all! An' yon plumber! Gude guide us, what's the courts comin' tae. Onyway, ye confused them wi' evidence. But Lord Bung was by ord'nar. Ye may thank your sakes it wasnae Deas or Ingles: they wad hae had Jaikson heels ower cran, ayther one o' them, afore he'd weel begude. I fand a cuttin o' the mōckery o' justice that I had and send

---

[1] Baxter noted: 'III to Thomson after his trial and Glorious Acquittal.'
[2] Asserting vehemently.
[3] Possibly parodying the name of George Young (1819–1907), Scottish judge; Judge of the Court of Session with the title of Lord Young 1874–1905.

it ye.[4] Ye can see what like it was wi' Deas; diffrent from Lord Bung – a true Lord him – a real honest Scotsman – the Lord bless him.

Thomas Johnstone

★To Cosmo Monkhouse[1]

16 March 1884   *La Solitude*

My dear Monkhouse, You see with what promptitude I plunge into correspondence; but the truth is, I am condemned to a complete inaction, stagnate dismally, and love a letter. Yours, which would have been welcome at any time, was thus doubly precious.[2]

Dover sounds somewhat shiveringly in my ears. You should see the weather *I* have – cloudless, clear as crystal, with just a punkah-draft of the most aromatic air, all pine and gum tree. You would be ashamed of Dover, sir; you would scruple to refer, sir, to a spot so paltry. To be idle at Dover is a strange pretension; pray, how do you warm yourself? If I were there I should grind knives or write blank verse, or – But at least you do not bathe? It is idle to deny it: I have – I may say I nourish – a growing jealousy of the robust, large-legged, healthy Britain-dwellers, patient of grog, scorners of the timid umbrella, innocuously breathing fog: all which I once was, and I am ashamed to say liked it. How ignorant is youth! grossly rolling among unselected pleasures; and how nobler, purer, sweeter, and lighter, to sip the choice tonic, to recline in the luxurious invalid chair, and to tread, well-shawled, the little round of the constitutional. Seriously, do you like to repose? Ye gods, I hate it. I never rest with any acceptation; I do not know what people mean who say they like sleep and that damned bedtime which, since long ere I was breeched, has rung a knell to all my day's doings and beings. Some people regimb at death; I do not regimb at death; what I regimb against is sleep and weariness. (I profess this is excellent Walt Whitman.) And when a man, seemingly sane, tells me he has 'fallen in love with stagnation', I can only say to him, 'You will never be a Pirate!' This may not cause any regret to Mrs Monkhouse; but in your own soul it will clang hollow – think of it!

---

[4] I have omitted the enclosure, a long mock account (parodying the legal reports in the *Scotsman*), of the trial of Johnstone, described as 'a solemn, dissipated looking man', before Lord Deas and the cross examination by the Solicitor General. It is headed 'Droll Scene in Court: Pettigrew *v.* Johnstone' and annotated, 'A prevarication of justice! T.J.'

[1] William Cosmo Monkhouse (1840–1901), civil servant, poet and art critic was a regular contributor to the *Magazine of Art*.

[2] Monkhouse, who had heard with great surprise from Henley that RLS would welcome a letter from him, wrote on 13 March, praising *Treasure Island*. He was staying at St Margaret's Bay, Dover, recovering from an illness and 'in love with stagnation'.

Never! After all boyhood's aspirations and youth's immoral day-dreams, you are condemned to sit down, grossly draw in your chair to the fat board, and be a beastly Burgess till you die. Can it be? Is there not some escape, some furlough from the Moral Law, some holiday jaunt contrivable into a Better Land? Shall we never shed blood? D—n! This prospect is too grey.

> Here lies a man who never did
> Anything but what he was bid;
> Who lived his life in paltry ease
> And died of commonplace disease.

To confess plainly, I had intended to spend my life (or any leisure I might have from Piracy upon the high seas) as the leader of a great horde of irregular cavalry, devastating whole valleys. I can still, looking back, see myself in many favourite attitudes; signalling for a boat from my pirate ship with a pocket-handkerchief,[3] I at the jetty end, and one or two of my bold blades keeping the crowd at bay; or else turning in the saddle to look back at my whole command (some five thousand strong) following me at the hand-gallop up the road out of the burning valley: this last by moonlight.

Et point du tout. I am a poor scribe, and have scarce broken a commandment to mention, and have recently dined upon cold veal! As for you (who probably had some ambitions), I hear of you living at Dover, in lodgings, like the beasts of the field. But in Heaven, when we get there, we shall have a good time, and see some real carnage. For Heaven is – must be – that great Kingdom of Antinomia, which Lamb saw dimly adumbrated in the *Country Wife*,[4] where the worm which never dies (the conscience) peacefully expires, and the sinner lies down beside the Ten Commandments. Till then, here a sheer hulk lies poor Tom Bowling, with neither health nor vice for anything more spirited than procrastination, which I may well call the Consolation Stakes of Wickedness; and by whose diligent practice, without the least amusement to ourselves, we can rob the orphan and bring down grey hairs with sorrow to the dust.

This astonishing gush of nonsense I now hasten to close, envelope, and expedite to Shakespeare's Cliff. Remember me to Shakespeare, and believe me, Yours very sincerely   Robert Louis Stevenson[5]

[3] Cf. p. 187, n. 2.
[4] Cf. Lamb's essay 'On the Artificial Comedy of the Last Century'.
[5] Monkhouse wrote a humorous reply (strangely dated 6 January): 'Your letter fills me with terror as to your spiritual condition . . . The miserable weakness of the concluding passage in which you try to make me believe that what you have written is intended for nonsense does not in the least deceive me. You were in earnest, Sir, . . . the phrase of "beastly burgess" could only have been coined by sincerity. . . . No writer of your ability . . . would have committed that terrible catachresis of a beast of the field residing in apartments . . . except under the stress of genuine emotion. Truly you are in a parlous state.'

*To Edmund Gosse

[*17 March 1884*]   *La Solitude*

My dear Gosse, Your office – office is profanely said – your bower upon
the leads is divine.[1] Have you, like Pepys, 'the right to fiddle' there?[2] I see
you mount the companion, barbiton in hand, and, fluttered about by city
sparrows, pour forth your spirit in a voluntary. Now when the spring
begins, you must lay in your flowers: how do you say about a potted
hawthorn? would it bloom? Wallflower is a choice pot-herb; lily-of-the-
valley, too, and carnation; and Indian cress trailed about the window, is
not only beautiful by colour but the leaves are good to eat. I recommend
thyme and rosemary for the aroma, which should not be left upon one
side; they are good quiet growths.

On one of your tables keep a great map spread out: a chart is still better
– it takes one further – the havens with their little anchors, the rocks,
banks and soundings, are adorably marine; and such furniture will suit
your ship-shape habitation. I wish I could see those cabins; they smile
upon me with the most intimate charm. From your leads, do you behold
St Paul's? I always like to see the Foolscap; it is London *per se* and no spot
from which it is visible is without romance. Then it is good company for
the man of letters; whose veritable nursing Pater-Noster is so near at hand.

I am all at a standstill; as idle as a painted ship,[3] but not so pretty. My
romance, which has so nearly butchered me in the writing, not even
finished; though so near, thank God, that a few days of tolerable strength
will see the roof upon that structure.[4] I have worked very hard at it, and
so do not expect any great public favour. *In moments of effort, one learns to
do the easy things that people like.* There is the golden maxim; thus one
should strain and then play, strain again and play again. The strain is for us,
it educates; the play is for the reader, and pleases. Do you not feel so? We
are ever threatened by two contrary faults: both deadly. To sink into what
my forefathers would have called 'rank conformity', and to pour forth
cheap replicas upon the one hand; upon the other, and still more insidi-
ously present, to forget that art is a diversion and a decoration, that no
triumph or effort is of value, nor anything worth reaching except charm.
Yours affectionately   R.L.S.[5]

---

[1] Colvin records that Gosse had written 'describing the office which he then occupied, a picturesque old-fashioned chamber in the upper stories of the Board of Trade'.
[2] In his essay on Pepys, RLS refers to Pepys as 'just the man to lose a night's sleep over some paltry question of his right to fiddle on the leads'. This seems not to be a direct quotation from the diary but a memory of the entries for 29–31 October 1660, when Pepys recorded his distress and lack of sleep because his neighbour locked the door to the leads.
[3] 'As idle as a painted ship/Upon a painted ocean' – Coleridge, 'The Ancient Mariner', Part II.
[4] RLS was able to tell Henley on 7 April, 'I have finished *Otto* and, by this master-stroke, driven the gaunt wolf from the door, where he was already licking his canines with a wrinkled smile.'
[5] Gosse replied on 7 May to what he called 'one of the most charming letters ever written.'

To W.E. Henley

[c. 8 April 1884]   [Hyères]

Dear Henley, The house was illuminated and a bonfire glowed in the southern night in honour of Yates in jail.[1]

> Long may he rot in prison grates,
> Pisonous, Pimping, Pandering Yates.

I beg to inform you that the name of the cycle is changed from *The Man in the Sealskin Coat*[2] to

THE HEAD CENTRE[3]

I beg to inform you that in the southern night before alluded to, I caught cold; that my eyes are on the mend and I hope soon to be able to read; that the *Head Centre* is on the jump . . . ;[4] that someday soon, I'll can tackle *Old Glory*;[5] that Coggie is immense; that I know where you will go to when you die, and now must wait until these pages dry. (Couplet.)

I wish Yates knew I had caught cold over my bonfire; I believe it would console him in his dungeon; and much as I dislike his trade I would not grudge him such alleviations. After all we are all gaol-birds loose; when I go, you may applaud also.

---

[1] Edmund Hodgson Yates (1831–94), novelist and journalist. On 2 April 1884 he was sentenced by the Lord Chief Justice, Lord Coleridge, to four months' imprisonment for libelling the Earl of Lonsdale in the society gossip columns of the *World* (which he had founded in 1874). He appealed against the sentence and it was confirmed in January 1885; because of ill-health he served only eight weeks of it. Fanny says that a candle was lit in each window and she, RLS and Valentine Roch 'clasped hands and danced round the fire, shouting and laughing'. Valentine Roch (?1861–1935), born in Switzerland of French parents, joined the Stevensons as housekeeper in May 1883 and stayed with them as servant and friend for the next six years, travelling as far as Honolulu. She later married a Scotsman, Thomas Brown and spent the rest of her life at Sonoma, California.

[2] The original name given to the collection of stories written in collaboration with Fanny and published in 1885 as *More New Arabian Nights: The Dynamiter*. The germ was evidently the dynamite explosion in the cloakroom at Victoria Station on 27 February 1884. Portmanteaus containing dynamite with clockwork mechanisms which had failed to operate were found the next day at other London railway stations. Fanny says that she made up the stories to amuse RLS during his illness.

[3] Name given to the leader of a Fenian group.

[4] Two or three words heavily deleted.

[5] A play by Henley, formerly called *Husband and Wife*, sent out by the hand of Miss Ferrier who was visiting RLS and Fanny.

You may be surprised to hear that I am now a great writer of verses: that is, however, so. I have the mania now like my betters, and faith if I live till I am forty I shall have a book of filthy rhymes like Pollock, Gosse or whom you please. Really I have begun to learn some of the rudiments of that trade, and have written three or four pretty enough pieces of octosyllabic nonsense, semi-serious, semi-smiling. A kind of prose Herrick, divested of the gift of verse, and you behold the Bard. But I like it.

If I am blown up, it will sell my life: Glory to Henley the great: infinite glory and gold. Pray on your two knees that I be exploded.

Furthermore about the Gold-lover.[6] I believe, . . . [*The rest of the MS is missing*]

To his Mother

[*19 April 1884*]   [*Hyères*]

My dear Mother, Mrs Ferguson has written a quite nice answer. We hasten to tell you this lest you should meet her. This communication is as clearly that of a lady, as the first was not.[1] How to reply I know not; but the great Cassandra[2] bids me be of good cheer and she will pull us through. The great Cassandra is in pretty good feather; I love her better than ever and admire her more; and I cannot think what I have done to deserve so good a gift. This sudden remark came out of my pen; it is not like me; but in case you did not know, I may as well tell you, that my marriage has been the most successful in the world. I say so, and being the child of my parents, I can speak with knowledge.[3] She is everything to me: wife, brother, sister, daughter and dear companion; and I would not change to get a goddess or a saint. So far, after, I think four years of matrimony.   R.L.S.

---

[6] RLS and Henley were exchanging ideas for the play which eventually became *Admiral Guinea* (1884).

[1] For reasons which remain obscure, Fanny had painted views of Royat and Hyères for two Edinburgh ladies – Mrs Ferguson Hume and Mrs MacQueen, but some dispute had arisen apparently over payment.

[2] Cassandra was one of TS's nicknames for Fanny because, like him, she usually took a gloomy view of the future.

[3] In November 1883 RLS had written to his mother: 'As for my wife, that was the best investment ever made by man; but "in our branch of the family" we seem to marry well.'

To W.E. Henley

I have been really ill for two days, hemorrhage, weakness, extreme nervousness that will not let me lie a moment, and damned sciatica o' nights; but today I am on the recovery. Time; for I was miserable. It is not often that I suffer, with all my turns and tumbles, from the sense of serious illness; and I hate it as I believe everybody does. And then the combination of not being able to read, not being allowed to speak, being too weak to write, and not wishing to eat, leaves a man with some empty seconds. But I bless God, it's over for now; today I am much mended.

Insatiable gulph, greedier than hell and more silent than the woods of Styx, have you or have you not, lost the dedication to the *Child's Garden?* Answer that plain question; as otherwise I must try to tackle to it once again.

Sciatica is a word employed much by Shakespeare in a certain connexion. 'Tis true, he was no physician; but as I read, he had smarted in the day. I, too, do smart. And yet this keen soprano agony, these veins of fire and bombshell explosions in the knee, are as nothing to a certain dull, drowsy pain I had when my kidneys were congested at Nice; there was death in that; the creak of Charon's rowlocks, and the miasmas of the Styx. I may say plainly, much as I have lost the power of bearing pain, I had still rather suffer much than die. Not only the love of life grows on me, but the fear of certain odd end-seconds grows as well. 'Tis a suffocating business, take it how you will; and Tyrrel and Forrest only bunglers.[1]

Well, this is an essay on death, or worse, on dying: to return to daylight and the winds, I perceive I have grown to live too much in my work and too little in life. 'Tis the dollars do it: the world is too much. Whenever I think I would like to live a little, I hear the butcher's cart resounding through the neighbourhood; and so to plunge again. The fault is a good fault for me; to be able to do so, is to succeed in life; and my life has been a huge success. I can live with joy and without disgust in the art by which I try to support myself; I have the best wife in the world (apologies to the Châtelaine; *accessit proxime*);[2] I have rather more praise and nearly as much coin as I deserve; my friends are many and true hearted. Sir, it is a big thing in successes. And if mine anchorage lies something open to the wind, Sciatica, if the crew are blind, and the captain spits blood, we

[1] Sir James Tyrrel arranged the murder of the Princes in the Tower and employed Dighton and Forrest to suffocate them (*Richard III*, IV, iii).

[2] She has come very near (or next). The phrase (usually written '*proxime accessit*') is used to indicate the person who has come second to the winner of a prize or scholarship.

cannot have all; and I may be patched up again, who knows? 'His timbers yet are (indifferently) sound, and he may float again.'

Thanks for the word on *Silverado*.[3] Is Chatto bust? *C'est trop drôle.* Yours ever   The Sciaticated Bard.

To P.G. Hamerton[1]

[April 1884]   *La Solitude*

My dear Hamerton, I have been in a very crazy state or I should long ago have answered your kind letter.[2] I have not been able to read at all, nor to write but a little, for ever so long; my eyes having played me a trick. In short I am one of the handsomest wrecks upon the shore of literature. However we keep the galley-fire alight and beat to quarters daily, as though she still ploughed the main full charged with England's thunder.

If you come south, do give us a visit. We cannot take you into the house for reasons best known to the architect. But we should be so pleased to see you and Mrs Hamerton, or yourself alone, and we could talk to you and give you some dinner, and find a room for you within hail. This is to be thought of: and if not now, then after, to be put ruthlessly in act. I think it not unlikely that I may fall on you this year; but all hangs upon my health, whose squirrel-like evolutions supplies me with unfailing entertainment. How little are we grateful to the Gods! The invalid-bore, that well-known person with the symptoms, is a most beautiful instance of the kindly compensations of our destiny.

I somewhat envy you your boating; I shall never be in a boat again, nor yet in a theatre, I fear; a short walk, a long talk – these are what is left me, and very good things too, at least the talk. For a short walk, with definite limits is against the very genius of walking. The amusement is either to ramble or to travel. New views, another hilltop – just down yon dingle – ha! but that wood, I must go so far! That is the spirit of the walker; and how can he attain to this in the square half mile around his house, much of it perhaps visible from his windows? Well, we have adjusting eyes and an adjustable mind. We change the sliding-scale of fancy; and even in my mile-long walks, I have at times got into so rich a vein of self-deception, that I had visited empires and continents when I returned. Life is the art

---

[3] Henley's review of *The Silverado Squatters* in the *Saturday Review* of 19 April.

[1] Philip Gilbert Hamerton (1834–94), artist and essayist who founded and edited *The Portfolio* 1869–94.

[2] Hamerton wrote a long letter to RLS on 22 March. In the course of it he said, 'my happiness is to go sailing on the Saône and stopping at little wayside inns as the wind lists'. He invited RLS to visit him at Autun.

of self-deception – is that new or old? I am a great self-deceiver; and a more valuable quality I know not.

Pray remember me kindly to yours, and believe me, my dear Hamerton, Yours very sincerely   Robert Louis Stevenson

To W.E. Henley

[? *2 May 1884*][1]   [*Hyères*]

TANDEM DESINO

I CANNOT read, work, sleep, lie still, walk, or even play patience. These plagues will overtake all damned silencists; among whom, from this day out, number

> the fiery indignator
> Roland Little Stevenson.
>
> I counted miseries by the heap,
> But now have had my fill,
> I cannot see, I do not sleep,
> But shortly I shall kill.
>
> Of many letters, here is a
> Full End.

Eructavit cor Timonis.

The loquacious man at peace.

> The last will and testament of
> a demitting correspondent.
>
> My indefatigable pen
> I here lay down forever. Men
> Have used, and left me, and forgot;
> Men are entirely off the spot;
> Men are a blague and an abuse;
> And I commit them to the deuce!
>   Roderick Lamond Stevenson
>
> I had companions, I had friends,
> I had of whisky various blends.
> The whisky was all drunk; and lo!
> The friends were gone for evermo!

---

[1] I have assumed that this is the letter written on the evening before RLS's major hemorrhage ('the eve of my blood'), subsequently found and sent to Henley under cover of the letter on p. 263.

And when I marked the ingratitude,
I to my maker turned, and spewed.

Randolph Lovel Stevenson

A pen broken, a subverted ink-pot.

Here endeth the Familiar Correspondence of R.L.S.

Explicuerunt Epistolae Stevensonianae Omnes.

All men are rot; but there are two—
Sidney, the oblivious Slade, and you—
Who from that rabble stand confest
Ten million times the rottenest.

R.L.S.

When I was sick and safe in gaol
I thought my friends would never fail.
One wrote me nothing; t'other bard
Sent me an insolent post card.

R.L.S.

Terminus: Silentia.

FINIS Finaliter finium

IF NOBODY WRITES TO ME I
SHALL DIE

I now write no more.

Richard Lefanu Stevenson
Duke of Indignation

Mark Tacebo,
Secretary

Isaac Blood
John Blind
Vain-hope Go-to-bed
Israel Sciatica } witnesses

The finger on the mouth.

★   ★   ★

On the night of 2/3 May Stevenson was attacked by the worst hemorrhage he had ever experienced. Fanny wrote later of the 'horror of that awful night' and described how RLS seeing her distress 'wrote on a paper to reassure me, while the blood was pouring "It is easy to die this way: no pain."' The next morning Fanny sent a telegram to Henley: 'Ask Mennell what to do for ruptured artery in lung. Much blood lost. Has taken much ergotine.' Henley immediately consulted Dr Mennell and telegraphed his advice to Fanny. Feeling that RLS's life was in danger and having no confidence in Dr Vidal, Henley, in consultation with Baxter and Bob Stevenson, decided to send Dr Mennell out to Hyères to take charge. Mennell arrived on 7 May and stayed for about a week. Under his treatment RLS, although still very weak, began to make progress towards recovery.

Fanny, relying on Dr Vidal's opinion, continued to believe that there had been a rupture of a large artery. Mennell's diagnosis was that no large artery had been broken 'but several small ones must have given way when the clot came up'; his view was that the bleeding had proceeded from the engorged (or congested) right lung. His advice was that RLS must take great care and 'have no excitement of any kind'. Fanny summed it up in a letter to her mother-in-law on 18 May: 'The doctor says keep him alive until he is forty and then, though a winged bird, he may live to ninety; but between now and forty he must live as though he were walking on eggs, and for the next two years, no matter how well he feels, he must live the life of an invalid.'

Although she was helped by Coggie Ferrier and later by a Mrs Louisa Burgess (who was at Hyères with her sick husband), the main burden fell on Fanny and she was, not surprisingly, almost overcome with worry, fatigue and loss of sleep. RLS was a difficult patient and would allow no one to touch him but his wife who hurt her back lifting him in and out of bed.

In the early days of RLS's illness the decision was taken not to tell his parents because it was feared that the news would have a serious effect on Thomas Stevenson's own precarious health. After they had been told there was the additional fear that they might insist on coming to Royat (where Stevenson planned, on Dr Mennell's advice, to convalesce) and that the excitement of their visit might kill Stevenson himself.

RLS made a slow recovery but by the beginning of June was well enough to make the journey to Royat. Fanny, who had written regularly to Henley and Baxter throughout the illness and was deeply appreciative of their help, wrote to Henley: 'I have fought with death hand to hand this bout, and it's victory so far, and I am stronger armed for the next fight . . .'

★   ★   ★

To Sidney Colvin

[*Late May 1884*]   [*Hyères*]

Many daughters have done virtuously but thou excellest them all.[1] All your steps are inspired; only, if there hath been no plural before me, by the immortal gods, I shall leave one behind me. *Envoys.*[2]

---

[1] Proverbs 31:29.

[2] RLS had sent Colvin the six Envoys as 'a kind of postscript to the *Child's Garden*'; Colvin had evidently replied that as applied to a poem the word could not be used in the plural. In his next

Here is a quaint thing. I have read *Robinson, Colonel Jack, Moll Flanders, Memoirs of a Cavalier, History of the Plague, History of the Great Storm, Scotch Church, and Union.* And there my knowledge of Defoe ends – except a book the name of which I forget about Peterborough in Spain – which Defoe obviously did not write and could not have written if he wanted. To which of these does B.J. refer?[3] I guess it must be the history of the Scottish Church. I jest, for of course I *know* it must be a book I have never read and which this makes me keen to read – I mean *Captain Singleton.* Can it be got and sent to me? If *T.I.* is at all like it, it will be delightful. I was just the other day, wondering at my folly in not remembering it when I was writing *T.I.* as a mine for pirate tips. *T.I.* came out of Kingsley's *At Last;* where I got the 'Dead Man's Chest'[4] – and that was the seed – and out of the great Captain Johnson's *History of Notorious Pirates.* The scenery is Californian in part, and in part *chic* – in this connexion, I might say *quid.* I was downstairs today! So now I am a made man – till the next time.

Florizel has left Royat I see;[5] so he and the Count of Arabia (my incognito title) shall not meet. Yours ever

There-is-a-fountain-filled-with-blood[6]

Stevenson

If it was *Captain Singleton,* send it to me, won't you?

To W.E. Henley

[*? June 1884*]   [*? Royat*]

Dear boy, I trust this finds you well; it leaves me so-so. The weather is so cold that I must stick to bed, which is rotten and tedious but can't be helped.

I find in the blotting book the enclosed, which I wrote to you the eve of my blood.[1] Is it not strange? That night, when I naturally thought I was

letter to Colvin RLS wrote: 'By the by, two days after your statement I found the plural used by the Rev. Cheyne in his preface to the psalms. Thou art too high and dry O Sidney Colvin!' *The Book of Psalms* translated by the Revd Thomas Kelly Cheyne appeared in 1884.
[3] Colvin notes: 'I had reported to Stevenson a remark made by me of his warmest admirers, Sir E. Burne-Jones, on some particular analogy, I forget what, between a passage of Defoe and one in *Treasure Island.*' The *Memoirs of Captain Carleton* (1728) dealing with Lord Peterborough's expedition to Spain, 1705, is now generally accepted as being by Defoe.
[4] In ch. 1 of his travel book about the West Indies (1871), Charles Kingsley refers briefly to The Dead Man's Chest as the name given by buccaneers to one of the islets in the Virgin Islands. The name is in fact Dead Chest Island; there is a Deadman's Bay on the nearby Peter Island.
[5] Florizel in *New Arabian Nights* was based on the Prince of Wales. Cf. p. 206.
[6] Cowper's hymn.
[1] The 'eve of my blood' must be the serious illness at the beginning of May: my guess is that the enclosure was the letter on p. 260.

coopered, the thought of it was much in my mind; I thought it had gone; and I thought what a strange prophecy I had made in jest, and how it was indeed like to be the end of many letters. But I have written a good few since and the spell is broken. I am just as pleased, for I earnestly desire to live. This pleasant middle age into whose port we are steering, is quite to my fancy. I would cast anchor here, and go ashore for twenty years, and see the manners of the place. Youth was a great time, but somewhat fussy. Now in middle age (bar lucre) all seems mighty placid. It likes me; I spy a little bright café in one corner of the port, in front of which I now propose we should sit down. There is just enough of the bustle of the harbour and no more; and the ships are close in, regarding us with stern-windows – the ships that bring deals from Norway and parrots from the Indies. Let us sit down here for twenty years, with a packet of tobacco and a drink, and talk of art and women. By the by, the whole city will sink, and the ships too, and the table, and we also; but we shall have sat for twenty years and had a fine talk; and by that time, who knows? exhausted the subject.

I send you a book which (or I am mistook) will please you; it pleased me. But I do desire a book of adventure – a romance – and no man will get or write me one. Dumas I have read and re-read too often; Scott, too, and I am short. I want to hear swords clash. I want a book to begin in a good way; a book, I guess, like *Treasure Island*, alas! which I have never read, and cannot though I live to ninety. I would God that some one else had written it! By all that I can learn, it is the very book for my complaint. I like the way I hear it opens; and they tell me John Silver is good fun. And to me it is, and must ever be, a dream unrealised, a book unwritten. O my sighings after romance, or even Skeltery, and O! the weary age which will produce me neither! Even *le bon Fortuné* has faded and gone out.[2] Once I could sing

> *Je me loue d'être né –*
> *Je l'affirme et je le signe.*
> *O que je suis Fortuné*
> *– Je le suis de ligne en ligne.*

But now the light is sinking; he is dull.

Chapter I

The night was damp and cloudy, the ways foul. The single horseman, cloaked and booted, who pursued his way across Willesden Common, had not met a traveller, when the sound of wheels——

---

[2] Fortuné du Boisgobey (1824–91), prolific author of sensational novels, and a great favourite of RLS's.

Chapter I

'Yes, sir,' said the old pilot, 'she must have dropped into the bay a little afore dawn. A queer craft she looks.'

'She shows no colours,' returned the young gentleman musingly.

'They're a-lowerin' of a quarter-boat, Mr Mark,' resumed the old salt. 'We shall soon know more of her.'

'Ay,' replied the young gentleman called Mark, 'and here, Mr Seadrift, comes your sweet daughter Nancy tripping down the cliff.'

'God bless her kind heart, sir,' ejaculated old Seadrift.——

Chapter I

The notary, Jean Rossignol, had been summoned to the top of a great house in the Isle St Louis to make a will; and now, his duties finished, wrapped in a warm roquelaure and with a lantern swinging from one hand, he issued from the mansion on his homeward way. Little did he think what strange adventures were to befall him!——

That is how stories should begin. And I am offered Husks instead.

What should be:	What is:
The Filibuster's Cache.	Aunt Anne's Tea Cosy.
Jerry Abershaw.	Mrs Brierly's Niece.
Blood Money: A Tale.	Society: A Novel

Celui qui a soif

He who asks for bread and they give him Henry James. By the by, the said Henry is better than ever; verges on a chief of works. 'The House Tellier'[3] is almost a chief of works, by the way; the garter scene being a perfect gem of purest ray serene. Very very funny and well seen.   R.L.S.

---

[3] Maupassant's short story 'La Maison Tellier' (1881).

IX. THREE YEARS IN BOURNEMOUTH
July 1884–August 1887

Stevenson and Fanny arrived in London from France on 1 July 1884 and joined his parents. He was not well enough to attend the matinée performance of *Deacon Brodie* (with E.J. Henley in the name part) at the Prince's Theatre the next day. His parents and Fanny were there and the play was enthusiastically received by an audience of what his mother called 'literary and artistic people' – Colvin, Gosse, Henry James, Leslie Stephen and Browning among them. The play was sympathetically reviewed but the critics made it clear that this was mainly due to the attraction of one of the authors' names rather than to any merit in the play.

After spending a few days at Richmond, and receiving conflicting advice from various doctors as to whether he should spend the winter in Britain or Davos, RLS decided to go down to Bournemouth to see Lloyd Osbourne who was at school there. On Saturday 12 July, in the pouring rain, Margaret Stevenson saw her son, Fanny, Valentine and the dog Bogue off on the train to Bournemouth from Waterloo Station.

A brief stay at the Highcliffe Hotel was followed by a move into lodgings and then into a boarding house called Wensleydale in West Cliff Gardens. In October RLS decided to spend the winter in Bournemouth and they took a furnished house called Bonallie Tower in Boscombe Park. By January 1885 the decision to settle in Bournemouth had been made and Thomas Stevenson bought his daughter-in-law a house which they renamed Skerryvore in honour of the lighthouse ('the noblest of all extant deep-sea lights') built by RLS's uncle Alan Stevenson; they moved in in April 1885.

For most of his three years in Bournemouth RLS lived the life of a chronic invalid, spending much of his time in bed plagued by colds and hemorrhages: a life he was later to sum up in a famous phrase as that of 'a pallid brute that lived in Skerryvore like a weevil in a biscuit'. These were, however, years of growing literary success and recognition, with the publication of, among other works, *Dr Jekyll and Mr Hyde*, *Kidnapped* and *A Child's Garden of Verses*.

To W.E. Henley[1]

[?17 July 1884]   *Highcliffe Hotel, Bournemouth*

Dear William Ernest Hart,[2] What is the reason of things? The Piratic and obscure Mennell came, interviewed my uncle, and then, without a word, fled, leaving me unadvised; since when I have not seen him. My uncle praised the pirate, said he agreed with him, said I was quite well, said my hemorrhage was all exaggeration (my wife's), said Mennell said so, said we were to throw the ergotine out of the window, said I might live in England: etc. The Simoom blew. It was wild weather.

Next day, being without word of Mennell (and so still!), I went up to Brunton on the chance. B. condemned out of hand, and says both lungs are affected seriously, and ordered me to the Alps in winter.

Then I came here, which is a pretty nice place (and a lovely journey), and I know nothing about anything, and as for Mennell, His tricks they are vain, His ways they are dark, His whole little game Is more than a lark.[3] In the words of his sacred Majesty King George the Third – what – what, what – why, why, why?[4] Can you throw any light? Did they quarrel, or did the pirate sell my uncle, or had he sold us, or did his courage collapse, and why did he bolt? I am dull and have a cold; real dull. About *Old Glory* I see much to say and, when I am less stupid, shall say it; but now! Unbroken clouds extend. Yours ever   R.L.S.

Of Bournemouth, Davos, Torquay, Mentone,
Nice, Cannes and Hyères Esq., Invalid.

---

[1] At Richmond on 9 July Dr Mennell and Dr George Balfour had given a favourable report on RLS's condition and agreed that he could stay in Britain. Fanny (the Simoom), convinced that RLS was spitting arterial blood (which they denied), had hurried him off to London to consult the distinguished physician Thomas Launder Brunton. He took a much less favourable view and advised that RLS should winter at Davos. Henley was indignant at the way Mennell had been treated. He replied to this letter on 18 July: 'What seems to have happened is what has happened before when the Simoom . . . has taken the war path. At a given moment everybody went off, completely off, his head. . . . The Simoom blew; the pirate retired to his tent as Achilles, and now declines to emerge . . . As for you, you started before eleven on Thursday morning for London, and there got Lauder-Bruntonised, thereby dismissing Mennell, and getting ordered out of England for the winter, which I take it, is what you wanted.'

[2] The review of *Deacon Brodie* in *Society* of 12 July concluded: 'The piece was excellently staged, and at the close, in answer to a unanimous call, the authors – Mr Robert Louis Stevenson and Mr William Ernest Hart – bowed their thanks to an applauding audience'.

[3] Cf. Bret Harte's 'Plain Language from Truthful James'.

[4] George III was ridiculed by contemporary satirists for his persistent questioning and his continued use of these words.

To his Father[1]

Bonallie Towers,
Branksome Park,
Bournemouth
(The three B's)

[5 November 1884]

My dear Father, Allow me to say, in a strictly Pickwickian sense,[2] that you are a silly fellow. I am pained indeed, but how should I be offended? I think you exaggerate; I cannot forget that you had the same impression of the *Deacon*, and yet, when you saw it played, were less revolted than you looked for; and I will still hope that the *Admiral* also is not so bad as you suppose. There is one point, however, where I differ from you very frankly; religion is in the world; I do not think you are the man to deny the importance of its rôle; and I have long decided not to leave it on one side in art. The opposition of the Admiral and Mr Pew is not, to my eyes, either horrible or irreverent; but it may be, and it probably is, very ill done: what then? this is a failure; better luck next time; more power to the elbow, more discretion, more wisdom in the design; and the old defeat becomes the scene of the new victory. Concern yourself about no failure; they do not cost lives, as in engineering; they are the *pierres perdues* of successes. Fame is (truly) a vapour; do not think of it; if the writer means well and tries hard, no failure will injure him, whether with God or man.

I wish I could hear a brighter account of yourself; but I am inclined to acquit the *Admiral* of too heavy a share in the responsibility. My very heavy cold is, I hope, drawing off; and the change to this charming house in the forest will I hope complete my re-establishment.

With love to all, believe me, Your ever affectionate

Robert Louis Stevenson

---

[1] Henley spent much of August and September at Bournemouth working with RLS on two plays, *Beau Austin* and *Admiral Guinea* with which they hoped to make their fortunes. These were privately printed by R. & R. Clark, the Edinburgh printers. Henley had sent TS an inscribed copy of the privately printed edition of *Admiral Guinea* on 29 October 1884. TS (who was depressed and ill) wrote to RLS on Sunday [2 November]:

> I hope you will not be horrified and I am sure you will not be angry when I say that the *Admiral* is far too much for me. The combination or at least close proximity of Nonconformist pious slang with the crawling obscenity of Pew is to me past all endurance and I must say that I cannot agree to pay for propagating such a production unless it can be altered . . . my intense solicitude for your fame compels me thus to write. Besides it is I think a vulgar offence against good taste . . . I know that independent of all other objections you would bring upon yourself a storm of indignant criticism which I really could not bear in my present state of health.

[2] In a debate at the Pickwick Club Mr Blotton calls Mr Pickwick 'a humbug', but explains that he 'had used the word in its Pickwickian sense . . . personally, he entertained the highest regard and esteem for the honourable gentleman' (ch. 1).

To Charles Baxter

11 November [1884]   *Bonallie Towers*

My dear Charles, I beg to inform you that I have already received Colvin's interest from him directly; I also beg to apologise for sinful delay about the enclosed receipt, which may still be interesting from an antiquarian point of view. I am in my new house, thus proudly styled, as you perceive; but the deevil a tower ava'[1] can be perceived (except out of window): this is not as it should be; one might have hoped, at least, a turret bogshop.

We are all vilely unwell. I put in the dark watches, imitating a donkey with some success but little pleasure; and in the afternoon I indulge in a smart fever, accompanied by aches and shivers. There is thus little monotony to be deplored; and what might still weigh upon me, my wife lightens by various inexplicable attacks, now in the pleasant morn, now at the noon of night. I, at least, am a *regular* invalid; I would scorn to bray in the afternoon, I would indignantly refuse the proposal to fever in the night. What is bred in the bone, will come out, sir, in the flesh; and the same spirit that prompted me to date my letter, regulates the hour and character of my attacks. I am Sir, Yours   Thomson

To Charles Baxter

[Postmark 13 November 1884][1]   *[Bournemouth]*

My dear Thomson, It's a maist remarkable fac', but nae shuner had I written yon braggin, blawin' letter aboot ma business habits, when bang! that very day, my hoast begude[2] in the aifternune! It is really remaurkable; it's prōvidenshle, I believe. The ink wasnae fair dry, the words werenae well ooten ma mouth, when bang, I got the lee. The mair ye think o't, Thomson, the less ye'll like the looks o't. Proavidence (I'm no sayin') is all verra weel *in its place*; but if proavidence has nae mainners, wha's to learn't? Proavidence is a fine thing; but hoo would you like proavidence to keep your till for ye? The richt place for proavidence is in the kirk; it has naething to do wi private correspondence between twa gentlemen, nor freendly cracks, nor a wee bit word o' sculduddery ahint the door, nor, in shoart, wi' ony *hole an' corner wark*, what I would call. I'm pairfec'ly willin' to meet in wi' proavidence, I'll be prood to meet in wi' him, when

---

[1] At all.
[1] The envelope is addressed to 'Mr Thomson (ex-precentor) care of Charles Baxter Esq., W.S.'.
[2] My cough began.

my time's come an' I cannae dae nae better; but *if he's to come skinking aboot my stair-fit*, damned, I micht as weel be deed for a' the comfort I'll can get in life. Cannae he no be made to understand that it's beneath him? Gosh, if I was in his business, I wouldnae steer my heid for a plain, auld ex-elder that, tak' him the way he tak's himsel, 's jist aboot as honest as he can weel afford, an' but for drink an' weemen an a wheen auld scandals, near forgotten noo, is a pairfeckly respectable and thoroughly decent man. An' if I fashed wi' him ava', it wad be kind o' handsome like; a pun-note under his stair door, a bottle o' auld, blended malt to his bit mornin', or a teshtymonial like yon ye ken sae weel aboot, but mair successfu'.

Dear Thomson, have I ony money. If I have, *send it's* for the loard's sake.   Johnson

To W.E. Henley

[14 November 1884]   [Bournemouth]

My dear boy, A thousand thanks for the Molière.[1] I have already read, in this noble presentment, *La Comtesse d'Escarbagnas, Le Malade Imaginaire,* and a part of *Les Femmes Savantes*; I say Poquelin took damned good care of himself: Argan and Chrysale, what parts! Many thanks also for John Silver's pistol; I recognise it; that was the one he gave Jim Hawkins at the mouth of the pit; I shall get a plate put upon it, to that effect.[2]

My birthday was a great success; I was better in health; I got delightful presents; I received the definite commission from the *P.M.G.* and began to write the tale;[3] and in the evening Bob arrived, a simple seraph. We have known each other ten years; and here we are too like the pair that met in the infirmary: why can we not mellow into kindness and sweetness like Bob? What is the reason? does nature, even in my octogenarian

---

[1] Henley wrote on 12 November: 'Tomorrow being your birthday, you will receive in memory thereof, a new and beautiful edition of the works of Poquelin. That you may be found reading it for thirty year to come is our heartfelt wish. . . . Next February, or January, we shall have been friends for ten years. Think of that, Master Brook! Ten years, dear boy, and all that in them is! – in ten years from now, I hope we shall have done a few good plays . . .' Molière's real name was Jean-Baptiste Poquelin. For 'Master Brook' see *The Merry Wives of Windsor*.

[2] Henley replied on 17 November: 'The pistol is a birthday gift from my brother Joe. . . . Of course when I gave it to Jim Hawkins, it was a flint; but, as you may see, it has since been converted. That proves its authenticity.' Joseph Warton, Henley's youngest brother, worked for a time as a draughtsman and finally as a rate-collector.

[3] RLS had agreed with Gosse to write for £40 a story for the *Pall Mall Gazette* Christmas Extra. 'Markheim' was originally submitted and set up in type but proved to be too short. RLS hastily finished 'The Body Snatcher' (begun at Pitlochry and previously called 'The Body Snatchers').

carcase, run too strong, that I must be still a bawler and a brawler and a treader upon corns? You, at least, have achieved the miracle of embellishing your personal appearance to that point that, unless your mother is a woman of even more perspicacity than I suppose, it is morally impossible that she can recognize you. When I saw you ten years ago, you looked rough and – ugly, kind of stigmatised, a look of an embittered political shoemaker; where is it now? You now come waltzing around like some light-hearted monarch; essentially jovial, essentially royal; radiant of smiles. And in the meanwhile, by a complementary process, I turn into a kind of hunchback with white hair! The devil.

Well, let us be thankful for our mercies; in these ten years what a change from the cell in the hospital, and the two sick boys in the next bed, to the influence, the recognition, the liberty and the happiness of today! Well, well; fortune is not so blind as people say; you dreed a good long weird;[4] but you have got into a fine green paddock now to kick your heels in. And I, too, what a difference; what a difference in my work, in my situation, and unfortunately, also in my health! But we need not complain of a pebble in the shoe, when by mere justice, one should rot in a dungeon.

Many thanks to both of you; long life to our friendship, and that means, I do most firmly believe, to these clay continents on which we fly our colours; good luck to one and all and may God continue to be merciful. Your old and warm friend   R.L.S.

To Henry James

8 December 1884   *Bonallie Towers*

My dear Henry James, This is a very brave hearing from more points than one.[1] The first point is that there is a hope of a sequel. For this I laboured. Seriously, from the dearth of information and thoughtful interest in the art of literature, those who try to practise it with any deliberate purpose run the risk of finding no fit audience. People suppose it is 'the stuff' that interests them: they think for instance that the prodigious fine thoughts and sentiments in Shakespeare impress by their own weight, not understanding that the unpolished diamond is but a stone. They think that

---

[4] Endured your fate.

[1] Henry James's essay 'The Art of Fiction' appeared in *Longman's Magazine* for September. RLS described it (in a letter to Miss Ferrier) as 'dreadful nonsense admirably said'. RLS's reply, 'A Humble Remonstrance', was published in the December *Longman's*. Henry James wrote on 5 December in response to RLS's article, sending him words 'of hearty sympathy, charged with the assurance of my enjoyment of everything you write. It's a luxury, in this immoral age, to encounter someone who *does* write – who is really acquainted with that lovely art.'

striking situations, or good dialogue are got by studying life; they will not rise to understand that they are prepared by deliberate artifice and set off by painful suppressions. Now, I want the whole thing well ventilated: for my own education and the public's; and I beg you to look as quick as you can, to follow me up with every circumstance of defeat where we differ, and (to prevent the flouting of the laity) to emphasize the points where we agree. I trust your paper will show me the way to a rejoinder; and that rejoinder I shall hope to make with so much art, as to woo or drive you from your threatened silence. I would not ask better than to pass my life in beating out this quarter of corn with such a seconder as yourself.

Point the second, I am rejoiced indeed to hear you speak so kindly of my work: rejoiced and surprised. I seem to myself, a very rude, left-handed countryman; not fit to be read, far less complimented, by a man so accomplished, so adroit, so craftsmanlike as you. You will happily never have cause to understand the despair with which a writer like myself considers (say) the park scene in 'Lady Barberina'.[2] Every touch surprises me by its intangible precision; and the effect when done, as light as syllabub, as distinct as a picture, fills me with envy. Each man among us prefers his own aim; and I prefer mine; but when we come to speak of performance, I recognize myself, compared with you, to be a lout and slouch of the first water.

Where we differ, both as to the design of stories and the delineation of character, I begin to lament. Of course, I am not so dull as to ask you to desert your walk; but could you not, in one novel, to oblige a sincere admirer, and to enrich his shelves with a beloved volume, could you not, and might you not, cast your characters in a mould a little more abstract and academic (dear Mrs Pennyman[3] had already, among your other work, a taste of what I mean) and pitch the incidents, I do not say, in any stronger, but in a slightly more emphatic key – as it were an episode from one of the old (so-called) novels of adventure? I fear you will not; and I suppose I must sighingly admit you to be right. And yet, when I see, as it were, a book of Tom Jones, handled with your exquisite precision and shot through with those sidelights of reflection in which you excel, I relinquish the dear vision with regret. Think upon it.

As you know I belong to that besotted class of man, the invalid; this puts me to a stand in the way of visits. But it is possible that some day you may feel that a day near the sea and among pinewoods would be a pleasant change from town. If so, please let us know; and my wife and I will be delighted to put you up, and give you what we can to eat and drink

[2] 'Lady Barberina' was serialised in the *Century*, May to July 1884 and published in book form in *Tales of Three Cities* in November 1884.
[3] In *Washington Square* (1881). The correct name is 'Penniman'.

(I have a fair bottle of claret). On the back of which, believe me, Yours
sincerely   Robert Louis Stevenson

P.S. I reopen this to say that I have re-read my paper, and cannot think
I have at all succeeded in being either veracious or polite. I know of
course, that I took your paper merely as a pin to hang my own remarks
upon; but alas! what a thing is any paper! what fine remarks can you not
hang on mine! how I have sinned against proportion and, with every
effort to the contrary, against the merest rudiments of courtesy to you!
You are indeed a very acute reader to have divined the real attitude of my
mind; and I can only conclude, not without closed eyes and shrinking
shoulders, in the well-worn words   Lay on Macduff!

To W.E. Henley

[c. 17 December 1884]   [Bournemouth]

Dear boy, Sargent has come and gone; I repeat what I said to Bob: he
represents me as a weird, very pretty, large-eyed, chicken-boned, slightly
contorted poet. He is not pleased; wants to do me again in several
positions; walking about and talking is his main notion. We both lost our
hearts to him: a person with a kind of exhibition manner and English
accent, who proves on examination, simple, bashful, honest, enthusiastic
and rude with a perfect (but quite inoffensive) English rudeness. *Pour
comble*, he gives himself out to be American.[1]

How comes it that you write telling me that Colvin is to see *P.M.G.*
and that Colvin, by a subsequent post, asks, all in the air, what I propose
to do with the *A.N's*?[2] This bewilders me. I hear from the Merry Andrew
that it looks like business with the Garding.[3] I am, Sir, Yours   Flint

---

[1] John Singer Sargent (1856–1925). This first portrait does not seem to have survived. In a letter
to his mother RLS wrote: 'Sargent just gone; a charming, simple, clever, honest young man: he
has delighted us. It appears Gladstone talks all the time about *Treasure Island*; he would do better
to attend to the imperial affairs of England.'

[2] RLS had proposed to Henley that *More New Arabian Nights* should be serialised in the *Pall
Mall Gazette*. Henley replied: 'The Archangel's question bewilders me. I dined with him
last Friday, and solemnly arranged, as I wrote, that he should sound Yates Thompson on
the subject of the *N.A.N.* as a possible *feuilleton*.' Thompson was owner of the *Pall Mall
Gazette*.

[3] Henley wrote on 17 December that he had seen Lang 'as Longman's emissary' about
publication of *A Child's Garden*. They offered '£30 (in advance) for the first thousand, and £20
per five hundred up to a total of 2500; after which, a new agreement, or a continuance
of the old, at your pleasure'. These terms were in the formal agreement dated 24 December
1884.

To Sidney Colvin[1]

[? 6 January 1885]   *[Bournemouth]*

Dear S.C., I have addressed a letter to the G.O.M. *à propos* of Villainton;[2] and I became aware, you will be interested to hear, of an overwhelming respect for the old gentleman. I can *blague* his failures; but when you actually address him, and bring the two statures and records to confrontation, dismay is the result. By mere continuance of years, he must impose; the man who helped to rule England before I was conceived strikes me with a new sense of greatness and antiquity, when I must actually beard him with the cold forms of correspondence. I shied at the necessity of calling him plain 'Sir'; had he been 'My Lord', I had been happier; no, I am no equalitarian: Honour to whom honour is due; and if to none, why, then, honour to the old!

These, O Slade Professor, are my unvarnished sentiments: I was a little surprised to find them so extreme, and therefore I communicate the fact.

Belabour thy brains, as to whom it would be well to question. I have a small space; I wish to make a popular book, nowhere obscure, nowhere, if it can be helped, unhuman. It seems to me the most hopeful plan to tell the tale, so far as may be, by anecdote. He did not die till so recently there must be hundreds who remember him, and thousands who have still ungarnered stories. Dear man, to the breach! up, soldier of the iron dook, up, Slades, and at 'em! (which, conclusively, he did *not* say: the at 'em–ic theory is to be dismissed). You know piles of fellows who must reek with matter; help, help!

I am going to try Happy-and-Glorious-long-to-reign-over us. True-blue, I am. H.-and-G. must remember things; and it is my belief, if my letter could be discreetly introduced, she would like to tell them; *pruritus scribendi, scabies reginarum.*[3] So I jest when I don't address my mind to it: when I do, shall I be smit louting to my knee, as before the G.O.M.? *Problème!* Yours ever   R.L.S.

---

[1] Colvin was appointed Keeper of Prints and Drawings at the British Museum in July 1883 but he does not seem to have taken up the position until 1884, when he left the Fitzwilliam Museum. He remained as Slade Professor until 1885.
[2] RLS had agreed to write a life of Wellington for Longman's shilling series of 'English Worthies' edited by Lang. The project never came to anything but part of a draft opening chapter was posthumously published in the Vailima and later collected editions. The letter to Gladstone was written but apparently never sent.
[3] The itch to write is the disease [scabies] of queens.

To John Addington Symonds

30 February 1885 [? 2 March]   *Bournemouth*

My dear Symonds, Yes, we have both been very neglectful. I had horrid luck; catching (from kind friends) two thundering influenzas in August and November; I recovered from the last with difficulty; also had great annoyance from hemorrhagic leaking; but have come through this blustering winter with some general success; in the house, up and down. My wife, however, has been painfully upset by my health. Last year of course was cruelly trying to her nerves; Nice and Hyères are bad experiences; and though she is not ill, the doctor tells me that prolonged anxiety may do her a real mischief. She is now at Hyères collecting our goods; and she has been ill there, which has upset my liver and driven me to the friendly Calomel; on which I now mainly live: it is the only thing that stops the bleeding, which seems directly connected with the circulation of the liver.

I feel a little old and fagged, and chary of speech, and not very sure of spirit in my work, but considering what a year I have passed, and how I have twice sat on Charon's pier-head, I am surprising. The doctors all seem agreed in saying that my complaint is quite unknown, and will allow of no prognosis.

My father has presented us with a very pretty house in this place, into which we hope to move by May.[1] My Child's verses come out next week. *Otto* begins to appear in April. *More New Arabian Nights* as soon as possible.[2] Moreover I am neck deep in Wellington – also: a story on the stocks: *The Great North Road*.[3] O, I am busy! Sam is at college in Edinburgh. That is, I think, all that can be said by way of news.

Have you read *Huckleberry Finn*? It contains many excellent things; above all, the whole story of a healthy boy's dealings with his conscience, incredibly well done.

My own conscience is badly seared; a want of piety; yet I pray for it, tacitly, every day; believing it, after courage, the only gift worth having; and its want, in a man of any claims to honour, quite unpardonable. The tone of your letter seemed to me very sound. In these dark days of public dishonour,[4] I do not know that we can do better than carry our private

---

[1] TS had bought a house as a present for Fanny and also paid for the cost of furnishing it. It was renamed Skerryvore.

[2] *A Child's Garden of Verses* was published on 6 March 1885 and *Prince Otto* began serialisation in the April *Longman's*. *More New Arabian Nights: The Dynamiter*, the story written in collaboration with Fanny, was published on 28 April.

[3] An unfinished, posthumously published novel.

[4] The news of the fall of Khartoum on 26 January (two days before the arrival of the relief force) reached England on 5 February and the death of Gordon was finally confirmed a week later. There was a great public outcry and much bitter criticism of Gladstone and his Government. Votes of censure were moved in both Houses of Parliament.

trials piously. What a picture is this of a nation! No man that I can see, on any side or party, seems to have the least sense of our ineffable shame: the desertion of the garrisons. I tell my little parable that Germany took England, and then there was an Indian Mutiny, and Bismarck said 'quite right: let Delhi and Calcutta and Bombay fall; and let the women and children be treated Sepoy fashion'; and people say: 'O, but that is very different!' and then I wish I were dead. Millais was painting Gladstone[5] when the news came of Gordon's death; Millais was much affected (this seems to throw a doubt on the truth of the anecdote); and Gladstone said: 'Why? *It is the man's own temerity!*' *Voilà le Bourgeois! le voilà nu!* But why should I blame Gladstone, when I too am a Bourgeois? when I have held my peace? Why did I hold my peace? Because I am a sceptic: i.e. a Bourgeois. We believe in nothing, Symonds: you don't, and I don't; and these are two reasons, out of a handful of millions, why England stands before the world dripping with blood and daubed with dishonour. I will first try to take the beam out of my own eye; trusting that even private effort somehow betters and braces the general atmosphere. See, for example, if England has shown (I put it hypothetically) one spark of manly sensibility, they have been shamed into it by the spectacle of Gordon. Impotent and small and (if you like) spiteful as it is, the mere fact of people taking their names off the Gordon Memorial Committee rather than sit thereon with Gladstone, is the first glimmer of a sense of responsibility that I have observed. Police Officer Cole is the only man that I see to admire. I dedicate my *New Arabs* to him and Cox,[6] in default of other great public characters. Yours ever most affectionately   Robert Louis Stevenson

To Edmund Gosse

[Postmark 12 March 1885]   *Bonallie Tower*

My dear Gosse, I was indeed much exercised how I could be worked into *Gray*; and lo! when I saw it, the passage seemed to have been written with a single eye to elucidate the. . . . worst? . . . . . well, not a very good poem of Gray's.[1] Your little life is excellent; clean, neat, efficient. I have read

---

[5] Millais' second portrait of Gladstone was exhibited at the Grosvenor Gallery in May.

[6] There were two dynamite explosions in the House of Commons on 24 January 1885. Police Constable William Cole was seriously injured when a burning charge of dynamite he was carrying away exploded in Westminster Hall. The Queen awarded him the Albert Medal for bravery and both Cole and Sergeant Thomas Cox (who was also injured) were commended and given various money testimonials. *The Dynamiter* was duly dedicated to them.

[1] Gosse's annotated school edition of *Selected Poems* of Thomas Gray, prefixed by a short memoir. Gosse annotated l. 40 of 'Ode on a Distant Prospect of Eton College' – 'And snatch a fearful joy' with a sentence from 'The Suicide Club' (*New Arabian Nights*, I, 35): 'Fear is the strong passion; it is with fear that you must trifle, if you wish to taste the intensest joy of living.'

many of your notes, too, with pleasure. It occurs to me that 'you was getting quite a little man.' Your connection with Gray was a happy circumstance; it was a suitable conjunction.

I did not answer your letter from the States, for what was I to say? I liked getting it, and reading it; I was rather flattered that you wrote it to me; and then I'll tell you what I did – I put it in the fire. Why? well, just because it was very natural and expansive; and thinks I to myself if I die one of these fine nights (there is a fountain filled with blood in my case,[2] in a very special sense) this is just the letter that Gosse would not wish to go into the hands of third parties.[3] Was I well inspired? And I did not answer it because you were on your high places, sailing with supreme dominion, and seeing life in a particular glory; and I was peddling in a corner, confined to the house, overwhelmed with necessary work, which I was not always doing well, and, in the very mild form in which the disease approaches me, touched with a sort of bustling cynicism. Why throw cold water? How ape your agreeable frame of mind? In short, I held my tongue.

I have now published on 101 small pages *The Complete Proof of Mr R.L. Stevenson's Incapacity to Write Verse: in a Series of Graduated Examples with Table of Contents*. I think I shall issue a companion volume of exercises: 'Analyse this poem. Collect and comminate the ugly words. Distinguish and condemn the *chevilles*. State Mr Stevenson's faults of taste in regard to the measure. What reasons can you gather from this example for your belief that Mr S. is unable to write any other measure?' They look ghastly in the cold light of print; but there is something nice in the little ragged regiment for all; the blackguards seem to me to smile; to have a kind of childish treble note that sounds in my ears freshly: not song, if you will, but a child's voice.

I was glad you enjoyed your visit to the States. Most Englishmen go there with a confirmed design of patronage, as they go to France for that matter; and patronage will not pay. Besides in this year of – grace, said I? – of disgrace, who should creep so low as an Englishman? It is not to be thought of that the flood[4] – ah '*Wordsworttus, mon maître de musique*', you would change your note were you alive today!

I am now a beastly householder, but have not yet entered on my domain. When I do, the social revolution will probably cast me back upon

[2] William Cowper's hymn.

[3] Gosse had been on a lecture-tour in America. His success had gone to his head. He wrote to the sculptor Hamo Thornycroft on 20 December 1884: 'We have enjoyed – but I must not be reported to have said it – the greatest social success that any Englishman of letters has enjoyed since Thackeray lectured in Boston.'

[4] The opening line of Wordsworth's sonnet, 'It is not to be thought of that the Flood/Of British freedom . . . should perish', written at the time of the threat of French invasion. At the end of the letter RLS misquotes the first line of another famous sonnet.

my dung heap. There is a person called Hyndman[5] whose eye is on me; his step is beHynd me as I go. I shall call my house Skerryvore when I get it: SKERRYVORE: *c'est bon pour la poéshie*. I will conclude with my favourite sentiment: 'The world is too much with thus.'

Robert Louis Stevenson
The Hermit of Skerryvore.

Author of *John Vane Tempest: a Romance, Herbert and Henrietta, or The Nemesis of Sentiment, The Life and Adventures of Colonel Bludyer Fortescue, Happy Homes and Hairy Faces, A Pound of Feathers and a Pound of Lead*, part author of *Minn's Complete Capricious Correspondent; a Manual of Natty, Natural and Knowing Letters*, and editor of the *Poetical Remains of Samuel Burt Crabbe, known as the Melodious Bottle-Holder*.

Uniform with the above:

The Life and Remains of the Reverend Jacob Degray Squab, author of *Heave-yo for the New Jerusalem. A Box of Candles; or the Patent Spiritual Safety Match*, and *A Day with the Heavenly Harriers*.

To Will H. Low

Bonallie Tower

13 March 1885

My dear Low, Your success has been immense. I wish your letter had come two days ago: *Otto*, alas! has been disposed of a good while ago; but it was only [the] day before yesterday that I settled the new volume of *Arabs*. However for the future, you and the sons of the deified Scribner are the men for me.[1] Really they have behaved most handsomely. I cannot lay my hand on the papers or I would tell you exactly how it compares with my English bargain; but it compares well. Ah! if we had that copyright, I do believe it would go far to make me solvent, ill health and all!

I wrote you a letter to the Rembrandt in which I stated my views about the dedication in a very brief form.[2] It will give me sincere pleasure;

---

[5] Henry Mayers Hyndman (1842–1921), Socialist leader, agitator and author; one of the founders of the Social Democratic Federation, 1881. Hyndman's speech at a demonstration by the unemployed organised by the Federation in London on 17 February had led the *Saturday Review* to declare that his Socialist propaganda with its incitement to assassination called for 'immediate and exemplary punishment'.

[1] With Low acting as their intermediary, the famous American publishers, Messrs Charles Scribner's Sons, had made a generous offer for *A Child's Garden*; they went on to become RLS's regular publishers in America.

[2] Low had moved from The Rembrandt to 3 Washington Square, North, New York. He had been commissioned to illustrate Keats's *Lamia* and had asked permission to dedicate the book to RLS.

and will make the second dedication I have received: the other being from John Addington Symonds.[3] It is a compliment I value much; I don't know any that I should prefer.

Confound the Balzacs. I wish I had thought of a lack of credit;[4] credit is all I have, and I am inclined to fancy others in the same case. 30 dollars = £6. loss on cheque etc. say £6.10. What a price! I believe I shall do best to send the books from here. I will hold off however, till I hear from you again; but if by the time this reaches you, you shall have still done nothing let me know and the books shall go from here. I hope the seeds and things of which I wrote can be sent to me without prepayment; if Vick draws a bill, I'll meet it at three days' sight.[5]

Bob has been staying with me in the character of sick-nurse while my wife was away. When I write I will upbraid him. You know, I suppose, that he is married and a father? highly uxorious and the most devoted parent? more improved than any man I ever knew or read of? but alas! deadly impecunious? Hence this burst into art criticism; his poverty but not his will consented;[6] and as the step is archi-necessary, and not grateful to the poor soul, I shall take the liberty of suppressing your message anent his inconsistency.[7] We really do not think he will ever make anything of painting; and we are all in a plot, sugaring him off on literature with many Jesuitical pretensions. If you wish to help, and you should ever see any merit in one of his papers that you could in conscience approve of, make him a complimentary letter. Of course he is yet awkward at the trade; has no facture, is bitter conscious of it; hates the slavery of writing; hates to give up the time when he should paint; but the one brings in something, the other nix; and I think it a good work to encourage him on. A little while ago, Henley and I remarked, about Bob, 'how strange it was that the cleverest man we knew, should be starving'. That was where it was. So please avoid chaff on that sore subject.

I am glad to hear you have windows to do; that is a fine business, I think; but alas, the glass is so bad nowadays; realism invading even that, as well as the huge inferiority of our technical resource corrupting every tint.

---

[3] Symonds dedicated *Wine, Women and Song* to RLS in 1884.
[4] To save himself the cost of postage RLS had asked Low to purchase a cheap edition of all of Balzac's works and send them to Nellie Sanchez. Low wrote that he had been unable to do this because they would cost about $30 and 'I have never been much harder up.'
[5] RLS had also asked Low to order for Fanny seeds of 'sugar peas, sweet corn, nutmeg, canteloupe melon' from James Vick, the famous firm of seed merchants of Rochester, New York.
[6] *Romeo and Juliet*, V.i.75.
[7] Low wrote: 'If you ever write to Bob give him my love, abuse him for not having answered a letter of mine written years ago. He shows an amount of entertaining erudition about the portraits by distinguished French painters in the current *Magazine of Art* ["Portraiture in France", a review in the February issue] with which I should not have credited him judging by his skit of past times to the effect that all painting was a mistake and that writing on painting still more so.'

Still anything that keeps a man to decoration is, in this age, good for the artist's spirit.

By the way, have you seen James and me on the novel? James, I think in the August or September – R.L.S. in the December *Longman*. I own I think the *école bête*, of which I am the champion, has the whip hand of the argument; but as James is to make a rejoinder, I must not boast. Anyway the controversy is amusing to see. I was terribly tied down to space, which has made the end congested and dull. I shall see if I can afford to send you the April *Contemporary* – but I daresay you see it anyway – as it will contain a paper of mine on style, a sort of continuation of old arguments on art in which you have often wagged a most effective tongue.[8] It is a sort of start upon my Treatise of the Art of Literature: a small, arid book that shall some day appear.

With every good wish from me and mine (should I not say 'she and hers'?) to you and yours, believe me, Yours ever

Robert Louis Stevenson

Do you see much of Morris Townsend? Are you next door to the Doctor's Daughter? Or does 'North' refer to another 'Washington Square' than Henry James's?[9]

I am sorry you can't show up this year. Before I can come, God will have to take some steps about my body, and Congress to give me copyright: as things are neither purse nor carcase can affront the Atlantic passage.   R.L.S.

I have written to Scribner's direct as I thought most polite: was this not right?

To his Father

	B.T.
	B.P.
20 March 1885	B.

My dear Father, It is certainly very annoying, but after all a great deal of water runs under the bridge. Are you surprised? Why? I do not know that I am; I *was* surprised when I thought you were going to get it. You must take one consideration with another; you were made the president, and

---

[8] 'On Style in Literature: Its Technical Elements'.
[9] A reference to two characters in Henry James's novel (1881): Morris Townsend jilts Catherine, Dr Sloper's daughter.

cried out it was too much honour;[1] you lose Peterhead[2] and cry out it is too much insult. 'We have piped unto you etc.'[3] Taking one consideration with another, this engineer's lot is chequered perhaps, but not so unhappy as it might be.[4] Let me direct your attention to his noble son, struggling under a ton's weight of dry-rot, and overwhelmed with incapacity to do his hand's darg.[5] Never was a man further removed from literature than I; yet I go on daily with my new boys' story (which is a very good story by the way, and which you will like, if ever I can write it, which seems almost too much to hope for. I have no name for it but only a title page like one of Defoe's: 'Memoirs of the Adventures of David Balfour; how he was kidnapped and cast away in the brig *Covenant* of Dysart; his journey in the wild Highlands; his acquaintance with Alan Breck Stewart and the sons of the notorious Rob Roy; with all that he suffered at the hands of his uncle Ebenezer Balfour of Shaws, wrongly so called: written by himself and now first set forth etc.' Whereof mair.

I think I have lost the thread. (Dry rot.) When Fanny may come, I cannot yet say.[6] Not till a little bit on in the week I think. You must let us know when you think of running down in time for Colvin to leave. Colvin is to be here from Monday to Friday. I wish we were all properly thankful for our mercies, but we none of us are: an ungrateful generation from the first, and like to stay so. Ever your affectionate son   R.L.S.

To Charles Baxter

[24 March 1885]   *[Bournemouth]*

Dear Thomson, It's extrōdnar; you an me in a Court of Law:[1] a place 'at I swure I wouldnae pit ma fit in for the Queen hersel'; and here we're

---

[1] With some reluctance TS had agreed in November 1884 to become President of the Royal Society of Edinburgh.

[2] Annotated by MIS: '*Apropos* of Peterhead Harbour.'

[3] 'We have piped unto you, and ye have not danced; we have mourned unto you, and ye have not lamented' – Matthew 11:17.

[4] Cf. the policeman's lot in Act II of Gilbert and Sullivan's *The Pirates of Penzance*. RLS saw the comic opera in San Francisco in May 1880 – his last visit to a theatre.

[5] A day's work.

[6] Fanny joined the Stevensons in London on 26 March and they spent the next few days buying furniture for Skerryvore.

[1] Baxter wrote to RLS on 20 March (in the character of Thomson):

> Man I'm fair to the wa' noo. Ye mind I wes aye ettlin at the law, hed aye a kin' o' hankerin for leetigation (Gōd knows 'ave hed ma bellyful syne) but that's no it. Weel efter the cairds was done for an' a' got oot o' Dumbarton (dam yon Bailie tae hell) I thocht I wad tak to the law, and no to be a burden tae ma freens, I just wheeped up canty and cosy to Lunnon but gosh me, they're ōn me aince mair, an' ye'll see in a swatch I cut oot o' *The Times* and sent to Jaikson to forward it ōn to ye, that the Law Society as the ca' themsels Gōds dam hes been on tie me. What to dae noo's mair than a can ask or think.

baith in't; an' the extrodnar pairt of it is that I cannae weel mak' out the richts and wrongs of it. But you and me must hae been innycent; there's nae doobt o' that. They had me up yince in a multiplepindin';[2] I had seen ower muckle o' thae games; sae nae suner had I taken the aith, than I said, 'My loard,' I says, 'it's proper that I should tell ye, at the first off go, how it stan's. There's a wheen folk that has a prejudice on my chara'ter,' I says, 'but, my loard, whatever for that,' I says, 'I'm innycent.' – 'Whae's accusin' you?' says he. – 'My loard,' I says, 'I div not know; and, my loard,' I says, 'I div not care.' And I lookit round the court like a lion. There was a wheen low writer lads that leugh; but the Judge, whae was a very decent spoken man (it wasnae Deas; it was yin I had never forgathered wi' afore; Muir,[3] I think, was the name of him) – he up, and says he, 'The gentleman,' he says, 'is labourin' under some mistak',' he says. 'My loard,' I says, 'there's been ower mony o' thae mistak's in my case; there was the trust mistak',' I says, 'and there was the Afeelyation mistak',' I says, 'and the till mistak', an' the plate mistak', an' the French cairds mistak',' I says, 'and now, to pit the tap to it, I'm accüsed o' multipplepindin! It's a thing,' I says, 'my loard, that I'm incapable of!' – 'My guid man,' says he, 'this is a ceevil case.' – 'My loard,' says I, 'the're all ceevil by their way of it; but yince ye're in the Dōck, nae mair civeelity for puir Johnstone.' – The loard turned to an aaadvikate: 'Mr Trayner,'[4] says he, 'cannae ye no get a better wutness?' – 'I'll try,' says he; and tauld me to step doun; and I never heard nae mair of it! I've aften thocht sinsyne if I had aye been as bauld at the first off-gang, mebbe I wad hae had less injustice. But ye see I was mōrally convinced that this yin was a shaam; and whiles I wasnae sae clear. There's a wheen awkwardnesses in the warld; and mony things are unco' sair to expleen. Nae doobt somebody had multiplepindit; but I'll tak my aith it wasnae me.

I'm muckle obleeged to ye for thon siller; and remain

Dear Johnstone	Dear Thamson
Yours	Yours
Thamson	Johns'one

---

[2] Multiplepoinding. A Scots legal term for an action raised by the holder of a fund or property to which there are several claimants. Baxter replied on 5 April: 'Man I fair pisht masel lauchin at the multiplepinding an' so did the Gōdkin. Ye're just donnert, it's no a crime or I wad hae committed it masel lang syne; it's a fōrm o' law an' ye sweer onything 'at comes intie yer heed. Gōd kens wha' it's a' fōr, but tha's hoo it is,' 'Godkin' was RLS's joke name for William Mitchell, Baxter's staid senior partner.
[3] David Mure, Lord Mure (1810–91), Lord Commissioner of Justiciary.
[4] John Trayner (1834–1929), advocate; Sheriff of Forfarshire.

To William Archer[1]

29 March 1885   *Bournemouth*

Dear Mr Archer, Yes, I have heard of you and read some of your work; but I am bound in particular to thank you for the notice of my verses.[2] 'There,' I said, throwing it over to the friend who was staying with me, 'it's worth writing a book to draw an article like that.' My friend (Sidney Colvin) was of the same mind; we debated who should be the author, and thought it must be Symonds in an unusually workmanlike humour: of no one else could we think, who had the requisite turn of style and turn of thought. Had you been as hard upon me as you were amiable, I try to tell myself I should have been no blinder to the merits of your notice. For I saw there, to admire and to be very grateful for, a most sober, agile pen: an enviable touch: the marks of a reader, such as one imagines for oneself in dreams, thoughtful, critical, and kind; and to put the top on this memorial column, a greater readiness to describe the author criticised than to display the talents of his censor.

I am a man *blasé* to injudicious praise (though I hope some of it may be judicious too), but I have to thank you for THE BEST CRITICISM I EVER HAD; and am therefore, dear Mr Archer, the most grateful crickee now extant.   Robert Louis Stevenson[3]

P.S. I congratulate you on living in the corner of all London that I like best.[4] *À propos*, you are very right about my voluntary aversion from the painful sides of life. My childhood was in reality a very mixed experience, full of fever, nightmare, insomnia, painful days and interminable nights; and I can speak with less authority of Gardens than of that other 'land of counterpane'. But to what end should we renew these sorrows? The sufferings of life may be handled by the very greatest in their hours of insight; it is of its pleasures that our common poems should be formed; these are the experiences that we should seek to recall or to provoke; and

---

[1] William Archer (1856–1924), Scottish dramatic critic, journalist, translator and editor of Ibsen.
[2] On reading Archer's unsigned review in the *P.M.G.* for 24 March RLS wrote a four-word letter: 'Now *Who* are you?' and addressed the envelope 'To the writer of the review on Mr Stevenson's verses for children, care of the Editor of the *Pall Mall Gazette*.' Archer replied on 27 March saying that the review was the first he had ever published on RLS's work: 'You may perhaps have heard my name from your friend and my valued acquaintance, W.E. Henley.'
[3] Archer was rather overcome by RLS's praise, responding on 2 April: 'If my notice of *A Child's Garden* gave you pleasure it only repaid some small part of a long-standing debt I owe you. . . . Believe me when I say that I regard your letter as one of the things that tend to reconcile a man to the journalistic house of bondage. I thank you for it from my heart.'
[4] Archer was living at 2 Queen Square Place, Bloomsbury.

I say with Thoreau, 'What right have I to complain, who have not ceased to wonder?'[5] and, to add a rider of my own, who have no remedy to offer.

R.L.S.

To W.E. Henley

[*?8 April 1885*]   [*Bournemouth*]

My dear Lad, That is all right, and a good job. I announce the good news to Henderson, whom I suppose they merely insulted for the keen, genial pleasure of the act: lovable dogs are they all: . . . .[1]

About coming down, you cannot get into us for a while as you may imagine: we are in a desperate vortex, and everybody most dead. I have been two days in bed with liver and slight bleeding.

Do you think you are right to send *Macaire* and the *Admiral* about? Not a copy have I sent, nor (speaking for myself personally) do I want sent. The reperusal of the *Admiral*, by the way, was a sore blow; eh, God man, it is a low, black dirty, blackguard, ragged piece: vomitable in many parts – simply vomitable. Pew is in places, a reproach to both art and man. But of all that afterwards. What I mean is that I believe in playing dark with second and third-rate work. *Macaire* is a piece of job-work, hurriedly buckled; might have been worse, might have been better; happy-go-lucky; act it, or-let-it-rot piece of business.[2] Not a thing, I think, to send in presentations. Do not let us *gober*[3] ourselves – and above all, not *gober* dam pot-boilers – and p.b.'s with an obvious flaw and hole in them, such as is our unrealised Bertrand in this one. But of this also, on a meeting.

I am not yet done with my proofs, I am sorry to say; so soon as I am, I must tackle *Kidnapped* seriously, or be content to have no bread, which you would scarcely recommend. It is all I shall be able to do to wait for the *Young Folks* money, on which I'll have to live as best I can till the Book comes in.

Plays at that rate, I do not think I can possibly look at before July; so let that be a guide to you in your views.[4] July or August or September or

---

[5] Thoreau's letter of 2 March 1842 to Mrs Lucy Brown ('complain' should be 'grieve'). RLS quotes the letter in his essay on Thoreau.

[1] About half a dozen words have been rubbed out. In March 1885 James Henderson had agreed to publish *Kidnapped* in *Young Folks* at 15s. a column. It finally began publication in the issue dated 1 May 1886.

[2] In January 1885 Herbert Beerbohm Tree (1853–1917), English actor (later a famous actor-manager) commissioned Henley and RLS to produce a new version of the French melodrama *Macaire*. There was much correspondence and negotiation but Tree finally withdrew from the venture. The play was privately printed in March 1885.

[3] French *gober*, to have a strong liking for, to think no end of; *se gober*, to be self-conceited.

[4] A week later RLS gave his considered views to Henley: 'I come unhesitatingly to the opinion that the stage is only a lottery, must not be regarded as a trade, and must never be preferred to

thereabouts: these must be our times, whichever we attack. I think you had better suspend a visit till we can take you in, and till I can speak. It seems a considerable waste of money; above all as just now, I could not even offer you meals, with my women in such a state of overwork. My father and mother have had to go to lodgings.[5] Post.   R.L.S.

To his Wife[1]

[c. 6 May 1885][2]   [Skerryvore]

My dear fellow, There's no place like home. Morning: went down to the pond and discussed with le Beaucox,[3] about the dam, the coasts etc; strolled in garden, flowers mighty pretty. Dined: Valentine and Agnes out on messages, your dear parent keeps house, sitting now in the porch, now out on the gravel, reading Meredith,[4] looking at rhododendrons and red hawthorn and hearing the piejohns, whirring about and saying damn; on return of maids, your d. p. goes out and visits Mrs Bellairs;[5] on his return receives the Bocox whom he pays, liquors and discusses flowers and trees and ponds and rights of way with: the Bocox dismissed he writes you this to cheer your unfortunate fat heart and to assure you of his love and friendship. Ever yours, my old, fat, pleasant, insane fellow

Robert Louis Stevenson

Valentine very pretty in her cap, and the pair quite a neat turn out.

To his Parents

[c. 10 May 1885]   [Skerryvore]

My dear people, There came here a lean, brown, bloodshot woman, claiming to be Fanny; I have taken her in provisionally. She had stolen much finery and her head ached.

---

drudgery. If money comes from any play, let us regard it as a legacy, but never count upon it in our income for the year.'
[5] In order to be out of the way while the move to Skerryvore took place.
[1] RLS and Fanny moved into Skerryvore in early April 1885. Skerryvore, on the brink of Alum Chine, was a two-storey yellow-brick house, closely covered with ivy and with a blue slate roof, set (in Graham Balfour's words) in 'half an acre of ground very charmingly arranged, running down from the lawn at the back, past a bank of heather into a chine or small ravine full of rhododendrons, and at the bottom a tiny stream'.
[2] Fanny had gone up to London with RLS's parents on 5 May.
[3] The gardener. Agnes was the maidservant. See p. 398, n. 8.
[4] Meredith's *Diana of the Crossways* was published on 16 February 1885.
[5] Wife of the Revd H.S.K. Bellairs, curate in charge of St Ambrose's Church, Westbourne. RLS later used the name in *The Wrecker*.

In the evening, James[1] brought along *The Times*, where on the latest intelligence page the enclosed notice was figuring.[2] This will do us much good; it should sell from five to ten thousand, I understand. I send some other notices, written by idiots; begging Mr Tommy's pardon – for it is plainly he who is the author of the one from *Society:*[3] I did not know he had gone in for journalism. Ever affectionate son   R.L.S.

This has been long delayed, but the Sam will have given you of our news,[4] and I am able to add two more reviews. The wine, I think *excellent.*

R.L.S.

To Anne Jenkin

[*14 or 15 June 1885*]   *Skerryvore*

My dear Mrs Jenkin, You know how much and for how long I have loved, respected and admired him;[1] I am only able to feel a little with you. But I know how he would have wished us to feel. I never knew a better man nor one to me more lovable; we shall all feel the loss more greatly as time goes on. It scarce seems life to me; what must it be to you? Yet one of the last things that he said to me was that from all these sad bereavements of yours,[2] he had learned only more than ever to feel the goodness and what we, in our feebleness, call the support of God; he had been ripening so much – to other eyes than ours, we must suppose, he was ripe, and try to feel it. I feel it is better not to say much more. It will be to me a great pride to write a notice of him:[3] the last I can now do. What more in any way I can do for you, please to think and let me know. For his sake and for your own, I would not be a useless friend; I know, you know me a most warm one; please command me or my wife, in any way. Do not trouble to write to me; Austin I have no doubt will do so, if you are, as I fear you will be, unfit.

My heart is sore for you. At least you know what you have been to

[1] Henry James went down to Bournemouth on 18 April and stayed for several weeks, visiting his invalid sister, Alice. He became a regular evening visitor to Skerryvore and a close friendship developed.

[2] A very favourable review of *The Dynamiter* in *The Times* of 9 May 1885. It begins: 'We are much inclined to wish that Mr Stevenson may spin out his *New Arabian Nights* to the length of their immortal originals.'

[3] A brief notice in *Society* of 9 May refers to 'these ridiculous nightmare stories'.

[4] Lloyd, who had been on holiday in Bournemouth, had just gone back to Edinburgh.

[1] Fleeming Jenkin died unexpectedly on 12 June 1885 after a minor operation.

[2] There had been a succession of family deaths: Mrs Jenkin's mother died on 19 May 1884 and her father on 14 January 1885; Jenkin's father died on 5 February 1885 and his mother on 8 February.

[3] RLS wrote an obituary notice in the *Academy* of 20 June 1885. He later contributed a Memoir of Jenkin to the two-volume collection of his *Papers Literary, Scientific, &c.* (Longmans, 1887), edited by Colvin and J.A. Ewing.

him; how he cherished and admired you, how he was never so pleased as when he spoke of you; with what a boy's love, up to the last, he loved you. This surely is a consolation. Yours is the cruel part: to survive; you must try and not grudge to him his better fortune, to go first. It is the sad part of such relations that one must remain and suffer; I cannot see my poor Jenkin without you. Nor you indeed without him; but you may try to rejoice that he is spared that extremity. Perhaps I (as I was so much his confidant) know even better than you can do, what your loss would have been to him, he never spoke of you, but what his face changed; it was – you were – his religion.

I write by this post to Austin and to the *Academy*. Yours most sincerely

Robert Louis Stevenson[4]

To Thomas Hardy[1]

Monday, 24 August [1885]   *Skerryvore*

Dear Sir, I expect to arrive in Dorchester tomorrow or next day; and if I shall be strong enough, I shall do myself the pleasure of calling on you – if not, I shall let you know at what inn I put up, and perhaps you will be kind enough to call on me? I think you must have heard of me from Gosse; – from whom, if the time had served, I could have got an introduction; but my acquaintance with your mind is already of so old a date, that I scarce felt such formalities were needed –; and if you should be busy or unwilling, the irregularity of my approach leaves you the safer retreat. Yours truly

Robert Louis Stevenson[2]

Thomas Hardy Esq.

[4] A week later RLS wrote: 'Dear me, what happiness I owe to both of you!'

[1] During the last week in August, RLS, Fanny, Lloyd and Katharine de Mattos set off to stay in 'cheap lodgings in a farmhouse on Dartmoor' (Fanny to MIS, 7 September). On the way they stayed for one night at the King's Arms Hotel in Dorchester and were among Hardy's first visitors at his new house at Max Gate. Fanny wrote to MIS on 10 September: 'Did I tell you that we saw Hardy the novelist at Dorchester? A pale, gentle, frightened little man, that one felt an instinctive tenderness for, with a wife – ugly is no word for it, who said "whatever shall we do?" I had never heard a living being say it before.' To Colvin she wrote: 'What very strange marriages literary men seem to make.'

[2] RLS and his party got no further than the New London Hotel, Exeter. Here, as Fanny wrote to Henley, RLS had 'a dreadful hemorrhage, only less bad than the one at Hyères'. She described RLS's 'mad behaviour' during his illness:

I think it must be the ergotine that affects his brain at such times. He is quite rational, now, I am thankful to say, but he has just given up insisting that he should be lifted into bed in a kneeling position, his face to the pillow, and then still kneeling he was lifted bodily around, and then a third time held up in the air while he drew out his feet. I never performed a feat as difficult. Every time I expected, if not to kill him, at least to snap his little bones somewhere.

To Sidney Colvin[1]

[*Late September/early October 1885*]   [*Skerryvore*]

Dear Colvin, So much the worse, and yet perhaps its better to wait till we can take you in to the Box. Do you remember a Mrs Montagu Blackett?[2] She introduced herself to us on your name; but has since confessed it was partly an imposture, as she only once met you for a week at Minto. She is very nice however; and her brother (or cousin) another Elliot, is supposed to know you well. She asked if you were married; I said you were not. I am however and my wife has a headache. The world is too much with us; and coin it grows so sparsely on the tree! (Scotch Ballad) I am pouring forth a penny (12 penny) dreadful; it is dam dreadful; they call it the Abbot George of Shaw (beg pardon: Scottish poesie) – I mean, they call it Doctor Jekyll, but they also call it Mr Hyde, Mr Hyde, but they also, also call it Mr Hyde.[3] I seem to bloom by nature – oh, by nature, into song; but for all my tale is silly it shall not be very long. So farewell, my noble Colvin, and if ever to our door You shall guide your pacing charger as repeatedly★ before, You shall find the face of welcome in the halls of Skerryvore.   R.L.S.

> ★So on mere poetic grounds, for the fancy of the bard
> Rather leaned to thinking metre and not reason was the card.

To Will H. Low

[*22 October 1885*]   *Skerryvore*

My dear Low, I trust you are not annoyed with me beyond forgiveness; for indeed my silence has been devilish prolonged.[1] I can only tell you that

---

[1] RLS returned home from Exeter on 12 September. Fanny wrote to Colvin the next day reporting that he had 'borne the journey wonderfully well'.

[2] Emma Mary, daughter of the Very Revd Gilbert Elliot, Dean of Bristol (who was a nephew of the first Earl of Minto), married (1862) Montagu Blackett (1826–66).

[3] RLS (as he relates in 'A Chapter on Dreams') had been racking his brains for two days for a plot. On the second night he 'dreamed the scene at the window, and a scene afterward split in two, in which Hyde, pursued for some crime, took the powder and underwent the change in the presence of his pursuers'. Fanny woke him from what she thought was a nightmare to be reproached with the words: 'Why did you wake me? I was dreaming a fine bogey tale.'

   Balfour (following Fanny and Lloyd's recollections) recorded that RLS wrote the first version of what was to become *Strange Case of Dr Jekyll and Mr Hyde* in three days, destroyed it after Fanny's criticism that he had missed the allegory, and prepared a second version in another three days. In later accounts Fanny and Lloyd claimed that the story was ready for the press in a further three days, but RLS's letters make it clear that several weeks were spent on the final version.

[1] RLS is replying to a letter from Low dated 3 June 1885.

I have been nearly six months (more than six) in a strange condition of collapse when it was impossible to do any work and difficult (more difficult than you would suppose) to write the merest note. I am now better, but not yet my own man in the way of brains and in health only so-so. I turn more towards the liver and dyspepsia business which is damned unpleasant and paralysing; I suppose I shall learn (I begin to think I am learning) to fight this vast, vague feather-bed of an obsession that now overlies and smothers me; but in the beginnings of these conflicts, the inexperienced wrestler is always worsted; and I own I have been quite extinct. I wish you to know, though it can be no excuse, that you are not the only one of my friends by many whom I have thus neglected; and even now, having come so very late into the possession of myself, with a substantial capital of debts, and my work still moving with a desperate slowness – as a child might fill a sandbag with its little handfuls – and my future deeply pledged, there is almost a touch of virtue in my borrowing these hours to write to you. Why I said 'hours' I know not; it would look blue for both of us, if I made good the word.

I was writing your address the other day, ordering a copy of my next, *Prince Otto*, to go your way. I hope you have not seen it in parts; it was not meant to be so read; and only my poverty (dishonourably) consented to the serial evolution.

I will send you (with this) a copy of the English edition of the *Child's Garden*. I have heard there is some vile rule of the post office in the States against inscriptions; so I send herewith a piece of doggerel which Mr Bunner may, if he thinks fit, copy on the fly-leaf.[2]

I have little news that would interest you. Bob gets along well with his literature, having much musical criticism for the *Saturday*, and hopes of more and of other work too; in painting, I do not think he advances to much success; the public is cold. I have a house now (and a fine house too; though it is small, it is dam comely; I should like you to see it) and it is largely decorated by Bobs, one of which is I think quite good; it certainly grows on me daily. Sargent was down again and painted a portrait of me walking about in my own dining room, in my own velveteen jacket and twisting, as I go my own moustache; at one corner a glimpse of my wife in an Indian dress and seated in a chair that was once my grandfather's, but since some months goes by the name of Henry James's for it was there the novelist loved to sit – adds a touch of poesy and comicality. It is, I think, excellent; but is too eccentric to be exhibited. I am at one extreme corner; my wife, in this wild dress and looking like a ghost, is at the extreme other end; between us an open door exhibits

---

[2] H.C. Bunner had sent RLS a copy of his *Airs from Arcady and Elsewhere* (1884) and asked in return for an English edition of *A Child's Garden*. RLS's verses to Bunner ('You know the way to Arcady') are dated 21 October 1885.

my palatial entrance hall and a part of my respected staircase. All this is touched in lovely, with that witty touch of Sargent's; but of course it looks dam queer as a whole.[3]

Pray let me hear from you and give me good news of yourself and your wife, to whom please remember me. Yours most sincerely, my dear Low

Robert Louis Stevenson

To his Father

24 October 1885   *Skerryvore*

My dear Father, A lower epistle I certainly never received but I consoled myself by the fact that I have received 'o' them' before now, and that the sun came out again after the cloud. I wish you were in better spirits and in stronger health of mind; but I must say I think there is something in the seasons which acts against the last. The great effort and the miserable results of my own attempts are enough to disgust a provost or anybody. I may be said, saving your presence, to be no better than a fool. I assure you only the top wheels of my brain have worked, except some three or four days, since we came to this house. This, at my age, is pretty annoying; but I bear up, sir, and have not yet fallen foul of the nonconformists, in your opinion of whom I will, however, follow you at a certain distance. I am disgusted, that is to say, with the whole body of the English people, and all other peoples; I think them not much good, and prefer a pound note to their opinion, which is indeed no opinion but a cry. The less a man troubles his heart about politics except to vote straight and quarrel with his most valued friends, the better. When I read at Nice that Graham was recalled from Suakin after all that butchery, I died to politics.[1] I saw that they did not regard what I regarded, and regarded what I despised; and I closed my account. If ever I could do anything, I suppose I ought to do it; but till that hour comes, I will not vex my soul. The people and the country have been the same in most ages; and yet they wars'le on.[2] One thing, however; are you going to vote for Goschen?[3] I am afraid that what happened in France will happen here, that the moderates will all be

---

[3] The portrait, painted in August 1885, was a gift by Sargent to RLS and remained in the possession of the family until Fanny's death. It was later owned by Mr and Mrs John H. Whitney. In a letter to MIS of 13 August, Fanny wrote: 'It is lovely . . . It is like an open box of jewels.'

[1] Cf. p. 247.

[2] Wrestle, struggle on.

[3] George Joachim Goschen (1831–1907), later Viscount Goschen, Liberal politician who won the seat at East Edinburgh in the November 1885 election. In an earlier letter RLS had called him 'the only candidate worth a rush that has stood for Edinburgh in my time'. He helped form the Liberal Unionists (1886) and subsequently served in Conservative administrations.

unseated and the two extremes left face to face. Yet remember the moderates are the cement and the means of compromise of politics. Support a moderate: support the necessary but.

My dear father, I pray God this finds you in a better and (pardon me) a braver spirit; and if you will let me suggest anything, I would breathe in your ear: Watch your liver! If I say nothing of lights, it is because of your professional acquaintance there.

We had a rare silly story of Charlie Robertson[4] the other night: however, until we hear his answer, it would not be fair to tell it; but from here, he smells to me like an ass. Ever your affectionate son

Robert Louis Stevenson

To W.E. Henley

[c. 25 October 1885]   [Skerryvore]

To Mr Henley ooralooralooralooraloo.

The wife arrived with her pulse at 102[1]
And a cat so lovely[2] I don't know what to do,
And biscuits so good I could eat them till all was blue
And sheets of *Otto* are ordered off to you
And I drink in sorrow the bile that I have to brew
And I shall be glad to learn it goes better with you
And I am your humble servant Robert Lou

is STEVENSON gone?

The cat's view is that my papers are the bog! This plan will never answer! When a cat comes in at the door, literature flies out of the window.[3] Not that there's much of it to fly from here. Parceque je swee le imbecile to such a point as few have yet attained: apparently, an indecent imbecile? This flattering tale! Go way, you naughty man! But the time is now beginning when I shall have to pay for my popularity. I have long expected it. When *you* find a friend beginning to get it (and you will see

---

[4] Charles Gray Robertson, editor of the *Court and Society Review*, was the son of General A.C. Robertson, an Edinburgh friend of the Stevensons. The 'story' is not known.
[1] Fanny had been staying with the Henleys in London.
[2] On 6 June 1899, commenting to Colvin on the selection of RLS's letters for publication, Henley wrote: 'If you have room for another, hunt out the charming note in which Lewis described the coming into his life of Ginger. It always pleased me; and, as the old cat's still alive, I don't see why he shouldn't live hereafter with the rest of us.' Henley told Archer in 1887: 'Ginger is a *semi*-Persian, not the genuine article. She [Fanny] bought him for ten bob at a Cat show at the [Crystal] Palace'.
[3] A parody of the proverb, 'When poverty comes in at the door, love flies out of the window.'

that, just as the praise has been exaggerated and beside the mark, so will the dispraise be) you may perhaps begin to change your vote for your unfriends, and not to delight (as I always think) childishly, in the weapons that a child can use and that can hurt a giant or an angel. Not that I am either; I am a careful, industrious and (apparently) an impure writer.[4] *Honi soit* the crowd – though I daresay it is true enough. Every defect in a man's character must out in his works, as a flaw in a window must make a mark on the wall; and nobody that I have yet heard of, took me for a white ribbon. That is not my weakness.

My wife has enjoyed her visit very much: Gingibber is HEAVENLY.

R.L.S.

To William Archer
(Slightly Abridged)

28 October 1885 [postmarked 29 October]   *Skerryvore*

Dear Mr Archer, I have read your paper with my customary admiration;[1] it is very witty, very adroit; it contains a great deal that is excellently true (particularly the parts about my stories and the description of me as an artist in life); but you will not be surprised if I do not think it altogether just. It seems to me, in particular, that you have wilfully read all my works in terms of my earliest; my aim, even in style, has quite changed in the last six or seven years; and this I should have thought you would have noticed. Again, your first remark upon the affectation of the italic names;[2] a practice only followed in my two affected little books of travel, where a typographical *minauderie* of the sort appeared to me in character; and what you say of it, then, is quite just. But why should you forget yourself and use these same italics as an index to my theology some pages further on? This is lightness of touch indeed; may I say, it is almost sharpness of practice?

[4] Henley replied on Tuesday (presumably 27 October): 'I don't understand your letter at all. What have I to do with your indecency? or with the over- or under praising you are like to get? where does childishness come in? *Enfin*, what's it all about?'

[1] 'Robert Louis Stevenson: His Style and his Thought' in *Time* for November 1885.

[2] In a footnote Archer refers to 'the eighteenth-century quaintness which Mr Stevenson introduces into his *Inland Voyage*, and *Travels with a Donkey*, by the typographical trick of italicising proper names' and quotes examples. Later he quotes RLS's remark in the preface to *An Inland Voyage* that the book 'contains not a single reference to the imbecility of *God's* universe' and comments: 'It is a characteristic of such optimism as Mr Stevenson's to do homage to God in capitals and italics, while refraining from any too curious consideration as to what is meant by that convenient term.' Elsewhere he writes: 'There are fashions in style as in everything else, and, for the moment, we are all agreed that the one great saving grace is "lightness of touch". Of this virtue Mr Stevenson is the accomplished model.' Archer uses the phrase many times in the course of his essay.

Excuse these remarks. I have been on the whole much interested, and sometimes amused. Are you aware that the praiser of this 'brave gymnasium', has not seen a canoe nor taken a long walk since '79? that he is rarely out of the house nowadays, and carries his arm in a sling?[3] Can you imagine that he is a back-slidden communist, and is sure he will go to Hell (if there be such an excellent institution) for the luxury in which he lives? And can you believe that, though it is gaily expressed, the thought is his hag and skeleton in every moment of vacuity or depression? Do you think that I believe in a future state? Can you conceive how profoundly I am irritated by the opposite affectation to my own when I see strong men and rich men bleating about their sorrows and the burthen of life in a world full of 'cancerous paupers', and poor sick children, and the fatally bereaved, ay, and down even to such happy creatures as myself who has yet been obliged to strip himself, one after another, of all the pleasures that he had chosen except smoking (and the days of that I know in my heart ought to be over) (I forgot eating, which I still enjoy)[4] and who sees the circle of impotence closing very slowly but quite steadily around him? In my view, one dank, dispirited word is harmful, a crime of *lèse-humanité*, a piece of acquired evil; every gay, every bright word or picture, like every pleasant air of music, is a piece of pleasure set afloat; the reader catches it and, if he be healthy, goes on his way rejoicing; and it is the business of art so to send him, as often as possible.

For what you say, so kindly, so prettily, so precisely, of my style, I must in particular thank you! though even here, I am vexed you should not have remarked on my attempted change of manner: seemingly this attempt is still quite unsuccessful! Well, we shall fight it out on this line if it takes all summer.

---

[3] After calling RLS an aggressive optimist Archer quotes from the Dedicatory Letter to *Virginibus Puerisque*.

> 'Times change,' says Mr Stevenson, 'opinions vary to their opposite, and still this world appears a brave gymnasium, full of sea-bathing, and horse-exercise, and bracing manly virtues.' There are some people on whom even sea-bathing and horse-exercise are apt to pall, and who fail to find a joy for ever in the practice of manly virtue; these, let us admit for the sake of the argument, are despicable persons, unworthy of regard. But what of those whose wishes are their only horses, who know more of sweat-baths than of sea-baths, and who are shut out from the exercise of any manly virtue, save that of renunciation? They, too, demonstrate the theorem of the liveableness of life, and that much more conclusively than the 'happy man or woman' who affords Mr Stevenson more gratification than a five-pound note. The happiness *must* be temporary, for under the best of circumstances it tends to wear itself out; the misery *may* be permanent, since it has no inherent tendency to decrease. If, then, the cancer-eaten pauper is as tenacious of existence as the horse-riding, sea-bathing virtuous athlete, is not he the true proof positive of the liveableness of life, which simply means the tenacity of our earliest, most mechanical habit? It is not Apollo-Goethe but Prometheus-Heine who demonstrates the liveableness of life.

[4] Added above as an afterthought.

And now for my last word: Mrs Stevenson is very anxious that you should see me, and that she should see you, in the flesh.[5] If you at all share in these views, I am a fixture. Write or telegraph (giving us time however to telegraph in reply, lest the day be impossible) and come down here to a bed and a dinner. What do you say, my dear critic? I shall be truly pleased to see you; and to explain at greater length what I meant by saying narrative was the most characteristic mood of literature,[6] on which point I have great hopes I shall persuade you. Yours truly

Robert Louis Stevenson[7]

To William Archer

[30 October 1885]   Skerryvore

Dear Mr Archer, You will see that I had already had a sight of your article and what were my thoughts.[1]

One thing in your letter puzzles me. Are you, too, not in the witness-box? And if you are why take a wilfully false hypothesis? If you knew I was a chronic invalid, why say that my philosophy was unsuitable to such a case? My call for facts is not so general as yours, but an essential fact should not be put the other way about.[2]

The fact is, consciously or not, you doubt my honesty; you think I am making faces, and at heart disbelieve my utterances. And this I am disposed to think must spring from your not having had enough of pain, sorrow and trouble in your existence. It is easy to have too much; easy also or possible to have too little: enough is required that a man may appreciate what elements of consolation and joy there are in everything, but abso-

---

[5] Fanny sent a separate letter pointing out that RLS knew 'more of sweat-baths than of sea-baths' and expressing their strong desire to meet Archer.

[6] In Part III of his essay on Thoreau, RLS says: 'He [Thoreau] was probably reminded by his delicate critical perception that the true business of literature is with narrative.' Archer calls this 'a widespread heresy'.

[7] Two postscripts omitted.

[1] Archer wrote on 29 October sending RLS a copy of his article, thus crossing in the post RLS's letter of 28 October.

[2] In his letter of 29 October Archer commented:

> I know that I am mis-representing you personally in making you out to be one of the robust nuisances whose 'aggressive optimism' springs from an ignorance of suffering . . . But it is precisely the absence of any hint of this [personal experience of illness and suffering] in your writings which leads me to adopt what I fear you will think the unsympathetic tone of the last part of my article. It seems to me that if a man says anything at all about life he should say all he knows. He is not bound to get into the witness-box, but once there he is upon oaths and must tell the truth, the whole truth and nothing but the truth. That is *my* view of the matter − you, I suppose, hold that one should at all costs prophesy smooth things, if one has no remedy to propose for what is rough in life.

lutely overpowering physical pain or disgrace, and how in almost all circumstances the human soul can play a fair part. You fear life, I fancy, on the principle of the hand of little employment. But perhaps my hypothesis is as unlike the truth as the one you chose. Well, if it be so, if you have had trials, sickness, the approach of death, the alienation of friends, poverty at the heels, and have not felt your soul turn round upon these things and spurn them under – you must be very differently made from me, and I earnestly believe from the majority of men. But at least you are in the right to wonder and complain.

To 'say all'? Stay here. All at once? That would require a word from the pen of Gargantua. We say each particular thing as it comes up, and 'with that sort of emphasis that for the time there seems to be no other'.[3] Words will not otherwise serve us; no, nor even Shakespeare, who could not have put *As You Like It* and *Timon* into one without ruinous loss both of emphasis and substance. Is it quite fair then to keep your face so steadily on my most light-hearted works, and then say I recognise no evil? Yet in the paper on Burns for instance, I show myself alive to some sorts of evil. But then perhaps they are not your sorts.

And again: 'to say all'? All: yes. Everything: no. The task were endless, the effect nil. But my all in such a vast field as this of life is what interests me, what stands out, what takes on itself a presence for my imagination or makes a figure in that little tricky abbreviation which is the best that my reason can conceive. That I must treat or I shall be fooling with my readers. That, and not the all of some one else.

And here we come to the division: not only do I believe that literature should give joy, but I see a universe, I suppose, eternally different from yours: a solemn, a terrible but a very joyous and noble universe; where suffering is not at least wantonly inflicted, though it falls with dispassionate partiality, but where it may be and generally is nobly borne; where, above all, *any brave man may make* out a life which shall be happy for himself and, by so being, beneficent to those about him. (This I believe; probably you don't: I think he may, with cancer.)[4] And if he fails, why should I hear him weeping? I mean if I fail, why should I weep? Why should *you* hear *me*?[5] Then to me morals, the conscience, the affections, and the passions are, I will own frankly and sweepingly, so infinitely more important than the other parts of life, that I conceive men rather triflers who become immersed in the latter; and I will always think the man who keeps his lip

---

[3] In his paper Archer quoted a sentence from Thoreau which RLS himself had quoted in his essay on Thoreau: 'No truth, we think, was ever expressed but with this sort of emphasis, that for the time there seemed to be no other.'

[4] This sentence (which I have placed in brackets) was added above the previous one as an afterthought.

[5] These three sentences were added at the side of the letter.

stiff, and makes 'a happy fireside clime'[6] and carries a pleasant face about
to friends and neighbours, infinitely greater (in the abstract) than an
atrabilious Shakespeare or a back-biting Kant or Darwin. No offence to
any of these gentlemen: two of whom probably (one for certain) came up
to my standard.

And now enough said: it were hard if a poor man could not criticise
another without having so much ink shed against him. But I shall still
regret you should have written on an hypothesis you knew to be untenable, and that you should thus have made your paper, for those who do
not know me, essentially unfair. The rich, fox-hunting squire speaks with
one voice; the sick man of letters with another. Yours very truly

Robert Louis Stevenson

(Prometheus-Heine *in minimis*)

P.S. Here I go again. To me, the medicine bottles on my chimney and
the blood on my handkerchief are accidents; they do not colour my view
of life, as you would know, I think, if you had experience of sickness; they
do not exist in my prospect; I would as soon drag them under the eyes of
my readers as I would mention a pimple I might chance to have (saving
your presence) on my bottom. What does it prove? what does it change?
it has not hurt, it has not changed me in any essential part; and I should
think myself a trifler and in bad taste if I introduced the world to these
unimportant privacies.

But again there is this mountain range between us: *that you do not believe
me.* It is not flattering, but the fault is probably in my literary art.[7]

To his Father[1]

5 December 1885   [*Skerryvore*]

My dear Father, Sorry to hear so poor an account of you. You must brace
up a little in the wind's eye, as I am engaged in doing. I am not yet out
of bed; but though I am rather disjaskit,[2] I have no very bad symptoms. It

---

6   'To make a happy fireside clime
                                                To weans and wife,
                                        That's the true pathos and sublime
                                                Of human life.'
                                                    – Burns, 'Epistle to Dr Blacklock', ix.

[7] RLS wrote a third letter to Archer on 1 November continuing the argument. MIS records that
Archer was at dinner at Skerryvore on 7 and 8 November – 'he is rather a wooden-faced young
man'.

[1] Corrected from MS at Yale.

[2] Depressed, dilapidated, exhausted.

was a very fine cold, stole upon me slowly, and I suppose it means to be as slow in going. The only thing you can do for me, is to be in better spirits and let me hear so. Ever your affectionate son   R.L.S.

No extra charge for correct date.

*To Katharine de Mattos

1 January 1886   .   [*Skerryvore*]

Dearest Katharine, Here, on a very little book and accompanied with your lame verses, I have put your name.[1] Our kindness is now getting well on in years; it must be nearly of age; and it gets more valuable to me with every time I see you. It is not possible to express any sentiment, and it is not necessary to try at least between us. You know very well that I love you dearly, and that I always will. I only wish the verses were better, but at least you like the story; and it is sent to you by the one that loves you – Jekyll and not Hyde.   R.L.S.

To his Parents

1 January 1886   *Skerryvore*

My dear people, Many happy returns of the day to you all; I am fairly well and in good spirits; and much and hopefully occupied with dear Jenkin's life. The enquiry in every detail, every letter that I read, makes me think

---

[1] *Strange Case of Dr Jekyll and Mr Hyde*, dedicated to Katharine de Mattos, was published on 9 January 1886. On 19 May 1885 RLS wrote the following verses for his wedding anniversary dinner at which Katharine as well as Henry James was a guest:

KATHARINE DE MATTOS
AVE!
Bells upon the city are ringing in the night;
High above the gardens are the houses full of light;
On the heathy Pentlands is the curlew flying free;
And the broom is blowing bonnie in the north countrie.

We cannae break the bonds that God decreed to bind,
Still we'll be the children of the heather and the wind;
Far away from home, O, it's still for you and me
That the broom is blowing bonnie in the north countrie!
                    R.L.S.

The second verse was printed in *Dr Jekyll* as part of the dedication, with the opening words amended to 'It's ill to loose the bands'.

of him more nobly. I cannot imagine how I got his friendship; I did not deserve it. I believe the notice will be interesting and useful.

My father's last letter, owing to the use of a quill pen and the neglect of blotting paper was hopelessly illegible. Everyone tried and everyone failed to decipher an important word on which the interest of one whole clause (and the letter consisted of two) depended.

I find I can make little more of this; but I'll spare the blots.

Dear people, Ever your loving son   R.L.S.

I will try again, being a giant refreshed by the house being empty. The presence of people is the great obstacle to letter-writing. I deny that letters should contain news (I mean mine – those of other people should). But mine should contain appropriate sentiments and humorous nonsense or nonsense without the humour. When the house is empty, the mind is seized with a desire – no that is too strong – a willingness to pour forth unmitigated rot, which constitutes (in me) the true spirit of correspondence. When I have no remarks to offer (and nobody to offer them to) my pen flies, and you see the remarkable consequence of a page literally covered with words and genuinely devoid of sense. I can always do that, if quite alone, and I like doing it; but I have yet to learn that it is beloved by correspondents. The deuce of it is, that there is no end possible but the end of the paper. My pen is literally flying: my mind quite vacant; and as the madman up the street was heard shouting aloud to all whom it may concern 'I owe no man anything, it's my own house, and the damned conscience is quite clear.' You see my breakneck course has led me to an anecdote (and a funny one) with which you might suppose I should be content to stop. Not so: nothing can bring me up but the paper running out; and as there is very little left of that, and not much chance of my bearing down on another anecdote – if I cannot stop writing – suppose you give up reading. It would all come to the same thing; and I think we should all be happier. As to my stopping to write the thing is impossible. I mean stopping[1] writing. Mighty little space now. This is very grave. The world is too much with us; and I am sure anything that flows tonight from my pen is little likely to alleviate its evils or to correct its errors. But who knows? Our lightest word has power to cheer the brawny Hottentot, and who can tell how many would be –

It may be as well to mention that I am not drunk.

---

[1] At this point RLS comes to the bottom of the page and continues sideways across the top of the first page. The last sentence is squeezed against the initials.

To Edmund Gosse

2 January 1886   *Skerryvore*

My dear Gosse, Thank you for your letter, so interesting to my vanity.[1]
There is a review in the *St Jingo*; which, as it seems to hold somewhat of
your opinion and is besides written with a pen and not a poker, we think
may possibly be yours.[2] The Prince has done fairly well in spite of the
reviews which have been bad; he was, as you doubtless saw, well slated in
the *Saturday*;[3] one paper reviewed it as a child's story;[4] another (picture my
agony) described it as a 'Gilbert comedy'. It was amusing to see the race
between me and Justin M'Carthy;[5] the Milesian has won by a length. That
is the hard part of literature. You aim high, and you take longer over your
work; and it will not be so successful as if you had aimed low and rushed
it. What the public likes is work (of any kind) a little loosely executed; so
long as it is a little wordy, a little slack, a little dim and knotless, the dear
public likes it: it should (if possible) be a little dull into the bargain. I know
that good work sometimes hits; but with my hand on my heart, I declare
I think it by an accident. And I know also that good work must succeed
at last; but that is not the doing of the public; they are only shamed into
silence or affectation. I do not write for the public; I do write for money,
a nobler deity; and most of all for myself, not perhaps any more noble but
both more intelligent and nearer home.

Let us tell each other sad stories of the bestiality of the beast whom we
feed. What he likes is the newspaper; and to me the press is the mouth of
a sewer, where lying is professed as from an university chair, and everything prurient, and ignoble, and essentially dull, finds its abode and pulpit.
I do not like mankind; but men, and not all of these – and fewer women.
As for respecting the race, and above all that fatuous rabble of burgesses
called 'the public', God save me from such irreligion; that way lies disgrace

---

[1] Gosse wrote on 25 December 1885: 'a Christmas letter about nothing at all, merely to recall
myself to your existence' – praising 'Markheim' in *Unwin's Annual* and reporting that Gladstone
had read *Treasure Island* 'over and over'.

[2] A review of *Prince Otto* in the *St James's Gazette* of 1 January 1886. Gosse replied on 4 January
that he had not written it.

[3] The *Saturday Review* of 21 November found it 'painful to have no words of praise to say of a
book by Mr Stevenson'. 'The author calls his book a romance, but the story deals with persons
who have no high or romantic aspirations . . . Tales of unsavoury court intrigue are not pleasant
to read even when the facts are real . . . In a work of imagination, and especially in a
"romance" . . . they seem oddly out of place.'

[4] The *Edinburgh Courant* reviewed the novel among the Christmas books for children.

[5] Justin M'Carthy (1830–1912), Irish politician, historian and novelist whose *Camiola* had just
been published.

and dishonour. There must be something wrong in me, or I would not be popular.

This is perhaps a trifle stronger than my sedate and permanent opinion. Not much, I think. As for the art that we profess and try to practise, I have never been able to see why its professors should be respected. They chose the primrose path; when they found it was not all primroses, but some of it brambly, and much of it uphill, they began to think and to speak of themselves as holy martyrs. But a man is never martyred in any honest sense in the pursuit of his own pleasure; and *delirium tremens* has none of the honour of the cross. We were full of the pride of life, and chose, like prostitutes, to live by a pleasure. We should be paid, if we give the pleasure we pretend to give; but why should we be honoured? We are whores, some of us pretty whores, some of us not, but all whores: whores of the mind, selling to the public the amusements of our fireside as the whore sells the pleasures of her bed.

Well, what's the odds? I'm a pretty sick whore anyway; though better than I have been. If there was a card for us, how few would be allowed to walk the streets? To the lock[6] with the fatted brain and the rancid imagination? – This is a gay letter: 1886 opens fairly.

You will have received Low's *Lamia*; how do you like it? I am very fond of two: 'Bathes unseen' and 'Into the green recessed woods'.

I hope some day you and Mrs Gosse will come for a Sunday; but we must wait till I am able to see people. – I am very full of Jenkin's life; it is painful yet very pleasant, to dig into the past of a dead friend, and find him, at every spadeful, shine brighter. I own as I read, I wonder more and more why he should have taken me to be a friend. He had many and obvious faults upon the face of him; the heart was pure gold. I feel it little pain to have lost him, for it is a loss in which I cannot believe; I take it, against reason, for an absence; if not today, then tomorrow, I still fancy I shall see him in the door, and then, now when I know him better, how glad a meeting! Yes, if I could believe in the immortality business, the world would indeed be too good to be true; but we were put here to do what service we can, for honour and not for hire; the sods cover us, and the worm that never dies, the conscience, sleeps well at last; these are the wages, besides what we receive so lavishly day by day; and they are enough for a man who knows his own frailty and sees all things in the proportion of reality. The soul of piety was killed long ago by that idea of reward. Nor is happiness, whether eternal or temporal, the reward that mankind seeks. Happinesses are but his wayside campings; his soul is in the journey: he was born for the struggle and only tastes his life in effort and

---

[6] I.e. the Lock-hospital for the treatment of venereal diseases (continuing the analogy of the 'sick whore').

on the condition that he is opposed. How then is such a creature, so fiery, so pugnacious, so made up of discontent and aspiration, and such noble and uneasy passions, how can he be rewarded but by rest? I would not say it aloud; for man's cherished belief is that he loves that happiness which he continually spurns and passes by; and this belief in some ulterior happiness exactly fits him. He does not require to stop and taste it; he can be about the rugged and bitter business where his heart lies; and yet he can tell himself this fairy tale of an eternal tea party, and enjoy the notion that he is both himself and something else; and that his friends will yet meet him, all ironed out and emasculate, and still be lovable; as if love did not live in the faults of the beloved only, and draw its breath in an unbroken round of forgiveness! But the truth is we must fight until we die, and when we die there can be no quiet for mankind but complete resumption into – what? – God, let us say – when all their desperate tricks will lie spell-bound at last.[7]

Here came my dinner and cut this sermon short. *Excusez.*   R.L.S.

To James Payn

2 *January 1886*   *Skerryvore*

Dear James Payn, Your very kind letter came very welcome; and still more welcome the news that you see Powell's tale.[1] I will now tell you (and it was very good and very wise of me not to tell it before) that he is one of the most unlucky men I know, having put all his money into a pharmacy at Hyères, when the cholera (certainly not his fault) swept away his customers in a body. Thus you can imagine the pleasure I have to announce to him a spark of hope, for he sits today in his pharmacy, doing nothing and taking nothing and watching his debts inexorably mount up. His address is, W.A. Powell, Pharmacie Anglaise, Hyères, Var, France.

To pass to other matters: your hand, you are perhaps aware, is not one of those that can be read running;[2] and the name of your daughter remains for me undecipherable. I call her, then, your daughter – and a very good

---

[7] In his reply Gosse wrote:

> It interests me very much to find you succumbing to this general tendency to take life so very seriously. I suppose you are right . . . But I cannot pretend that I follow you, except civilly and for sympathy's sake . . . I have no anxiety about my soul . . . I am not without terror, sometimes, at the idea of this sensual sufficiency in life coming to an end; I have no idea how the spiritual world would look to me, for I have never glanced at it since I was a child and was gorged with it. You will perhaps see how oddly your serious letter has affected me; I am made rather sullen, frightened a little, by your earnestness.

[1] 'A Run of Luck in the Var', published in *Cornhill* October 1886.
[2] Cf. John Keble's hymn, 'There is a book, who runs may read'.

name, too – and I beg to explain how it came about that I took her
house.[3] The hospital was a point in my tale; but there is a house on each
side. Now the true house is the one before the hospital: is that No. 11?
If not, what do you complain of? If it is, how can I help what is true?
Everything in the *Dynamiter* is not true; but the story of the Brown Box
is, in almost every particular; I lay my hand on my heart, and swear to it.
It took place in that house in 1884; and if your daughter was in that house
at the time, all I can say is she must have kept very bad society.

But I see you coming. Perhaps your daughter's house has not a balcony
at the back? I cannot answer for that; I only know that side of Queen
Square from the pavement and the back windows of Brunswick Row.
Thence I saw plenty of balconies (terraces rather); and if there is none
to the particular house in question, it must have been so arranged to
spite me.

I now come to the conclusion of this matter. I address three questions
to your daughter

1° Has her house the proper terrace?

2° Is it on the proper side of the hospital?

3° Was she there in the summer of 1884?

You see I begin to fear that Mrs Desborough may have deceived me on
some trifling points, for she is not a lady of peddling exactitude. If this
should prove to be so, I will give your daughter a proper certificate; and
her house property will return to its original value.

Can man say more? Yours very truly   Robert Louis Stevenson

I saw the other day that the Eternal had plagiarised from *Lost Sir
Massingberd*: Good again, sir! I wish he would plagiarise the death of
Zero.[4]

---

[3] Payn's third daughter, Alicia Isobel (died 1898), married (1885) G.E. Buckle, editor of *The
Times*. She had (in Colvin's words) 'laughingly remonstrated, through her father, on recognising
some features of her own house in Queen Square, Bloomsbury, in the description of that
tenanted by the fair Cuban' in 'Desborough's Adventure: The Brown Box' in *The Dynamiter*.

[4] In Payn's *Lost Sir Massingberd* (1864) the wicked baronet Sir Massingberd Heath mysteriously
disappears. Several years later his skeleton is found in the hollow trunk of an oak-tree; he had
apparently climbed into the tree to watch for poachers, fallen through and been unable to escape
or to attract attention. *The Times* of 29 December 1885 reported that a ten-year-old boy,
Edward Light, of Bedminster near Bristol had been found in a starving and emaciated condition
in the hollow of an old elm-tree after being missing for nearly a week. He had run away from
home, got through an opening in the tree, taken his shoes and stockings off, and fallen asleep;
in the morning, his feet were badly frost-bitten and he was so benumbed with the cold that he
could not get out. After six days his moaning was heard by children playing nearby.

Zero accidently blows himself up at Euston Station with his own dynamite in the closing
pages of *The Dynamiter*.

To his Father
(Slightly Abridged)

[*25 January 1886*]   [*Skerryvore*]

My dear Father, Many thanks for a letter quite like yourself. I quite agree
with you and had already planned a scene of religion in *D. Balfour*; the
Society for the Propagation of Christian Knowledge furnishes me with a
catechist whom I shall try to make the man. I have another catechist, the
blind, pistol-carrying highway robber, whom I have transferred from the
Long Island to Mull.[1] I find it a most picturesque period, and wonder
Scott let it escape. The *Covenant* is lost on one of the Torrans, and David
is cast on Earraid, where (being from inland) he is nearly starved before he
finds out the island is tidal. Then he crosses Mull to Torosay, meeting the
blind catechist by the way; then crosses Morven from Kinlochaline to
Kingairloch, where he stays the night with the good catechist; that is
where I am; next day he is to be put ashore in Appin, and be present at
Colin Campbell's death.

Today I rest, being a little run down. Strange how liable we are to
brain fag in this scooty[2] family! But as far as I have got, all but the last
chapter, I think David is on his feet, and (to my mind) a far better story
and far sounder at heart than *Treasure Island*.

I have no earthly news, living entirely in my story and only coming out
of it to play patience. The Shelleys are gone;[3] the Taylors kinder than can

---

[1] RLS's source was *Travels in the Western Hebrides from 1782 to 1790* (1793) by the Revd John L.
Buchanan, who worked as a missionary in the Hebrides on commission from the Society for
Propagating Christian Knowledge. In ch. X (244) Buchanan describes

> Questors, . . . that go about from house to house, teaching the children the Creed, the
> Commandments, &c. by rote, in the evenings, they are not only useless, but many of them
> worthless drunkards. There is a blind bully of this order in *Uist*, who in order to escape
> contempt, and secure respectful attention both to his person and his doctrines, carries about
> with him, wherever he goes, loaded pistols. As he is remarkably strong, as well as full of
> courage, though blind, few people are fond of grappling with him.

On p. 241 he describes another catechist on the island of Harris: '. . . an old blind beggar, of
fourscore years and upwards, who is led by the hand by any boy or girl, or other person who
will have the goodness to do so, from village to village, or from door to door'.

[2] Worthless, insignificant (Scots).

[3] Sir Percy Florence Shelley (1819–89), son of the poet, married (1849) Jane St John, *née* Gibson
(1820–99), widow of Charles St John. Sir Percy pursued many hobbies including private
theatricals, yachting and amateur photography. Lady Shelley was a formidable defender of her
father-in-law's reputation and maintained a shrine of MSS and relics at their home, Boscombe
Manor. MIS recorded her first meeting with RLS: 'When Lou comes into the room she gives
a start and says "Shelley!"'

be imagined.[4] The other day, Lady Taylor drove over and called on me; she is a delightful old lady and great fun. I mentioned a story about the Duchess of Wellington which I had heard Sir Henry tell; and though he was very tired, he looked it up and copied it out for me in his own hand. The Vandergrifter is pretty vandergrifty; I am well, only for this touch of over-work which annoys me but does me no harm I think.

I do trust Bath may do the trick; but I suspect the great thing is rest.[5] Mind your allowance; stick to that: if you are too tired, go to bed; don't call in the aid of the enemy, for as long as you are in this state, an enemy it is and a dangerous one. Believe me, Ever your most affectionate son

Robert Louis Stevenson[6]

To his Father

27 January [*1886*]   *Skerryvore*

My dear Father, Yesterday we were both abed, and today I am up but the Vandergrifter (that heraldic animal) still *couchant*. It is very odd. I have had a cold; now when I take a cold of my own taking the derangement is always gastric and biliary, with congestion; never catarrhal. If I get a cold from another – it is always catarrhal, and I can do nothing with it. Here is a pleasant medical mystery for your by-hours.

I am at *David* again, and have just murdered James Stewart semi-historically.[1] I am now fairly in part two: the Highland part. I don't think it will be so interesting to read, but it is curious and picturesque.

I weary to hear from you.

Scott says it is important YOU SHOULD BE IN THE HIGH PARTS OF BATH. The lower are damp and not worth a twopenny – (*vide* Duke of Wellington *passim.*[2]) Is not that a delightful saying of the Duke in his old age: 'I don't care a damn - I haven't time not to do right.'[3]

---

[4] Sir Henry Taylor (1800–1886) had a distinguished career as a civil servant in the Colonial Office and was famous in his day for *Philip van Artevelde* (1834) and other verse dramas. He married (1839) Theodosia Alice Spring Rice (1817–91), daughter of the first Lord Monteagle. RLS and Fanny also became friends of their two unmarried daughters, Ida Alice Ashworth (1850–1929) and Una Mary Ashworth (1857–1922). They both wrote a few minor novels, and Ida later wrote a number of biographies. Una Taylor's *Guests and Memories* (1924) gives an interesting account of her parents and the visitors to 'The Roost', their villa at Bournemouth.

[5] On 16 January TS had been ordered three months' complete rest by his doctors. The Stevensons went to Bath on 22 January 1886.

[6] Postscript omitted.

[1] Ch. 17 of *Kidnapped*.

[2] The *OED* cites Macaulay (letter of 8 March 1849): 'How they settle the matter I care not, as the Duke [of Wellington] says, one twopenny damn.'

[3] In May 1840, acting on the principle that party considerations should not apply when the national interest was at stake, Wellington dismayed the Tories and delighted the Whig

I have tried the religious part once – and failed. Shall try again. Ever affectionate son   R.L.S.

My last went to Post Office.

To Charles Baxter

14 February 1886   *Skerryvore*

My dear Charles, I have at last a moment to write to you; it is already my ninth letter this mortal day, and I have other two to write, so be lenient and try to be grateful.

First, business: I enclose three bills, which you might pay; £20 you might remit to me here; and I don't know, but I almost half think we might invest the hundred. I am afraid to do it; I know it will evoke sleeping bills, and I'll just have to sell again; and that indeed is why I have so long delayed. But if there is anything very good to do with a small sum like that, you might perpend and advise me.

So far so well. I am going, if you will allow me, to dedicate my next book to you. I think I ought to let you know because you are a damned professional man, and it might not suit your book. It's not indecent, nor irreligious; in fact it is a kind of a boy's story; and as far as it has gone Henley and my wife and I all think well of it. What's mair, Sir, it's Scōtch: no strong, for the sake o' they pock-puddens,[1] but jist a kitchen o't, to leeven the wersh, sapless, fushionless, stotty, stytering South-Scotch they think sae muckle o'.[2] Its name is Kidnaaaped; or Memoyers of the Adventyers of Darvid Balfour in the year seventeen hunner and fifty wan. There's nae sculduddery aboot that, as ye can see for yoursel. And if you hae no objection, I would like very much to put your name to it.[3]

Government by speaking strongly in support of British actions in China in opposition to the criticisms made by Lord Stanhope. A few days later the diarist Charles Greville commented to him that 'he must be aware there were many of his own people who were . . . annoyed and provoked at his speech'. The Duke replied: 'I know that well enough, and I don't care *one damn*. I was afraid Lord Stanhope would have a majority, and *I have not time not to do what is right.*' Entry for 26 May 1840 in *The Greville Memoirs (Second Part)* (1885) I, 288.

[1] A contemptuous (later jocular) Scottish nickname for an Englishman. See p. 145, n. 3.

[2] 'kitchen' – seasoning (cf. *Kidnapped*, ch. 23); 'wersh' – tasteless; 'fushionless' – lacking pith or spirit; 'stotty' and 'stytering' – staggering, tottering.

[3] Baxter replied on 16 February: 'There is nothing in the world that would give me a greater pleasure than what you propose. I think it is a beautiful practice putting a friend's name on a book. It is like a handgrasp that lives for ever. A book lives while we are dead, and it does seem something that the memory of a friendship which I think my dear boy has been singularly uncrossed by cloud should somewhere live embalmed in a kindly message from one to another.'

And now see here, I *long* to see 'Brashiana'. Do please send them to me. Remember I have never seen them but just a few at a time as I sent them, and I have a real homesickness for these children of my Muse. (Damn this hair![4] Hurray! gone; why, now I am myself again.) Send me the copy, and I swear you shall have them again.

My wife is at Bath, and gives me good news of my father, who is (she thinks) more hipped than hurt. She is not very well herself, but the change (by last accounts) had done some good. I have acidity beyond comprehension or belief; I am a bottle of vinegar with the heart burn; and my brain is a kind of chaste and spotless cotton wool. As I fear this letter well displays. Let me hear on all these many points. And believe me, my dear old man, Yours affectionately   Robert Louis Stevenson

To Edmund Gosse

[*17 February 1886*]   [*Skerryvore*]

Dear Gosse, *Non, c'est honteux!* for a set of shambling lines[1] that don't know whether they're trochees or what they are, that you or any of the crafty ones would blush all over if you had so much as thought upon, all by yourselves, in the water-closet. But God knows, I am glad enough of five pounds; and this is almost as honest a way to get it as plain theft, so what should I care? Ever yours   R.L.S.

To Henry James
(*Joint Letter with Fanny Stevenson*)

[*25 February 1886*]   *Skerryvore*

[*Fanny begins*]
My dear Mr James, A magic mirror has come to us which seems to reflect not only our own plain faces, but the kindly one of a friend entwined in the midst of all sorts of pleasant memories. Louis felt that verse alone would fitly convey his sentiments concerning this beautiful present, but his muse, I believe, has not as yet responded to his call. As for me, to whom the gift of song has been denied in common with the modest hen canary, I can only attempt to express my thanks in plain prose.

[4] In the pen-nib.
[1] RLS had sent Low some verses ('Damned bad lines in return for a beautiful book'), beginning 'Youth now flees on feathered foot', in acknowledgement of the gift of *Lamia*, dedicated to him. They were published in the *Century* for May 1886 and reprinted in *Underwoods*.

The above, as you will easily perceive, is the present aspect of the side wall of our drawing room, correctly and carefully drawn. Miss Taylor's beautiful work, Mr Lemon's adorable picture of horses, the magic mirror, Sargent's picture of Louis, and the copy of Chatterton.[1]

[*RLS continues*]

At this stage, my wife was (or should have been) removed to an asylum. I have not fallen quite so low, for I reserve my verses. When they go, you will know that Skerryvore lies cold and smokeless, and the mirror represents only the walls and furniture. I scorn to try to express myself in prose. But there is no doubt you are a fine fellow and the mirror lovely. More, when the Muse shall countenance,[2] and meantime a thousand thanks from Yours affectionately

★(Hen) Robert Louis Stevenson

★You see my state of idiocy: I began to sign this 'Henry James': The asylum yawns for me   R.L.S.

[1] William Archer's article on Skerryvore in the *New York Critic* of 5 November 1887 describes Arthur Lemon's *Landscape with Horses*, a copy by Miss Una Taylor 'of what purports to be an authentic portrait of Chatterton, with hard by it an imposing piece of flower-embroidery, framed and glazed by the same accomplished lady'. Arthur Lemon (1850–1912), English painter and pupil of Carolus-Duran.
[2] The poem, sent to James on 7 March and later published as *Underwoods* XVIII, 'The Mirror Speaks', concludes:

> Now with an outlandish grace,
> To the sparkling fire I face
> In the blue room at Skerryvore;
> And I wait until the door
> Open, and the Prince of men,
> Henry James, shall come again.

To Edward Purcell

27 February 1886   *Skerryvore*

Dear Sir, I seem to gather than I have afforded you some amusement;[1] please, then, return the compliment and pursue your study of Fielding indicated once in the *Academy*. I have used the word 'amusement'; it is here deceptive; I shall look forward with the keenest interest to such a treat. I do beg of you to do as you said you would not, and give us (what I think you are the most capable of giving) a moral-scape of Henry Fielding.

To what is less important: my extreme sympathy for your critical utterances and your remarkable sleuthhound critical finesse (marred, as I must sometimes think it is, by a certain protervity, as of a strong man rejoicing in a paradox) has not lost anything, as you may well believe, by your kind notice. I write to you as to one whom I have long known, and with a familiarity that must surprise you; but I have been so long your reader that I feel myself almost an acquaintance.

First. As to my adaptation. I had no idea what a cruelly bold adapter I was, till I found the whole first part of *Treasure Island* in what I had not read (I believe, but I am not sure) for nearly twenty years: Washington Irving's 'Treasure Seekers'.[2] How you found out the book on Hayti remains to me a mystery.[3]

Second. What you say about the confusion of my ethics, I own to be all too true.[4] It is, as you say, where I fall, and fall almost consciously. I have the old Scotch Presbyterian preoccupation about these problems; itself morbid; I have alongside of that a second, perhaps more – possibly

---

[1] In a review in the *Academy* of 27 February 1886, Purcell referred to his unfavourable review of *Virginibus Puerisque* in 1881 (see p. 198, n. 5). He found *Prince Otto*, although containing 'some things of rare beauty and sweetness' disappointing, 'but it still towers above its rivals'. He praised *The Dynamiter* as a masterpiece – 'no modern English book contains such a profusion and superfluity of talent'.

[2] In 'My First Book' RLS later wrote: 'It is my debt to Washington Irving that exercises my conscience, and justly so, for I believe plagiarism was rarely carried farther. I chanced to pick up the *Tales of a Traveller* some years ago . . . and the book flew up and struck me; Billy Bones, his chest, the company in the parlour, the whole inner spirit and a good deal of the material detail of my first chapters – all were there, all were the property of Washington Irving.' The reference is to Part IV 'The Money-Diggers', ch. 3, 'Wolfert Webber, or Golden Dreams'.

[3] 'I wondered how anyone could invent the Story of the Fair Cuban. I wonder still more, since I lit on a certain heavy book about Hayti, how such prose could be sublimated into such fiction.' The book was *Hayti or The Black Republic* (1884) by Sir Spenser St John.

[4] 'We have no right to demand his scheme of human life; but this is certain, that his puzzling enigmatic ethics, whether they be individual, or whether they are a true reflection of a present transitional state of society, are the real hindrance to his aim of producing a great romance worthy of his genius.'

less – morbid element – the dazzled incapacity to choose, of an age of transition. The categorical imperative is ever with me, but utters dark oracles. This is a ground almost of pity. The Scotch side came out plain in *Dr Jekyll*; the XIXth century side probably baffled me even there, and in most other places baffles me entirely. Ethics are my veiled mistress;[5] I love them, but I know not what they are. Is this my fault? Partly, of course, it is; because I love my sins like other people. Partly my merit, because I do not take, and rest contented in, the first subterfuge.

Third. Of all who would change *Otto*, I need not tell you I am the first. But it is too late. The fate of that little book is cast. Yet I may be allowed to say, to one like yourself, that I think I set myself too hard a task and fell between the two stools – treating too realistically the figures of the court-life, von Rosen and Gondremark, or at least failing to make the two ends of the book dovetail.

Fourth. For God's sake, dear sir, do not compare me to Scott. I know well you wrote in sincerity, but it was in one of your hasty moments. I know Scott's novels to be full of sawdust, but they are full besides of organic blood, and built for posterity. I admire your friend who can re-read Scott and cannot read *Prince Otto*; and I think the difference lies deeper, far deeper, than your kind humour led you to indicate.[6] It lies in the genius, human, quiet, solid, smiling, unperturbed, of Sir Walter; not in changing phases of opinion. It lies also (as you say, truly enough) in the fact that Sir Walter was a good man, and a good man content with a more or less conventional solution, whereas I am only a man who would be content to be good if I knew what goodness was – and could lay hold of it. It lies far more in that incomparable art, more perhaps dramatic than merely literary, which gave us Mucklebackit and (my namesake) Steenson.[7]

But that I should have been the occasion of a generous error on the part of a critic like you, is to me, and will ever be to me, a source of pride; and I have much pleasure in signing myself, Your obliged

Robert Louis Stevenson

---

[5] Purcell quoted this phrase in his review of *Weir of Hermiston* in the *Academy*, 27 June 1896.

[6] Purcell referred to a friend who could not read *Prince Otto*, yet again and again plodded through Scott's 'ponderous stories'. Scott's strength, he suggested was that his mind was 'quite made up about the right and wrong of most things and persons' and he could 'describe and judge them steadily, without excitement or misgiving'. Comparing Scott and RLS he wrote: 'Equal in imagination, the one is strengthened and disciplined to prolonged flights by his perfect assimilation of conventional principles; the other's course, rapid, erratic and interrupted, displays far deeper insight, far keener perception, far bolder genius – a genius brilliant but seemingly troubled, because it ventures into a world ignored by Scott, where all is doubt and difficulty.'

[7] In *The Antiquary* and *Redgauntlet*.

To John Addington Symonds[1]

[*Early March 1886*]   *Skerryvore*

My dear Symonds, If we have lost touch it is (I think) only in a material sense; a question of letters not hearts. You will find a warm welcome at Skerryvore from both the light keepers; and indeed we never tell ourselves one of our financial fairy tales, but a run to Davos is a prime feature. I am not changeable in friendship; and I think I can promise you you have a pair of trusty well-wishers and friends in Bournemouth; whether they write or not is but a small thing; the flag may not be waved, but it is there.

Jekyll is a dreadful thing, I own; but the only thing I feel dreadful about is that damned old business of the war in the members.[2] This time it came out; I hope it will stay in, in future.

Raskolnikoff is the greatest book I have read easily in ten years; I am glad you took to it. Many find it dull; Henry James could not finish it: all I can say is, it nearly finished me. It was like having an illness. James did not care for it because the character of Raskolnikoff was not objective; and at that I divined a great gulf between us and, on further reflection, the existence of a certain impotence in many minds of today, which prevents them from living *in* a book or a character, and keeps them standing afar off, spectators of a puppet show. To such I suppose the book may seem empty in the centre; to the others it is a room, a house of life, into which they themselves enter, and are tortured and purified. The Juge d'Instruction, I thought, a wonderful, weird, touching, ingenious creation. The drunken father, and Sonia, and the student friend, and the uncircumscribed, protoplasmic humanity of Raskolnikoff, all upon a level that filled me with wonder. The execution also, superb in places. Another has been translated: *Humiliés et Offensés*. It is even more incoherent than *Le Crime et le Châtiment*; but breathes much of the same lovely goodness, and has passages of power. Dostoieffsky is a devil of a swell to be sure.[3] Have

---

[1] Written in reply to a letter from Symonds dated 3 March 1886 which begins: 'At last I have read *Dr Jekyll*. It makes me wonder whether a man has the right so to scrutinise "the abysmal deeps of personality". It is indeed a dreadful book, most dreadful because of a certain moral callousness, a want of sympathy, a shutting out of hope . . . As a piece of literary work, this seems to me the finest you have done . . . But it has left such a deeply painful impression on my heart that I do not know how I am ever to turn to it again.' The letter concludes: 'Goodbye. I seem to have quite lost you. But if I come to England I shall try to see you.'

[2] Cf. 'Your lusts that war in your members' – James 4:1.

[3] Symonds had praised *Raskolinkow*, a German translation (1882) of Dostoevsky's *Crime and Punishment* (1866). RLS had read a French translation, *Le Crime et le Châtiment*, which he had received from Henry James, with the pages only partially cut. He had also read a French translation of *The Insulted and the Injured* (1861). Both French translations appeared in 1884. RLS wrote to Henley in November 1885:

you heard that he became a stout, imperialist conservative? It is interesting to know. To something of that side, the balance leans with me also in view of the incoherency and incapacity of all. The old boyish idea of the march on Paradise being now out of season, and all plans and ideas that I hear debated being built on a superb indifference to the first principles of human character, a helpless desire to acquiesce in anything of which I know the worst assails me. Fundamental errors in human nature of two sorts stand on the skyline of all this modern world of aspirations. First, that it is happiness that men want; and second, that happiness consists of anything but an internal harmony. Men do not want, and I do not think they would accept, happiness; what they live for is rivalry, effort, success – the elements our friends wish to eliminate. And on the other hand, happiness is a question of morality – or of immorality, there is no difference – and conviction. Gordon was happy in Khartoum, in his worst hours of anger and fatigue; Marat was happy, I suppose, in his ugliest frenzy; Marcus Aurelius was happy in the detested camp; Pepys was pretty happy, and I am pretty happy on the whole, because we both somewhat crowingly accepted a *via media*, both liked to attend to our affairs and both had some success in managing the same. It is quite an open question whether Pepys and I ought to be happy; on the other hand there is no doubt that Marat had better be unhappy. He was right (if he said it) that he was '*la misère humaine*', cureless misery – unless perhaps by the gallows. Death is a great and gentle solvent; it has never had justice done it, no, not by Whitman. As for those crockery chimney-piece ornaments, the bourgeois (*quorum pars*)[4] and their cowardly dislike of dying and killing, it is merely one symptom of a thousand how utterly they have got out of touch of life. Their dislike of capital punishment and their treatment of their domestic servants are for me the two flaunting emblems of their hollowness.

God knows where I am driving to. But here comes my lunch.

Which interruption happily for you seems to have stayed the issue. I have now nothing to say, that had formerly such a pressure of twaddle. Pray don't fail to come this summer. It will be a great disappointment now it has been spoken of, if you do. Yours ever

Robert Louis Stevenson

Dostoieffsky is of course simply immense: it is not reading a book, it is having a brain fever, to read it. The Judge is to me the greatest stroke of genius of all; I adore the Judge. Would you like to read another of his: *Humiliated and Offendended* it is not as good as *The Cream and the Shattiment*, but has great merit, too, has *Humiliated and Offendended* and the author Dustimuffsky is not only a man of genius, but a dam good fellow and a credit to the race, and in these days of Zolaism he shines like a star.

[4] '*Et quorum pars magna fui*' (and of which I was a major part), Virgil, *Aeneid*, II. 6.

To William Archer

[c. *9 March 1886*]   [*Skerryvore*]

My dear Archer, What am I to say? I have read your friend's book with
singular relish.[1] If he has written any other, I beg you will let me see it;
and if he has not, I beg him to lose no time in supplying the deficiency.
It is full of promise; – but I should like to know his age. There are things
in it that are very clever; to which I attach small importance; it is the shape
of the age. And there are passages, particularly the rally in presence of the
Zulu king, that show genuine and remarkable narrative talent – a talent
that few will have the wit to understand, a talent of strength, spirit,
capacity, sufficient vision, and sufficient self-sacrifice, which last is the
chief point in a narrator.

As a whole, it is (of course) a fever dream of the most feverish. Over
Bashville the footman I howled with derision and delight; I dote on
Bashville – I could read of him forever; *de Bashville je suis le fervent*; there
is only one Bashville, and I am his devoted slave; *Bashville est magnifique,
mais il n'est guère – possible.* He is the note of the book. It is all mad, mad
and deliriously delightful; the author has a taste in chivalry like Walter
Scott's or Dumas's, and then he daubs in little bits of socialism; he soars
away on the wings of the romantic griphon – even the gryphon, as he
cleaves air, shouting with laughter at the nature of the quest – and I
believe in his heart he thinks he is labouring in a quarry of solid granite
realism.

It is this that makes me – the most hardened adviser now extant – stand
back and hold my peace. If Mr Shaw is below five-and-twenty, let him go
his path; if he is thirty, he had best be told that he is a romantic, and
pursue romance with his eyes open; – or perhaps, he knows it; – God
knows! – my brain is softened.

It is HORRID FUN. All I ask is more of it. Thank you for the
pleasure you gave us, and tell me more of the inimitable author.

(I say, Archer, my God, what women!) Yours very truly

Robert Louis Stevenson

1 part Charles Reade: 1 part Henry James or some kindred author, badly
assimilated: $\frac{1}{2}$ part Disraeli (perhaps unconscious): $1\frac{1}{2}$ parts struggling, over-
laid original talent: 1 part blooming, gaseous folly. That is the equation as

[1] *Cashel Byron's Profession*, Bernard Shaw's first published novel, but the fourth of his novels in
order of composition, was published in February 1886, stereotyped from the pages of the
Socialist monthly *To-Day* in which it had been serialised. Archer reviewed the book enthusiastically in the *P.M.G.* and Henley wrote to RLS: 'Who the devil is Bernard Shaw. I've been at
him all morning: with astonishment and delight.'

it stands. What it may be, I don't know, nor any other man. *Vixere fortes*[2] – O, let him remember that – let him beware of his damned century; his gifts of insane chivalry and animated narration are just those that might be slain and thrown out like an untimely birth by the Daemon of the Epoch. And if he only knew how I had adored the chivalry! Bashville! – O *Bashville! j'en chortle* (which is fairly polyglot).   R.L.S.[3]

To Sidney Colvin

[*17 March 1886*]   *Skerryvore*

My dear Colvin, My wife says she'll copy my letter to Gosse but I don't believe her. Briefly as far as concerns you, I have put the matter in his hands, leaving you thus shockingly used upon all sides; but I am not afraid of that, and will risk, upon your custodianic person, any extreme of formal ill-usage, sure that you know my heart and will understand my motives. I don't suppose Gosse will do it; but I leave it in his power.[1] I have done him the compliment to be honest; it will pain me much if he should feel this, and I suppose he must. I regret my step; and yet it is not quite unimportant that I should not be daubed in the States, where there may be sleeping serpents or at the best, sleeping dogs. I have no wish to be publicly unfrocked and catalogued; I don't think it dignified, I don't think it comfortable and (in my case) I'll be damned if I think it safe.

---

[2] '*Vixere fortes ante Agamemnon Multi . . .*' (Many brave men lived before Agamemnon) Horace, *Odes*, IV.ix.25.

[3] Archer replied on 10 March: 'Your diagnosis of Shaw's case is delicious. I look forward to reading it to him – it will infuriate him and do him all the good in the world. I am always assuring him that he is an *a priori* novelist, which he doesn't like at all; but to be told that he is a sentimentalist and romanticist will drive the shaft three barbs deeper . . . I think you're wrong by the way, in attributing any part of his idiosyncrasy to imitation. He has read one or two of Charles Reade's books but with no special attention or admiration. I am almost sure that he has never read a line of Henry James or any of his school, and I am pretty certain he knows no more of Disraeli than I do, who once read *Coningsby* and proceeded to forget it as quickly as possible.' Shaw came to tea with Archer and heard RLS's opinion on 10 March.

[1] RLS had inadvertently offended Gosse, a notoriously touchy individual, and had written him a long apologetic letter. Not knowing that Gosse had already planned to write a biographical article on him for the *Century*, RLS had suggested that Colvin should do it. Nothing came of the project. In the course of his letter to Gosse RLS wrote:

> To begin with, this whole affair of the biographical treatment of people in their lifetime, goes sore against my heart. I admit it is a good form of advertisement; and I am no such self-deceiver as to suppose this does not weigh with me, for I earnestly wish my books to sell. In every other way, it shocks me. I think the public should know nothing from behind the scenes, until the man himself is out of reach of hurt; and when I have been applied to for biographical details, I have always either refused or (which I think best) sent a list of such facts as a diligent reader of the newspapers might have gathered for himself. Hence the first news of this paper (kindly as I know it was meant and good as it would be for my pocket) was far from an unmingled pleasure.

But all this is as God wills.

I have been reading the Vth and VIth *Aeneid* – the latter for the first time – and am overpowered. That is one of the most astonishing pieces of literature, or rather it contains the best, I ever met with. We are all damned small fry, and Virgil is one of the tops of human achievement; I never appreciated this; you should have a certain age to feel this; it is no book for boys, who grind under the lack of enterprise and dash, and pass ignorantly over miracles of performance that leave an old hoary-headed practitioner like me stricken dumb with admiration. Even as a boy, the sibyl would have bust me; but I never read the VIth till I began it two days ago; it is all fresh and wonderful; do you envy me? If only I knew any Latin! If you had a decent edition with notes – many notes – I should like weel to have it; mine is a damned Didot, with not the ghost of a note, type that puts my eyes out, and (I suspect) no very splendid text – but there the carnal feelings of the man who can't construe are probably parents to the suspicion.

My dear fellow, I would tenfold rather come to the Monumong;[2] but my father is an old man; and if I go to town, it shall be (this time) for his pleasure. He has many marks of age, some of childhood; I wish this knighthood business would come off, though even the talk of it has been already something; but the change (to my eyes) is thoroughly begun; and a very beautiful, simple, honourable, high-spirited and childlike (and childish) man is now in process of deserting us piece-meal. *Si quis piorum*[3] – God knows, not that he was pious, but he did his hand's-darg or tried to do it; and if not, well it is a melancholy business. Yours ever

R.L.S.[4]

To W.E. Henley

[*Mid-April 1886*]   *Smedley's Hydro, Matlock Bridge*[1]

Dam fools!

Get Zola's *L'Oeuvre*! It is dreary, but – it *is* Youth and Art.
No: it is dam fine – I say it – and sign myself by my name
John Marcus Dodd

---

[2] RLS jokingly referred to Colvin's official residence at the British Museum as 'The Monument'.
[3] Tacitus, *Agricola*, ch. 46. The opening words of Tacitus's valediction to his father-in-law: 'If there is any mansion for the spirits of the just, if, as the wise aver, great souls do not perish with the body, quiet O Father, be your rest!'
[4] RLS and Fanny joined his parents at Bacon's Private Hotel, 5 Fitzroy Square on 25 March.
[1] As RLS wanted to help take care of his father he accompanied him to this Hydropathic in Derbyshire. TS was ill and depressed and the experiment was not a success. After a few days RLS was glad to let his mother come up to Matlock and take over and to return to Skerryvore.

The first four or five chapters are like being young again in Paris; they woke me like a trumpet. Does Bob remember the martyrdom of St Stephen with petits-pains? the man who misused his old mistress? The very moral of him is in here.[2]

To his Father

[*May 1886*]   *Skerryvore*

My dear Father, The *David* problem has today been decided. I am to leave the door open for a sequel if the public take to it; and this will save me from butchering a lot of good material to no purpose. Your letter from Carlisle[1] was pretty like yoursel, sir, as I was pleased to see; the hand of Jekyll, not the hand of Hyde. I am for action quite unfit,[2] and even a letter is beyond me; so pray take these scraps at a vast deal more than their intrinsic worth. I am in great spirits about *David*, Colvin agreeing with Henley, Fanny and myself in thinking it far the most human of my labours hitherto. As to whether the long-eared British public may take to it, all think it more than doubtful; I wish they would, for I could do a second volume with ease and pleasure, and Colvin thinks it sin and folly to throw away David and Alan Breck upon so small a field as this one. Ever your affectionate son   R.L.S.

To Messrs R. & R. Clark[1]

5 June 1886   *Skerryvore*
Messrs R. & R. Clark

Dear Sirs, What has become of me and my donkey?[2] She was never a fast traveller, but she has taken longer to come through Hanover Street than

[2] In ch. 3 of *The Wrecker*, RLS (drawing upon memories of the same incident) described a visit by Loudon Dodd and Pinkerton to an unpleasant student who showed them a huge painting of 'St Stephen, wallowing in red upon his belly . . . and a crowd of Hebrews in blue, green, and yellow, pelting him – apparently with buns'. To Pinkerton's disgust, the artist described how he had kicked his discarded mistress downstairs and pelted her with stones.
[1] The Stevensons left Matlock on Monday 10 May, stayed at Carlisle on Tuesday night and arrived home on 12 May.
[2] RLS notes in another letter that the lines 'I am for action quite unfit,/Either of exercise or wit' were his father's favourite quotation. They are a slight misquotation of, 'I am for action now unfit,/Either of Fortitude or Wit' from Samuel Butler, *Hudibras*, Part I, canto III.
[1] The Edinburgh printers.
[2] A new edition (520 copies) of *Travels with a Donkey*, printed from the stereotype plates acquired from Kegan Paul, was published on 21 June 1886 with a new title-page bearing the Chatto and Windus imprint.

to cross the Gévaudan. There must be carrots in your office. Please see to
it, and let me hear. Yours truly   Robert Louis Stevenson

To Sidney Colvin

[? 28 June 1886]   [Skerryvore]

My dear Colvin, I am in bed again – bloudie Jackery and be damned to
it. Sam is better, I think; and money matters better; only my rascal carcase
and the muddy and oily lees of what once was my immortal soul are in
a poor, pitiful and damnable condition.

I think I sour on the game about the *Garden* a good deal.[1] I rather think
I stand to lose; and the best plan is to let things be as they are. I cannot
find Bazett[2] his bill? Will you send me a note of the total?

> Litany
> Damn my moral character
> - - - - - conscience
> - - - the political situation
> - - - you
> - - - me
> - - - *Le Prince de Galles* and
> - - - Gladstone

I am a kind of a dam home ruler, worse luck to it; I would support
almost anything but that bill. How am I to vote?[3] Great Caesar's Ghost![4]
Ever yours   R.L.S.

O! 'The Travelling Companion' won't do;[5] I am back on it entirely; it
is a foul, gross, bitter, ugly daub, with lots of stuff in it, and no urbanity
and no glee and no true tragedy – to the crows with it, a carrion tale! I

---

[1] Apparently a proposal for an illustrated edition.
[2] Colvin's brother, Bazett David Colvin (1842–?), B.A. Trinity College, Cambridge 1864.
[3] Following the defeat of Gladstone's Home Rule Bill, Parliament had been dissolved and the
election campaign was in full swing. Voting began on 1 July. The Liberals were defeated and the
Conservatives, under Lord Salisbury, took office.
[4] The oath used by Tom in ch. 29 of Mark Twain's *The Adventures of Tom Sawyer* (1876).
[5] In 'A Chapter on Dreams' RLS refers to it as an earlier story on the theme of 'man's double
being': '"The Travelling Companion", which was returned by an editor [Longman] on the plea
that it was a work of genius and indecent, and which I burned the other day on the ground that
it was not a work of genius, and that *Jekyll* had supplanted it.' The story, first planned in July
1881, was certainly underway in September 1883. RLS wrote to Chatto on 28 June asking him
to withdraw it from the projected volume of short stories, *The Merry Men*.

will do no more carrion. I have done too much in this carrion epoch; I will now be clean or see myself damned; and by clean I don't mean any folly about purity, but such things as a healthy man with his bowels open shall find fit to see and speak about without a pang of nausea. I am, Yours

A repentant Dankist

The lakeists, the drainists, the brookists and the riverites; let me be a brookist, *faute de mieux*.
I did enjoy myself in town and was a thousand fold the better of it.[6]

John Marchmont Sepulchre
William King (of Janes)
Mathieu Pierre Devis de la Bavette

To Bob Stevenson

[c. 10 July 1886]   *Skerryvore*

My dear Bob, I am not so noble a pickler as I used to be, having been seduced by some very good pickling music, which led me to one finger:[1] Gluck's Gavotte from *Don Juan*, Boccherini's celebrated minuet,[2] and some gavottes and games of Bach; most delightful stuff. All the noble pickling I have done of late, is the persistent, ingloriously unsuccessful attempt to play the first return – A passage B passage A passage, – of The Muttons, celebrated gavotte by Père Martini.[3] I can fish along with either hand pretty jolly, but on putting them together I become like Martha careful and troubled.[4] There is in me something nobly impatient or (call it) 'aughty, and I refuse to deal with any second part that seems to have no being of its own. For instance I fished out *l'amo, l'amo* air de *Bellini*;[5] then with great labour learned the bass by a Booseyite,[6] and found it far

[6] RLS had stayed with Colvin at the British Museum earlier in the month.
[1] Bob wrote on Thursday (8 July):

> I have heard about you from Henley and that you are pickling honourably at the instrument. Honourably I say because of your lofty attitude towards the pickler's art. The one finger pickler, much as I esteem him, is a poor trifler compared with such as you who I understand never fail to sit down with both hands neatly on the board even if you have to play an *Adagio Molto* when the composer has written *Prestissimo*. I never thought to welcome you to the Kingdom of Heaven in this way and still less as a kind of first class cadet.

[2] Luigi Boccherini (1743–1805), prolific composer of chamber music.
[3] 'Les Moutons', a gavotte by Giovanni Battista Martini (1706–84), known as 'Padre Martini', a Franciscan friar who was a composer and a famous teacher of music.
[4] Luke 10: 41.
[5] 'L'amo, l'amo, e m'è più cara,' sung by Tebaldo in Act I of Bellini's opera *I Capuletti ed i Montecchi* (1830).
[6] Boosey and Co., the well-known London music publishers, founded by Thomas Boosey in 1816; in 1930 through amalgamation they became Messrs Boosey and Hawkes.

from repaying, returned indeed with a gush of relief to one finger. This is damping to the beginner; music shouldn't be printed unless it has an air in every part. *Dixi*. Else the pickler is swindled.

I now understand why you were so idle in boyhood's breezy: the pianner is the consolation of idleness; I never wish to do anything but pickle. Henley has really been my ruin as a pickler; I entrusted him with money, and he filled my house with Bach. Now I adore Batch, but Batch is a gentleman who forces the pickler to one finger. I have now sent for Litolff's *Album Classique for the Young*[7] which I hope may contain things good enough to lead me on and easy enough to encourage the other hand. Martini (though) is easy; and some day years from now I shall know something about him and his muttons. Why Muttons? Do you know the Muttons? Do you know Boccherini? Are you on the jump? O pickling, chaste exploit! I am a pickler, O! Wha wouldnae pickle? (Scotch air) *Ich bin ein pickler treu* (German air) *Pickleur charmant, picklerez-vous toujours?* (Romance by Boilgod).[8]

I wish you would come down. When could you? Yours   Le Pickleur

> He pickled low, he pickled loud
> He recked not of the smiling crowd,
> Over a score confused and curly
> He pickled late, he pickled early.
> He pickled slow; he pickled fast –
> At least he hoped he might at last;
> He pickled wrong; he pickled right –
> At least he hoped at last he might.
> He pickled up, he pickled down
> And was the bugbear of his town.

Two *Kidnappeds* will come to you; one is for Lemon whose address[9] I forgot. Head gone.

To Sidney Colvin

[c. *10 July 1886*]   *Skerryvore*

Dear Custodian, I sent a letter to B.D. Colvangle Esq, containing a *blank cheque*. For God's sake what has become of it. I may be ruined; his clerk

---

[7] The Litolffs, music publishers of Brunswick, were pioneers in the production of cheap editions of the classics.
[8] François Adrien Boïeldieu (1775–1834), French composer of comic operas.
[9] RLS first wrote, then deleted 'name'.

may have levanted with the swag. For the love of Budgett,[1] let us have the truth and that right early. I have turned my bottom on Bloudy-Jackerie, and am now gay, free, and obnoxious. *Je ne vis que pour le piano*; on the which I labour like an idiot as I am. You should hear me labouring away at Martini's celebrated, beroomed gavotte or Boccherini's beroomed, famous minuet. I have 'beroomed' on the brain, and sign myself, Sir,

> The Beroomed Stevenson

> To the Highly-geborn
> > Beroomed
> > > Custodian
> > > > Sidney S. Colvangle
> > > > > *These*
> > in a hell of a hurry
> > > Spur! Spur! Spurrey!

> > > Where is now the Père Martini?
> > > Where is Bumptious Boccherini?
> > > Where are Hertz and Crotch[2] and Batch?
> > > – Safe in bed in Colney Hatch?[3]

To Alison Cunningham

[*16 July 1886*]   [*Skerryvore*]

My dear Cummy, Herewith goes my new book[1] in which you will find some places that you know; I hope you will like it: I do. The name of the girl at Limekilns (as will appear if the sequel is ever written) was Hastie,[2] and I conceive she was an ancestress of yours; as David was no doubt some kind of relative of mine. I have no time for more, but send my love; and remembrances to your brother. Ever your affectionate

> R.L.S.

---

[1] Samuel Budgett (1794–1851), prosperous Bristol merchant and philanthropist, noted for his piety. A biography of him, *The Successful Merchant*, by William Arthur was very popular. RLS refers to him scornfully in 'Virginibus Puerisque I', and 'Crabbed Age and Youth'.
[2] Henri Herz (1803–88), Austrian-born pianist and composer who lived in Paris; William Crotch (1775–1847), English organist, pianist and composer, who was a child prodigy.
[3] The London County Lunatic Asylum was opened in this Middlesex hamlet in 1851.
[1] *Kidnapped* was published on 14 July. Cummy's copy is inscribed 'Alison Cunningham/from her boy/The Author/Skerryvore/July 16th 1886'.
[2] Alison Hastie (duly named in *Catriona*, the sequel to *Kidnapped*) rows David and Alan Breck across the Forth. Hastie was the maiden name of Cummy's mother.

*To his Mother

[*10 August 1886*]   *British Museum*

My dear Mother, We are having a capital holiday, and I am much better, and enjoying myself to the nines. Richmond[1] is painting my portrait. Today I lunch with him, and meet Burne-Jones; tonight Browning dines with us. That sounds rather lofty work, does it not? His path was paved with celebrities. Tomorrow we leave for Paris, and next week, I suppose, or the week after, come home.[2] Address here, as we may not reach Paris. I am really very well. Ever your affectionate son   R.L.S.

*To Theodore Watts-Dunton

[*Early September 1886*]   *Skerryvore*

Dear Mr Watts, The sight of the last *Athenaeum* reminds me of you, and of my debt, now too long due. I wish to thank you for your notice of *Kidnapped*; and that not because it was kind, though for that also I valued it, but in the same sense as I have thanked you before now for a hundred articles on a hundred different writers. A critic like you is one who fights the good fight, contending with stupidity, and I would fain hope not all in vain; in my own case, for instance, surely not in vain.

What you say of the two parts in *Kidnapped* was felt by no one more painfully than by myself. I began it partly as a lark, partly as a pot-boiler; and suddenly it moved, David and Alan stepped out from the canvas, and I found I was in another world.[1] But there was the cursed beginning, and a cursed end must be appended; and our old friend Byles the butcher[2] was

---

[1] William Blake Richmond (1842–1921), portrait painter. Richmond's sketch in oils is in the National Portrait Gallery.

[2] RLS and Fanny spent a week or ten days in Paris, staying with Will H. Low and his wife. Henley was also in Paris with Anna.

[1] In his review of *Kidnapped* in the *Athenaeum* of 14 August 1886, Watts-Dunton wrote:

> [In] the mind of every true story-teller the story passes through two stages – the stage when the group of situations is conceived or, as we say, 'invented', and the stage when they are really imagined, when the inventor's mind has become as familiar with them as though he had actually lived in them. Not till it has reached the latter stage can imaginative work in any art become vital and, so to speak, organic. . . . Now of *Kidnapped* the Highland portions alone are imagined. . . . In the Highland portions the imagination is of an exceedingly high and rare kind.

Earlier in the review he wrote: 'As a picture of the state of Scotland after 1745 we do not hesitate to say that there is nothing in history and nothing in fiction equal to these remarkable chapters.'

[2] In ch. 71 of *Middlemarch*, Mrs Dollop, landlady of the public house, gossiping about Lydgate's possible involvement in the sudden death of Raffles, comments that the previously very poor

plainly audible tapping at the back door. So it had to go into the world, one part (as it does seem to me) alive, one part merely galvanised: no work, only an essay. For a man of tentative method, and weak health, and a scarcity of private means, and not too much of that frugality which is the artist's proper virtue, the days of sinecures and patrons look very golden: the days of professional literature very hard. Yet I do not so far deceive myself as to think I should change my character by changing my epoch; the sum of virtue in our books is in a relation of equality to the sum of virtues in ourselves; and my *Kidnapped* was doomed, while still in the womb and while I was yet in the cradle, to be the thing it is.

And now to the more genial business of defence. You attack my fight on board the *Covenant*:[3] I think it literal. David and Alan had every advantage on their side – position, arms, training, a good conscience; a handful of merchant sailors, not well led in the first attack, not led at all in the second, could only by an accident have taken the round-house by attack; and since the defenders had firearms and food, it is even doubtful if they could have been starved out. The only doubtful point with me is whether the seamen would have ever ventured on the second onslaught; I half believe they would not; still the illusion of numbers and the authority of Hoseason would perhaps stretch far enough to justify the extremity. I am, dear Mr Watts, your very sincere admirer

Robert Louis Stevenson

To the Montagnon Children[1]

5 October 1886   *Skerryvore*

Dear Sirs
and   }
Dear Mesdames

---

doctor is 'so flushed o' money as he can pay off Mr Byles the butcher as his bill has been running on for the best o' joints since last Michaelmas was a twelvemonth.'

[3] Watts-Dunton argued that stories written for boys can contain scenes of action 'free from the restraints of imaginative logic' necessary in fiction for adults. An illustration of this is the fight in the roundhouse where Alan Breck can be shown 'fighting and conquering an entire ship's crew of reckless desperadoes and fire-eaters . . . single-handed save for the aid of a boy who knows not how to handle sword or pistol. Such incidents as these, which are perfectly legitimate in a boys' story, would be absurd in a story for adults.'

[1] Written in reply to a fan-letter from the children of Louis William Montagnon of Marlborough House, Cheltenham. The letter (in the hand of Mabel but signed by all four admirers) is dated 'Thursday' 30 September 1886:

Dear Mr Stevenson, We have read *Kidnapped*, And we like it so much that we want to ask you to write some more about David and Alan. We have read and enjoyed *Treasure Island* often, but we all like *Kidnapped* best, we think Alan and David such noble characters. My

Thank you for your very pleasant letter. I have every intention to start Alan and David once again on their adventures; but what you have heard is true, I am often ill and unfit to work; Alan, besides, and David too, have views of their own and sometimes sulk; so that when it will be done and my pair of friends get fairly into the open air again, is more than I can say. The last time I had a talk with them, they seemed to me in great force; Ebenezer and Mr Campbell were not quite so well, I should not wonder if they were to die soon; but I shall tell them that Miss Daisy Montagnon is interested in their career, and who knows? this may pull them together. Believe me, Yours kindly   Robert Louis Stevenson

To Miss Mabel S.B. ⎞
   Master Louis L. ⎟
   Miss Daisy E.   ⎬ Montagnon
   and   ⎟
   Master Denis J. ⎠

To Auguste Rodin[1]

[*December 1886*]   *Skerryvore*

Mon cher ami, Il y a bien longtemps déjà que je vous dois des lettres par dizaines; mais bien que je vais mieux, je ne vais toujours que doucement. Il a fallu faire le voyage à Bournemouth comme une fuite en Egypte, par crainte des brouillards qui me tuaient; et j'en ressentais beaucoup de fatigue. Mais maintenant celà commence à aller, et je puis vous donner de mes nouvelles.[2]

---

sister would like to hear more about Mr Campbell and Ebenezer. We hope what we have heard is not true – that you are often very ill, and that we have not troubled you by writing. We are yours gratefully

                                                       Mabel S.B. Montagnon
                                                       Louis L. Montagnon
                                                       Daisy E. Montagnon
                                                       Denis J. Montagnon

The two boys were educated at Cheltenham College. Louis Langlois Montagnon (1873–1904) went on to Hertford College, Oxford; his brother Denis John (1878–1945) became a tea-planter in India.

[1] During his stay in Paris RLS had visited Rodin's studio to watch him at work on his bust of Henley. The two men took a great liking to each other and a friendly correspondence followed. This is one of three known letters from RLS to Rodin. In September RLS defended Rodin in *The Times* against the charge of being 'the Zola of sculpture'.

[2] In mid-October RLS and Fanny came up to London to stay with Colvin at the British Museum. RLS caught a cold on arrival and stayed in bed for several weeks. On 25 November he was ordered back to Bournemouth for fear of the London fogs. Rodin had heard from Henley that RLS had been in London.

Le Printemps[3] est arrivé, mais il avait le bras cassé, et nous l'avons laissé, lors de notre fuite, aux soins d'un médecin-de-statues. Je l'attends de jour en jour; et ma maisonette en resplendira bientôt. Je regrette beaucoup le dédicace; peut-être, quand vous viendrez nous voir, ne serait-il pas trop tard de l'ajouter? Je n'en sais rien, je l'espère. L'oeuvre, c'est pour tout le monde; le dédicace est pour moi. L'oeuvre est un cadeau, trop beau même; c'est le mot d'amitié qui me le donne pour de bon. Je suis si bête que je m'embrouille, et me perds; mais vous me comprendriez je pense.

Je ne puis même pas m'exprimer en Anglais; comment voudriez vous que je le pourrais en Français? Plus heureux que vous, le Némésis des Arts ne me visite pas sous le masque du désenchantement; elle me suce l'intelligence et me laisse bayant les corneilles, sans capacité mais sans regret; sans ésperance, c'est vrai, mais aussi, dieu merci, sans désespoir. Un doux étonnement me tient; je ne m'habitue pas à me trouver si bûche, mais je m'y résigne; même si celà durait, ce ne serait pas désagréable – mais comme je mourrais certainement de faim, ce serait tout au moins regrettable pour moi et ma famille.

Je voudrais pouvoir vous écrire; mais ce n'est pas moi qui tient la plume – c'est l'autre, le bête, celui qui ne connaît pas le Français, celui qui n'aime pas mes amis comme je les aime, qui ne goûte pas aux choses de l'art comme j'y goûte; celui que je renie, mais auquel je commande toujours assez pour le faire prendre la plume en main et écrire des tristes bavardages. Celui-là, mon cher Rodin, vous ne l'aimez pas; vous ne devez jamais le connaître. Votre ami, qui dort à présent, comme un ours, au plus profond de mon être, se réveillera sous peu. Alors, il vous écrira de sa propre main. Attendez-lui. L'autre ne compte pas; ce n'est qu'un secretaire infidèle et triste, à l'âme gelée, à la tête-de-bois.

Celui qui dort est toujours, mon cher ami, bien à vous; celui qui écrit est chargé de vous en faire part et de signer de la raison sociale.

Robert Louis Stevenson et Triple-Brute

Translation

My dear friend, I have owed you dozens of letters for a very long time, but although I am getting better I still have to take things gently. I had to make the journey to Bournemouth like the flight into Egypt for fear that the fogs would kill me; and I felt extremely tired. But now things begin to improve and I can give you my news.

'Le Printemps' has arrived, but it had a broken arm, and we left it, at the time of our flight, in the care of a statue-doctor. I am expecting it any

---

[3] The plaster group, twenty-five inches high, was sold after Fanny's death. The inscription (added later) reads: 'À R.L. Stevenson, au sympathique artiste, fidèle ami, et cher poète, Rodin.'

day and my little house will soon be resplendent with it. I very much regret the dedication; perhaps, when you come to see us, it will not be too late to add it? I don't know about such things, but I hope not. The work is for everyone; the dedication is for me. The work is a present, too beautiful a one even; it is the word of friendship that gives it to me for good. I am so stupid that I'm getting muddled and lost here; but you will understand me, I think.

I cannot even express myself in English; how can you expect me to manage it in French? I am more fortunate than you in that the Nemesis of the Arts does not visit me under the mask of disenchantment; she saps my intelligence and leaves me gaping foolishly, without ability but without regret; without hope, it's true, but also, thank God, without despair. I'm still slightly surprised; I haven't got used to finding myself such a blockhead, but I'm resigning myself to it; even if it should last, it wouldn't be disagreeable, but since I would certainly die of hunger, it would be at the very least regrettable for me and my family.

I wish I could write to you, but it isn't me who holds the pen – it's the other one, the stupid one, who doesn't know French, who doesn't love my friends as I love them, who doesn't appreciate things of art as I appreciate them; he whom I disavow, but whom I control sufficiently to make him take up a pen and write this twaddle. That creature, dear Rodin, you do not like; you must never know him. Your friend, who is asleep just now, like a bear, in the depths of my being, will awaken before long. Then he will write to you in his own hand. Wait for him. The other one doesn't count; he is only a poor unfaithful secretary with a cold heart and a wooden head.

He who is sleeping is always, my dear friend, yours; he who writes is commissioned to inform you of the fact and to sign under his trade name
Robert Louis Stevenson and Triple-Brute

To Lady Taylor

[23 December 1886]   *Skerryvore*

My dear Lady Taylor, This is to wish you all the salutations of the year, with some regret that I cannot offer them in person; yet less than I had supposed. For hitherto your flight to London seems to have worked well; and time flies and will soon bring you back again.[1] Though time is ironical, too; and it would be like his irony if the same tide that brought you back, carried me away. That would not be, at least, without some meeting.

[1] The Taylors (while retaining the house in Bournemouth) had moved to London in November.

I feel very sorry to think the book to which I have put your name will be no better, and I can make it no better. The tales are of all dates and places; they are like the fox, the goose and the cabbage of the ferryman;[2] and must go floating down time together as best they can. But I am after all a (superior) penny-a-liner; I must do, in the Scotch phrase, as it will do with me; and I cannot always choose what my books are to be, only seize the chance they offer to link my name to a friend's. I hope the lot of them (the tales) will look fairly disciplined when they are clapped in binding; but I have a fear they will be but an awkward squad. I have a mild wish that you at least would read no farther than the dedication.

I suppose we have all been reading Dowden.[3] It seems to me a really first rate book, full of justice, and humour without which there can be no justice; and of fine intelligence besides. Here and there, perhaps a trifle precious; but this is to spy flaws in a fine work. I was uneasy at my resemblances to Shelley; I seem but a Shelley with less oil, and no genius; though I have had the fortune to live longer and (partly) to grow up. He was growing up. There is a manlier note in the last days; in spite of such really sickening aberrations as the Emilia Viviani business;[4] a business, which (if you can figure such a character as a hysterical man of sense) would have set him screaming. The last phrase is sadly involved: I mean the man of sense would have screamed. I try to take a humorously-genial view of life; but Emilia Viviani, if I have her detested name aright, is too much for my philosophy. I cannot smile when I see all these grown folk waltzing and piping the eye about an insubordinate and perfectly abominable schoolgirl, as silly and patently as false as Blanche Amory.[5] I really think it is one of these episodes that make the angels weep.

With all kind regards and affectionate good wishes to and for you and yours, believe me, Your affectionate friend   Robert Louis Stevenson

To Henry James[1]

[c. 23 December 1886]   [Skerryvore]

All the salutations!

[2] *The Merry Men* is dedicated to Lady Taylor. The reference is to the old poser of how the ferryman could get all three across the river without the fox eating the goose and the goose eating the cabbage.

[3] Edward Dowden's two-volume biography of Shelley had just appeared.

[4] Emilia Viviani was the young Italian girl with whom Shelley was infatuated.

[5] The selfish little shrew in Thackeray's *Pendennis*.

[1] James wrote from Florence on 19 December 1886 about his preparations for an essay on RLS (eventually published in the *Century* for April 1888). He asked when *The Merry Men* would be published – 'if there be such a thing as an advance copy I fain would grasp it'. RLS's letter is written on the half-title of proofs of *The Merry Men*.

My dear James, I send you the first two sheets of the new volume, all that
has yet reached me. The rest shall follow in course. I am really a very fair
sort of a fellow all things considered, have done some work; a silly Xmas
story (with some larks in it) which won't be out till I don't know when.[2]
I am also considering a volume of verse, much of which will be cast in my
native speech, that very dark oracular medium. I suppose this is a folly, but
what then? As the nurse says in Marryat, 'It was only a little one.'[3] We
have good news so far of the Samuel boy, but his supplies seem to have
hopelessly miscarried: ('if you want a thing done, entrust it to a friend who
is a man of business') and he may have held his hat by now upon a Badian[4]
wayside. My wife is peepy and dowie:[5] two Scotch expressions with
which I will leave you to wrestle unaided, as a preparation for my poetical
works. She is a woman (as you know) not without art: the art of
extracting the gloom of the eclipse from sunshine; and she has recently
laboured in this field not without success or (as we used to say) not
without a blessing. It is strange: 'we fell out my wife and I'[6] the other
night; she tackled me savagely for being a canary-bird; I replied
(bleatingly) protesting that there was no use in turning life into King Lear;
presently it was discovered that there were two dead combatants upon the
field, each slain by an arrow of the truth, and we tenderly carried off each
other's corpses.[7] Here is a little comedy for Henry James to write! The
beauty was each thought the other quite unscathed at first. But we had
dealt shrewd stabs. You say nothing of yourself, which I shall take to be
good news. Archer's note has gone.[8] He is, in truth, a very clever fellow
that Archer, and I believe a good one. It is a pleasant thing to see a man
who can use a pen; he can; really says what he means, and says it with a
manner; comes into print like one at his ease, not shame-faced and wrong-
foot-foremost like the bulk of us. Well, here is luck, and here are the
kindest recollections from the canary-bird and from King Lear, from the
Tragic Woman and the Flimsy Man.

Robert Ramsay Fergusson Stevenson

[2] 'The Misadventures of John Nicholson', published in *Yule Tide* (Cassell's Christmas annual),
December 1887.
[3] The excuse made by the nurse for her illegitimate baby in ch. 3 of *Mr Midshipman Easy*.
[4] I.e. Barbadian. Lloyd had gone on holiday to the West Indies. A letter of credit (probably
arranged by Bazett Colvin) had failed to reach him.
[5] Sad, mournful, dismal.
[6] Tennyson, 'The Princess', Part II, Introductory Song, l. 3.
[7] Colvin asked for James's advice before publishing this letter in 1911. James replied on 5 January
1911: 'Fanny S. will be a bigger fool than I ever took her for if she resents the lively description
of their domestic broil. It helps to commemorate her and makes her interesting – and just so,
I feel sure, she will rejoice'. In a letter about this time to Colvin, Fanny wrote: 'Mrs S. as gay
as a lark, but somehow I get very black and low spirited in the continual canary-bird-like
cheerfulness with which she fills the atmosphere. I suppose it is very degraded of me, no doubt
it is. I am in a fit of black gloom.'
[8] James had asked RLS to forward a note from him to William Archer asking for information
about his article on RLS.

[Postscript by Fanny]

It is odd, but the 'doleful woman' became such through too much cheerful society, too long continued nothing more serious than that. She sends you all good wishes. Ever the D.W.

To Henry James

[24 January 1887]   [Skerryvore]

My dear James, My bloody health has played me it in once more in the absurdest fashion, and the creature who now addresses you is but a stringy and white-faced *bouilli* out of the pot of fever: sub-acute rheumatism, whispers the doctor: the congested kidney, the genial pleuritic rub, the familiar recalcitrant liver, the aching constipated gall-duct, the swimming headache, and the devil to pay in every corner of the economy. I suppose (to judge by your letter) I need not send you these sheets, which came during my collapse by the rush.[1] I am on the start with three volumes, that one of tales, a second one of essays and one of – ahem – verse. This is a great order is it not? After that I shall have empty lockers. All new work stands still; I was getting on well with *Jenkin* when this blessed malady unhorsed me, and sent me back to the dung-collecting trade of the republisher. I shall re-issue *Virginibus Puerisque* as vol. I of *Essays*, and the new vol. as vol. II of ditto: to be sold however separately. This is but a dry maundering; however I am quite unfit – 'I am for action quite unfit Either of exercise or wit.'[2] My father is in a variable state; many sorrows and perplexities environ the house of Stevenson, my mother shoots north at this hour on business of a distinctly rancid character, my father (under my wife's tutory) proceeds tomorrow to Salisbury,[3] I remain here in my bed and whistle; in no quarter of heaven is anything encouraging apparent, except that the good Colvin comes to the hotel here on a visit. This dreary view of life is somewhat blackened by the fact that my head aches; which I always regard as a liberty on the part of the powers that be. This is also my first letter since my recovery. God speed your laudatory pen!

My wife joins in all warm messages. Yours   R.L.S.

---

[1] Proofs of *The Merry Men*. James had written from Florence on 21 January acknowledging RLS's December letter. He had decided to begin 'my genial tribute to your "exceptional powers"' without waiting for publication of *The Merry Men*.

[2] See p. 315, n.2.

[3] MIS's visit to Edinburgh was to collect papers connected with a dispute between TS and his nephews David and Charles over their remuneration from the family firm, against the background that because of his prolonged illness TS was doing none of the work but continuing to draw the lion's share of the profits. Fanny accompanied TS on a brief visit to Salisbury on 25 January.

To Bob Stevenson[1]

[February 1887]   *[Skerryvore]*

My dear Bob, I had already discovered the key to the D minor.[2] I am now sending works daily to Una Taylor; she is very pedantic and correct and washes my head over every note; I think it excellent work. I have sent for some primers also; I give up all advanced ideas: I mean to write two parts correctly first of all. I am in bed, so can't try what you say; your great speech in the case of dominant *versus* subdominant was pronounced, by all in court, convincing. When I have written two parts without a flaw, O then! Four parts, I think I scarce aspire to. Every time I try to write four parts, madness seizes on me; they are so obstinate, so stiff, so mulish, and the world so bubbles over with consecutive fifths. Yet it is a delightful idea, if it could be done; which it can't. I must say the pickler's life is a very sweet one. I lie in bed here with a musical slate, and labour at four parts till the world goes round me; damnable $\frac{6}{4}$ springing upon me unprepared, the ambitious leading note clambering upwards when every human tie demands that he shall descend, the fifths crowding thick upon my poor defences, the note that should be at the bottom invariably – ay, invariably – at the top. *Quelle vie, mes amis, O quelle vie!* If one could only have a piano in bed; but then one would never get up. Those who despise the pickler do not love art; they may love music, *je ne dis pas*; they don't love art. The delight of finding out what is what in an art, [is] surely as great as that of practising it mangily as most men must.

In the course of time, I shall persecute you with some more: just now, I am humbled into petty labours. Yours ever   R.L.S.

To James A.H. Murray[1]

[c. 21 February 1887]   *Skerryvore*

Dear Sir, That proof was never read; hence these tears.

Please read 'horror of the charnel *ocean*', which sounds very strange without its connection, but need not delay the dictionary maker.

---

[1] An example of a number of letters written to Bob and Una Taylor at this time about RLS's efforts to write music.

[2] In a long letter (which can be dated February 1887) Bob commented on a piece of music sent to him: 'I find chief fault in the want of contrast of the second subject and the manner in which its appearance in the key of the Tonic at C fritters away its appearance in the dominant at D.'

[1] James Augustus Henry Murray (1837–1915), Scottish philologist and lexicographer; knighted 1908. He became famous as the planner and editor of the great *Oxford English Dictionary* from 1879; he had completed half the editorial work at his death. Murray wrote to RLS on 19 February 1887 saying that he and his helpers were puzzled by the word 'brean' in the phrase 'the

I live and long for your dictionary. Ah, why was I not born later! Yours
very truly   Robert Louis Stevenson

Dr Murray.

To Mary Mapes Dodge[1]

5 April 1887   *Skerryvore*

Dear Madam, I have to thank you for two volumes of *St Nicholas*, in
which I found and read with indescribable amusement and delight, *Little
Lord Fauntleroy*.[2] It is the most pickthank business to find fault with
anything so daintily humorous and prettily pathetic; and yet I could wish
the author had conceived the tale one touch more humanly. By making
Fauntleroy this piece of sheer perfection, she has missed the delicious *scène-
à-faire*: the scene when the boy misbehaves, and our wicked earl becomes
in turn his teacher in goodness. If you think the authoress would value the
appreciation of a brother craftsman, it would be kind in you to communicate the news of my pleasure.

And now to business: I have a story in prospect; but my hero is a liar
and I think that would not please the readers of *St Nicholas*. On the other
hand, I have half clear before me a set of juvenile fantastic stories, partly
founded on making men of various kinds of beasts and insects: 'The
Adventure of the Invasion of Blind Men' (a warfaring ant idea), 'The City
of Little Men', 'The Tree Top Folk', etc. I should likely call the lot the
Voyages of Somebody or other (name not found) and there would be
fables and small stories intercalated. How if I contributed these as they
came to *St Nicholas*?[3] They would be self-contained, and might run to
(say) two to four numbers. (All this very much in the air). I should ask you
to give me say a couple of dozen proofs in a brochure form, in plenty of
time, so that I might get a title page put and publish first here to keep my
copyright. And I should think that a matter of £2 a column (taking your
column at about 500 words) would not be too much for you to pay. I
should not care, I think, to accept less; and indeed I am doubtful if I

horror of the charnel brean' in 'The Merry Men' as published in *Cornhill* for June 1882; he asked
whether RLS could tell them 'anything about the meaning and source of the word'. His
granddaughter records that RLS's letter was one of those that Murray liked to show to visitors
to his Scriptorium at Oxford (see K.M.E. Murray, *Caught in the Web of Words*, 1977).
[1] Mary Mapes Dodge (1831–1905) American author of children's stories, including *Hans Brinker;
or, the Silver Skates* (1865). She was the editor of *St Nicholas*, a monthly magazine for children
1873–1905.
[2] This immensely popular children's story by Frances Hodgson Burnett was serialised in *St Nicholas*
November 1885–October 1886.
[3] Nothing came of this project.

should not do better to bring them out in book form at once. But if I were to publish the tales from time to time in your pages, it would be a way to induce me to continue.

I wonder if you observed the singular resemblance between a tale of Mr Howells (with very droll and clever illustrations by a little girl) and one contributed by my wife (while still Mrs Osbourne) to *St Nicholas* in the year '78 or '79?[4] The similarity is striking. I am, dear Madam, Very truly yours   Robert Louis Stevenson

Mrs Mary Mapes Dodge.

To Will H. Low[1]

My dear Low, The fares to London may be found in any continental Bradshaw or sich; from London to Bournemouth impoverished parties who can stoop to the third class, get their ticket for a matter of 10s, or as my wife loves to phrase it 'a half a pound'. You will also be involved in a 3/- fare to get at Skerryvore; but this I daresay friends could help you in on your arrival; so that you may reserve your energies for the two tickets – costing the matter of a pound – and the usual gratuities of porters. This does not seem to me much; considering the intellectual pleasures that await you here, I call it dirt cheap. I *believe* the third class from Paris to London (via Dover) is *about* 40 francs; but I cannot swear. Suppose it to be fifty.

	frcs
50 × 2 = 100	100
The expense of spirit or spontaneous lapse of coin on the journey, at 5 frcs a head. 5 × 2 = 10	10
Victuals on ditto, at 5 frcs a head. 5 × 2 = 10	10
Gratuity to stewardess, in a case of severe prostration, at 3 francs	3
One night in London, on a modest footing, say 20	20
Two tickets to Bournemouth at 12.50. 12.50 × 2 = 25	25

---

[4] Fanny's story 'Too Many Birthdays' appeared in *St Nicholas* for July 1878 under the signature 'Fanny M. Osborne'. W.D. Howells's story 'Christmas Every Day' was published in the magazine for January 1886.

[1] Low wrote to RLS from Florence on 1 April 1887 about a planned visit to Skerryvore. In the course of it he wrote: 'It would facilitate matters for me if I had some little idea of the probable cost of the journey from Paris to Skerryvore via Calais to Dover. *Will you induce the practical member of your family to write us on this subject, the sooner the better.*'

Porters and general devilment, say 5   5
Cabs in London, say 2 shillings. Cab in Bournemouth,
   3 shillings = 5 shillings = 6 frcs 25 . . . .   6.25

frcs. 179.25

or, the same in pounds. £7.3.6½

or, the same in dollars. $35.45.

if there be any arithmetical virtue in me. I have left out dinner in London
in case you want a blow out which would come extry, and with the aid
of *vangs fangs* might easily double the whole amount, above all if you have
a few friends to meet you.

In making this valuable project, or budget, I discovered for the first
time a reason (frequently overlooked) for the singular costliness of travelling with your wife. Anybody would count the tickets double; but how
few would have remembered − or indeed has anyone ever remembered?
− to count the spontaneous lapse of coin double also. Yet there are two
of you, each must do his daily leakage, and it must be done out of your
travelling fund. You will tell me perhaps that you carry the coin yourself;
my dear sir, do you think you can fool your maker? Your wife has to lose
her quota; and by God she will − if you kept the coin in a belt. One thing
I have omitted; you will lose a certain amount on the exchange; but this
even I cannot foresee, as it is one of the few things that vary with the
money a man has. I also omitted (there being a lady in the case) 4 sous for
cabinets modernes at Paris. But this you can add when you are quite alone.
I am, dear Sir, Yours financially   Samuel Budgett

A copy of the book goes.[2] It has been to the West Injies seeking Sam
and missing him.[3]

★To Anne Jenkin

15 or 16 April (the hour not being known) [1887]   *Skerryvore*

My dear Mrs Jenkin, It is I know not what hour of the night; but I cannot
sleep, have lit the gas, and here goes.

First, all your packet arrived; I have dipped into the Schumann already
with great pleasure. Surely in what concerns us there is a sweet little

---

[2] Low had asked for a copy of *The Merry Men* before he left Florence as he intended to have it
rebound there.

[3] Low replied on 12 April 1887: 'I was mistaken in the identity of the practical member of the
family; what a pity that you should waste yourself on literature.' The Lows came to London *en
route* for the USA but were unable to meet RLS because of his summons to Edinburgh and his
father's death.

chirrup; the *Good Words* arrived in the morning just when I needed it,[1] and the famous notes that I had lost were recovered also in the nick of time.

And now I am going to bother you with my affairs: premising, first, that this is *private;* second, that whatever I do the *Life* shall be done first, and I am getting on with it well; and third, that I do not quite know why I consult you, but something tells me you will hear with fairness.

Here is my problem. The Curtin women are still miserable prisoners;[2] no one dare buy their farm of them, all the manhood of England and the world stands aghast before a threat of murder. (1) Now, my work can be done anywhere; hence I can take up without loss a back-going Irish farm, and live on, though not (as I had originally written) in it: First Reason. (2) If I should be killed, there are a good many who would feel it; writers are so much in the public eye, that a writer being murdered would attract attention, throw a bull's-eye light upon this cowardly business: Second Reason. (3) I am not unknown in the States, from which the funds come that pay for these brutalities; to some faint extent, my death (if I should be killed) would tell there: Third Reason. (4) *Nobody else is taking up this obvious and crying duty*: Fourth Reason. (5) I have a crazy health and may die at any moment, my life is of no purchase in an insurance office, it is the less account to husband it, and the business of husbanding a life is dreary and demoralising: Fifth Reason.

I state these in no order, but as they occur to me. And I shall do the like with the objections.

First Objection: It will do no good; you have seen Gordon die, and nobody minded; nobody will mind if you die. This is plainly of the devil. Second Objection: You will not even be murdered, the climate will miserably kill you, you will strangle out in a rotten damp heat, in congestion, etc. Well, what then? It changes nothing: the purpose is to brave crime; let me brave it, for such time and to such an extent as God allows. Third Objection: The Curtin women are probably highly uninteresting females. I haven't a doubt of it. But the Government cannot, men will not, protect them. If I am the only one to see this public duty, it is to the public and the Right I should perform it – not to Mesdames Curtin. Fourth Objection: I am married. 'I have married a wife!'[3] I seem to have heard it before. It smells ancient; what was the context? Fifth

---

[1] *Good Words*, May 1886, contained 'Reminiscences of My Later Life' by Mary Howitt, recording a visit to the Jenkins; it is quoted in ch. IV of the *Memoir*.

[2] There were widespread disturbances in Ireland during this period. On 13 November 1885 a gang of 'moonlighters' had attacked the farm of John Curtin in County Kerry demanding arms. During the fighting Curtin was mortally wounded but succeeded in shooting one of the gang. In retaliation, the Curtin family were boycotted and subjected to harassment and persecution.

[3] Luke 14:20.

Objection: My wife has had a mean life (1), loves me (2), could not bear to lose me (3). (1) I admit: I am sorry. (2) But what does she love me for? and (3) she must lose me soon or late. And after all, because we run this risk, it does not follow we should fail. Sixth Objection: My wife wouldn't like it. No, she wouldn't. Who would? But the Curtins don't like it. And all those who are to suffer if this goes on, won't like it. And if there is a great wrong, somebody must suffer. Seventh Objection: I won't like it. No, I will not; I have thought it through, and I will not. But what of that? And both she and I may like it more than we suppose. We shall lose friends, all comforts, all society: so has everybody who has ever done anything; but we shall have some excitement, and that's a fine thing, and we shall be trying to do the right, and that's not to be despised. Eighth Objection: I am an author with my work before me. See Second Reason. Ninth Objection: But am I not taken with the hope of excitement? I was at first. I am not much now. I see what a dreary, friendless, miserable, God-forgotten business it will be. And anyway, is not excitement the proper reward of doing anything both right and a little dangerous? Tenth Objection: But am I not taken with a notion of glory? I daresay I am. Yet I see quite clearly how all points to nothing coming, to a quite inglorious death by disease and from the lack of attendance; or even if I should be knocked on the head, as these poor Irish promise, how little any one will care. It will be a smile at a thousand breakfast-tables. I am nearly forty now; I have not many illusions. And if I had? I do not love this health-tending, housekeeping life of mine. I have a taste for danger, which is human, like the fear of it. Here is a fair cause; a just cause; no knight ever set lance in rest for a juster. Yet it needs not the strength I have not, only the passive courage that I hope I could muster, and the watchfulness that I am sure I could learn.

Here is a long midnight dissertation; with myself; with you. Please let me hear. But I charge you this: if you see in this idea of mine the finger of duty, do not dissuade me. I am nearing forty, I begin to love my ease and my home and my habits, I never knew how much till this arose; do not falsely counsel me to put my head under the bed-clothes. And I will say this to you: my wife, who hates the idea, does not refuse. 'It is nonsense,' says she, 'but if you go, I will go.' Poor girl, and her home and her garden that she was so proud of! I feel her garden most of all, because it is a pleasure (I suppose) that I do not feel myself to share.

1. Here is a great wrong.
2.   "   a growing wrong.
3.   "   a wrong founded on crime.
4.   "   crime that the Government cannot prevent.
5.   "   crime that it occurs to no man to defy.
6. But it has occurred to me.

7. Being a known person, some will notice my defiance.
8. Being a writer, I can *make* people notice it.
9. And, I think, *make* people imitate me.
10. Which would destroy in time this whole scaffolding of oppression.
11. And if I fail, however ignominiously, that is not my concern. It is, with an odd mixture of reverence and humorous remembrances of Dickens, be it said – it is A-nother's.[4]

And here, at I cannot think what hour of the morning, I shall draw up, and remain, Yours, really in want of a little help   R.L.S.

Sleepless at midnight's dewy hour.
　　　　〃　　　　　　〃　witching　〃
　　　　〃　　　　　　〃　maudlin　〃
　　　　　　　　　　　　　　etc.

Next morning

Eleventh Objection: I have a father and mother. And who has not? Macduff's was a rare case; if we must wait for a Macduff. Besides, my father will not perhaps be long here. Twelfth Objection: The cause of England in Ireland is not worth supporting. *À qui le dites-vous?* And I am not supporting that. Home Rule, if you like. Cause of decency, the idea that populations should not be taught to gain public ends by private crime, the idea that for all men to bow before a threat of crime is to loosen and degrade beyond redemption the whole fabric of man's decency.[5]

To Alison Cunningham

16 April 1887   *Skerryvore*

My dearest Cummy, As usual I have been a dreary bad fellow and not written for ages; but you must just try to forgive me, to believe (what is

---

[4] In *Martin Chuzzlewit*, Augustus Noddle constantly refers to Mercy Pecksniff (with whom he is in love) as 'another's'.
[5] RLS commented further in a letter to Mrs Jenkin in late April:

> You misunderstood me in one point: I always hoped to found such a society: that was the outside of my dream, and would mean entire success. *But* – I cannot play Peter the Hermit. In these days of the Fleet Street journalist, I cannot send out better men than myself, with wives or mothers just as good as mine, and sisters (I may at least say) better, to a danger and a long-drawn dreariness that I do not share. My wife says it's cowardice; what brave men are the leader-writers! Call it cowardice; it is mine. Mind you, I *may* end by trying to do it by the pen only; I shall not love myself if I do; and is it ever a good thing to do a thing for which you despise yourself? – even in the doing? And if the thing you do is to call upon others to do the thing you neglect? I have never dared to say what I feel about men's lives, because my own was in the wrong: shall I dare to send them to death? The physician must heal himself; he must honestly *try* the path he recommends: if he does not even try, should he not be silent?

The project was overtaken by his father's death.

the truth) that the number of my letters is no measure of the number of times I think of you, and to remember how much writing I have to do. The weather is bright but still cold; and my father, I am afraid, feels it sharply. He has had, still has rather, a most obstinate jaundice, which has reduced him cruelly in strength and really upset him altogether. I hope, or think, he is perhaps a little better; but he suffers much, cannot sleep at night for the continual itching that accompanies the complaint, and gives John[1] and my mother a severe life of it to wait upon him. My wife is I think a little better, but no great shakes. Sam has come back from the West Indies much stronger in health; not, I fear, any better in his eyes. But he has very pluckily made up his mind to the worst, is learning to write with a typewriter; and even if he does go blind, will bear it, I hope, like a man.[2] I keep mighty respectably myself. We had Isabella, as you will have heard, a great deal in the house: she is wonderful, she seems no older to me than when I was a laddie, and that is some while ago now. Coolin's Tombstone is now built into the front wall of Skerryvore, and poor Bogue's (with a Latin inscription also) is set just above it. Poor, unhappy, wee man, he died, as you must have heard, in fight; which was what he would have chosen; for military glory was more in his line than the domestic virtues.[3] I believe this is about all my news, except that, as I write, there is a blackbird singing in our garden trees, as it were at Swanston. I would like fine to go up the burnside a bit, and sit by the pool and be young again – or no, be what I am still, only there instead of here, for just a little. Did you see that I had written about John Todd? In this month's *Longman* it was; if you have not seen it, I will try and send it you. Some day climb as high as Halkerside for me (I am never likely to do it for myself) and sprinkle some of the well water on the turf. I am afraid it is a Pagan rite, but quite harmless, *and ye can sain it wi' a bit prayer.* Tell the Peewies that I mind their forbears well. My heart is sometimes heavy and sometimes glad to mind it all. But for what we have received, the Lord make us truly thankful. Don't forget to sprinkle the water and do it in my name; I feel a childish eagerness in this.

Remember me most kindly to James and with all sorts of love to yourself, Believe me, Your laddie   Robert Louis Stevenson

[1] John Cruickshank, employed as a valet to help look after TS.

[2] In April 1886 Lloyd had had to withdraw from his examination in Edinburgh because of threatened blindness. Although RLS still calls him 'Sam' to Cummy he had decided to use his second name 'Lloyd' because of fears of scandal about his father Sam Osbourne who had mysteriously disappeared and was never heard of again.

[3] Coolin, RLS's Skye terrier, given to him when he was seven years old, was killed in 1869. His tombstone was moved from Swanston Cottage to Skerryvore. In April 1886, having been injured in a fight with another dog, Bogue was sent to a dogs' infirmary for treatment. Before he had recovered he broke loose, attacked a dog more powerful than himself and so perished.

P.S. I suppose Mrs Reid ought to see the paper about her man;[4] judge of that, and if you think she would not dislike it, buy her one for me, and let me know. The article is called 'Pastoral': in *Longman's Magazine* for April. I will send you the money; I would today but it's the Sabbie day,[5] and I cannae.   R.L.S.

Remembrances from all here

To Sidney Colvin[1]

[*Late May 1887*]   [*17 Heriot Row*]

My Dear S.C., At last I can write a word to you. Your little note in the *P.M.G.* was charming;[2] I have written 4 pp. in the *Contemporary*, which Bunting found room for,[3] they are not very good; but I shall do more for his memory in time.

About the death, I have long hesitated, I was long before I could tell my mind; and now I know it and can but say that I am glad. If we could have had my father, that would have been a different thing. But to keep that changeling – suffering changeling,[4] any longer, could better none and nothing. Now he rests; it is more significant, it is more like himself; he will begin to return to us in the course of time as he was and as we loved him.

My favourite words in literature, my favourite scene – 'O let him pass,'[5] – Kent and Lear – was played for me here in the first moment of my

---

[4] 'Pastoral' celebrates the Swanston shepherd John Tod (1809–81) and 'Mrs Reid' was presumably a slip of the pen; John Reid was farm grieve (bailiff or overseer) at Swanston.

[5] Since Sunday was on 17 April, RLS either added the postscript on that day or misdated his letter.

[1] The seriously ill TS went home to Edinburgh from Bournemouth on 21 April. RLS was sent for and arrived on 6 May but his father did not recognise him. He died on 8 May and the funeral took place on 13 May. RLS, who had caught a cold on the journey north, was too ill to attend.

[2] In his letter of condolence of 10 May Colvin mentioned the paragraph he had written for the *Pall Mall Gazette* of that date.

[3] Sir Percy William Bunting (1836–1911), editor of the *Contemporary Review* 1882–1911. RLS's essay 'Thomas Stevenson' in the June *Contemporary* was reprinted in *Memories and Portraits*.

[4] Cf. RLS's 'The Last Sight', the last six lines of a long (unpublished) poem about his father, *Songs of Travel* XLIII (in *Collected Poems*):

> Once more I saw him. In the lofty room,
> Where oft with lights and company his tongue
> Was trump to honest laughter, sate attired
> A something in his likeness. 'Look!' said one,
> Unkindly kind, 'look up, it is your boy!'
> And the dread changeling gazed on me in vain.

[5] *King Lear*, V.iii.314.

return. I believe Shakespeare saw it with his own father. I had no words; but it was shocking to see. He died on his feet, you know; was on his feet the last day, knowing nobody – still he would be up. This was his constant wish; also that he might smoke a pipe on his last day, that was not quite granted, but he did smoke a cigarette on the Wednesday. The funeral – abominable business, as ever I saw – would have pleased him: it was the largest private funeral in man's memory here.[6]

We have no plans; and it is possible we may go home without going through town. I do not know; I have no views yet, whatever; nor can have any at this stage of my cold and my business. Ever yours   R.L.S.[7]

To Sidney Colvin

[? 3 June 1887]   *[Skerryvore]*

My dear Colvin, This is to announce to you, what I believe should have been done sooner, that we are at Skerryvore. We were both tired, and I was fighting my second cold, so we came straight through by the west.[1]

We have a butler: by God! He doesn't buttle, but the point of the thing is the style. When Fanny gardens, he stands over her and looks genteel.[2] He opens the door, and I am told waits at table. Well, what's the odds; I shall have it on my tomb: 'He ran a butler.'

> He may have been this and that
> A drunkard or a guttler,
> He may have been bald and fat;
> At least he kept a butler.

[6] MIS recorded that there were more than one hundred people at the funeral and forty to fifty carriages.

[7] RLS wrote to Henley:

> Time enough has past for me to see how I stand; and I am glad: glad for his sake, glad for mine, that poor, suffering, altered face is gone, that stumbling tongue looking no longer in vain for the old brilliant words. It is my chief feeling. All I regret is that he did not get his title; I will never forgive the London clique for that: Douglass a Sir and a F.R.S., and my father nothing – because he lived in Edinburgh. Well, all that matters to him no more, and to me only a little.

Sir James Douglass, the English engineer designed and built the new Eddystone lighthouse.

[1] RLS and Fanny left Edinburgh on 31 May. They were accompanied by TS's valet John, but he proved an unsatisfactory servant and was soon dismissed.

[2] RLS told his mother: 'We were thrilled by the pleasant spectacle of Fanny on her knees gardening, and John, with his hands behind his back, looking on; he looked much like a gentleman. The scene lasted the better part of an afternoon, and a faint rumour of mirth went from house to house along Alum Chine. On some hint of this coming to F.'s ears, she said, with dignity: "There was nothing there I could trust John to do." '

> He may have sprung from ill or well
>   From Emperor or sutler;
> He may be burning now in Hell;
>   On earth he kept a butler.

I want to tell you also that I have suppressed your poem.[3] I shall send it you for yourself, and I hope you will agree with me that it was not good enough in point of view of merit and a little too intimate as between you and me. I would not say less of you, my friend, but I scarce care to say so much in public while we live. A man may stand on his own head; it is not fair to set his friend on a pedestal.

The verses are now at press;[4] I have written a dam fine ballad;[5] and I am, dear S.C., Ever yours   Tomnoddy

Fanny Stevenson to her Mother-in-Law
(Extracts)

Thursday [23 June 1887]   *Skerryvore*

My dear Mrs Stevenson, . . . We have had our American guest, and Louis is enchanted with him.[1] We gave him the worst dinner that ever millionaire ate, and I was horribly mortified in consequence. He came on the Jubilee day,[2] so we could change nothing. In the afternoon Agnes came to me in the garden with a very haggard countenance to say that the pudding (a cold one) was finished and cooling in the cellar. 'It looks very well,' she said – 'in the cellar.' 'That's very nice,' said I. 'I put it in the cellar,' continued Agnes anxiously. 'Well,' said I, 'that's all right.' 'I put the fish in the cellar, too,' persisted Agnes. 'That's the right place to put it,' said I. There was a pause, and then Agnes broke out with 'The cat's got the

---

[3] The poem 'To—' beginning 'I knew thee strong and quiet like the hills' describing Colvin as 'the perfect friend' was eventually published as *Songs of Travel* XXI.

[4] *Underwoods* was published on 15 August.

[5] 'Ticonderoga'. One of the manuscripts is written on the back of part of the essay on Thomas Stevenson. It was published in the December 1887 issue of *Scribner's*.

[1] Charles Fairchild (1838–1910) was a younger brother of General Lucius Fairchild, the distinguished American soldier and diplomat. Originally a lawyer, he became a wealthy Boston banker and businessman; he was a partner in the banking and stockbroking firm of Lee, Higginson and Co., and President of the Fairchild Paper Co.; in 1895 he established the New York banking house of Charles Fairchild and Co. A friend and patron of Sargent, he commissioned him to paint a portrait of RLS as a present for his wife Elizabeth (1845–1924), who was an admirer of Stevenson's writings. This well-known work, now in the Taft Museum, Cincinnati, showing RLS sitting in a wicker-work chair with a cigarette in his right hand, was painted in late April 1887; it was long thought to be the first Sargent painting of 1884. It is reproduced on the jacket of this volume.

[2] Queen Victoria's Jubilee was celebrated on 21 June.

fish, and eaten it all up!' I turned in dismay, knowing no more fish was procurable, when I perceived Valentine had come out too, and was regarding me with a curious expression. 'This is unpleasant,' I said to her. 'I am so glad Agnes has told you,' cried Valentine, 'I hadn't the courage.' 'After all,' said I, 'I suppose we can do well enough without the fish.' 'The fish!' exclaimed Valentine; 'it wasn't the fish I meant! I forgot to order the cream yesterday, and as I have arranged for a white vegetable soup, I don't know how to make it without cream; also, there is the whipped cream for the pudding, which it must have.'

The millionaire drank, as we knew, nothing but hock, and we had no hock in the cellar. The day before, Louis sent John to get some sample bottles in Bournemouth. By some mistake, when the day came, there was but one bottle of indifferent hock. On the same train with the millionaire came, to my horror, Teddy Henley, without a word of warning. I could not, somehow, receive him with much cordiality.

Well, we sat down to dinner; the soup, doctored up by Valentine, was brought; in her excitement she had gone on salting it so that it was like sea brine, and excoriated the mouth. There was nothing to do but send it away. The joint was placed before me; I had told Valentine to see that it was really small young lamb, and not half-grown sheep as we had had the last time. When John lifted the cover I could have burst into tears. It was a leg the size of a kitten's, and could positively, so far as size went, have been served upon this sheet of paper. There were plenty of peas, and potatoes, but nothing to follow but some hastily improvised custard in very small cups. Fortunately your cheese was still to the fore, and it was pathetic to hear both Mr Fairchild and Teddy praise the cheese which they ate until for shame's sake they had to leave off. Louis, knowing about the hock guarded it jealously from Lloyd and Teddy, the latter of whom discovered at an early hour that hock was not for him. As to Lloyd, the unseductive fluid was removed from him by force. I believe Valentine and John wept together in the pantry. Can you conceive of a more mortifying fiasco? Such a thing never happened to me before, and I thought it couldn't, so was all unprepared.

The millionaire had a special train sent down to take him back to London. He is a sweet fellow, and is going to arrange all our travelling plans from New York to the west, and find out exactly where we had better go,[3] and about a house to live in, and all that. . . . The Fairchilds spend the summers at Newport which is the most fashionable place in America. They have a cottage there . . . They propose we go directly there . . . Dear love to you all   Fanny

[3] Following his father's death RLS and his family were (on the advice of his doctors) making plans to go to America for the winter; at this time Colorado was the favoured destination.

To Sidney Colvin

19 August 1887   *Skerryvore*

My dear Colvin, I wanted to write to you again today, and the post is gone, and I have not yet had the time to write a word: so much remained to be attended to, so much still remains over. Here I am in this dismantled house hoping to leave tomorrow, yet still in doubt; this time of my life is at an end: if it leaves bitterness in your mind, what kind of a time has it been? I send this, on the chance, to the B.M. I shall be (it seems) at Armfield's Finsbury tomorrow afternoon and till Monday. If you can find it in your heart to forgive me, I shall go with the more peace.[1] If not, my dear old friend, time will bring it about. There was no essential unkindness in any of our minds; some muddle, some trouble, there was, and it has spattered you; no more. I wish we could have left with a Godspeed; but if that may not be, I know you will forgive us before long. I discount it, I will not let myself think harm. I have told Fanny, who was cut to the heart with fear and alarm, that I would disculpate her. It was certainly not her doing, beyond muddling; wherein I cannot excuse her; and if we have grown to count on your indulgence very largely, yours is the fault. I wish I had a word of peace to take to her tomorrow; I may have it by tomorrow's post; and anyway I count upon your affection, already so often proved to one so unworthy, to overclimb this fault also; and however it may prove, I am still your most grateful, most admiring and most affectionate friend, without change – perhaps not without enough – but with enough of affection to make this letter hard indeed to write, and enough of faith, even if nothing came before we sail, to sail with a sure hope of some kind word upon the other side. Yours, my dear soul, from the bottom of my heart   R.L.S.

The last day – the last evening – in the old house – with a sad, but God knows, nowise a bitter heart; I wish I could say with hope.

To Adelaide Boodle[1]

[? 21 August 1887]   *[South Place Hotel, Finsbury]*

My dear Miss Boodle, I promise you the paper-knife shall go to sea with me; and if it were in my disposal, I should promise it should return with

---

[1] Colvin stayed at Bournemouth 11–13 August; the cause of the disagreement is unknown.

[1] Adelaide Ann Boodle (1858–1934) was the sixth of the seven daughters of Edward Boodle (1800–1873), a London barrister, and his wife Julia Barrie whom he married in 1847. A few years after her husband's death Mrs Boodle and her daughters came to Bournemouth because Adelaide was threatened with lung trouble; they lived at Lostock in the Poole Road in genteel

me too. All that you say, I thank you for very much; I thank you for all the pleasantness that you have brought about our house; and I hope the day may come when I shall see you again in poor old Skerryvore, now left to the natives of Canada, or to worse Barbarians, if such exist. I am afraid my attempt to jest is rather *à contre-coeur*. Good-bye – *au revoir* – and do not forget, Your friend   Robert Louis Stevenson

poverty as neighbours of RLS. Adelaide became a devoted friend and *protegée* of the Stevensons: RLS gave her lessons in the art of writing and she joined in his music-making by playing the violin. Her *RLS and his Sine Qua Non* (1926) gives an affectionate account of life at Skerryvore.

X. SECOND VISIT TO AMERICA: THE QUARREL WITH HENLEY
August 1887–June 1888

A succession of friends and relatives called at the South Place Hotel, Finsbury on 20 and 21 August 1887 to say good-bye. They included William Archer, Henry James, Gosse, Henley, Coggie Ferrier, Katharine de Mattos, Aunt Alan and Cummy. Colvin (who had been out of town) returned late on Sunday evening and stayed the night at the hotel. He relates how on Monday 22 August he accompanied Stevenson and his party – comprising Fanny, Margaret Stevenson, Lloyd Osbourne and the maid Valentine Roch – to the London docks to see them embark on the *Ludgate Hill*: 'Leaving the ship's side as she weighed anchor, and waving farewell to the party from the boat which landed me, I little knew what was the truth, that I was looking on the face of my friend for the last time.'

Fanny had booked the passage on the advice of Colvin's brother, Bazett, but no one had realised that the *Ludgate Hill* was a cattle-boat due to call at Le Havre for a cargo of over a hundred horses and a consignment of apes for American zoos. In spite of this, and the gales and continual stormy seas, Stevenson was in high spirits, and was in his element visiting and giving champagne to the sea-sick passengers. He was busy with the proofs of *Memories and Portraits*, dedicating the book to his mother from 'S.S. *Ludgate Hill* within sight of Cape Race'.

On arrival in New York on Wednesday 7 September Stevenson and his party were greeted on the quayside by Will H. Low and Edward L. Burlingame, editor of *Scribner's Magazine*,[1] and by a reporter from the *New York Herald* who soon singled out 'a tall gentleman wearing a short velvet jacket and a peculiarly low cut hat.' RLS was also handed a telegram from Charles Fairchild (see p. 338) inviting him to stay at the Victoria Hotel as his guest until he was ready to go to the Fairchild house at Newport; a carriage from the hotel was waiting. Stevenson went straight to bed but managed to give interviews to some of the journalists anxious to meet the author of *Dr Jekyll and Mr Hyde*.

---

[1] Edward Livermore Burlingame (1848–1922), son of Anson Burlingame, US congressman and diplomat. He accompanied his father to Peking as secretary at the age of seventeen and completed his education at Heidelberg. He joined Scribner in 1879 and was editor of *Scribner's Magazine* 1886–1914; he was literary adviser to the firm until his death.

The next day it was decided that as the cold RLS had caught in the final stages of the voyage was still bad, he should start at once for Newport with Valentine and Lloyd. Fanny and Margaret Stevenson moved to a cheaper hotel, the Hotel St Stephen, and stayed on in New York in order to attend the first production in that city of T.R. Sullivan's dramatisation of *Dr Jekyll and Mr Hyde* with Richard Mansfield, at the Madison Square Theatre on 12 September.[2] They joined RLS in Newport on 14 September.

To Sidney Colvin

[c. *18 September 1887*]   *Newport, R.I. U.S.A.*[1]

My dear Colvin, So long it went excellent well, and I had a time I am glad to have had; really enjoying my life; there is nothing like being at sea, after all. And O why have I allowed myself to rot so long on land? – But on the Banks I caught a cold, and I have not yet got over it. My reception here was idiotic to the last degree; if Jesus Christ came, they would make less fuss. It is very silly and not pleasant, except where humour enters; and I confess the poor interviewer lads pleased me. They are too good for their trade; avoided anything I asked them to avoid; and were no more vulgar in their reports than they could help. I liked the lads.

We have had a doubtful time. I am still with the kind Fairchilds, as are Fanny and Valentine; my mother and Lloyd in a neighbouring Quaker boarding house. Do not blame Fanny if my feeble pen takes up the tale; she is much run down with all our worries.[2] Today I am really much on the mend; but have a good deal of leeway to make up.

O it was lovely on our stable-ship, chock full of stallions; she rolled heartily, rolled some of the fittings out of our stateroom, and I think a

---

[2] Thomas Russell Sullivan (1849–1916), American author, playwright and adaptor of plays, wrote to RLS in June 1886 and obtained permission to dramatise *Dr Jekyll*. He later visited RLS at Saranac. Richard Mansfield (1854–1907), the American actor, scored a great success in the name part, and it became one of his most famous rôles. While RLS was in America Mansfield made small monthly payments to him; RLS wrote to the *New York Sun* in March 1888 to publicise this and to record that Sullivan's version was 'fully authorised' by him.

[1] The Fairchilds had a summer residence at 94 Washington Street, Newport. Maude Howe Elliott wrote in *This Was My Newport* (Cambridge, Mass., 1944): '... I carried flowers from Oak Glen to Robert Louis Stevenson during his Newport sojourn. Stevenson was very ill during the visit, and was rarely visible – spending his days lying full length on a couch, wrapped in a scarlet dressing-gown, smoking endless cigarettes, and at times pouring forth a stream of talk that left his listeners tingling with the thrill of his rare and exquisite personality.'

[2] Fanny wrote to Dora Williams: 'Here we are at Newport stopping with very delightful millionaires, who are spoiling us beautifully ... We had a very bad passage, and it did not do me very much good. I was pretty ill in New York, and had to for the first time in my life, let Louis go away from me when he was bad too.'

more dangerous cruise (except that it was summer) it would be hard to imagine. But we enjoyed it to the mast head, all but Fanny; and even she perhaps a little. When we got in, we had run out of beer, stout, curaçao, soda-water, water, fresh meat and (almost) of biscuit. But it was a thousandfold pleasanter than a great big Birmingham liner like a new hotel; and we liked the officers, and made friends with the quartermasters, and I (at least) made a friend of a baboon (for we carried a cargo of apes) whose embraces have pretty near cost me a coat. The passengers improved and were a very good specimen lot, with no drunkard, no gambling that I saw, and less grumbling and backbiting than one would have asked of poor human nature. Apes, stallions, cows, matches, hay, and poor men-folk all or almost all came successfully to land. Yours ever   R.L.S.

To Sidney Colvin[1]

[*24 September 1887*]   [*Hotel St Stephen, New York*]

My dear S.C., Your delightful letter has just come, and finds me in a New York hotel, waiting the arrival of a sculptor (St Gaudens)[2] who is making a medallion of yours truly and who is (to boot) one of the handsomest and nicest fellows I have often seen. I caught a cold on the Banks; fog is not for me; nearly died of interviewers and visitors, during twenty-four hours in New York; cut for Newport with Lloyd and Valentine, a journey like Fairy Land for the most engaging beauties, one little rocky and pine-shaded cove after another, each with a house and a boat at anchor, so that I left my heart in each and marvelled why American authors had been so unjust to their country; caught another cold on the train; arrived at Newport to go to bed and to grow worse, and to stay in bed until I left again; the Fairchilds proving during this time kindness itself, Mrs Fairchild very intense and very handsome and a trifle like Una Taylor in character, Mr Fairchild simply one of the most engaging men in the world, and one of the children, Blair,[3] *aet.* ten, a great joy and amusement in his solemn adoring attitude to the author of *Treasure Island* – here I was interrupted by the arrival of my sculptor — I withdraw

---

[1] RLS and Fanny returned to New York on 19 September by the evening boat.

[2] Augustus Saint-Gaudens (1848–1907), American sculptor of Franco-Irish parentage. He is best known in England for the statue of Lincoln in Parliament Square, London. A close friend of Will H. Low's, he became a devoted admirer of RLS. He was making preliminary studies for the well-known medallion in bas-relief of RLS sitting up in bed reading and smoking a cigarette. In a modified form, with a couch substituted for the bed and a pen for the cigarette, this became the basis of the memorial in St Giles's Cathedral, Edinburgh. MIS records that sittings began on 23 September.

[3] Blair Fairchild (1877–1933), fifth child and third son of Charles and Elizabeth Fairchild. He became a composer and lived mainly in Paris.

calling him handsome; he is not quite that, his eyes are too near together; he is only remarkable looking, and like an Italian *cinque-cento* medallion; I have begged him to make a medallion of himself and give me a copy — I will not take up the sentence in which I was wandering so long; but begin fresh. I was ten or twelve days at Newport; then came back convalescent to New York; Fanny and Lloyd are off to the Adirondacks to see if that will suit; and the rest of us leave Monday (this is Saturday) to follow them up. I hope we may manage to stay there all winter. I have a splendid appetite and have on the whole recovered well after a mighty sharp attack. I am now on a salary of £500 a year for twelve articles in *Scribner's Magazine* on what I like; it is more than £500 but I cannot calculate more precisely. You have no idea how much is made of me here; I was offered £2000 for a weekly article[4] – eh hé, how is that, but I refused that lucrative job. They would drive even an honest man into being a mere lucre-hunter in three weeks; to make me *se gober*[5] is I think more difficult: I have my own views on that point and stick to them. The success of *Underwoods* is gratifying.[6] I thought the *St Jingo* was about as near the mark as any; you see the verses are sane, that is their strong point, and it seems it is strong enough to carry them.

A thousand thanks for your grand letter. Ever yours   R.L.S.

To Henry James

[*6 October 1887*]   [*Saranac Lake*][1]
I know not the day; but the month it is
the drear October by the ghoul haunted
woodland of Weir.[2]

My dear Henry James, This is to say *First*: the voyage was a huge success. We all enjoyed it (bar my wife) to the ground; sixteen days at sea with a cargo of hay, matches, stallions and monkeys, and in a ship that rolled like God Almighty, and with no style on, and plenty of sailors to talk to, and the endless pleasures of the sea – the romance of it, the sport of the scratch

---

[4] S.S. McClure (see p. 347) was commissioned by Joseph Pulitzer of the *New York World* to offer RLS $10,000 a year for a short weekly article.

[5] French *se gober* – to be self-conceited.

[6] In his letter Colvin had referred to favourable reviews of *Underwoods* in the *Pall Mall Gazette, St James's Gazette, The Times* and the *Athenaeum.*

[1] Saranac Lake in the Adirondacks was a well-known area for sufferers from tuberculosis. Here in 1884 the American physician Edward Livingston Trudeau (1848–1915), a pioneer in tuberculosis research and treatment, and himself a sufferer from the disease, founded the Adirondack Cottage Sanatorium and established the first laboratory devoted to research on the subject. Trudeau paid few professional visits to RLS and found no active symptoms of tuberculosis.

[2] Cf. Poe, 'Ulalume'.

dinner and the smashing crockery, the pleasure – an endless pleasure – of balancing to the swell: well, it's over.

Second, I had a fine time, rather a troubled one, at Newport and New York; saw much of and liked hugely, the Fairchilds, St Gaudens the sculptor, Gilder of the *Century*, – just saw the dear Alexander[3] – saw a lot of my old and admirable friend Will Low, whom I wish you knew and appreciated – was medallioned by St Gaudens – and at last escaped to

Third, Saranac Lake, where we now are, and which I believe we mean to like and pass the winter at. Our house – emphatically 'Baker's'[4] – is on a hill, and has a sight of a stream turning a corner in the valley – bless the face of running water! – and sees some hills too, and the paganly prosaic roofs of Saranac itself: the Lake, it does not see, nor do I regret that; I like water, (fresh water I mean) either running swiftly among stones or else largely qualified with whisky. As I write, the sun (which has been long a stranger) shines in at my shoulder; from the next room, the bell of Lloyd's type-writer makes an agreeable music, as it patters off (at a rate which astonishes this experienced novelist) the early chapters of a humorous romance;[5] from still further off – the walls of Baker's are neither ancient nor massive – rumours of Valentine about the kitchen stove come to my ears; of my mother and Fanny, I hear nothing for the excellent reason that they have gone sparking off, one to Niagara one to Indianapolis[6] – People complain that I never give news in my letters. I have wiped out that reproach.

But now, *Fourth*, I have seen the article;[7] and it may be from natural partiality, I think it the best you have written. O – I remember the Gautier, which was an excellent performance; and the Balzac, which was good; and the Daudet,[8] over which I licked my chops; but the R.L.S. is better yet. It is so humorous, and it hits my little frailties with so neat (and so friendly) a touch; and Alan is the occasion for so much happy talk; and

---

[3] John White Alexander (1856–1915), American painter, had visited Skerryvore in July 1886 to do a portrait of Stevenson for the *Century Magazine*. His drawing was reproduced in the issue for April 1888, with Henry James's essay.

[4] The Stevensons had rented part of the house belonging to a man called Andrew Baker at Saranac Lake; it is now preserved as a Stevenson Museum. MIS describes it: 'The house is built of wooden boards, painted white, with green shutters, and a verandah round it. It belongs to a guide, who takes parties into the woods for shooting and fishing excursions; he usually has boarders, but he and his wife have agreed to give over to us part of the house, their own portion being entirely shut off by double doors.'

[5] The story first called *The Finsbury Tontine*, then *A Game of Bluff*, finally became *The Wrong Box*.

[6] Fanny left on 6 October to visit her mother and sister Josephine Thomas at Danville, Indiana; MIS accompanied her as far as Niagara.

[7] The article on RLS which finally appeared in the *Century* for April 1888; it was reprinted in *Partial Portraits* (1888).

[8] James's articles on Gautier and Balzac were published in *French Poets and Novelists* (1878); the one on Daudet in the *Century* for August 1883 and in *Partial Portraits*.

the quarrel is so generously praised.[9] I read it twice, though it was only some hours in my possession; and Low, who got it for me from the *Century*, sat up to finish it ere he returned it; and, Sir, we were all delighted. Here is the paper out, nor will anything, not even friendship, not even gratitude for the article, induce me to begin a second sheet; so here with the kindest remembrances and the warmest good wishes, I remain, Yours affectionately   R.L.S.

To S.S. McClure[1]

[c. 20 October 1887]   [*Saranac Lake*]

Dear Mr McClure, *The Black Arrow* has come, and I believe I see my way to make something of it for your purpose; I dare not say before January; I think not unlikely by that time.[2] This I hope will please you; though once more, I must beg you to observe that I tie myself to no date; having done that before and lived to repent it too often.

On the other hand, I am very sorry, but I must beg off letting you print the essays.[3] I find, if I do so, I shall involve myself in real difficulties with my publishers; and I am sure you will regard this as a sufficient excuse, and pardon me my precipitance at the time and my present enforced resiliation. If you are able to announce a story, I think it should console you. Yours very truly   Robert Louis Stevenson

---

[9] 'Alan Breck, in *Kidnapped*, is a wonderful picture of the union of courage and swagger; the little Jacobite adventurer, a figure worthy of Scott at his best, and representing the highest point that Mr Stevenson's talent has reached . . .' Later James writes: 'Such a scene as the episode of the quarrel of the two men on the mountain-side is a real stroke of genius, and has the very logic and rhythm of life . . . The author's vision of it has a profundity which goes deeper, I think, than *Dr Jekyll.*'

[1] Samuel Sidney McClure (1857–1949) came to the USA as a poor immigrant boy from Ireland and fought his way to success in popular journalism as editor and publisher with great energy, flair and enthusiasm. He began his pioneer newspaper syndicate in 1884 and founded and edited *McClure's Magazine* 1893–1912; he was the original of Pinkerton in *The Wrecker*. In *My Autobiography* (1914) McClure describes how on a visit to England in search of material for his syndicate he had written to RLS in February 1887 but had had no reply. Lloyd called on McClure in New York explaining that RLS had mislaid the letter. As a result McClure and his wife Hattie visited RLS at the Hotel St Stephen. It must have been at this meeting that RLS rejected an offer to contribute a weekly article to the *New York World*.

[2] RLS had agreed to let McClure publish *The Black Arrow* (which had never appeared in book form) through his syndicate and had obtained the relevant issues of *Young Folks*. It was duly syndicated in March 1888, with the opening chapters omitted, as *The Outlaws of Tunstall Forest*. Later in the year the book itself was published by Scribner's and Cassell's.

[3] RLS had originally agreed to let McClure syndicate three of the essays from the forthcoming *Memories and Portraits* but cried off at Scribner's request.

To George Iles[1]

[29 October 1887]   [Saranac Lake]

Dear Mr Iles, The undersigned was born in 1850, November the 13th, in the city of Edinburgh. He was always sick when he was a child. You will find a good deal of autobiographical matter in the new volume of Essays *Memories and Portraits*, soon to be issued by Charles Scribner's Sons.[2] He – O hang this! I – was educated for a civil engineer, on my father's design, and was at the building of harbours and lighthouses, and worked in a carpenter's shop and a brass foundry, and hung about wood yards and the like. Then it came out that I was learning nothing; and on being tightly cross-questioned during a dreadful evening walk, I owned I cared for nothing but literature. My father said that was no profession; but I might be called to the Bar, if I chose; so, at the age of 21, I began to study law. Two years after, I met Sidney Colvin, who took me up and introduced my work. My first paper appeared just after I was 23, in the *Portfolio*, under the harmless anagram of L.S. Stoneven: it was called 'Roads'. My second, written that same winter at Mentone, came out in *Macmillan*: it has been reprinted: 'Ordered South'. It took me pretty near three months to write, I imagine. Nobody had ever such pains to learn a trade as I had; but I slogged at it, day in, day out; and I frankly believe (thanks to my dire industry) I have done more with smaller gifts than almost any man of letters in the world. My first story (that I have dared to reprint) was 'Will o' the Mill', written in France; though the scenery is a kind of hash-up of the Murzthal in Baden and the Brenner Pass in the Tyrol, over which I went when I was twelve.[3] The next was 'A Lodging for the Night', written concurrently with my study on Villon, in *Men and Books*. The first 'New Arabian Nights' (properly so called) was begun at the Burford Bridge inn (see 'A Gossip on Romance', in the forthcoming volume) where I stayed to be near George Meredith; they were continued in London, Edinburgh, Paris, Barbizon and finished at Le Monastier (see *Travels with a Donkey*) – all within about five months: this will give a notion of my roving ways. That same autumn, I wrote 'Providence and the Guitar', part at London, part in Cambridge: so that year saw me quite the story teller. It was that same spring that I had brought out *The Inland*

---

[1] George Iles (1852–1942), Canadian author, was born in Gibraltar and went to Canada as a child. For some years up to 1887 he was manager of the Windsor Hotel in Montreal. He then went to New York and spent the rest of his life in literary work; he wrote and edited a number of books on scientific subjects.

[2] The American edition of *Memories and Portraits* appeared on 2 December; the English edition on 21 November. A second edition of *Virginibus Puerisque* was issued at the same time.

[3] On their 'Grand Tour' in 1863, the Stevensons travelled by coach through the Brenner Pass to Innsbruck on 10 May.

Voyage, my first volume. 'The Pavilion on the Links' was begun in London, finished in Monterey, California. *Treasure Island*, begun at Braemar, finished at Davos; the whole in two bursts of about fifteen days each, my quickest piece of work. *Kidnapped* was all written at Bournemouth, inside of a year: probably five months actual writing, and one of these months entirely over the last chapters which had to be put together, without interest or inspiration, almost word by word, for I was entirely worked out: *Kidnapped*, you may like to know, appears to me infinitely my best, and indeed my only good, story. *Prince Otto* was written at Hyères: it took me about five months, in the inside of a year, not counting the first chapter, which was written before at Kingussie: *Otto* was my hardest effort, for I wished to do something very swell, which did not quite come off: whole chapters of *Otto* were written as often as five and six times, and one chapter, that of the Countess and the Princess, eight times by me and once by my wife – my wife's version was the second last. 'The Treasure of Franchard' was mostly written at Kingussie. *Jekyll*, 'Olalla', 'Markheim', were all written at Bournemouth. *The Dynamiter* begun in Hyères, finished at Bournemouth. 'Thrawn Janet' at Kinnaird near Pitlochrie: 'The Merry Men', begun at Pitlochrie, finished at Davos. My life of Fleeming Jenkin, now in the press, is another child of Bournemouth. *The Silverado Squatters* hails from Hyères: *Travels with a Donkey* from Edinburgh: *Inland Voyage* from Edinburgh, and Dieppe.

In a very early number of *Scribner's Magazine*, you will find something about my dreams.[4]

Here is enough gossip, I hope; if you want more, let me know. Yours very truly   R.L.S.

Note, if you like, that all my considerable stories were done at two breaks. I have to leave off and forget a tale for a little; then I can return upon it fresh and with interest revived.[5]

To James B. Carrington[1]

[c. 4 November 1887]   [Saranac Lake]

To the Reader

If I receive another proof of this sort, I shall return it at once with the general direction:'See MS.' I must suppose my system of punctuation to

---

[4] 'A Chapter on Dreams', the first of the twelve essays commissioned by Scribner's, appeared in *Scribner's Magazine* for December 1887.

[5] Fanny added a note – 'Here is the bit of condensed biography I promised you' – referring to meeting Iles in Montreal.

[1] When he published this note in *Scribner's* in August 1927 Carrington described himself as a 'cub proof and MS reader'. The proof is probably that of 'A Chapter on Dreams'. When returning

be very bad; but it is mine; and it shall be adhered to with punctual exactness, by every created printer who shall print for me.

Robert Louis Stevenson

To William Archer[1]

[c. 10 November 1887]   [Saranac Lake]

William Archer Esq.

Sir, You have done the deed.[2] You have confused the Blue Room with the Red in Skerryvore: a fault for which pardon is impossible. God, sir, do you suppose me so impotent a workman that I should say a mirror faced the fire when in truth it only faced a window?[3] No, Mr Archer; blood is what I require. Besides, sir, I play with more than one finger on the piano;[4] the difficulty about my playing is that I cannot go quicker than – say – *adagio assai*; but that is a different matter; and I can use any number of fingers (and hands, sir) if you let me go at my own pace.

We feel your references to the food keenly; your devotion to heavy meals sounds strangely, let me tell you, in a pessimist; Captain's Biscuit should be good enough – is too good, for a pessimist.[5]

My wife is furious at your insinuation that she is a negress.[6] What if she be, sir? It is better to be a negress than a pessimist.

And then, Mr Archer, I had always heard you were so incorruptible; and I find you, in your reference to my moustache, lending yourself to a low private vengeance on the part of Henley.[7] And what, sir, if I have but

---

it to Burlingame RLS wrote: 'Herewith the proof, which I trust will put your printers on their mettle. Possibly a word from you might help: depict me as a man of a congested countenance and the most atrabilious disposition; you will only anticipate the truth, for if they go on making hay of my punctuation, I shall surely have a stroke.'

[1] RLS is commenting on Archer's article, 'Robert Louis Stevenson at "Skerryvore"' in the *Critic* (New York) of 5 November 1887. The article was written at Henley's invitation and he sent Archer much material.

[2] Cf. *Macbeth*, II.ii.16.

[3] Archer wrongly called the 'blue room' the dining-room and the 'red room' the drawing-room. In his poem 'The Mirror Speaks' (see p. 307, n. 2), RLS describes the mirror as facing 'the sparkling fire'.

[4] 'The piano is another of his resources, his performances with one finger being truly surprising.'

[5] Archer says that the dinner-table is 'not precisely a "groaning board"' and that 'heavy suppers are unknown at Skerryvore': 'Those who will may brace their nerves with whiskey (or claret) and apollinaris, or may, like Mr Pecksniff, promote cheerfulness by taking a captain's biscuit.'

[6] '[Mrs Stevenson's] features are clear-cut and delicate, but marked by unmistakeable strength of character; her hair of an unglossy black and her complexion darker than one would expect in a woman of Dutch-American race. I have heard her speak of a Moorish strain in her ancestry, whether seriously or in jest I know not.'

[7] 'He still has the air and manner of a young man, for illness has neither tamed his mind, nor aged his body. It has left its mark, however, in the pallor of his long oval face, with its wide-set eyes, straight nose and thin-lipped sensitive mouth, scarcely shaded by a light moustache, the jest and scorn of his more ribald intimates.'

little? If my moustaches reached from pole to pole, they could not rescue my Immortial Soul.

Much you know of Mrs Stevenson's strength of character; but you may have an opportunity of learning more. A black woman, who feeds her friends on Captain's Biscuit!

No, sir, the whole thing cries to Heaven for vengeance: therefore tremble, for illness has neither tamed the mind nor aged the body of Yours

R.L.S.

And none can mistake the strength of character of *the negress.*[8]

P.S. My entrance hall is no narrower than your own – Sneck up![9]

P.P.S. My wife is not so graphic a narrator as her husband – this is to sow wanton discord in a quiet family.

P.P.P.S. My house is not unpretending: I give you the lie, sir.

P.P.P.P.S. My sanctum is NOT cheerful: – it is as dreary as a boot jack.

P P P P P P P P P P P

Goes

     slavering   My limp fingers! – how about your limp nose?[10]

     mad

To John Paul Bocock[1]

Private

Dear Mr Bocock, (1) The shanty in *Treasure Island* is my own invention entirely; founded on the name of one of the Buccaneer Islets – the Dead Man's Chest. A good collection of shanties has been recently published in England; it has been reviewed in the *Saturday Review,* within a few months, so you may run it down by consulting a file of that paper.[2]

---

[8] The words 'the negress' are in Fanny's hand. She wrote to Archer in December that she thought the article 'admirably done, and in perfect taste . . . I cannot put by the fancy that Louis's silly letter to which he made me sign my name, gave the effect of our really being annoyed by the article'.

[9] Go hang! Cf. *Twelfth Night,* II.iii.101.

[10] 'He now sits at the foot of the table rolling a limp cigarette in his long limp fingers.'

[1] John Paul Bocock (1856–1903), journalist who contributed stories, essays and poems to periodicals in New York and Philadelphia. A collection of his poetry was posthumously published as *Book Treasures of Maecenas* (1904).

[2] Frederick J. Davis and Ferris Tozer, *Sailor's Songs: or, Shanties* (1887). The review in the *Saturday Review* of 27 August 1887 (probably by Henley) quoted RLS's 'terrifying and desperate stave' as an example of what might be achieved if shanties were written by poets.

(2) 'The Suicide Club' had no ground; it was reached in my mind by a process of reasoning, in talk with a friend; yet oddly enough the idea, I learn has been twice used before in literature; and since then (say the newspapers, if you believe one word you see in them) such a club has actually existed, and came to singular failure, somewhere in Austro-Hungary.

(3) See my paper on Villon in *Studies of Men and Books*; you will find there also, the proper name of M. Longnon's book, which is the great authority.

(4) Confound it, Mr Bocock, neither you nor the public have anything to do with that.

(5) Your prominent dramatic critic, writing like a journalist, has written like a braying ass; what he meant is probably quite different and true enough – that the book is ugly and the allegory too like the usual pulpit fudge and not just enough to the modesty of facts. You are right as to Mansfield: Hyde was the younger of the two. He was not good looking however; and not, Great Gods! a mere voluptuary. There is no harm in a voluptuary; and none, with my hand on my heart and in the sight of God, none – no harm whatever – in what prurient fools call 'immorality'. The harm was in Jekyll, because he was a hypocrite – not because he was fond of women; he says so himself; but people are so filled full of folly and inverted lust, that they can think of nothing but sexuality. The Hypocrite let out the beast Hyde – who is no more sexual than another, but who is the essence of cruelty and malice, and selfishness and cowardice: and these are the diabolic in man – not this poor wish to have a woman, that they make such a cry about. I know, and I dare to say, you know as well as I, that bad and good, even to our human eyes, has no more connection with what is called dissipation than it has with flying kites. But the sexual field and the business field are perhaps the two best fitted for the display of cruelty and cowardice and selfishness. That is what people see; and these they confound.

(7) The dream and how it came, and how much it gave me, you will find in an early number of *Scribner's Magazine*: December, I believe, or January at latest.

Thank you for your account of Mansfield. By the way, the name is Lloyd OSBOURNE. Yours truly   Robert Louis Stevenson

John Paul Bocock Esq.

I need not say this letter is not for publication; you can use my facts, not my language; but indeed the distinction is made here chiefly to explain the word private at the top, or you might suppose I was feeding you with an empty spoon.   R.L.S.

To Sidney Colvin

[c. 20 November 1887][1]   [*Saranac Lake*]

My dear Colvin, This goes to say that we are all fit, and the place is very bleak and wintry, and up to now has shown no such charms of climate as Davos, but it is a place where men eat and where the cattarh (catarrh, cattarrh or cattarrhh) appears to be unknown. I walk in my verandy in the snaw, sir, looking down over one of those dabbled wintry landscapes that are (to be frank) so chilly to the human bosom, and up at a gray, English – nay, *mehercle*, Scottish – heaven; and I think it pretty bleak; and the wind swoops at me round the corner, like a lion and fluffs the snow in my face; and I could aspire to be elsewhere; but yet I do not catch cold, and yet, when I come in, I eat. So that hitherto, Saranac, if not deliriously delectable, has not been a failure; nay, from the mere point of view of the wicked body, it has proved a success. But I wish I could still get to the woods; alas, *nous n'irons plus au bois*,[2] is my poor song; the paths are buried, the dingles drifted full, a little walk is grown a long one; till spring comes, I fear the burthen will hold good.

I get along with my papers for Scribner not fast, nor so far specially well; only this last, the fourth one (which makes a third part of my whole task) I do believe is pulled off after a fashion. It is a mere sermon; 'Smith opens out';[3] but it is true, and I find it touching and beneficial, to me at least; and I think there is some fine writing in it, some very apt and pregnant phrases. 'Pulvis et Umbra',[4] I call it; I might have called it a Darwinian Sermon, if I had wanted. Its sentiments although parsonic will not offend even you, I believe. The other three papers, I fear, bear many traces of effort, and the ungenuine inspiration of an income at so much per essay, and the honest desire of the incomer to give good measure for his money. Well, I did my damdest anyway.

We have been reading H. James's *Roderick Hudson*, which I eagerly press you to get at once; it is a book of a high order – the last volume in

---

[1] On Saturday 19 November MIS recorded: 'Fine snow falls almost all day. Lou has two walks on the verandah and quite enjoys it.' The next day she noted: 'Snow all day. Can't get to church.'

[2] The first line of a poem by Theodore de Banville, itself based on an earlier nursery rhyme, in *Les Stalactites*. RLS used it as the title of a rondeau, beginning 'We'll walk the woods no more', sent to Mrs Sitwell in August 1875.

[3] 'Smith opens out his cauld harangues/On practice and on morals'. Burns in *The Holy Fair* (xiv) thus refers to RLS's great-grandfather on his mother's side, Dr George Smith of Galston, Ayr (1748–1823). Colvin notes that 'against Stevenson himself, in his didactic moods, the passage was often quoted by his friends when they wished to tease him'.

[4] Published in the April *Scribner's*. The phrase *'pulvis et umbra sumus'* (we are dust and shadow) comes from Horace, *Odes* IV.vii.16.

particular is really a stodger. I wish Meredith would read it. It took my breath away.[5]

I am at the seventh book of the *Aeneid*, and quite amazed at its merits (also very often floored by its difficulties). The Circe passage at the beginning, and the sublime business of Amata with the simile of the boy's top – O, Lord, what a happy thought! – have specially delighted me.

Verse 136. *Et geniumque loci primamque deorum*
Tellurem Nymphasque.

I wish you would explain: '*primam*' gets away with me altogether. Also verse 381, is '*manus*' used (as I humbly, even tremulously conjecture) for the boy himself?[6] – '*inscia impubesque manus stupet supra*'

  – 'And wondering how it spins,
   Forgets to whip.' imitation by Ancient Author.

 I am, dear sir, Your respected friend   John Gregg Gillson,
                  J.P., M.R.I.A., etc.

To Sidney M. Colvin Esq.
Brutish Muzeum, London, England, *et per contra.*

To Charles Scribner

[*15 December 1887*]   [*Saranac Lake*]

My dear Mr Scribner, I think I am on the way to meet your views. For I have got a story begun with an eye to you: as soon as I have some pages well in advance I will send it you to be set up in England and copyrighted as a pamphlet: *The Master of Ballantrae* is its name. I telegraphed you today for the *Memoirs of the Chevalier Johnstone, on which I depend*; I cannot go on without it.[1] I have to ask you now for works that will enable me to touch

---

[5] RLS wrote to Henry James on the same day describing how they were all enjoying *Roderick Hudson*, James's first novel (1875): 'In the silence of the snow, the afternoon lamp has lighted an eager fireside group; my mother reading, Fanny, Lloyd and I delighted listeners.'

[6] Colvin replied on 4 December: '"*primamque deorum Tellurem*" simply means that Tellus (feminine) was the oldest of the gods . . . "*manus*" means band or troop, a common usage: there isn't one "*puer*" but a lot, "*pueri*", above, l. 379, if you notice.'

[1] In 'The Genesis of *The Master of Ballantrae*' RLS described how walking one night on the verandah at Saranac, the first ideas for a novel came to him – 'a singular case of a buried and resuscitated fakir' often told him by his uncle John Balfour – 'the next moment I had seen the circumstance transplanted from India and the tropics to the Adirondack wilderness and the stringent cold of the Canadian border'. Later, while 'groping for the fable and the characters required', he remembered 'a story conceived long before on the moors between Pitlochry and Strathairdle, conceived in the Highland rain, in the blend of the smell of heather and bog-plants, and with a mind full of the *Atholl Correspondence* and the *Memoirs of the Chevalier de Johnstone*'. James, Chevalier de Johnstone (1719–?1800) was aide-de-camp to the Young Pretender. Extracts from his *Memoirs* were published in 1820 and the full version in 1870. In the telegram RLS also asked for Charles Johnson's *Lives of Notorious Pirates*, which he had used when writing *Treasure Island*.

on colonial life here about 1760. I want any traveller's book of early days; the best you can recommend. I want Dr Eggleston's book[2] if that be out; and how about somebody called McMasters.[3] A journey in the woods at that date (1760–70) I have to make, can anything be produced? A missionary of that time: a military report of an expedition: what not? Likewise, I have to deal (Save us and bless us, how like me!) with Buccaneers on the coast of the U.S. (1764 – and around) and if you can help me, why so much the better. Cooper's *Water Witch*,[4] I believe, is somewhere about my date: I might look at that. But that is apart: what I want is *originals*.

You see I am now quite cheerful; I mean to make this up to you, which is the best way out, and so let us be happy.[5] Yours very sincerely

Robert Louis Stevenson

To Sidney Colvin

[24 December 1887]   *[Saranac Lake]*

My dear Colvin, Well, I say nought of the *homunculus*; but vim is a good Scottish at least – if not (as I am tempted to think) a good English, word; never a thought of Latin was in my mind; I used a current and a very general and a very definite colloquialism.[1] Thank you for your

---

[2] Edward Eggleston (1837–1902), American author, wrote a series of papers in the *Century* from November 1882 to April 1885 designed to form 'A History of Life in the Thirteen Colonies'. They were not published in book form.

[3] John Bach McMaster (1852–1902), who wrote a notable social and economic history, *A History of the People of the United States* (8 vols, 1883–1913).

[4] James Fenimore Cooper's romance of piracy, *The Water Witch* (1830), is set in New York at the close of the seventeenth century.

[5] On 1 November, overlooking the fact that he had promised to let Scribner's have the American rights for all his future work, RLS had signed an agreement with McClure that he would let him have for American serial publication 'the next story I finish of the same character as *Kidnapped*'. RLS wrote several letters of apology to Charles Scribner for his 'unhappy oversight'.

[1] In his letter of 4 December (in reply to RLS's November letter) after explaining the passages in the *Aeneid*, Colvin wrote:

And now we are on Latinity – what the dickens have you been at with your Latin in *Memories and Portraits*? In 'The Manse' for example . . . you must needs go and decline the plural of *homunculus*, and give us *homunculos*, and not only so, but 'of these *homunculos*' where of course it ought to be *homunculorum* if anything. Similarly in another essay ['Talk and Talkers I'] you have 'with or by this *vim*', where equally of course it ought if anything to be *vi*, not objective but ablative. But the rule is that when you borrow a Latin word in an English sentence that way, you don't decline it at all, but treat it like an English word, content yourself with the nominative for all cases alike, *homunculi* (or better homunculuses) and *vis*. Please have *homunculos* and *vim* altered on the plates, they look comic. *Explicit dissertatio Bummkopfii.*

In the Edinburgh Edition Colvin printed 'homunculi' and 'vigour'.

explanations. I have done no more Virgil since I finished the VII book, for I have first been eaten up with Taine,[2] and next have fallen head over heels into a new tale: *The Master of Ballantrae*. No thought have I now apart from it. And I have got along up to p. 92 of the draught with great interest. It is to me a most seizing tale; there are some fantastic elements; the most is a dead genuine human problem – human tragedy, I should say rather. It will be about as long (I imagine) as *Kidnapped*. *Dramatis personae*:

(1) My old Lord Durrisdeer.
(2) The Master of Ballantrae, *and*
(3) Henry Durie, *his sons.*
(4) Clementina,[3] *engaged to the first, married to the second.*
(5) Ephraim Mackellar, *land steward at Durrisdeer and narrator of the most of the book.*
(6) Francis Burke, Chevalier de St Louis, *one of Prince Charlie's Irishmen and narrator of the rest.*

Besides these, many instant figures, most of them dumb or nearly so: Jessie Brown, the whore, Captain Crail, Captain McCombie, our old friend Alan Breck, our old friend Riach (both only for an instant), Teach the pirate (vulgarly Blackbeard); John Paul and Macconochie, servants at Durrisdeer. The date is from 1745 to '65 (about). The scene near Kirkcudbright, in the States and for a little moment in the French East Indies. I have done most of the big work, the quarrel, duel between the brothers, and announcement of the death to Clementina and my Lord – Clementina, Henry, and Mackellar (nicknamed Squaretoes) are really very fine fellows; the Master is all I know of the devil; I have known hints of him, in the world, but always cowards; he is as bold as a lion, but with the same deadly, causeless duplicity I have watched with so much surprise in my two cowards. 'Tis true, I saw a hint of the same nature in another man who was not a coward; but he had other things to attend to; the Master has nothing else but his devilry. Here come my visitors . . . and have now gone, or the first relay of them; and I hope no more may come. For mark you, sir, this is our 'day' – Saturday, as ever was; and here we sit, my mother and I, before a huge wood fire and await the enemy with the most steadfast courage; and without snow and grayness; and the woman Fanny in New York, for her health which is far from good; and the lad Lloyd at the inn in the village because he has a cold; and the handmaid Valentine abroad in a sleigh upon her messages; and tomorrow Xmas and no

---

[2] Hippolyte Taine (1828–93), *Les Origines de la France Contemporaine* (6 vols, 1875–94); vols 2–4 cover the French Revolution.
[3] She later became 'Alison'.

mistaky. Such is human life: *la carrière humaine*. I will enclose, if I remember, the required autograph.[4]

I will do better, put it on the back of this page. Love to all, and mostly my very dear Colvin, to yourself. For whatever I say or do, or don't say or do, you may be very sure I am, Yours always affectionately   R.L.S.

To Henry James

[*Late January 1888*]   [*Saranac Lake*]

My dear, delightful James, To quote your heading to my wife; I think no man writes so elegant a letter, I am sure none so kind; unless it be Colvin, and there is more of the stern parent about him. I was vexed at your account of my admired Meredith: I fear what you say of Mariette is too true;[1] I wish I could go and see him; as it is I will try to write; and yet (do you understand me?) there is something in that potent, *genialisch* affectation that puts me on the strain even to address him in a letter. He is not an easy man to be yourself with: there is so much of him, and the veracity and the high athletic intellectual humbug are so intermixed.[2] I read with indescribable admiration your 'Emerson'. I begin to long for the day when these portraits of yours shall be collected; do put me in. But 'Emerson' is a higher flight. Have you a 'Tourgueneff'?[3] You have told me many interesting things of him, and I seem to see them written, and forming a graceful and *bildende* sketch. (I wonder whence comes this flood of German – I haven't opened a German book since I teethed.) My novel is a tragedy, four parts out of six or seven are written, and gone to Burlingame. Five parts of it are sound, human tragedy, done with a brevity and a winged persaltatory step in which I have excelled myself. The last one or two, I regret to say are not so soundly designed: I almost hesitate to write them; they are very picturesque, but they are fantastic, they shame, perhaps degrade, the beginning. I wish I knew; that was how the tale came to me however. I got the situation; it was an old taste of

---

[4] Colvin, unwilling to part with any more of RLS's letters and MSS, asked him to provide an autograph for Eleanor, daughter of the poet and anthologist, Frederick Locker-Lampson and widow of Lionel Tennyson, younger son of the poet.

[1] Marie Eveleen (1871–1933), later Mrs Sturgis, Meredith's daughter by his second wife.

[2] Colvin annotated: 'Alluding to a kind of lofty, posturing way of G.M.'s in mind and speech, quite different from any real insincerity.' Before publishing this letter in 1911, Colvin consulted James. James replied on 5 January 1911: 'By the same token don't hesitate to print the passage about Meredith *tel quel* – leaving the "humbugging" untouched. The word isn't invidiously but pictorially and caressingly used – as with a rich, or vague, loose synthetic suggestion. Who in the world is there today to complain of it. *Voilà*.'

[3] 'The Life of Emerson' (*Macmillan's Magazine*, December 1887) was reprinted in *Partial Portraits* (1888), together with 'Ivan Turgénieff' (*Atlantic Monthly*, January 1884) and the essay on RLS.

mine: the older brother goes out in the '45, the younger stays; the younger of course gets title and estate and marries the bride designate of the elder – a family match, but he (the younger) had always loved her, and she had really loved the elder. Do you see the situation? Then the devil and Saranac suggested this *dénouement*, and I joined the two ends in a day or two of constant feverish thought, and began to write. And now – I wonder if I have not gone too far with the fantastic. The elder brother is an INCUBUS; supposed to be killed at Culloden, he turns up again and bleeds the family of money; on that stopping he comes and lives with them, whence flows the real tragedy, the nocturnal duel of the brothers (very naturally and indeed, I think, inevitably arising) and second supposed death of the elder. Husband and wife now really make up, and then the cloven hoof appears. For the third supposed death and the manner of the third reappearance is steep; steep, sir. It is even very steep, and I fear it shames the honest stuff so far; but then it is highly pictorial, and it leads up to the death of the elder brother at the hands of the younger in a perfectly cold-blooded murder of which I wish (and mean) the reader to approve. You see how daring is the design. There are really but six characters and one of these episodic and yet it covers eighteen years, and will be I imagine the longest of my works. Yours ever   R.L.S.

To Joseph B. Gilder[1]

1 March 1888   *Saranac Lake*

Dear Mr Gilder, I understand you dined with my wife at St Gaudens's in company with some gentleman (name forgotten by my wife, whose memory is a scandal to her native land) who had a pair – or knew where to get a pair – of the lightest spectacles in New York City and (it seems to be believed) in the world. It is the address of this maker of light spectacles that we now pant for. Can you fish it out – do you think? It sounds vague I know, but – Well, if you can, telegraph it up to us and materially oblige, Yours very truly   Robert Louis Stevenson

J.B. Gilder Esq.

P.S. My wife *thinks* that the gentleman who knew about the address of the man who makes light spectacles, was born at sea; which may help to identify him, and will at least breezily remind you of Peter Piper and the House that Jack Built.[2]   R.L.S.

---

[1] Joseph B. Gilder (1858–1936), brother of Richard Watson Gilder; founder with his sister, Jeanette Leonard Gilder, of the *Critic* 1881, and co-editor 1881–1906.
[2] RLS later commented: 'a more admirable example of my wife's intellectual method I never met'. The makers were Meyrowitz Bros of New York; the spectacles were apparently for Lloyd.

To W.E. Henley

[? *22 March 1888*]   [*Saranac Lake*]

My dear Henley, I write with indescribable difficulty; and if not with perfect temper, you are to remember how very rarely a husband is expected to receive such accusations against his wife.[1] I can only direct you to apply to Katharine and ask her to remind you of that part of the business which took place in your presence and which you seem to have forgotten; she will doubtless add other particulars which perhaps you may not have heard – such as that she refused to collaborate on my wife's version of the tale, and when she agreed it was to be written, asked that a copy might be sent her; she will also, I have no doubt, lend you the copy of her original story from which you will be reminded how the matter stands.

I am sorry I must ask you to take these steps; I might take them for myself had you not tied my hands by the strange step of marking your letter 'private and confidential'.[2] An accusation of this gravity, you must suffer me to say, should not have been made without leaving me free to communicate with Katharine. I wish I could stop here. I cannot. When you have refreshed your mind as to the facts, you will, I know, withdraw what you have said to me; but I must go further and remind you, if you have spoken of this to others, a proper explanation and retractation of what you shall have said or implied to any person so addressed, will be necessary.

From the bottom of my soul, I believe what you wrote to have been merely reckless words written in forgetfulness and with no clear

---

[1] The spark that set off the famous quarrel with Henley was his long letter of 9 March 1888. In the course of it Henley made, almost casually, the accusation that Fanny was guilty of plagiarism in publishing under her own name (in the March 1888 *Scribner's*) a short story, 'The Nixie', based on an earlier story by RLS's cousin, Katharine de Mattos: 'I read "The Nixie" with considerable amazement. It's Katharine's; surely it's Katharine's? The situation, the environment, the principal figure – *voyons!* There are even reminiscences of phrase and imagery, parallel incident – *que sais-je?* It is all better focussed, no doubt; but I think it has lost as much (at least) as it has gained; and why there wasn't a double signature is what I've not been able to understand.' RLS and Fanny claimed that Katharine had in effect given up the story and consented to Fanny's use of it (although RLS, in a later letter, admitted to Baxter that Katharine's consent had been an unwilling one and he had asked Fanny not to write the story); Henley was convinced that Fanny was guilty and that the story should have had both their names on it. The rights and wrongs cannot now be determined. The issue for RLS was that Henley had been disloyal as a friend in making such an accusation, and he saw it as the latest example of what he regarded as Henley's penchant for stirring up trouble behind his back and speaking ill of him to his friends. RLS agonised at length over the affair in his letters to Baxter and made himself ill with distress and bitterness. In this selection it is not possible to give more than a sample of these. Baxter showed himself a wise and calm counsellor and helped steer RLS safely through this emotional crisis.

[2] In his letter Henley wrote at length of his own feelings of weariness and depression; this would have justified the 'private and confidential' marking quite apart from the reference to Fanny.

appreciation of their meaning; but it is hard to think that any one – and least of all, my friend – should have been so careless of dealing agony. To have inflicted more distress than you have done would have been difficult. This is the sixth or seventh attempt I make to write to you; and I will now only add that I count upon you immediately applying to Katharine for the facts, and await your answer with the most painful expectation.

You will pardon me if I can find no form of signature; I pray God such a blank will not be of long endurance   Robert Louis Stevenson

To Charles Baxter

[22 March 1888]   *[Saranac Lake]*

My dear Charles, I am going to write what I should not, and shall probably not send; but in the melancholy that falls upon me, I must break out at least upon paper. I fear I have come to an end with Henley; the Lord knows if I have not tried hard to be a friend to him, the Lord knows even that I have not altogether failed. There is not one of that crew that I have not helped in every kind of strait, with money, with service, and that I was not willing to have risked my life for; and yet the years come, and every year there is a fresh outburst against me and mine. If the troubles that have been brewed for me in Shepherd's Bush had been taken out of my last years, they would have been a different season. And I have forgiven, and forgiven, and forgotten and forgotten; and still they get their heads together and there springs up a fresh enmity or a fresh accusation. Why, I leave to them – and above all to Henley – to explain: I never failed one of them. But when they get together round the bowl, they brew for themselves hot heads and ugly feelings.

But this, as I say, I have known and suffered under long; I knew long ago, how Henley tried to make trouble for me, and I not only held my peace, when I had the evidence; I willingly forgave also; for I understood all his nature, and much of it I love. And I would have gone on forgiving, too, or so I think *ad libitum*; but unless this business comes to a termination I dare scarcely hope, it is what I cannot pass over; even as it is, the best reconciliation to be hoped will be largely formal. If this letter go, which I much question, and I am sure it had better not – I shall put you in no false position by calling it private; I shall only ask you to judge, and to be wiser in what you do with it than I am in writing it. It is hard for me to recognize my old friends falling away from me; whatever my defects, I do not think they have changed; but I daresay I deceive myself and I have indeed altered for the worst; if I have not, some singular feeling springs spontaneously in the bosom of those whom I love. For God's sake, don't let us . . . But hush upon that.

You will tell me this is another case of the tact of the elephant: I know it is or hope it is; but the tact of that animal applied to one's wife is a little difficult to stand. . . .[1]

So much I must say; in case I send this: it stands on an accusation brought against my wife of a description to cut both of us to the soul, couched – well that is nothing, and sent to me in a letter marked 'private and confidential', with directions it was to be communicated to no one and immediately burned. The baseness of this special form of the anonymous letter, I feel sure he was unaware of; though I remember him branding the same conduct in another person – Gosse. Of course, it is not a thing to be respected; yet I have so far respected it that I have written to him, instead of to the principal, in the first place. I also still refrain from dwelling on the nature of the charge (it cuts especially deep as he had means of knowing exactly how it stood) until he shall have a chance of doing what he ought. But this much I do wish to say: to get an acknowledgement of the way in which the facts really are, is my first purpose. And whatever you do, pray do nothing that may compromise my hope of getting this. You see why I do not mark this letter private, yet if you decide you should communicate any idea of its nature to Henley, pray at least consider this great need of our position.

I cannot say it is anger that I feel, but it is despair. My last reconciliation with Henley is not yet a year old; and here is the devil again. I am weary of it all – weary, weary, weary. And this letter was (so the writer said) intended to cheer me on a sick-bed! May God deliver me from such consolations; I slept but once last night, and then woke in an agony, dreaming I was quarrelling with you; the miserable cold day was creeping in, and I remembered you were the last of my old friends with whom I could say I was still on the old terms. Dear Charles, either you are a very magnanimous fellow, or the others have not been very[2]

caetera desunt[3]

Since above I have dined and continue scribbling, and will say for myself that I am a stout friend and eager to help anyone. It seems to me that little feverish crowd expect too much from me, and are (some of them) willing to repay too little: not that I have ever to my knowledge asked from them anything but some little attention to my feelings. I see that in the revulsion produced by this 'private and confidential' of Henley's, and my fear of placing you in any false position to him, I shall have probably deceived you as to my attitude and wish. I would infinitely prefer you should remain outside of this entirely; the last thing I desire for

[1] A sentence of about a dozen words heavily scored through. It seems to read in part, 'The worst . . . is . . . forgiven as time passes.'
[2] RLS crossed out the words 'careful of' and broke off in mid-sentence.
[3] The rest is wanting.

your sake, for his and for mine, is that you should appear to know of it; and in the frame of mind in which I find myself, I have but one clear thought – the desire of wresting an acknowledgement of how the facts stand – and can offer – can certainly procure – no reconciliation. It will probably come to a smash; and I shall have to get you to give the poor creature an allowance, pretending that it comes from Hamilton Bruce[4] or – anybody but me. Desert him I could not: my life is all bound about these thorns; but whether I can continue to go on cutting my hands and my wife's hands, is quite another question. I think – and I think – and when I recall all – although I see myself in a thousand ways unwise and (as my way is) sometimes harsh, and often foolish with my mouth – I do seem to see a record of a not ungenerous friendship upon my side. The tale of the plays which I have gone on writing without hope, because I thought they kept him up, is of itself something; and I can say he never knew – and never shall know – that I thought these days and months a sacrifice. On the other side, there have been, I think there still are, some warm feelings; they have never been warm enough to make him close his mouth, even where he knew he could hurt me sorely, even to the friends whom he knew I prized: to you, I know not: to others, I do know, and have long buried the knowledge. I know the man, I loved him; I have shown it; even in the hardest trial, when I risked his anger on the drink business. I have not changed my thoughts of him, not even, I believe, my heart. Last winter, my illness was largely the work of his persistent unkindness: I thought it was over; it begins again in this staggering attack; and the bottom of my thoughts is, that we shall be better apart. The old intimacy is impossible, on the old terms. I see not the call I have to pursue a friendship that is so fruitful of the cruellest pains to me, and that risks, if it has not already lost me, other friends.

I should be unjust to you, if I did not say heartily and plainly and with the profoundest honesty, that to you I believe he is a sincere friend; I never heard him speak of you except in terms of love; God forbid that my weak need to pour out my distresses should in any way cloud the friendship of you two – more happy! But to me – whether by my own fault, or through some not quite unnatural jealousy, or from the influence of lesser persons – he has been of late so miserably changed that I have had little but bitterness from our acquaintance, and indeed I think I should rather call it our estrangement. About what it began I never knew; he assured me last spring, it was through no fault of mine but because of matters personal to himself – and I was so impressed by the depth and

---

[4] Robert Tyndale Hamilton Bruce (1848–99), wealthy Edinburgh businessman and collector (whose wealth was derived from a chain of bakeries in Glasgow). He was one of the founders and backers of the *Scots Observer*; Henley later dedicated his poem 'Invictus' to his memory.

recentness of the estrangement that I was far from inviting further confidence; he so assured me, right or wrong, and for the first time, after more than a year, I had a day or so of genuine pleasure. It has not lasted long, this reconciliation. If the first quarrel (of which I never understood one word) was not my fault, God knows I think this one is not. But what exasperates me in this clique is that they foment these things in my absence. Since I left (I would not say it to them – I may to you) I think not one of them has had anything but money from me; and here again they have sprung up one of their little bitter cabals in my absence and my silence. It is a process essentially weariful, and I perceive no possible end to it; but a judicious distance – no longer in space, which avails me nothing – but in heart, which will at least save me further lacerations. If I give the business up for a bad job and stand apart, I fear it is but a little I shall lose, and what I shall gain in peace I cannot estimate.

So far, sometimes I own in rising moments of irritation, on the whole in a miserable soberness, I have written. Whether to send or not, who knows? After this, you are the last of my old friends to whom I dare pour forth a feeling. God! Can it be my blame? Two of them have married wives who love me not;[5] there I may a little stand excused; and for Henley – well, a man is no judge in his own quarrel; yet I am strangely in error or I am on the whole on the right side of that account. It is damned hard not to weep, my boy, at this back-look; but I have better to do, and must be calm for others. I believe, a little quite unconscious jealousy and the influence of a person who shall be nameless explains all: to you, I do devoutly believe, he will be the old affectionate, fine, big heart of a fellow whom we have both loved: as for me – I despair. Thank you for paying Clark. Traquair will not call, the thing had been previously mismanaged. Yours ever   R.L.S.

P.S. I may deceive you on one point: with Colvin I have never had a cloud: it is *ad hoc* that I cannot write to him; I dare not complain to him of Henley, for I do not think – I am sure he does not really like the man: you, who do, whatever you may think of me or of his conduct, can make the due allowances; and my complaint will not injure Henley – for Lord! we both know him!

And on another: I have used the phrase 'principal'. In case Henley should communicate with you and name names, do not be led to suppose that I think 'the principal' was aware of the affair. That would be to me an inconceivable meanness.   R.L.S.

Well, I send it. Take it for what it is: a very desolate cry![6]

5 Presumably Bob and Simpson.
6 Written across the top of the letter, probably just before posting on 23 March.

To Elizabeth Anne Ferrier

[c. 23 March 1888]   [Saranac Lake]

My dearest Coggie, I wish I could find the letter I began to you some
time ago when I was ill; but I can't, and I don't believe there was much
in it anyway. We have all behaved like pigs and beasts and barn-door-
poultry to you; but I have been sunk in work, and the lad is lazy and blind
and has been working too, and as for Fanny she has been (and still is)
really unwell. I had a mean hope you might perhaps write again before I
got up steam; I could not have been more ashamed of myself than I am,
and I should have had another laugh.

   They always say I cannot give news in my letters: I shall shake off that
reproach. On Monday, if she is well enough, Fanny leaves for California
to see her friends;[1] it is rather an anxiety to let her go alone, but the doctor
simply forbids it in my case, and she is better anywhere than here − a
bleak, blackguard, beggarly climate, of which I can say no good except
that it suits me and some others of the same or similar persuasions whom
(by all rights) it ought to kill. It is a form of Arctic St Andrews, I should
imagine; and the miseries of forty degrees below zero with a high wind
have to be felt to be appreciated. The grayness of the heavens here is a
circumstance eminently revolting to the soul; I have near forgot the aspect
of the sun. − I doubt if this be news; it is certainly no news to us. My
mother suffers a little from the inclemency of the place, but less on the
whole than would be imagined. Among other wild schemes we have been
projecting yacht voyages; and I beg to inform you that Cogia Hassan[2] was
cast for the part of passenger. They may come off! − Again this is not
news.[3] The lad? Well the lad wrote a tale this winter, which appeared to

---

[1] Fanny left for San Francisco on Monday 26 March.

[2] Cogia Houssain is the captain of the forty thieves in the story of 'Ali Baba' in *The Arabian Nights*.
In her letter of condolence after RLS's death, Miss Ferrier wrote to Fanny: 'I can never forget
all your goodness to me and the many happy days we had in France and at Bournemouth when
you were Follenfat and I was Cogia Hassan.'

[3] MIS records that RLS first began to plan a yacht trip in order to amuse Lloyd when he was
suffering from toothache: 'and they discuss all the arrangements even to where the piano is to
stand in the saloon, how many rifles and other instruments of war they are to have, and where
they are to be hung. Many pleasant hours are passed in this way . . .' McClure became drawn
into the discussions during his visits: on 18 January 1888 MIS wrote in her diary that he was
'most anxious to join in the yacht scheme'. McClure sent books and sailing directories and on
10 March he wrote formally to RLS from New York: 'Should you go upon a yacht cruise, or
other expedition, this year or next year, and should you write letters descriptive of your
experiences and observations for publication, I will undertake to sell such letters to syndicates of
newspapers (or such other periodicals as we may agree upon), in all countries where such sales
can be effected.' RLS was to get three-quarters of gross receipts. When Fanny left for San
Francisco it was agreed that she should look into the possibility of hiring a suitable yacht but
clearly future plans were very uncertain.

me so funny that I have taken it in hand, and some of these days you will receive a copy of a work entitled

A Game of Bluff
by
Lloyd Osbourne
and
Robert Louis Stevenson

Otherwise he (the lad) is much as usual, very intelligent, very florid in manner – but they have the indecency to say that comes from me, the plainest man in Europe! – and with the same high degree of practical incompetency that you and Katharine deplored upon your travels. There remains I believe, to be considered only R.L.S., the house-bond, prop, pillar, bread-winner and bully of the establishment. Well I do think him much better; he is making piles of money; the hope of being able to hire a yacht ere long dances before his eyes; otherwise he is not in very high spirits at this particular moment, though compared with last year at Bournemouth an angel of joy.

And now is this news, Cogia? or is it not? It all depends upon the point of view, and I call it news; though not so excellent as your noble sketch of the aristocratic parolee with a taste for narratives, and of your unflagging efforts to supply her. The devil of it is, my dear Hassan, that I can think of nothing else, except to send you all our loves, and to wish exceedingly you were here to cheer us all up. But we'll see about that on board the yacht. Your affectionate friend   Robert Louis Stevenson

To his Wife

[c. 4 April 1888]   [Saranac Lake]

My dearest girlie, I have not written to you for some days: all my energies have gone in writing and destroying letters to Katharine; but I have now decided after two sleepless nights to do nothing. And if (as I believe they will) things take the worst course, simply to let 'silence be the rest'. I see no other way out of it, either with health or dignity; and you may be sure I have not come to this hastily. I envy you flimsy people who rage up so easily into hate; the days go, and this is the more dreadful to me. Excuse my little bitterness with 'flimsy'; it is a tap in return for many thousands, and I don't believe it, dearest. Enough that this is a dreadful misery, and I am surprised if any good came of it.

I enclose my letters and – I can write no more; even that short reference to this affair has bowled me quite over.

Well, this is the next morning. I have slept and I wash my hands of
these hobgoblin figures, once my friends, for just now. But indeed I find
it hard to think or write of anything else; and my work is at a stand. Not
so my piping, which takes up hours of God's valuable time;[1] but there is
nothing lost about that – you must prepare for the heavenly choir.
Bandmann, my mother has told you about: a heavenly old gentleman, to
be sure; simple and gamesome as a child, wild as a boy of twenty, you
would have lost your heart to him outright.[2] I was really mashed; so we
all were; even the judicious Lloyd was enthusiastic, always a refreshing
sight in itself. Love to Belle and her respected offspring.[3] I trust your
money has turned up. The bank was stupid about it, and I had to
telegraph, but they then despatched it at once, so you should not have to
wait long.

I have not had time to miss you; when I am alone I think of nothing
but the one affair. Say nothing of it to anyone, please. If things go to the
worst, we must bear this in mere silence. I am, my dear, Your   Louis

Please say which of the enclosed you prefer – light or dark.

To S.R. Crockett[1]

Address c/o Charles Scribner's Sons,
743 Broadway, New York

[c. 10 April 1888]   [Saranac Lake]

Dear Minister of the Free Kirk at Penicuik, – for O, man, I cannae read
your name! – that I have been so long in answering your delightful letter
sits on my conscience badly.[2] The fact is I let my correspondence accumul-
ate until I am going to leave a place; and then I pitch in, overhaul the

---

[1] At this time both RLS and Lloyd were playing tin whistles and RLS was writing music. He
wrote to Miss Boodle: 'I may be said to live for these instrumental labours now; but I have
always some childishness on hand.'
[2] Daniel Edward Bandmann (1837–1905), Austrian-born actor, who had produced a rival dramatic version of *Dr Jekyll and Mr Hyde* in New York, visited Saranac on 2 April to try to
persuade RLS to accept payment; RLS refused because he had authorised Mansfield's play.
[3] In September 1882 Joe Strong was commissioned by John D. Spreckels, son of Claus Spreckels,
founder of the Oceanic Steamship Company and owner of extensive sugar plantations in
Hawaii, to go out to Honolulu to make paintings of island life to decorate the company offices.
Joe and Belle settled in Honolulu. In 1887 because of the 'revolution' of June/July 1887 Belle
and her son Austin had returned temporarily to San Francisco.
[1] Samuel Rutherford Crockett (1859–1914), minister of the Free Church, Penicuik 1886,
achieved literary success with *The Stickit Minister* (1893) and followed it up with a great many
romances and historical novels including *The Lilac Sunbonnet* (1894) and *The Raiders* (1894); he
resigned from the ministry 1895. He was immensely proud of his correspondence with RLS,
calling it his 'poor patent of nobility' and later exaggerated the extent and intimacy of it.
[2] Crockett wrote a 'fan' letter to RLS on 7 September 1887 on stationery bearing the printed
address 'Free Church Manse, Penicuik, N.B.'

pile, and my cries of penitence might be heard a mile about. Yesterday I despatched thirty-five belated letters; conceive the state of my conscience, above all as the Sins of Omission (see boyhood's guide, the Shorter Catechism) are in my view the only serious ones: I call it my view, but it cannot have escaped you that it was also Christ's. However, all that is not to the purpose; which is to thank you for the sincere pleasure afforded by your charming letter. I get a good few such; how few that please me at all, you would be surprised to learn – or have a singularly just idea of the dulness of our race; how few that please me as yours did, I can tell you in one word – *None*. I am no great kirkgoer, for many reasons – and the sermon's one of them, and the first prayer another, but the chief and effectual reason is the stuffiness – I am no great kirkgoer, says I, but when I read yon letter of yours, I thought I would like to sit under ye. And then I saw ye were to send me a bit buik, and says I, I'll wait for the bit buik, and then I'll mebbe can read the man's name, and onyway I'll can kill twa birds wi' ae stane. And, man! the buik was ne'er heard tell o'!³

That fact is an adminicle of excuse for my delay.

And now, dear Minister of the illegible name, thanks to you, and greeting to your wife, and may you have good guidance in your difficult labours, and a blessing on your life.   Robert Louis Stevenson

(No just so young sae young's he was, though –
I'm awfae near forty, man)⁴

Don't put 'N.B.' on your paper: put *Scotland*, and be done with it. Alas, that I should be stabbed in the house of my friends!⁵ The name of my native land is not *North Britain*, whatever may be the name of yours.

R.L.S.

To Mark Twain

[c. *12 April 1888*]   [*Saranac Lake*]

My dear Mark Twain, I should have written a great while ago to the author of *Huckleberry Finn* – a book which I have read four times, and am quite ready to begin again tomorrow. I think you will like to hear this: I got *Huckleberry* when I was pretty ill at Bournemouth, my first winter

---

³ Crockett had promised to send a copy of his book of poems *Dulce Cor* (1886) published under the pseudonym Ford Berêton. In his long reply dated 23 April 1888 to this letter, Crockett explained that the book had been returned from Bournemouth marked 'Left the country, left no address'; he sent RLS another copy.

⁴ Crockett: 'You will see that I am younger even than you – the only fault which I'm consciously mending.'

⁵ Cf. Zechariah 13:6, 'wounded in the house of my friends'.

there; read it straight through, began again at the beginning and read it straight through again without a break. Just at this juncture, down comes a Distinguished Painter to do my portrait;[1] he was very refined and privately French; and when I insisted that *Huckleberry* was to be read aloud at the sittings, he *wilted*, sir. But I told him he had to face it, and he did, and I believe it did him good. I think he supposed I should have had Baudelaire read aloud to me.

Another anecdote, my father (who died last year) was a man who rarely looked at a new book: *Guy Mannering* was his great stand-by and some Latin theologians; the rest was all science. One night however, he had some painful complaint, could not sleep, and fell upon my copy of the *Innocents at Home*.[2] Next morning, he told me he had to put it aside. 'I was frightened,' he said, 'I was positively frightened; it cannot be safe for a man of my time of life to laugh so much.' What finished him was the cards, whisky and tobacco business.

All this, which comes to pen so readily, has nothing to do with my present purpose, which is merely to say that I am now leaving my Patmos and shall be from Thursday next for about a week in the St Stephen's Hotel, East 11th Street, N.Y. (pray keep the address secret – I cannot see many people) where if you are in the way, I should be rejoiced to see you.[3] If this can't be managed, in the course of six weeks or two months from then, it is I think conceivable that my wife and I – my wife is an old Californian – might push as far as Hartford just to behold Huckleberry's grandfather – his father is in the tale, we know him already, thank you!

c/o Scribner's Sons will always find me.

Greeting!   Robert Louis Stevenson[4]

★ *To Sidney Colvin*

[? 7 May 1888]   *Union House, Manasquan, New Jersey*[1]

My dear Colvin, We are here at a delightful country inn, like a country French place, the only people in the house, a cat-boat[2] at our disposal, the

[1] Sargent's visit in December 1884.

[2] The English title of the second volume of *Roughing It*.

[3] Mark Twain replied on 15–17 April: 'I will run down and see you . . . and thank you for writing *Kidnapped* and *Treasure Island* and for liking *Huckleberry*'. Twain recorded in his *Autobiography* (New York, 1924), that he and RLS spent 'an hour or more' talking on a bench in Washington Square.

[4] RLS arrived in New York on 16 April and stayed at the St Stephen's Hotel for the next fortnight.

[1] RLS (in his mother's words) 'feeling tired and out of sorts' said that he must leave New York at once. On Low's recommendation they went on 2 May to stay at the Union House, an inn near the mouth of the river Manasquan in New Jersey, run by Mr and Mrs Wainwright. The Lows spent much time with them.

[2] Described by Balfour as 'A rather broad and shallow boat, with a centre-board, and a single mast stepped at the extreme point of the bow'.

sea always audible on the outer beach, the lagoon as smooth as glass, all
the little, queer, many coloured villas standing shuttered and empty; in
front of ours, across the lagoon, two long wooden bridges; one for the rail,
one for the road, sounding with intermittent traffic. It is highly pleasant,
and a delightful change from Saranac. My health is much better for the
change; I am sure I walked about four miles yesterday, one time with
another – well, say three and a half; and the day before, I was out for four
hours in the cat-boat, and was as stiff as a board in consequence. More
letters call. Yours ever   R.L.S.

To Lady Taylor

[c. *15 May 1888*]   [*Manasquan*]

My dear Lady Taylor, I have to announce our great news. On June 15th
we sail from San Francisco in the schooner yacht *Casco*, for a seven
months' cruise in the South Seas.[1] You can conceive what a state of
excitement we are in; Lloyd perhaps first; but this is an old dream of mine
which actually seems to be coming true, and I am sun-struck. It seems
indeed too good to be true; and that we have not deserved so much good
fortune. From Skerryvore to the Galapagos is a far cry! And from poking
in a sick-room all winter to the deck of one's own ship, is indeed a
heavenly change.

All these seven months I doubt if we can expect more than three mails
at the best of it; and I do hope we may hear something of your news by
each. I have no very clear views as to where the three addresses ought to
be, but if you hear no later news, Charles Scribner's Sons will always have
the run of our intended movements. And an early letter there would
probably catch us at the Sandwich Islands. Tahiti will probably be the
second point; and (as I roughly guess) Quito the third. But the whole
future is invested with heavenly clouds.

I trust you are all well and content, and have good news of the Shelleys,
to whom I wish you would pass on ours. They should be able to
sympathise with our delight.

---

[1] MIS recorded on 9 May: 'Hear tonight that we are to get the yacht *Casco* at San Francisco for
a cruise.' On 12 May she noted: 'It is all settled about the *Casco*. We are to sail from San
Francisco for a seven month cruise on the 15th of June.' Low remembered the arrival of a
telegram from Fanny which was read aloud at lunch and RLS's despatch of an immediate reply.
Writing many years later, Lloyd purported to give the texts: 'Can secure splendid sea-going
schooner yacht *Casco* for seven hundred and fifty a month with most comfortable accommodation for six aft and six forward. Can be ready for sea in ten days. Reply immediately Fanny.'
'Blessed girl, take the yacht and expect us in ten days. Louis.'

Now I have all my miserable *Scribner* articles to rake together in the inside of a fortnight; so you must not expect me to be more copious. I have you all in the kindest memory, and am, Your affectionate friend

Robert Louis Stevenson

Remember me to Aubrey de Vere.[2]

To his Wife

[c. *15 May 1888*]   [*Manasquan*]

My dearest fellow, This will not reach you till some time after our wedding day, which as usual has taken me aback; but I mean to send you a despatch on the day itself, and this is for dessert. Not that I think so much of that day; if I had some other dates, I would think more of them: that of the day when I looked through the window,[1] or the day when I came to see you in Paris after the first absence, for example. But the marriage day we know, and it was a mighty good day too, for me: for you, I wish I was sure. It would have been better, if I my health had been so, that I do believe. The longer I go on, the more I think the worst of me is my health. 'The longer you live the more you come to see the truth of the old adage –' My dear, if I had the date of the day when you said that I would think more of it, God bless you!

What is to be done about Unger's[2] proposal to go with us? It would be an awful nuisance, I think; it is dreadful to have anybody but ourselves. And yet of course he has claims. Should we take him to the Sandwiches and leave him there to come back by packet? Do what you think best. If you think we ought, let's take him for better for worse; but my heart repines at it.

Next day

I meant to have gone on this morning but have worked up to a late hour – and very well, and must finish and get out. God bless you, my dearest Fanny, I send you a kiss and some letters, and the liveliest dog picture over which I have laughed till I can laugh no more. Yours

Louis

---

[2] Aubrey Thomas de Vere (1814–1902), Irish poet and author, a cousin of Lady Taylor and a frequent visitor to her home.

[1] RLS here lends support to the traditional story that he fell in love with Fanny when first seeing her in the lamplight through the open window of the inn at Grez.

[2] Frank Unger, a San Francisco friend.

To Charles Baxter
(Slightly Abridged)

[*21 May 1888*]   [*Manasquan*]

My dear, I have had a sore mail. You were right; and Henley should not have written. I send you his letter; and I must ask you somehow or other to get me out of the task of answering it.[1] I will own frankly this tread of the elephant's foot is too heavy for me. You will observe that . . .[2] my delicacy in never referring to my wife's miserable position is construed (I must suppose) as a tacit condemnation; *that to me, a married man, he writes a letter of reconciliation which I could never dare to show my wife*! I have been even using my wife ill, by my treatment of this matter; but this passes the measure. Henley and Katharine may make their peace with *her* if they are able. I am weary of trying to think and plan, and suppress letters, for their sake; not one thought do they give to me. And you must try to explain to him that for his sake and mine, I must simply not be supposed to have received the enclosed specimen of correspondence. Explain to him also, if you are able, that when a man in a matter of this description does not dwell on his wife's feelings, the suppression does not imply that she is dead. But I feel he will never understand. . . .[3]

O, I go on my journey with a bitter heart. It will be best for all, I daresay, if the *Casco* goes down with me. For there's devilish little left to live for. And don't think me ungrateful, my dear; God bless you, for your kindness and your wisdom. And would God I had had your letter before I wrote. For this wooden incapacity to understand any feeling that can inspire one word of my correspondence or one act of my life, is the sorest blow of all.

By the same mail I had a pencil note from Katharine, also enclosed; along with my answer.[4] I do not know whether it is that I am 'weary of

---

[1] Henley wrote a carefully worded letter on 7 May, confessing that RLS's letter had convicted him 'of a piece of real unkindness, unworthy of myself and our old tried friendship', regretting 'the cruel blunder I made in opening my mind to you . . . I should, I know now, have said nothing'. He denied that he 'struck to hurt' and continued: 'I thought the matter one of little consequence. It seemed right that you should know how it looked to myself, and that there might well be the end of it. I was elbows deep in the business from the first, and had (I thought) a right to make remarks. . . . That I had any feeling of unfriendliness is what I want now explicitly to deny.' When sending the letter to Baxter RLS annotated it: 'His original position carefully saved throughout; (1) and yet I gave him my word as to certain matters of fact; (2) and yet the letter (in consequence of this) can never be shown to my wife; (3) and yet, even if he still thinks as he did, I think a kind spirit would have even lied. R.L.S.'

[2] Eight lines (about fifty-five words) deleted. All deletions noted were made by RLS.

[3] About five words deleted.

[4] In her letters Katharine (who was Henley's protégée) had refused to confirm RLS's version of events. In this brief note she wrote: 'That was best. I am afraid to speak or breathe. There is devilry in the air.' RLS replied:

well-doing'.[5] I think not. I think I perceive that I injure these people by treating them with too great delicacy, which they misconstrue – and what drives me wild, misconstrue to the disadvantage of my wife.

O, Henley's letter! I cannot rise from it. What does the man think? Has he ever met a human being on his way through life? – Well, well, here I am writing all night again, with all my arrears of work on hand, and within nine days of leaving for San Francisco. This business has been my headstone; I will never be reconciled to life – O, I speak wildly – but it will never be the same to me. Katharine has behaved in a manner that I shall leave herself to qualify if she please; Henley, poor devil, seems unable to understand a single impulse of my heart or a single necessity of my position; he seems also quite unable to believe my plain word. . . .[6] Well, I mean to beat the crowd. I *will* have a good time on the *Casco*; it means a hard heart; well, harden it, O Lord! and let's be done.

Lord, man! I can't help loving him either. I would give a leg that this were blotted out, and I could sit down with him as of yore. . . .[7] Does he suppose my wife *enjoyed* this business? God, what a want – what a corpse-like want of thought – for others, this displays! Don't you see me going to my wife and showing her this letter, and——read it!

Truly, I have found in myself wonderful things, but I believe in my widest flights of unconcern for my neighbours, I never flew one third of this. But the affair is back in your hand. The trouble is, dear Charles, and this I feel wretched about; they will have to put off Rodin to next year.[8] I lost more than a month over this business; I had this chance of a schooner, which I thought I might enjoy – and I mean to, if the devil's in it – and which might do me good; and I am in dreadful arrears. I have still two articles which must be done in eight days,[9] a feat I know not how to accomplish; and in short – the Rodin must go over to next year. For I cannot do it on board.

[*22 May*] Next day; the sensible part here begins.

Of other business – I have the pretty complete certainty that the

---

Up to this moment you have never had one word of reproach from me. I must say now it had been 'best' if you had called to memory, when Henley came to see you, that which I myself so vividly remember. By so doing you might have saved me a friendship of which I have great need; and you would have saved yourself, when your better nature speaks, cruel reproaches. . . . I know, and you know, how you have used my wife. I know, and you know, how when this matter came up you failed me with Henley.

[5] Galatians 6:9.
[6] Six lines (about thirty-five words) deleted.
[7] Four lines (about twenty words) deleted.
[8] RLS had promised to write an article on Rodin for the *Art Journal* for which Henley was acting as advisory editor; this never materialised.
[9] Presumably the last two essays for *Scribner's*, 'The Education of an Engineer' (November) and 'A Christmas Sermon' (December).

£2,000 will carry me well through my seven months. What you have in hand, and what we may hope you shall receive in the interim from publishers, Skerryvore, etc., may thus collect, and should amount to something ere my return. If I come back in any health I should make another £300 in six weeks by finishing my novel *The Master of Ballantrae*. Pretty soon after, Lloyd and I should have one of our ships at the harbour mouth. And these should go far to keep us for the year, so that (what I am particularly anxious to manage) the *Casco* letters[10] may go towards repayment of the capital now borrowed. I shall think it unlucky if I cannot get from ten to fifteen hundred out of them, and this should go (or a great part of it should) toward the hole made in capital. I now find myself in debt to my heirs, for I scarce think myself entitled to decrease the little stock. . . .[11]

As to Henley's letter, then, you will try to explain to him, as kindly as you can, what it appears to me are its defects, and how from the nature of these defects, it is better I should not be supposed to have received it. I cannot describe with what disappointment I read it; but upon this, you will not dwell. My plan, in not receiving it, and not answering it, is to keep the door open for the return of friendship. I could not write to himself, and point out to him the position in which he leaves me as to my wife; because I am too proud to do so, and because if I tried I should but open the wound. I lay the burthen, then, upon your shoulders; and should I receive any letters from W.E.H. before I have heard from you, I shall act upon your original proposal and send them to you unopened.[12]

He says he was 'in the business from the first'. He was in it enough to have known a little more as I reminded him, were he not under an influence which I fear is (just now at least) an evil one. But it is true: I know how easy he is to lead.

You will hear from me again ere I sail, my dear Charles, I trust in better spirits.

I cannot say I think I act harshly. I am trying to do the best for all. The Lord knows there is in my soul this morning no hatred and no anger; a very weary disappointment, a dread of the future, and a doubt of all – that is my sentiment. With my voyage in front of me – the dream of a life realised – I must still say Would God I had died at Hyères! I have never been well enough since then to enjoy life as I once did; I have had a considerable success, which is a disappointing circumstance in life, believe

[10] The Letters on the South Seas to be syndicated by McClure. McClure wrote from London on 31 May that he hoped to be able to get $300 per letter.
[11] One paragraph omitted.
[12] On 27 April, having obtained Henley's agreement, Baxter wrote to RLS seeking his agreement 'that all direct correspondence shall cease between you, for a period of six months, and shall not be resumed without my leave'.

me; and – well, now, I feel as if I were moving among bladders. For either I am a very unjust judge, or I am being hardly used by those whom I loved and tried to serve.

Your kindness, your countenance and the affection you show to me, my dear, has been of the most incalculable support, and I thank you again and again, and am – O, I hope – Ever yours   R.L. Stevenson

Because I say nothing of my wife's position and my wife's feelings, you at least will not misunderstand me. There are things of which a man cannot write; but dear God, that he must feel. And think of my wooden Henley! I shall scarce get an answer to this before I am on the sea: if all goes well. Better address to Scribner's, and I shall hear at our first *escale*.
                                                                                          R.L.S.

To my wife, I shall (God forgive me) pretend that your plan has held all the time, and that I have not communicated with Henley. So here you see I am still tricking and lying for him, and he cannot think once of my position. It is indeed disheartening. Words cannot describe my weariness of life. And yet it seems it would have been so easy for Henley to have made his letter presentable! Lloyd is in a great state of doubt too; hating to go to sea without a friendly hail! to Henley; and yet not knowing how or whether.

Some of the first of this letter, being the usual steam escape, I have deleted in a cooler moment.   R.L.S.

★*To Homer Saint-Gaudens*[1]

27 May 1888   *Manasquan*

Dear Homer St Gaudens, Your father has brought you this day to see me, and he tells me that it is his hope that you may remember the occasion. I am going to do what I can to carry out his wish; and it may amuse you, years after, to see this little scrap of paper and to read what I here write. I must begin by testifying that you yourself took no interest whatever in the introduction, and in the most proper spirit, displayed a single-minded ambition to get back to play. And this I thought an excellent and admirable point in your character. You were also (I use the past tense, with a view to the time when you shall read, rather than to that when I am writing) a very pretty boy and (to my European views) startlingly self-

---

[1] Homer Schiff Saint-Gaudens (1880–1958), stage director for the American actress Maude Adams 1908–1917; Director of Fine Arts, Carnegie Institute, Pittsburgh 1922–50; writer and lecturer on the arts.

possessed. My time of observation was so limited that you must pardon me if I can say no more: what else I remarked, what restlessness of foot and hand, what graceful clumsiness, what experimental designs upon the furniture, was but the common inheritance of human youth. But you may perhaps like to know that the lean, flushed man in bed, who interested you so little, was in a state of mind extremely mingled and unpleasant: harassed with work which he thought he was not doing well, troubled with difficulties to which you will in time succeed, and yet looking forward to no less a matter than a voyage to the South Seas and the visitation of savage and of desert islands. Your father's friend

Robert Louis Stevenson

★   ★   ★

Stevenson, his mother, Lloyd and Valentine returned briefly to New York and on 2 June they left for San Francisco to join the *Casco*. They travelled by rail across the U.S.A. via Chicago and Council Bluffs in some luxury. Fanny joined them at Sacramento and they reached San Francisco on 7 June. For the first few days RLS remained in bed at the Occidental Hotel but a flurry of preparations began.

The formal agreement to charter the *Casco* was signed with her owner Dr Samuel Merritt[1] on 21 June 1888. Under it RLS chartered the yacht for seven months 'for a cruise to various islands in the Pacific Ocean, including the Galapagos,[2] Marquesas, Society, Sandwich and other Islands which in the judgement of the Captain . . . can be visited with safety'. He agreed to pay $3500 for the seven months plus 'the entire cost of the cruise including the victualling, manning and all expenses'. It was also agreed that 'the present Captain A.H. Otis' should remain in command of the yacht during the cruise and that RLS would 'respect his views in regard to the sailing and general management of the yacht'.

Stevenson was still bitterly preoccupied with the quarrel with Henley and in the course of his farewell letter to Baxter he wrote:

My dear Charles, Here I am in my berth, and pretty sick; I cannot recover from this affair, though crossing the continent picked me up for the time; and I long to get to sea. Shall I ever return? I have no great

---

[1] Samuel Merritt (1822–90), came to San Francisco from his native Maine in 1849. He practised as a doctor and made a fortune in property deals; he later moved to Oakland and became Mayor (1867–69). Balfour says that until he met RLS, Merritt distrusted the proposed arrangements but after their interview (on 14 June) he agreed that they should go ahead: 'I'd read things in the papers about Stevenson, and thought he was a kind of crank; but he's a plain, sensible man that knows what he's talking about just as well as I do.'

[2] The original idea of going to the Galapagos Islands was dropped, at Fanny's insistence, because of the risk of being becalmed for several weeks in the intense heat of the tropics.

mind to see England any more, I must confess; but time is a great healer. . . .

Good-bye, my dear old fellow: We all send you the kindest wishes, and whether or not we ever meet again, you stand near in my heart.

It is easy to send a last word to you; but just in case of accidents, I wish to send one to W.E.H. also. These words will do: 'Auld Lang Syne.' To Katharine, if I come again no more, I send these: 'It is never too late to repent and make amends.' But these are of course only testamentary.

Good-bye to yourself. Yours ever affectionately

Robert Louis Stevenson

I am going to have a job to manage and enjoy myself; but I'll try!

XI. THE CRUISE OF THE CASCO
THE MARQUESAS, PAUMOTUS, TAHITI
July 1888–January 1889

At 5 a.m. on the morning of 28 June 1888 the tug *Pelican* towed the *Casco* through the Golden Gate out of San Francisco Bay into the waters of the Pacific Ocean. After twenty-two days at sea and a voyage of three thousand miles, the yacht dropped anchor on 20 July in Anaho Bay in Nuka Hiva, the largest of the Marquesas Islands.

In the opening paragraph of *In the South Seas* Stevenson later described the mood in which he set out:

> For nearly ten years my health had been declining; and for some while before I set forth upon my voyage, I believed I was come to the afterpiece of life, and had only the nurse and undertaker to expect. It was suggested that I should try the South Seas; and I was not unwilling to visit like a ghost, and be carried like a bale, among scenes that had attracted me in youth and health.

The *Casco* was a graceful two-masted schooner yacht, ninety-four feet in length, of seventy-four tons burden. Captain Albert H. Otis began the voyage (in Balfour's words) 'with a supreme contempt for his new employers, [and] ended it as an intimate and valued friend'. RLS later drew his portrait in *The Wrecker* as Captain Nares. There was a crew of four deck-hands plus the cook.

In the few letters written to his friends during this period Stevenson made no attempt to provide a detailed account of his experiences. All his literary energies until he reached Tahiti were devoted to his journal, 'The Cruise of the *Casco*', which has never been fully published. From it he later quarried Parts I and II of the South Seas Letters syndicated by McClure in 1891 and posthumously published in 1896 as *In the South Seas*. Unfortunately RLS discontinued this journal when he reached Tahiti and he never wrote the account of Tahiti he planned.

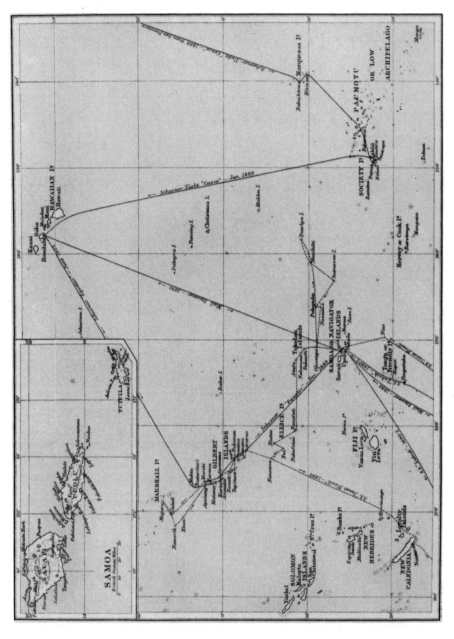

Stevenson's journeys in the South Seas from 1888 to 1893. (*In the South Seas*, Tusitala edition, 1924)

To Charles Baxter[1]

7 a.m. 6 September 1888
with a dreadful pen   *Yacht* Casco, *at sea, near the Paumotus*[2]

My dear Charles, Last night as I lay under my blanket in the cockpit,[3] courting sleep, I had a comic seizure. There was nothing visible but the southern stars, and the steersman there out by the binnacle lamp; we were all looking forward to a most deplorable landfall on the morrow, praying God we should fetch a tuft of palms which are to indicate the Dangerous Archipelago; the night was as warm as milk; and all of a sudden, I had a vision of – Drummond Street. It came on me like a flash of lightning; I simply returned thither, and into the past. And when I remembered all that I hoped and feared as I pickled about Rutherford's[4] in the rain and the east wind; how I feared I should make a mere shipwreck, and yet timidly hoped not; how I feared I should never have a friend far less a wife, and yet passionately hoped I might; how I hoped (if I did not take to drink) I should possibly write one little book etc., etc. And then, now – what a change! I feel somehow as if I should like the incident set upon a brass plate at the corner of that dreary thoroughfare, for all students to read, poor devils, when their hearts are down.[5] And I felt I must write one word to you. Excuse me if I write little: when I am at sea, it gives me a headache; when I am in port, I have my diary crying, 'Give, give."[6] I shall have a fine book of travels, I feel sure; and will tell you more of the South Seas after very few months than any other writer has done – except Herman Melville perhaps, who is a howling cheese.[7] Good luck to you, God bless you. Your affectionate friend   R.L.S.

Love to Henley and Simpson and Bob, if you see him.

---

[1] The letter was mislaid and not posted until 19 June 1889. Baxter noted receipt on 22 July 1889.
[2] The *Casco* sailed from Hiva-oa in the Marquesas Islands on the morning of 4 September on a dangerous voyage through many coral atolls bound for Fakarava in the Paumotu (or Tuamotu) Archipelago, also known as the Dangerous or Low Archipelago. RLS describes his experiences in *In the South Seas*, Part II, ch. I, 'Atolls at a Distance'.
[3] RLS had adopted the 'dangerous practice' of sleeping 'on deck upon the cockpit bench' with the steersman for company.
[4] The pub in Drummond Street known as 'The Pump' frequented by Edinburgh students.
[5] A bronze plaque, bearing a quotation from this letter, was unveiled on the wall at the end of Drummond Street by a group of admirers of RLS on 11 September 1995.
[6] Cf. the two daughters of the horseleach in Proverbs 30:15.
[7] A compliment. RLS had earlier praised Musset as 'an inconceivable cheese'. Andrew Lang remembered RLS's 'boyish habit of slang': 'I *think* it was he who called Julius Caesar "the howlingest cheese who ever lived".' Melville's novel *Typee* (1846) takes place in Nuka Hiva.

To Sidney Colvin

21 September 1888   *Fakarava, Low Archipelago*

My dear Colvin, Only a word. Get out your big atlas; and imagine a straight line from San Francisco to Anaho, the N.E. corner of Nuka Hiva, one of the Marquesas Islands; imagine three weeks there; imagine a day's sail on August 12 round the Eastern end of the Island to Tai-o-hae the capital; imagine us there till August 22nd; imagine us skirt the east side of Ua-pu – perhaps Roua-Poa on your atlas – and through the Bordelais Straits to Taaha-uku in Hiva-Oa, where we arrive on the 23rd; imagine us there until September 4th, when we sailed for Fakarava, which we reached on the 9th, after a very difficult and dangerous passage among these isles. Tuesday, we shall leave for Taïti where I shall knock off and do some necessary work ashore. It looks pretty bald on the atlas; not in fact; nor I trust in the 130 odd pp. of diary which I have just been looking up for these dates: the interest, indeed, has been *incredible*. I did not dream there were such places or such races. My health has stood me splendidly; I am in for hours wading over the knees for shells; I have been five hours on horseback:[1] I have been up pretty near all night, waiting to see where the *Casco* would go ashore, and with my diary all ready – simply the most entertaining night of my life.[2] Withal I still have colds; I have one now, and feel pretty sick too; but not as at home: instead of being in bed for instance I am at this moment sitting snuffling and writing in an undershirt and trousers; and as for colour, hands, arms, feet, legs and face, I am browner than the berry; only my trunk and the aristocratic spot on which I sit, retains the vile whiteness of the north.

Please give my news and kind love to Henley, Henry James, and any whom you see of well-wishers. Accept from me the very best of my affection: and believe me ever yours   The Old Man Virulent[3]

7 October   *Taïti*[4]

Never having found a chance to send this off, I may add more of my news: my cold took a very bad turn, and I am pretty much out of sorts at

---

[1] The journey with Brother Michel at Hiva-oa on 27 August described in *In the South Seas*, Part I, ch. XIV, 'In a Cannibal Valley'.

[2] The night of 8 September on the dangerous voyage to Fakarava.

[3] Colvin says that this form of signature 'alludes to the fits of uncontrollable anger to which he was often in youth, but by this time hardly ever subject: fits occasioned sometimes by instances of official stolidity or impertinence . . . more often by acts savouring of cruelty, meanness, or injustice'.

[4] The *Casco* sailed from Fakarava on 25 September and cast anchor in Papeete Harbour, Tahiti on 27 September. After a few nights at the Hôtel de France, RLS and Fanny moved into a small house. By this time he was seriously ill with a bad cough and threatenings of hemorrhage. When he felt slightly better he began to write letters.

this particular, living in a little, bare one-twentieth-furnished house, sur-rounded by mangos etc. All the rest are well, and I mean to be soon. But these Taïti colds are very severe and, to children, often fatal; so they were not the thing for me. Yesterday the brigantine came in from S.F. so we can get our letters off soon. Yesterday night, my dear, my wife and I conversed about you thus. 'My chief reason', said I, 'for wishing to go back to England is to see Colvin.' 'It's my only reason,' said she. There are in Papeete at this moment, in a little wooden house with grated veran-dahs, two people who love you very much; and one of them is

Robert Louis Stevenson

To Sidney Colvin

16 October 1888   *Taïti*

My dear Colvin, The *courrier*[1] for San Francisco departs tomorrow morning bearing you some kind of a scratch. This much more important packet will travel by way of Auckland. It contains a ballant;[2] and I think a better ballant than I expected ever to do. I can imagine how you will wag your pow over it; and how ragged you will find it, etc.[3] But has it not spirit all the same? and though the verse is not all your fancy painted it, has it not some life? and surely as narrative, the thing has considerable merit! Read it, get a typewritten copy taken, and send me that and your opinion to the Sanguishes. I know I am only courting the most excruci-ating mortification; but the real cause of my sending the thing is that I could bear to go down myself, but not to have much MS go down with me. To say truth, we are through the most dangerous; but it has left in all minds a strong sense of insecurity, and we are all for putting eggs in various baskets.

We leave here soon, bound for Uahine, Raiatea, Bora-Bora[4] and the Sanguishes.

> O how my spirit languishes
> To step ashore on the Sanguishes;
> For there my letters wait
> There shall I know my fate.
> O how my spirit languidges
> To step ashore on the Sanguidges.

[1] French mail-boat.
[2] 'The Feast of Famine' first published in *Ballads* (1890). The MS is dated 5–16 October 1888.
[3] Colvin: 'I never very much admired his South Sea ballads for any quality except their narrative vigour, thinking them unequal and uncertain both in metre and style.'
[4] In the Leeward Islands. The plan to visit these islands *en route* for Hawaii was later abandoned.

18th I think

We shall leave here if all is well on Monday. I am quite recovered, astonishingly recovered. It must be owned these climates and this voyage have given me more strength than I could have thought possible. And yet the sea is a horrible place, stupefying to the mind and poisonous to the temper; the sea, the motion, the lack of space, the cruel publicity, the villainous tinned foods, the sailors, the captain, the passengers – but you are amply repaid when you sight an island, and drop anchor in a new world.[5] Much trouble has attended this trip, but I must confess more pleasure. Nor should I ever complain; as in the last few weeks, with the curing of my illness indeed, as if that were the bursting of an abscess, the cloud has risen from my spirits and to some degree from my temper. Do you know what they called the *Casco* at Fakarava? The Silver Ship. Is that not pretty? Pray tell Mrs Jenkin, *die silberne Frau*, as I only learned it since I wrote her.[6] I think of calling the book by that name: *The Cruise of the Silver Ship*: so there will be one poetic page at least – the title. At the Iles Sangwish, we shall say farewell to the S.S. with mingled feelings. She is a lovely creature: the most beautiful thing at this moment in Taïti.

Well, I will take another sheet, though I know I have nothing to say. You would think I was bursting: but the voyage is all stored up for the book, which is to pay for it, we fondly hope; and the troubles of the time are not worth telling; and our news is little. Would you like to know what we hear in Taïti? I am drunk all day long; the captain was drunk at Tai-o-hae, and struck one of the ladies (I never heard which) and I arose in my might, thrust and locked him into his cabin, and went out and hired the Baron von der Goltz[7] for mate. And this was well thought upon, for he was a man suited to the manners of the ship; and if I ever was sober, which is to be doubted, there can be no doubt about the Baron. He visited me this afternoon; he was clean shaved and fatherly, and he held my hand (partly for steadiness) and wept, did the Baron; but words failed him to communicate the cause of his sorrows. It may have been because we discharged him on our arrival here. That makes four we have paid off: the cook, two hands and the Baron; but the Baron was the greatest of these. He is one of the handsomest men in the world: sixty years old, and

---

[5] RLS wrote to William Archer on 17 October: 'The voyage has agreed well with all; it has had its pains, and its extraordinary pleasures; nothing in the world can equal the excitement of the first time you cast anchor in some bay of a tropical island, and the boats begin to surround you, and the tattooed people swarm aboard.'

[6] When the Jenkin family were on holiday in Austria, Mrs Jenkin had been called *die silberne Frau* from some silver ornaments she was wearing (cf. RLS's *Memoir*, ch. VI).

[7] Georges Henry Goltz (1826–1912), a German-born sailor and merchant of Polish origin who worked on ships in the area and was living with his family at Tai-o-hae. Fanny, in a letter to Dora Williams, says that he was 'continually referring to his very genteel extraction' and was familiarly known as the Baron.

never sober, to see him stand on the bowsprit to con the ship, was really to see the young Apollo. But in these isles drink seems only to pickle people. Death is so busy with the natives, that he has no time to harpoon Europeans.

Interview on board the *Casco*:
Captain: 'Hullo, Mr Goltz, you are drunk.' *The Baron*: 'Do you mean to insinuate that I have been drinking?' *Captain*: 'I know nothing about that but you're drunk.' *The Baron* (with passion): 'Speak to me kindly, Captain, or I shall weep!'

Here I conclude (October 24th, I think) for we are now stowed, and the Blue Peter metaphorically flies.

⋆   ⋆   ⋆

On 24 October 1888 the *Casco* left Papeete and sailed round to Taravao on the south side of Tahiti on a dangerous and unpleasant journey whose worst moments were later recalled in a letter to Bob (p. 391); they arrived on the 25th. The climate was unhealthy and RLS grew steadily worse. Fanny bravely determined to move him to the village of Tautira, a difficult journey of some sixteen miles through dense forests and across many streams. On 28 October, following an earlier journey of reconnaissance, she managed, with the help of Lloyd and Valentine to get him there and to rent a suitable house.

The day after RLS and Fanny had arrived at Tautira, the Princess Moë,[1] hearing there was a sick foreigner in the village 'whose wife was troubled because he would not eat' brought him a South Seas delicacy, a dish of raw fish with *miti* sauce (coconut milk, mixed with lime-juice and sea-water) which she had prepared herself; for the next few days she continued to bring him or send him special dishes. Fanny later told Balfour: 'I feel that she saved Louis's life. He was lying in a deep stupor when she first saw him, suffering from congestion of the lungs and in a burning fever.' A few days later, as RLS began to gain strength, the Princess arranged for him and Fanny to move into the house of the sub-chief of the village, the splendid Teriitera usually called Ori a Ori (1838–1916), deacon of the Protestant church, with whom (as the letters show) they became great friends. Another friend was the chief Ariie a Teraimano, described by the historian Henry Adams (see p. 429) as 'a conventional official, with a

---

[1] Princess Moë (died 1891) was the widow of the dissolute King Tamatoa of Raiatea (1842–81). When she left Tautira on 5 November (she returned later) RLS gave her the poem 'To an Island Princess' (*Songs of Travel*, XXIX). All the contemporary accounts by European visitors such as Pierre Loti and Lord Pembroke bear witness to her beauty and charm.

round face', an educated man who spoke French and had been to Paris; he usually acted as interpreter, since Ori spoke only Tahitian.

Meanwhile the *Casco* had sailed round the peninsula of Taiarapu and anchored off Tautira on 3 November. By 6 November his mother wrote home that 'Louis is fairly well again, and is able to go for a little walk from time to time; but he is terribly thin and white.' On 7 November she gave a feast on board to the local women who had befriended her in the church and prayers were duly said for the safety of the ship. The next day Captain Otis discovered that the main-mast of the *Casco* was riddled with dry-rot; on 11 November the vessel limped back to Papeete for repair. Three weeks later it was discovered that the other mast was rotten and so departure from Tautira was further delayed.

★ ★ ★

To Thomas Archer

[*? 18 December 1888*][1]   *Tautira, Island of Tahiti*

Dear Tomarcher, This is a pretty state of things! seven o'clock and no word of breakfast! And I was awake a good deal last night, for it was full moon, and they had made a great fire of cocoa-nut husks down by the sea, and as we have no blinds or shutters this kept my room very bright. And then the rats had a wedding or a schoolfeast under my bed. And then I woke early, and I have nothing to read except Virgil's *Aeneid*, which is not good for an empty stomach, and a Latin dictionary, which is good for naught, and by some humorous accident, your dear papa's article on Skerryvore. And I read the whole of that, and very impudent it is, but you must not tell your dear papa I said so, or it might come to a battle in which you might lose either a dear papa or a valued correspondent, or both, which would be prodigal. And still no breakfast; so I said 'Let's write to Tomarcher.'

This is a much better place for children than any I have hitherto seen in these seas. The girls (and sometimes the boys) play a very elaborate kind of hopscotch.[2] The boys play horses exactly as we do in Europe; and have very good fun on stilts trying to knock each other down, in which they

---

[1] William Archer's only child Thomas (1885–1918), who called himself 'Tomarcher', was a highly imaginative boy who invented a country called Peona and a large family of imaginary brothers and sisters. He was killed in the First World War. There is an affectionate account of him in Shaw's essay on Archer, reprinted in *Pen Portraits and Reviews* (1931).

[2] MIS wrote to her sister: 'He is in the very midst of the large village, and the life of it goes on all around him; the little girls even play special games of hopscotch . . . before his window to amuse him'.

do not often succeed. The children of all ages go to church and are allowed to do what they please, running about the aisles, rolling balls, stealing mamma's bonnet and publicly sitting on it, and at last going to sleep in the middle of the floor. I forgot to say that the whips to play horses, and the balls to roll about the church – at least I never saw them used elsewhere – grow ready made on trees; which is rough on toy-shops. The whips are so good that I wanted to play horses myself; but no such luck! my hair is gray, and I am a great, big, ugly man. The balls are rather hard, but very light and quite round. When you grow up and become offensively rich, you can charter a ship in the port of London, and have it come back to you entirely loaded with these balls; when you could satisfy your mind as to their character, and give them away when done to your uncles and aunts. But what I really wanted to tell you was this: besides the tree top toys (Hush-a-by, toy-shop on the tree-top!), I have seen some real *made* toys, the first hitherto observed in the South Seas.

This was how. You are to imagine a four-wheeled gig; one horse; in the front seat two Tahiti natives, in their Sunday clothes, blue coat, white shirt, kilt (a little longer than the Scotch) of a blue stuff with big white or yellow flowers, legs and feet bare; in the back seat me and my wife, who is a friend of yours; under our feet, plenty of lunch and things; among us a great deal of fun in broken Tahitian, one of the natives, the sub-chief of the village being a great ally of mine. Indeed we have changed names; so that he is now called Rui, the nearest they can come to Louis, for they have no l and no s in their language.[3] Rui is six feet three in his stockings, and a magnificent man. We all have straw hats, for the sun is strong. We drive between the sea, which makes a great noise, and the mountains; the road is cut through a forest mostly of fruit trees, the very creepers, which take the place of our ivy, heavy with a great and delicious fruit, bigger than your head and far nicer, called Barbedine.[4] Presently we came to a house in a pretty garden, quite by itself, very nicely kept, the doors and windows open, no one about, and no noise but that of the sea. It looked like a house in a fairy-tale; and just beyond we must ford a river, and there we saw the inhabitants. Just in the mouth of the river, where it met the sea waves, they were ducking and bathing and screaming together like a covey of birds: seven or eight little naked brown boys and girls as happy as the day was long; and on the banks of the stream beside them real toys – toy ships, full rigged; and with their sails set, though they were lying in the dust on their beam ends. And then I knew for sure they were all

---

[3] The exchange of names took place on 21 November on the day of a village feast given by RLS. RLS took Ori's Christian name Teriitera. The journey described is probably that to visit Tati Salmon on 24–6 November (see below).

[4] Also spelled barbadine, the gourd-like edible fruit of the giant granadilla, a tropical member of the passion-flower family.

children in fairy-story, living alone together in that lonely house with the only toys in all the island; and that I had myself driven, in my four-wheeled gig, into a corner of the fairy-story, and the question was should I get out again? But it was all right: I guess only one of the wheels of the gig had got into the fairy-story; and the next jolt the whole thing vanished, and we drove on in our seaside forest as before, and I have the honour to be Tomarcher's Valued Correspondent, Teriitera, Which he was previously known as   Robert Louis Stevenson

To Sidney Colvin

14 January 1889. Twenty days out from Papeete   *Yacht* Casco *at Sea*

Yes, sir, all that, and only (for a guess) in 4° north or at the best 4°30′, though already the wind seems to smell a little of the North Pole. My handwriting you must take as you get for we are sprawling along through a nasty swell, and I can only keep place at the table by means of a foot against the divan: the unoccupied hand meanwhile assuring the ink-bottle. As we begin (so very slowly) to draw near to seven months of correspondence, we are all in some fear; and I want to have letters written before I shall be plunged into that boiling pot of disagreeables which I constantly expect at Honolulu. What is needful can be added there.

   We were kept two months at Tautira in the house of my dear old friend Ori a Ori, till both the masts of this invaluable yacht had been repaired. It was all for the best: Tautira being the most beautiful spot, and its people the most amiable, I have ever found. Besides which, the climate suited me to the ground; I actually went sea bathing almost every day, and in our feasts (we are all huge eaters in Taiarapu) have been known to apply four times for pig. And then again I got wonderful materials for my book, collected songs and legends on the spot: songs still sung in chorus by perhaps a hundred persons, not two of whom can agree on their translation; legends, in which I have seen half-a-dozen seniors sitting in conclave and debating what came next. Once I went a day's journey to the other side of the island to Tati, the high chief of the Tevas – *my* chief that is, for I am now a Teva and Teriitera at your service – to collect more and correct what I had already.[1] In the meanwhile I got on with my work,

---

[1] Tati Salmon (1850–1918), hereditary high chief of the Tevas at Papara, the greatest and oldest native family in Tahiti, was educated in England and was an authority on Tahitian legends and poetry. He was one of the ten children of Alexander Salmon, an Anglo-Jewish trader who married the famous Teva chiefess Ariitaimai (1821–97); her memoirs were edited by Henry Adams who became friendly with Tati and other members of the Salmon family when he visited Tahiti in 1891.

almost finished *The Master of Ballantrae*[2] which contains more human work
than anything of mine but *Kidnapped* – and wrote the half of another
ballad, 'The Song of Rahéro',[3] on a Taiarapu legend of my own clan, sir
– not so much fire as 'The Feast of Famine', but promising to be more
even and correct. But the best fortune of our stay at Tautira was my
knowledge of Ori himself: one of the finest creatures extant. The day of
our parting was a sad one. We deduced from it a rule for travellers: not
to stay two months in one place: which is to cultivate regrets.

At last our contemptible ship was ready: to sea we went, bound for
Honolulu and the letter bag, on Christmas Day;[4] and from then to now
have experienced every sort of minor misfortune, squalls, calms, contrary
winds and seas, pertinacious rains, declining stores, till we came almost to
regard ourselves as in the case of Vanderdecken.[5] Three days ago our luck
seemed to improve, we struck a leading breeze, got creditably through the
doldrums and just as we looked to have the N.E. trades and a straight run,
the rains and squalls and calms began again about midnight, and this
morning, though there is breeze enough to send us along, we are beaten
back by an obnoxious swell out of the north. Here is a page of complaint;
when a verse of thanksgiving had perhaps been more in place. For all this
time we must have been skirting past dangerous weather, in the tail and
circumference of hurricanes, and getting only annoyance where we should
have had peril, and ill-humour instead of fear.

I wonder if I have managed to give you any news this time? or whether
the usual doom hangs over my letter? 'The midwife whispered, Be thou
dull!'[6] or at least inexplicit. Anyway I have tried my best, am exhausted
with the effort, and fall back into the land of generalities. I cannot tell you
how often we have planned our arrival at the Monument: two nights ago,
the 12 January, we had it all planned out, arrived in the lights and whirl
of Waterloo, hailed a hansom, span up the Waterloo Road, over the
Bridge, etc., etc., and hailed the Monument gate in triumph and with
indescribable delight. My dear Custodian, I always think we are too
sparing of assurances; Cordelia is only to be excused by Regan and
Goneril in the same nursery: I wish to tell you that the longer I live, the

---

[2] *The Master of Ballantrae* began serialisation in *Scribner's* in November 1888. E. L. Burlingame
wrote to RLS on 22 January acknowledging receipt the day before of 'the precious seventh
instalment of *The Master*'. Chapters VIII–X, drafted in Tahiti were completed and sent to
Burlingame from Honolulu on 5 February.

[3] Dedicated to Ori a Ori and published in *Ballads*. Fanny says that he heard the legend from the
Princess Moë and Tati Salmon.

[4] The *Casco* (after many false hopes) reached Tautira on 22 December, and finally weighed anchor
at 2.30 p.m. on Christmas Day.

[5] In the legend of The Flying Dutchman; RLS had recently read Marryat's treatment of the story
in *The Phantom Ship*.

[6] Cf. Dryden, *Absolom and Achitophel*, Part II, ll. 476–7: 'The midwife laid her hand on his thick
skull,/With this prophetic blessing: *Be thou dull*'.

more dear and the more respected do you become to me. You see devilish little of the respect, say you; I know you do, nor much of the affection. And yet both are there; nor does my heart own any stronger sentiments. If the bloody schooner didn't send me flying in every sort of direction at the same time, I would say better what I feel so much; but really if you were here, you would not be writing letters, I believe; and even I, though of a more marine constitution, am much perturbed with this bobbery and wish – O ye Gods, how I wish that it was done, and we had arrived, and I had Pandora's Box (my mail-bag) in hand, and was in the lively hope of something eatable for dinner instead of salt horse, tinned mutton, duff without any plums, and pie fruit, which now make up our whole repertory. Ah Pandora's Box! I wonder what you will contain. As like as not, you will contain but little money; if that be so, we shall have to return to Frisco in the *Casco*, and thence by sea via Panama to Southampton: where we should arrive in April. I would like fine to see you on the tug: ten years older both of us than the last time you came to welcome Fanny and me to England, but I, if all goes well, in better health, and you glad to see Fanny this time, and she I can promise you burning to see you. If we have money, however, we shall do a little differently; send the *Casco* away from Honolulu empty of its high born lessees, for that voyage to Frisco is one long dead beat in foul and at least in cold weather; stay awhile behind, follow by steamer, cross the States by train, stay awhile in New York on business, and arrive probably by the German Line in Southampton. But all this is a question of money. We shall have to lie very dark awhile to recruit our finances: what comes from the book of the cruise, I do not want to touch until the capital is repaid.[7]

---

[7] RLS could not find this letter on arrival in Honolulu and it was not posted until 9 May 1889.

XII. FIVE MONTHS IN HAWAII
January–June 1889

The *Casco* had a difficult journey from Tautira to Honolulu and was delayed by about two weeks. They were becalmed for several days within sight of land, living on short rations as food supplies ran out. Stevenson's mother recorded their arrival on Thursday 24 January:

> At last we pass through the reef and cast anchor in Honolulu harbour at 3.30 p.m. . . . Joe and Belle and Austin came on board at once and Belle takes hysterics when she finds it really is her mother. She had boarded two wrong yachts before. Louis goes straight to the Hawaiian Hotel to see his letters. I go with Belle to her house and we all dine at the Hotel (Captain too) – it seems to us the finest meal we have ever eaten.

Joe and Belle Strong and their son Austin (by now eight years old) had lived in Honolulu since September 1882 (see p. 366, n. 3). The Stevenson party joined the Strongs at 40 Emma Street, the home of Henry F. Poor and his mother, Mrs Caroline Bush, where they were staying.[1] A few days later, on 27 January, in search of greater peace and quiet, RLS and Fanny moved to Poor's bungalow, Manuia Lanai, at Waikiki, about three miles out of Honolulu. Waikiki was then a country district of rice fields, coconut groves, a white sandy beach and a few scattered summer residences.

The Strongs and their friends were members of the 'Royal set' surrounding Kalakaua, the last King of Hawaii. David Kalakaua (1836–91), a chief who was elected king in 1874, had fought a losing battle for political power against the Reform (or Missionary) Party, dominated by American business interests, and the 'Bayonet Constitution' of 1887 had shorn him of most of his authority; the struggle was to end in 1893 with the deposition of his sister and successor, Queen Liliuokalani, and annexation by the United States at the end of the century. Despite the corruption and scandal that characterised his regime, Kalakaua himself was a man of great personal charm and ability, deeply interested in Hawaiian history and legend: RLS was later to describe him as an 'amiable, far from

---

[1] Henry F. Poor (1856–99), part-Hawaiian official was Superintendent, Postal Savings Bank, Honolulu. He was secretary of an ill-fated Hawaiian Mission to Samoa in 1887, of which Strong was official artist. His mother, Mrs Caroline Bush (1836–1914) was regarded as 'a woman of considerable social prestige'. For her birthday on 3 March 1889 RLS wrote the verses beginning 'Dear Lady, tapping at your door'.

unaccomplished, but too convivial sovereign'. RLS and Lloyd were formally presented to the King at Iolani Palace on 26 January and they spent that afternoon at the King's Boat House where they were adorned with wreaths, drank champagne, played whist and had their photographs taken. The King visited the *Casco* on the afternoon of 1 February. He was given champagne, sherry and cake; RLS read 'Ticonderoga', Captain Otis played the accordion, Belle danced and Lloyd sang 'The Dollars of Peru' (a poem written by RLS in Tahiti). Two days later Henry Poor gave a *luau* or native feast at Manuia Lanai in honour of RLS, with Kalakaua and Princess Liliuokalani as chief guests. Fanny presented the King with a golden pearl and RLS read a specially written poem, 'To Kalakaua' (*Songs of Travel*, XXX). Stevenson and the King were soon on friendly terms and Kalakaua tried very hard to persuade RLS to settle in Hawaii.

As early as 2 February RLS had decided to send the *Casco* back to San Francisco. On 5 February his mother noted in her diary: 'Louis finds that he can hire the house next to Mr Poor's at Waikiki for a few months so he determines to send away the *Casco* and settle down here and make a little money to take us home.' At this period letters took a week to reach San Francisco, a further week to cross the States to New York and about ten days to cross the Atlantic to London or Edinburgh. There were usually two deliveries and collections of mail in Honolulu each month by the regular mail steamers.

To Bob Stevenson

Not to get to print: Private[1]
February 1889   *Honolulu, Hawaiian Islands*

My dear Bob, My extremely foolhardy venture is practically over. How foolhardy it was I don't think I realised. We had a very small schooner, and like most yachts overrigged and oversparred, and like many American yachts on a very dangerous sail plan. Her head sails thus: A. jib and stay foresail in one, giving us no light and safe headsail, for even reefed it was

---

[1] RLS had been annoyed by the publication in the *Scotsman* of a private letter from Lloyd to Baxter from Tahiti.

a formidable bit of canvas, and (what is far worse) carrying the forestay outboard on the bowsprit: B. is the flying jib, working you see on the same identical stick (bowsprit, jib-boom and flying jib-boom in one) which thus had to bear a horrid strain and was the key of the ship. In a head sea, the Captain and I used to watch that stick with interest. The waters we sailed in are of course entirely unlighted and very badly charted; in the Dangerous Archipelago through which we were fools enough to go, we were perfectly in ignorance of where we were for a whole night and half of the next day, and this in the midst of invisible islands and rapid and variable currents; and we were lucky when we found our whereabouts at last. We have twice had all we wanted in the way of squalls; once, as I came on deck, I found the green sea over the cockpit coamings and running down the companion like a brook to meet me; at that same moment the foresail sheet jammed and the Captain had no knife; this was the only occasion on the cruise that ever I set a hand to a rope, but I worked like a Trojan, judging the possibility of hemorrhage better than the certainty of drowning. Another time I saw a rather singular thing: our whole ship's company as pale as paper from the Captain to the cook: we had a black squall astern on the port and a white squall ahead to starboard; this complication passed off innocuous, the black squall only fetching us with its tail, and the white one slewing off somewhere else. Twice we were a long while (days) in the close vicinity of hurricane weather; but again luck prevailed and we saw none of it. These are dangers incident to these seas and small craft. What was an amazement, and at the same time, a powerful stroke of luck, both our masts were rotten, and we found it out – I was going to say in time, but it was stranger and luckier than that. The head of the mainmast hung over so that hands were afraid to go to the helm; and less than three weeks before – I am not sure it was more than a fortnight – we had been nearly twelve hours beating off the lee shore of Eimeo (or Moorea, next island to Tahiti) in half a gale of wind with a violent head sea; she would neither tack nor wear once, and had to be boxed off with the mainsail; you can imagine what an ungodly show of kites we carried – and yet the mast stood. The very day after that, in the southern bight of Tahiti, we had a near squeak, the wind suddenly coming calm; the reefs were close in, with my eye! what a surf! the pilot thought we were gone, and the Captain had a boat cleared, when a lucky squall came to our rescue. My wife, hearing the order given about the boats, remarked to my mother: 'Isn't that nice? We shall soon be ashore!' Thus does the female mind unconsciously skirt along the verge of eternity. Our voyage up here was most disastrous, calms, squalls, head sea, waterspouts of rain, hurricane weather all about, and we in the midst of the hurricane season, when even the hopeful builder and owner of the yacht had pronounced these seas unfit for her. We ran out of food, and were quite given up for lost in Honolulu: people had ceased to speak to Belle about the *Casco*, as a deadly subject.

But the perils of the deep were a part of the programme; and though I am very glad to be done with them for a while and comfortably ashore, where a squall does not matter a snuff to any one, I feel pretty sure I shall want to get to sea again ere long. The dreadful risk I took was financial, and double headed: First, I had to sink a lot of money in the cruise, and if I didn't get health, how was I to get it back? I have got health to a wonderful extent; and as I have the most interesting matter for my book, bar accidents, I ought to get all I have laid out and a profit. But second (what I own I never considered till too late) there was the danger of collisions, of damages and heavy repairs, of disablement, towing and salvage; indeed the cruise might have turned round and cost me double. Nor will this danger be quite over, till I hear the yacht is in San Francisco; for though I have shaken the dust of her deck from my feet, I fear (as a point of law) she is still mine till she gets there.[2]

From my point of view, up to now, the cruise has been a wonderful success. I never knew the world was so amusing. On the last voyage we had grown so used to sea life that no one wearied, though it lasted a full month; except Fanny who is always ill.[3] All the time, our visits to the islands have been more like dreams than realities: the people, the life, the beachcombers, the old stories and songs I have picked up, so interesting; the climate, the scenery and (in some places) the women so beautiful. The women are handsomest in Tahiti; the men in the Marquesas: both as fine types as can be imagined. Lloyd reminds me, I have not told you one characteristic incident of the cruise from a semi-naval point of view. One night we were going ashore in Anaho Bay; the most awful noise on deck, the breakers distinctly audible in the cabin; and there I had to sit below, entertaining in my best style a negroid native chieftain much the worse for rum! You can imagine the evening's pleasures.

This naval report on cruising in the South Seas would be incomplete without one other trait. On our voyage up here, I came one day into the dining room, the hatch in the floor was open, the ship's boy was below with a baler and two of the hands were carrying buckets as for a fire: this meant that the pump had ceased working.

One stirring day was that in which we sighted Hawaii. It blew fair but very strong; we carried jib, fore sail and mainsail, all single-reefed, and she carried her lee rail under water and flew. The swell, the heaviest I have ever been out in − I tried in vain to estimate the height, I am sure *at least*

[2] MIS recorded that the *Casco* sailed for San Francisco on 14 February.
[3] In a letter of 20 January 1889 MIS noted: 'Fanny suffers a good deal from sea-sickness and declares that when only she reaches Honolulu, she is going *ashore* and never means to leave it again'.

fifteen feet – came tearing after us about a point and a half off the wind. We had the best hand – old Louis – at the wheel; and really he did nobly, and had noble luck, for it never caught us once. At times, it seemed we must have it; Louis would look over his shoulder with the queerest look, and draw down his neck into his shoulders; and then it missed us somehow, and only sprays came over our quarter, turning the little outside lane of deck into a mill race as deep as to the cockpit coamings. I never remember anything more delightful and exciting. Pretty soon after, we were lying absolutely becalmed under the lee of Hawaii, of which we had been warned; and the Captain never confessed he had done it on purpose, but when accused, he smiled. Really I suppose he did quite right, for we stood committed to a dangerous race; and to bring her to the wind would have been rather a heart-sickening manoeuvre.

This naval report I should think would interest Walter Simpson, Baxter, Colvin, perhaps Walter Pollock, perhaps Hole.[4] Anyway, as I shall never write the stuff again, I wish you would start these two sheets round to any friend whom you think it would amuse. O, I feel sure Frewen Jenkin and his mother would like to see them.

Address Scribner's Sons, New York, unless sure to reach here before April 1st.

To Charles Baxter

[*Postmark 8*] *March 1889*   *Honolulu*

My dear Charles, At last I have the accounts: the doer has done excellently and in the words of Galpin,[1] 'I reciprocate every step of your behaviour.' Only upon one point would I protest, in re my mother. (1) The house is hers; she might live in it, if she chose and pay no rent to the Trust: therefore if she lets it, the rent is hers and (in my contention) the Trust has nothing to do with it. But (2) suppose you have some argument I do not follow which disposes of No. 1, I cannot see how you are to charge her with the rent received for the use of the house during the winter *before* my father's death. It was let then to meet extra expenses in the south; the extra expenses were incurred by my father; why then is my mother to be charged with the covering sum? I see no answer to that anyway. And still if I am dull, and there should be a reason, I should like to make up my

---

[4] William B. Hole (1846–1917), the Edinburgh painter and etcher who had been a fellow-actor with RLS in the Jenkin theatricals. He provided drawings for the illustrated edition of *Kidnapped* (1887) and was working on *The Master of Ballantrae* (in its serialised form) for *Scribner's*. The illustrations to *The Master* appeared in the first American book edition and in later English editions.

[1] Thomas Dixon Galpin of Cassell's with whom RLS was corresponding about *The Master of Ballantrae*.

mother's money to what it was. Possibly we had better wait to decide this
till we meet, so that I can make sure I follow. – The £5 and £20 paid on
account of my mother is all right: let it slide. I used to embezzle from her:
turn about is fair play.

Quite right you were of course, about Bob, Henley, and the book of
verses.[2] Let Bob's interest slide, it's only an annoyance to him and
bookkeeping for your clerks: to me it would not make the change of a
hair. I send a letter for Bob in your care as I don't know his Liverpool
address,[3] by which (for he is to show you part of it) you will see we have
got out of this adventure – or hope to have – with wonderful fortune. I
have the retrospective horrors on me when I think of the liabilities I
incurred; but thank God, I think I'm in port again, and I have found one
climate in which I can enjoy life. Even Honolulu is too cold for me; but
the South Isles were a heaven upon earth to a poor catarrhal party like
Johns'one. We think, as Tahiti is too complete a banishment, to try
Madeira. It's only a week from England, good communications; and I
suspect in climate and scenery not unlike my own dear islands; in people,
alas, there can be no comparison. But friends could go; and I could come
in summer; so I should not be quite cut off.

Lloyd and I have finished a story, *The Wrong Box*. If it is not funny, I'm
sure I don't know what is.[4] I have split over writing it. Since I have been
here, I have been toiling like a galley slave: three numbers of *The Master*
to rewrite; five chapters of *The Wrong Box* to write and rewrite; and about
five hundred lines of a narrative poem to write rewrite and re-rewrite.
Now I have *The Master* waiting me for its continuation – two numbers
more: when that's done I shall breathe.

This spasm of activity has been chequered with champagne parties.
Happy and Glorious, *Hawaii Ponoi nana i Kou moi* (Native Hawaiians, dote
upon your monarch!) – Hawaiian God Save the King – (in addition to my
other labours I am learning the language with a native *moonshee*). Kalakaua
is a terrible companion; a bottle of fizz is like a glass of sherry to him; he
thinks nothing of five or six in an afternoon as a whet for dinner. Look
here, Van Laun, Edmonstone, Charles Mackay, and Sam Bough[5] – he
could have taken all four, one up, another down: as for you, you poor
creature, he could settle you before breakfast. You should see a photo-

[2] Baxter was paying an allowance (on behalf of RLS) to Bob and Henley.
[3] Bob was Professor of Fine Arts at University College, Liverpool 1889–93. The atmosphere of
genteel conformity was too much for him and he resigned.
[4] RLS had revised and rewritten eleven chapters of Lloyd's story *The Game of Bluff* and left them
with Scribner's. In Tahiti he asked Burlingame to send him a typed copy of these chapters
together with the rest of Lloyd's original. In Honolulu, RLS renamed the story *The Wrong Box*,
revised the typescript, and rewrote the remaining five chapters from Lloyd's original. He sent it
to Burlingame on 5 March asking $5000 for 'all rights in the States' and adding, 'Yachting is a
great pleasure, but expensive.'
[5] Henri Van Laun (1820–96), author and teacher of French, translator of Molière's plays. He was

graph of our party after an afternoon with H.H.M.: my! what a crew! The proud drunkenness of Lloyd, the soppy swan-neckery of R.L.S., my mother – let us draw a veil, till you see it. Yours ever affectionately

Robert Louis Stevenson

I enclose one of many Income Tax things I have received. What's owing?

[*Fanny adds*]

My dear friend, This is only to show that my heart is in the right place, though my body is not. It, alas, should [be] in Tautira with my well-beloved 'savages', as they are fond of calling themselves. I am really better than I have been for some time. I *believe* the thing in my throat is gone, though I am nervous about it, and imagine that it is coming back when it is not.[6] Louis is wonderful, and Lloyd is quite the literary man. It was very saddening to hear of poor Mrs Henley's death,[7] and most unexpected. I hope she passed away with as much comfort as one may. She had not too much in life. I had meant to write to Anna, congratulating her on the new acquisition,[8] but somehow I can't write letters. My love to you all.

F.V. de G.S.

★ *To Adelaide Boodle*

6 April 1889[1]   *Honolulu*

My dear Miss Boodle, The family seems to say I am the man, or rather, mine is the voice; for as to gratitude, we are all in a concatenation. Nobody writes a better letter than my Gamekeeper;[2] so gay, so pleasant,

---

French master at the Edinburgh Academy, 1869–74. In 'Memoirs of Himself' (dictated at Vailima) RLS described Van Laun and his drinking companions: 'that big, gross, fat, black, hyperbolical, and entirely good-humoured adventurer, Van Laun . . . I suppose he has long since gone, where most of his old friends had preceded him, to the paradise of drinkers. There he will find his former afternoon society complete; poor Sam Bough, poor Edmonstone the publisher, poor Mackay the jeweller, all victims to the kindly jar.'

[6] Before leaving San Francisco Fanny had had an operation for the removal of a throat tumour.

[7] Emma Henley (Henley's mother) died 25 October 1888, aged sixty, of heart disease and chronic bronchitis. RLS's poem 'In Memoriam E.H.' was published in the *Scots Observer*, 11 May 1889 and reprinted in *Songs of Travel*.

[8] Henley's daughter, Margaret Emma Henley – 'The Golden Child' – was born on 4 September 1888. She died on 11 February 1894 and the light went out of his life. In his letter of sympathy RLS wrote: 'There is one thing I have always envied you, *and that I envy you still.*'

[1] Although dated 6 April most of this letter must have been written on Sunday 7 April. MIS recorded that this was Lloyd's twenty-first birthday and there was a guest at dinner. Breakfast with the King at the Palace was on 8 April.

[2] When the Stevensons left Skerryvore, Fanny asked Miss Boodle to keep an eye on the pigeons and the stray cats which visited the garden. RLS asked her to send weekly letters – 'Thus these

so engagingly particular, answering (by some delicate instinct) all the
questions she suggests. It is a shame you should get such a poor return as
I can make, from a mind essentially and originally incapable of the art
epistolary. I would let the paper-cutter[3] take my place; but I am sorry to
say the little wooden seaman did after the manner of seamen and deserted
in the Societies. The place he seems to have stayed at – seems, for his
absence was not observed till we were near the equator – was Tautira; and
I assure you he displayed good taste, Tautira being as 'nigh hand heaven'
as a paper-cutter or anybody has a right to expect.

I think all our friends will be very angry with us, and I give the grounds
of their probable displeasure bluntly: we are not coming home for another
year. My mother returns next month.[4] Fanny, Lloyd and I push on again
among the islands on a trading schooner the *Equator*.[5] first to the Gilbert
group, which we shall have an opportunity to explore thoroughly; then if
occasion serve to the Marshalls and Carolines; and if occasion (or money)
fail, to Samoa, and back to Tahiti. I own we are deserters, but we have
excuses. You cannot conceive how these climates agree with the wretched
house-plant of Skerryvore; he wonders to find himself sea-bathing, and
cutting about the world loose, like a grown-up person. They agree with
Fanny too, who does not suffer from her rheumatism; and with Lloyd
also. And the interest of the islands is endless. And the sea, though I own
it is a fearsome place, is very delightful. We had applied for places in the
American missionary ship, the *Morning Star*, but this trading schooner is a
far preferable idea, giving us more time and a thousandfold more liberty;
so we determined to cut off the missionaries with a shilling.[6]

Do you know that I got the *Mystery in Scarlet* after all? I wonder if
through you? But I got it, and liked it hugely – far better than I ever
expected; and see that Mr Errym (query Merry) had a genuine influence
on me, and wish I had his talent, above all in sketching girls.[7]

---

chronicles became "Reports of the Skerryvore Preserves"; the sender turned automatically into
a gamekeeper, and the receiver into an absentee squire' (Boodle, *RLS and his Sine Qua Non*).
[3] The gift made by Miss Boodle when RLS left Skerryvore; RLS made several references to it in
other letters to her.
[4] MIS left Honolulu on the steamer *Umatilla* on 10 May.
[5] The trading schooner *Equator* (owned by Wightman Brothers, San Francisco) had survived on
the high seas the hurricane which devastated the warships in Apia harbour on 15–16 March and
had been the first ship to reach Apia. It had gone on to Tutuila to advise the *Alameda* (bound
from Australia to San Francisco) and John Wightman Jr had transferred to the *Alameda* which
reached Honolulu on 6 April. RLS must have made the chartering arrangements with him.
[6] Lloyd later recalled how they had all dreaded the 'frightful' drawbacks of a voyage on the
Morning Star: 'no smoking, not a drink, no profanity; church, nightly prayer-meetings, and an
enforced intimacy with the most uncongenial of people'.
[7] In his essay 'Popular Authors' (*Scribner's*, July 1888), RLS celebrated near-forgotten authors,
among them Malcolm J. Errym, pseudonym of James Malcolm Rymer (1804–?82), prolific
author of penny-dreadfuls, including *Varney the Vampire* (1847). RLS had asked if any reader
could send him a copy of his favourite Errym novel, *The Mystery in Scarlet* (1850).

The Sandwich Islands do not interest us very much; we live here, oppressed with civilisation, and look for good things in the future. But it would surprise you if you came out tonight from Honolulu (all shining with electric lights, and all in a bustle from the arrival of the mail, which is to carry you these lines) and crossed the long wooden causeway along the beach, and came out on the road through Kapiolani park, and seeing a gate in the palings, with a tub of goldfish by the wayside, entered casually in. The buildings stand in three groups by the edge of the beach, where an angry little spitfire sea continually spirts and thrashes with impotent irascibility; the big seas breaking further out upon the reef. The first is a small house, with a very large summer parlour, or *lanai* as they call it here, roofed, but practically open. There you will find the lamps burning and the family sitting about the table, dinner just done; my mother, my wife, Lloyd, Belle, my wife's daughter, Joe Strong, her husband, Austin her child, and tonight (by way of rarity) a guest. All about the walls our South Sea curiosities, war clubs, idols, pearl shells, stone axes, etc.; and the walls are only a small part of a *lanai*, the rest being glazed or latticed windows, or mere open space. You will see there no sign of the Squire, however; and being a person of a humane disposition, you will only glance in over the balcony railing at the merry-makers in the summer parlour, and proceed further afield after the Exile. You look round, there is beautiful green turf, many trees of an outlandish sort that drop thorns – (look out, if your feet are bare – but I beg your pardon you have not been long enough in the South Seas) – and many oleanders in full flower. The next group of buildings is ramshackle, and quite dark; you make out a coach-house door, and look in – only some cocoanuts; you try round to the left and come to the sea front, where Venus and the moon are making luminous tracks on the water, and a great swell rolls and shines on the outer reef; and here is another door – (all these places open from the outside) – and you go in, and find photography, tubs of water, negatives steeping, a tap, and a chair and an ink-bottle, where my wife is supposed to write; round a little further, a third door, entering which you find a picture of Joe Strong's upon the easel and a table sticky with paints; a fourth door admits you to a sort of court, where there is a hen sitting – I believe on a fallacious egg. No sign of the Squire in all this. But right opposite the studio door you have observed a third little house, from whose open door lamplight streams and makes hay of the strong moon-light shadows. You had supposed it made no part of the grounds, for a fence runs round it lined with oleander; but as the Squire is nowhere else, is it not just possible he may be here. It is a grim little wooden shanty, cobwebs bedeck it; friendly mice inhabit its recesses; the mailed cockroach walks upon the wall, so also, I regret to say, the scorpion: herein are two pallet beds, two mosquito curtains, strung to the pitch-boards of the roof,

two tables laden with books and manuscripts, three chairs, and (in one of
the beds) one Squire busy writing to yourself, as it chances, and just as this
moment somewhat bitten by mosquitoes. He has just set fire to the insect
powder, and will be all right in no time; but just now he contemplates
large white blisters, and would like to scratch them, but knows better. The
house is not bare; it has been inhabited by *Kanakas* and (you know what
children are!) the bare wood walls are pasted over with pages from the
Graphic, *Harper's Weekly*, etc. The floor is matted, and I am bound to say
the matting is filthy. There are two windows and two doors, one of which
is condemned; on the panels of that last a sheet of paper is pinned up, and
covered with writing. I cull a few plums.

'A duck-hammock for each person.

A patent organ like the commandant's at Tai-o-hae.

Cheap and bad cigars for presents.

Revolvers.

Permanganate of potass.

Liniment for the head and sulphur.

Fine tooth-comb.'

What do you think this is? Simply life in the South Seas foreshortened.
These are a few of our *desiderata* for the next trip, which we jot down as
they occur.

There I have really done my best and tried to send something like a
letter: one letter, in return for all your dozens. Pray remember us all to
yourself, Mrs Boodle, the rest of your house, Mary Ann and her chicks,
and the blonde Agnes.[8] I do hope your mother will be better when this
comes. I shall write and give you a new address when I have made up my
mind as to the most probable, and I do beg you will continue to write
from time to time and give us airs from home. That you will keep your
eye on our poor Watts folk I know very well; and if anything goes far
amiss with that estimable crowd, please apply to Charlie Baxter, who has
a discretion from me, and will not turn a cold ear to a proper tale of
remedial distress in that quarter. Tomorrow (think of it) I must be off by
a quarter to eight to drive in to the palace and breakfast with his Hawaiian
Majesty at 8.30; I shall be dead indeed. Please give my news to Scott:[9] I

---

[8] Mary Ann Watts, the housekeeper at Skerryvore and her daughter, the young maidservant
Agnes. RLS had written to both Baxter and Miss Boodle in May 1888 instructing that provision
be made for Mrs Watts (who had a drunken husband) in case of need.

[9] Thomas Bodley Scott (1851–1924). RLS's doctor at Bournemouth, took up general practice in
Bournemouth about 1876 and spent the rest of his life there, dying during his term of office as
Mayor of Bournemouth. In his dedication of *Underwoods* to many doctors, RLS paid a special
tribute to 'one name I have kept on purpose to the last, because it is a household word with
me . . . that of my friend Thomas Bodley Scott'.

trust he is better; give him my warm regards, he is a good fellow. To you we all send all kinds of things, and I am the absentee Squire

Robert Louis Stevenson

To James Bain[1]

April 1889   *Honolulu*

Dear Mr Bain, I pray you in the first instance to continue keeping up my serials against my return which is relegated to 1890. Present your accounts to Mr Baxter, Edinburgh, with whom I believe you are already in relation.

In the second place, and this is more important, I wish you to get *Treasure Island, Kidnapped, The New Arabian Nights* (*1st Series*) and *The Merry Men*: the two first illustrated; to have them bound for me, as you know how and no man better, and to have on the binding of each, these words,

> H.R.H.
> Kaiulani   (KAIULANI)
> from
> R.L.S.

elegantly imprimpted.

The little lady in question is the 'Little Princess' of Hawaii[2] – a pretty and engaging Royal Highness; and as soon as you can get the books bound, they are to be sent to this address: H.R.H. Princess Kaiulani, c/o Mrs T.R. Walker, c/o T.H. Davies Esq.,[3] Sundown, Hesketh Park, Liverpool.

Pray give this trivial affair (to which I attach a real importance) your kind attention.

---

[1] James Bain (1829–94), RLS's regular bookseller at No. 1 Haymarket, London.

[2] Princess Victoria Kaiulani (born 1875) was the daughter of Archibald Scott Cleghorn (1835–1910), an Edinburgh-born Scot, originally a merchant in Honolulu and later Collector General of Customs, and Princess Miriam Likelike (1851–87), a sister of King Kalakaua. RLS was a frequent visitor to Cleghorn's beautiful estate of Ainahau in Waikiki and often sat talking to the Princess Kaiulani under a giant banyan tree. Kaiulani left Honolulu on 10 May (on the same steamer as MIS) in the care of Mrs Thomas Rain Walker, wife of the British Vice-Consul, to go to school in England. RLS commemorated their friendship in the verses 'Written in April to Kaiulani in the April of her age' beginning 'Forth from her land to mine she goes' (*Songs of Travel*, XXXI). Kaiulani wrote to RLS on 7 August 1889, thanking him for the books: 'I hope that by the time I have finished school I will be able to fulfil the position you offered me as your secretary.' The Princess, who became heir-apparent after Kalakaua's death, returned to Hawaii in 1897 and died there of pneumonia in 1899.

[3] Theo H. Davies, whose firm was one of the largest sugar-factors and merchants in Honolulu, acted as Kaiulani's guardian in England.

I wish this letter to serve you also as a letter of introduction to Mr Cleghorn, the father of the little lady, who may possibly turn up next year, and desire some books. If you can help him in any way I shall be the better pleased.

These are far latitudes from which I address you; not at all within hail of the Haymarket; but you will gather that your name, the name of the only bookseller in the world – so far as I know the world, has arisen in conversation even in the islands of Hawaii. A year or so from now I shall hope to drop in for one of my usual passing visits; but between whiles I trust I shall have been in strange places. I am, dear Mr Bain, Yours truly

Robert Louis Stevenson

To Will H. Low

Highly Private and Confidential
[? *20 May 1889*]   [*Honolulu*]

My dear Low, As you (and I) anticipated the little trouble with the Scribs has upon my side quite blown over. They have accepted my terms; it appears that they did not mean, or I did not understand, their letter; and as I wrote mine to them upon an *open verdict*, to meet either emergency, and have since written to assure Burlingame of my affectionate regard (a sentiment which I really entertain) I trust all is for the best in the Best of POSSIBLE worlds.[1] I assure you I am very sensible of what I owe to their upright and liberal views; besides I am personally (as declared above) highly partial to my Burlingame;[2] and these little equinoctial gales 'keep me warm and make them grow'. I am sorry they should ever occur for my own sake, and theirs: they are maladies incidental to correspondence, I dare say.[3] So that '*autant en emportent les vents!*' is my motto; and I will spare you any reference to *les vieilles lunes* or *les neiges d'antan*[4] out of consideration for your age and general bearing. I should not have written

---

[1] Scribner's had originally offered $5000 for *The Wrong Box* including all rights in both countries. RLS had written an indignant reply to Burlingame accepting this sum for the American rights only, and asking Burlingame, if he did not agree, to hand the MS to Low. At the same time he asked Low, in that event, to take the MS to Longmans for them to handle in both countries; Longmans had already agreed to publish the English edition. Before RLS's letter had been sent Burlingame had in fact already written offering with some misgiving $5000 for the American rights only.

[2] In his letter of 28 April (to which this is a reply) Low had referred to Burlingame's distress over the misunderstanding: 'Of one thing, which you probably know as well as I, I can assure you that independently of business relations Burlingame . . . [has] a hearty personal regard for you.'

[3] RLS deleted: 'and if they [the Scribs *written above*] had a faint air of trying to take an advantage of me, I daresay I have had such an air myself, in the course of my life, and meant no harm'.

[4] The first quotation is from Villon's '*Ballade des Seigneurs du Temps Jadis*' (the second ballade '*en vieil françois*') and the third from his '*Ballade des Dames du Temps Jadis*'.

even so much, and you see I have put out a part of it; these are matters for speech, not correspondence; to touch on them with the careless pen of the letter writer, is to prepare fresh quarrels; and I make no doubt that both Burlingame and I wrote otherwise than we intended. Assure him however he is a man whom I truly like; and it would make a hole in my daily comfort if I fell out with him even slightly. – The goods have come; many daughters have done virtuously, but thou excellest them all,[5] O Wilhelmina Low! J.D. Strong is crazy over his water colours: the chromos seem calculated to debase art in the South Seas for the next half century; we are all highly obliged.[6] – I have at length finished *The Master*; it has been a sore cross to me; but now he is buried, his body's under hatches – his soul, if there is any hell to go to, gone to Hell;[7] and I forgive him; it is harder to forgive Burlingame for having induced me to begin the publication, or myself for suffering the induction. – Yes, I think Hole has done finely; it will be one of the most adequately illustrated books of our generation; he gets the note, he tells the story – *my* story: I know only one failure – the Master standing on the beach. – You must have a letter for me at Sydney till further notice. Remember me to Mrs Will H., the Godlike Sculptor,[8] and any of the faithful: Faxon first of all.[9] What a comfort it is when a man's a gentleman! If you want to cease to be a republican, see my little Kaiulani, as she goes through – but she is gone already. You will die a red: I wear the colours of that little royal maiden: *Nous allons chanter à la ronde, si vous voulez!*[10] only she is not blonde by

---

[5] Proverbs 31:29.

[6] As he explained in his letter of 28 April, Low had sent, at Lloyd's request, 'a lot of material and chromos galore. He can ruin the artistic taste of the countless future generations of Polynesia with 'em.'

[7] Cf. the last two lines of Dibdin's 'Tom Bowling': 'For, though his body's under hatches, /His soul is gone aloft'.

[8] Saint-Gaudens. Low explains that during a conversation between RLS, Low and Saint-Gaudens, reference had been made to Saint-Gaudens' accidental avoidance of the nude. To fortify him in his resolve to repair the omission, Low quoted from Emerson's poem 'Painting and Sculpture':

> The sinful painter drapes his goddess warm,
> Because she still is naked, being dressed:
> The godlike sculptor will not so deform
> Beauty, which limbs and flesh enough invest.

The lines took RLS's fancy and thereafter he referred to Saint-Gaudens as the 'God-like sculptor'.

[9] William Bailey Faxon (1849–1941), New York artist. He had visited RLS in his New York hotel and accompanied Low on visits to Manasquan.

[10] Cf. the second verse of Fortunio's song in Act II, scene 3 of Alfred de Musset's comedy *Le Chandelier* (1835):

> 'Nous allons chanter à la ronde,
> Si vous voulez,
> Que j'adore, et qu'elle est blonde
> Comme les blés.'

The song was set to music by Offenbach when the comedy was first performed at the Comédie-Française (of which he was musical director) in 1850.

several chalks, though she is but a half blood, and the wrong half Edinburgh Scots like mysel'. But, O Low, I love the Polynesian: this civilisation of ours is a dingy, ungentlemanly business; it drops out too much of man, and too much of that the very beauty of the poor beast: who has his beauties in spite of Zola and Co. As usual here is a whole letter with no news; I am a bloodless, inhuman dog; and no doubt Zola is a better correspondent. Long live your fine old English Admiral – yours I mean – the U.S.A. one at Samoa;[11] I wept tears and loved myself and mankind when I read of him: he is not too much civilised. And there was Gordon too; and there are others, beyond question. But if you could live, the only white folk, in a Polynesian village; and drink that warm light *vin du pays* of human affection, and enjoy that simple dignity of all about you[12] – I will not gush, for I am now in my fortieth year, which seems highly unjust, but there it is, Mr Low. And the Lord Enlighten your affectionate

R.L.S.

To Sidney Colvin

[*Early June 1889*][1]   [*Honolulu*]

My dear Colvin, I am just home after twelve days' journey to Molokai, seven of them at the leper settlement, where I can only say that the sight of so much courage, cheerfulness and devotion, strung me too high to mind the infinite pity and horror of the sights. I used to ride over from Kalawao to Kalaupapa (about three miles across the promontory, the cliff-wall, ivied with forest and yet inaccessible from steepness, on my left) go

---

[11] Lewis Ashfield Kimberly (1830–1902), Rear Admiral in the US Navy, whose three warships were wrecked in the Samoan hurricane; he led the cheers from his flagship *Trenton* as the British *Calliope* steamed to safety.

[12] RLS spent a week (27 April–3 May) at Hookena on the Kona Coast, the west coast of the island of Hawaii in the home of an ex-judge. He wrote to Baxter on 9 May:

> I have just been a week away alone on the lee coast of Hawaii, the only white creature in many miles, riding 5 1/2 hours one day, living with a native, seeing poor lepers shipped off to Molokai, hearing native causes and giving my opinion as *amicus curiae* as to the interpretation of a statute in English: a lovely week among God's best – at least God's sweetest works – Polynesians. It has bettered me greatly. If I could only stay there the time that remains, I could get my work done and be happy; but the care of a large, costly, and no' just preceesely forrit-gaun family keeps me in vile Honolulu where I am always out of sorts, amidst heat and cold and cesspools and beastly *haoles*. What is a *haole*? You are one; and so, I am sorry to say, am I. After so long a dose of whites, it was a blessing to get among Polynesians again even for a week.

[1] RLS sailed from Honolulu on 21 May to visit the leper settlement on the island of Molokai. On landing at Kalaupapa the next morning he went, partly on foot and partly on horseback, to Kalawao to stay at the guest house there.

to the Sisters' Home[2] which is a miracle of neatness, play a game of croquet with seven leper girls (90° in the shade), get a little old-maid meal served me by the Sisters, and ride home again, tired enough but not too tired. The girls all have dolls, and love dressing them. You who know so many ladies delicately clad, and they who know so many dressmakers, please make it known it would be an acceptable gift to send scraps for doll dress-making to The Reverend Sister Maryanne, Bishop Home, Kalaupapa, Molokai, Hawaiian Islands.

I have seen sights that cannot be told, and heard stories that cannot be repeated: yet I never admired my poor race so much, nor (strange as it may seem) loved life more, than in the settlement. A horror of moral beauty broods over the place: that's like bad Victor Hugo, but it is the only way I can express the sense that lived with me all these days. And this even though it was in great part Catholic, and my sympathies flew never with so much difficulty as towards Catholic virtues. The pass-book kept with heaven stirs me to anger and laughter. One of these Sisters calls the place 'The ticket office to heaven'. Well, what is the odds? They do their darg, and do it with kindness and efficiency incredible; and we must take folk's virtues as we find them, and love the better part. Of old Damien,[3] whose weaknesses and worse perhaps I heard fully, I think only the more. It was a European peasant: dirty, bigoted, untruthful, unwise, tricky, but superb with generosity, residual candour and fundamental good humour: convince him he had done wrong (it might take hours of insult) and he would undo what he had done and like his corrector better. A man, with all the grime and paltriness of mankind; but a saint and hero all the more for that. The place as regards scenery, is grand, gloomy and bleak. Mighty mountain walls descending sheer along the whole face of the island into a sea unusually deep; the front of the mountain ivied and furred with clinging forest, one viridescent cliff: about half way from east to west, the low, bare, stony promontory edged in between the cliff and the ocean: the two little towns (Kalawao and Kalaupapa) seated on either side of it, as bare almost as bathing machines upon a beach; and the population – gorgons and chimaeras dire.[4] All this tear of the nerves I bore admirably;

[2] The Home for leper girls at Kalaupapa was founded by Charles R. Bishop, a wealthy Honolulu banker. It was run by a group of Franciscan Sisters of Syracuse, New York, led by Mother Marianne Kopp (1836–1918), an American (of German birth) who went to Molokai in 1888 and served there for the rest of her life. On his arrival RLS handed her the poem 'To Mother Maryanne', published in slightly revised form as *Songs of Travel* XXXII. After his return to Honolulu, RLS sent the Home a grand piano.

[3] Joseph de Veuster – Father Damien (1840–89), the famous Belgian Roman Catholic missionary priest – went to Molokai in 1873 and devoted the rest of his life to caring for the lepers and improving conditions at the settlement. Damien had died from leprosy on 15 April.

[4] 'Gorgons, and Hydras, and Chimaeras dire' – Milton, *Paradise Lost*, II, 628.

and the day after I got away, rode twenty miles along the opposite coast and up into the mountains: they call it twenty, I am doubtful of the figures: I should guess it nearer twelve; but let me take credit for what residents allege; and I was riding again the day after.[5] So I need say no more about my health. Honolulu does not agree with me at all; I am always out of sorts there, with slight headache, blood to the head, constipation, etc.; I had a good deal of work to do and did it with miserable difficulty; and yet all the time I have been gaining strength as you see, which is highly encouraging. By the time I am done with this cruise I shall have the material for a very singular book of travels: masses of strange stories and characters, cannibals, pirates, ancient legends, old Polynesian poetry; never was so generous a farrago. I am going down now to get the story of a shipwrecked family, who were fifteen months on an island with a murderer: there is a specimen.[6] The Pacific is a strange place, the nineteenth century only exists there in spots; all round, it is a no man's land of the ages, a stir-about of epochs and races, barbarisms and civilisations, virtues and crimes.

It is good of you to let me stay longer, but if I had known how ill you were, I should be now on my way home.[7] I had chartered my schooner and made all arrangements before (at last) we got definite news. I feel highly guilty; I should be back to insult and worry you a little. Our address till further notice is to be c/o R. Towns & Co., Sydney. New South Wales, isn't it? That is final; I only got the arrangement made yesterday; but you may now publish it abroad. Give my love to George and Hester;[8] to yourself my dear fellow, we send (all of us) all that we have of affection and respect. When we did not know what was wrong, and feared there might be all kinds of trouble, Lloyd stopped drinking stout lest money should be wanted for you. *Sponte sua*, I knew nothing of it till the other day, or would have protested. I think you would like to know this; and how our whole house regards you from the oldest to the youngest – if

[5] After leaving the leper settlement on 28 May RLS travelled round the coast on board ship. He then went ashore and made a number of visits involving journeys on horseback. He rejoined the ship and arrived back in Honolulu on 1 June.

[6] Captain F.D. Walker and the crew of the *Wandering Minstrel* were shipwrecked on Midway Island in February 1888. They found a seaman, Adolph Jorgensen, already living there who had been abandoned by the shipwrecked crew of another vessel, *General Seigel*, when they escaped by boat, because they suspected him of murder. Walker and his crew were eventually rescued by Captain C. Johnson of the schooner *Norma*, who brought them to Honolulu on 6 April 1889. The story, which had strange undercurrents, gave RLS and Lloyd the germ of the plot for *The Wrecker*.

[7] RLS had been worried to find no letter from Colvin awaiting him on his arrival in Honolulu. Colvin appears to have had a serious breakdown in health and had been receiving treatment in Paris from Jean-Martin Charcot, the French physician famous for his study of nervous diseases.

[8] George and Hester Went. George Went (1819–93), is described by Colvin as 'my old faithful servant, as he had been my father's before me; no scholar, but one of the shrewdest of natural wits'.

Lloyd can be called young. One thing I have to beg; if money is wanted in any way, you are to go at once to Charles Baxter;[9] what do I care for money, my dear fellow? or what need you? It would be too hard, because neither you nor I are Skimpoles,[10] we should let any essential right be pretermitted for a mere appearance. Save yourself just now; spare yourself; save yourself till we meet again; and when we come to the Monument door, you will have made our family happy. Remember me to Mrs Sitwell; Henry James (who is a good fellow indeed, and a man that I find one grows to love) and William Archer, if you see him. It is strange, I think these are the best of my London friends; and both (the men I mean) quite new – O, I did not mean to exclude Meredith or Lang. And say something kind to Gosse: *poverino*. Here is a lot of copy; I will shut up for the meantime.

To James Payn

13 June 1889   *Honolulu*

My dear James Payn, I get sad news of you, here, at my off-setting for further voyages;[1] I wish I could say what I feel. Sure there was never any man less deserved this calamity; for I have heard you speak time and again, and I remember nothing that was unkind, nothing that was untrue, nothing that was not helpful, from your lips. It is the ill-talkers that should hear no more. God knows I know no word of consolation; but I do feel your trouble. You are the more open to letters now; let me talk to you for two pages; I have nothing but happiness to tell; and you may bless God you are a man so sound-hearted that (even in the freshness of your calamity) I can come to you with my own good fortune unashamed – and secure of sympathy. It is a good thing to be a good man, whether deaf or whether dumb; and of all our fellow craftsmen (whom yet they count a jealous race) I never knew one but gave you the name of honesty and kindness: come to think of it gravely, this is better than the finest hearing. We are all on the march to deafness, blindness, and all conceivable and fatal disabilities; we shall not all get there with a report so good. – My

---

[9] Colvin's brother Bazett had gambled away all the family money and left his mother destitute, save for what Colvin could provide. RLS agreed to help him keep up his insurances. From 1889 Baxter appears to have paid (on RLS's behalf) an annual premium of £137 on Colvin's life assurance policy of £2000 to provide for his mother in the event of his death. Before he sailed in the *Casco* RLS had told Baxter that help had to be provided if necessary – '*however I may have to raise the money to do it with*'.

[10] Harold Skimpole, the selfish irresponsible character in Dickens's *Bleak House* who sponges on his friends.

[1] Colvin notes that the 'sad news' was Payn's 'ill-health and increasing deafness'.

good news is a health astonishingly reinstated. This climate; these voyagings; these landfalls at dawn; new islands peaking from the morning bank; new, forested harbours; new, passing alarms of squalls and surf; new interests of gentle natives, – the whole tale of my life is better to me than any poem. I am fresh just now from the saddest sojourn on this beautiful earth: a week at the leper settlement of Molokai, playing croquet with seven leper girls, sitting and yarning with old, blind, leper beachcombers in the hospital, sickened with the spectacle of abhorrent suffering and deformation amongst the patients, touched to the heart by the sight of lovely and effective virtues in their helpers: no stranger time have I ever had, nor any so moving; I do not think it a little thing to be deaf, God knows, and God defend me from the same! – but to be a leper, or one of the self-condemned, how much more awful! and yet there is a way there also. 'There are Molokais everywhere,' said Mr Dutton,[2] Father Damien's dresser; you are but new landed in yours; and my dear and kind adviser, I wish you, with all my soul, that patience and courage which you will require. Think of me meanwhile on a trading schooner bound for the Gilbert Islands, thereafter for the Marshalls, with a diet of fish and cocoanut before me; a barrel-organ (Mrs Stevenson); a magic lantern; a flageolet (Herr Stevenson); a guitar (Signor Strong, my son-in-law) and a talopatch[3] (Mr Osbourne, my stepson) – possibly a Chinese fiddle (Ah Foo – my Chinese servant)[4] to make up my band – bound on a cruise of – well, of investigation to what islands we can reach, and to get (some day or other) to Sydney – where a letter addressed in the care of R. Towns & Co., will find me sooner or later; and if it contains any good news, whether of your welfare or the courage with which you bear the contrary, will do me good. Yours affectionately (although so near a stranger)

Robert Louis Stevenson

---

[2] Ira Barnes ('Brother Joseph') Dutton (1843–1931), an American who served in the Civil War and became a Roman Catholic convert in 1883. He went to Molokai in 1886 and spent the rest of his long life in devoted service to the lepers.

[3] A ukulele. Fanny wrote to Colvin on 21 May: 'Lloyd, also takes a native instrument, something like a banjo, called a taropatch fiddle.'

[4] Ah Foo (sometimes spelled Ah Fu) joined the *Casco* in the Marquesas (when the previous cook was discharged for drunkenness). He stayed on with RLS (to whom he was devoted) in Hawaii and on the *Equator*.

XIII. PACIFIC VOYAGES:
THE CRUISE OF THE EQUATOR;
SAMOA AND SYDNEY;
THE CRUISE OF THE JANET NICOLL
June 1889–September 1890

The *Equator* sailed from Honolulu on 24 June 1889. Balfour describes the departure: 'At the last moment two fine carriages drove down at full speed to the wharf and there deposited King Kalakaua and a party of his native musicians. There was but a minute for good-bye and a parting glass [of champagne]. The king returned to shore and stood there waving his hand, while from the musicians, lined up on the very edge of the wharf, came the tender strains of a farewell.' The 'pigmy trading schooner' of sixty-two tons register, under the command of Captain Dennis (Denny) Reid – characterised by Fanny as 'a small, fiery Scotch-Irishman, full of amusing eccentricities, and always a most gay and charming companion' – spent the next six months voyaging through the Gilbert Islands, southward towards Samoa.

The Gilbert Islands (formerly also known as the Kingsmill Group and now called Kiribati) form a chain of some sixteen small, low-lying coral islands and atolls situated very close to the equator. At this time they were still governed by native kings or chiefs and were little visited save by trading vessels. Stevenson and his party spent two considerable periods ashore. The first of these was at Butaritari where the *Equator* arrived on 13 July and where the Stevensons lived, in the Wightman compound, for over a month; passing their evenings in the *Sans Souci* bar owned by Adolf Rick, a Prussian, who had lived at Butaritari for nine years as manager of the Wightman Brothers' trading store. From Butaritari the *Equator* travelled to Apaiang and thence to Apemama where the Stevensons made their second considerable stay ashore. RLS's own very full account of his experiences at both places is given in Parts IV and V of *In the South Seas*.

To Sidney Colvin

22 August 1889   Schooner Equator, *Apaiang Lagoon*[1]

My dear Colvin, The missionary ship is outside the reef trying (vainly) to get in; so I may have a chance to get a line off. I am glad to say I shall be home by June next for the summer, or we shall know the reason why. For God's sake, be well, and jolly for the meeting: I shall be, I believe, a different character from what you have seen this long while. This cruise is up to now a huge success, being interesting, pleasant and profitable. The beachcomber is perhaps the most interesting character here; the natives are very different, on the whole, from Polynesians: they are moral, stand-offish (for good reasons) and protected by a dark tongue. It is delightful to meet the few Hawaiians (mostly missionaries) that are dotted about, with their Italian *brio* and their ready friendliness. The whites are a strange lot, many of them good kind pleasant fellows, others quite the lowest I have ever seen even in the slums of cities. I wish I had time to narrate to you the doings and character of three white murderers (more or less proven) I have met;[2] one, the only undoubted assassin of the lot, quite gained my affection in his big home out of a wreck, with his New Hebrides wife in her savage turban of hair and yet a perfect lady, and his three adorable little girls in Rob Roy Macgregor dresses, dancing to the hand organ, per-forming circus on the floor with startling effects of nudity, and curling up together on a mat to sleep, three sizes, three attitudes, three Rob Roy dresses, and six little clenched fists: the murderer meanwhile brooding and gloating over his chicks, till your whole heart went out to him, and yet his crime on the face of it was dark: disembowelling in his own house, an old man of seventy and him drunk.

It is lunch time, I see, and I must close up with my warmest love to you. I wish you were here to sit upon me when required. Ah, if you were but a good sailor! I will never leave the sea I think; it is only there that a Briton lives; my poor grandfather, it is from him I inherit the taste, I fancy, and he was round many islands in his day; but I, please God, shall beat him at that before the recall is sounded. Would you be surprised to learn that I contemplate becoming a ship-owner?[3] I do; but it is a secret.

---

[1] A large atoll in the Gilbert Group. The *Equator* arrived there on 21 August and RLS and Fanny spent the next night on shore.

[2] From 17–20 August the *Equator* was at the island of Mariki, where according to Lloyd they met Peter Grant 'the supposed poisoner – an ill-looking fellow enough'.

[3] Both Lloyd and Fanny relate RLS's project to buy a schooner, half-yacht and half-trader to be called the *Northern Light*. Fanny says that elaborate plans were made with the enthusiastic co-operation of Captain Reid (who was to command the vessel), but that RLS dropped the scheme after closer experience of the dishonest aspects of South Sea trading. The same project seems to be referred to in Lloyd's diary as the *Brig Skerryvore*.

Life is far better fun than people dream who fall asleep among the
chimney stacks and telegraph wires. Ever yours, my dear fellow

Robert Louis Stevenson

Love to Henry James and others near.

[*30 September 1889*]   '*Equator Town*', Apemama[4]

No *Morning Star* came, however: and so now I try to send this to you
by the schooner *J.L. Tiernan*. We have been about a month ashore,
camping out in a kind of town the king set up for us; on the idea that I
was really a 'Big Chief' in England. He dines with us sometimes and sends
up a cook for a share of our meals when he does not come himself. This
sounds like high living: alas, undeceive yourself. Salt junk is the mainstay;
a low island, except for cocoanuts, is just the same as a ship at sea: brackish
water, no supplies, and very little shelter.[5] The king is a great character; a
thorough tyrant, very much of a gentleman, a poet, a musician, a historian
or perhaps rather more a genealogist – it is strange to see him lying in his
house among a lot of wives (nominal wives) writing the History of
Apemama in an account book –; his description of one of his own songs,
which he sang to me himself, as 'about sweethearts, and trees and the sea
– and no true, all-the-same lie', seems about as compendious a definition
of lyric poetry as a man could ask. Timpanok is here the great attraction:
all the rest is heat and tedium, and villainous dazzle, and yet more
villainous mosquitoes. We are like to be here however many a long week
before we get away, and then Whither? A strange trade this voyaging: so
vague, so bound-down, so helpless. Fanny has been planting some vegetables, and we have actually onions and radishes coming up: ah, onion-
despiser, were you but awhile in a low island, how your heart would leap
at sight of a coster's barrow! I think I could shed tears over a dish of
turnips. No doubt we shall all be glad to say farewell to low islands; I
had near said forever. They are very tame; and I begin to read up the
directory, and pine for an island with a profile, a running brook, or were
it only a well among the rocks. The thought of a mango came to me early
this morning and set my greed on edge; but you do not know what a
mango is, so –

[4] According to Lloyd's diary, the *Equator* left Apaiang on 25 August and reached the island of
Apemama (or Abemama) on 30 August. RLS established friendly relations with the formidable
tyrant Tembinok' and he allowed the party to stay there while the *Equator* went off on trading
visits to other islands. Squalls and adverse winds delayed its return and at one point it was feared
that the ship had been lost. RLS's classic account of Tembinok' and life in Apemama must be
read in Part V of *In the South Seas*. Tembinok' died in 1891, and the following year the Gilberts
became a British Protectorate.
[5] In the South Seas the contrast is between the 'high' islands of volcanic origin, and the 'low'
islands – atolls of coral formation comprising a ring-shaped reef enclosing a lagoon.

I have been thinking a great deal of you and the Monument of late and even tried to get my thoughts into a poem, hitherto without success. God knows how you are: I begin to weary dreadfully to see you: well, in nine months, I hope; but that seems a long time. I wonder what has befallen me too, that flimsy part of me that lives (or dwindles) in the public mind; and what has befallen *The Master*,[6] and what kind of a Box *The Wrong Box* has been found?[7] It is odd to know nothing of all this. We had an old woman to do devil work for you about a month ago, in a Chinaman's house on Apaiang. (August 23rd or 24th) You should have seen the crone with a noble masculine face, like that of an old crone, a body like a man's (naked all but the feathery female girdle), knotting cocoanut leaves and muttering spells: Fanny and I, and the good captain of the *Equator*, and the Chinaman and his native wife and sister-in-law, all squatting on the floor about the sibyl; and a crowd of dark faces watching from behind her shoulder (she sat right in the doorway) and tittering aloud with strange, appalled, embarrassed laughter at each fresh adjuration. She informed us you were in England, not travelling and now no longer sick; she promised us a fair wind the next day, and we had it; so I cherish the hope she was as right about Sidney Colvin. If so, here's a blow for Blavatsky.[8]

The shipownering has rather petered out since I last wrote, and a good many other plans beside. For I have had trouble with my poor bad child (Joe Strong) and have had to reform my battalions.[9] People are unco' hard to help in this world; and particularly them that willnae help theirsels. I had to depose the creature from taking photographs any more; which (under the circumstances) would have killed a man of any virile pride. But a few days sullens, a sense of the blessedness of being idle, and a sop to his vanity in the shape of an order for a picture, have made all right for him, and I doubt if he feel much awkwardness – or any. Well, we have all our faults; at least I have plenty, which I dislike worse than Joe's, at times. Only he does no more business for, or with, me. I would rather pay him handsomely to keep hands off.

Health? Fanny very so-so: Lloyd laid up with the curse of these islands, a sore that will not heal: Joe peaked and pallid and unshaven; and I pretty

[6] After a great struggle RLS had completed *The Master of Ballantrae* on 20 May before leaving for Molokai; it was published in September.

[7] RLS sent the final instalment of proofs of *The Wrong Box* to Burlingame on 18 June, but Scribner's had already published the novel on 5 June without waiting for RLS's considerable revisions and corrections.

[8] Helena Petrovna Blavatsky (1831–91) founded the Theosophical Society in 1875. The Society for Psychical Research had shown that many of her miracles and claims of occult powers were fraudulent.

[9] Lloyd noted in his diary on 25 September an 'ugly and silly exhibition over the flashlight. Collapse of all our hope in our friend.' The next day he wrote: 'We tip the black-spot on J.D.S. with all its accompaniments. I take over the photograph business.'

right upon the whole, and getting through plenty work: I know not quite how, but it seems to me not bad and in places funny.

South Sea Yarns:[10]

1. *The Wrecker*   ⎫   by R.L.S.
2. *The Pearl Fisher* ⎬   and
3. *The Beachcombers* ⎭   Lloyd O.

The Pearl Fisher part done lies in Sydney. It is *The Wrecker* we are now engaged upon; strange ways of life, I think, they set forth: things that I can scarce touch upon, or even not at all, in my travel book; and the yarns are good I do believe. *The Pearl Fisher* is for the *New York Ledger*:[11] the yarn is a kind of *Monte Cristo* one. *The Wrecker* is the least good as a story, I think; but the characters seem to me good. *The Beachcombers* is more sentimental. These three scarce touch the outskirts of the life we have been viewing; a hot-bed of strange characters and incidents: Lord, how different from Europe or the Pallid States! Farewell. Heaven knows when this will get to you. I burn to be in Sydney and have news.

To his Mother

Schooner Equator, *at sea*
Sunday 1 December 1889   *240 miles from Samoa*

My dear Mother, We are drawing (we fondly hope) to the close of another voyage like that from Tahiti to Hawaii: we sailed from Butaritari on the 4th November,[1] and since then have lain becalmed under cataracts of rain, or kicked about in purposeless squalls. We were sixteen souls in this small schooner, eleven in the cabin; our confinement and over-crowding in the wet weather was excessive; we lost our foretopmast in a squall; the sails were continually being patched (we had but the one suit) and with all attention, we lost the jib topsail almost entirely and the staysail and main sail are far through. To complete the discomfort, we have carried a very wild weather-glass; a daily fall of fifteen-hundredths in four hours, followed by a corresponding rise, and on one occasion

---

[10] The title was duly given in the Edinburgh Edition to the group of stories which included *The Wrecker* and *The Ebb-Tide* (the final title for *The Pearl Fisher*). No more is heard of *The Beachcombers*.

[11] In March 1888 McClure had brought Robert Bonner, proprietor of the *New York Ledger*, to Saranac and RLS and Lloyd had agreed to write a story for the *Ledger*. Various works were projected, among them *Fighting the Ring* and *The Gaol Bird*, but they were soon abandoned. At Honolulu Lloyd began drafting *The Pearl Fisher* and his opening chapters were highly praised by RLS.

[1] Lloyd noted that the *Equator* came back on 19 October and that they left Apemama on the 25th. They briefly returned to Butaritari and had a 'big spree ashore'. Adolf Rick decided to sail with them to Samoa.

accompanied by the fall of the thermometer to 79° at noon, kept us on
the *qui-vive*. I wonder: are you already so far out of key with the South
Seas, that 79° at noon will seem warm to you? You should have seen the
great coats out! I myself wore two wool undershirts, a knitted waistcoat –
the gift of the king of Apemama, and a flannel blazer: and I was seriously
thinking of a flannel shirt, when the cold let up. My birthday was a great
event: Mr Rick, the agent of the firm at Butaritari, who makes on this trip
one of the eleven beings in the cabin, had his on the twelfth; so we had
two days festivity, champagne, music, the capture of sharks, dolphins and
skipjack – mighty welcome additions to our table; Ah Fu (at my elbow in
the traderoom door) begs me to add that two little land-birds joined the
ship and stayed some twenty hours. The log says, '13th. Throughout this
day dead calm with heavy rain; sometimes very light westerly airs; and
very strong easterly current.' Of course we had no observation, but our
position next day was 179° 35'E, 6° 58'N: which could not be far out, as
that was a calm also. On the evening of my birthday, all hands came in the
cabin to make me a compliment; the long American sailor (called *The
Fisherman's Child*, after a doleful ditty that he sings) was at the wheel:
compeared, Ta Toma, tall powerful Hawaiian, about twenty; Teu Tău,
Apaiang islander, perhaps thirteen; Charlie Selth, San Franciscan, of
Scotch origin, and very like our Agnes, fifteen; La, Honolulu stowaway,
perhaps thirteen; Georgie (called George Muggery Bowyer, Esq.)
Hawaiian, the ship's infant – age, perhaps nine – his little jacket shrunk
almost up to his nipples, his little breeches (once they were trousers)
leaving bare his knees below and a part of his hips above; how they stayed
on, nobody can guess. Both marines of the after guard were at table,
Fanny, Lloyd, Joe, and I; Captain Dennis Reid, Greenock, twenty-five;
Adolf Rick, Gallician, born in Prussia, forty-three; Paul Leonard, twenty-
eight, Prussian, known as the *Passenger to Mariki*[2] – towards which island,
like a will o' the wisp, he has been sailing in this *Equator* for nine weeks,
and will sail at least half as many more, and yet he has twice sighted it, and
then the wind failed, the westerly current took charge, and farewell
Mariki!; Tom Thomson, but his name is Ole Somethingson, Norwegian,
our mate, the tavern keeper on Mariki,[3] thirty. In the background, our

[2] Paul Hoeflich (also called Paul Leonard), a trader at Butaritari, took passage (with his merchandise) on the *Equator* for the nearby island of Marakei (spelled Mariki by RLS). Because of
contrary winds and heavy seas the schooner was unable to make a landing there and Hoeflich
was forced to travel on to Samoa. Here he bought a piece of land and, after settling his affairs
in the Gilberts, returned in 1891 and set up in business in Apia as a mineral water manufacturer;
he also had an estate near Vailima.

[3] Evidently a slip of the pen. 'Norwegian Tom' was, as RLS relates in *In the South Seas*, the bar-
keeper of the *Sans Souci* at Butaritari. His real name appears to have been Ole Thollesen. Fanny
says that a number of the crew including 'little Muggeree Bowyer' died of influenza on the
return voyage to San Francisco and that La the Hawaiian was swept overboard in a storm.

cook and steward, the great Ah Fu, Sana, China, and Murray MacCallum,[4] son of a Free Kirk minister on the Clyde – Mr Swan[5] has been in his father's house – aged maybe twenty. To this congregation, in the small, lamplighted, tossing cabin, nine feet square, with the compass and the binnacle lantern inside on a bracket on the after bulkhead, and the steersman looking down at us through an eyeshaped aperture, like an arrow loophole – add the incessant uproar of the tropic rain, the dripping leaks, the slush on the floor, and the general sense that we were nowhere in particular and drifting anywhere at large; and there is my thirty-ninth birthday! Charlie Selth was the spokesman of the crew, and made a neat little speech of a sentence; and you should have seen the row of brown faces, tailing down from Ta Toma to George. Georgie comes aft every morning to get from the Captain his 'Boia' – a thrashing; it is quite solemnly gone through on both sides, and I must candidly declare is the only duty the child has, or at least attends to. From this word, his family name of Bowyer has been deduced by the Heralds of the *Equator*; the middle name 'Muggery' is (something like) a native word; and the whole thing gives very much the effect of an heir to a baronetcy.

We had a fine alert once; a p.d.[6] reef ahead – three positions indicated, our own disputed – a very heavy sea running – the boats cleared and supplied with bread and water, our little packets made (medicines, papers, and woollen clothes) and the poor passenger for Mariki trying rather ruefully to insure his little all which was on board. It was rather fun going to bed that night; though (had we struck the reef) the boat voyage of four or five hundred miles would have been no joke.

Fanny has stood the hardships of this rough cruise wonderfully; but I do not think I could expose her to 'another of the same'. I have been first rate; though I am now done for lack of green food. Joe is, I fear, really ill; and Lloyd has bad sores in his leg. We shall send Joe on to Sydney by the first steamer; and L., Fanny and I shall stay on awhile (time quite vague) in Samoa. Write to Sydney. We shall turn up in England by May or June. Ever your affectionate son   R.L.S.

★   ★   ★

[4] Thomson Murray MacCallum (died in California 1957) was born in New Zealand and lived and worked in Samoa before making his way to San Francisco and securing the job of ship's cook on the *Equator*. Fanny described him as 'a runaway college lad who knew Greek, but was an indifferent hand with the pots and pans'. He and Ah Fu spent alternate weeks in the galley vying with each other to produce new dishes. In old age he recorded his memories of the voyage in *Adrift in the South Seas, including Adventures with Robert Louis Stevenson* (Los Angeles, 1934).
[5] William Swan (1818–94), Professor of Natural Philosophy at St Andrews University, 1859–80. He and TS were cousins (their mothers were sisters) and close and lifelong friends.
[6] Position doubtful.

The *Equator* reached Apia on 7 December 1889. Almost twenty years later, the Revd W.E. Clarke of the London Missionary Society remembered his first impressions of its passengers (though strangely he does not mention Joe Strong):

> Making my way along the 'Beach' – the sandy track with its long straggling line of 'stores' and drink saloons – I met a little group of three European strangers – two men and a woman. The latter wore a print gown, large gold crescent earrings, a Gilbert-island hat of plaited straw, encircled with a wreath of small shells, a scarlet silk scarf round her neck, and a brilliant plaid shawl across her shoulders; her bare feet were encased in white canvas shoes, and across her back was slung a guitar. The younger of her two companions was dressed in a striped pyjama suit – the undress costume of most European traders in these seas – a slouch straw hat of native make, dark blue sun-spectacles, and over his shoulders a banjo. The other man was dressed in a shabby suit of white flannels that had seen many better days, a white drill yachting cap with prominent peak, a cigarette in his mouth, and a photographic camera in his hand. Both the men were bare-footed. They had evidently, just landed from the little schooner now lying placidly at anchor, and my first thought was that, probably, they were wandering players *en route* to New Zealand, compelled by their poverty to take the cheap conveyance of a trading vessel.

Clarke soon learned that they were 'educated and refined gentlefolk' and he himself became the closest of RLS's friends among the missionaries.[1]

A very different friend was the American trader, H.J. Moors, who took Stevenson under his wing and became one of his main informants in his extensive research into the recent history of Samoa.[2]

★   ★   ★

---

[1] William Edward Clarke (1854–1922) was ordained in 1882; in the same year he married Ellen Allanson (died 1946) and sailed for Samoa. He served as missionary for the London Missionary Society in Apia 1883–5 and again from 1888–95 when he returned to England and resigned from the Society. He rejoined and saw temporary service in Samoa 1917–20. His Samoan name was 'Talati' and RLS put him into 'The Beach of Falesá' as the missionary Tarleton.

[2] Harry Jay Moors (1854–1926) was an American trader (born in Detroit) who from modest beginnings built up a highly successful business with a network of trading stores and extensive plantations. As a young man he worked for the Hawaiian Government, recruiting plantation labourers in the Gilbert Islands and for three years he was a junior partner of a rather dubious German merchant E.A. Grevsmühl, before setting up on his own account in Apia in 1886. By 1907 the *Cyclopedia of Samoa* could describe him as the sole owner of the second most important planting and trading enterprise in Samoa, the largest individual taxpayer in the islands, and as importer of merchandise and exporter of copra one of the most important merchants in the South Pacific. He played an active part in Samoan politics and was a warm supporter of Mataafa. His *With Stevenson in Samoa* (1910) contains some useful information but is not always accurate.

To Lady Taylor

20 January 1890   *Apia, Samoa*

My dear Lady Taylor, I shall hope to see you in some months from now, when I come home – to break up my establishment – I know no diminutive of the word. Your dreadful daughters cast a spell upon me; they were always declaring I was a winged creature and would vanish into the uttermost isle; and they were right, and I have made my preparations. I am now the owner of an estate on Upolu, some two or three miles behind and above Apia; three streams, two waterfalls, a great cliff, an ancient native fort, a view of the sea and lowlands, or (to be more precise) several views of them in various directions, are now mine. It would be affectation to omit a good many head of cattle; above all as it required much diplomacy to have them thrown in, for the gentleman who sold to me was staunch. Besides all this, there is a great deal more forest than I have any need for; or to be plain, the whole estate is one impassable jungle, which must be cut down and through at considerable expense. Then the house has to be built; and then (as a climax) we may have to stand a siege in it in the next native war.[1]

I do feel as if I was a coward and a traitor to desert my friends; only, my dear lady, you know what a miserable corrhyzal[2] (is that how it is spelt?) creature I was at home; and here I have some real health, I can walk, I can ride, I can stand some exposure, I am up with the sun, I have a real enjoyment of the world and of myself; it would be hard to go back again to England and to bed; and I think it would be very silly. I am sure it would; and yet I feel shame, and I know I am not writing like myself. I wish you knew how much I admired you, and when I think of those I must leave, how early a place your name occupies. I have not had the pleasure to know you very long; and yet I feel as if my leaving England were a special treachery to you, and my leaving you a treachery to myself.

---

[1] Fanny wrote a very long gossipy letter to Colvin on the same day about their experiences on board the *Equator* and in Samoa, gingerly breaking the news of the decision to buy an estate in Samoa:

> You told me when we left England that if we found a place where Louis was really well, to stay there. It really seems that anywhere in the South Seas will do . . . Well, just as we had made up our minds that Samoa was our choice we discovered by accident the very piece of land that seemed to have been made to order for us . . . This tract consists of between three and four hundred acres, part of it table land of the richest deep virgin soil: more than enough for a large plantation.

The legal deed for the purchase of the Vailima estate is dated 10 January 1890; it is signed by the vendor, William Johnson, and RLS. The purchase price was ten Chile dollars per acre. At the rates then in force this gives a total price of about $ (American) 2250 (£450).

[2] Coryza (from the Greek) is the medical term for the running of the nose which accompanies a cold in the head; the adjective is RLS's own.

I will only ask you to try to forgive me: for I am sure I will never quite forgive myself. Somebody might write to me in the care of R. Towns & Co., Sydney, New South Wales, to tell me if you can forgive. But you will do quite right if you cannot. Only let me come and see you when I do return, or it will be a lame home-coming.

My wife suffered a good deal in our last, somewhat arduous voyage; all our party indeed suffered except myself; and my poor son-in-law I fear, is to die. I ought to say, I hope; for the dear, good fellow is unfit for life, which can only be the cause of suffering or humiliation to himself and his friends; and, like many of us, he is very fit to die and leave a green and pleasant memory – a kindly memory – not a man's perhaps, but a wingless, fallen angel's: you must know the type, beloved, and justly beloved, through endless annoyances and disappointments. Fanny is now better, but she is still no very famous success in the way of health; and with the probable trouble before us of Strong's death, and the certain labour of our expatriation, I feel a little anxious.

All the while I have been writing, I have had another matter in my eye; of which I scarce like to speak: you know of course that I am thinking of Sir Percy and his widow.[3] The news has reached me in the shape of a newspaper cutting, I have no particulars. He had a sweet, original nature; I think I liked him better than ever I should have liked his father; I am sorry he was always a little afraid of me; if I had had more chance, he would have liked me too, we had so much in common, and I valued so much his fine soul, as honest as a dog's, and the romance of him, which was like a dog's too, and like a poet's at the same time. If he had not been Shelley's son, people would have thought more of him; and yet he was the better of the two, bar verses.

Please tell my dear Ida and Una that we think much of them, as well as of your dear self, and believe me, in words which you once allowed me to use (and I was very much affected when you did so), your affectionate friend   Robert Louis Stevenson

To his Mother

[*Postmark 5 March 1890*]   *Union Club, Sydney*[1]

My dear Mother, I understand the family keeps you somewhat informed. For myself, I am in such a whirl of work and society, I can ill spare a

---

[3] Sir Percy Shelley died on 6 December 1889. RLS wrote a letter of condolence to his widow.
[1] The Stevensons reached Sydney, from Apia, on 13 February.

moment. My health is excellent, and has been here tried by abominable wet weather and (what's waur) dinners and lunches. As this is like to be our metropolis, I have tried to lay myself out to be sociable with an eye to yoursel'. Several niceish people have turned up: Fanny has an evening, but she is about at the end of the virtuous effort, and shrinks from the approach of any fellow creature.

Have you seen Hyde's (Dr not Mr) letter about Damien? That has been one of my concerns; I have an answer in the press;[2] and have just written a difficult letter to Damon,[3] trying to prepare him, for what (I fear) must be to him extremely painful. The answer is to come out as a pamphlet: of which I make of course a present to the publisher. I am not a cannibal, I would not eat the flesh of Dr Hyde —;[4] and it is conceivable it will make a noise in Honolulu. I have struck as hard as I knew how; nor do I think my answer can fail to do away (in the minds of all who see it) with the effect of Hyde's incredible and really villainous production. What a mercy I was not this man's *guest* on the *Morning Star*! I think it would have broke my heart.

Time for me to go![5] More anon. With love   R.L.S.

---

[2] In the months following Father Damien's death there had been controversy in the religious press between Protestants and Catholics about the extent of his contribution to the relief of lepers at Molokai. Against this background the Revd Charles M. Hyde of Honolulu, a prominent member of the American Board of Missions, wrote a private letter to the Revd H.B. Gage (a Presbyterian minister), in response to his enquiries, attacking Damien's character, morals and motives. He concluded that Damien 'was not a pure man in his relations with women, and the leprosy of which he died should be attributed to his vices and carelessness'. Gage promptly published this letter in a San Francisco religious paper and it was widely copied in the religious press throughout the world. Soon after his arrival in Sydney, RLS's attention was drawn to Dr Hyde's letter, as reprinted in the Sydney *Presbyterian*. In a white-heat of indignation RLS wrote his famous *Father Damien: An Open Letter to the Reverend Dr Hyde of Honolulu*. This pamphlet was privately printed in Sydney and presentation copies were sent out on 27 March. Henley published it in the *Scots Observer* of 3 and 10 May 1890.
[3] The Revd Francis (Frank) Williams Damon (1852–1915), one of the missionaries of the American Board of Missions in Honolulu whom both RLS and Fanny had liked very much. Damon and his colleague Dr Hyde had been involved in RLS's plan to become a passenger on the missionary ship, the *Morning Star*.
[4] In September 1890 RLS wrote to Andrew Chatto (who published *Father Damien*): 'The letter to Dr Hyde is yours, or any man's. I will never touch a penny of remuneration; I do not stick at murder, I draw the line at cannibalism, I could not eat a penny roll that piece of bludgeoning had gained for me.'
[5] 'Time for us to go!' is the chorus of the sea shanty sung by Pew in *Admiral Guinea*.

To Sidney Colvin[1]

[*30 April 1890*]   S.S. Janet Nicoll, *off Upolu*[2]

My dearest Colvin, I was sharply ill at Sydney, cut off, right out of bed,
in this steamer on a fresh island cruise, and have already reaped the benefit.
We are excellently found this time, on a spacious vessel, with an excellent
table; the captain, supercargo, our one fellow passenger, etc., very nice;
and the charterer, Mr Henderson, the very man I would have chosen.[3]
The truth is, I fear, this life is the only one that suits me; so long as I cruise
in the South Seas, I shall be well and happy – alas no, I do not mean that
and *absit omen*! – I mean that, so soon as I cease from cruising, the nerves
are strained, the decline commences, and I steer slowly but surely back to
bedward. We left Sydney, had a cruel rough passage to Auckland for the
Janet is the worst roller I was ever aboard of, I was confined to my cabin,
ports closed, self shied out of the berth, stomach (pampered till the day I
left on a diet of perpetual eggnogg) revolted at ship's food and ship's
eating, in a frowsy bunk, clinging with one hand to the plate, with the
other to the glass, and using the knife and fork – (except at intervals) with
the eyelid. No matter: I picked up hand over hand. After a day in
Auckland, we set sail again; were blown up in the main cabin with
calcium fires, as we left the bay:[4] Let no man say I am unscientific; when
I ran, on the alert, out of my stateroom, and found the main cabin
encarnadined with the glow of the last scene of a pantomime, I stopped
dead. 'What is this?' said I. 'This ship is on fire, I see that; but why a

---

[1] RLS's serious illness in Sydney forced him to abandon his plan to travel to Britain – the passages
had already been booked on a ship leaving on 19 April. Instead Fanny managed, after great
difficulties, to secure passages for RLS, Lloyd and herself on the *Janet Nicoll*, an iron screw
steamer of about 600 tons, due to leave Sydney for the Islands under charter to Messrs
Henderson and Macfarlane of Auckland, a well-known trading firm. The Strongs were left
behind in Sydney. Fanny's diary of the voyage was published in abridged form as *The Cruise of
the 'Janet Nichol' among the South Sea Islands* (1915); she consistently misspelt the name.
   The *Janet Nicoll* sailed on 11 April and the three months' cruise took in the Gilbert and Ellice
Islands and the Marshalls.
[2] Fanny's diary shows that the *Janet Nicoll* was off Upolu on 30 April. They went ashore at Apia
that evening and visited Vailima the next morning.
[3] The captain was Ernest Henry, 'a very mild German', and the supercargo was Ben Hird (died
1896), a well-known trader and 'character' with a wide knowledge of the South Seas; RLS
greatly enjoyed his skill as a teller of yarns. The passenger was Jack Buckland (known as 'Tin
Jack'), a handsome, happy-go-lucky young man, the original of the 'Remittance Man' Tommy
Hadden in *The Wrecker*. According to Fanny, he had a certain yearly fixed income which he
usually spent in 'a wild burst of dissipation' in Sydney; for the rest of the year he was a copra-
trader in the Gilbert Islands. RLS dedicated *Island Nights' Entertainments* to Henderson, Hird and
Buckland.
[4] Fanny tells how Jack Buckland bought fireworks, including ten pounds of 'calcium fire' with
fumes, for the entertainment of his native retainers, in Auckland. The fireworks exploded on 20
April just as the ship was leaving Auckland harbour.

pantomime?' And I stood and reasoned the point, until my head was so muddled with the fumes that I could not find the companion. A few seconds later, the captain had to enter crawling on his belly, and took days to recover (if he has recovered) from the fumes. By singular good fortune, we got the hose down in time and saved the ship, but Lloyd lost most of his clothes and a great part of our photographs was destroyed. Fanny saw the native sailors tossing overboard a blazing trunk; she stopped them in time, and behold! it contained my manuscripts. Thereafter we had three (or two) days fine weather; then got into a gale of wind, with rain and a vexatious sea. As we drew in to our anchorage in a bight of Savage Island,[5] a man ashore told me afterward, the sight of the *Janet Nicoll* made him sick; and indeed it was rough play, though nothing to the night before. All through this gale I worked four to six hours *per diem*, spearing the ink bottle like a flying fish, and holding my papers together as I might. For of all things, what I was at was history: the Samoan business; and I had to turn from one to another of three piles of manuscript notes, and from one page to another in each, until I should have found employment for the hands of Briareus.[6] All the same this history is a godsend for a voyage; I can put in time getting events coordinated and the narrative distributed, when my much-heaving numskull would be incapable of finish or fine style. At Savage, we met the missionary barque, *John Williams*; I tell you it was great day for Savage Island. The path up the cliffs was crowded with gay islandresses (I like that feminine plural) who wrapped me in their embraces, and picked my pockets of all my tobacco, with a manner something between a whore and a child, which a touch would have made revolting, but as it was, was simply charming like the Golden Age. One pretty, little, stalwart minx, with a red flower behind her ear, had gone through me with extraordinary zeal; and when, soon after, I missed my matches, I accused her (she still following us) of being the thief. After some delay, and with a subtle smile, she produced the box, and gave me *one match*, and put the rest away again. Too tired to add more. Your most affectionate

R.L.S.

To Charles Baxter

[*Late July 1890*][1]   *Hotel Sebastopol, Noumea*

My dear Charles, I have stayed here a week while Lloyd and my wife continue the voyage in the *Janet Nicoll*; this I did partly to see the convict

---

[5] The ship anchored off Savage Island (or Niue) on 26 April and stayed several days.
[6] The hundred-handed monster in Greek mythology.
[1] The *Janet Nicoll* arrived at Noumea, capital and chief port of the French colony of New Caledonia, on 26 July 1890 and left the next day. It reached Sydney on 4 August.

system,[2] partly to shorten my stay in the extreme cold – hear me! with my extreme! *moi qui suis originaire d'Edimbourg*! – of Sydney at this season. I am feeling very seedy, utterly fatigued and overborne with sleep; I have a fine old gentleman of a doctor who attends and cheers and entertains, if he does not cure me; but even with his ministrations I am almost incapable of the exertion sufficient for this letter; and I am really, as I write, falling down with sleep. What is necessary to say, I must try to say shortly. Lloyd goes to clear out our establishments:[3] pray keep him in funds, if I have any; if I have not, pray try to raise them. Here is the idea: to install ourselves, at the risk of bankruptcy, in Samoa. It is not the least likely it will pay (although it may) – but it is almost certain it will support life with very few external expenses. If I die, it will be an endowment for the survivors; at least for my wife and Lloyd, and my mother, who might prefer to go home, has her own. Hence, I believe I shall do well to hurry my installation. The letters are already in part done: in part done is a novel for *Scribner*; in the course of the next twelve months, I should receive a considerable amount of money. I am aware I had intended to pay back to my capital much of this; I am now of opinion I should do foolishly. Better to build the house, and have a roof and farm of my own; and thereafter, with a livelihood assured, save and repay; than to go on, living expensively and paying back capital which makes only a modest return. I am in hopes you will share this view. The price of the house will be considerable: many expenses have to be faced before we have cattle, feed, and vegetables. On the other hand, once faced there is my livelihood, all but books and wine, ready in a nutshell; and it ought to be more easy, and it would be certainly (by all the laws of arithmetic) less expensive, to save and to repay; afterward. Excellent, say you, but will you save? and will you repay? I do not know, said the Bell of Old Bow. But, on the other hand, will you tell me how much I shall lose, if I delay building my house and mounting my plantation, and must live at heck and manger,[4] paying three prices for one, after I have paid back the money, and while I economise, under this drain, the fresh capital necessary for the installation? It seems clear to me.

Have you paid back what I owe to Simpson? Please guide Lloyd all you can. We see him go, Fanny and I, with sinkings. He is not – well – not a man of business.

---

[2] In ch. 3 of *The Ebb-Tide* RLS referred to 'those white, shaved men, in their dust clothes and straw hats, prowling around in gangs in the lamplight at Noumea'. The convict settlement was established in 1864.

[3] Following their return to Sydney, Lloyd left for England to make arrangements to sell Skerryvore and to ship the furniture and possessions out to Samoa. He sailed on *R.M.S. Austral* on 18 August 1890 and reached England on 25 September.

[4] In comfortable circumstances, in plenty. Heck (Scots) is a rack for fodder.

The deuce of the affair is that I do not know when I shall see you and Colvin. I guess you will have to come and see me; many a time already we have arranged the details of your visit in the yet unbuilt house on the mountain. I shall be able to get decent wine from Noumea. We shall be able to give you a decent welcome, and talk of old days. *À propos* of old days, do you remember still the phrase we heard in Waterloo Place?[5] I believe you made a piece for the piano on that phrase. Pray, if you remember it, send it me in your next. If you find it impossible to write correctly, send it me *à la récitative*, and indicate the accents. Do you feel (you must) how strangely heavy and stupid I am? I must at last give up and go sleep; I am simply a rag.

The morrow. I feel better, but still dim and groggy. Tonight I go to the governor's; such a lark – no dress clothes – twenty-four hours' notice – able-bodied Polish tailor – suit made for a man with the figure of a puncheon – same hastily altered for self with the figure of a bodkin – front flaps of coat descending to *pudenda* – sight inconceivable. Never mind: dress clothes, 'which nobody can deny', and the officials have been all so civil that I liked neither to refuse nor to appear in mufti. Bad dress clothes only prove you are a grisly ass; no dress clothes, even when explained, indicate a want of respect. I wish you were here with me to help me dress in this wild raiment, and to accompany me to M. Noel-Pardon's.

My dear Charles, it is a very poor affair to (what is called) succeed. My faults, whatever they were, were taken very easily by my friends till I had (what is called) succeeded: then the measure was changed. What I have gained is an invitation to the governor's in New Caledonia; what I have lost, you can see in what I wrote last night, when I mentioned you and Colvin – and you two only. Even Bob writes to me with an embarrassment which communicates itself to my answers. Our relation is too old and close to be destroyed; I have forgiven him too much – and he me – to leave a rupture possible; but there it is – the shadow. I bore you with these regrets. But I did not ever care for much else than my friends; and some they are dead etc., and I am at the end of the world from what remains: gone, all are gone.[6] I cannot say what I would not give, if there came a knock now at the door, and you came in. I guess Noel-Pardon would go begging, and we might burn the £200 dress clothes in the back garden for a bonfire; or what would be yet more expensive and more humorous, get them once more expanded to fit you, and when that was done a second time cut down for my gossamer dimensions.

I hope you never forget to remember me to your father: who has always a place in my heart, as I hope I have a little in his. His kindness

[5] Cf. p. 127.
[6] Cf. the last verse of Lamb's 'The Old Familiar Faces': 'How some they have died, and some they have left me, . . . All, all are gone, the old familiar faces.'

helped me infinitely when you and I were young; I recall it with gratitude and affection in this town of convicts at the world's end. There are very few things, my dear Charles, worth mention; on a retrospect of life, the day's flash and colour, one day with another, flames, dazzles and puts to sleep; and when the days are gone, like a fast-flying thaumatrope, they make but a single pattern. Only a few things stand out, and among these, most plainly to me – Rutland Square.

I don't know if it will cut you to the heart as it does me; but the Boehm flageolet has gone (presumably with the heat) out of tune. A, B♭, B, C, C♯ have all run together; C♯ certainly flat, and most of the others I think sharp: all at least run into 'pie', and the pipe smiles in the face of the performer. I dare not play now; it is bad enough to play inconceivably ill; when the pipe itself is out of tune, the offence is capital. I believe I show in these words that I am not quite so much out of gear as I was last night; yet I still struggle with somnolence and make but an imperfect fight of it, and when I walk it is still on aching legs. Possibly the long voyage, and so long ship's food, explain my state; but I feel unusually useless. My loneliness has a certain pleasure. Ever, my dear Charles, Your affectionate friend   Robert Louis Stevenson

On my arrival at Sydney, I shall doubtless find a letter: this is to be ready before, and to go first of all, should there be a mail on the move. P.S. Just returned from trying on the dress clo'. Lord, you should see the coat: it stands out at the waist like a bustle, the flaps cross in front, the sleeves are like bags.[7]

To Henry James

[19 August 1890]   *Union Club, Sydney*

My dear Henry James, Kipling is too clever to live.[1] *The Beast Human* I had already perused in Noumea, listening the while to the strains of the convict band. He is a Beast; but not human, and to be frank, not very

---

[7] RLS left Noumea on the *S.S. Stockton* on 2 August and reached Sydney on 7 August.
[1] In a letter of 21 March 1890, referring to RLS's expected return to England, James wrote: 'We'll tell you all about Rudyard Kipling – your nascent rival . . . the star of the hour.' He enclosed a book by Kipling, presumably *Soldiers Three*. After working as a journalist in India, Rudyard Kipling (1865–1936) had arrived in London in October 1889 and achieved great literary success with what Henry James described to RLS as 'remarkable Anglo-Indian and extraordinarily observed barrack life – Tommy Atkins – tales'. *Plain Tales from the Hills, Soldiers Three* and five other collections of short stories, which had appeared two years earlier in India, were reissued in London in 1890.

interesting.[2] 'Nervous maladies: the homicidal ward', would be the better name: O, this game gets very tedious.

Your two long and kind letters have helped to entertain the old, familiar sickbed. So has a book called *The Bondman*, by Hall Caine;[3] I wish you would look at it. Here is a man who improves very rapidly. He has read some Victor Hugo; but if I am not in error, he has genius. I am not half-way through yet. I have just read a lover's parting between Michael and Greeba, and do you know? it seemed to me all there: the note, sir, the desired note. Read the book, and communicate your views. Hall Caine, by the way, appears to take Hugo's view of History and Chronology. (*Later*, the book doesn't keep up; it gets very wild.)

A heavy cold fit is on me over my letter to Dr Hyde. I think it brutal and cruel: *la Bête Humaine, quoi!* I wish I had regained my temper ere I wrote it. It took me four months to regain my temper; by which you may see what a healthy sort of anger it was. I generally recover my temper in ten minutes, and almost without exception in twenty-four hours. But Dr Hyde had the art to touch me on the raw; and the consequence is that I've been unjust to him, and am now sorry.

I must tell you plainly – I *can't* tell Colvin – I do not think I shall come to England more than once, and then it'll be to die. Health I enjoy in the tropics; even here, which they call sub or semi-tropical, I come only to catch cold. I have not been out since my arrival; live here in a nice bedroom by the fireside, and read books and letters from Henry James, and send out to get his *Tragic Muses*,[4] only to be told they can't be had as yet in Sydney; and have altogether a placid time. But I can't go out! The thermometer was nearly down to 50° the other day: no temperature for me, Mr James: how should I do in England? I fear not at all. Am I very sorry? You may conceive how Colvin weighs on my mind; I feel it the worst kind of desertion; but yet, to go home and get buried, would not help him greatly.[5] I am sorry about Henry James, old Lady Taylor, about four more people in England, and one in the States. And outside of that,

---

[2] Zola's recently published *La Bête Humaine*. On 28 April 1890 James wrote: 'I sent you a new Zola the other day – at a venture: but I have no confidence that I gratified a curiosity. I haven't read *The Human Beast* – one knows him without that – and I am told Zola's account of him is dull and imperfect.'

[3] Thomas Henry Hall Caine (1853–1931), phenomenally successful popular novelist. *The Bondman* had just appeared.

[4] *The Tragic Muse* was published in June 1890. On 21 March James referred to it as 'the longest and most careful novel I have ever written'; on 28 April he promised to send RLS a copy – 'I can't (spiritually) afford *not* to put the book under the eye of the sole and single Anglo-Saxon capable of perceiving – though he may care for little else in it – how well it is written.'

[5] On 21 March 1890, while expressing his joy at RLS's improved health, James had written of the 'long howl of horror' that had gone up from all his friends 'on the question of Samoa and expatriation': 'Your return will probably do dear old Colvin more good than any other remedy . . . Don't disappoint him – don't fail him.'

I simply prefer Samoa. These are the words of honesty and soberness.[6] (I am fasting from all but sin, coughing, *The Bondman*, a couple of eggs and a cup of tea.) I was never fond of towns, houses, society or (it seems) civilisation. Nor yet it seems was I ever very fond of (what is technically called) God's green earth. The sea, islands, the islanders, the island life and climate, make and keep me truly happier. These last two years I have been much at sea, and I have *never wearied*, sometimes I have indeed grown impatient for some destination; more often I was sorry that the voyage drew so early to an end; and never once did I lose my fidelity to blue water and a ship. It is plain then that for me, my exile to the place of schooners and islands can be in no sense regarded as a calamity. But for Colvin perhaps it may be. I am glad you know him now: it makes him less lonely by one; for as you doubtless have found out, in the midst of that bustle of society, the man is almost dead alone. Almost none know him, he has a husk; inside, it is good meat, but the husk is by most teeth invincible.

I believe both you and Colvin are eminent sea-sickists: could you not both come and visit us? They say sea sickness is so good for the liver. Well, well, that is to be spoken of later on.

Good-bye just now: I must take a turn at my proofs.

N.B. Even my wife has weakened about the sea. She wearied, the last time we were ashore, to get afloat again. Yours ever   R.L.S.

To Sidney Colvin

[August 1890]   *Union Club, Sydney*

My ever dear Colvin, I have just arrived from New Caledonia, following Fanny and Lloyd who continued on in the *Janet Nicoll* and were very nearly lost on the Australian Coast. I have read some of your letters; not all; not having quite courage.[1] My dear friend, you are our beloved; my wife never had a thought of being vexed – if I tell you that she cried all night after reading your letter, it is simply to give you a measure of what she thinks of your opinion. And yet she knew all the time that you scarce

---

[6] An echo of Acts 26: 25.

[1] In *Memories and Notes* Colvin explains that the news that RLS was buying a property in Samoa

was a rude shock to those who loved him and were looking forward eagerly to his return. . . . In spite of the fine work he had done during his voyages, I persuaded myself that from living permanently in that outlandish world and far from cultivated society both he and his writing must deteriorate, and wrote warning him as much in plain terms. Translating unconsciously my own need and desire for his company into a persuasion that mine was needed, as of old, for criticism and suggestion to him in his work, and that he no longer valued it, I wrote reproachfully, pleading against and prophesying evil from his purpose.

meant all; she – and I – understand you as you understand me. But one thing vexes me. You have not got my letter: I only remember how I began: that if you could forgive me, I could never forgive myself. I do not know if these were the exact words, they were the exact sentiment and the words near by. I must tell you too, when it became more and more clear to me that I ought to stay in the tropics: my one trouble was about you. (If you have missed all my letters ask to see Charles Baxter's). I said to Fanny: I cannot bear to stay here, I must go home to Colvin. She said: He made me promise to keep you in any place that suited your health; it would be cruel to go home and lose your health; it would be sham kindness, it would be to doubt what he said. I am sure, had my letter not miscarried, you would not have dreamed I was indifferent.

Enough said on that. Yes, these phrases in the Hyde letter were abominable; I had long since found them out, and withered under them; but the thing was written, printed and distributed, ere I had recovered my temper: you see I was already months behind time, and thought of little but of being speedy.

I sit here with three flannels on, in a good bedroom with a fire and am scarce warm; if I open the door, I shiver; the thought of England this autumn, as you thought, is quite beside the question: But anyway we had given it up before I saw your letter, as soon as I had a slight blood spitting on the *Janet Nicoll*. I have done well on that voyage; sixteen Letters – at least, not that, but the draught of sixteen chapters of my book, from which thirteen or fourteen Letters will be selected – go home to be set up: which Lloyd who goes soon after will get you to correct.[2] Please remember, the printer five times out of ten prints my OR as AS, and bear in mind it does not enter into my view of English, any more than I believe it does into yours, to use AS for OR: although I know the thing is done by persons laying claim to human stature. Besides the Letters finished I have some twelve or fourteen drafted in more or less distinct form; on the same voyage I did nothing to *The Wrecker*, but solved the problem of the far more important *Pearl Fisher*, none of which had been yet done except by Lloyd; who is of course quite incapable of turning the ugliness of this rugged, harsh and really striking tale. I got it, I do hope, set upon its legs; the difficulty was to put the hero up, I think I have done it. I believe only a Pharisee will blame him his mistakes.

We had a very interesting voyage for some part; it would have been delightful to the end – though never so delightful – as you go westward, the charm of the people wanes and at last dies – had my health held out.

---

[2] The first fifteen chapters of *The South Seas* were privately printed in London by Cassell's, 12 November 1890, in an edition of twenty-two copies. Two copies were sold to secure copyright, a few given to friends and the rest were cut up for use in newspaper syndication.

That it did not, I attribute to savage hard work in a wild cabin heated like the Babylonian furnace, four plies of blotting paper under my wet hand and the drops boiling from my brow. For God's sake, don't start in to blame Fanny; often enough, she besought me not to go on: but I did my work while I was a bedridden worm in England, and please God I shall do my work until I burst. I do not know any other virtue I possess; and indeed there are few others I prize alongside of it. Only, one other I have: I love my friends, and I don't like to hear the most beloved of all casting doubt on that affection. Did you not even get the verses I sent you from Apemama? I guess they were not A.1. verses; but they expressed something you surely could not doubt.[3] But perhaps all my letters have miscarried? A sorrow on correspondence! If this miscarry too? We shall be well off at last. See here: if by any chance this should come to your hand, of which I now begin to despair – nothing can have reached you, or you could not reproach me with coldness – but if this (by some exception) reach you: understand once and for all, that since my dear wild noble father died, no head on earth, and not my wife's, is more precious to my thought than yours. I do not know if you know what I thought of him; I think of you, my honoured and beloved friend, equally and with a kindred spirit. When first I heard you were not well, it was my first impulse to come straight back. Fanny prevented me; or rather, I say not well – we passed near a night debating it – and we persuaded each other, you would be little pleased if I did so extreme a step.

When it came to the Samoa business, I was averse, only for your sake; had I known I could not make out my visit, I do not suppose I would ever have consented, dearly as I wished to stay in that place which is so agreeable to my wishes and where I enjoy such excellent health – or have enjoyed, I would not boast. I could not foresee this dreary cold in spring, could I? But all this talk is useless. Know this: I love you; and since I am speaking plainly for once, I bind it upon you as a sacred duty, and upon another beside you: should you be dangerously ill, I must be summoned. I will never forgive you, nor her, if I am not. So long as there is not danger, I do well – do I not? – to consider conditions necessary to my work and health. I have a charge of souls; I keep many eating and drinking; my continued life has a value of its own; and I cannot but feel

---

[3] The poem beginning 'I heard the pulse of the besieging sea', published as 'To S.C.' in *Songs of Travel* XXXVII. In his letter of 2 December 1889 RLS wrote: 'My dear fellow, now that my father is done with his troubles, and 17 Heriot Row no more than a mere shell, you and that gaunt old Monument in Bloomsbury are all that I have in view when I use the word home; some passing thoughts there may be of the rooms at Skerryvore, and the blackbirds in the chine on a May morning; but the essence is S.C. and the Museum.'

it. But I have to see you again. That is sure. And – how strangely we are made! – I can see no harm in my dying like a burst pig upon some outlandish island, but if you died, without due notice and a chance for me to come and see you, I should count it a disloyalty: no less.[4]

[4] In a long and affectionate postscript Fanny explained RLS's improvement in health in the South Seas and particularly in Samoa, and his severe illness in Sydney. She concluded:

> Dear friend, because I make my sacrifice with flowers on my head and point out the fine views on the way do not think it is no sacrifice, and only for my own pleasure. The Samoan people are picturesque, but I do not like them. I do not trust them. My time must be so arranged as not to clash with them. I shall be able to get no servants but cannibal black boys, runaways and discontents from the German plantations. A great part of the housework I shall have to do myself, and most of the cooking. The land *must* produce food enough for us all, or we shall have nothing to eat. I must also manage that. Oh it makes me tired to speak of it; and I never feel well there. I don't want to complain. I am not complaining, really, only telling you. There is one thing more. If a letter should come saying that you were dead it would kill Louis on the spot. If ever there is any danger of that (and I pray God not) tell us, for Louis might as well, then, go to you and die with you as away from you.

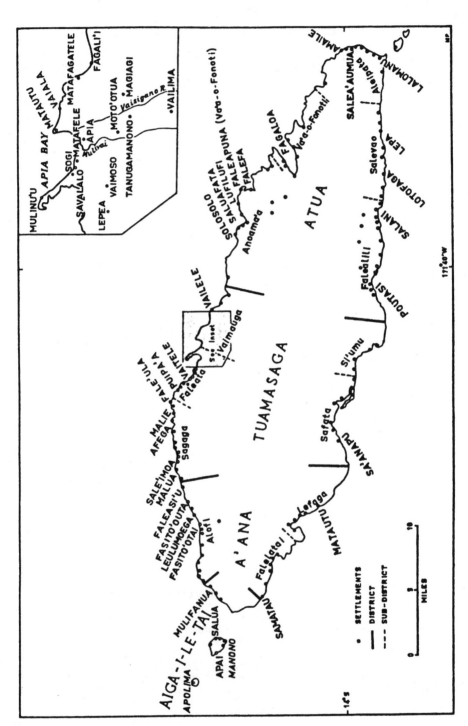

Island of Upolu, Samoa. (R.P. Gilson, *Samoa 1830 to 1900*, Oxford University Press, Melbourne, 1970)

XIV. THE FIRST TWO YEARS AT VAILIMA
September 1890–December 1892

For the last four years of his life Stevenson made his home on his estate of Vailima, nearly six hundred feet above sea-level, in the hills about three miles inland from Apia, the chief town and port of Upolu, the most important of the three principal islands comprising Samoa.

RLS and Fanny reached Apia from Sydney on 15 September 1890 and moved into Vailima. During their absence H.J. Moors had arranged for a small cottage to be built on the estate for the Stevensons to live in pending the planning and construction of a larger house. Here they lived for the first few months under the most primitive conditions. A valuable record of how they looked to an outside observer (albeit a prejudiced and snobbish one) is provided by the letters written by Henry Adams,[1] who with his companion John La Farge paid his first visit to Vailima on the afternoon of 16 October:

> At last we came out on a clearing dotted with burned stumps exactly like a clearing in our backwoods. In the middle stood a two-story Irish shanty with steps outside to the upper floor, and a galvanised iron roof. A pervasive atmosphere of dirt seemed to hang around it, and the squalor like a railroad navvy's board hut. As we reached the steps a figure came out that I cannot do justice to. Imagine a man so thin and emaciated that he looked like a bundle of sticks in a bag, with a head and eyes morbidly intelligent and restless. He was costumed in very dirty striped cotton pyjamas, the baggy legs tucked into coarse knit woollen stockings, one of which was bright brown in color, the other a purplish dark tone. With him was a woman who retired for a moment into the house to reappear a moment afterwards, probably in some change of costume, but, as far as I could see, the change could have consisted only in putting shoes on her bare feet. She wore the usual missionary nightgown which was no cleaner than her husband's shirt and drawers, but she omitted the stockings. Her complexion and

---

[1] Henry Adams (1838–1918), distinguished American historian, grandson and great-grandson of American presidents. Following the suicide of his wife (for whom Saint-Gaudens designed a famous memorial) he travelled widely in Japan and the South Seas. His companion was John La Farge (1830–1910), American painter and worker in stained glass. They arrived in Samoa in October 1890 and left at the end of January 1891. In an often quoted comment, Adams foolishly opined that RLS's 'squalor' was 'somehow due to his education' and that his 'early associates were all second-rate'.

eyes were dark and strong, like a half-breed Mexican. . . . When conversation fairly began, though I could not forget the dirt and discomfort, I found Stevenson extremely entertaining.

In another letter he described RLS and Fanny as looking like 'queer birds': 'He seems never to rest, but perches like a parrot on every available projection, jumping from one to another, and talking incessantly. The parrot was very dirty and ill-clothed as we saw him, being perhaps caught unawares, and the female was in rather worse trim than the male.'

By April 1891 the new house had been built and they were able to move in after a fashion. In May, in a letter to his Aunt Jane, RLS summarised what had been achieved: '[W]hen I look round on this place, which Fanny and I came to some eight months back and found a trackless forest, and see clearings, houses, stables, paths, and food trees everywhere rising, I am surprised at our success. It was a tough job; and Fanny had the heavy end of it . . .'

Stevenson's mother arrived on 16 May and the next day she wrote a description of the house to her sister:

> . . . The house really looks very nice indeed. The outside is painted a sort of peacock blue, and the roof and verandahs a red, that goes very well with it; the dining-room is very pretty and comfortable, the walls hung with *tapa*, the native cloth, which gives an effect of tapestry. There are large sliding-doors, more than half glass, opening on to the verandah, which looks out over the harbour; a smaller glass door opens to the back, and a large double window to the west. The kitchen proper is quite a separate erection at the back, which will eventually be connected with the house by a covered way; but opening from the back verandah is a capital pantry and store-closet, with an American stove in it that can be used for emergencies or special occasions. I think my room is delightful, although in time I am to have even better quarters; it is at present a sitting- and bed-room in one, but the two portions are to be divided by Japanese bead screens, coming from Sydney. I have both sliding-doors and a double window giving on to the verandah that looks towards the sea; and at the 'sitting-room' end the walls are hung with the flags we used on board the *Casco*, the 'red ensign' on the one side, the 'stars and stripes' on the other, and Kalakaua's royal standard in the middle. Above the standard there is a fine piece of *tapa* from Savage Island, painted with an elaborate pattern and in the centre the word *soifau*, which means *welcome*. The floor is covered with beautiful white Samoan mats, very soft and thick to the tread; the walls and roof are painted pale green, and over my table is hung a lovely branching tree of pink and white coral. . . . The rest of the upper floor is divided into Louis's library and their bedroom. The

library is shelved all round and painted green, like my room, but everything in it is as yet in a state of chaos.

A week later Joe, Belle and Austin Strong arrived from Sydney; Lloyd had already returned from England, where he had arranged for the packing and despatch to Samoa of the furniture and household effects from Skerryvore. The Vailima household was complete.

In reading Stevenson's letters from Samoa it has to be remembered that they took about a month to reach Britain. The mail steamers of the Oceanic Line, plying between San Francisco and Sydney via Honolulu and Auckland made a monthly delivery and collection of mailbags in Samoa.

Stevenson's life in Samoa cannot be fully understood without some background knowledge of the political situation, bedevilled by the competing interests of the three Great Powers and complicated by the rivalries between the Samoan chiefs. RLS himself told the complex story of German intervention in Samoan affairs and the involvement of Britain and the United States in his *A Footnote to History* (1892). German political interference stemmed from the fact that they had major commercial interests, greater than those of any other Power, in the form of large plantations of coconut trees producing copra for the valuable export trade.[2] In August 1887 the Germans with a display of naval power (they had five warships in Apia Bay), deposed and deported the rightful Samoan King, Malietoa Laupepa, and installed in his stead their own puppet-king, Tupua Tamasese. Samoan opposition to Tamasese and German control rallied round another Samoan chief, Mataafa Iosefo. Mataafa declared war against Tamasese and was himself elected king under the title of 'Malietoa' (a Samoan title of special honour). In the course of the conflict there was, by accident, a skirmish between a German naval landing party and a band of Mataafa's men at Fangalii in December 1888 in the course of which eighteen Germans were killed and a number wounded: this affront to their national pride coloured the future German attitude to Mataafa. During this period of unrest the German Consul assumed in effect autocratic powers and there was much resentment and a serious risk of military conflict between the three Great Powers. At this dangerous point the hurricane of 16 March 1889 wrecked (with great loss of life) six of the seven warships crowded into Apia Bay, and the risk was averted.

At the proposal of the German Government, a Conference on Samoan Affairs was held in Berlin from April to June 1889 and an agreement was

[2] German commercial interests in Samoa were managed by a firm called Deutsche Handels- und Plantagen-Gesellschaft der Südsee-Inseln zu Hamburg. In his letters RLS usually called it the German Firm, but it was also called 'the D.H. and P.G'. It was the biggest trading firm in the South Seas.

reached between the three Powers for their tripartite control of the Government of Samoa. The complicated administrative arrangements were set out in the Final Act of the Conference signed on 14 June 1889, but not formally ratified by the three Powers (mainly because of delays by the US Senate) until 12 April 1890. They can be summarised as follows:

A Supreme Court was established under a Chief Justice of Samoa. He was the key figure in the new arrangements: in addition to his legal duties he was to act as arbiter in various possible matters of dispute and to advise the Government on legislation.

The Municipality of Apia (largely occupied by the white residents), which had been abolished by the Germans, was re-established as neutral territory. It was to be managed by a Council of six residents under the chairmanship of the President of the Municipal Council who was also to act as adviser to the King.

A Land Commission comprising one representative from each of the Three Powers was set up to investigate all claims by foreigners to the ownership of land in Samoa and to register the titles of claims judged to be valid. It was to be assisted by a Natives' Advocate representing Samoan interests.

The Consuls of the three Powers retained their considerable powers and intervened regularly on behalf of their own Governments. The Chief Justice, Conrad Cedercrantz did not reach Samoa until the end of December 1890 (see p. 446) and the President of the Council, Baron Senfft von Pilsach, four months later in April 1891 (see p. 462). In the event, both of these officials proved completely unsuitable for their difficult tasks, and RLS's letters to *The Times* were concerned with their incompetence and the impropriety of some of the administrative and legal decisions.

The new arrangements agreed in Berlin were designed more for the protection of the interests of the Great Powers than for the needs of the Samoans and failed to solve the main problem – the traditional rivalries over the kingship between the Samoan high chiefs. At the first session of the Berlin Conference the German Government announced that Malietoa Laupepa would be released from his exile in the Marshall Islands: he arrived back in Upolu in August 1889, a broken and demoralised man and seems to have accepted without protest the decision of the leading Samoan chiefs, at a meeting in October, that the popular Mataafa should be elected king. At this time the Samoans were unaware of the decision of the three Powers in Berlin. After recognising 'the free right of the natives to elect their Chief or King', Article I went on to recognise Malietoa Laupepa as the legal King. The decision to restore Laupepa was ostensibly because of the risk of civil war, but the real reason was the

German insistence that Mataafa was unacceptable because of his responsibility for the death of German sailors. On the instructions of their Governments the three Consuls in Apia gave effect to the Conference decision by issuing a proclamation on 8 November 1889 annulling the election of Mataafa and requiring the re-election of Laupepa. The Samoans gave way and on 5 December 1889, two days before RLS first arrived in Apia on board the *Equator*, Malietoa was formally recognised by the three Powers as the King of Samoa.

When Stevenson settled in Samoa in September 1890 an uneasy truce existed between Laupepa and Mataafa. The growing unrest culminated in Mataafa's withdrawal to Malie in May 1891 and his establishing himself as a rival King. RLS saw Laupepa, although a gentle and likeable man, as a weak and ineffective ruler, manipulated by his European advisers whereas Mataafa was strong and able, and had been elected under Samoan traditions. Throughout RLS's object was to encourage reconciliation between the two rivals and thus prevent bloodshed, but as the letters show his efforts were in vain. To his distress fighting broke out in July 1893; Mataafa was defeated and sent into exile.

Note on Samoan spelling

In written Samoan the break or catch in the voice characteristic of the language known as the 'glottal stop' is represented by an inverted comma or apostrophe. Stevenson rarely used this symbol either in his letters or in *A Footnote to History*. I have followed him in printing, for example, 'Mataafa' rather than the more correct 'Mata'afa', 'Mulinuu' rather than 'Mulinu'u', and so on. For the sake of consistency I have corrected or standardised his or Belle's spelling of Samoan in a few cases.

To Sidney Colvin[1]
(Abridged)

Monday 2 [actually 3] November 1890 *In the mountain, Apia, Samoa*

My dear Colvin, This is a hard and interesting and beautiful life that we lead now: our place is in a deep cleft of Vaea Mountain, some six hundred feet above the sea, embowered in forest, which is our strangling enemy and which we combat with axes and dollars. I went crazy over outdoor work, and had at last to confine myself to the house, or literature must have gone by the board. *Nothing* is so interesting as weeding, clearing and path-making: the oversight of labourers becomes a disease: it is quite an

---

[1] This is the first of the *Vailima Letters* published by Colvin, in expurgated form, in 1895.

effort not to drop into the farmer; and it does make you feel so well. To come down covered with mud and drenched with sweat and rain after some hours in the bush, change, rub down, and take a chair in the verandah, is to taste a quiet conscience. And the strange thing that I remark is this: if I go out and make sixpence, bossing my labourers and plying the cutlass or the spade, idiot conscience applauds me: if I sit in the house and make twenty pounds, idiot conscience wails over my neglect and the day wasted. For near a fortnight I did not go beyond the verandah; then I found my rush of work run out, and went down for the night to Apia; put in Sunday afternoon with our Consul,[2] a nice 'young man', dined with my friend Moors in the evening, went to church – no less – at the white and half white church – I had never been before and was much interested – the woman I sat next *looked* a full blood native, and it was in the prettiest and readiest English that she sang the hymns; back to Moors, where we yarned of the islands, being both wide wanderers, till bed time; bed, sleep, breakfast, horse saddled; round to the Mission, to get Mr Clarke to be my interpreter; over with him to the King's, whom I have not called on since my return; received by that mild foozle and fossil, have some interesting talk with him about Samoan superstitions and my land – the scene of a great battle in his (Malietoa-Laupepa's) youth – the place which we have cleared the platform of his fort – the gulley of the stream full of dead bodies – the fight rolled off up Vaea mountain-side; back with Clarke to the Mission; had a bit of lunch and consulted over a queer point of missionary policy, just arisen, about our new Town Hall and the balls there – too long to go into, but a quaint example of the intricate questions which spring up daily in the missionary path: rum trade the missionaries' – wants more sense than running an hotel.

Then off up the hill: Jack very fresh, the sun (close on noon) staring hot, the breeze very strong and pleasant; the ineffable green country all round – gorgeous little birds (I think they are humming birds, but they say not) skirmishing in the wayside flowers. About a quarter way up I met a native coming down with the trunk of a cocoa palm across his shoulder; his brown breast glittering with sweat and oil: '*Talofa*' – '*Talofa, alii* – You see that white man. He speak for you.' – 'White man he gone up here?' – '*Ioe*' (Yes) – '*Tofã, alii*' – '*Tofã, soi fua!*' I put on Jack up the steep path, till he is all as white as shaving stick – Brown's euxesis,[3] wish I had some

– past Tanugamanono, a bush village – see into the houses as I pass – they are open sheds scattered on a green – see the brown folk sitting there, suckling kids, sleeping on their stiff wooden pillows – then on through the wood path – and here I find the mysterious white man (poor devil!) with his twenty years certificate of good behaviour as a book-keeper, frozen out by the strikes in the colonies, come up here on a chance, no work to be found, big hotel bill, no ship to leave in – and come up to beg twenty dollars because he heard I was a Scotchman: offering to leave his portmanteau in pledge. Settle this, and on again; and here my house comes in view, and a war whoop fetches my wife and Henry (or Simelē) our Samoan boy on the front balcony: and I am home again, and only sorry that I shall have to go down again to Apia this day week. Curses on it, I could, and would, dwell here unmoved; but there are things to be attended to.

Never say, I don't give you details and news. That is a picture of a letter.

I have been hard at work since I came: three chapters of *The Wrecker*, and since that, eight of the South Sea book, and along and about and in between, a hatful of verses. Someday I'll send the verse to you, and you'll say if any of it is any good. I have got in a better vein with the South Sea book, as I think you will see: I think these chapters will do for the volume without much change. Those that I did on the *Janet Nicoll*, under the most ungodly circumstances, I fear will want a lot of suppling and lightening; but I hope to have your remarks in a month or two upon that point. It seems a long while since I have heard from you. I do hope you are well. I am wonderful, but tired from so much work: 'tis really immense what I have done: in the South Sea book I have fifty pages copied fair, some of which has been four times and all twice written: certainly 250 pp. of solid scriving inside a fortnight; but I was at it by seven A.M. till lunch, and from two till four or five, every day; between whiles, verse and blowing on the flageolet; never outside. If you could see this place! but I don't want anyone to see it till my clearing is done, and my house built. It will be a home for angels.

So far I wrote after my bit of dinner, some cold meat and bananas, on arrival. Then out to see where Henry and some of the men were clearing the garden; for it was plain there was to be no work today indoors, and I must set in consequence to farmering. I stuck a good while on the way up; for the path there is largely my own handiwork, and there were a lot of sprouts and saplings and stones to be removed. Then I reached our clearing just where the streams join in one; it had a fine autumn smell of burning, the smoke blew in the woods, and the boys were pretty merry and busy. Now I had a private design.

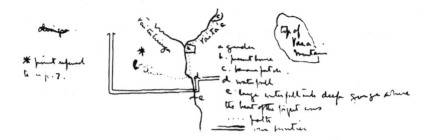

The Vaita'e I had explored pretty far up; not yet the other stream the Tuluiga (g = nasal n, as ng in sing); and up that, with my wood knife, I set off alone. It is here quite dry; it went through endless woods; about as broad as a Devonshire lane, here and there crossed by fallen trees; huge trees overhead in the sun, dripping lianas and tufted with orchids; tree ferns; ferns depending with air roots from the steep banks; great arums – I had not skill enough to say if any of them were the edible kind, one of our staples here; hundreds of bananas, another staple – and alas! I had skill enough to know all of these for the bad kind that bears no fruit. My Henry moralised over this the other day: how hard it was that the bad banana flourished wild; and the good must be weeded and tended; and I had not the heart to try to tell him how fortunate they were here, and how hungry were other lands by comparison. The ascent of this lovely lane of my dry stream filled me with delight. I could not but be reminded of old Mayne Reid;[4] as I have been more than once since I came to the tropics; and I thought, if Reid had been still living, I would have written to tell him that, for me, *it had come true*; and I thought, forby, that, if the Great Powers go on as they are going, and the Chief Justice delays, it would come truer still; and the war conch will sound in the hills, and my home will be inclosed in camps, before the year is ended. And all at once – mark you, how Mayne Reid is on the spot – a strange thing happened. I saw a liana stretch across the bed of the brook about breast high, swung up my knife to sever it, and – behold, it was a wire! On either hand it plunged into thick bush; tomorrow I shall see where it goes and get a guess perhaps of what it means; today I know no more than – there it is. A little higher the brook began to trickle; then to fill. At last, as I meant to do some work upon the homeward trail, it was time to turn. I did not return by the stream; knife in hand, as long as my endurance lasted I was to cut a path in the congested bush. At first it went ill with me; I got badly stung as high as the elbows by the stinging plant; I was nearly hung in a

---

[4] Mayne Reid (1818–83), prolific and highly popular author of adventure stories, was one of RLS's boyhood favourites.

tough liana – a rotten trunk giving way under my feet: it was deplorable bad business, and an axe – if I dared swing one – would have been more to the purpose than my cutlass. Of a sudden things began to go strangely easier; I found stumps, bushing out again; my body began to wonder, then my mind; I raised my eyes and looked ahead; and by George, I was no longer pioneering – I had struck an old track overgrown, and was restoring an old path. So I laboured till I was in such a state that Carolina Wilhelmina Skeggs could scarce have found a name for it.[5] Thereon desisted; returned to the stream; made my way down that stony track to the garden, where the smoke was still hanging and the sun was still in the high tree tops, and so home. Here fondly supposing my long day was over, I rubbed down: exquisite agony; water spreads the poison of these weeds; I got it all over my hands, on my chest, in my eyes, and presently, while eating an orange, à la Rarotonga, burned my lip and eye with orange juice. Now, all day, our three small pigs had been adrift, to the mortal peril of our corn, lettuce, onions, etc.; and as I stood smarting on the back verandah, behold the three piglings issuing from the wood just opposite. Instantly I got together as many boys as I could – three, and got the pigs penned against the rampart of the sty, till the others joined; whereupon we formed a cordon, closed, captured the deserters, and dropped them, squealing amain, into their strengthened barrack: where, please God they may now stay! Perhaps you may suppose the day now over: you are not the head of a plantation, my juvenile friend. Politics succeeded: Henry got adrift in his English, Bene was too cowardly to tell me what he was after: result I have lost seven good labourers, and had to sit down and write to you to keep my temper. Let me sketch my lads: Henry – Henry has gone down to town or I could not be writing to you – this were the hour of his English lesson else – when he learns what he calls 'long expleshions' or 'your chief's language' for the matter of an hour and a half – Henry is a chiefling from Savaii; I once loathed, I now like and – pending fresh discoveries – have a kind of respect for Henry. He does good work for us; goes among the labourers, bossing and watching; helps Fanny; is civil, kindly, thoughtful; O si sic semper![6] But will he be 'his sometime-self throughout the year'? Anyway he has deserved of us; and he must disappoint me sharply ere I give him up. Bene – or Peni – Ben, in plain English – is supposed to be my ganger; the Lord love him! God made a truckling coward: there is his full history. He cannot tell me what he wants; he dare not tell me what is wrong; he dare not transmit my orders or translate my censures. And with all this, honest, sober,

---

[5] The lady in ch. 9 of Goldsmith's The Vicar of Wakefield who observed that 'by the living jingo, she was all of a muck of a sweat'.
[6] If it were always so.

industrious, miserably smiling over the miserable issue of his own unman-
liness. Paul[7] – a German – cook and steward – a glutton of work – a
splendid fellow: drawbacks, three: (1) no cook, (2) an inveterate bungler;
a man with twenty thumbs, continually falling in the dishes, throwing out
the dinner, preserving the garbage: (3) a dr— well, don't let us say that –
but we daren't let him go to town, and he – poor, good soul – is afraid
to be let go. Lafaele (Raphael) a strong dull, deprecating man:[8] splendid
with an axe or if watched; the better for a row, when he calls me 'Papa'
in the most wheedling tones; desperately afraid of ghosts, so that he dare
not work alone up in the banana patch – see map. The rest are changing
labourers; – and tonight, owing to the miserable the obscene cowardice of
Peni – who did not venture to tell what the men wanted – which was no
more than fair – all are gone – and my weeding in the article of being
finished! Pity the sorrows of a planter. I am, Sir, Yours, and be jowned to
you   The Planter
                                                               R.L.S.

Tuesday 3rd [actually 4]

I begin to see the whole scheme of letter writing; you sit down every
day and pour out an equable stream of twaddle.

This morning all my fears were fled; and all the trouble had fallen to
the lot of Peni himself, who deserved it; my field was full of weeders; and
I am again able to justify the ways of God. All morning I worked at the
South Seas, and finished the chapter I had stuck upon on Saturday. Fanny,
awfully hove-to with rheumatics and injuries received upon the field of
sport and glory, chasing pigs, was unable to go up and down stairs; so she
sat upon the back verandah, and my work was chequered by her cries:
'Paul, you take a spade to do that – dig a hole first – *If you do that, you'll
cut your foot off!* – Here, you boy, what you do there? You no got work?
You go find Simelē; he give you work. Peni, you tell this boy he go find
Simelē; suppose Simelē no give him work, you tell him go way. I no want
him here. That boy no good.' *Peni* (from the distance in reassuring tones)
'All right, sir!' *Fanny* (after a long pause) 'Peni, you tell that boy go find
Simelē! I no want him stand here all day. I no pay that boy. I see him all
day. He no do nothing.' Luncheon: beef, soda scones, fried bananas,
pineapple in claret, coffee. Try to write a poem; no go. Play the flageolet.
Then sneakingly off to farmering and pioneering. Four gangs at work on
our place: a lively scene; axes crashing and smoke blowing: all the knives

---

[7] Paul Einfürer. In her diary Fanny explained that Paul, the German 'pantry man' from the *Lübeck*,
had stayed on in Apia and applied to the Stevensons for work.
[8] Lloyd says that Lafaele was a middle-aged Futuna Islander who had spent many years of his life
on a whale-ship, the captain of which had kidnapped him when a boy.

are out. But I rob the garden party of one without a stock, and you should see my hand – cut to ribbons. Now I want to do my path up the Vaituluiga single-handed, and I want it to burst on the public complete. Hence, with devilish ingenuity, I begin it at different places; so that if you stumble on one section, you may not even then suspect the fulness of my labours. Accordingly, I started in a new place, below the wire and hoping to work up to it. It was perhaps lucky I had so bad a cutlass, and my smarting hand bid me stay; before I had got up to the wire; but just in season, so that I was only the better of my activity, not dead beat as yesterday. A strange business it was, and infinitely solitary: away above, the sun was in the high tree tops; the lianas noosed and sought to hang me; the saplings struggled, and came up with that sob of death that one gets to know so well; great soft, sappy trees fell at a lick of the cutlass; little tough switches laughed at and dared my best endeavour. . . . Just at the right time I returned: to wash down, change, and begin this snatch of letter before dinner was ready, and to finish it afterward, before Henry has yet put in an appearance for his lesson in 'long explessions'. Dinner: stewed beef and potatoes, baked bananas, new loaf bread hot from the oven, pineapple in claret. These are great days; we have been low in the past; but now are we as belly-gods, enjoying all things.

Wednesday

Hist. Vailima resumed.

A gorgeous evening of after-glow in the great tree-tops and behind the mountain, and full moon over the lowlands and the sea, inaugurated a night of horrid cold. To you effete denizens of the so-called temperate zone, it had seemed nothing; neither of us could sleep; we were up seeking extra coverings, I know not at what hour – it was as bright as day, the moon right over Vaea – near due west, the birds strangely silent, and the wood of the house tingling with cold: I believe it must have been 60°! Consequence: Fanny has a headache and is wretched, and I could do no work. (I am trying all round for a place to hold my pen; you will hear why later on: this to explain penmanship). I wrote 2 pp., very bad –, no movement, no life or interest; then I wrote a business letter; then took to tootling on the flageolet, till glory should call me farmering. . . . Then turned my attention to the path. I could not go into my bush path for two reasons: first, sore hands; second, had on my trousers and good shoes. Lucky it was. Right in the wild lime hedge which cuts athwart us just homeward of the garden, I found a great bed of *kuikui* – sensitive plant – our deadliest enemy. A fool brought it to this island in a pot, and used to lecture and sentimentalize over the tender thing. The tender thing has now taken charge of this island, and men fight it, with torn hands, for bread and life. A singular insidious thing, shrinking and biting like a weasel; clutching by its roots as a limpet clutches to a rock. As I fought him, I bettered some verses in my poem, 'The Woodman':[9] the only thought I gave to letters. Though the *kuikui* was thick, there was but a small patch of it; and when I was done, I attacked the wild lime, and had a hand to hand skirmish with its spines and elastic suckers. . . . Suddenly quoth Lafaele: 'Somebody he sing out.' — 'Somebody he sing out? All right, I go.' And I went and found they had been whistling and 'singing out' for long, but the fold of the hill and the uncleared bush shuts in the garden, so that no one heard; and I was late for dinner, and Fanny's headache was cross; and when the meal was over, we had to cut up pineapple which was going bad, to make jelly of; and the next time you have a handful of broken blood blisters, apply pineapple juice, and you will give me news of it, and I request a specimen of your hand of write five minutes after — the historic moment when I tackled this history. My day so far. . . .

Friday — I think

I have been too tired to add to this chronicle, which will at any rate give you some guess of our employment. All goes well; the *kuikui* — (think of this mispronunciation having actually infected me to the extent of misspelling! *Tuitui* is the word by rights) — the *tuitui* is all out of the paddock a fenced park between the house and boundary. Peni's men start today on the road; the garden is part burned, part dug; and Henry at the head of a troop of underpaid assistants is hard at work clearing. The part clearing you will see from the map; from the house run down to the stream side, up the stream nearly as high as the garden, then back to the star which I have just added to the map. My long silent contests in the forest have had a strange effect on me. The unconcealed vitality of these vegetables, their exuberant number and strength, the attempts — I can use no other word — of lianas to enwrap and capture the intruder, the awful silence; the knowledge that all my efforts are only like the perform- ance of an actor, the thing of a moment, and the wood will silently and swiftly heal them up with fresh effervescence; the cunning sense of the *tuitui*, suffering itself to be touched with wind-swayed grasses and not minding — but let the grass be moved by a man, and it shuts up; the whole silent battle, murder and slow death of the contending forest — weighs upon the imagination. My poem 'The Woodman' stands; but I have taken refuge in a new story, which just shot through me like a bullet in one of my moments of awe, alone in that tragic jungle.

[9] Published as *Songs of Travel*, XXXIX.

The High Woods of Ulufanua
1. A South Sea Bridal. 2. Under the Ban. 3. Sāvao and Fa'avao. 4. Cries
in the High Wood. 5. Rumour full of Tongues. 6. The Hour of Peril. 7.
The Day of Vengeance.

It is very strange, very extravagant, I daresay; but it's varied, and
picturesque, and has a pretty love affair, and ends well. *Ulufanua* is a lovely
Samoan word, *ulu* = grove, *fanua* = land, grove land – 'the tops of the
high trees'. *Sāvao*, 'sacred to the wood', and *Fa'avao*, 'wood-ways', are the
names of two characters. *Ulufanua* the name of the supposed island.[10]

I am very tired and rest off today from all but letters; Fanny is quite
done up; she could not sleep last night, something it seemed like asthma
– I trust not. I suppose Lloyd will be about, so you can give him the
benefit of this long scrawl. Never say that I *can't* write a letter; say that I
don't. Yours ever, my dearest fellow   R.L.S.[11]

To Charles Baxter

[*Postmark 6 December 1890*]   [*Vailima*]

My dear Charles, I wonder if you ever receive any of my letters; I see you
miss many; and I have myself lost so much that I now take the precaution
of registering. This is disagreeable matter. I have at least received word
from Lloyd: one letter – others are lost I suppose. From it I gather that
Henley has not been to call on my mother.[1] I have taken a good deal from
Henley for myself and my wife, for a wife counts on the same plane as her
husband; this treatment of an old lady, recently bereaved and very lonely,
I refuse to pass over, the supplies are stopped. He may go and beg from
whom he pleases; no threepenny piece of mine goes near him. His
disloyalty as a friend has long been very plain to me. What a picture, when
in the midst of our trouble, I send McClure to him – McClure who had
heard from us nothing but Henley's praise – and the uncivil fellow

---

[10] This story was written in due course as 'The Beach of Falesá'.

[11] A long postscript and a 'Supplementary Page' omitted.

[1] Lloyd wrote a long letter to RLS and Fanny from Edinburgh on 13 October 1890 describing
meetings with friends and relatives: 'Down last night to Henley's. A shade less boisterous and
noisy than I remember him – greyer too, and even more bitter and intolerant. . . . He has never
been to call on Aunt Maggie – confound him!' In a later letter from London on 26 October
he wrote of him at greater length: 'He has alienated every friend, save Hamilton Bruce, Bob
and C.B. – and his usual dreary little court of duffers and tongue-tied incapables'; according to
Sir Walter Simpson, Henley, who was on an income of £800 a year, had recently borrowed
£200 from Baxter and was in a fair way to alienate him, too – 'And Bruce keeps open house
for him, submits to boundless extravagances – and is sure to find it intolerable in the long run.'
For Hamilton Bruce, see p. 362, n. 4.

receives my guest with dispraise of myself; and what a contrast is the
conduct of McClure, who never breathed a word in betrayal of Henley,
and continues to give me news of him as though all were well; so that
I only hear of this by a back way.[2] And yet that is what I have been
accustomed to accept, and accepted. The treatment of my mother stands
on a different base; it is so cruelly small to an old woman very much alone;
I have a loyalty to her also; he has chosen to strike me there; and I am
done with him for time and for eternity.

You will kindly communicate to him the enclosed scrap of paper: on
second thoughts I will post it myself. Here are the terms:

'The man who did not care to call upon my mother returning alone
and bereaved to the empty roof of my father, is – in the name of him dead
and of her living – dead to me forever. Farewell.'

Explicit Amicitia.

My mother also did not tell me; everyone seeks to save me pain, save
Henley alone. But he has given me the last pang. Should he write to me,
I will enclose his letter unopened. I have supped full of him. What would
my father say, ye Gods, if he could but know? I think he – W.E.H. – had
some entertainment in his time in that poor house: the fire is a little cold;
he might have made a visit of digestion to the widow, now when the
mirth has ceased.

I am so moved with living rage that I can think of nothing else. You
seem to be doing as I would have you; to judge from Lloyd's letter. A
thousand thanks. I do not think this breach should make you think me
variable in my affections. Change the thing; suppose your father were
dead, you in a far part of the world, your mother returning alone to
Rutland Square, and I keeping camp unmoved in Heriot Row. Would
you accept such conduct? I know you better. And yet, if I have tried you
– and I fear I have – it has not been as Henley has tried me. It was an ill
day for me when I saw him: all that was pleasant in the past but augments
my bitterness this hour. I am, my dear Charles, Yours ever affectionately
and gratefully   R.L.S.

Next day

Of course the first note is condemned; I give you a copy of the
substitute:

[2] In his autobiography, McClure says that he went to London in 1888, on business connected
with his syndicate, bearing letters of introduction from RLS to Baxter, Henley, Colvin, Henry
James and others: 'I found most of Stevenson's set very much annoyed by the attention he had
received in America. There was a note of detraction in their talk which surprised and, at first,
puzzled me. Henley was particularly emphatic.' The one most marked exception to 'this
dissenting chorus' was Henry James. In a letter dated 9 October 1890, Lloyd wrote of Colvin:
'He is vastly attached to the incandescent McClure; it was as we supposed – W.E.H. ran you
down before the Little Man, and a flare up ensued on Pink's [i.e. McClure's] part – I believe
it was this that started the Colvingular attachment.'

'I hear you have not thought fit to call on my mother since her return. I think my father tried to make you welcome in that house; he is gone, the house is empty; it would have been very fit you should have paid your respects to his widow – perhaps, if you had called to mind some of the past, you would have thought it kind to visit my mother. Had I been so indifferent, we should never have met. I will say no more; I do not wish to part in harshness from so old a friend and one bound up with the memories of so much joy and sorrow. But let the parting if you please, be final. R.L.S.'

I have no more anger; I am simply weary of the incubus. He must feel it strange after all to receive, and to have earned, such a farewell, in that city of Edinburgh, where I made myself no sluggish friend to him.[3]

To Henry James

29 December 1890   *Vailima*

My dear Henry James, It is terrible how little everybody writes, and how much of that little disappears in the capacious maw of the Post Office. Many letters both from and to me, I now know to have been lost in transit: my eye is on the Sydney Post Office, a large ungainly structure with a tower, as being not a hundred miles from the scene of disappearance; but then I have no proof. *The Tragic Muse* you announced to me as coming; I had already ordered it from a Sydney bookseller; about two months ago he advised me that his copy was in the post; and I am still tragically museless.

News, news, news. What do we know of yours? What do you care for ours? We are in the midst of the rainy season, and dwell among alarms of hurricanes, in a very unsafe little two storied wooden box 650 feet above and about three miles from the sea beach. Behind us, till the other slope of the island, desert forest, peaks and loud torrents; in front green slopes to the sea, some fifty miles of which we dominate. We see the ships as they go out and in to the dangerous roadstead of Apia; and if they lie far out, we can even see their topmasts while they are at anchor. Of sounds

---

[3] RLS went over the ground again in a letter to Baxter in late February 1891, and commented:

> As for Henley, what a miss I have of him. The charm, the wit, the vigour of the man, haunt my memory; my past is all full of his big presence and his welcome, wooden footstep: let it be a past henceforward: a beloved past, without continuation. I had a letter from him the other day in which he signed himself 'my old friend'. I accept the phrase: I am his old friend; I was, not am, his friend. The affair is ended, the record closed; without ill will on my side and without irritation.

In August 1891 he confessed to Baxter: 'H.'s conduct to my mother was only the last straw. I had been nettled and worried for years before by his strange attitude behind my back, and though I forgave, I could not truly forget.'

of men, beyond those of our own labourers, there reach us at very long
intervals, salutes from the warships in harbour, the bell of the cathedral
church, and the low of the conch shell calling the labour boys on the
German plantations. Yesterday, which was Sunday – the *quantième* is most
likely erroneous; you can now correct it – we had a visitor – Baker of
Tonga.[1] Heard you ever of him? He is a great man here; he is accused of
theft, rape, judicial murder, private poisoning, abortion, misappropriation
of public moneys – oddly enough, not forgery nor arson: you would be
amused if you knew how thick the accusations fly in this South Sea world.
I make no doubt my own character is something illustrious; or if not yet,
there is a good time coming.

But all our resources have not of late been Pacific. We have had
enlightened society: La Farge the painter, and your friend Charles Adams:
a great privilege – would it might endure. I would go oftener to see them,
but the place is awkward to reach on horseback; I had to swim my horse
the last time I went to dinner, and as I have not yet returned the clothes
I had to borrow, I dare not return in the same plight: it seems inevitable
– as soon as the wash comes in, I plump straight into the American
Consul's shirt or trousers! They, I believe, would come oftener to see me,
but for the horrid doubt that weighs upon our commissariat department;
we have *often* almost nothing to eat; a guest would simply break the bank;
my wife and I have dined on one avocado pear; I have several times dined
on hard bread and onions; what would you do with a guest at such narrow
seasons? eat him? or serve up a labour boy fricasseed?[2] However we do
meet and I enjoy it much.

Work? work is now arrested; but I have written I should think about
thirty chapters of the South Sea book, they will all want rehandling I
daresay; gracious, what a strain is a long book! The time it took me to
design this volume, before I could dream of putting pen to paper was

---

[1] Shirley Waldemar Baker (1835–1903), Wesleyan missionary who became a friend and adviser of
King George Tupou I of Tonga (1797–1893) and was created Prime Minister in 1880 after
resigning in disgrace from the Missionary Society. As virtual dictator he guided the development
of Tonga into a modern sovereign state recognised by the Great Powers. Widespread disorders
followed the establishment of an independent Free Church of Tonga in 1885 and the adherents
of the old Wesleyan Church were fiercely persecuted. There was an attempt to assassinate Baker
in 1887 and after further unrest, Baker – whose activities both as missionary and politician were
the subject of much scandal and controversy – was deported from Tonga in July 1890 by Sir
John Bates Thurston (1836–97), Governor of Fiji and British High Commissioner for the
Western Pacific. RLS and Fanny had stayed with Moors over Christmas and Baker and his son
had been guests for dinner on Christmas Day. RLS wrote to Colvin about him: 'Baker's
appearance is not unlike John Bull in a cartoon, with very small sly eyes, and very oily Wesleyan
manners.'

[2] In his reply dated 18 February 1891 James wrote: 'Your loneliness and your foodlessness, my
dear Louis, bring tears to my eyes ... Don't eat up Mrs Louis, whatever you do. You are
precious to literature – but she is precious to the affections ...'

excessive. And then think of writing a book of travels on the spot; when I am continually extending my information, revising my opinions, and seeing the most finely finished portions of my work come part by part in pieces. Very soon I shall have no opinions left. And without an opinion, how to string artistically vast accumulations of fact? Darwin said no one could observe without a theory;[3] I suppose he was right, 'tis a fine point of metaphysic; but I will take my oath, no man can write without one – at least the way he would like to. And my theories melt, melt, melt, and as they melt the thaw-waters wash down my writing, and leave unidea'd tracts – wastes instead of cultivated farms.

Kipling is by far the most promising young man who has appeared since – ahem – I appeared. He amazes me by his precocity, and various endowment. But he alarms me by his copiousness and haste. He should shield his fire with both hands, 'and draw up all his strength and sweetness in one ball.' ('draw all his strength, and all his sweetness up into one ball'? I cannot remember Marvell's words.)[4] So the critics have been saying to me; but I was never capable of – and surely never guilty of – such a debauch of production. At this rate his works will soon fill the habitable globe; and surely he was armed for better conflicts than these succinct sketches and flying leaves of verse? I look on, I admire, I rejoice for myself; but in a kind of ambition we all have for our tongue and literature, I am wounded. If I had this man's fertility and courage, it seems to me I could leave a pyramid.

Well, we begin to be the old fogies now; and it was high time *something* rose to take our places. Certainly Kipling has the gifts; the fairy god-mothers were all tipsy at his christening: what will he do with them?

I am going to manage to send a long letter every month to Colvin: which I daresay, if it is ever of the least interest, he will let you see. My wife has had an abscess in her ear; but she is now better, and I hope will be reasonably right. We are a very crazy couple to lead so rough a life; but we manage excellently: she is handy and inventive, and I have one quality, I don't grumble. The nearest I came was the other day; when I had finished dinner, I thought awhile; then had my horse saddled, rode down to Apia, and dined again – I must say with unblunted appetite; that is my best excuse. Good-bye, my dear James, find an hour to write to us and register your letter. Yours affectionately   R.L.S.

---

[3] In the autobiographical chapter included in *The Life and Letters of Charles Darwin* (1887) by his son Francis Darwin, Darwin says at one point in his research that led to *The Origin of Species* that he had collected facts without a theory but later he says that he had 'at last got a theory by which to work'.

[4] RLS wrote the words in brackets above his first attempt to remember Marvell's 'To his Coy Mistress' – 'Let us roll all our strength, and all/Our sweetness, up into one ball'.

To his Mother

[*2 January 1891*]   [*Vailima*]

My dear Mother, I should have been at Melbourne to meet you;[1] but my
proofs did not come,[2] and I have been obliged to begin building. Let both
the boys come right straight on here: bringing each a camp bed with wire
– Lloyd knows the kind, a mattress, mosquito bars[3] and two blankets. We
can put *them* up, and they will really be a help to us in our struggles with
man and beast and nature; I have a special wish to have Tommy here; if
he knows nothing of leprosy, let him try and get a book about it in
Melbourne or Sydney.

We must just make no recriminations from one side or the other. None
of us seem to have understood the gulph that severed us; and I never
dreamed you were to leave so early, and so many of your letters have
miscarried, that I still know almost nothing. We are totally averse to your
coming here before April at the soonest, but I'll manage to come down
and meet you at Auckland, if the coins permit, so as to return with you.
Fanny is pretty seedy; I am fairly fit; but not getting on with work as I
could wish, which damps me all round. However I shall bull-dose it
through, I suppose. The Chief Justice is come.[4] I have not yet met, but
seen, him; he is a fine *looking* fellow – but the proof of the pudding. It was
a mercy he came when he did or we should have been in war before the
end of the month. (This is January 2nd 1891, ma'am.) Petty squabbles
diversify the political horizon as the custom is: the white men are mostly
fools, and the natives all children: we may still be able to receive you
with the clash of arms; but if the C.J. chooses and knows, I think it may
be still averted. Had he come six months ago, it would have been an
easier task.

We have many bothers, I need scarcely say; but I do hope before April
to have a kind of house to put you in. More I cannot say. The whole
upper story is for Fanny and me: the lower story has a sitting-room and
your quarters and kitchen and pantry. Your quarters are not very grand
but you can arrange about your own when we build next. The main thing

---

[1] MIS arrived in Melbourne on 16 January 1891, accompanied by Lloyd and her nephew, Dr
Thomas Balfour. Thomas Stevenson Balfour (1868–1912), son of MIS's brother Dr George
Balfour, had recently qualified as a doctor. He stayed with relatives in Australia and did not
travel on to Vailima.

[2] Of *The Wrecker*. RLS was pressing Burlingame to begin publication of the uncompleted novel
in *Scribner's*. Publication began in August 1891.

[3] Mosquito bar is an American term for a kind of mosquito net: a curtain of thin gauze.

[4] Otto Conrad Waldemar Cedercrantz (1854–1932), Assistant Judge of the Swedish Court of
Appeal was, failing agreement by the three Powers, nominated in October 1890 by the King of
Sweden and Norway to be the Chief Justice of Samoa. He arrived in Samoa on 30 December
1890 on board the steamer *Alameda*.

just now was to insure my study and a place of congregation and good verandahs; Joe and Bell and Austin, we shall clap in the house we are now in, and Lloyd will have to camp in one of our outbuildings – say, the chicken house! The expense of building up here is ungodly; it is getting up the stuff that kills. I should never have believed what it would come to; and what annoys me, I know my neglect makes it dearer. But what can I do? I have to stick to my work, when I am able; that is, after all, more important: it is a pity we had not King[5] or Lloyd here from the start. It would have saved money in the long run and infinite botheration. Installation on a South Sea Island is not all roses, by several fathoms.

Up to Wednesday night I had fully meant to meet you or I would have been preparing a letter. Then the failure of the proofs decided me; and anyway last month has been very near a blank as to work, and it seemed a pity to mangle another – so I judged the proofs to settle it. I believe the grisly Letters have begun;[6] the cart is at my heels; but I have a good start, and with anything like luck should not be bothered the least. I have now sent, as well as I remember twenty-seven, or one more than the half, and the year of publication began only yesterday. Then there's the vile *Wrecker:* and I have to go to a ball tomorrow in Apia! *have* to, for it's a German Ball, and I must go to show goodwill: I wish they were all in Davy Jones's Bosom. I nearly wrote Billy Jones[7] – and you have never even heard of Billy Jones, or his cousin:[8] these be great mysteries, and belong to the Line Islands, of which you are no citizen. I trust you will like Upolu; I know you cannot help liking Vailima; it is really a lovely spot. Ever your affectionate son R.L. Stevenson

To Adelaide Boodle

17 January 1891   *Dampfer* Lübeck, *between Apia and Sydney*

My dear Miss Boodle, I was going to pretend I was amused; it is more honest to confess I was annoyed. Sorry you could not come; annoyed for

---

[5] Arthur Aris King took passage on the *Janet Nicoll* on one of the Line Islands *en route* for Sydney and a journey home to England to visit his family. RLS engaged him to help Lloyd with the packing and shipping of their furniture and belongings from Bournemouth to Samoa. He travelled back with Lloyd and worked for a time at Vailima. He seems to have lived originally at Pingelap (or Pingalap) in the Caroline Islands. He later married a half-caste girl and settled in Savaii.

[6] *The South Seas*, syndicated by McClure, began publication in the *Daily Telegraph* (Sydney) on 24 January 1891 and the *Auckland Star* on 31 January. These appearances (unrecorded by the bibliographers) are slightly earlier than the publication in the *Sun* (New York) from 1 February and in *Black and White* (London) from 6 February.

[7] RLS wrote, then deleted 'Bill' before writing 'Davy Jones'.

[8] According to Fanny, Jack Buckland had 'a sort of partner at Nanouti, known as "Billy Jones's cousin" . . . a man with a big head and one hand blown off by dynamite'. He was Charles Jones who died in 1890 leaving a native wife and young daughter.

your reasons. I have no doubt your friend is a good man, and I have no doubt he is a good adviser, and he may be practically right. But I should not like to think a friend of mine held seriously these opinions. Consider a while. Who are those whom we respect, who do a fair day's work in life, and keep their blood pure by exercise? The most that I have known do not sit in your friend's church; many of the best Christians sit in none. Christ himself and the twelve apostles seem to me (*chétif*) to have gone through this rough world without the support of the Anglican communion. The man whom I most admire, perhaps with but one exception in this world, a missionary here, and a hero, exists and does well without the Anglican sacrament.[1] God is no churchman, my dear lady; and no clergyman. The world is great and rough; he is nearest to the right divinity who can accept that greatness and that roughness. The quiet chancel – to call it quiet, though I know it often rings with the dissensions of the vestrymen and curates – is no school of life. In the forecastle, on the mast, in the ranks, and upon the field of battle, men may be denied the sacraments, I think they learn some knowledge, I am very sure God does not deny to them his countenance. I daresay your friend advised you very well; I daresay he used that reason which came uppermost, as men may, as they often must, do; but I pray you, do not take for a gospel this schismatic doctrine. Value your church, it will be so much the more to you a means of grace, I may not doubt: acceptation is a talisman. But do not for that cause undervalue that which is without; the great world in which we live and try vainly to do well, and the far greater part of which is quite a stranger to the consolations of your sect; and the far greater universe, which we dimly conceive to surround us, and in which I do not dream we can suppose the Church of England to be largely, or at least exclusively, reproduced. I smile a little bitterly when I think of my friends in these poor islands, native Christians, white missionaries, and plain irreligious laymen like myself; and then of the myriads in the other planets, who strive doubtless like ourselves to do their duty; and then (next) of my friend Miss Adelaide who cannot trust herself in the hands of God without the assistance of the Church of England, as arranged very largely by John Knox and finally defined by Act of Parliament. Perhaps it may help you to share with me a little – or to excuse a little – my annoyance, if I remind you that all my ancestors, for as far back as I can trace them, or with a very

---

[1] James Chalmers (1841–1901), Scottish missionary and explorer. After working at Rarotonga (where he was given the native name of 'Tamate') 1867–76, he went to New Guinea in 1877 and spent most of the rest of his life there exploring and establishing new missionary posts in conditions of great hardship and danger among very savage tribes. In April 1901 he and a fellow missionary were killed and eaten by savages at Dopima in the Gulf of Papua. RLS met Chalmers on board the *Lübeck* taking him to Samoa in September 1890, and developed a great admiration and affection for him, describing him to Colvin as 'a man that took me fairly by storm; for the most attractive, simple, brave, and interesting man in the whole Pacific'.

few exceptions, were denied, and somehow managed to breast through this life without the privilege of that communion on which you, and your friend, would set so high a value. I believe they did well; doubtless better than I; possibly as well – some of them – as your friend. I am pained that a friend of mine should conceive life so smally as to think she leaves the hand of her God, because she leaves a certain clique of clergymen and a certain scattered handful of stone buildings, some of them with pointed windows, most with belfries, and a few with an illumination of the Ten Commandments on the wall. I have forgot Milton's exact words; they are something to this purpose: 'Do not take the living God for a buzzard.'[2]

Whenever I speak of religion to those whom I value, I find myself embarrassed. I use phrases in one sense which they doubtless understand in another. As I have been here so disagreeable, and used the language of annoyance – it might almost seem of reproof – let me clear my feet: I do believe with my heart and soul in a God, and a righteous God: what he wants of me, with what measure he will serve me, I know not, and I do not think it is my business to inquire, convinced it will be right. For prettified religion that would pretend the world is not a tragic battlefield, and for petty religion that takes the name and attributes of God for an election ticket, I have no earthly patience. It cannot be good, it cannot be manly or womanly, to feed ourselves with these illusions. Face the gross facts; if you be pure, you will be the more pure; if you be brave, the more courageous. The ostrich and the sectarian have their place in the scheme of things; let the bandmaster intervene, and suggest they are 'a passing note'.

Now that I have unburthened myself, my dear gamekeeper, let me pass on to our news. My wife and I have had a rough time in our cabin on the mountains; one night we must sit in the dark, the wind would not suffer any light, and so loud was the roar of the rain and the beating boughs on the roof, that we must sit in silence also; I confess it was a tedious evening. May I suggest that in such hours (when any moment may turn you adrift in the storm under a shower of iron roof plates) there is a communion impossible in any chapel of ease, even in any cathedral? You are then alone with God: with one face of him, that is: which he who blinks, blinks at his peril.

The other day I left my wife alone with an inheritance of trouble, such as you can scarce imagine, of wood to be hauled up the mountain – and iron, forby; of roads that the rain removes and we must repair; of native workmen, who will not work; and sailed on the *Lübeck*, whose paper you now handle, to meet my mother and Lloyd in Sydney. 1500 miles from

---

[2] Milton, *Eikonoklastes*, ch. 1: 'those who thought no better of the living God than of a buzzard idol'. Milton is using 'buzzard' in the sense of 'stupid'.

port, in the great desert Pacific and in the hurricane season, we broke a
crank-shaft. It is almost incredible, but so well have things been managed
by the officers, so excellently has the wind served us, that we hope to be
in Sydney only four days late. Perhaps you would be inclined to say by the
kindness of Providence; in my present, not quite assuaged condition of
annoyance, I would beg you to be done for ever with such partial fancies.
The world, the universe, turns on vast hinges, proceeds on a huge plan:
you, and me, and the Church of England, are all – I potently believe it –
used for good; but we are all – and this I know – as the dust of the
balances. The loss or the salvation of the *Lübeck* was weighed and was
decided in the hour of birth of the universe; the interesting case of R.L.S.
and his wife alone on Upolu, and his mother waiting to meet him in the
colonies, and his friend Adelaide Boodle expecting a letter – and a nicer
letter than this, no doubt – in Bournemouth, were all out of court before
the first world span, a sphere, in space; we are the cranks of a huge
machine – I do believe – of righteousness; we are there to suffer and to
be broken, I am convinced, for a good end. That churches may sustain us,
I am the last to deny, though one of the last to feel; in so far, we are right
to cherish and respect them; but a church is not the universe and can
never be the house of the Great God. See how you have excited the
squire that he should practically rail at his gamekeeper till this voluminous
paper is exhausted! I must say that, for the cause of annoyance, I did not
read your letter to an end. Doubtless you decided right; doubtless your
friend knows well; it is not that I am hurt: I am only hurt when the brave
friends I know and love, and the good forbears I respect somewhat on
trust, are 'unchurched' by one who is my friend. Ever yours affectionately

Robert Louis Stevenson[3]

---

[3] Miss Boodle's reply has not survived, but in a letter of 9 February 1893 she referred to it as 'the
one letter from you that ever hurt me' and confirmed that it had changed her attitude. RLS
wrote to her in April or May 1891 apologising for having expressed his views 'somewhat
roughly':

> God forbid, I should seem to judge for you on such a point; it was what you seemed to set
> forth as your reasons that fluttered my old Presbyterian spirit – for mind you, I am a child
> of the Covenanters – whom I do not love, but they are mine after all, my fathers and my
> mothers – and they had their merits too, and their ugly beauties, and grotesque heroisms,
> that I love them for, the while I laugh at them; but in their name and mine, do what you
> think right, and let the world fall.

Later in the letter RLS commented:

> What a strange idea, to think me a Jew-hater! Isaiah and David and Heine are good enough
> for me; and I leave more unsaid. Were I of Jew blood, I do not think I could ever forgive
> the Christians; the ghettos would get in my nostrils like mustard or lit gunpowder. Just so
> you, as being a child of the Presbytery, I retain – I need not dwell on that. The ascendant
> hand is what I feel most strongly; I am bound in and in with my forbears; were he one of
> mine, I should not be struck at all by Mr Moss of Bevis Marks, I should still see behind him

Do not be amazed at the registration; so many of our letters have miscarried that I now register all.

To Sidney Colvin[1]
(Abridged)

Friday 19 [actually 20] March [1891]   *[Vailima]*

My dear S.C., You probably expect that now I am back at Vailima, I should resume the practice of the diary letter. A good deal is changed. We are more;[2] solitude does not attend me as before; the night is passed playing Van John[3] for shells; and what is not less important I have just recovered from a severe illness, and am easily tired.

I will give you today. I sleep over in one of the lower rooms of the new house, where my wife has recently joined me. We have two beds, an empty case for a table, a chair, a tin basin, a bucket and a jug; next door in the dining-room, the carpenters camp on the floor, which is covered with their mosquito nets. Before the sun rises, at 5.45 or 5.50, Paul brings me tea, bread and a couple of eggs; and by about six I am at work. I work in bed – my bed is of mats, no mattress, sheets or filth – mats, a pillow and a blanket – and put in some three hours. It was 9.5 this morning when I set off to the streamside to my weeding; where I toiled, manuring the ground with the best enricher, human sweat, till the conch shell was blown from our verandah at 10.30. At eleven we dine; about half-past twelve I tried (by exception) to work again, could make nothing on't, and by one was on my way to the weeding, where I wrought till three. Half-past five is our next meal, and I read Flaubert's *Letters* till the hour came around; dined, and then Fanny having a cold, and I being tired, came over to my den in the unfinished house, where I now write to you, to the tune of the carpenters' voices, and by the light – I crave your

Moses of the Mount and the Tables and the shining face. We are all nobly born; fortunate those who know it; blessed those who remember.

Bevis Marks, in the City of London is the oldest synagogue in Britain. When Moses came down from Mount Sinai bearing the stone tablets of the Commandments 'the skin of his face shone' (Exodus 34:29, 30).

[1] When RLS arrived in Sydney on 20 January his mother travelled from Melbourne to join him. She persuaded him to stay on for a month to await the repair of the *Lübeck*. He caught a cold and then became seriously ill. In consequence, MIS postponed her planned visit to New Zealand in order to accompany him back to Samoa. The *Lübeck* reached Apia on 1 March and MIS had her first sight of Vailima. But, as Fanny wrote in her diary, 'the close quarters, continuous rain, and general discomfort were too much for her'; she left for Sydney on the *Lübeck*'s return journey on 3 March to carry out her visit to New Zealand.

[2] Because of Lloyd's arrival.

[3] Slang for the card game *Vingt-et-un*, a favourite with RLS and his family.

pardon – by the twilight of three vile candles filtered through the medium
of my mosquito bar. Bad ink being of the party, I write quite blindfold;
and can only hope you may be granted to read that which I am unable to
see while writing.

I said I was tired; it is a mild phrase; my back aches like toothache;
when I shut my eyes to sleep, I know I shall see before them – a
phenomenon to which both Fanny and I are quite accustomed – endless
vivid deeps of grass and weed, each plant particular and distinct, so that I
shall lie inert in body and transact for hours the mental part of my day
business, choosing the noxious from the useful. And in my dreams I shall
be hauling on recalcitrants, and suffering stings from nettles, stabs from
citron thorns, fiery bites from ants, sickening resistances of mud and slime,
evasions of slimy roots, dead weight of heat, sudden puffs of air, sudden
starts from birdcalls in the contiguous forest – some mimicking my name,
some laughter, some the signal of a whistle; and living over again at large
the business of my day.

Though I write so little, I pass all my hours of fieldwork in continual
converse and imaginary correspondence. I scarce pull up a weed, but I
invent a sentence on the matter to yourself; it does not get written; *autant
en emportent ly vents*;[4] but the intent is there, and for me (in some sort) the
companionship. Today for instance we had a great talk. I was toiling, the
sweat dripping from my nose in the hot fit after a squall of rain;
methought you asked me – frankly, was I happy. Happy (said I), I was
only happy once: that was at Hyères; it came to an end from a variety of
reasons, decline of health, change of place, increase of money, age with his
stealing steps:[5] since then, as before then, I know not what it means. But
I know pleasure still; pleasure with a thousand faces, and none perfect, a
thousand tongues all broken, a thousand hands and all of them with
scratching nails. High among these I place this delight of weeding out here
alone by the garrulous water, under the silence of the high wood, broken
by incongruous sounds of birds. And take my life all through, look at it
fore and back, and upside down, – though I would very fain change
myself, I would not change my circumstances – unless it were to bring
you here. And yet God knows perhaps this intercourse of writing serves
as well; and I wonder, were you here indeed, would I commune so
continually with the thought of you: I say I wonder for a form; I know,
and I know I should not.

So far and much further, the conversation went, while I groped in
slime after viscous roots, nursing and sparing little spears of grass, and

---

[4] The refrain from Villon's Ballade (see p. 400, n. 4).
[5] The First Gravedigger in *Hamlet* V.i.79–80, quoting inaccurately from a poem by Thomas, Lord
Vaux (1510–56), 'The Aged Lover Renounceth Love'.

retreating (even with outcry) from the prod of the wild lime. I wonder if anyone had ever the same attitude to nature as I hold, and have held for so long? This business fascinates me like a tune or a passion; yet all the while I thrill with a strong distaste. The horror of the thing, objective and subjective, is always present to my mind; the horror of creeping things, a superstitious horror of the void and the powers about me, the horror of my own devastation and continual murders. The life of the plants comes through my fingertips, their struggles go to my heart like supplications. I feel myself blood boltered; then I look back on my cleared grass, and count myself an ally in a fair quarrel, and make stout my heart.

It is but a little while since I lay sick in Sydney, beating the fields about the navy and Dean Swift and Dryden's Latin hymns;[6] judge if I love this reinvigorating climate, where I can already toil till my head swims and every string in the poor jumping jack (as he now lies in bed) aches with a kind of yearning strain, difficult to suffer in quiescence.

As for my damned literature, God knows what a business it is, grinding along without a scrap of inspiration or a note of style. But it has to be ground; and the mill grinds exceeding slowly though not particularly small. The last two chapters have taken me considerably over a month, and they are still beneath pity. This I cannot continue, time not sufficing; and the next will just have to be worse. All the good I can express is just this: some day, when style revisits me, they will be excellent matter to rewrite. Of course my old cure of a change of work would probably answer; but I cannot take it now. The treadmill turns; and with a kind of desperate cheerfulness, I mount the idle stair. I have not the least anxiety about the book; unless I die, I shall find the time to make it good; but the Lord deliver me from the thought of the Letters. However the Lord has other things on hand; and about six tomorrow, I shall resume the consideration practically, and face (as best I may) the fact of my incompetence and disaffection to the task. Toil I do not spare; but fortune refuses me success. We can do more, Whatever-his-name-was, we can deserve it.[7] But my mis-desert began long since, by the acceptation of a bargain quite unsuitable to all my methods.

Saturday [21 March]

. . . Today I have not weeded, I have written instead from six till eleven, from twelve till two . . .; a damned Letter is written for the third

---

[6] French 'battre les champs', to wander in mind. RLS was seriously ill with fever for two days in Sydney. In his delirium he was remembering in a nonsensical way two books he had recently read, a life of Swift, and Scott's life of Dryden in which he had (wrongly) attributed to the poet translations of two Latin hymns.

[7] ''Tis not in mortals to command success,/But we'll do more, Sempronius; we'll deserve it' – Addison, Cato, I.ii.43.

time; I dread to read it, for I dare not give it a fourth chance – unless it be very bad indeed. Now I write to you from my mosquito curtain, to the song of saws and planes, and hammers, and wood clumping on the floor above; in a day of heavenly brightness; a bird twittering near by; my eye, through the open door, commanding green weeds, two or three forest trees casting their boughs against the sky, a forest-clad mountain-side beyond, and close in by the door-jamb, a nick of the blue Pacific. It is March in England, bleak March, and I lie here with the great sliding doors wide open in an undershirt and p'jama trousers, and melt in the closure of mosquito bars, and burn to be out in the breeze. A few torn clouds – not white, the sun has tinged them a warm pink, swim in heaven. . . .

Sunday

When I had done talking to you yesterday, I played on my pipe till the conch sounded, then went over to the old house for dinner, and had scarce risen from table ere I was submerged with visitors. The first of these despatched, I spent the rest of the evening going over the Samoan translation of my 'Bottle Imp' with Claxton the missionary;[8] then to bed, but being upset I suppose by these interruptions, and having gone all day without my weeding, not to sleep. For hours I lay awake and heard the rain fall, and saw faint, faraway lightning over the sea, and wrote you long letters which I scorn to reproduce. This morning Paul was unusually early; the dawn had scarce begun when he appeared with the tray and lit my candle; and I had breakfasted and read (with indescribable sinkings) the whole of yesterday's work, before the sun had risen. Then I sat and thought, and sat and better thought. It was not good enough, nor good; it was as slack as journalism, but not so inspired; it was excellent stuff misused, and the defects stood gross on it like humps upon a camel. But – could I, in my present disposition, do much more with it? in my present pressure for time, were I not better employed doing another one about as ill, than making this some thousandth fraction better? Yes, I thought; and tried the new one, and behold – I could do nothing: my head swims, words do not come to me, nor phrases; and I accepted defeat, packed up my traps, and turned to communicate the failure to my esteemed corres-

---

[8] 'The Bottle Imp', translated into Samoan by the Revd A.E. Claxton, was published under the title 'O Le Fagu Aitu' in O Le Sulu Samoa (The Samoan Torch), the missionary magazine of which he was editor, May–August and October–December 1891. The original appeared in the New York Herald, 8 February 1891 and in Black and White, 28 March 1891.

The Revd Arthur Edward Claxton (1862–1941), was ordained in 1885; in the same year he married Frances Alice Clarke (1866–1916) and went out to Samoa as a missionary for the L.M.S. In May 1890 he was moved to Apia from Savaii, and among other duties was in charge of English services in the Church for white residents. From 1891 to 1893 he was Natives' Advocate on the Land Commission and (as later letters will show) involved in a bitter controversy with RLS. In 1895–1921 he served as a missionary in China.

pondent. I think it possible I overworked yesterday: well, we'll see tomorrow, or perhaps try again later. It is indeed the hope of trying later that keeps me writing to you. If I take to my pipe, I know myself – all is over for the morning. Hurray, I'll correct proofs! . . .

★To W. Craibe Angus[1]

April 1891   *Vailima*

Dear Mr Angus, Surely I remember you! It was W.C. Murray[2] who made us acquainted, and we had a pleasant crack. I see your poet is not yet dead. I remember even our talk – or you would not think of trusting that invaluable *Jolly Beggars* to the treacherous posts, and the perils of the sea, and the carelessness of authors.[3] I love the idea, but I could not bear the risk. However –

> Hale be your heart, hale be your fiddle –[4]

it was kindly thought upon.

My interest in Burns is, as you suppose, perennial. I would I could be present at the exhibition, with the purpose of which I heartily sympathise; but the *Nancy* has not waited in vain for me,[5] I have followed my chest, the anchor is weighed long ago, I have said my last farewell to the hills and the heather and the lynns; like Leyden;[6] I have gone into far lands to die, not stayed like Burns to mingle in the end with Scottish soil. I shall not even return like Scott for the last scene. Burns Exhibitions are all over. 'Tis a far cry to Lochawe from tropical Vailima.[7]

> But still our hearts are true, our hearts are Highland,
> And we in dreams behold the Hebrides.[8]

[1] William Craibe Angus (died 1899), a well-known Glasgow picture and fine-art dealer, was a noted Burns collector. He conceived the idea and was the main organiser of the Burns Exhibition held in Glasgow in 1896 to commemorate the centenary of the poet's death.

[2] Presumably William Cleghorn Murray, W.S. (1837–?).

[3] Angus's copy of Burns's *The Jolly Beggars* (Glasgow, 1799), autographed by RLS on the title page, was exhibited at the 1896 Exhibition, as was a copy of the 1787 edition of Burns's *Poems* also autographed by RLS.

[4] Burns, 'Epistle to Captain William Logan', l. 13.

[5] In 1796 Burns planned to emigrate to Jamaica on board the *Nancy*.

[6] John Leyden (1775–1811), Scottish physician, poet and orientalist, who assisted Scott in compiling *Minstrelsy of the Scottish Border*. He worked for the East India Company in India and the East Indies, and died in Java.

[7] 'It's a far cry to Lochow (Lochawe)' explained by Scott (in *A Legend of Montrose*, ch. 13) as 'a proverbial expression of the [Campbells], meaning that their ancient hereditary domains lay beyond the reach of an invading enemy'.

[8] 'Canadian Boat Song', ll. 9–10. The first line quoted should read, 'Yet still the blood is strong, the heart is Highland'. The authorship of the poem (first published in *Blackwood's*, September 1829) is disputed but it has been attributed to the Scottish novelist John Galt.

When your hand is in, will you remember our poor Edinburgh Robin? Burns alone has been just to his promise; follow Burns, he knew best, he knew whence he drew fire – from the poor, white-faced, drunken, vicious boy that raved himself to death in the Edinburgh madhouse. Surely there is more to be gleaned about Fergusson, and surely it is high time the task was set about. I may tell you (because your poet is not dead) something of how I feel; we are three Robins who have touched the Scots lyre this last century. Well, the one is the world's, he did it, he came off, he is for ever; but I and the other – ah! what bonds we have – born in the same city, both sickly, both vicious,[9] both pestered, one nearly to madness, one to the madhouse, with a damnatory creed; both seeing the stars and the dawn, and wearing shoe-leather on the same ancient stones, under the same pends, down the same closes, where our common ancestors clashed in their armour, rusty or bright. And the old Robin, who was before Burns and the flood, died in his acute, painful youth, and left the models of the great things that were to come; and the new, who came after, outlived his green-sickness, and has faintly tried to parody the finished work. If you will collect the strays of Robin Fergusson, fish for material, collect any last re-echoing of gossip, command me to do what you prefer – to write the preface – to write the whole if you prefer: anything, so that another monument (after Burns's) be set up to my unhappy predecessor on the causey of Auld Reekie. You will never know, nor will any man, how deep this feeling is; I believe Fergusson lives in me. I do; but tell it not in Gath, every man has these fanciful superstitions, coming, going, but yet enduring; only most men are so wise (or the poet in them so dead) that they keep their follies for themselves. I am, yours very truly   Robert Louis Stevenson

To Henry Clay Ide[1]

[*19 June 1891*]   [*Vailima*]

Dear Mr Ide, Herewith please find the DOCUMENT which I trust will prove sufficient in law. It seems to me very attractive in its eclecticism; Scots, English and Roman law phrases are all indifferently introduced and

---

[9] RLS, misled by the prejudices of the early biographers, is too severe in his references to Fergusson's dissipation.

[1] Henry Clay Ide (1844–1921), American lawyer and public official. He arrived in Apia on 16 May 1891, following his appointment as American Land Commissioner. He was later Chief Justice of Samoa (1893–97), Governor-General of the Philippines (1906), and US Minister to Spain (1909–13). In *A Footnote to History* RLS described Ide as 'a man of character and intelligence'.

a quotation from the works of Haynes Bayly can hardly fail to attract the indulgence of the Bench. Yours very truly   Robert Louis Stevenson

[*Enclosure*]

I, Robert Louis Stevenson, Advocate of the Scots Bar, author of *The Master of Ballantrae* and *Moral Emblems*, stuck civil engineer, sole owner and patentee of the Palace and Plantation known as Vailima in the island of Upolu, Samoa, a British Subject, being in sound mind and pretty well I thank you in body:

In consideration that Miss A.H. Ide, daughter of H.C. Ide, in the town of St Johnsbury, in the county of Caledonia, in the State of Vermont, United States of America, was born, out of all reason, upon Christmas Day, and is therefore, out of all justice, denied the consolation and profit of a Proper Birthday;[2]

And considering that I, the said Robert Louis Stevenson, have attained an age when O, we never mention it,[3] and that I have now no further use for a birthday of any description;

And in consideration that I have met H.C. Ide, the father of the said A.H. Ide, and found him about as white a Land Commissioner as I require;

Have transferred and *do hereby transfer* to the said A.H. Ide, *All and Whole* my rights and privileges in the thirteenth day of November, formerly my birthday, now, hereby, and henceforth, the birthday of the said A.H. Ide, to have, hold, exercise and enjoy the same in the customary manner, by the sporting of fine raiment, eating of rich meats and receipt of gifts, compliments and copies of verse, according to the manner of our ancestors;

And I direct the said A.H. Ide to add to her said name of A.H. Ide the name Louisa − at least in private; and I charge her to use my said birthday with moderation and humanity, *et tamquam bona filia familiae*, the said birthday not being so young as it once was and having carried me in a very satisfactory manner since I can remember;

And in case the said A.H. Ide shall neglect or contravene either of the above conditions, I hereby revoke the donation and transfer my rights in

---

[2] Ide had told RLS that his daughter Annie was unhappy because her birthday fell on Christmas Day. RLS's 'Gift' of his birthday became a popular journalistic story and many accounts of it have been published. Annie Ide (1879−1945) and her two sisters accompanied their father to Samoa in 1893 and were soon on friendly terms with the Vailima household; Annie and Belle became lifelong friends. She married (1906) as his third wife the Irish-American lawyer and Congressman William Bourke Cockran (1854−1923).

[3] Cf. the once popular song 'Oh! No! We Never Mention Her' by Thomas Haynes Bayley.

the said birthday to the President of the United States of America for the time being:[4]

In witness whereof I have hereto set my hand and seal this nineteenth day of June in the year of grace eighteen hundred and ninety-one.

Robert Louis Stevenson
I.P.D.[5]

Witness: Lloyd Osbourne
Witness: Harold Watts[6]

To Sidney Colvin
(Slightly Abridged)

[24 or 25 June 1891]   [Vailima]

My dear Colvin, I am so hideously in arrears that I know not where to begin. However here I am a prisoner in my room, unfit for work, incapable of reading with interest, and I may try to catch up a bit. We have a guest here; a welcome guest: my Sydney music master, whose health broke down, and who came with his remarkable simplicity, to ask a month's lodging. He is newly married, his wife in the family way: beastly time to fall sick. I have found, by good luck, a job for him here, which will pay some of his way; and in the meantime he is a pleasant guest, for he plays the flute with little sentiment but great perfection, and endears himself by his simplicity. To me, especially; I am so weary of finding people approach me with precaution, pick their words, flatter, and twitter; but the muttons of the good God are not at all afraid of the lion. They take him as he comes, and he does not bite – at least not hard. This makes us a party of 1, 2, 3, 4, 5, 6, 7, 8, at table; deftly waited on by Mary Carter, a very nice Sydney girl, who served us at our boarding-house and has since come on[1] – how long she will endure this exile is another story; and gauchely waited on by Faauma, the new left-handed wife of the famed Lafaele, a little creature in native dress of course and beautiful as a

---

[4] It is related that US President William H. Taft (who knew the Ides in the Philippines) entered into the joke by formally enquiring whether the birthday was being properly celebrated.

[5] In praesentia dominorum – In presence of the Lords (of Session). Under Scottish law the letters I.P.D. are added to the signature of the presiding Judge in the Court of Session to indicate that he has signed in the presence of the other judges.

[6] Harold Watts, RLS's flageolet teacher in Sydney, had just arrived in Apia and was staying at Vailima.

[1] MIS's maid, who arrived with the Strongs on 24 May. She stayed on at Vailima until May 1892.

bronze candlestick, so fine, clean and dainty in every limb; her arms and her little hips in particular masterpieces. The rest of the crew may be stated briefly: the great Henry Simelē, still to the front; King, of the yellow beard, rather a disappointment – I am inclined, on this point, to republican opinions; Ratke, a German cook, good – and Germanly bad, he don't make *my* kitchen;[2] Paul, now working out his debts outdoors; Emma, a strange weird creature – I suspect (from her colour) a quarter white – widow of a white man, ugly, capable, a really good laundress; Java – yes, that is the name – they spell it Siava, but pronounce it, and explain it Java – her assistant, a creature I adore for her plain, wholesome, bread-and-butter beauty. An honest, almost ugly, bright good-natured face; the rest (to my sense) very exquisite; the inside of Java's knees, when she kilts her *lava-lava* high, is a thing I never saw equalled in a statue. She comes steering into my room of a morning, like Mrs Nickleby, with elaborate precaution; unlike her, noiseless.[3] If I look up from my work, she is ready with an explosive smile. I generally don't, and wait to look at her as she stoops for the bellows, and trips tiptoe off again, a miracle of successful womanhood in every line. The worst of civilisation is that you never see a woman. Hence my continual preference of the male, of which I used to grow ashamed. I am not ashamed of it now; it was good taste; for when you see a woman undeformed, you recognise the rights of mankind. Sometimes, when I look at Java, I am glad I am elderly and sick and overworked. Then again I am amused to find plain, healthy Java pass in my fancy so far before pretty, young Faauma. I observed Lloyd the other day to say that Java must have been lovely 'when she was young'; and I thought it an odd word, of a woman in the height of health, not yet touched with fat, though (to be just) a little slack of bust.

Our party you know: Fanny, Lloyd, my mother,[4] Bell, Joe Strong and 'the babe' – as we call him – Austin. . . .[5] We have now three instruments;

---

[2] Cf. 'I will make my kitchen' in RLS's (then unpublished) poem 'I will make you brooches' (*Songs of Travel* XI).

[3] In ch. 55 of *Nicholas Nickleby*, Mrs Nickleby enters Madeline Bray's sick-room 'with an elaborate caution, calculated to discompose the nerves of an invalid rather more than the entry of a horse-soldier at full gallop'; and makes 'every board creak and every thread rustle as she moved stealthily about'. Fanny in her diary of 30 June described the 'special delight' with which she and RLS watched Java's 'dramatic display of carefulness' every morning:

> she lifts one long shapely brown leg high in the air, looks for a suitable resting spot for her foot, comes down light as a feather on one toe, lifting the other leg with the same slow and graceful sweep; and so she moves about all her work. Her body she holds reverently bent forward, following the catlike movements of her leg with a corresponding swing of the arm. Upon her face, all the while, is a bright set smile, like that of an acrobat.

[4] MIS arrived from Auckland on 16 May. RLS told Colvin the next day: 'My mother has arrived, young, well and in good spirits. By desperate exertions, which have wholly floored Fanny, her room was ready for her, and the dining-room fit to eat in.'

[5] Colvin erased the next three lines (about fifty words) from the MS, evidently some reference to the Strongs. Joe, Belle and their son Austin arrived on 24 May. The cottage in which RLS and

Boehm flageolet, flute, and B♭ clarinet; and we expect in a few days our piano. This is a great pleasure to me: the band-mastering, the playing, and all. As soon as I am done with this stage of a letter, I shall return, not being allowed to play, to band-master, being engaged on an attempt to arrange an air with effect for the three pipes. And I'll go now, by jabers.

3 July

A long pause: occasioned, first by some days' hard work: next by a vile quinsey, if that be the way to spell it. But today I must write. For we have all kinds of larks on hand. The wars and rumours of wars begin to take consistency, in so much that we have loaded the weapons this morning, and inspected the premises with a view to defence. Of course it will come to nothing; but as in all stories of massacres, the one you don't prepare for is the one that comes off. All our natives think ill of the business; none of the whites do.[6] According to our natives the demonstration threatened for today or tomorrow is one of vengeance on the whites – small wonder – and if that begins, where will it stop? Anyway I don't mean to go down for nothing, if I can help it; and to amuse you I will tell you our plans. . . .[7]

Date Unknown [c. 13 July]

Well, nothing as yet, though I don't swear by it yet. There has been a lot of trouble, and there still is a lot of doubt as to the future; and those who sit in the chief seats, who are all excellent, pleasant creatures, are not, perhaps, the most wise of mankind. They actually proposed to kidnap and deport Mataafa; a scheme which would have loosed the avalanche at once. But some human being interfered and choked off this pleasing scheme.[8] You ask me in yours just received, what will become of us, if it comes to

Fanny had lived until the new house was built was dismantled and re-erected on a new site for them. It was called 'Chateau Fort' or 'Pineapple Cottage'.

[6] On Sunday 31 May, Mataafa, after attending service in the R.C. Church in Apia, was taken by his followers to the village of Malie (some seven miles down the coast to the west) for the purpose of making him King in opposition to Malietoa Laupepa. According to Samoan custom, the village had the right of conferring the royal title of Malietoa. This was therefore a symbolic act by which Mataafa again claimed the kingship. There were fears that fighting would begin and there was a flurry of activity by the white officials. In spite of all efforts and protests Mataafa remained at Malie, living in regal state, but not provoking conflict nor, apart from this one major act of defiance, disobeying the laws.

[7] I have omitted a paragraph in which RLS explained, with the aid of a rough sketch, how he proposed to garrison and defend the house. The weapons available were 'eight revolvers and a shotgun and swords galore'.

[8] A scheme allegedly proposed by the Revd A.E. Claxton to Harold Sewall on 8 July that Mataafa should be decoyed to Apia and there arrested. According to H.J. Moors, the story was for months the common talk in Apia. R.L.S. (without naming names) put it into A Footnote to History. Harold Marsh Sewall (1860–1924) was American Consul-General in Samoa, 1887–90 and 1891–2; he was later US minister to Hawaii 1897–8.

war? Well, if it is a war of the old sort, nothing. It will mean a little bother, and a great deal of theft, and more amusement. But if it comes to the massacre lark, I can only answer with the Bell of Old Bow.[9] You are to understand that, in my reading of the native character, every day that passes is a solid gain. They put in the time public speaking; so wear out their energy, develop points of difference and exacerbate internal ill-feeling. Consequently, I feel less apprehension of difficulty now, by about a hundredfold. All that I stick to, is that if war begins, there are ten chances to one we shall have it bad. The natives have been scurvily used by all the white Powers without exception; and they labour under the belief, of which they cannot be cured, that they defeated Germany. This makes an awkward complication. . . .

[*18 July*]

Date unknown, but it's post day, and July, and the rude inclement depth of winter, and the thermometer was 68° this morning and a few days ago it was 63°, and we have all been perishing with cold. All still seems quiet. Your counterfeit presentments are all round us: the pastel over my bed, the Dew-Smith[10] over my door, and the 'celebrity' on Fanny's table. It looks very celebrated, and very military, and very well. I wish it were, on this point, more consistent with your bulletins; but this must be as it must, since it may not as it should. My room is now done, and looks very gay and chromatic, with its blue walls and my coloured lines of books.

To Sidney Colvin
(Abridged)

Sunday 5? [6] September 1891   [*Vailima*]

My dear Colvin, Yours from Lochinver has just come.[1] You ask me if I am ever homesick for the Highlands and the Isles. Conceive that for the last month I have been living there between 1786 and 1850, in my grandfather's diaries and letters. I *had* to take a rest; no use talking; so I put in a month over my *Lives of the Stevensons* with great pleasure and profit and some advance; one chapter and a part drafted. The whole promises

---

[9] 'I'm sure I don't know' ('I do not know' in some versions) in the nursery rhyme 'Oranges and Lemons'.

[10] A photograph by Albert George Dew-Smith (1848–1903), a Cambridge friend of Colvin who also took a famous photograph of RLS.

[1] Colvin wrote to RLS from Lochinver, Sutherlandshire, on 4 August 1891 (a few pages of what was evidently a long letter survive – the only one to do so from this period).

well. Chapter I. Domestic Annals. Chapter II. The Northern Lights. Chapter III. The Bell Rock. Chapter IV. A Family of Boys. Chapter V. The Grandfather. VI. Alan Stevenson. VII. Thomas Stevenson. My materials for my great-grandfather are almost null; for my grandfather copious and excellent. Name, a puzzle. *A Scottish Family, A Family of Engineers, Northern Lights, The Engineers of the Northern Lights: a Family History.*[2] Advise; but it will take long. Now, imagine if I have been homesick for Barrahead and Island Glass, and Kirkwall, and Cape Wrath, and the Wells of the Pentland Firth; I could have wept.

Now for politics. I am much less alarmed. I believe the *malo* – *raj*, Government – will collapse and cease like an overlain infant, without a shot fired. They have now been months here on their big salaries – and Cedercrantz, whom I specially like as a man, has done nearly nothing, and the Baron, who is a well-meaning ass, has done worse.[3] They have these huge salaries, and they have all the taxes; they have made scarce a foot of road, they have not given a single native a position – all to beachcombers, they have scarce laid out a penny on Apia and scarce a penny on the King. They have forgot they were in Samoa or that such a thing as Samoans existed and had eyes and some intelligence. The Chief Justice has refused to pay his customs! The President proposed to have an expensive house built for himself, while the King, his master, has none! The German Consul[4] to whom I expressed my opinion that this was one of the most disgraceful things I had ever heard of, bleated: 'But there is still some doubt about it – he *may* mean to pay a rent.' 'Exactly,' said I, 'and if the man were not insane, there would be no doubt on such a point.' At which Schmidt could but agree. This house bust me. I had stood aside, and been a loyal and above all a silent subject, up to then; but now I snap my fingers at their *malo*. It is damned, and I'm damned glad of it. And this is not all. Last *Wainui*, when I sent Fanny off to Fiji,[5] I hear the wonderful news that the Chief Justice is going to Fiji and the colonies to improve his mind. I showed my way of thought to his guest, Count Wachtmeister,[6] whom I have sent to you with a letter – he will tell you all our news. Well, the

---

[2] The work remained unfinished at RLS's death. The first three chapters were posthumously published by Colvin as *Records of a Family of Engineers* in the Edinburgh Edition (1896). Chs 4, 5 and 6 survive in MS in incomplete and unrevised form. They were privately printed in part by J. Christian Bay (Chicago, 1929).

[3] Baron Arnold Senfft von Pilsach (1859–1919), described as 'a superior employé' in the Prussian Government Service, was nominated by the German Government in October 1890 to the post of President of the Municipal Council of Apia. After long delays the appointment was approved by the other two Governments and the Baron and his wife finally arrived in Apia on 26 April 1891. He had married (earlier in 1891) Laura Betty Dorothea von Gaudecker (1867–1936).

[4] Emil Schmidt, the German Vice-Consul. Later (1894–6) he became President of the Municipal Council. He was a difficult man and made many enemies.

[5] Fanny, who had not been well, left on 7 August.

[6] Probably Count Hans Wachtmeister (1828–1905), Swedish travel writer.

Chief Justice stayed, but they said he was to leave yesterday. I had intended to go down and see and warn him. But the President's house had come up in the meanwhile, and I let them go to their doom, which I am only anxious to see swiftly and (if it may be) bloodlessly fall.

Thus I have in a way withdrawn my unrewarded loyalty. Lloyd is down today with Moors to call on Mataafa; the news of the excursion made a considerable row in Apia and both the German and the English Consuls besought Lloyd not to go. But he stuck to his purpose, and with my approval. It's a poor thing if people are to give up a pleasure party for a *malo* that has never done anything for us but draw taxes, and is going to go pop, and leave us at the mercy of the identical Mataafa, whom I have not visited for more than a year and who is probably furious.

The sense of my helplessness here has been rather bitter; I feel it wretched to see this dance of folly and injustice and unconscious rapacity go forward from day to day, and to be impotent. I was not consulted – or only by one man and that on particular points; I did not choose to volunteer advice, till some pressing occasion; I have not even a vote, for I am not a member of their blooming Municipality;[7] and the short and the long is if the Consulship could be got for me at the next vacancy, I would take it gladly, for I see now that (whether or not I have much common sense) I have it above the most of my contemporaries here; and I might possibly be useful, and I would always have a weight in my hand to throw into a trembling scale. As for trying to make my way or gain influence among the crew here on the beach, never. I feel in my thought something boil with the scorn of politicians. I could go round the beach, and rat, and flatter, and bear tales, and earwig, and intrigue, and play the rancid game of popularity; and my dear man, I wouldn't think I was fit to write to you as one friend to another. I see democracy here on the least scale, perhaps in no very favourable example. It's an ugly picture.

What ails you, miserable man, to talk of saving material? I have a whole world in my head, a whole new society to work, but I am in no hurry; you will shortly make the acquaintance of the Island of Ulufanua, on which I mean to lay several stories: 'The Bloody Wedding',[8] possibly 'The High Woods' – O it's so good, 'The High Woods', but the story is craziness, that's the trouble – a political story, 'The Labour Slave' etc. Ulufanua is an imaginary island; the name is a beautiful Samoan word for the *top* of a forest, *ulu* = leaves or hair, *fanua* = land. The ground or country of the leaves. 'Úlufánua the isle of the sea', read that verse

---

[7] Vailima fell just outside the boundary of the Municipality. MIS recorded that RLS tried to get it included because he thought it would 'give him a better chance of getting a proper road made'.

[8] The idea for the story, based on a recent murder case, came to RLS during a visit to Pago Pago in March 1891. No more is heard of it.

dactylically and you get the beat; the u's are like our double oo: did ever you hear a prettier word? (and I'm afraid I'll have to give up Ulufanua, they say it has a bawdy meaning!) . . .

I have just interrupted my letter and read through the chapter of 'The High Woods' that is written, a chapter and a bit, some sixteen pages, really very fetching; but what do you wish? The story is so wilful, so steep, so silly – it's a hallucination I have outlived, and yet I never did a better piece of work, horrid, and pleasing, and extraordinarily *true*: it's sixteen pages of the South Seas: their essence. What am I to do? Lose this little gem – for I'll be bold, and that's what I think it – or go on with the rest which I don't believe in, and don't like, and which can never make aught but a silly yarn? Make another end to it? Ah, yes, but that's not the way I write; the whole tale is implied; I never use an effect when I can help it, unless it prepares the effects that are to follow; that's what a story consists in. To make another end, that is to make the beginning all wrong. The *dénouement* of a long story is nothing; it is just a 'full close', which you may approach and accompany as you please – it is a coda, not an essential member in the rhythm: but the body and end of a short story is bone of the bone and blood of the blood of the beginning. Well, I shall end by finishing it against my judgement; that fragment is my Delilah. Golly, it's good. I am not shining by modesty; but I do just love the colour and movement of that piece so far as it goes.

I cannot say how amazed I was to hear of your fishing. And you saw the *Pharos*, thrice fortunate man; I wish I dared go home, I would ask the Commissioners to take me round for old sake's sake, and see all my family pictures once more from the Mull of Galloway to Unst. However all is arranged for our meeting in Ceylon, except the date and the blooming pounds. . . .

Our life is now wholly changed: Lloyd, Bell and Joe do the cooking, a vast improvement and a huge economy. We have had nine luncheon and dinner parties since this change, and a tenth is due day after tomorrow.

Evening

Lloyd has returned. Peace and war were played before his eyes at heads or tails. A German was stopped with levelled guns; he raised his whip; had it fallen, we might have been now in war. Excuses were made by Mataafa himself. Doubtless the thing was done – I mean the stopping of the German – a little to show off before Lloyd. Meanwhile Haggard[9] was up

---

[9] Bazett Michael Haggard (1847–99), barrister, brother of Rider Haggard, was the British representative on the Samoan Land Commission, which formally began its activities on 1 June. Although very able, his increasing drunkenness later caused problems.

here, telling the C.J. was really gone for five or eight weeks[10] and begging me to write to *The Times* and denounce the state of affairs; many strong reasons he advanced; and Lloyd and I have been since his arrival and Haggard's departure, near half an hour debating what should be done. Cedercrantz is gone; it is not my fault; he knows my views on that point – alone of all points; he leaves me with my mouth sealed. Yet this is a nice thing that because he is guilty of a fresh offence – his flight – the mouth of the only possible influential witness should be closed? I do not like this argument. I look like a cad, if I do in the man's absence, what I could have done in a more manly manner in his presence. True; but why did he go? It is his last sin. And I, who like the man extremely – that is the word – I love his society – he is intelligent, pleasant, even witty, a gentleman – and you know how that attaches – I loathe to seem to play a base part; but the poor natives – who are like other folk, false enough, lazy enough, not heroes, not saints – ordinary men damnably misused – are they to suffer because I like Cedercrantz, and Cedercrantz has cut his lucky?[11] This is a little tragedy, observe well – a tragedy! I may be right, I may be wrong in my judgement; but I am in treaty with my honour. I know not how it will seem tomorrow. Lloyd thought the barrier of honour insurmountable, and it is an ugly obstacle. . . .

Tuesday [8 September]

One more word about the *South Seas* in answer to a question I observe I have forgotten to answer. The Tahiti part has never turned up, because it has never been written. As for telling you where I went or when, or anything about Honolulu, I would rather die; that is fair and plain. How can anybody care when or how I left Honolulu? This is (excuse me) childish. A man of upwards of forty cannot waste his time in communicating matter of that degree of indifference. The Letters, it appears, are tedious; by God, they would be more tedious still if I wasted my time upon such infantile and sucking-bottle details. If ever I put in any such detail, it is because it leads into something or serves as a transition. To tell it for its own sake, never! The mistake is all through that I have told too much; I had not sufficient confidence in the reader, and have overfed him: and here are you anxious to learn how I – O, Colvin! Suppose it had made a book, all such information is given to one glance of an eye by a

---

[10] The three Consuls wrote a formal joint letter to Cedercrantz on 1 September asking him not to leave during the political crisis and pointing out that under the Treaty it was not possible to delegate his responsibilities. In spite of this, he left for Fiji on 5 September and went on to Australia. He later sought to justify his two months' absence by stating that he was studying the system of administration in Fiji and the system of registration of land titles in Melbourne.

[11] To cut or make one's lucky is a slang phrase meaning to get away, escape or decamp.

map with a little dotted line upon it. But let us forget this unfortunate
affair.[12]

Wednesday [9 September]

Yesterday I went down to consult Clarke, who took the view of delay.
Has he changed his mind already? I wonder: here at least is the news.
Some little while back some men of Manono – what is Manono? – a
Samoan rotten borough, a small isle of huge political importance, heaven
knows why, whose handful of chiefs make half the trouble in the country
– some men of Manono (which is strong Mataafa) burned down the
houses and destroyed the crops of some Malietoa neighbours. The President went there the other day and landed alone on the island, which (to
give him his due) was plucky. Moreover he succeeded in persuading the
folks to come up and be judged on a particular day in Apia. That day they
did not come; but did come the next and to their vast surprise were given
six months' imprisonment and clapped in gaol. Those who had
accompanied them, cried to them on the streets as they were marched to
prison: 'Shall we rescue you?' The condemned, marching in the hands of
thirty men with loaded rifles, cried out 'No!' And the trick was done. But
it was ardently believed a rescue would be attempted; the jail was laid
about with armed men day and night; but there was some question of
their loyalty; and Ulfsparre, commandant of the forces, a very nice young
beardless Swede, became nervous and conceived a plan. How if he should
put dynamite under the jail and in case of an attempted rescue blow up
prison and all? He went to the President who agreed; he went to the
American man-of-war for the dynamite and machine, was refused, and got
it at last from the wreckers.[13] The thing began to leak out, and there arose
a muttering in town. People had no fancy for amateur explosions for one
thing. For another, it did not clearly appear that it was legal; the men had
been condemned to six months' prison, which they were peaceably
undergoing; they had not been condemned to death. And lastly, it seemed
a somewhat advanced example of civilisation to set before barbarians. The
mutter in short became a storm, and yesterday, while I was down, a
schooner was chartered and the prisoners were suddenly banished to the
Tokelaus. Who has changed the sentence? We are going to stir in the

---

[12] Colvin reported that *Black and White* had tried to 'get off their bargain' because they found the
South Seas Letters 'too monotonous'. Colvin suggested that when they were published in book
form, RLS might 'set right the places where you leave us puzzled as to the course, order and
geography of your voyages'. He was puzzled as to what had happened to the Tahitian chapters:
'the consequence is a grisly gap between the Marquesan and the Hawaiian chapters'.

[13] MIS noted that Bazett Haggard came up to Vailima on 8 September and told them of the
dynamite affair. The wreckers were the men demolishing the warships wrecked in the 1889
hurricane.

dynamite matter; we do not want the natives to fancy us consenting to such an outrage.

[14 or 15 September]

Fanny has returned from her trip and on the whole looks better.[14] 'The High Woods' are under way and their name is now 'The Beach of Falesá,' and the yarn is cured. I have about thirty pages of it done; it will be fifty to seventy I suppose. No supernatural trick at all; and escaped out of quite easily: can't think why I was so stupid for so long. Mighty glad to have Fanny back to this Hell of the South Seas as the German Captain called it. What will Cedercrantz think, when *he* comes back? To do him justice, had he been here, this Manono hash would not have been. Here is a pretty thing. When Fanny was in Fiji all the Samoa and Tokelau folks were agog about our 'flash' house; but the whites had never heard of it.

Robert Louis Stevenson
Author of 'The Beach of Falesá'

To Sidney Colvin
(Abridged)

28 September [1891]   *[Vailima]*

My dear Colvin, Since I last laid down my pen I have written and re-written 'The Beach of Falesá': something like sixty thousand words of sterling domestic fiction; (the story you will understand is only half that length); and now I don't want to write any more again for ever, or feel so; and I've got to overhaul it once again to my sorrow; I was all yesterday revising and found a lot of slacknesses and (what is worse in this kind of thing) some literaryisms. One of the puzzles is this: it is a first person story: a trader telling his own adventure in an island; when I began I allowed myself a few liberties, because I was afraid of the end; now the end proved quite easy and could be done in the pace; so the beginning remains about a quarter tone out (in places); but I have rather decided to let it stay so. The problem is always delicate; it is the only thing that worries me in first person tales, which otherwise (quo' Alan) 'set better wi' my genius'.[1] There is a vast deal of fact in the story, and some pretty good comedy. It is the first realistic South Sea story; I mean with real South Sea character and details of life; everybody else who has tried, that I have seen, got

---

[14] MIS recorded that Fanny returned on board the *Lübeck* on the evening of 14 September, bringing back 'lots of plants and flowers'.

[1] Cf. *Kidnapped*, ch. 9: 'It doesn't set my genius.'

carried away by the romance and ended in a kind of sugar candy sham epic, and the whole effect was lost – there was no etching, no human grin, consequently no conviction. Now I have got the smell and look of the thing a good deal. You will know more about the South Seas after you have read my little tale, than if you had read a library. As to whether anyone else will read it, I have no guess. I am in an off time; but there is just the possibility it might make a hit; for the yarn is good and melo-dramatic, and there is quite a love affair – for me; and Mr Wiltshire (the narrator) is a huge lark, though I say it. But there is always the exotic question; and everything, the life, the place, the dialects – traders' talk, which is a strange conglomerate of literary expressions and English and American slang, and Beach de Mar, or native English – the very trades and hopes and fears of the characters, are all novel and may be found unwel-come to that great, hulking, bullering whale, the public.

Since I wrote, I have been likewise drawing up a document to send in to the President; it has been dreadfully delayed, not by me, but today they swear it will be sent in. A list of questions about the dynamite report are herein laid before him, and considerations suggested why he should answer.

5 [6] October

Ever since my last scratch I have been much chivvied about over the President business; his answer has come and is an evasion accompanied with a schoolboy insolence, and we are going to try to answer it. I drew my answer and took it down yesterday, but one of the signatories wants another paragraph added, which I have not yet been able to draw and as to the wisdom of which I am not yet convinced. Been off about two hours about the clause, and a worse business. . . .

Next day 7 October, the right day

. . . We are all in rather a muddled state with our President affair. I do loathe politics; but at the same time, I cannot stand by and have the natives blown in the air treacherously with dynamite. They are still quiet; how long this may continue I do not know, though of course by mere prescription the Government is strengthened, and is probably insured till the next taxes fall due. But the unpopularity of the whites is growing. My native overseer, the great Henry Simelē, announced today that he was 'weary of whites upon the beach. All too proud,' said this veracious witness. One of the proud ones had threatened yesterday to cut off his head with a bush knife! There are 'native outrages': honour bright, and setting theft aside, in which the natives are active, this is the main stream of irritation. The natives are generally courtly, far from always civil; but really gentle and with a strong sense of honour of their own, and certainly quite as much civilised as our dynamiting President.

We shall be delighted to see Kipling.[2] I go to bed usually about half-past eight, and my lamp is out before ten. I breakfast at six. We may say roughly we have no soda-water on the island, and just now truthfully no whisky. I *have* heard the chimes at midnight; now no more, I guess. *But* – Fanny and I as soon as we can get coins for it, are coming to Europe, not to England: I am thinking of Royat. Bar wars. If not, perhaps the Apennines might give us a mountain refuge for two months or three in summer. How is that for high? But the money must be all in hand first.

13 October

How am I to describe my life these last few days? I have been wholly swallowed up in politics; a wretched business, with fine elements of farce in it too, which repay a man in passing, involving many dark and many moonlight rides, secret councils which are at once divulged, sealed letters which are read aloud in confidence to the neighbours, and a mass of fudge and fun, which would have driven me crazy ten years ago and now makes me smile.

On Friday, Henry came and told us he must leave and go to 'my poor old family in Savaii': why? I do not quite know – but I suspect to be tattooed – if so then probably to be married and we shall see him no more. I told him he must do what he thought his duty. We had him to lunch, drank his health, and he and I rode down about twelve. When I got down, I sent my horse back to help bring down the family later. My own afternoon was cut out for me; my last draft for the President had been objected to by some of the signatories – not enough 'hell-hound' and 'atheist' –. I stood out, and one of our small number accordingly refused to sign. Him I had to go and persuade, which went off very well after the first hottish moments; you have no idea how stolid my temper is now. By about five the thing was done; and we sat down to dinner at the Chinaman's – the Verrey or Doyen's[3] of Apia – Gurr and I, at each end, as hosts: Gurr's wife, – Fanua, late maid of the village – her (adopted) father and mother, Seumanu and Faitulia,[4] Fanny, Bell, Lloyd, Joe, Austin,

[2] Kipling, who was in Australia and New Zealand in 1891, had announced before leaving England that he intended to visit RLS. In his autobiography, *Something of Myself* (1937), Kipling says that when he was in Auckland 'the captain of the fruit-boat, which might or might not go to Samoa at some time or another, was so devotedly drunk' that he abandoned the idea and went to India.

[3] Verry's, a famous French restaurant in Regent Street, London, is mentioned in *The Wrong Box*, ch. 9. Ledoyen was in the Avenue des Champs Elysées, in Paris.

[4] Edwin William Gurr (1863–1933) was born in Tasmania but was educated in New Zealand, where he studied law and was a schoolteacher for a short time. On coming to Samoa he studied law and qualified as a barrister, meanwhile working as a banker (Hayhurst, Gurr & Co.). In 1892 he became Natives' Advocate on the Land Commission and was active in Samoan politics. From

and Henry Simelē, his last appearance. Henry was in a kilt of gray shawl, with a blue jacket, white shirt and black neck tie, and looked like a dark genteel guest in a Highland shooting box. Seumanu (opposite Fanny, next Gurr) is chief of Apia, a rather big gun in this place, looking like a large, fatted military Englishman, bar the colour. Faitulia, next me, is a bigger chief than her husband. Henry is a chief too – his chief name, Iiga (Ee-eeng-a) he has not yet 'taken' because of youth. We were in fine society, and had a pleasant meal time with lots of fun. Then to the Opera – I beg your pardon, I mean the Circus. We occupied the first row in the reserved seats, and there in the row behind were all our friends – Captain Foss[5] and his Captain-Lieutenant, three of the American officers – very nice fellows, the doctor, etc. – so we made a fine show of what an embittered correspondent of the local paper called 'the shoddy aristocracy of Apia'; and you should have seen how we carried on, and how I clapped, and Captain Foss hollered '*wunderschön!*' and threw himself forward in his seat, and how we all in fact enjoyed ourselves like schoolchildren, Austin not a shade more than his neighbours. Then the circus broke up and the party went home, but I stayed down, having business on the morrow.

The next days were very largely passed trying to make up my mind how to write to *The Times*.[6] It is now done, true enough, not false I mean – but quite un*true*; not telling for instance how this mild, wild little creature is as civil as a trick terrier, painfully eager to please – and came here (the poor soul) on his wedding jaunt with a pretty little wife no bigger than himself; and how there is no fault to find with him but mere

1900 to 1908 he was Secretary of Native Affairs and Chief District Judge in American Samoa. He returned to Western Samoa from Tutuila in 1924 and became one of the leaders of the Samoan *Mau* movement, opposing the New Zealand administration, and first editor of the *Samoan Guardian*. For these activities he was deported by the New Zealand Governor in 1928 for five years.

Gurr's marriage to Fanua took place in January 1891 at the British Consulate and (according to Gurr) RLS made a speech at the wedding breakfast. Henry Adams (who makes several references to Fanua in his letters) was at the reception. Fanua (who died in 1917) became a close friend of Belle's and was a great favourite at Vailima where she and her husband were frequent visitors.

Seumanutafa was the hero of the March 1889 hurricane. In return for his efforts in rescuing sailors from the American warship *Trenton*, the US Government presented him with a 'double-banked whaleboat, with its fittings'.
[5] Of the German warship *Sperber*.
[6] In his letter to *The Times*, dated 12 October (and published 17 November), RLS set out the story of the 'dynamite scandal' and enclosed a copy of the correspondence with the Baron Senfft von Pilsach, including an appeal signed by RLS and other leading white residents (H.J. Moors and E.W. Gurr among them) seeking information and reassurances about the rumours of the purchase and threatened use of dynamite against the prisoners. The Baron gave evasive and unsatisfactory replies and refused to deny the rumours. In his letter RLS ridiculed the Baron and his antics: 'Such an official I never remember to have read of, though I have seen the like, from across the footlights and the orchestra, evolving in similar figures to the strains of Offenbach.'

folly, and the dynamite was no doubt never intended to be used, and the man is too dull to see what harm his threat could do, but thought it bold and cunning, the poor soul! Such a difference between politics and history, between a letter to *The Times* and a chapter I shall write some day if I am spared, and make this little history-in-a-teapot living. . . .

To Sidney Colvin
(Extracts)

Monday 24 [actually 26] October [1891]   [*Vailima*]

My dear Carthew[1] – See what I have written, but it's Colvin I'm after – I have written two chapters, about 30 pp. of *Wrecker* since the mail left, which must be my excuse, and the bother I've had with it is not to be imagined; you might have seen me the day before yesterday weighing British sov's and Chile dollars to arrange my treasure chest. And there was such a calculation not for that only, but for the ship's position and distances when – but I am not going to tell you the yarn – and then as my arithmetic is particularly lax, Lloyd had to go over all my calculations; and then as I had changed the amount of money, he had to go over all *his* as to the amount of the lay; and altogether a bank could be run with less effusion of figures than it took to shore up a single chapter of a measly yarn. However it's done, and I have but one more or at the outside two to do, and I am Free! and can do any damn thing I like.

Before falling on politics, I shall give you my day. Awoke somewhere about the first peep of day, came gradually to, and had a turn on the verandah before 5.55, when 'the child' (an enormous Wallis Islander) brings me an orange; at six, breakfast; six-ten to work; which lasts till at 10.30, Austin comes for his history lecture. This is rather dispiriting because he ain't a bright child; but education must be gone about in faith – and charity; both of which pretty nigh failed me today about (of all things) Carthage. Eleven, luncheon; after luncheon in my mother's room, I read Chapter XXIII of *The Wrecker*; then Belle, Joe, Lloyd, and I go up and make music furiously till about two (I suppose) when I turn into work again till four; fool from four to half past, tired out and waiting for the bath hour: 4.30, bath; 4.40 eat two heavenly mangoes on the verandah and see the boys arrive with the pack horses. Five, dinner; smoke, chat on verandah, then hand of cards, and at last at eight, come up to my room with a pint of beer and a hard biscuit, which I am now consuming, and as soon as they are consumed I shall turn in. Such are the innocent days of this ancient and out-worn sportsman; today there was no weeding,

---

[1] Norris Carthew, the key character in the closing chapters of *The Wrecker*.

usually there is however, edged in somewhere. My books for the moment are a crib to *Phaedo*, and the second book of Montaigne; and a little while back I was reading Frederic Harrison – *Choice of Books* etc.[2] – very good indeed, a great deal of sense and knowledge in the volume, and some very true stuff, *contra* Carlyle, about the eighteenth century. A hideous idea came over me that perhaps Harrison is now getting *old*. Perhaps you are. Perhaps I am. O, this infidelity must be stared firmly down. I am about twenty-three – say twenty-eight –; you about thirty, or, by'r lady, thirty-four; and as Harrison belongs to the same generation, there is no good bothering about him.

Here has just been a fine alert; I gave my wife a dose of chlorodyne. 'Something wrong,' says she. 'Nonsense,' said I. 'Embrocation,' said she. I smelt it, and – it smelt very funny. I think it's just gone bad, and tomorrow will tell. Proved to be so.[3] . . .

Wednesday – November 10th or 11th [actually 11th] – and I am ashamed to say mail day. *The Wrecker* is finished, that is the best of my news; it goes by this mail to Scribner's, and I honestly think it a good yarn on the whole and of its measly kind. The part that is genuinely good is Nares, the American sailor; that is a genuine figure; had there been more Nares it would have been a better book; but of course it don't set up to be a book – only a long tough yarn with some pictures of the manners of to-day in the greater world – not the shoddy sham world of cities, clubs and colleges – but the world where men still live a man's life. The worst of my news is the influenza; Apia is devastate; the shops closed, a ball put off etc. – as yet we have not had it at Vailima, and who knows? we may escape. None of us go down, but of course the boys come and go.

Your letter had the most wonderful 'I told you so' I ever heard in the course of my life. Why, you madman, I wouldn't change my present installation for any post, dignity, honour or advantage conceivable to me. It fills the bill; I have the loveliest time. And as for wars and rumours of war, you surely know enough of me to be aware that I like that also a thousand times better than decrepit peace in Middlesex? I do not quite like politics; I am too aristocratic, I fear, for that. God knows, I don't care who I chum with: perhaps like sailors best; but to go round and sue and

---

[2] Frederic Harrison (1831–1923), *The Choice of Books and other Literary Pieces* (1886).
[3] Fanny related the incident in her diary for 28 October:

> I am in a horrid state from the drug given me by Uncle George's advice for what is supposed to be an aneurysm inside my head. The beating in my head is already much less distressing, but my eyes and nose are swollen and I have a continual brow ache and not much sleep. Uncle George recommended chlorodyne. Louis gave me a dose, as he thought, night before last, but it turned out to be something else, tasting like an embrocation of some sort; unless possibly the stuff had gone bad.

sneak to keep a crowd together – never. My imagination, which is not the
least damped by the idea of having my head cut off in the bush, recoils
aghast from the idea of a life like Gladstone's, and the shadow of the
newspaper chills me to the bone. Hence my late eruption was interesting
but not what I like. All else suits me in this (killed a mosquito) A one
abode. . . .

To H.B. Baildon[1]

[*? October or November 1891*]   *Vailima*

My dear Baildon, This is a real disappointment. It was so long since we
had met I was curious to see where time had carried and stranded us.[2] Last
time we saw each other, it must have been all ten years ago, we were new
to the thirties, it was only for a moment, and now we're in the forties, and
before very long we shall be in our graves. Sick and well, I have had a
splendid life of it, grudge nothing, regret very little – and there only some
little pison corners of misconduct for which I deserve hanging and must
infallibly be damned – and, take it all over, damnation and all, would
hardly change with any man of my time, unless perhaps it were Gordon
or our friend Chalmers: a man I admire for his virtues, love for his faults,
and envy for the really A.1. life he has, with every thing that heart – my
heart, I mean – could wish. It is singular to think you will read this in the
gray metropolis;[3] go the first gray, east windy day into the Caledonian
Station, if it looks at all as it did of yore; I met Satan there. And then go
and stand by the cross, and remember the other one – him that went
down – my brother, Robert Fergusson. It is a pity you had not made me
out and seen me as the patriarch and planter. I shall look forward to some
record of your time with Chalmers; you can't weary me of that fellow; he
is as big as a house, and far bigger than any church, where no man warms
his hands. Do you know anything of Thomson? of Boyd, Ferryman,
Williamson, Kinloch, John Young *et al?*[4] As I write Williamson's name,

[1] Henry Bellyse Baildon (1849–1907), the son of an Edinburgh chemist, became Lecturer in
English at Vienna University and at University College, Dundee. He and RLS were fellow-
pupils in 1864–5 at a day school for backward or delicate boys in Frederick Street, Edinburgh,
run by Robert Thomson. They collaborated in a school magazine, first called *The Trial* and later
Jack o' Lantern.

[2] Baildon and his sister Frances had visited Australia and then stayed with the missionary James
Chalmers and his wife Elizabeth (to whom they were distantly related) in New Guinea in
August 1891. A plan to visit Samoa had fallen through.

[3] Tennyson, 'The Daisy', l. 105 – 'gray metropolis of the North'.

[4] The names must be those of fellow pupils at Robert Thomson's school. Boyd may be Alexander
Scheviz Boyd (1848–89), son of John Boyd, Edinburgh publisher, who was at the Academy
1860–61. Augustus Hamilton Ferryman (1850–1909) was at the Academy 1865–6. John George

mustard rises in my nose;[5] I have never forgiven that weak, amiable boy a little trick he played me, when I could ill afford it: I mean that whenever I think of it some of the old wrath kindles, not that I could hurt the poor soul, if I got the world with it. And old Nicholson? Is he still afloat? Harmless bark! I gather you aren't married yet, since your sister, to whom I ask to be remembered, goes with you. Did you see a silly tale, 'John Nicholson's Predicament' – or some such name – in which I had made free with your house at Murrayfield?[6] There is precious little sense in it, but it might amuse. Cassell's published it – in a thing called *Yule Tide* years ago; and nobody that I ever heard of reads or has ever seen *Yule Tide*; it is addressed to a class we never meet – readers of Cassell's series and that class of conscientious chaff. And my tale was chaff; but I don't recall that it was conscientious. Only there's the house at Murrayfield and a dead body in it, forby: no extra charge. Glad the ballads amused you. They failed to entertain a coy public: at which I own I wondered. Not that I set much account by my verses, which are the verses of Prosator; but I do know how to tell a yarn, and two of the yarns were great. 'Rahéro' is for its length, I think, a perfect folk tale; savage and yet fine, full of a tail foremost morality, ancient as the granite rocks; if the historian not to say the politician could get that yarn into his head, he would have learned some of his A.B.C. But the average man at home cannot understand antiquity; he is sunk over the ears in Roman civilisation; and a tale like that of 'Rahéro' falls on his ears inarticulate. The *Spectator* said there was no psychology in it; that interested me much; my grandmother (as I used to call that able paper – and an able paper it is, and a fair one) cannot so much as observe the existence of savage psychology when it is placed before it. I am at bottom a psychologist and ashamed of it; the tale seized me one third because of its picturesque features, two-thirds because of its astonishing psychology; and the *Spectator* says there's none.[7] I am going on with a lot of island work, exulting in the knowledge of a new world – 'a new created world'[8] and new men; and I am sure my income will Decline and Fall Off. For the effort of comprehension is death to the intelligent public, and sickness to the dull.

Smyth Kinloch (1849–1910) was at the Academy 1858–61 and at Edinburgh University where he was a member of the Speculative Society; he succeeded his father as 2nd Baronet 1881 and was MP for East Perthshire 1889–1903. G. Williamson was an American boy at the school, probably George Millar Williamson (1849–1921), an early Stevenson collector.

[5] An Anglicisation of the French phrase meaning to lose one's temper.

[6] Baildon's home, Duncliffe, Murrayfield is the scene of the murder in 'Misadventures of John Nicholson' (*Yule Tide*, December 1887).

[7] R.H. Hutton, in an unsigned review of *Ballads* in the *Spectator* of 3 January 1891, singled out for praise two passages in 'The Song of Rahéro' but generally found the Ballads disappointing. Cf. p. 173, n. 3.

[8] Milton, *Paradise Lost*, VII. 554.

I do not know why I pester you with all this truck; above all, as you deserve nothing. I give you my warm *Talofa*. Write me again when the spirit moves you. And some day, if I still live, make out the trip again, and let us hob-a-nob with our grey pows on my verandah. Yours sincerely

Robert Louis Stevenson

To Charles Baxter
(Abridged)

[9 or 10 November 1891]   [Vailima]

Dear Charles, . . .

[After two paragraphs on financial and business matters]

3. Haith![1] I believe that's a'. By this time, I suppose you will have heard from McClure, and 'The Beach of Falesá' will be decided for better for worse.[2] The end of *The Wrecker* goes by this mail, an awfae relief. I am now free and can do what I please. What do I please? I kenna. I'll bide a wee. There's a child's history in the wind; and there's my grandfather's life begun; and there's a history of Sāmoa in the last four or five years begun[3] – there's a kind of sense to this book: it may help the Sāmoans, it may help me, for I'm bound on the altar here for anti-Germanism. Then there's *The Pearl Fisher* about a quarter done; and there's various short stories in various degrees of incompleteness. Deil, there's plenty grist; but the mill's unco slaw! Tomorrow or next day, when the mail's through, I'll attack one or other, or maybe something else. All these schemes begin to laugh at me, for the day's far through, and I believe the pen grows heavy. However, I believe *The Wrecker* is a good yarn of its poor sort, and it is certainly well nourished with facts; no realist can touch me there; for by this time I do begin to know something of life in the XIXth century, which no novelist either in France or England seems to know much of.

You must have great larks over Masonry.[4] You're away up in the ranks now and (according to works that I have read) doubtless design

---

[1] A mild oath (Scots) equivalent to 'Faith!'.

[2] RLS sent 'The Beach of Falesá' to Baxter in October asking him to negotiate serial rights with McClure and suggesting it might be brought out as a small volume through Cassell's and Scribner's. On 19 December Baxter signed an agreement with Robert McClure (McClure's brother and London agent) giving McClure serial rights to the story for all countries for £500. RLS must have been in touch independently with Cassell's, for on 9 December they signed an agreement for the sole UK rights to publish a volume the size of *Kidnapped* or *The Master of Ballantrae* to include 'The Beach of Falesá' and other stories: the volume to be called *Beach de Mar* 'or some such title'.

[3] Published as *A Footnote to History*.

[4] Baxter was First Principal of the Naval and Military Royal Arch Chapter No. 40 in Edinburgh, 1889–90. The following year he described himself as Senior Grand Deacon of Scotland. RLS

assassinations and kiss – I believe it is the devil's arse? But I am an outsider; and I have a certain liking for a light unto my path which would deter me from joining the rank and file of so vast and dim a confraternity. At your altitude it becomes (of course) amusing and – perhaps – useful. Yes I remember the L.J.R., and the constitution and my homily on Liberty and yours on Reverence which was never written – so I never knew what reverence was. I remember I wanted to write Justice also; but I forget who had the billet. My dear papa was in a devil of a taking;[5] and I had to go out to lunch – to meet the Wigans[6] at Ferriers – in a strangely begrutten[7] state, which was *infra dig.* for a homilist on liberty. It was about four, I suppose, that we met in the Lothian Road – had we the price of two bitters between us? questionable!

All you say of Henley I feel; I cannot describe the sense of relief and sorrow with which I feel I am done with him.[8] No better company in God's earth, and in some ways a fine fellow, a very fine one. But there has been too much hole-and-cornering, and cliquing, and sweltering; too much of the fizz and cackle of the low actor lot; and of late days, with all sorts of pleasant and affecting returns of friendship when we met, too much and a too visibly growing jealousy of me. It made my life hard; now it leaves it a good bit empty. *Et puis après?* So they both died and went out of the story; and I daresay young fellows short of a magazine article in the twentieth century (if our civilisation endures) will expose the horrid R.L.S. and defend and at last do justice to the misused W.E.H. For he is of that big, round, human, faulty stamp of man that makes lovers after death. I bet he has drunk more, and smoked more, and talked more sense, and quarrelled with more friends, than any of God's creatures; and he has written some A.1. verses – talking of that – man alive!–

---

wrote to him in August: 'Your portrait and thrilling Masonic biography delighted us all beyond measure. Would I were a Mason and tippled in a lodge – and all the other Masons, attended in obeisance – O would I were a Mason, deep in Masonic dodge.'

[5] Baxter wrote of the close links that bound Masons together:

'Tis a strange craft and the more interesting the more you see and know; for four years after I joined it I saw nothing in it; now I see everything. . . . I should like some day to 'make' you. You would enjoy it. The L.J.R. was curiously enough not altogether dissimilar. Do you remember the fatal ritual I invented and the *awful* scene that followed on its discovery? I still remember meeting you in the Lothian Road and hearing the terrible news that fell from your blanched lips. I also remember a sensation as if my knees were melting. That was the way terror affected *me.*

For the L.J.R. see p. 21, n. 7.

[6] Conceivably Alfred Wigan (1814–78) and his wife Leonora (1805–84), well-known actors of the period. MIS recorded seeing them with RLS at the theatre on 8 November 1871 and finding them 'great fun'.

[7] Tear-stained.

[8] Baxter wrote: 'Henley's swelled head is more swelled than ever, but I have smoked the pipe of peace. I can't help the old feeling when I see him . . . I think you would feel the very same.'

4. Your bookseller – (I have lost his letter – I mean the bloody maid has, arranging my room – and so have to send by you) – wrote me a letter about Old Bailey Papers. Gosh, I near swarfed;[9] dam'd man, I near hand dee'd o't. It's only yin or twa volumes I want; say 500 or 1000 pp. of the stuff; and the worthy man (much doubting) proposed to bury me in volumes. Please allay his rage, and apologise that I have not written him direct: his note was civil and purposelike. And please send me a copy of Henley's *Book of Verses*; mine has disappeared. . . .   R.L.S.

To Adelaide Boodle[1]

4 January 1892   *Vailima*

My dear Adelaide, We were much pleased with your letter and the news of your employment. Admirable, your method. But will you not run dry of fairy stories? Please salute your pupils, and tell them that a long, lean, elderly man who lives right through on the under side of the world, so that down in your cellar you are nearer him than the people in the street, desires his compliments. This man lives in an island which is not very long and extremely narrow. The sea beats round it very hard, so that it is difficult to get to shore. There is only one harbour where ships come, even that is very wild and dangerous; four ships of war were broken there a little while ago, and one of them is still lying on its side on a rock clean above water, where the sea threw it as you might throw your fiddle-bow upon the table. All round the harbour the town is strung out, it is nothing but wooden houses, only there are some churches built of stone, not very large, but the people have never seen such fine buildings. Almost all the houses are of one story. Away at one end lives the King of the whole country. His palace has a thatched roof which stands upon posts; it has no walls, but when it blows and rains, they have Venetian blinds which they let down between the posts and make it very snug. There is no furniture, and the King and the Queen and the courtiers sit and eat on the floor which is of gravel: the lamp stands there too, and every now and then it is upset. These good folks wear nothing but a kilt about their waists, unless to go to church or for a dance or the New Year or some great occasion. The children play marbles all along the street; and though they are generally very jolly, yet they get awfully cross over their marbles, and cry and fight like boys and girls at home. Another amusement in country

[9] Swooned (Scots).

[1] This letter and two others later in the year were written for girls – addressed by RLS as 'The Children in the Cellar' – in a convalescent home in Kilburn that Miss Boodle was helping to manage.

places is to shoot fish with a little bow and arrow. All round the beach there is bright shallow water, where the fishes can be seen darting or lying in shoals. The child trots round the shore and wherever he sees a fish, lets fly an arrow and misses, and then wades in after his arrow. It is great fun (I have tried it) for the child, and I never heard of it doing any harm to the fishes: so what could be more jolly?[2] The road up to this lean man's house is uphill all the way and through forests; the forests are of great trees not so much unlike the trees at home, only here and there are some very queer ones mixed with them, cocoanut palms, and great forest trees that are covered with blossom like red hawthorn but not near so bright; and from all the trees thick creepers hang down like ropes and nasty-looking weeds that they call orchids grow in the forks of the branches; and on the ground many prickly things are dotted, which they call pineapples: I suppose every one has eaten pineapple drops.

On the way up to the lean man's house you pass a little village, all of houses like the King's house, so that as you ride through you can see everybody sitting at dinner, or if it be night, lying in their beds by lamplight; for all these people are terribly afraid of ghosts and would not lie in the dark for any favour. After the village, there is only one more house, and that is the lean man's. For the people are not very many and live all by the sea, and the whole inside of the island is desert, woods and mountains. When the lean man goes into this forest, he is very much ashamed to say it, but he is always in a terrible fright. The wood is so great and empty and hot, and it is always filled with curious noises; birds cry like children and bark like dogs, and he can hear people laughing and felling trees, and the other day (when he was far in the woods) he heard a great sound like the biggest mill-wheel possible going with a kind of dot-and-carry-one movement like a dance. That was the noise of an earthquake away down below him in the bowels of the earth, and that is the same thing as to say away up towards you in your cellar in Kilburn. All these

---

[2] In his account of a visit to Tutuila in March 1891, RLS described the harbour at Pago Pago (Pango Pango):

Or yet again you may be accompanied in your walk by bronze gentlemen, equipped with bow and arrow to chase fish. The sport is pleasing and humane; the little hunters patter on the margin of the beach, stand and gaze on outlying rocks, or wade in the bright shallows; the innocuous arrow is at times discharged and recovered, and the fish scorn to withdraw. For in this method of chase, the situation is reversed, and the hunter has the exercise, the quarry the sport. Pango Pango is not popular with gentlemen of the American navy. They say it is hot, feverish and dull. The days weigh upon them in this mountain anchorage; they prefer even Apia; and are said to languish for the joys of poker. I may be morose, perhaps effeminate – but I could walk a lifetime on these shores, and if I must condescend to any pastime, let me rather pursue fish and recover bloodless arrows.

('Tutuila: The American Harbour'. Published in the *Auckland Star*, 30 January 1892, as part of *The South Seas*, but never reprinted.)

noises make him feel lonely and scared, and he doesn't quite know what he is scared of. Once when he was just about to cross a river, a blow struck him on the top of his head and knocked him head-foremost down the bank and splash into the water. It was a nut, I fancy, that had fallen from a tree, by which accidents people are sometimes killed. But at the time he thought it was a black boy.

Aha, say you, and what is a black boy? Well, there are here a lot of poor people who are brought here from distant islands to labour as slaves for the Germans. They are not at all like the King or his people, who are brown and very pretty; but these are black as negroes and as ugly as sin, poor souls, and in their own lands they live all the time at war and cook and eat men's flesh. The Germans thrash them with whips to make them work, and every now and then, some run away into the bush, as the forest is called, and build little sheds of leaves, and eat nuts and roots and fruits, and dwell there by themselves in the great desert. Sometimes they are bad and wild and come down on the villages and steal and kill; and people whisper to each other that some of them have gone back to their horrid old habits, and catch men and women in order to eat them. But it is very likely not true; and the most of them are only poor, stupid, trembling, half-starved, pitiful creatures like frightened dogs. Their life is all very well when the sun shines as it does eight or nine months in the year. But it is very different the rest of the time. The wind rages here most violently. The great trees thrash about like whips; the air is filled with leaves and great branches flying like birds; and the sound of the trees falling shakes the earth. It rains too as it never rains at home. You can hear a shower while it is yet half a mile away, hissing like a showerbath on the forest; and when it comes to you, the water blinds your eyes, and the cold drenching takes your breath away as though some one had struck you. In that kind of weather it must be dreadful indeed to live in the woods, one man alone by himself. And you must know that, if the lean man feels afraid to be in the forest, the people of the island and the black boys are much more afraid than he. For they believe the woods to be quite filled with spirits; some are like pigs, and some are like flying things; but others (and these are thought the most dangerous) come in the shape of beautiful young women and young men, beautifully dressed in the island manner, with fine kilts and fine necklaces and crowns of scarlet seeds and flowers. Woe betide, he or she who gets to speak with one of these! They will be charmed out of their wits, and come home again quite silly, and go mad and die. So that the poor black boy must be always trembling and looking about for the coming of the women-devils.

Sometimes the women-devils go down out of the woods into the villages, and here is a tale the lean man heard last year. One of the islanders was sitting in his house and he had cooked fish. There came along the road two beautiful young women, dressed as I told you, who came into his house and asked for some of his fish. It is the fashion in the islands always to give what is asked, and never to ask folk's names. So the man gave them fish and talked to them in the island, jesting way. And presently he asked one of the women for her red necklace; which is good manners and their way; he had given the fish and he had a right to ask for something back. 'I will give it you by and by,' said the woman, and she and her companion went away, but he thought they were gone very suddenly, and the truth is they had vanished. The night was nearly come, when the man heard the voice of the woman crying that he should come to her and she would give the necklace. And he looked out, and behold she was standing calling him from the top of the sea, on which she stood as you might on the table. At that fear came on the man; he fell on his knees and prayed; and the woman disappeared. It was known afterwards that this was once a woman indeed, but should have died a thousand years ago, and has lived all that while as a devil in the woods beside the spring of a river. *Sau-mai-afe* – Sow-my-affy – is her name, in case you want to write to her.

If by any accident, your cellar should be able to understand this, and it should at all amuse them, it will be continued in our next, and the house of the lean man and his servants and his ox and his ass – he has neither the one nor the other, but a thriving bullcalf (if you please) of which all stand in horror – shall be faithfully described. I am alarmed about giving you stories, for Polynesian stories are generally pretty grim; but I'll try some; and perhaps this sort of chatter may amuse equally. Take care of yourself and keep your bow rosined. Give the babes *Maggie Lauder*[3] with my compliments; I think it will raise enthusiasm in a Kilburn cellar. All well here but Lloyd, who is being despatched for a change,[4] and Fanny who ails a good bit. Ever your friend   Tusitala (tale-writer)
                                                                                    alias
                                                                      Robert Louis Stevenson

To Sidney Colvin
(Extracts)

[*Thursday 18 February 1892*]   [*Vailima*]

My dear Colvin, This has been a busyish month for a sick man. First, Faauma – the bronze candlestick, whom otherwise I called my butler –

---

[3] The Scottish song, with verses beginning, 'Wha wad-na be in love/Wi' bonnie Maggie Lauder?' sometimes attributed to Francis Sempill.
[4] Lloyd went on holiday to San Francisco.

bolted from the bed and bosom of Lafaele, the Archangel-Hercules, prefect of the cattle. There was the deuce to pay, and Hercules was inconsolable and immediately started out after a new wife, and has had one up on a visit, but says she has 'no conversation', and I think he will take back the erring and possibly repentant candlestick; whom we all devoutly prefer, as she is not only highly decorative but good-natured, and if she does little work makes no rows. I tell this lightly, but it really was a heavy business; many were accused of complicity, Lafaele was really very sorry. I had to hold beds of justice – literally – seated in my bed and surrounded by lying Samoans seated on the floor; and there were many picturesque and still inexplicable passages. It is hard to reach the truth in these islands. . . . Before I sleep this night I have a confession to make. When I was sick[1] I tried to get to work to finish that Samoa thing; wouldn't go; and at last in the colic time, I slid off into *David Balfour*,[2] some 50 pp. of which are drafted, and like me well. Really I think it is spirited; and there's a damned heroine that (up to now) seems to have attractions: *absit omen*! David, on the whole, seems excellent. Alan does not come in till the tenth chapter, and I am only at the eighth, so I don't know if I can find him again; but David is on his feet, and doing well, and very much in love, and mixed up with the Lord Advocate and the (untitled) Lord Lovat, and all manner of great folk. And the tale interferes with my eating and sleeping. The join is bad; I have not thought to strain too much for continuity; so this part be alive, I shall be content. But there's no doubt David seems to have changed his style, de'il ha'e him! And much I care, if the tale travel! . . .

[*Wednesday*] 2 *March*

Since I last wrote, fifteen chapters of *David Balfour* have been drafted, and five *tiré au clair*. I think it pretty good; there's a blooming maiden that costs anxiety – she is as virginal as billy; but David seems there and alive, and the Lord Advocate is good, and so I think is an episodic appearance of the Master of Lovat. In Chapter XVII I shall get David abroad – Alan went already in Chapter XII. The book should be about the length of *Kidnapped*; this early part of it, about D.'s evidence in the Appin case, is more of a story than anything in *Kidnapped*, but there is no doubt there comes a break in the middle and the tale is practically in two divisions. In the first James More and the M'Gregors, and Katriona, only show; in the second, the Appin case being disposed of, and James Stewart hung, they

---

[1] In the full letter RLS describes how on a journey from Apia in the tropical rain he was 'drenched like a drowned man' and in consequence was 'laid down with diarrhoea and threatenings of Samoa colic for the inside of another week'.

[2] The sequel to *Kidnapped* (published in England as *Catriona*).

rule the roast and usurp the interest – should there be any left. Why did I take up *David Balfour*? I don't know. A sudden passion. . . .

This morning, our cook-boy having suddenly left – injured feelings[3] – the archangel was to cook breakfast. I found him lighting the fire before dawn; his eyes blazed, he had no word of any language left to use, and I saw in him (to my wonder) the strongest workings of gratified ambition. Napoleon was no more pleased to sign his first treaty with Austria than was Lafaele to cook that breakfast. All morning, when I had hoped to be at this letter, I slept like one drugged, and you must take this (which is all I can give you) for what it is worth.

D.B.:
Memoirs of his Adventures at Home and Abroad

The Second Part: where are set forth the misfortunes in which he was involved upon the Appin Murder; his troubles with Lord Advocate Prestongrange; captivity on the Bass Rock; journey into France and Holland; and singular relations with James More Drummond or MacGregor, a son of the notorious Rob Roy.

Chapters

I. A Beggar on Horseback. II. The Highland Writer. III. I go to Pilrig. IV. Lord Advocate Prestongrange. V. Butter and Thunder. VI. I make a Fault in Honour. VII. The Bravo. VIII. The Heather on Fire. IX. I begin to be haunted with a Red-headed Man. X. The Wood by Silvermills. XI. On the march again with Alan. XII. Gillane Sands. XIII. The Bass Rock. XIV. Black Andie's Tale of Tod Lapraik. XV. I go to Inverary.

That is it, as far as drafted. Chap. IV, V, VII, IX and XIV, I am specially pleased with; the last being an episodical bogie story about the Bass Rock told there by the Keeper.

To Sidney Colvin
(Abridged)

9 March [*1892*]   [*Vailima*]

My dear S.C., Take it not amiss if this is a wretched letter. I am eaten up with business. Every day this week I have had some business impediment – I am even now waiting a deputation of chiefs about the road – and my

---

[3] According to MIS, Talolo had been involved with Lafaele's wife, and when she left Vailima Talolo also had to be sent away.

precious morning was shattered by a polite old scourge of a *faipule* –
Parliament man – come begging. All the time *David Balfour* is skelping
along. I began it the 13th of last month; I have now twelve chapters, 79
pp, ready for press, or within an ace, and by the time the month is out one
half should be completed, and I'll be back at drafting the second half.
What makes me sick is to think of Scott turning out *Guy Mannering* in
three weeks! What a pull of work: heavens, what thews and sinews! And
here am I my head spinning from having only rewritten seven not very
difficult pages – and not very good when done. Weakling generation. It
makes me sick of myself, to make such a fash and bobbery over a rotten
end of an old nursery yarn, not worth spitting on when done. Still, there
is no doubt I turn out my work more easily than of yore; and I suppose
I should be singly glad of that. And if I got my book done in six weeks;
seeing it will be about half as long as a Scott, and I have to write
everything twice, it would be about the same rate of industry. It is my fair
intention to be done with it in three months; which would make me
about one half the man Sir Walter was for application and driving the dull
pen. Of the merit we shall not talk; but I don't think *Davie* is *without*
merit.

12 March

And I have this day triumphantly finished fifteen chapters 100 pp. –
being exactly one-half (as near as anybody can guess) of *David Balfour*, the
book to be about a fifth as long again (altogether) as *Treasure Island*: could
I but do the second half in another month! But I can't, I fear; I shall have
some belated material arriving by next mail, and must go again at the
History. Is it not characteristic of my broken tenacity of mind, that I should
have left Davie Balfour some five years in the British Linen Company's
office,[1] and then fall on him at last with such vivacity? But I leave you
again; the last (fifteenth) chapter ought to be rewrote, or part of it, and I
want the half completed in the month, and the month is out by midnight;
though to be sure last month was February, and I might take grace. These
notes are only to show I hold you in mind, though I know they can have
no interest for man or God or animal. . . .

25 March

Heaven knows what day it is, but I am ashamed, all the more as your
letter from Bournemouth of all places – poor old Bournemouth! – is to

---

[1] The last words of *Kidnapped* bring David Balfour 'to the very doors of the British Linen
Company's bank'; the first sentence of *Catriona* (*David Balfour*) describes how he 'came forth of
the British Linen Company'.

hand, and contains a statement of pleasure in my letters which I wish I could have rewarded with a long one. What has gone on? A vast of affairs of a mingled, strenuous, inconclusive, desultory character: much waste of time, much riding to and fro, and little transacted or at least peracted.

Let us give you a review of the present state of our live stock. Six boys in the bush under Joe Strong, who is now a most industrious admirable overseer, the best I ever saw, with far more pride in the work than ever he took in painting. Six souls about the house. Talolo, the cook, returns again today, after an absence and a cloud on his (private character) which has cost me about twelve hours of riding, and I suppose eight hours solemn sitting in council.[2] 'I am sorry indeed for the Chief Justice of Samoa,' I said; 'it is more than I am fit for to be Chief Justice of Vailima'. Lauilo is steward. . . . Steward's assistant and washman, Arrick, a New Hebridee black boy, hired from the German firm; not so ugly as most, but not pretty neither, not so dull as his sort are but not quite a Crichton.[3] When he came first, he ate so much of our good food, that he got a prominent belly. We still chaff him about being thrashed, and he quite believes that is on the cards. 'This what they give black boys on the plantation?' asked Joe showing him a stock-whip. 'No, got plenty string,' says Arrick. Which we translate 'cat-o-nine tails'. But we have no slavery, of course, you understand; and this is the so-called nineteenth century. Kitchen assistant: Tomas, Thomas in English, a Fiji man, very tall and handsome, moving like a marionette with sudden bounds and rolling his eyes with sudden effort. Washerwoman and precentor: Helen, Tomas's wife. This our weak point; we are ashamed of Helen, the cook-house blushes for her, they murmur there at her presence. She seems all right; she is not a bad-looking, strapping wench, seems chaste, is industrious, has an excellent taste in hymns – you should have heard her read one aloud the other day, she marked the rhythm with so much gloating, dissenter sentiment. What is wrong then? says you. Low in your ear – and don't let the papers get hold of it – she is of no family. None, they say; literally, a common woman. Of course, we have out-islanders, who *may* be villains; but we give them the benefit of the doubt, which is impossible with Helen of Vailima, our blot, our pitted speck. The pitted speck I have said is our precentor. It is always a woman who starts Samoan song; the men who sing second, do not enter for a bar or two. Poor, dear Faauma, the

---

[2] On 21 March Lafaele agreed to let Talolo come back and RLS went to Apia the next day to try to arrange this. MIS records Talolo's return on 26 March.

[3] Belle described Arrick to Stoddard as 'a continual joy' as a comic character. He could 'breathe into the glasses to polish them, and hand around soup with his thumb in the dish, and bring in a bottle of wine using his nose as a cork; and endless tricks of that kind, with such amiability and sweetness that nobody gets angry with him' (letter of 15 April 1892). Sir James Crichton (1560–82), a Scottish prodigy of scholarly and knightly accomplishments, was given the epithet 'The Admirable'. Barrie wrote his play about a paragon of a butler in 1902.

unchaste, the extruded Eve of our Paradise, knew only two hymns; but Helen seems to know the whole repertory, and the morning prayers go far more lively in consequence. Lafaele, provost of the cattle. The cattle are: Jack, my horse, quite converted, my wife rides him now and he is as steady as a doctor's cob; Tifanga Jack, a circus horse, my mother's piebald, bought from a passing circus; Bell's mare, now in childbed or next door, confound the slut!; Musu, – amusingly translated the other day 'don't want to', literally cross, but always in the sense of stubbornness and resistance – my wife's little dark brown mare, with a white star on her forehead, whom I have been riding of late to steady her – she has no vices but is unused, skittish and uneasy, and wants a lot of attention and humouring; lastly (of saddle horses) Joe's Luna – not the Latin *moon*, the Hawaiian *overseer*, but it's pronounced the same – a pretty little mare too, but scarce at all broken, a bad bucker, (threw Joe the other day), and has to be ridden with a stock-whip and be brought back with her rump criss-crossed like a clan tartan. The two carthorses, now only used with pack-saddles; two cows, one in the straw (I trust) tomorrow, a third cow, the Jersey – whose milk and temper are alike subjects of admiration – she gives good exercise to the passing saunterer and refreshes him on his return with cream; two calves, a bull and a cow; God knows how many ducks and chickens, and for a wager not even God how many cats. Twelve humans, seven horses, five kine: is not this Babylon the Great which I have builded? Call it Subpriorsford.[4] . . .

The Lang story,[5] will have very little about the treasure, the Master will appear, and it is to a great extent a tale of Prince Charlie *after* the '45, and a love story forbye: the hero is a melancholy exile, and marries a young woman who interests the prince, and there is the devil to pay. I think the Master kills him in a duel, but don't know yet, not having yet seen my second heroine. No – the Master doesn't kill him, they fight, he is wounded, and the Master plays *deus ex machina*. I *think* just now of calling it *The Tail of the Race*; no – heavens! I never saw till this moment – but of course nobody but myself would ever understand Mill-Race, they would think of a quarter-mile. So – I am nameless again. My melancholy young man is to be quite a Romeo. Yes I'll name the book for him: *Dyce of Ythan* – pronounce Eethan.

[4] A joking reference to Scott's country home at Abbotsford; a subprior is two down from an abbot.
[5] In November 1891 Andrew Lang wrote to RLS outlining a plot for a possible story involving Charles Edward, the Young Pretender, at Avignon, the intrigues to make him King of Poland and the return of Alan Breck to Scotland to dig up treasure. This became the basis for RLS's unfinished romance, *The Young Chevalier*. RLS changed his mind several times about the name of the hero.

Dyce of Ythan
by R.L.S.

O, Shovel, Shovel waits his turn, he and his ancestors.[6] I would have tackled him before but my State Trials have never come. So that I have now quite planned:–

Dyce of Ythan. (Historical. 1750)
Sophia Scarlet. (Today).
The Shovels of Newton French. (Historical. 1650 to 1830).

and quite planned and part written:–

The Pearl Fisher. (Today) (with Lloyd, a machine)
David Balfour. (Historical 1751)

And by a strange exception for R.L.S. all in the third person except *D.B.*

[*Tuesday 29 March*]

I don't know what day this is now (the 29th), but I have finished my two chapters, IXth and Xth, of *Samoa* in time for the mail and feel almost at peace. The Xth was the hurricane, a difficult problem; it so tempted one to be literary; and I feel sure the less of that there is in my little handbook, the more chance it has of some utility. Then the events are complicated, seven ships to tell of, and sometimes three of them together; O it was quite a job. But I think I have my facts pretty correct, and for once, in my sickening yarn, they are handsome facts: creditable to all concerned; not to be written of – and I should think scarce to be read without a thrill. I doubt I have got no hurricane into it, the intricacies of the yarn absorbing me too much. But there – it's done somehow, and time presses hard on my heels. The book, with my best expedition, may come just too late to be of use. In which case I shall have made a handsome present of some months of my life for nothing and to nobody. Well, through Her the most ancient heavens are fresh and strong.[7]

---

[6] At Bournemouth in 1886 and at Saranac in November 1887 RLS had planned a romance of the Peninsular War called *The Adventures of Henry Shovel*. The first three chapters were posthumously published in the Vailima Edition (1923). At Vailima (as he told Colvin in February 1891) RLS planned to combine this with another story *The Adventures of John Delafield* (of 1882) into 'a strange kind of novel' to be called *The Shovels of Newton French*. This was never written, but several pages of notes survive.

[7] Wordsworth, 'Ode to Duty': 'And the most ancient heavens, through Thee, are fresh and strong.'

30th [March]

After I had written you, I reread my hurricane which is very poor; the life of the journalist is hard, another couple of writings and I could make a good thing I believe, and it must go as it is! But of course, this book is not written for honour and glory, and the few who will read it may not know the difference. Very little time. I go down with the mail shortly, dine at the Chinese restaurant and go to the Club to dance with islandresses. Think of my going out once a week to dance.[8]

Politics are on the full job again, and we don't know what is to come next. I think Laupepa seems quite played out and therewith the whole treaty *raj*. They have taken to bribing the *faipule* men (Parliament men) to stay in Mulinuu,[9] we hear; but I have not yet sifted the rumour. I must say I shall be scarce surprised if it prove true; these rumours have the knack of being right. Our weather this last month has been tremendously hot, not by the thermometer, which sticks at 86° but to the sensation: no rain, no wind, and this the storm month. It looks ominous and is certainly disagreeable.

No time to finish. Yours ever   R.L.S.

To Sidney Colvin
(Extracts)

[*Vailima*]

[*The extracts come from a letter begun on 1 May 1892*]

Tuesday [17 May]

Yesterday came yours. Well, well, if the dears prefer a week, why I'll give them ten days, but the real document, from which I have scarcely varied, ran for one night.[1] I think you seem scarcely fair to Wiltshire who

---

[8] Earlier in the month RLS and Fanny had been persuaded to establish a social club – (in RLS's words) 'a sort of weekly ball for the half-castes and natives, ourselves to be the only whites'. MIS records: 'Lou dances every dance and rides home at twelve p.m. having started soon after lunch.'

[9] In *A Footnote to History* RLS describes Mulinuu, the western horn of Apia bay, as 'a flat windswept promontory, planted with palms, backed against a swamp of mangroves, and occupied by a rather miserable village'. Mulinuu was the traditional seat of the Samoan Government.

[1] The notorious sham marriage certificate in 'The Beach of Falesá', which was worrying Cassell's. In RLS's MS, Uma is 'illegally married' to Wiltshire 'for one night' and he is 'at liberty to send her to hell next morning'. In *An Island Nights' Entertainments*, Cassell's substituted 'one week' for 'one night' and 'to hell when he pleases' for the second phrase. Scribner's, in the American edition, omitted the first phrase and printed 'to send her packing when he pleases' for the

had surely, under his beastly ignorant ways, right noble qualities. And I think perhaps you scarce do justice to the fact that this is a piece of realism *à outrance* nothing extenuated or adorned. Looked at so, is it not, with all its tragic features, wonderfully idyllic, with great beauty of scene and circumstance? And will you please to observe that almost all that is ugly is in the whites? I'll apologise for Papa Randall if you like; but God! if I told you the whole truth – for I did extenuate there! and he seemed to me essential as a figure, and essential as a pawn in the game, Wiltshire's disgust for him being one of the small, efficient motives in the story. Now it would have taken a fairish dose to disgust Wiltshire. Again, the idea of publishing 'The Beach' substantively is dropped – at once, both on account of expostulation, and because it measured shorter than I had expected. And it was only taken up, when the proposed volume *Beach de Mar*, petered out. It petered out thus: the chief of the short stories got sucked into *Sophia Scarlett* – I give you the two T's, though I prefer the look of it without – and *Sophia* is a book I am much taken with; and mean to get to, as soon as but not before I have done *David Balfour* and *The Young Chevalier*. So you see you are like to hear no more of the Pacific or the XIXth century for awhile. *The Young Chevalier* is a story of sentiment and passion, which I mean to write a little differently from what I have been doing – if I can hit the key; rather more of a sentimental tremolo to it. It may thus help to prepare me for *Sophia*, which is to contain three ladies, and a kind of a love affair between the heroine and a dying planter who is a poet! large orders for R.L.S.[2]

O! about the Consulate, I thought we had quite decided to do nothing till the pestilent book came out, and we saw if it did not damn me forever. 'Tis now done, bless God! and I am a free man. O, the German taboo is quite over; no soul attempts to support the C.J. or the President; they are past hope; the whites have just refused their taxes – I mean the Council has refused to call for them, and if the Council consented, nobody would pay; 'tis a farce, and the curtain is going to fall briefly. Consequently in my *History*, I say as little as may be of the two dwindling stars. Poor devils! I

second. C.K. Shorter felt it his 'duty', as 'the editor of a family newspaper', to omit the certificate completely from the serial version published in the *Illustrated London News*. Ironically enough, the suspect phrases had already been published in RLS's account of 'marriages' between native women and white traders in the Gilbert Islands in the newspaper serialisation of *The South Seas*. On 1 February RLS had told Colvin that he had refused the 'plaintive request' sent to him by McClure 'to make the young folks married properly before "that night" '. He commented: 'This is a poison bad world for the romancer, this Anglo-Saxon world; I usually get out of it by not having any women in at all.'

[2] RLS had written enthusiastically to Colvin on 1 February 1892 about his ideas for *Sophia Scarlet* – 'a *regular novel*; heroine and hero, and false accusation, and love and marriage, and all the rest of it – all planted in a big South Sea plantation run by ex-English officers'. This never got beyond the planning stage, but a fifteen-page outline, dictated to Belle, exists, summarising the first ten chapters.

liked the one, and the other has a little wife, now lying in![3] There was no man born with so little animosity as I. When I heard the C.J. was in low spirits and never left his house, I could scarce refrain from going to him. Yet the man is a rogue. It was a fine feeling to have finished the *History*; there ought to be a future state to reward me for that grind! It's not literature, you know; only journalism, and pedantic journalism. I had but the one desire, to get the thing as right as might be, and avoid false concords – even if that! And it was more than there was time for. However there it is: done. And if Samoa turns up again, my book has to be counted with, being the only narrative extant. Milton and I – If you will kindly excuse the juxtaposition – harnessed ourselves to strange wagons, and I at least will be found to have plodded very soberly with my load. There is not even a good sentence in it; but perhaps – I don't know, it may be found an honest, clear volume.

Wednesday

Never got a word set down, and continues on Thursday 19th May, his own marriage day as ever was. . . .

Other news: well, for a single glimpse of family difficulties. Joe is in black disgrace; and Lloyd, who is continually led by Joe into all sorts of misjudgements, is cooking his remorse (as usual after a fresh unmasking of that false god) to our deep depression and at the same time covert amusement. Poor Joe is not altogether an agreeable inmate, though on the whole I suppose he tries to behave. The wheels go roughest there, or I should rather say deepest, for it is a sloughy surface, trick upon trick, and lie within lie, in fathomless duplicity. Fanny and my mother have tiffs occasionally; when they seem to me to be alternately in the wrong. It is no joke to tell Fanny that I think so, when her turn comes; but it has had to be done. Luckily neither of them rasp or harbour malice; they just have a big row, and shake down again. More than enough of this.

I have celebrated my holiday from *Samoa* by a plunge at the beginning of *The Young Chevalier*; I am afraid my touch is a little broad in a love story; I cannot mean one thing and write another. If I have got to kill a man, I kill him good; and if my characters have to go to bed to each other – well, I want them to go. As for women, I am no more in any fear of them: I can do a sort all right, age makes me less afraid of a petticoat; but I am a little in fear of grossness. However there's David Balfour's love affair, that's all correct – might be read out to a mothers' meeting – or a daughters' meeting, and would be thought delicate by a strumpet, who seems always (in spite of Shakespeare) to have the finer sense. The difficulty in a love yarn, which dwells at all on love, is the dwelling on

---

[3] The Baron Senfft's wife gave birth to a son (Heinrich) on 19 May 1892.

one string; it is manifold, I grant, but the root fact is there unchanged, and the sentiment being very intense and already very much handled in letters, positively calls for a little pawing and gracing. With a writer of my prosaic literalness and pertinency of point of view, this all shoves towards grossness – possibly even towards the far more damnable *closeness*. This has kept me off the sentiment hitherto, and now I am to try: Lord! Of course Meredith can do it, and so could Shakespeare; but with all my romance, I am a realist and a prosaist, and a most fanatical lover of plain physical sensations plainly and expressly rendered; hence my perils. To do love in the same spirit as I did (for instance) D. Balfour's fatigue in the heather; my dear sir, there were grossness ready made! And hence, *how* to sugar? Of course, I mean something different from the false fire of Hardy – as false a thing as ever I perused, unworthy of Hardy and untrue to all I know of life.[4] If ever I do a rape, which may the almighty God forfend! you would hear a noise about my rape, and it should be man that did it. However I have nearly done with Marie Madeleine, and am in good hopes of Marie Salomé, the real heroine – the other is only a prologuial heroine to introduce the blame' hero.

Friday [20 May]

Anyway the first prologuial episode is done, and Fanny likes it. There are only four characters, Francis Blair of Balmile (Jacobite Lord Gladsmuir) my hero; the Master of Ballantrae; Paradon, a wine seller at Avignon; Marie Madeleine his wife. These two last I am now done with, and I think they are successful; and I hope I have Balmile on his feet; and the style seems to be found. It is a little charged and violent; sins on the side of violence; but I think will carry the tale. I think it is a good idea so to introduce my hero being made love to by an episodic woman. Consider this point, please and answer: – I loathe adjectives in titles: Dare I say 'The Chevalier', when my story never touches on The Chevalier de St Georges *ipse*, but only on the Young One? Do consider, and reply. This queer tale – I mean queer for me – has taken a great hold upon me. Where the devil shall I go next? This is simply the tale of a *coup de tête* of a young man and a young woman, with a nearly, perhaps a wholly, tragic sequel, which I desire to make thinkable right through, and sensible; to make the reader, as far as I shall be able, eat and drink and breathe it. Marie-Salomé des Saintes-Maries is, I think, the heroine's name; she has to *be* yet: *sursum corda!* So has the Young Chevalier, whom I have not yet touched, and who comes next in order. Characters: Balmile, or Lord Gladsmuir, *comme vous voulez*; Prince Charlie; Earl Marischal; Master of Ballantrae; and a spy,

---

[4] Hardy's *Tess of the D'Urbervilles* (1891).

and Dr Archie Campbell and a few nondescripts; then of women, Marie Salomé, and Flora Blair: seven at the outside; really four full lengths, and I suppose a half dozen episodic profiles. How I must bore you with these ineptitudes! Have patience. I am going to bed; it is (of all hours) eleven. I have been forced in (since I began to write to you) to blatter to Fanny on the subject of my heroine, there being two *cruces* as to her life and history: how came she alone? and how far did she go with the Chevalier? The second must answer itself when I get near enough to see. The first is a back-breaker. Yet I know there are many reasons why a *fille de famille*, romantic, adventurous, ambitious, innocent of the world, might run from her home in those days; might she not have been threatened with a convent? might there not be some Huguenot business mixed in? Here am I, far from books: if you can help me with a suggestion, I shall say God bless you. She has to be new run away from a strict family, well justified in her own wild but honest eyes, and meeting these three men, C.E., Marischal, and Balmile, through the accident of a fire at an inn. She must not run from a marriage, I think; it would bring her in the wrong frame of mind.[5] Once I can get her, *sola*, on the highway, all were well with my narrative. Perpend. And help if you can.[6]. . .

27th Mail Day [actually 25 May]

And I don't know that I have much to report. I may have to leave for Malie as soon as these mail packets are made up.[7] 'Tis a necessity (if it be one) I rather deplore. I think I should have liked to lazy; but I daresay all it means is the delay of a day or so in tacking back to *David Balfour*; that respectable youth chides at being left (where he is now) in Glasgow with the Lord Advocate, and after five years in the British Linen, who shall blame him? I was all forenoon yesterday down in Apia, dictating and Lloyd typewriting, the conclusion of *Samoa*; and then at home correcting till the dinner bell; and in the evening again till eleven of the clock. This morning I have made up most of my packets, and I think my mail is all ready but two more, and the tag of this. I would never deny (as D.B. might say) that I was rather tired of it. But I have a damned good dose of the devil in my pipe-stem atomy; I have had my little holiday outing in

---

[5] Added as an afterthought at the side of the paragraph.

[6] RLS wrote no more of this novel although it was still 'on the stocks' in November. Colvin published the Prologue and the beginning of ch. 1 in the Edinburgh Edition (1897).

[7] RLS, concerned at the possibility of conflict, was trying to urge the rival Kings to come to some peaceful arrangement. He visited Malietoa Laupepa but the attempt to arrange a private interview fell through. He determined to visit Mataafa at Malie. The full letter recounts two visits during May, the first with both Fanny and Belle (who were thought to be his two wives). The third expedition to Malie (foreseen in this letter) took place on 27 May; RLS, accompanied by his mother and Belle went to a feast given by Mataafa.

my kick at *The Young Chevalier*, and I guess I can settle to *David Balfour* tomorrow or Friday like a little man. I wonder if any one had ever more energy upon so little strength? I know there is a frost; the *Samoa* book can only increase that – I can't help it, that book is not written for me but for Miss Manners; but I mean to break that frost inside two years, and pull off a big success, and vanity whispers in my ear that I have the strength. If I haven't, whistle ower the lave o't![8] I can do without glory, and perhaps the time is not far off when I can do without coin. It is a time coming soon enough anyway; and I have endured some two and forty years without public shame, and had a good time as I did it. If only I could secure a violent death, what a fine success! I wish to die in my boots; no more land of counterpane[9] for me. To be drowned, to be shot, to be thrown from a horse – ay, to be hanged, rather than pass again through that slow dissolution. Yet I don't believe I should commit suicide, I *think* I'm afraid of that, I could not tell you why. I fancy this gloomy ramble is caused by a twinge of age; I put on an undershirt yesterday (it was the only one I could find) that barely came under my trousers; and just below it, a fine healthy rheumatism has now settled like a fire in my hip. From such small causes, do these valuable considerations flow!

I shall now say adieu, dear Sir, having ten rugged miles before me and the horrors of a native feast and parliament without an interpreter, for today I go alone. Yours ever   R.L.S.

To Henry James

[*? 25 May 1892*]   [*Vailima*]

My dear Henry James, From this perturbed and hunted being expect but a line, and that line shall be but a whoop for Adela.[1] O she's delicious, delicious; I could live and die with Adela – die, rather the better of the two; you never did a straighter thing, and never will.

David Balfour, second part of *Kidnapped*, is on the stocks at last; and is not bad, I think. As for *The Wrecker*, it's a machine, you know; don't expect aught else:[2] a machine, and a police machine; but I believe the end

---

[8] A Scots air used by Burns as the title and refrain of a song and as the refrain of a chorus in 'The Jolly Beggars'.

[9] The title of one of the poems in *A Child's Garden*.

[1] Adela Chart is the heroine of James's short story 'The Marriages', included in *The Lesson of the Master*. James sent the 'little volume of tales which I lately put forth' to RLS at the same time as a letter dated 19 March 1892.

[2] In his letter James explains, 'I have still had the refinement not to read *The Wrecker* in the periodical page ... Trust me, however, to taste you in long draughts as soon as I can hold the book.'

is one of the most genuine butcheries in literature; and we point to our machine with a modest pride – as the only police machine without a villain. Our criminals are a most pleasing crew, and leave the dock with scarce a stain upon their character.

What a different line of country to be trying to draw Adela, and trying to write the last four chapters of *The Wrecker*! Heavens, it's like two centuries; and ours is such rude, transpontine business, aiming only at a certain fervour of conviction and sense of energy and violence in the men; and yours is so neat and bright and of so exquisite a surface! Seems dreadful to send such a book to such an author; but your name is on the list. And we do modestly ask you to consider the chapters on the *Norah Creina* with the study of Captain Nares, and the forementioned last four, with their brutality of substance and the curious (and perhaps unsound) technical manoeuvre of running the story together to a point as we go along, the narrative becoming more succinct and the details fining off with every page.

Sworn affidavit of R.L.S.

No person now alive has beaten Adela: I adore Adela and Her Maker. Sic subscrib: Robert Louis Stevenson

A Sublime Poem to follow.[3]

> Adela, Adela, Adela Chart
> What have you done to my elderly heart?
> Of all the ladies of paper and ink
> I count you the paragon, call you the pink.
>
> The word of your brother depicts you in part:
> 'You raving maniac!' Adela Chart;
> But in all the asylums that cumber the ground,
> So delightful a maniac was ne'er to be found.
>
> I pore on you, dote on you, clasp you to heart,
> I laud, love, and laugh at you, Adela Chart,
> And thank my dear maker the while I admire
> That I can be neither your husband nor sire.
>
> Your husband's, your sire's were a difficult part;
> You're a byway to suicide, Adela Chart;
> But to read of, depicted by exquisite James,
> O, sure you're the flower and quintessence of dames.

R.L.S.

---

[3] Written at the bottom of the page, with instructions to 'p.t.o.'

Eructavit cor meum[4]

My heart was inditing a goodly matter about Adela Chart.

[5]Though oft I've been touched by the volatile dart,
To none have I grovelled but Adela Chart.
There are passable ladies, no question, in art –
But where is the marrow of Adela Chart?
I dreamed that to Tyburn I fared in the cart –
I dreamed I was married to Adela Chart:
From the first I awoke with a palpable start,
The second dumbfounded me, Adela Chart!

Another verse bursts from me, you see; no end to the violence of the
Muse. *C'est Venus tout entier!*[6]

To Charles Baxter

[*First part dictated to Belle*][1]
[*18 July 1892*]   *Vailima Plantation*

My dear Charles, Enclosed is the slip filled up. I shall try to remember the
set of Samoan stamps;[2] but look here, if I forget this time, keep me up to
the mark in future.

Awfully glad you have got a good man for the *Davy Balfour* maps. As
for your news of the presentation of Lady Simpson of Strathavon the
whole family fell in swaths about the apartment, but man why didn't ye
no send us the *Gentlewoman*?[3] You will never be forgiven until this is
done. An irate amanuensis here interrupts with a countenance deformed
with fury and says 'Why don't you tell him there is no book stall in
Apia?'

---

[4] The opening words of Psalm 45 – 'My heart is inditing of a good matter'. The Revised Version
has 'overfloweth with a goodly matter'.

[5] This last verse is squeezed in the margins and across the top of the letter.

[6] Racine, *Phèdre*, I. iii.

[1] On 20 June 1892, because of writer's cramp, RLS began dictating letters to Belle. Thereafter she
became his amanuensis and he dictated many letters and some literary work (e.g. *St Ives* and *Weir
of Hermiston*) to her.

[2] RLS was supplying Baxter's sons with sets of Samoan stamps. Baxter wrote to RLS on 15
November: 'The children . . . thank you immensely for the princely supply of Samoan stamps
just received. The $\frac{1}{2}$ d. stamps especially are sufficient to make a collector's fortune.'

[3] 'Lady Simpson of Ballabraes, presented [at court] by Mrs Struth, had a magnificent train in rich
cream brocade, arranged from left shoulder with plumes of feathers; cream duchesse satin
petticoat, trimmed in festoons of chiffon and feathers; diamond ornaments. Miss Florence
Fitzgerald, presented by Lady Simpson, was much admired' (*Gentlewoman*, 4 June 1892). Among
the photographs of the ladies presented there was one of Miss Fitzgerald.

Perhaps you will understand our situation better if I tell you this. I have been now for some time contending with powers and principalities[4] and I have never once seen one of my own letters to *The Times*. So when you see something in the papers that you think might interest the exiles of Upolu – how much more if you see anything that you know will convulse them, like my lady's picture in the *Gentlewoman* – do not think twice, out with your saxpence, and send it flying to Vailima.

Of what you say[5] – amanuensis called to the cook-house – of the past, eh, man, it was a queer time, and awful miserable, but there's no sense in denying it was awful fun, and life? – yes, sir, it was deadly living. Do you mind the youth in Highland garb and the tableful of coppers? Do you mind the SIGNAL of Waterloo Place?[6] – Hey, how the blood stends[7] to the heart at such a memory! – Ha'e ye the notes o't? Gie's them – Gude's sake, man, gie's the notes o't; I mind ye made a tüne o't an' played it on your pinanny; gie's the notes. Dear Lard: that past.

Glad to hear Henley's prospects are fair; his new volume[8] is the work of a real poet. He is one of those who can make a noise of his own with words, and in whom experience strikes an individual note. There is perhaps no more genuine poet living, bar the Big Guns. In case I cannot overtake an acknowledgement to himself by this mail, please let him hear of my pleasure and admiration.[9] How poorly Kipling compares! K. is all smart journalism and cleverness; it is all bright and shallow and limpid like a business paper – a good one, *s'entend*; but there is no blot of heart's blood and the Old Night;[10] there are no harmonics, there is scarce harmony, to his music; and in Henley – all of these: a touch, a sense within sense, a sound outside the sound, the shadow of the inscrutable,

---

[4] Cf. Ephesians 6:12.

[5] The rest of the letter is in RLS's own hand.

[6] Cf. p. 127.

[7] Leaps, bounds (Scots).

[8] *The Song of the Sword and Other Verses* (published April 1892). It included (apart from the title poem) four 'London Voluntaries' and twenty-five 'Rhymes and Rhythms'.

[9] RLS wrote to Henley on 1 August, signing himself, 'Your old friend and present huge admirer':

> I have not received the same thrill of poetry since G.M.'s *Joy of Earth* volume, and 'Love in a Valley'; and I do not know that even that was so intimate and deep. Again and again, I take the book down, and read, and my blood is fired as it used to be in youth. . . . I did not guess you were so great a magician; these are new tunes, this is an undertone of the true Apollo; these are not verse, they are poetry – inventions, creations, in language.

[10] Cf. 'Chaos and old Night' – Milton, *Paradise Lost*, I. 543.

eloquent beyond all definition. The first 'London Voluntary' knocked me wholly. Ever yours affectionately, my dear Charles

Robert Louis Stevenson

Kind memories to your father and all friends.

To Sidney Colvin
(Extracts)

[*Dictated to Belle*]
[*Tuesday 9*] *August* [*1892*]   *Vailima*

My dear Colvin, You will have no letter at all this month and it is really not my fault. I have been saving my hand as much as possible for *Davy Balfour*, only this morning I was getting on first rate with him, when about half-past nine there came a prick in the middle of the ball of my thumb and I had to take to the left hand and two words a minute. I fear I slightly exaggerate the speed of my left hand; about a word and a half in the minute – which is dispiriting to the last degree,

Your last letter with the four excellent reviews and the good news about *The Wrecker* was particularly welcome. I have already written to Charles Baxter about the volume form appearance of 'The Beach of Falesá'. In spite of bad thumbs and other interruptions I hope to send to Baxter by this mail the whole first part (a good deal more than half) of *David Balfour* ready for press. This is pretty satisfactory, and I think ought to put us beyond the reach of financial catastrophe for the year. Yet we have mismanaged one piece of business, which will certainly let us in for a piece of unexpected extravagance. Strong, whom I hoped to have now seen the back of forever is still amongst us – at least on the beach here – and likely so to continue.[1] I could not satisfy this gentleman with the allowance and travelling terms I had to offer him; he asked me among other things for money to buy a piece of land in Japan; and when I finally refused, in a sudden fit of nobility he broke off the negotiation and

---

[1] On 15 July 1892 Belle obtained a divorce from Joe Strong against a background of anger and bitterness about his behaviour. Colvin destroyed the relevant part of RLS's letter to him about it, but the facts were summarised by Fanny when she resumed her diary on 23 December 1892:

> About the time I stopped writing we found Joe Strong out in various misdeeds: robbing the cellar and store-room at night with false keys. In revenge, when he found that he was discovered, he went round to all our friends in Apia and spread slanders about Belle. We turned him away and applied for a divorce for Belle, which was got with no difficulty, as he had been living with a native woman of Apia as his wife ever since he came here – an old affair begun when he was here before. Also, he had been in an intrigue with Faauma. He came up here late one night to beg forgiveness and ask to be taken back. I was so shocked at seeing him that I had an attack of angina, which seems to remain with me. Louis was made sole guardian of the child, who has been sent to Nelly to school.

announced he would depend upon himself. This is cheap, but alas nasty. Since the mountain will not go away from Mahomet, Mahomet accompanied by his family proposes to go away from the mountain; and we shall all probably make a little trip to Tahiti in October. But *D.B.* must be finished first.

You say nothing whatever about your health. Indeed I am an ass to apologize for my letter, your own pottering correspondence being entirely occupied either with preachments or taffy. The last was taffy but it is usually the other way. A cousin of mine Graham Balfour arrived along with your last.[2] It was rather a lark. Fanny, Belle and I stayed down at the hotel two nights expecting the steamer, and we had seven horses down daily for the party and the baggage. These were on one occasion bossed by Austin, age eleven. 'I'm afraid I cannot do that now', said he in answer to some communication, 'as I am taking charge of the men here.' In the course of the forenoon he took 'his' men to get their lunch, and had his own by himself at the Chinese restaurant. What a day for a boy. The steamer came in at last on Saturday morning immediately after breakfast. We three were out at the place of anchorage in the hotel boat as she came up, spotting rather anxiously for our guest, whom none of us had ever seen. We chose out some rather awful cads and tried to make up our mind to them; they were the least offensive yet observed among an awful crew of cabin passengers; but when the Simon Pure[3] appeared at last upon the scene he was as nice a young fellow as you would want. Followed a time of giddy glory – one crowded hour of glorious life[4] – when I figured about the deck with attendant shemales in the character of *the* local celebrity, was introduced to the least unpresentable of the ruffians on board, dogged about the deck by a diminutive Hebrew with a Kodak the click of which kept time to my progress like a pair of castanets, and filled up in the Captain's room on iced champagne at 8.30 of God's morning. The Captain in question, Cap. Morse,[5] is a great South Sea character, like

[2] Thomas Graham Balfour (1858–1929), destined to become RLS's close friend and his official biographer, was the only child of Thomas Graham Balfour, a nephew of RLS's grandfather Lewis Balfour, and his wife Georgina. RLS had met and liked them during a visit to Cockfield Rectory in 1870. On leaving Oxford, Balfour qualified as a barrister but never practised. His life-work was in the field of education; he was Director of Education for Staffordshire 1903–26 and served on many official committees. He was knighted in 1917.

Following his father's death in 1891, Balfour was free to travel. Because of his interest in Japanese art he decided to visit Japan and having got so far he wrote to RlS suggesting a visit to Vailima.

[3] The real or genuine person. Simon Pure was a Quaker in Mrs Susannah Centlivre's comedy *A Bold Stroke for a Wife* (1718). Another character impersonates him during the play for his own ends but the 'real Simon Pure' turns up at the end. Scott used the phrase in *Guy Mannering*, ch. 56.

[4] 'One crowded hour of glorious life Is worth an age without a name' – Scott's motto for ch. 34 of *Old Mortality*, since identified as being from a poem by Thomas Osbert Mordaunt.

[5] Captain Hiram G. Morse of the *S.S. Alameda*, one of the mail-steamers plying between San Francisco and Australia.

the side of a house and the green-room of a music hall, but with all the saving qualities of the seaman. . . . The whole celebrity business was particularly characteristic; the Captain has certainly never read a word of mine; and as for the Jew with the Kodak, he had never heard of me till he came on board. . . .

[*10 August*]

Graham Balfour the new cousin and Lloyd are away with Clarke the Missionary on a school inspecting *malanga*,[6] really perhaps the prettiest little bit of opera in real life that can be seen, and made all the prettier by the actors being children. I have come to a collapse this morning on *D.B.*; wrote a chapter one way, half re-copied it in another, and now stand halting between the two like Buridan's donkey.[7] These sorts of *cruces* always are to me the most insoluble, and I should not wonder if *D.B.* stuck there for a week or two. This is a bother for I understand McClure talks of beginning serial publication in December.[8] If this could be managed, what with *D.B.*, the apparent success of *The Wrecker*, 'Falesá', and some little pickings from *Across the Plains* – not to mention, as quite hopeless, *The History of Samoa* – this should be rather a profitable year, as it must be owned it has been a busy one. The trouble is, if I miss the December publication, it may take the devil and all of a time to start another syndicate. I am really tempted to curse my conscientiousness. If I had not recopied *Davie* he would now be done and dead and buried; and here I am stuck about the middle, with an immediate publication threatened and the fear before me of having after all to scamp the essential business of the end. At the same time, although I love my *Davy*, I am a little anxious to get on again on *The Young Chevalier*. I have in nearly all my works been trying one racket: to get out the facts of life as clean and naked and sharp as I could manage it. In this other book I want to try and megilp them altogether in an atmosphere of sentiment, and I wonder whether twenty-five years of life spent in trying the one thing will not make it impossible for me to succeed in the other. However it is the only

---

[6] In ch. 1 of *A Footnote* RLS explained: 'When people form a party and go from village to village, junketing and gossipping they are said to go on a *malanga*. Their songs have announced their approach ere they arrive; the guest house is prepared for their reception; the virgins of the village attend to prepare the kava bowl and entertain them with the dance; time flies in the enjoyment of every pleasure which an islander conceives.' Europeans later adopted the word to describe a visit or tour.

[7] The famous problem, traditionally ascribed to the Medieval French philosopher, about the ass placed between a bundle of hay and a pail of water who dies of hunger and thirst because he cannot choose between them. In another version the ass is undecided between two bundles of hay.

[8] *David Balfour* was serialised in *Atalanta* (a magazine for girls), December 1892 to September 1893. It was also syndicated by McClure in a number of newspapers.

way to attempt a love story. You can't tell any of the facts, and the only chance is to paint an atmosphere.

Fanny has been very ill, or I would say so if she were anybody else. But somehow she is such a hand at getting diseases and not seeming to be so much the worse for them after all, that whatever she springs upon me, I cannot feel as anxious as I ought. In the last eight months she has started an aneurism in her head, for which we luckily knew the treatment, and she seems a good deal better. In the last three weeks, and in consequence of the beastly rows and scenes heretofore depicted, she sprung angina pectoris on us. But I believe a single attack of that is not uncommon; such was my father's case, and I hope it will be here. . . .

15 August

On the Saturday night Fanny and I went down to Haggard's to dine and be introduced to Lady Jersey.[9] She is there with her daughter Lady Margaret and her brother Captain Leigh, a very nice stupid kind of glass-in-his-eye kind of fellow.[10] It is to be presumed I made a good impression; for the meeting has had a most extraordinary sequel. Fanny and I slept in Haggard's billiard room which happens to be Lloyd's bungalow. In the morning she and I breakfasted in the back parts with Haggard and Cap. Leigh, and it was then arranged that the Captain should go with us to Malie on the Tuesday under a false name; so that Government House at Sydney [might] by no possibility be connected with a rebel camp. [11]On Sunday afternoon up comes Haggard in a state of huge excitement: Lady J. insists on going, too, in the character of my cousin; I write her a letter under the name of Miss Amelia Balfour, proposing the excursion; and this morning up comes a copy of verses from Amelia. I wrote to Mataafa announcing that I should bring two cousins instead of one, that the second was a lady, unused to Samoan manners, and it would be a good thing if she could sleep in another house with Kalala.[12] Send a copy of this to Amelia, and at the same time make all arrangements, dating my letter 1745. We shall go on ahead on the Malie Road; she is to follow with Haggard and Captain Leigh, and overtake us at the ford of the Gase-Gase where Haggard will return, and the rest of us pursue our way to rebeldom.

[9] Margaret Elizabeth Leigh (1849–1945), daughter of the 2nd Baron Leigh, married (1872) Victor Albert George Child-Villiers (1845–1915), 7th Earl of Jersey, who was Governor of New South Wales 1890–93. Haggard had met her in Sydney and invited her to visit Samoa. There is a biography of Lady Jersey by her granddaughter, Lady Violet Powell (1978).

[10] Lady Margaret Child-Villiers (1875–1959) married (1898) the 7th Baron Dynevor. Violet Powell says that 'she openly declared to the next generation [that she] fell in love with Stevenson'. Rupert Leigh (1856–1919) was at this time a Captain in the 15th Hussars and one of Lord Jersey's ADCs.

[11] The next part of the letter is in RLS's hand.

[12] Mataafa's natural daughter; he was unmarried.

This lark is certainly huge. It is all nonsense that it can be concealed; Miss Amelia Balfour will be at once identified with the Queen of Sydney, as they call her; and I would not in the least wonder if the visit proved the signal of war. With this I have no concern, nor yet with the feelings of the Earl of Jersey; I am not his wife's keeper, and the thing wholly suits my book and fits my predilections for Samoa. Moreover, how do I know (whatever I may think probable) that she is not acting on a suggestion of her husband's? What a pity the mail leaves, and I must leave this adventure to be continued in our next![13] But I need scarcely say that all this is deadly private. I expect it all to come out, not without explosion, only it must not be through me or you. By the bye, do you know Lady J.? I thought you knew everybody except people in the South Seas. We had a visit yesterday from a person by the name of Count Nerli[14] who is said to be a good painter also a drunkard and a sweep, and looks it. Altogether the aristocracy clusters thick about us. In which radiant light, as the mail must now be really put up, I leave myself until next month. Yours ever

R.L.S.

To Charles Baxter
(Slightly Abridged)

[*Dictated to Belle*]
11 August 1892   *Vailima*

My dear Charles, Herewith please receive a considerable portion of *David Balfour*.[1] McClure has been behaving in a particularly annoying and shilly-shallying manner. His own old unsolicited offer was sixteen hundred pounds for serial rights. I am now done with the bargaining, and place it in your hands. In my belief, sixteen hundred is a fair figure and I should propose (while leaving you discretion) to refuse anything under fifteen hundred.[2] Suppose Samuel to fail in reaching this figure my advice would

---

[13] Belle concludes the letter.

[14] Count Girolamo Pieri Nerli (1860–1926), son of an Italian nobleman and an English mother (daughter of Shelley's friend, Thomas Medwin). He arrived in Australia in 1885 and lived there and in New Zealand for many years. MIS records that RLS gave Nerli ten sittings for his portrait 15 September to 3 October. His original oil painting of RLS appears to be the one in the Scottish National Portrait Gallery in Edinburgh; there are duplicates in the Writers' Museum, Edinburgh, and at Yale. There are also a bewildering number of sketches and studies in oil, water-colour, pastel, charcoal and pencil but it is not clear how many of these were done from life.

[1] In the postscript RLS noted that he was sending 'in three envelopes 147 pages of *David Balfour*'.

[2] RLS had in effect promised on 1 November 1887 that McClure should have the serial rights (p. 355, n 5). Baxter eventually secured £1600 from McClure for these rights.

be to put the whole affair *quoad* serial rights in the hands of A.P. Watt,[3] to whom, instead of your idea of sealed offers, I feel rather inclined to intrust those books in the future for which I have not otherwise arranged.

Apropos of 'The Beach of Falesá' I reply to you, although I believe it's through Colvin I have received the proposal. You will kindly communicate to him my answer. The B. of F. is *simply not* to appear along with 'The Bottle Imp', a story of a totally different scope and intention, to which I have already made one fellow, and which I design for a substantive volume.[4] If on the other hand Cassell shall choose to publish it by itself, I would remind the lot of you that this was my own original proposal, which I have seen no reason to change, and which I should be rather glad to see come in operation.

As for the news about Etta I only wish there were any possible means of communicating directly to herself my sympathy. I think it is really one of the most dastardly things I ever heard of, and I am now rather a connoisseur in dastards.[5] I cannot remember whether I told you last mail the news of our domestic revolution – talking of dastards. I shall enclose in this the papers from the Consulate to be added to the archives.[6] Doubtless anyway you will have heard some details through Colvin. But what in God's name could have happened to Eva. The animosity of women is always an extraordinary study; but when I remember that I once

---

[3] Alexander Pollock Watt (1834–1914) claimed to have founded the profession of literary agent; he acted for many major authors including Hardy and Kipling.

[4] Cassell's had gone ahead, at Colvin's suggestion, with plans to publish the two stories in one volume; an announcement in the *Scotsman* of 4 August said that it would be ready 'towards the end of August'. Publication was delayed because of problems over the sham marriage contract (see p. 487, n. 1), complicated by Baxter's absence abroad. Baxter passed an extract of this letter on to Cassell's and the firm's General Manager Wemyss Reid wrote to RLS on 4 October, explaining the background and agreeing to respect his wishes. Reid sent RLS a copy of the proof-volume Cassell's had already set up. This is the so-called 'Trial Issue'.

[5] Sir Walter Simpson was formally married to Anne Fitzgerald Mackay (Etta) on 13 January 1881, but there was an earlier irregular Scottish marriage. When their illegitimate daughter, Florence Fitzgerald was presented at Court with her mother on 18 May 1892 she was described as her niece. Baxter wrote to RLS on 1 July 1892:

> I told you Lady Simpson and Flo. Fitzg. had been presented. As I expected they were blown upon, but you will never guess by whom. There is one Mrs Clifton, a kind of cousin of the Simpsons' mother, I don't suppose you ever knew her. Impelled by a sense of Duty to Her Queen, she denounced Lady Simpson as an ex-mistress of six years standing, an adventuress, and a liar, and Flo as her illegitimate child. This in a letter to the Lord Chamberlain, adding that the brother and sister '*at whose request she wrote*' felt deeply pained at the insult offered to Her Majesty by one of their family. Unexpectedly to them no doubt the Lord Chamberlain's office furnished us with a copy of their letter, and it was put to Eva and Willie whether they adopted it, which they did! Can you conceive anything more vile? Well there has been an awful shindy, and I have done what I could to help, but of course it wasn't much.

'Eva and Willie' were Simpson's sister (p. 174, n. 2) and brother (p. 27, n. 6), who were opposed to the marriage. His daughter was Ethel Lucy Florence Mackay (1875–1955) who married (1908) Sir Arthur Willert, *Times* correspondent and later a Foreign Office official.

[6] Baxter noted that these papers (evidently dealing with the Strong divorce) did not arrive.

seriously dreamed of marrying that underhand virago my heart wells over
with gratitude.

The beginning of your letter was exceedingly dreary and bad reading.
You say you care for nobody which I take the liberty of denying, and that
nobody cares for you, to which I take the freedom to present the lie
direct. However that humour is no doubt long blown by; and I can assure
you if I had written during some of the pleasing episodes of the revolution
– say no longer ago than last Thursday when I was chewing the bitterness
of its last episode I might have appeared to you almost as weariful a
creature as you showed to me. And believe me the worst of what can
have been troubling you can have been but a flea-bite compared to the
mouth-deep mires in which our family has been wading for six weeks. I
wish I could say it was quite over but owing to mismanagement on
our side the unwelcome presence is likely to be continued on our island.
The worst of it at least *is* over, and I do not believe that there is remaining in the hand of Fortune any such disgusting drug to be again
administered.

Glad you saw Colvin. I wish you would tell me how you thought him
looking. You and he are the last of the Romans and it appears that one of
these Romans must be rapidly aging. At least I hear by the means of an
Academy schoolboy that 'an old gentleman to whom I dedicated all my
books' recently presented the Rector with a choice of two of my photographs. If this be really you, and I cannot see who else it could refer to,
it is enough to cure us all of existence.[7] I remain, My dear old gentleman,
Your ancient tottering but Faithful friend   Robert Louis Stevenson[8]

To Lady Jersey

14 August 1745   [*Vailima*]

To Miss Amelia Balfour.

My dear Cousin, We are going an expedition to leeward on Tuesday
morning. If a lady were perhaps to be encountered on horseback – say,
towards the Gase-Gase river – about six A.M., I think we should have an
episode somewhat after the style of the '45. What a misfortune, my dear
cousin, that you should have arrived while your cousin Graham was
occupying my only guest chamber – for Osterley Park[1] is not so large in

---

[7] Baxter replied on 15 November: 'I was the old gentleman. I saw the picture the other day on
the wall of the Big Hall and it does everybody credit. It is an enlargement of the Boston one
which I think the best of all.'
[8] Postscript on financial matters omitted.
[1] Lord Jersey's family home in Middlesex, now owned by the National Trust.

Samoa as it was at home – but happily our friend Haggard has found a corner for you!

The King over the Water – the Gase-Gase water – will be pleased to see the clan of Balfour mustering so thick around his standard.

I have (one serious word) been so lucky as to get a really secret interpreter, so all is for the best in our little adventure into the Waverley Novels. I am, Your affectionate cousin   Robert Louis Stevenson

P.S. Observe the stealth with which I have blotted my signature, but we must be political *à outrance*.

To Sidney Colvin
(Abridged)

[*19 August 1892*]   [*Vailima*]

My dear Colvin, This is Friday night, the (I believe) 18th or 20th August or September. I shall probably regret tomorrow having written you with my own hand like the Apostle Paul.[1] But I am alone over here in the workman's house, as we now call the ex-Strong chalet, where I and Belle and Lloyd and Austin are pigging; the rest are at cards in the main residency. I have not joined them because 'belly belong me' has been kicking up, and I have just taken 15 drops of laudanum.

On Tuesday, the party set out – self in white cap, velvet coat, cords and yellow half boots, Belle in a white kind of suit and white cap to match mine, Lloyd in white clothes and long yellow boots and a straw hat, Graham in khakis and gaiters, Henry (my old overseer) in blue coat and black kilt, and the great Laafaele with a big ship-bag on his saddle-bow. We left the mail at the P.O., had lunch at the hotel, and about 1.50 set out westward to the place of tryst. This was by a little shrunken brook in a deep channel of mud, on the far side of which in a thicket of low trees, all full of moths of shadow and butterflies of sun, we lay down to await her ladyship. Whisky and water, then a sketch of the encampment for which we all posed to Belle, passed off the time until 3.30. Then I could hold in no longer. Thirty minutes late. Had the secret oozed out? were they arrested? I got my horse, crossed the brook again, and rode hard back to the Vaea cross roads, whence I was aware of white clothes glancing in the other long straight radius of the quadrant. I turned at once to return to the place of tryst; but Haggard, insane with secrecy and romance, overtook me, almost bore me down, shouting 'Ride, ride!' like a hero in

[1] I Corinthians 16:21: 'The salutation of me Paul with mine own hand.' Cf. II Thessalonians 3:17.

a ballad. Lady Margaret and he were only come to show the place; they returned, and the rest of our party, reinforced by Captain Leigh and Lady Jersey, set on for Malie. The delay was due to Haggard's infinite, and deliciously infinitesimal, precautions, leading them up lanes, by back ways, and then down again to the beach road a hundred yards further on.

It was agreed that Lady Jersey existed no more; she was now my cousin Amelia Balfour. That relative and I headed the march; she is a charming woman, all of us like her extremely after trial on this somewhat rude and absurd excursion. And we Amelia'd or Miss Balfour'd her with great but intermittent fidelity. When we came to the last village, I sent Henry on ahead to warn the King of our approach and amend his discretion, if that might be. As he left I heard the villagers asking *Which was the great lady?* And a little further at the borders of Malie itself, we found the guard making a music of bugles and conches. Then I knew the game was up and the secret out. A considerable guard of honour, mostly children, accompanied us; but for our good fortune, we had been looked for earlier, and the crowd was gone.

Dinner at the King's; he asked me to say grace, I could think of none – never could. Graham suggested *Benedictus Benedicat*, at which I leaped. We were nearly done, when old Popo inflicted the Atua howl (of which you have heard already) right at Lady Jersey's shoulder.[2] She started in fine style. – 'There,' I said, 'we have been giving you a chapter of Scott, but this goes beyond the Waverley Novels.' After dinner, *kava*.[3] Lady J. was

---

[2] In an account to Colvin in May of an earlier visit to Mataafa, RLS described Popo as 'the highest talking-man in Samoa, having in his gift the name of *Tuiatua*, King of Atua, the windward province of Upolu'. The King's drinking of *kava* was hailed by Popo and his son 'with a singular ululation, perfectly new to my ears; it means (to the expert) "Long live Tuiatua"; to the inexpert, is a mere voice of barbarous wolves'. RLS put the following verse below a drawing by Belle in the booklet they gave to Lady Jersey:

> Eighty the years of his body, and how much more of his mind
> Vigorous yet and erect, with an aquiline face designed
> Like Dante's, he who had worshipped feathers and shells, and wood,
> As a pillar alone in the desert that points where a city stood,
> Survived the world that was his, playmates and gods and tongue –
> For even the speech of his race had altered since Popo was young.
> And ages of time and epochs of changing manners bowed,
> And the silent hosts of the dead wondered and muttered aloud
> With him, as he bent and marvelled, a man of the time of the Ark,
> And saluted the ungloved hand of the Lady of Osterley Park.

The Samoid, Book XIII

[3] A drink made from the grated root of the *ava* or *kava* plant (*Piper methysticum*, a pepper plant). The formal making and consumption of *kava* played an important part on all ceremonial occasions, including the greeting of visitors. In olden times the root was chewed by the *Taupo* (a virgin of rank in each village) who spat it into a wooden bowl, poured water over it and then left it to ferment.

served before me, and the King *drank last*; it was the least formal *kava* I ever saw in that house – no names called, no show of ceremony. All my ladies are well trained; and when Belle drained her bowl, the King was pleased to clap his hands. Then he and I must retire for our secret interview to another house. He gave me his own staff and made me pass before him; and in the interview which was long and delicate, he twice called me *Afioga*. Ah, that leaves you cold, but I am Samoan enough to have been moved. *Susuga* is my accepted rank; to be called *Afioga* – Heavens! what an advance – and it leaves Europe cold. But it staggered my Henry. The first time it was complicated '*lana Susuga* ma *lana Afioga* – His Excellency *and* His Majesty'; the next time plain Majesty. Henry then begged to interrupt the interview and tell who he was – he is a small family chief in Savaii, not very small – 'I do not wish the King,' says he, 'to think me a boy from Apia.' On our return to the palace we separated. I had asked for the ladies to sleep alone; that was understood; but that Tusitala – his *Afioga* Tusitala – should go out with the other young men, and not sleep with the highborn females of his family – was a doctrine received with difficulty. Lloyd and I had one screen, Graham and Leigh another, and we slept well.

In the morning I was first abroad before dawn; not very long, already there was a stir of birds. A little after, I heard singing from the King's chapel – exceeding good – and went across in the hour when the east is yellow and the morning bank is breaking up, to hear it nearer. All about the chapel, the guards were posted, and all saluted Tusitala. I could not refrain from smiling: 'So there is a place too,' I thought, 'where sentinels salute me.' Mine has been a queer life.

Belle and Lady Jersey had a good time, she is quite unaffected and unfussy and it must have been funny to see the pair brushing their teeth outside the house, with the night guard squatted in front looking in. Breakfast was rather a protracted business. And that was scarce over when we were called to the great house (now finished – recall your earlier letters) to see a royal *kava*. This function is of rare use; I know grown Samoans who have never witnessed it. It is besides, as you are to hear, a piece of prehistoric history, crystallised in figures, and the facts largely forgotten; an acted hieroglyph. The house is really splendid; in the rafters in the midst, two carved and coloured model birds are posted; the only thing of the sort I have ever remarked in Samoa, the Samoans being literal observers of the Second Commandment. At one side of the egg our party sat. a = Mataafa, b = Lady J, c = Belle, d = Tusitala, e = Graham, f = Lloyd, g = Captain Leigh, h = Henry, i = Popo. The x's round are the high chiefs, each man in his historical position. One side of the house is set apart for the King alone; we were allowed there as his guests and Henry as an interpreter.

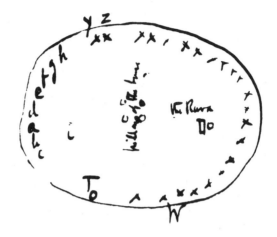

It was a huge trial to the lad, when a speech was made to me which he must translate, and I made a speech in answer which he had to orate, full-breathed, to that big circle; he blushed through his dark skin, but looked and acted like a gentleman and a young fellow of sense. Then the *kava* came to the King; he poured one drop in libation, drank another, and flung the remainder outside the house behind him. Next came the turn of the old shapeless stone marked T. It stands for one of the King's titles, Tamasoalii; Mataafa is Tamasoalii this day, but cannot drink for it; and the stone must first be washed with water, and then have the bowl emptied on it. Then – the order I cannot recall – came the turn of Y. and Z., two orators of the name of Malietoa; the first took his *kava* down plain, like an ordinary man; the second must be packed to bed under a big sheet of *tapa*, and be massaged by anxious assistants and rise on his elbow groaning to drink his cup. W., a great hereditary war man, came next; five times the cup-bearers marched up and down the house, and passed the cup on, five times it was filled and the general's name and titles heralded at the bowl, and five times he refused it (after examination) as too small. It is said this commemorates a time when Malietoa at the head of his army suffered much for want of supplies. Then this same military gentleman must *drink* five cups one from each of the great names: all which took a precious long time. He acted very well, haughtily and in a society tone *outlining* the part. The difference was marked when he subsequently made a speech in his own character as a plain God-fearing chief. A few more high chiefs, then Tusitala; one more, and then Lady Jersey; one more, and then Captain Leigh, and so on with the rest of our party – Henry of course excepted. You see in public, Lady Jersey followed me – just so far was the secret kept.

[Monday 29 August]

Then we came home; Belle, Graham and Lloyd to the Chinaman's, I with Lady Jersey, to lunch; so, severally home. Thursday I have forgotten: Saturday, I began again on *Davie*; on Sunday, the Jersey party came up to call and carried me to dinner. As I came out, to ride home, the search-lights of the *Curaçoa* were lightening on the horizon from many miles away, and next morning she came in.[4] Tuesday, was huge fun: a reception at Haggard's. All our party dined there; Lloyd and I in the absence of Haggard and Leigh, had to play aide-de-camp and host for about twenty minutes, and I presented the population at Apia at random but (luck helping) without one mistake. Wednesday we had two middies to lunch.[5] Thursday we had Eeles and Hoskyn (Lieutenant and doctor – very, very nice fellows – simple, good and not the least dull) to dinner.[6] Saturday, Graham and I lunched on board; Graham, Bell, Lloyd dined at the Gurrs; and Austin and the *whole* of our servants went with them to an evening entertainment: the more bold returning by lantern light. Yesterday, Sunday, Bell and I were off by about half-past eight, left our horses at a public house, and went on board the *Curaçoa* in the wardroom skiff; were entertained in the wardroom; thence on deck to the service, which was a great treat; three fiddles and a harmonium and excellent quire, and the great ship's company joining: on shore in Haggard's big boat to lunch with the party. Thence altogether to Vailima, where we read aloud a Ouida Romance we have been secretly writing; in which Haggard was the hero, and each one of the authors had to draw a portrait of him or herself in a Ouida light. Leigh, Lady J., Fanny, R.L.S., Bell and Graham were the authors. Lady J. is to have it printed, so I'll send you a copy; some of it is good, though I daresay it would scarce amuse outsiders; the fun is the large amount of truth.[7] In my chapter and in Belle's there is *nothing* but the truth, and in Fanny's only two or three crackling false-hoods: the effect is only given by the abuse of language.

[4] HMS *Curaçoa*, a screw cruiser of 2380 tons, built in 1877, arrived in Australia in August 1890 and was based at Sydney. Its officers were to become special favourites of the Vailima household.

[5] MIS notes the visit on 24 August of Claud Denison Burney and George E. Nares, two midshipmen from the *Curaçoa*. Burney, who was to become a favourite visitor, was promoted to Lieutenant in 1897 but was dismissed from the Navy in 1902 after a court-martial. Nares was a son of Admiral Sir George Nares, the Arctic explorer.

[6] Charles Gerald Sheperd Eeles (1854–1940) entered the Navy in 1866 and retired with the rank of Captain in 1903. During the Egyptian campaign (1884) he was engaged on hydrographic work and a bay in the Red Sea was named after him. Donald Templeton Hoskyn (1857–1938) joined the Navy as a surgeon in 1883 and retired with the rank of Surgeon Rear Admiral in 1917.

[7] *An Object of Pity or The Man Haggard*. A Romance By Many Competent Hands. Imprinted at Amsterdam. Lady Jersey had this 'Ouida Romance' privately printed at Sydney in a very small number of copies. Haggard himself countered with *Objects of Pity: or, Self and Company*. By a Gentleman of Quality.

In the midst of this gay life, I have finally recopied two chapters, and drafted for the first time three, of *Davie Balfour*. But it is not a life that would continue to suit me, and if I have not continued to write to you, you will scarce wonder. And today we all go down again to dinner, and tomorrow they all come up to lunch! The world is too much with us. But it now nears an end, today already the *Curaçoa* has sailed; and on Saturday or Sunday, Lady Jersey will follow them in the mail steamer. I am sending you a wire by her hands as far as Sydney, that is to say either you or Cassell, about 'Falesá':[8] I will not allow it to be called *Uma* in book form, that is not the logical name of the story. Nor can I have the marriage contract omitted; and the thing is full of misprints abominable. 'The STAVE (*store*) was in front full of the finest' (which should be, as the context clamours, POOREST). Then 'ignorant of the natives', instead of the NATIVE, which is the point of the story.[9] Also your omission of the little copra story seems to me very illogical; that is the preparatory note to Case, and the whole tale: the reader must be shown how far men go, and Case has gone, to get copra; and though you dislike the name of that merchandise, you might have borne ten lines for so obvious a purpose.[10] In the picture, Uma is rot; so is the old man and the negro; but Wiltshire is splendid, and Case will do. It seems badly illuminated, but this may be printing. How have I seen this first number? Not through your attention, guilty one! Lady Jersey had it, and only mentioned it yesterday. Secrecy and Indiscretion mark your steps.

I ought to say, how much we all like the Jersey party. Leigh is very amusing in his small way. Lady Margaret is a charming girl. And Lady Jersey is in all ways admirable: so unfussy, so plucky, so very kind and gracious.[11] My boy Henry was enraptured with the manners of the

---

[8] Lady Jersey says that the telegram, sent from Auckland, contained 'strict injunctions to "follow Uma line by line"'. 'The Beach of Falesá' was serialised in the *Illustrated London News* from 2 July to 6 August 1892.
[9] These misreadings of RLS's hand were corrected in the English first edition of *Island Nights' Entertainments* but two of them ('finest' and 'natives') survive in American editions and collected editions derived from them. They were still in the Penguin edition of 1979.
[10] RLS did not restore this passage in the book edition. It was first published (from the MS) in Barry Menikoff, *Robert Louis Stevenson and 'The Beach of Falesá'* (1984).
[11] Fanny did not share RLS's enthusiasm. In her diary she wrote:

> The Jerseys have been and gone, trailing clouds of glory over the island... They were a selfish 'champagne Charley' set, with the exception of the daughter, Lady Margaret Villiers, a tall, leggy, awkward young girl of the best English sort; gracious and gentle, and simple with the pretty simplicity of youth. Lady Jersey tall and leggy and awkward, with bold black eyes and sensual mouth; very selfish and greedy of admiration, a touch of vulgarity, courageous as a man, and reckless as a woman.

In a letter to Mrs Sitwell, Fanny wrote: 'She [Lady Jersey] is [Kipling's] Mrs Hauksbee exactly, and didn't like me.'

Tamaitai Sili (chief lady). Among our other occupations, I did a bit of a supposed epic describing our tryst at the ford of the Gase-gase; and Belle and I made a little book of caricatures and verses about incidents on the visit: Lady Margaret mobbed by a lot of dwarfish snobs at the reception; old Popo, the ex-heathen, kissing Lady Jersey's hand at Mataafa's; Lady J. and I riding home from Malie, she on Haggard's lean, tall horse, I on my fat, little Jack.[12] . . .

Sunday 4 September

. . . Mail came Friday, and a communication from yourself much more decent than usual, for which I thank you. Glad *The Wrecker* should so hum; but Lord, what fools these mortals be! So far yesterday, the citation being wrung from me by remembrance of many reviews. I have now received all 'Falesá', and my admiration for that tale rises, I believe it is in some ways my best work; I am pretty sure, at least, I have never done anything better than Wiltshire. Pray note, in case still in time, it was from Tarleton's 'HEAD' not his 'HAND' that Case took the dollar; and that the schoolboy sorcerer, referred to in the Devilwork chapter, was made to 'BUM' not to 'HUM'. The pictures are excellent, and Wiltshire a real inspiration. O! also in devilwork chapter, 'high and steep and full of cliffs. *Up* to the west side of the wall.' The two sentences are made to run on. Last chapter, Uma 'HUMPED herself', not BUMPED.[13]

Monday 13 [actually 12] September 1892

On Wednesday the Spinsters of Apia gave a ball to a select crowd. Fanny, Belle, Lloyd and I rode down, met Haggard by the way, joined company with him, and as we neared his house – passed Joe. Neither Belle nor I recognised him till he was actually up to us; it is strange, I never recognise him now. Dinner with Haggard, and thence to the ball. The Chief Justice appeared, looking cropped, genial and squinty[14]; it was immediately remarked, and whispered from one to another, that he and I had the only red sashes in the room, – and they were both of the hue of blood, sir, blood. He shook hands with myself and all the members of my family, which was infinite bad taste, but of course, in a ballroom not to be

---

[12] RLS's *Samoid*, Canto XII is prefixed to ch. 2 of *An Object of Pity*. The little book of three drawings by Belle with accompanying verses by RLS, presented by them to Lady Jersey, is in the National Library of Scotland.

[13] Two of these misreadings – 'hum' and 'bumped' – went into the first American edition and survive in later reprints.

[14] Henry Adams, on first meeting Cedercrantz in January 1891, described him as having 'one eye that seems to be fixed, and glares perversely into space'.

refused. Then the cream came, and I found myself in the same set of a quadrille with his honour. We dance here in Apia a most fearful and wonderful quadrille, I don't know where the devil they fished it from; but it is rackety and prancing and embrace-atory beyond words; perhaps it is best defined in Haggard's expression of a gambado. When I and my great enemy found ourselves involved in this gambol, and crossing hands, and kicking up, and being embraced almost in common by large and quite respectable females, we – or I – tried to preserve some rags of dignity, but not for long. The deuce of it is that, personally, I love this rogue; his eye speaks to me, I am pleased in his society, he is beautiful to me – *very* beautiful. We exchanged a glance, and then a grin; the rogue took me in his confidence; and through the remainder of that prance, we pranced for each other. Hard to imagine any position more ridiculous: a week before he had been trying to rake up evidence against me by brow-beating and threatening a half-white interpreter; that very morning, I had been writing most villainous attacks upon him for *The Times*; and we meet and smile, and – damn it! like each other.[15] Have I then no morality? He hasn't I know, but I have, and do my best to damn the man and drive him from these islands; but the weakness endures – I love him. This is a thing I would despise in anybody else; but when I think of the C.J.'s cock eye, I cannot be too hard upon myself. It is a strange thing to say of a gross, bulky Swede of some forty summers; but he has the charm of a funnily-pretty girl; and he is so jolly insidious and ingratiating! No, sir, I can't dislike him; but if I don't make hay of him, it shall not be for want of trying. . . .

Five more chapters of *Davie* 22 to 27, go to Baxter. All love affair; seems pretty good to me. Will it do for the young person? I don't know; since 'The Beach', I know nothing, except that men are fools and hypocrites, and I know less of them than I was fond enough to fancy.

---

[15] RLS wrote to Cedercrantz on 13 September complaining about the way in which he had tried to frighten 'the British half-caste Charles Taylor' (employed by Moors as his clerk) by threats of deportation, in an attempt to obtain information about RLS's dealings with Mataafa. Taylor had accompanied RLS as his interpreter on two of his visits to Malie in May. RLS's letter to *The Times*, dated 14 September (and published on 17 October 1892), made a number of criticisms of Cedercrantz's actions.

*To the Revd S.J. Whitmee[1]

[*26 September 1892*]   [*Vailima*]

My dear Count Whitmee, I have just finished a novel,[2] which you will
understand if you consider it's like a hundred and twenty sermons on end
– I simply cannot put my mind to Samoan or anything else. I am like an
empty bag. I can, and I will, do nothing. Your unfruitful pupil

Tusitala

To Ida Taylor
(Slightly Abridged)

[*Dictated to Belle*]
7 October 1892   *Vailima*

My dear Ida, I feel very much the implied reproof in yours just received;
but I assure you there is no fear of our forgetting either Una or yourself,
or your dear mother, who was one of the women that I have most
admired and loved in the whole of my way through life. The truth is that
Fanny writes to nobody and that I am on the whole rather overworked.
I compose lots of letters to lots of unforgotten friends, but when it comes
to taking the pen between my fingers there are many impediments. Hence
it comes that I am now writing to you by an amanuensis, at which I know
you will be very angry. Well, it was Hobson's choice. A little while ago
I had very bad threatenings of scrivener's cramp; and if Belle (Fanny's
daughter of whom you remember to have heard) had not taken up the
pen for my correspondence, I doubt you would never have heard from
me again except in the way of books. I wish you and Una would be so

---

[1] Samuel James Whitmee (1838–1925) had worked in Samoa as an L.M.S. missionary 1863–78.
When Claxton was appointed Natives' Advocate, the Society asked Whitmee to return to
Samoa 'to take charge of work among the foreign residents in Apia and to co-operate in a special
mission among native churches'. He arrived in Apia in December 1891 and left in 1893. At first,
RLS described him to Colvin as having 'the oily gloating utterance of the typical dissenter, a
thing which none of my family from my grandfather down has been able to listen to and live'.
Later he came to respect him. Whitmee was an expert in the Samoan language and from June
onwards RLS arranged to have lessons from him every Monday afternoon.
[2] RLS wrote to Colvin on 30 September:

> With *David Balfour*, I am very well pleased; in fact these labours of the last year – I mean
> 'Falesá' and *D.B.*, not *Samoa* of course – seem to me to be nearer what I mean than anything
> I have ever done – nearer what I mean by fiction; the nearest thing before was *Kidnapped*.
> I am not forgetting *The Master of Ballantrae*, but that lacked all pleasureableness, and hence
> was imperfect in essence. So you see, if I am a little tired, I do not repent.

good as [to] write to us now and then even without encouragement. An unsolicited letter would be almost certain (sooner or later depending on the activity of the conscience) to produce some sort of an apology for an answer. . . .

Fanny has not been at all well for a good long time. You remember she had always a method of starting unexpected complaints – all the old ones are quite gone, but she has a new stock, one of them really very alarming. However I think even that is getting better and she promises to be altogether a very fitting wife for a man who has himself been called 'Mother Hubbard's dog'.

If you carry out your design of settling in London you must be sure and let us have the new address. I swear we shall write some time. And if the interval be long you must just take it on your own head for prophesying horrors. You remember how you always said we were but an encampment of Bedouins, and that you would awake some morning to find us fled for ever. Nothing unsettled me more than these ill-judged remarks. I was doing my best to be a sedentary semi-respectable man in a suburban villa; and you were always shaking your head at me and assuring me (what I knew to be partly true) that it was all a farce. Even here, when I have sunk practically all that I possess, and have good health and my fill of congenial fighting, and could not possibly get away if I wanted ever so – even here and now the recollection of these infidel prophecies rings in my ears like an invitation to the sea. *Tu l'as voulu!*

I know you want some of our news, and it is all so far away that I know not where to begin. We have a big house and we are building another – pray God that we can pay for it.[1] I am just reminded that we have no less than eight several places of habitation in this place, which was a piece of uncleared forest some three years ago. I think there are on my pay rolls at the present moment thirteen human souls, not counting two washerwomen who come and go. In addition to this I am at daggers drawn with the Government, am going to have a lawsuit with a worthless missionary,[2] have had my correspondence stopped and opened by the Chief Justice – it was correspondence with the so-called Rebel King, – and have had boys examined and threatened with deportation to betray the secrets of my relations with the same person. In addition to this I might direct attention to those trifling exercises of the fancy, my literary works, and I hope you won't think that I am likely to suffer from ennui. Nor is Fanny any less active. Ill or well, rain or shine, a little blue indefatigable figure is to be observed howking about certain patches of

---

[1] With some reluctance (to Baxter he called it 'a dam folly') RLS had agreed, largely at his mother's request, to build a new wing onto the house. MIS agreed to pay £500 out of the total estimated cost of £1200.
[2] Arthur Claxton. See below.

garden. She comes in heated and bemired up to the eyebrows, late for every meal. She has reached a sort of tragic placidity. Whenever she plants anything new the boys weed it up. Whenever she tries to keep anything for seed the house boys throw it away. And she has reached that pitch of a kind of noble dejection that she would almost say she did not mind. Anyway her cabbages have succeeded. Talolo (our native cook, and a very good one too) likened them the other day to the head of a German; and even this hyperbolical image was grudging. I remember all the trouble you had with servants at the Roost. The worst of them were nothing to the trances that we have to go through here at times, when I have to hold a bed of justice, and take evidence which is never twice the same, and decide, practically blindfold, and after I have decided have the accuser take back the accusation in block and beg for mercy for the culprit. Conceive the annoyance of all this when you are very fond of both.

Kindest love from all of us to yourself and Una. Your affectionate friend   Robert Louis Stevenson

To Charles Baxter
(Abridged)

[*Dictated to Belle*]
7 October 1892   *Vailima*

My dear Charles, The deuce and all — here have been nearly two months and not a word from you, and now turns up your letter of [   ][1] via Sydney! I hope to goodness we can manage to avoid this the next few months. The whole of *David Balfour* should now or in a few days be in your hands, I trust in time.[2] To tell you the truth I am most unhappy that I have got embarked in the building of this new house, and I know there is going to be the deuce to pay to get to the year's end. As if all were not enough, it seems I am in for a libel action. An accursed ruffian, a missionary by the vile name of Arthur Claxton, of whom I narrated semi-anonymously a pleasing anecdote in the *Footnote to History*, has taken the thing amiss. I am fighting it just now by merely procrastinatory measures, having retained both the lawyers. As we are both British subjects it can go first before the Consul here as Deputy Commissioner, thence to Fiji to the High Commission Court, and thence, alas, to the Privy Council. It will scarcely escape your powerful intellect that this may come to something short, not to say sweet. I am not really troubling about it, because when

[1] Left blank in MS but presumably a reference is intended to Baxter's letter of 3 August.
[2] From a later reference it seems that RLS sent off the end of *David Balfour* by the same mail as this letter.

all is done it can never be more than a pecuniary cast-back, and I am not
ashamed of anything that I have done. At the same time, in conjunction
with the new house it makes not at all the kind of year that I like to look
forward to; and I wish you would sit down and thoroughly consider my
financial position. Is there anything that I can do to meet this sudden
strain? Please let me know by return all that you can to give me a clear
view of the prospects at home and any suggestion you can make as to
what I could be doing to raise the wind. It is too intensely annoying that
I should have been kicked into the new house at such a period, when
I might otherwise have faced the missionary and all his works with
composure.

The exact nature of the man's action I cannot find out. The story told
of him in the *Footnote* is the A. and B. story of the man who proposed a
treachery to the American Consul, and I *suppose* it is on that issue he
means to attack. I have never yet received any copy of the book and seem
to have lost the proofs of that part; so that I cannot be certain of what
words I used; still I believe I shall have a good chance to come scatheless,
as the truth of the story can be proved and proved again. It is at the same
time possible that he may intend to take action on a private letter to
himself in which I said I must either break relations with him or cease to
respect myself. On this, since I was unguarded enough to show a copy of
it to one of the man's colleagues, I fear his action would be better
grounded. But the real trouble is this – the man being a missionary will get
any amount of subscriptions to carry on the lawsuit and I suspect very few
to pay the expenses in case he should lose. So that I imagine in the end
R.L.S. must pay the piper. I will keep you posted month by month on all
new developments.[3]

I am quite of opinion that twenty per cent is a very handsome payment
from a publisher; and I confess that since I have a little studied the subject,
the bulk of the complaints against that very uninteresting class of men
seem to me either groundless or grossly exaggerated.[4]

Suppose that I am not wrong, that it will be difficult for you to meet
the bills announced to you for the building of the new house and that you

[3] See p. 460, n. 8. The allegations against Claxton were investigated by a Missionary Committee
in Apia. H.J. Moors (who had sent an account of the incident to L.M.S. headquarters in London
and was also threatened by Claxton with legal action), RLS and others gave evidence to the
Committee in October and were cross-examined by Claxton. Sewall, the American Consul
(who had left Samoa), wrote his version of the interview with Claxton and confirmed the
essential truth of the story. In spite of this, in July 1893 the L.M.S. Directors in London accepted
Claxton's denials and said they believed him to be 'entirely innocent'. By this time Claxton had
left Samoa and did not serve there again. Ironically enough, in old age he became the respected
Chairman of the RLS Club, London.
[4] On 3 August Baxter wrote about publishing agreements: 'From independent enquiries I've made
it seems that 25% is too high a rate to make a publisher have a decent profit . . . my advice from
an ex-publisher is not to go beyond 20%. And I am quite prepared to try that on with Cassell's.'

agree with me as to the possibility of a serious expenditure immediately impending from the lawsuit – I wish, so as to avoid possible delay, to put myself entirely into your hands. In that case any bargain that you can find to make for me I will accept. If time be of its essence, try to get the time as long as possible; but if it has got to be short I shall have to fill the bill. Understand, any sort of work on any sort of terms and at any humanly possible period. The one thing I cannot have happen is to get altogether stuck; and as I am particularly well and working very easily the chance is a good one. Of course all this is written in a vast ignorance as to the state of my affairs; but I hope you will manage in your answer to make that entirely plain to me. I see that my account in Sydney is already far lower than is wholesome – and I fear I must ask you to feed it. I do not like to say with how much for I know so little of how I stand; but if it be at all feasible I should like to have three hundred pounds at least paid into their English branch. The name of the bank, I suppose you remember, is the 'Bank of Australasia'. Yours ever   R.L. Stevenson

To J.M. Barrie[1]

[*The beginning dictated to Belle*]
1 November 1892   *Vailima Plantation*

Dear Mr Barrie, I can scarce thank you sufficiently for your extremely amusing letter. No, *The Auld Licht Idylls* never reached me. I wish it had and I wonder extremely whether it would not be good for me to have a pennyworth of the Auld Licht pulpit.[2] It is a singular thing that I should live here in the South Seas under conditions so new and so striking, and yet my imagination so continually inhabit that cold old huddle of gray hills from which we come. I have just finished *David Balfour*. I have another book on the stocks, *The Young Chevalier* which is to be part in France and part in Scotland and to deal with Prince Charlie about the year 1749; and now what have I done but begun a third which is to be all moorland together and is to have for a centrepiece a figure that I think you will appreciate – that of the immortal Braxfield. Braxfield himself is my *grand*

[1] James Matthew Barrie (1860–1937) was at this time a successful journalist, who had published collections of articles, *Auld Licht Idylls* (1888) and *A Window in Thrums* (1889). His first major novel, *The Little Minister*, had appeared in October 1891 but fame as a dramatist was still to come. As a young man he had used the pseudonym 'Gavin Ogilvy'. RLS wrote what he thought was his first letter to Barrie in February 1892, but Barrie reminded him that they had in fact exchanged letters in about 1884. This is RLS's third letter to Barrie from Vailima, written in reply to a letter from him of 25 September 1892.
[2] In his letter Barrie said that he had sent RLS in America a copy of *Auld Licht Idylls*. The kirk Barrie had described had now been taken down 'and the pulpit bought by a native who lets you sit in it for a penny'.

premier − or since you are so much involved in the British drama, let me say my heavy lead.[3]

Yon was an exquisite story about the barrow,[4] but I think I can beat it. In a little tale of mine, the slashed and gaping ruins of which appeared recently in the *Illustrated London News*, a perfect synod of appalled editors and apologetic friends had sat and wrangled over the thing in private with astonishing results. The flower of their cuts was this. Two little native children were described as wriggling out of their clothes and running away mother-naked. The celestial idiots cut it out.[5] I wish we could afford to do without serial publication altogether. It is odd that Hardy's adventure with the barrow and mine of the little children should happen in the same year with the publication and success of *Tess*. Surely these editor people are wrong.

Your description of your dealings with Lord Rintoul are frightfully unconscientious.[6] You should never write about anybody until you persuade yourself at least for the moment that you love him: above all anybody on whom your plot revolves. It will always make a hole in the book; and if he have anything to do with the mechanism, prove a stick in your machinery. But you know all this better than I do and it is one of your most promising traits that you do not take your powers too seriously. *The Little Minister* ought to have ended badly; we all know it did; and we are infinitely grateful to you for the grace and good feeling with which you lied about it. If you had told the truth, I for one could never have forgiven you. As you had conceived and written the earlier parts, the truth about the end, though indisputably true to fact, would have been a lie or what is worse a discord in art. If you are going to make a book end badly, it must end badly from the beginning. Now your book began to end well. You let yourself fall in love with, and fondle, and smile at your puppets. Once you had done that your honour was committed − at the cost of truth to life you were bound to save them. It is the blot on *Richard*

---

[3] RLS wrote to Colvin on 29 October listing the characters for his projected new novel in which the leading character, Adam Weir, Lord Hermiston, was to be based on Robert MacQueen, Lord Braxfield (1722–99), the Scottish 'Hanging Judge' notorious for his brutality and coarseness, who became Lord Justice-Clerk in 1788. At that stage he favoured either *The Lord Justice-Clerk* or *Lord Justice-Clerk Hermiston* as the title, but other possibilities were *Weir of Hermiston*, *The Two Kirsties of the Cauldstaneslap* or *The Four Black Brothers*. The story was to be set 'about Hermiston in the Lammermuirs or in Edinburgh. *Temp.* 1812'.

[4] Barrie, giving his views on *Tess of the D'Urbervilles*, wrote: 'In the book Angel carries the milkmaids across the river in his arms one at a time (Hardy would like to do this), but the paper [the *Graphic*] in which it appears thought this improper, and made him wheel them across in a barrow.'

[5] The phrase occurred in the MS of ch. 2 of 'The Beach of Falesá'. RLS restored it (evidently from memory) in a slightly different place in the book.

[6] RLS had written to Barrie on 20 June praising *The Little Minister*, but pointing out that Lord Rintoul was 'a lay figure perfectly unrealized and extremely imperfectly credible'. In his reply Barrie wrote: 'As for the earl, I never brought him on . . . without first kicking him round the room.'

Feverel,[7] for instance, that it begins to end well; and then tricks you and ends ill. But in that case, there is worse behind; for the ill-ending does not inherently issue from the plot – the story *had*, in fact, *ended well* after the great last interview between Richard and Lucy – and the blind, illogical bullet which smashes all has no more to do between the boards than a fly has to do with the room into whose open window it comes buzzing. It might have so happened; it needed not; and unless needs must, we have no right to pain our readers. I have had a heavy case of conscience of the kind about my Braxfield story. Braxfield – only his name is Hermiston – has a son who is condemned to death; plainly there is a fine tempting fitness about this; and I meant he was to hang. But now on considering my minor characters, I saw there were five people who would – in a sense who must – break prison and attempt his rescue. They were capable hardy folks too, who might very well succeed. Why should they not then? Why should not young Hermiston escape clear out of the country? and be happy, if he could, with his – but soft! I will not betray my secret or my heroine. Suffice it to breathe in your ear that she was what Hardy calls (and others, in their plain way, don't) a Pure Woman. Much virtue in a capital letter – such as yours was.

Write to me again in my infinite distance. Tell me about your new book. No harm in telling *me*; I am too far off to be indiscreet, there are too few near me who would care to hear. I am rushes by the riverside, and the stream is in Babylon; breathe your secrets to me fearlessly; even if the Trade Wind caught and carried them away, there are none to catch them nearer than Australia, unless it were the Tropic Birds. In the unavoidable absence of my Amanuensis, who is buying eels for dinner, I have thus concluded my despatch, like St Paul, with my own hand.

And in the inimitable words of Lord Kames, Faur ye weel, ye bitch![8]
Yours very truly   Robert Louis Stevenson

To Dora Norton Williams

[*Dictated to Belle*]
2 November 1892   *Vailima*

My dear Mrs Williams, I thank you very heartily for your kindness to Austin,[1] and the interesting letter that you sent to Fanny. I know she

---

[7] RLS takes over from Belle.

[8] Robert Chambers recorded in his *Traditions of Edinburgh* (1847), that the Scottish Judge Lord Kames (1696–1782), famous for his coarse humour, said farewell to his colleagues a few days before his death in a solemn speech, but 'at the door of the court-room, he turned about, and casting them a last look, cried, in his usual familiar tone: "Fare ye a' weel, ye bitches!" '.

[1] In September 1892 Austin Strong had been sent to stay with Fanny's widowed sister, Nellie Sanchez in Monterey, so that he could go to school there. Louis Sanchez was Nellie's son, celebrated in one of the Envoys to *A Child's Garden*.

intends to answer herself; but in a long continuance of years, and even more emphatically of late, I have learned to rely very little on her intentions in the matter of correspondence. Besides as is not unusually the case with me when I am really polite, I am after hooking you into doing me another service. Xmas draws near, the Middy is away in California, and it will no doubt be considered a step of propriety on the part of their Uncle Louis if he send them a proper reminder of the season. Now how is their Uncle Louis to do that in a place where there are no shops and anything that is for sale costs a hundred per cent better than it ought? Plainly the only thing left for him to do is to throw himself upon the assistance of a trustworthy friend in San Francisco. And who should that be Ma'am but yourself? I should like them to have some books – I suggest two of Captain Mayne Reid's, *The Plant Hunters* and *The Cliff Climbers*[2] – but please remember this, if you can't get *The Cliff Climbers* you must on no account whatever give them *The Plant Hunters*, for I have no wish that they should suffer as I remember to have done myself in childhood. There were two other books of Mayne Reid's that I read with great delight when I was about their age, *The Young Voyageurs* and *The Young Jägers*. Each has a sequel, but I'll be dashed if I can recollect the names, and in this case the books will do very well alone.[3] Now let us suppose you were able to get these four. Two of them – say the two first mentioned – to go to Austin, and two to Louis. So much expended, I will leave you to make up at your own sweet will fifteen dollars' worth of assorted truck, the same to be packed in a box and addressed in a bold hand

To Messieurs

Austin Strong

and

Louis Sanchez

from

Uncle Louis

At the same time, as I do not desire to go bust over this business, I see that I must slightly correct the directions given above. The sum – pardon my enthusiasm – the munificent sum of fifteen dollars is to be an outside figure, and to cover the price of the books and the expense of carriage. My heart relents. The carriage shall be met specifically – and the present eloquent epistle is to serve, if Mr Young[4] will be so good, as an order upon him for the fifteen dollars aforesaid, *and* in addition for the carriage

---

[2] First published in 1857 and 1864 respectively.

[3] In fact, *The Young Voyageurs* (1853) was the sequel to *The Boy Hunters* (1852); *The Young Jägers* (1856) was the sequel to *The Bush Boys* (1855). MIS records that his Aunt Jane read *The Young Jägers* to RLS at Colinton in the spring of 1857 and that in playing with his toy-gun he subsequently imitated the adventures of its boy hero ('I'm just hunting blawboks [antelopes]').

[4] E.B. Young, Fanny's solicitor in San Francisco.

of the box to the two young gentlemen, and your own legitimate expenses during the anxious period of choice. By legitimate expenses I do not refer merely to car-tickets, I must insist in addition that you shall drink my health – perhaps, after having finished the perusal of this letter, you will think fit to remember my reason also – in anything that you please down as low as ice-cream soda. The period we shall suppose to be about seven days before Xmas – at which time I on my side will reciprocate the compliments and the health of Dora Norton Williams will be feelingly proposed and enthusiastically toasted in the unassuming halls of Vailima.

I am my dear Mrs Wums (as Austin spells it) the jibbering remains of what once was, Your friend   R.L. Stevenson

To Henry James

5 December 1891 [1892][1]   *[Vailima]*

My dear James, How comes it so great a silence has fallen? The still small voice of self-approval whispers me it is [not] from me. I have looked up my register and find I have neither written to you nor heard from you since June 22nd, on which day of grace that invaluable work began. This is not as it should be. How to get back? I remember acknowledging with rapture *The Lesson of the Master*, and I remember receiving *Marbot*:[2] was that our last relation?

Hey, well! – anyway, as you may have probably gathered from the papers I have been in devilish hot water and (what may be new to you) devilish hard at work. In twelve calendar months, I finished *The Wrecker*, wrote all of 'Falesá' but the first chapter, wrote (well, much of)[3] the *History of Samoa*, did something here and there to my life of my grandfather, and began And Finished *David Balfour*. What do you think of it for a year? Since then, I may say I have done nothing, beyond draft three chapters of another novel: *The Justice-Clerk*, which ought to be a snorter and a blower[4] – at least if it don't make a spoon, it will spoil the horn of an Aurochs (if that's how it should be spellt).

[1] James replied on 17 February 1893 to 'My dear distant Louis' pointing out the error in the date – 'not 1891 – my dear time-deluded islander: it is enviable to see you so luxuriously "out" '.

[2] James had written on 15 April 1892 sending 'the magnificent *Mémoires de Marbot*'. The *Mémoires* by Baron de Marbot (3 vols, 1891) relate his dashing (and some thought fictitious) adventures as a soldier of Napoleon. They provided the basis for Conan Doyle's *The Exploits of Brigadier Gerard*.

[3] RLS first wrote and deleted 'all'; substituted 'almost all' and finally wrote 'well, much of' above it.

[4] A reference to a favourite RLS story of the mate of a whaler who sights 'a snorter and a blower' and is annoyed by the lack of 'civility' shown by the captain when he seeks permission to lower a boat and give chase.

On the hot water side, it may entertain you to know that I have been actually sentenced to deportation by my friends on Mulinuu, C.J. Cedercrantz and Baron Senfft von Pilsach. The awful doom, however, declined to fall, owing to Circumstances over Which. I only heard of it (so to speak) last night. I mean officially, but I had walked among rumours. The whole tale will be some day put into my hand and I shall share it with humorous friends.

It is likely, however, by my judgment, that this epoch of gaiety in Samoa will soon cease; and the fierce white light of history will beat no longer on yours sincerely and his fellows here on the beach. We ask ourselves whether the reason will more rejoice over the end of a disgraceful business, or the unregenerate man more sorrow over the stoppage of the fun. For, say what you please, it has been a deeply interesting time. You don't know what news is, nor what politics, nor what the life of man, till you see it on so small a scale and with your own liberty on the board for stake. I would not have missed it for much. And anxious friends beg me to stay at home and study human nature in Brompton drawing-rooms! *Farceurs!* And anyway you know that such is not my talent. I could never be induced to take the faintest interest in Brompton *qua* Brompton or a drawing-room *qua* a drawing-room. I am an Epick Writer with a k to it, but without the necessary genius.

Hurry up with another book of stories. I am now reduced to two of my contemporaries, you and Barrie – O and Kipling! I did like Haggard's *Nada the Lily*; it isn't great but it's big.[5] As for Hardy – you remember the old gag? – Are you wownded, my lord? – Wownded, 'Ardy – Mortually, my lord? – Mortually, 'Ardy – Well, I was mortually wounded by *Tess of the Durberfields*.[6] I do not know that I am exaggerative in criticism; but I will say *Tess* is one of the worst, weakest, least sane, most *voulu* books I have yet read. Bar the style, it seems to me about as bad as Reynolds[7] – I maintain it – Reynolds: or to be more plain, to have no earthly connexion with human life or human nature; and to be merely the unconscious portrait of a weakish man under a vow to appear clever, or a rickety schoolchild setting up to be naughty and not knowing how. I should tell you in fairness I could never finish it; there may be the treasures of the Indies further on; but so far as I read, James, it was (in one word) damnable. *Not alive, not true,* was my continual comment as I read;

---

[5] Henry Rider Haggard (1856–1925) was encouraged by the success of *Treasure Island* to write *King Solomon's Mines* (1885); RLS had written to him to praise it for its 'flashes of a fine weird imagination'. It was followed by many other popular romances including *She*. RLS wrote to him to praise *Nada the Lily* (1892) as 'A.1'.

[6] The dialogue between Captain Hardy and Nelson in popular dramatic representations of the death of Nelson.

[7] George William MacArthur Reynolds (1814–79), editor of the *London Journal*, wrote a series of sensational novels including *The Mysteries of London* (1845–50).

and at last – *not even honest!* was the verdict with which I spewed it from my mouth.[8] I write in anger? I almost think I do; I was betrayed in a friend's house – and I was pained to hear that other friends delighted in that barmecide feast. I cannot read a page of Hardy for many a long day, my confidence is gone. So that you and Barrie and Kipling are now my Muses Three. And with Kipling, as you know, there are reservations to be made. And you and Barrie don't write enough. I should say I also read Anstey when he is serious,[9] and can almost always get a happy day out of Marion Crawford[10] – *ce n'est pas toujours la guerre,*[11] but it's got life to it and guts, and it moves, and it isn't *Tess* anyway.[12] Did you read *The Witch of Prague?* Nobody could read it twice, of course; and the first time even, it was necessary to skip. *E pur si muove.*[13] But Barrie is a beauty, *The Little Minister* and the *Window in Thrums,* eh? Stuff in that young man; but he must see and not be too funny. Genius in him, but there's a journalist at his elbow – there's the risk. Look, what a page is the glove business in the *Window!* knocks a man flat; that's guts, if you please.

Why have I wasted the little time that is left with a sort of naked review article? I don't know, I'm sure. I suppose a mere ebullition of congested literary talk. I am beginning to think a visit from friends would be due. Wish you could come!

Let us have your news anyway, and forgive this silly stale effusion.
Yours ever   Robert Louis Stevenson

---

[8] Cf. Revelations 3:16.

[9] Thomas Anstey Guthrie (1856–1934), the humorous writer who used the pseudonym 'F. Anstey' was well known for *Vice Versa* (1882). RLS had recently read *The Pariah* (1889), written in a more serious vein.

[10] Francis Marion Crawford (1854–1909), American novelist who lived much of his life in Italy. He wrote more than forty popular romances and historical novels, including *The Witch of Prague* (1891). RLS wrote to him in April 1890 sending him his 'salutations and thanks' for his work.

[11] A reminiscence of Maréchal Bosquet's comment on the charge of the Light Brigade: '*C'est magnifique, mais ce n'est pas la guerre.*'

[12] James had written on 19 March 1892; 'The good little Tommy Hardy has scored a great success with *Tess of the d'Urbervilles,* which is chock-full of faults and falsity and yet has a singular beauty and charm.' In the reply to RLS's letter above James wrote:

> I grant you Hardy with all my heart and even with a certain quantity of my boot-toe. I am meek and ashamed where the public chatter is deafening – so I bowed my head and let *Tess of the D.'s* pass. But oh yes, dear Louis, she is vile. The pretence of 'sexuality' is only equalled by the absence of it, and the abomination of the language by the author's reputation for style. . . . On the other hand I can't go with you three yards in your toleration either of Rider Haggard or of Marion Crawford.

[13] But yet it does move. The remark traditionally attributed to Galileo after his recantation before the Inquisition in 1632 of his belief that the earth moves round the sun.

XV. THE LAST TWO YEARS AT VAILIMA January 1893–December 1894

By the New Year of 1893 the addition to Vailima had been completed. In his biography Balfour gives a good description of how the house looked in the last two years of Stevenson's life:

The house of Vailima was built of wood throughout, painted a dark green outside, with a red roof of corrugated iron, on which the heavy rain sounded like thunder as it fell and ran off to be stored for household purposes in the large iron tanks. The building finally consisted of two blocks of equal size, placed, if I may use a military phrase in this connection, in échelon. . . .

After December 1892 the downstairs accommodation consisted of three rooms, a bath, a storeroom and cellars below, with five bedrooms and the library upstairs. On the ground-floor, a verandah, twelve feet deep, ran in front of the whole house and along one side of it. Originally there had been a similar gallery above in front of the library, but it so darkened that room as to make it almost useless for working. Stevenson then had half of the open space boarded in, and used it as his own bedroom and study, the remainder of the verandah being sheltered, when necessary, by Chinese blinds. The new room was thus a sort of martin's nest, plastered as it were upon the outside of the house; but except for being somewhat hot in the middle of the day, it served its purpose to perfection. A small bedstead, a couple of bookcases, a plain deal kitchen table and two chairs were all its furniture, and two or three favourite Piranesi etchings and some illustrations of Stevenson's own works hung upon the walls. On one side was a locked rack containing half-a-dozen Colt's rifles for the service of the family in case they should ever be required. One door opened into the library, the other into the verandah: one window, having from its elevation the best view the house afforded, looked across the lawns and pasture, over the tree-tops, out to the sapphire sea, while the other was faced by the abrupt slope of Vaea. The library was lined with books, the covers of which had all been varnished to protect them from the climate. . . .

The chief feature within was the large hall that occupied the whole of the ground-floor of the newer portion of the house – a room some fifty feet long and perhaps five and thirty wide, lined and ceiled with varnished redwood from California. Here the marble bust of old Robert Stevenson twinkled with approval upon many a curiously combined company, while a couple of Burmese gilded idols guarded the two posts of the big staircase leading directly from the room to the upper floor. . . . In one corner was built a large safe, which, being continually replenished from Apia, rarely contained any large amount of money at a time, but was supposed by the natives to be the prison of the Bottle Imp, the source of all Stevenson's fortune. In this room hung J.S. Sargent's portrait of Stevenson and his wife, Sir George Reid's portrait of Thomas Stevenson, two reputed Hogarths which the old gentleman had picked up, two or three of R.A.M. Stevenson's best works, a picture of horses by Mr Arthur Lemon, and – greatly to the scandal of native visitors – a plaster group by Rodin.

In a series of notes on life at Vailima sent to W.H. Triggs, a New Zealand journalist, on 3 December 1893, RLS summarised the main activities of the members of the family.

Here is the correct hierarchy of Vailima. *Suum cuique tribuere.*[1]

Mr Osbourne is the bookkeeper, general business manager, and looks after the overseer and his gang of outside boys.

Mrs Stevenson, agriculturalist, in correspondence with Kew, gardens at Honolulu, Brisbane, Florida, etc., is general referee on all matters of science. Special charge of her own two experimental gardens. General supervision of all the additions and improvements; for example, has just engineered a court of cement between the house and kitchen, working with her hands, when her tongue failed her. Also doctor.

Mrs Strong acts as my amanuensis and has the charge of the house-hold and house and kitchen boys. Thanks to her training, whereas we began with an Australian table-maid, German cook, etc., we are now equally well served and better by a set of Samoan boys.

Mr Stevenson may be described as playing the part of veiled prophet in general. He rarely appears upon the scene unless someone has misbehaved; you must not be led into the idea that these are frequent occasions or the misdemeanours serious. The boys are awfully good on the whole. . . .

To his Mother[1]

[*Dictated to Belle*]
27th [*January*] 1893   *Vailima*

My dear Mother, This is being written in your new room which I at present occupy and am bound to say is a boss chamber. I come to be here,

---

[1] To allot to everyone his duties. The phrase (from Cicero) is written at the side of the page.
[1] MIS left Samoa on 1 January 1893 and spent some time visiting relatives in Australia before returning to Edinburgh. She went to arrange for 17 Heriot Row to be sold and the furniture shipped out to Vailima.

owing to the simple piratical act of turning Fanny out of her bed and sticking her into mine, my new chamber having proved untenable in the afternoon when it is sunny. She and I and the Amanuensis have thus the whole new palace to ourselves roosting here under the roof like three bats, and below us the really vast expanse of the hall entirely empty save for the safe built into one corner. The colour of the varnish you will I think be rejoiced to hear has turned out beyond expectation, ruddier and blonder than I had dreamed it would, and lighting up at night in a highly mysterious manner. They say that from the outside – I have not seen this, being on the sick-list – the glitter and sparkle of the lamps is heavenly. Belle's room is swept and garnished,[2] the rest of us being rather in the pig. It looks deliciously bright and unexpected, and delightfully unlike that blooming contrivance a bedroom. Altogether this new house has supplied a felt want; and now that it is paid for I can be vain about it with a clear conscience. It and its inhabitants have been made the subject of some bee-eautiful poetry which (if you are good) you may someday be privileged to see.[3] You are in it! With characteristic fickleness I have begun a new novel since you left, about ten chapters of it are done.[4] I have dictated it to Belle – part of it, when it was thought better I should not speak, in the deaf and dumb alphabet. I think I ought to charge *extry* for this book! on the principle of the parties who paint pictures with their toes.

The influenza, which you were so obliging as to leave behind you, played the deuce with the household. We once had seven cases down at the same time, two of them, mine and Misifolo's, pretty bad. You should have seen Henry going round at night emptying the slops and praying with the patients. As soon as the others began to pick up, this admirable evangelist lay down with it himself and it was suspected he had been a good while ailing. But all the boys were as good as gold and Sina[5] too who has risen in consequence very much higher in our esteem. Umslopogaas[6] – this is the name the slopman now bears – has been a very changeable officer – but Henry's tenure of the place has doubtless done a great deal to raise it in men's estimation. We have a real chief working for us – a village chief, none of your family fellows. The day after Henry lay down, what should I see enter my apartment but a procession, the real

---

[2] Matthew 12:44 and Luke 11:25.

[3] The sequence of poems about 'The Family' published posthumously.

[4] RLS wrote to Colvin on 24 January: 'I must tell you that in my sickness I had a huge alleviation and began a new story. This I am writing by dictation, and really think it is an art I can manage to acquire. . . . The story is to be called *St Ives*.' On 30 January he gave a list of twenty-nine chapters. He also asked both Colvin and Baxter for source-books, particularly about fashions for the year 1814. Belle's first reference in her journal is on 13 January – 'one of the most delightful days of my life' – when she took dictation from 8 a.m until 4 p.m.

[5] Talolo's wife, known as the Minx.

[6] A joking reference to the Zulu warrior whose exploits are recounted in Rider Haggard's *Allan Quatermain*, *Nada the Lily* and other romances.

living village chief in the character of Umslopogaas and bearing a bucket, and Sina, looking mighty sick, but with the most gracious and society bearing, marshalling him from utensil to utensil?

The guests have gone (so to speak) to glory. I can only say that we find their memory sweeter than their presence. They proved to be a pair of exceptionally silly women who took more pains to cut their own noses off than I should have thought possible. Things got strained towards the end of the visit, the family kissed and sat down to a kind of love-feast behind their departing backs. However, all's well that ends well, and they were not bad people, only fools, and not the kind of fools that we are.[7]

They being gone, and the invalids all restored, we hope to see the Clarkes up next week. The Frasers who were here through all our troubles showed themselves very hard and very little inclined to help. The history of their decline and fall in the public estimation was thus: Belle was the first to cast them off, closely followed by Fanny with a loud report. Lloyd still clung on to the note of the banjo that startles the deep;[8] and we had all managed so well to conceal our growing disgust that when that young gentleman at last joined the band of unbelievers, he actually supposed he was the first. I need not tell you that when he did turn, he turned and rent. Indeed, it was his defection, or rather the awful manner of it, that finally and suddenly, though in the most smiling manner, relieved us of our guests.

Owing to the influenza, I may say we have seen nothing of anybody since you left. Haggard only once, and then but the wreck of him, Gurr and Fanua only once, and nobody else that I can remember except the youthful Willis[9] and the constant Ahrens.[10] This made it dullish for the F.'s – to do them justice. The new Tivoli is said to be a failure before it is finished. Partsch[11] has given it up, and the still small voice of flying and (it

[7] Mrs Fraser and her actress daughter, Marie, arrived in Apia from Australia in November 1892 and stayed several months in Samoa. Marie, an actress of limited ability, played a few parts on the London stage in 1890/91 and toured in Australia in 1892 and 1893. They were regular visitors to Vailima in November and December 1892, and at the end of the year, because they were having difficulties with their landlord, RLS invited them to stay; RLS and Fanny moved into the new house to make room for them.

[8] An echo of an (untraced) quotation in *The Ebb-Tide*, Part III 'The Pearl-Fisher': 'For my voice has been tuned to the note of the gun/That startles the deep when the combat's begun.'

[9] Alex Willis, a Canadian carpenter, married to Laulii, an attractive Samoan girl, who was a great favourite of the Vailima household.

[10] Wilhelm Ahrens. Belle wrote to Charles Stoddard on 21 January 1893: 'I have a devoted lover of twenty-two – one of the clerks of the German Firm who sends me notes and flowers by a faithful black boy. It is a very innocent affair (*and therefore novel to me!*) but it makes life a little more interesting.'

[11] George W. Partsch (1850–1933), a German from Hamburg who spent his life in the South Seas, first as mate on a schooner in Tahiti, then as a trader in Tonga and a supercargo in the Gilbert and Ellice Islands. He was a hotel-keeper in Apia for ten years from 1889 and ended up as an auctioneer and general commission agent in Apia.

is to be trusted) lying rumour breathes the name of J.D.S.[12] as his successor! Moors and Carruthers[13] have had a quarrel but are both standing on
the same ticket for the Municipal Council. Tom Kenna, the man who was
to have worked the machine at the blowing up of the jail, was drowned
the other day in the harbour while drunk. Poor dear old Taylor was his
companion but happily escaped. O! the constant Ahrens, à propos of boots,
remarked that three Germans were never collected together in Apia but
what they fell to talk of R.L.S. Is this glory? Anyway that's the news – and
I think you might say thank you!

Remember me to May[14] and with much love to your dear self in which
all jine. Believe me, Ever your affectionate   R.L.S.[15]

[In RLS's own hand]
Same day but later

Your enchanting letter just arrived; and O! to think of you and dear
Jack Buckland careering about Sydney! But he is a good, lovable, little
rascal, is he not?[16]

You see I did my best to give you our piddling news. But we have not
your opportunities nor your literary talents – more's the sorrow. Belle, the
only valid hand, is away after Mentz this afternoon. And we'll hope he can
come.[17] And at least shall have done something civil. The Lord look upon
you – you are a grand fist at a letter! Ever   R.L.S.

★To The Editor of The Times

[c. 15] February 1893   Samoa

Sir, Will you allow me to bring to the notice of your readers the Sedition
(Samoa) Regulation, 1892, for the Western Pacific, and, in particular, the
definition in section 3?[1]

---

[12] Joe Strong.
[13] Richard Hetherington (1844–c.1909), barrister-in-law and solicitor in Apia. The son of a
    Melbourne clergyman, he came to Samoa from Fiji in 1877. He added Carruthers to his name
    in 1888 on succeeding to an estate. He had a Samoan wife and his descendants are still living
    in Samoa.
[14] MIS was staying with her niece Marion (May) Wilson Scott in Melbourne.
[15] The last three words and the initials are by RLS with flourishes to fill up the page.
[16] MIS's '1st Epistle to the Vailimans' was begun on board the Lübeck on 5 January and completed
    in Sydney on 15 January. In her letter and her diary MIS relates how Jack Buckland lunched
    and dined with her and took her to the theatre.
[17] MIS had said that Captain Mentz of the Lübeck would like to be invited to Vailima.
[1] As an enclosure to this letter The Times printed in full the 'Regulation for the Maintenance of
    Peace and Good Order in Samoa' made by Sir John Thurston, British High Commissioner for
    the Western Pacific, on 29 December 1892 and coming into force on 1 January 1893.

My letters have been complained of, my statements called in question, and I was content to wait until facts and the publication of official papers should justify me. This new style of controversy appears more barbarous. I am content to take that also. If any further scandal happen I shall take the freedom to report it to your paper and endure my three months in Apia Gaol with as much patience as I may.

But I think these are new experiences for a British subject. I think this is a new departure in British legislation. I ask myself how it would be liked

Under section 1 any British subject found guilty of 'sedition towards the Government of Samoa' was liable to a fine not exceeding ten pounds, or to imprisonment without hard labour for 'not more than three months, with or without a fine not exceeding ten pounds'.

In section 3 the expression 'sedition towards the Government of Samoa', was defined as embracing 'all practices, whether by word, deed, or writing, having for their object to bring about in Samoa discontent or dissatisfaction, public disturbance, civil war, hatred or contempt towards the King or Government of Samoa or the laws or constitution of the country, and generally to promote public disorder in Samoa'.

Besides his letter to *The Times* RLS also wrote formal letters complaining about the definition of sedition to Lord Ripon, the Colonial Secretary and Lord Rosebery, the Foreign Secretary (see p. 566). In fact, before receipt of RLS's protest the authorities had agreed that this definition was far too drastic and should be amended. Because of delay in implementing their decision (the Colonial Office had mislaid the file) it appeared that it was RLS's letter, appearing in *The Times* on 4 April and provoking widespread unfavourable comment against the Regulation in the world press, which had spurred the Government into action.

On 15 April Lord Ripon wrote to Sir John Thurston telling him that the Regulation was 'much too general in its character and comprises acts which should not be made penal'. He instructed him to redefine sedition in section 3 in more harmless terms as embracing all practices 'having for their object to bring about in Samoa public disturbance, or civil war, and generally to promote public disorder in the country'.

Meanwhile, a Parliamentary Question on the subject had been garbled in press reports to the effect that Thurston 'had been instructed to greatly modify the opposition towards Mr R.L. Stevenson the novelist'. Thurston sent an angry telegram to the Colonial Office denying that he had had any relations with RLS, but going on to characterise him as a mischievous man with a morbid desire for notoriety with 'secret and personal objects'; he thought there was a risk that rebel chiefs might believe that RLS's advice was countenanced by the British Government and expressed the view that all meddling must be dealt with firmly. The Colonial Office acted quickly and decisively. On 14 April a telegram was despatched to Thurston ordering him to take no steps against RLS and to await receipt of additional instructions. This was followed the next day by a long and measured rebuke from Lord Ripon. He appreciated that the presence in Samoa of such an eminent writer whose comments inevitably attracted attention could be a source of embarrassment to the authorities, and that some Samoans might form an incorrect idea of RLS's status and authority. It could not be denied that the present position in Samoa invited criticism and much that RLS had published had been justified. A writer of RLS's 'established popularity and high distinction' could hardly be presumed to be influenced by 'the desire for notoriety' or by 'secret and personal objects'. The amendment Thurston had been instructed to make probably took RLS's conduct out of the purview of the Regulation but if in future Thurston considered it necessary to take action against him, he was instructed to report the details to the Colonial Office and await instructions from the Government. The next day the Chief Secretary of the Colonial Office told Colvin what had happened and on 17 April Colvin passed the news to Baxter with the comment that Thurston had 'had a wigging'; Colvin no doubt sent the information out to RLS.

Formal letters were sent to RLS from both the Colonial Office and the Foreign Office setting out the amendment to the definition of sedition. RLS received what he called the 'glorious document' in May and characterised the affair as 'a famous victory'.

at home – in Ireland, for example – and I am curious to learn what will be thought of it even as applied to British residents in that singular limbo, the Western Pacific. The High Commission has done good service in the past; it was created to deal with anomalous circumstances which exist no longer. I wonder if its existence or nature are generally understood; and I wonder whether this last instance of its power and discretion will be palatable to the Government of England. I am, Sir, Your obedient servant

Robert Louis Stevenson

To Sidney Colvin[1]

Bad pen, bad ink, bad light,   S.S. Mariposa, *at sea.*
bad blotting paper   Apia due by daybreak
[29 March 1893]   tomorrow.
9 P.M.

My dear Colvin, Have had an amusing but tragic holiday, from which we return in disarray: Fanny, quite[2] sick, but I think slowly and steadily mending. Belle in a terrific state of dentistry troubles which now seem calmed and myself with a succession of gentle colds out of which I at last succeeded in cooking up a fine pleurisy. By stopping and stewing in a perfectly airless stateroom I seem to have got rid of the pleurisy. Poor Fanny had very little fun of her visit, having been most of the time on a diet of maltine and slops – and this while the rest of us were rioting on oysters and mushrooms. Belle's only devil in the hedge was the dentist. As for me I was entertained at the General Assembly of the Presbyterian Church; likewise at a sort of artistic club of a very rowdy character;[3] made speeches at both and may therefore be said to have been like Saint Paul, all things to all men.[4] I have an account of the latter racket which I meant to have enclosed in this. The pianist who was the president[5] became so much excited[6] that he did not leave the club till 3 A.M. and was believed

---

[1] As part of his convalescence after his illness (influenza followed by two hemorrhages) RLS decided to take 'a month's lark' in Sydney. RLS, Fanny and Belle left Apia on 18 February and reached Sydney on 28 February; MIS joined them on 2 March. They left on 20 March and arrived back in Apia on the 30th.
[2] Belle took over at this point.
[3] RLS made a short speech at the General Assembly of the Presbyterian Church of New South Wales when he had lunch with them on 14 March. He made another short speech on 16 March when he was guest of honour at a lunch given by the Cosmopolitan Club, Sydney.
[4] I Corinthians 9:22.
[5] Henri Kowalski (1841–1916), French pianist and composer of Polish and Irish descent, who settled in Sydney in 1885.
[6] The rest of the letter is in RLS's own hand.

to be sick in bed next day. Saw a good deal of the Wises and Threlfalls[7] (did you know Threlfall in Cambridge – a friend of Dew's?) Had some splendid photos taken, likewise a medallion by a French sculptor:[8] met Graham who returned with us as far as Auckland. Have seen a good deal too of Sir George Grey;[9] he has gone down the Gladstone Hill; but what a wonderful old historic figure to be walking on your arm and recalling ancient events and instances! It makes a man small, and yet the extent to which he approved what I had done – or rather have tried to do – encouraged me. Sir George is an expert at least, he knows these races, he is not a small *employé* with an inkpot and a *Whitaker*.

Take it for all in all: it was huge fun: even Fanny had some lively sport at the beginning: Belle and I all through. We got Fanny a dress on the sly, made to fit Belle, gaudy black velvet and Duchesse lace. And alas! she was only able to wear it once. But we'll hope to see more of it at Samoa; it really is lovely. Both dames are royally outfitted in silk stockings etc. We return, as from a raid, with our spoils and our wounded. When Belle was at her worst – just before she let a passenger draw her tooth with a piece of silk – no forceps on board, of course! – she confessed that the thought of her silk stockings sustained her. I am now very dandy; I announced two years ago that I should change. Slovenly youth, all right – not slovenly age. So really now I am pretty spruce: always a white shirt, white necktie, fresh shave, silk socks, O a great sight! No more possible.			R.L.S.

To Sidney Colvin
(Abridged)

[? 1 April 1893]							[Vailima]

. . .[1] You seem to hint that *Davie* is not finished in the writing; which cuts me; and yet I think you deceive yourself. To me, I own, it seems in

---

[7] Bernhard Ringrose Wise (1858–1916), Australian barrister who was Attorney-General for New South Wales 1887–8 and 1899–1904; Q.C. 1898; Agent-General for N.S.W. in London 1915. RLS first met him in Sydney in February 1890. His brother-in-law, Richard Threlfall (1861–1932), English physicist and chemical engineer (who was knighted 1917) was Professor of Physics at Sydney University 1886–99. On his return to England he joined a major firm of chemical manufacturers and did important work in the manufacture of phosphorus and helium; he was the first director of the Chemical Research Laboratory, Teddington. His wife, Evelyn Agnes Baird (died 1929) was a sister of Wise's wife, Lilian Margaret Baird.
[8] Pierre Emile Leysalle (born 1847), was Professor of Sculpture at Geneva for ten years and exhibited at the Paris Salon 1873–1905. It is not known what happened to his portrait of RLS. RLS told Saint-Gaudens that it was 'thought in my family to be a good likeness of Mark Twain'.
[9] Sir George Grey (1812–98), an early explorer of Australia and colonial governor. He became a famous 'elder statesman' of New Zealand politics; Governor of New Zealand 1845–53 and 1861–7 and Prime Minister 1877–9. RLS visited him in Auckland on 24 February.
[1] I have omitted a long series of detailed replies by RLS to Colvin's comments and queries on the proof-sheets of *David Balfour* (*Catriona*). RLS did a considerable amount of revision to the original text serialised in *Atalanta* December 1892–September 1893.

the proof a very pretty piece of workmanship. David, himself, I refuse to discuss; he *is*. The Lord Advocate, I think a strong sketch of a very difficult character, James More sufficient; and the two girls very pleasing creatures. But O dear me, I came near losing my heart to Barbara! I am not quite so constant as David, and even he – well, he didn't know it, anyway! 'Tod Lapraik' is a piece of living Scots; if I had never writ anything but that and 'Thrawn Janet', still I'd have been a writer. The defects (of *D.B.*) are inherent, I fear. But on the whole I'm far indeed from being displeased with the tailie. One thing is sure, there has been no such drawing of Scots character since Scott; and even he never drew a full length like Davie, with his shrewdness and simplicity, and stockishness and charm. Yet, you'll see, the public won't want it; they want more Alan. Well, they can't get it. And readers of *Tess* can have no use for my David, and his innocent but real love affairs. Much I care.

I found my fame much grown on this return to civilisation. *Digito monstrari*[2] is a new experience; people all looked at me in the streets in Sydney; and it was very queer. Here of course, I am only the white chief with the Great House to the natives; and to the whites, either an ally or a foe. It is a much healthier state of matters. If I lived in an atmosphere of adulation, I should end by kicking against the pricks. O my beautiful forest, O my beautiful, shining, windy house, what a joy it was to behold them again! No chance to take myself seriously here. . . .

Thursday 5 [6] April

Well, there's no disguise possible: Fanny is not well, and we are miserably anxious. I may as well say now that for no,[3] nearly eighteen months there has been something wrong; I could not write of it; but it was very trying and painful – and mostly fell on me. Now, we are face to face with the question: what next? The doctor has given her a medicine; we think it too strong, yet dare not stop it; and she passes from death-bed scenes to states of stupor. Ross,[4] doctor in Sydney, warned me to expect trouble, so I'm not surprised; and happily Lloyd and Belle and I work together very smoothly, and none of us get excited. But it's anxious; Isla Sitwell[5] is due to arrive on a visit tomorrow. Last night, I called a council of war. It was plainly impossible to expose Fanny to a stranger; so we decided to send him on by the same steamer that brings him, and for

---

[2] To be pointed out with the finger (i.e. to be famous) – Persius, *Satires*, i. 28.
[3] RLS first wrote 'nearly'; crossed it through and wrote 'more than' above, then reverted to 'no, nearly'.
[4] Elsey Fairfax Ross (1857–1902), a well-known Sydney physician.
[5] Isla Ernest Hurt Sitwell (1870–95), son of Isla Ashley Sitwell (1841–80) and Sidney May Beckwith Wilson (1841–1908), daughter of MIS's sister Marion. He had been staying with his uncle Lewis Wilson in New Zealand.

Lloyd in the meanwhile to play host to him at the hotel. It is very disagreeable to have to do; but I think you can see how helpless we are to do better. Of course, as you understand, the clouds may rise tomorrow and all be well; but then they mayn't. I am stupid and tired and have done little even to my proofs. It is awful good these children are so good to me; or I'd be in a horrid pickle. I am really far better off now than I was eighteen months ago, when this was beginning; I felt so dreadfully alone then. You know about F. there's nothing you can say is *wrong*, only it ain't *right*; it ain't *she*; at first she annoyed me dreadfully; now of course, that one understands, it is more anxious and pitiful.

Later. 1.30

The doctor has been. 'There is no danger to life,' he said twice. – 'Is there any danger to mind?' I asked. – 'That is not excluded,' said he. Since then I have had a scene with which I need not harrow you; and now again she is quiet and seems without illusions. 'Tis a beastly business.

You see though I have written you so fully all these months, I have scarce been frank but kept my inmost trials to myself. At first it only seemed a kind of set against *me*; she made every talk an argument, then a quarrel; till I fled her, and lived in a kind of isolation in my own room. The thing was of course complicated by that damned Joe, who kept everybody by the ears. Then it was that Belle began to make herself my helper, to my unspeakable comfort. Next came the last misbehaviour of Joe, which wrought up Fanny dreadfully and did her no end of harm. There followed Lady Jersey's visit, of which I gave you the white side; at home, it was a wretched period. It was then first that I began to have a suspicion of the truth. The last was a hell of a scene which lasted all night – I will never tell anyone what about, it could not be believed, and was so unlike herself or any of us – in which Belle and I held her for about two hours; she wanted to run away. Then we took her to Sydney; and the first few weeks were delightful: her voice quiet again – no more of that anxious shrillness about nothing, that had so long echoed in my ears. And then she got bad again. Since she has been back, also she has been kind – querulously so, but kind. And today's fit (which was the most insane she has yet had) was still only gentle and melancholy. I am broken on the wheel, or feel like it. Belle and Lloyd are both as good as gold. Belle has her faults and plenty of them; but she has been a blessed friend to me.

Friday 7th

I am thankful to say the new medicine quieted her at once; and she has been entirely reasonable and very nice since she took it. A crape has been removed from the day for all of us. To make things better, the morning is ah! such a morning as you have never seen; heaven upon earth for sweetness, freshness, depth upon depth of unimaginable colour, and a huge silence broken at this moment only by the far-away murmur of the Pacific and the rich piping of a single bird. We have got her back to her own room where Belle sleeps with her. Belle and I are to take watches all day, off and on, to be with her: Lloyd is off to meet the visitor. You can't conceive what a relief this is. It seems a new world. She has such extraordinary recuperative power, that I do hope for the best. I am as tired as man can be. This is a great trial to a family, and I thank God it seems as if ours was going to bear it well. And O! if it only lets up, it will be but a pleasant memory. We are all seedy, bar Lloyd: Fanny, as per above; self nearly extinct; Belle, utterly overworked and bad toothache; Cook, down with a bad foot; Butler, prostrate with a bad leg. Eh, what a faim'ly! But it's all right, so long as we hang together!

Saturday

Lloyd down on the beach waiting for dratted visitors;[6] Belle practically in bed with what seems to be threatenings of rheumatic fever; however, Fanny, I hope really on the mend. She seems quite herself this day, and has eaten, and for the first time in three weeks not complained of the food. I keep pretty cheery and good, but it isn't good for proofs. The doctor, when here yesterday, refused a prognosis; but I believe she will come to the wind after all – I have seen so much of her power of going down and coming up again. I was just passing between the two sick rooms like a see-saw for about an hour: awful lucky F. is so much better when B. lies down; but now F. is completely asleep, and B. is feeling and looking on the mend (she had a chill when I could find neither her pulse nor her heart, drat her) and reading a book. So here am I back in my den and prattling to you.

Sunday

Gray heaven, raining torrents of rain, occasional thunder and lightning. Everything to dispirit; but my invalids are really on the mend. Belle seems all right again, bar toothache. Fanny, now nearly two-thirds through a 24 hours stoppage of her medicine, is still quite herself, and calm and quiet; so that really seems to speak of improvement. The rain roars like the sea; in the sound of it there is a strange and ominous suggestion of an approaching tramp; something nameless and measureless seems to draw near, and strikes me cold, and yet is welcome. Anything is welcome but the one horror of madness! I lie quiet in bed today, and think of the

[6] Graham Balfour and Isla Sitwell.

universe with a good deal of equanimity. I have, at this moment, but the one objection to it: the *fracas* with which it proceeds. I do not love noise; I am like my grandfather in that; and so many years in these still islands has ingrained the sentiment perhaps. Here are no trains; only men pacing barefoot. No carts or carriages; at worst the rattle of a horse's shoe among the rocks. Beautiful silence; and so soon as this robustious rain takes off, I am to drink of it again by oceanfuls.

Monday [10 April]

The approaching tramp must have been Isla's. The whole of my family, with the single glowing exception of myself, took up the romantic and pitiful view of this young gentleman (whom I have never seen – he had an opportunity to dine with a Duchess[7] when I was in Auckland, and preferred that to making the acquaintance of the kinsman whom he was about to visit – I have no toleration for such un-licked cubs – a snob should know his manners). That being so, and Fanny still keeping steady (and now over her 24 hours intermission of the medicine), and beginning to threaten screechiness about the poor sick boy driven from our doors, and all the world in the same tale – I swallowed my tongue, and he's to be installed today. I gave way, wrote the necessary letter, Belle objected to the letter – I admit rightly, I wrote another – the boy was despatched, and I gave way to my rage. A stranger in the house in the midst of my[8]

16 April

Several pages of this letter destroyed as beneath scorn; the wailings of a crushed worm; matter in which neither you nor I can take stock. Fanny is distinctly better, I believe all right now; I too am mending, though I have suffered from crushed wormery, which is not good for the body and damnation to the soul. . . .

The decay of the Vicar feebly consoled me for the news of George.[9] Isla seems a decent enough boy; I have extended to him a languid sceptre;

---

[7] Alice Anne (1847–1931), daughter of Sir Graham Graham-Montgomery, 3rd Baronet, of Stobo Castle, and widow of the 3rd Duke of Buckingham and Chandos whom she married in 1885 (and who died in 1889); she later married Earl Egerton of Tatton. In 1892/93 she made a tour of Australia, New Zealand and North America and published an acccount of her travels as *Glimpses of Four Continents* (1894). She joined the *Mariposa* at Auckland and travelled with RLS on their return journey to Apia. In a letter to his mother RLS described her as 'rather a wild, violent eccentric Scotchwoman': 'Fanny and the Duchess rather fell in love; nobody else could stand – I was going to say either of them, but I mean Her Grace.'

[8] The text breaks off mid-sentence at the end of a page and the letter resumes at a new page headed 3.

[9] Because of ill-health (he was suffering from dropsy) the Revd Albert Sitwell had resigned his living as Vicar of Minster; he died in January 1894. George Went, Colvin's family servant, had died.

and really Fanny is well enough not to make it awkward. I feel tonight a baseless anxiety to write a lovely poem *à propos des bottes de ma grandmère, qui etaient à revers.* I see I am idiotic. I'll try the poem.

17th

... The poem did not get beyond plovers and lovers. I am still, however, harassed by the unauthentick Muse; if I cared to encourage her – but I have not the time, and anyway we are at the vernal equinox. It is funny enough, but my pottering verses are usually made (like the gawd-gifted organ voice's)[10] at the autumnal; and this seems to hold at the Antipodes. There is here some odd secret of Nature. I cannot speak of politics: we wait and wonder. It seems (this is partly a guess) Ide won't take the C.J.-ship,[11] unless the islands are disarmed: damn his fat head for it! And that England hesitates and holds off. By my own idea, strongly corroborated by Sir George, I am writing no more letters. But I have put as many irons in against this folly of the disarming as I could manage. It did not reach my ears, till nearly too late. What a risk to take! What an expense to incur! and for how poor a gain! Apart from the treachery of it. My dear fellow, politics is a vile and a bungling business. I used to think meanly of the plumber; but how he shines beside the politician!

Thursday [20 April]

A general, steady advance; Fanny really quite chipper and jolly[12] – self on the rapid mend, and with my eye on *forests* that are to fall – and my finger on the axe, which wants stoning.

Saturday 22

Still all for the best; but I am having a heart-breaking time over *David*. I have nearly all corrected. But have to consider, 'The Heather on Fire', 'The Wood by Silvermills', and the last chapter. They all seem to me off colour; and I am not fit to better them yet. No proof has been sent of the

---

[10] Tennyson, 'Milton: Alcaics', l. 3.

[11] The three Powers had decided in November 1892 that the two discredited Treaty officials – Cedercrantz and Senfft von Pilsach – should be replaced, but the official announcement was not made until May 1893. There were lengthy negotiations before agreement was reached about their successors. Henry Clay Ide, the former American Land Commissioner, had been offered the position of Chief Justice and eventually accepted it.

[12] The various setbacks in Fanny's slow recovery were chronicled in a letter RLS wrote to his mother 17–22 April. By 21 April she was much better and he wrote: 'Last night, the cats woke both her and me about ten, Belle was not yet in bed; so we all three sat in my room and had some grog and a cigarette, and were as jolly as sand boys. It was delightful: Fanny was as nice as possible, and did not seem ill one particle. Yesterday, too, she went all round her garden with an umbrella, and quite tired me out following her.'

title, contents, or dedication. By the by, remind Messrs Cassell they are under an agreement to me to print the whole list of my works on the inside of the false title; they seem too prone to forget this; and must be kept up to the line. Remember it is the *whole of my works*; not merely those published by Cassell.

To J.M. Barrie

[*Dictated to Belle*][1]
2 or 3 April 1893   *Vailima*

My dear Barrie, Tit for tat.[2] Here follows a catalogue of my menagerie:

R.L.S.
The Tame Celebrity.
Native name, *Tusi Tala*.

Exceedingly lean, dark, rather ruddy – black eyes (drawing-book eyes – *Amanuensis*) crow's-footed, beginning to be grizzled, general appearance of a blasted boy – or blighted youth – or to borrow Carlyle on De Quincey 'Child that has been in hell.'[3] Past eccentric – obscure and O no we never mention it – present, industrious respectable and fatuously contented. Used to be very fond of talking about Art, don't talk about it any more. Is restrained by his family from talking about Origin of Polynesian Race. Really knows a good deal but has lived so long with aforesaid family and foremast hands, that you might talk a week to him and never guess it. (This is the grossest injustice – what that man knows about *chiffons* is something wonderful, and he never tires of it. *Am.*) Friendly grocer in Sydney: 'It has been a most agreeable surprise to meet you Mr Stevenson. I would never have guessed you were a literary man.' Name in family, The Tame Celebrity. Cigarettes without intermission except when coughing or kissing. Hopelessly entangled in apron strings. Drinks plenty. Curses some. Temper unstable. Manners purple on an emergency, but liable to trances. Essentially the common old copybook gentleman of commerce: if accused of cheating at cards, would feel bound to blow out's brains, little as he would like the job. Has been an invalid for ten years, but can boldly claim that you can't tell it on him. (When he's well he looks like a brown boy with an uncertain temper, but when

---

[1] The letter is decorated by Belle's sketches of the people described.

[2] In his letter of 29 January 1893, Barrie had given a humorous description of himself.

[3] 'When he sat, you would have taken him [De Quincey] by candlelight for the beautifullest little child; blue-eyed, blonde-haired, sparkling face, – had there not been a something, too, which said, "*Eccovi*, this Child has been in Hell"' (Carlyle, *Reminiscences*, ed. C.E. Norton, 1887, II, 152).

he is ill he's a rose-garden invalid with a sainted smile. *Am.*) Given to explaining the universe. Scotch, sir, Scotch.

Fanny V. de G. Stevenson.
The Weird Woman.
Native name, *Tamaitai*.

This is what you will have to look out for, Mr Barrie. If you don't get on with her, it's a pity about your visit. She runs the show. Infinitely little, extraordinary wig of gray curls, handsome waxen face like Napoleon's, insane black eyes, boy's hands, tiny bare feet, a cigarette, wild blue native dress usually spotted with garden mould. In company manners presents the appearance of a little timid and precise old maid of the days of prunes and prism; you look for the reticule. (But wouldn't be surprised to find a dagger in her garter, *Am.*) Hellish energy; relieved by fortnights of entire hibernation. Can make anything from a house to a row, all fine and large of their kind. My uncle, after seeing her for the first time: 'Yes Louis, you have done well. I married a besom[4] myself and have never regretted it.' Mrs Fraser (*et pour cause*): 'She has the indomitable will of Richelieu.' (Reminds me of Madam Esmond in *The Virginians*. *A.*) Doctors everybody, will doctor you, cannot be doctored herself. The Living Partizan: A violent friend, a brimstone enemy. Imaginary conversation after your visit: 'I like Mr Barrie. I don't like anybody else. I don't like anybody that don't like him. When he took me in to dinner he made the wittiest remark I ever heard. "Don't you think" he said "the old fashioned way – etc."' Is always either loathed or slavishly adored; indifference impossible. The natives think her uncanny and that devils serve her. Dreams dreams, and sees visions.

Isobel Stewart Strong.
Your humble servant the Amanuensis.
Native Name, *Teuila*.

Believed on the beach to be my illegitimate daughter by a Morocco woman.[5] When we wish to please her we say she is slender. Rich dark colour; taken in Sydney for an islander. Eyes enormous and particoloured, one and three-fifths brown the other two-fifths golden. She

---

[4] Mis-spelled 'bizzom' by Belle. The Scots word 'besom' (a broom) is also used as a term of contempt for a woman. Rosaline Masson (*Life*), says that 'it indicates she is a little tart in temper, and what might be described as "a handful".'

[5] In a letter of 21 [February] 1893 to Charles Stoddard, Belle referred to the gossip of the beach that she was a half-caste – 'Louis's illegitimate daughter by a Moorish woman': 'Louis was delighted with the idea. . . . Introduces me as his daughter, and when he talks about old days in Morocco he is magnificent. He tells me long tales about my mother which invariably wind up with "She was a damned fine woman!"'

> Her long dark hair deep as her knees
> And thrid with living silver sees –

unpublished poem – ahem![6] Has made a hussar[7] blush: fact. Doesn't go in
for intellect – still less for culture – (Unfair! 'Life is a positive mixture of
heterogeneous changes both simultaneous and successive in co-
respondence to external sequences and co-existences.'[8] Written from
memory. How is that for intellect?   *Am.*) When a cultured person, trying
to establish relations with her, asked if over-education were not the curse
of the present century, she replied 'Yes. I feel it myself. When I lie awake
nights and think how much I know it makes me tired.'[9] Reads nothing
but novels; likes these good; e.g. *Little Minister* and *The Pariah*; couldn't
read *Tess*.[10] With her spelling you are already acquainted; my prices are
coming down since I began to employ her. Caricatures cleverly. Thing she
likes best in the world, dress for herself and others – rather adornment.
Will arrange your hair and stick flowers about you till you curse. Meaning
of her native name, The Adorner of the Ugly. Even a stiff six feet two
English guest learned to kneel daily for his wreath, and the native boys go
to her to have their ties put on. Runs me like a baby in a perambulator,
sees I'm properly dressed, bought me silk socks and made me wear them,
takes care of me when I am sick, and I don't know what the devil she
doesn't do for me when I'm well, from writing my books to trimming
my nails. (I tried once to shave him too, but that alas was a failure.   *Am.*)
Has a growing conviction that she is the author of my works. Manages the
house and the house boys who are very fond of her. An unaffected Pagan,
and worships an idol with lights and flowers. Does all the haircutting of
the family. Will cut yours, and doubtless object to the way you part it.
Mine has been reorganised twice.

Lloyd Osbourne.
The Boy.
Native name, *Loia.*

Six foot. Blond. Eyeglasses. British eyeglasses too. Address varying
from an elaborate civility to a freezing haughtiness. Decidedly witty.

---

[6] RLS's poem 'Mother and Daughter', written in January 1893.

[7] Rupert Leigh (see pp. 499, n. 10).

[8] A misquotation from Herbert Spencer's *Principles of Biology.*

[9] Belle recorded this conversation with Flora Shaw (see p. 561, n. 5) on the *Mariposa*. She added
that a fellow-passenger, the Duchess of Buckingham, laughed 'like one who had been listening
to more intellectual conversation than she wanted, and had yet been unable to stop it'.

[10] Belle wrote to Stoddard on 20 June 1892: 'Have you read *The Pariah* by Anstey and *The Little
Minister* by Barrie . . . They are the books that have excited conversation at dinner lately – *Tess*
by Hardy is repudiated with scorn by all hands. Lloyd and I read it (3 solid volumes) because
the press called it immoral but it's a poor made tale'.

Astonishingly ignorant – the original young man whose education was neglected, and it was I who neglected it – yet somehow you would almost never find it out. (I never have.   *Am.*) Has seen an enormous amount of the world for his age. Keeps nothing of youth but some of its intolerance. Unexpected soft streak for the forlorn. When he is good he is very very good, but when he is cross he is horrid.[11] Of Dutch ancestry, and has spells known in the family as 'Cold blasts from Holland'. Exacting with the boys, and yet they like him. Rather stiff with his equals, but apt to be very kindly with his inferiors. The only undemonstrative member of the family, which otherwise wears its heart upon both sleeves; and except for my purple patches, the only mannered one. Has tried to learn fifteen instruments; has learned none but is willing to try another tomorrow. *Signe particulier*: when he thrums or tootles on any of these instruments, or even turns a barrel-organ, he insists on public and sustained applause, and the strange thing is he doesn't seem to demand any for his stories. This trait is supposed to be unique. He is his mother's curly headed boy.

Family Life.

The Boy, the Amanuensis and the Tame Celebrity all play on instruments, and all ill. But you need not applaud the two last; little they'll reck if you'll let them play on. Conversation, surprisingly free, at times embarrassingly so when guests are present. General character of life: a solid comfortable selfishness – guests preferred to be selfish also. N.B. No attention paid to guests. Clothing. You may find Loia in pajamas of which he has lost the string, soaked through and bedaubed with mud; or you may find him in white coat, tie and shirt, gaudyish sash, and excruciatingly elegant riding breeches and boots; to say nothing of silver mounted riding whip and sapphire studs. Take me at the present moment, and my costume consists of one flannel undershirt and one pair of striped pajama trousers all told – I beg your pardon, I forgot two rings and one cigarette, but you see the process is exhaustive. On the other hand you might find me in cords and fancy boots, with a velvet jacket chosen by the Amanuensis to the exact shade of harmony. My wife's usual dress will scarcely bear to be dwelt upon; but sir, when you told her the old-fashioned way etc., she was in black velvet and duchesse lace, and I will trouble you for how she looked. The career of the Amanuensis would require a pen more accomplished than mine. Her effects are various, sometimes gaudy. Now she is to be seen in bare feet with toe-rings, and anon she is troubling the world with silk stockings, and these are sometimes blue. *Absit omen*. Her frocks and my wife's are all (to do the creatures justice) on the same pattern, the native pattern, and fully more

---

[11] Cf. the verses, attributed to Longfellow, about the little girl 'who had a little curl/Right in the middle of her forehead.'

like chemises. But the Amanuensis calls in turn into the field every colour known under heaven; she goes through similar changing phases with her hair of which there is so much that the combinations and permutations are practically inexhaustible; and after each fresh make-up she appears among us for approval and weeps if it be withheld. (There are different ways of withholding approval. One way 'You look much prettier with your hair dressed low.' Another 'With your hair on top you look like a moon faced idiot with water on the brain.' It is then I cry – and so would you.   *Am.*) Thus we go up, up, up, and thus we go down, down, down. And you can see for yourself it is a somewhat dressy spot though not at all like Piccadilly.

Another thing you must be prepared for – and that is the arrival of strange old shell-back guests out of every quarter of the island world, their mouths full of oaths for which they will punctiliously apologise, their clothes unmistakeably purchased in a trade room, each probably followed by a dusky bride. These you are to expect to see hailed with acclamations, and dragged in as though they were dukes and duchesses. (But do you drag in dukes and duchesses?   *Am.*) For though we may be out of touch with 'God knows what', we are determined to keep in touch with Apemama and the Marquesas.

Miss Fraser gave a really neat and convincing representation of J.M.B. sitting in a large chair and saying *h'm*.[12] It was the only clever thing I ever saw her do or could ever suppose her doing. (To me she described you enthusiastically but somewhat vaguely as 'a dear!'   *Am.*) Your doubts as to her vitality were probably grounded.[13] She is the only actor I ever knew who did not care even to talk about the stage.

By the bye a passage in the above has nearly blown up this family. It was faithfully submitted to all concerned and admitted to be on the whole a faithful and unvarnished account; but after a series of painful discussions we have decided to recall the word 'selfishness'. Loia prefers the phrase 'a *Wuthering Heights* impatience'. You may take it at that.

And now my dear fellow I want to thank you very heartily for your last letter. That you should have telegraphed to the States, and that you and Anstey should have dined together in honour of the better news, has infinitely touched me.[14] I am quite sure that I know you and quite sure that you know me. People mayn't be like their books, they *are* their

[12] In his letter Barrie had given a comic playlet describing his visit to Vailima in which all he had said was 'h'm'.

[13] Barrie: 'I await Miss Fraser's imitation of you with impatience. When she played in my dramar I never was quite sure whether she was alive.' She had a part in the one and only performance on 16 April 1891 of *Richard Savage*, Barrie's first play written with H.B. Marriot-Watson.

[14] Barrie, troubled by a press report from San Francisco of RLS's serious illness in January 1893, had cabled to America to check the facts. When he learned from others that RLS was well he and Anstey had dined together to celebrate the good news.

books. All that we want to do now is to meet – again. Do try and bring this visit about before anything happens; and to show that my eccentric family are at one with me in the invitation here follow the signatures of all

Fanny V. de G. Stevenson
Isobel Strong
Lloyd Osbourne
Robert Louis Stevenson

★To Arthur Conan Doyle[1]

[Probably dictated to Belle]
5 April 1893   Vailima

Dear Sir, You have taken many occasions to make yourself agreeable to me, for which I might in decency have thanked you earlier. It is now my turn; and I hope you will allow me to offer you my compliments on your very ingenious and very interesting adventures of Sherlock Holmes. That is the class of literature that I like when I have the toothache. As a matter of fact, it was a pleurisy I was enjoying when I took the volume up; and it will interest you as a medical man to know that the cure was for the moment effectual. Only the one thing troubles me: can this be my old friend Joe Bell?[2] I am, Yours very truly   Robert Louis Stevenson

P.S. And lo, here is your address supplied me here in Samoa! But do not take mine, O frolic fellow Spookist, from the same source; mine is wrong.[3]   R.L.S.

[1] Arthur Conan Doyle (1859–1930), as he told RLS in his reply, was born in Edinburgh and received his medical training at Edinburgh University. He was knighted 1902. He himself set great store by his historical novels like *The White Company* (1891) and *The Refugees* (1893) but to his chagrin achieved his greatest literary fame through the creation of Sherlock Holmes. The short stories about Holmes began publication in the *Strand Magazine* in July 1891; the first twelve were collected in book form as *The Adventures of Sherlock Holmes* (October 1892). A second series, still appearing in the *Strand* at the time of this letter, was collected as *The Memoirs of Sherlock Holmes* (1894). RLS put a reference to Holmes into ch. 7 of *Weir of Hermiston*. Doyle had written 'Mr Stevenson's Methods in Fiction', a long essay in the *National Review*, January 1890, praising in particular his short stories and calling 'The Pavilion on the Links' the 'high-water mark of his genius'. He wrote an enthusiastic reply to RLS on 30 May, repeating his praise of 'The Pavilion' and thanking him 'for all the pleasure you have given me during my lifetime – more than any other living man has done'.
[2] Doyle responded: 'I'm so glad Sherlock Holmes helped to pass an hour for you. He's a bastard between Joe Bell and Poe's Monsieur Dupin (much diluted). I trust that I may never write a word about him again. I had rather that you knew me by my *White Company*. I'm sending it on the chance that you have not seen it . . .' Joseph Bell (1837–1911), one of the best-known Edinburgh surgeons of his day, was Consulting Surgeon to the Edinburgh Royal Infirmary for fifteen years.
[3] The 'List of Members and Associates' appended to the *Proceedings of the Society for Psychical Research* 1893 gave RLS's address as 'Vailinia Plantation'.

To S.R. Crockett

17 May 1893   *Vailima*

Dear Mr Crockett, I do not owe you two letters, nor yet merely one, sir! The last time I heard of you, you wrote about an accident, and I sent you a letter to my lawyer, Charles Baxter, which does not seem to have been presented: as I see nothing of it in his accounts.[1] Query, was that lost? I should not like you to think I had been so unmannerly and so inhumane. If you have written since, your letter also has miscarried, as is much the rule in this part of the world, unless you register.

Your book is not yet to hand, but will probably follow next month.[2] I detected you early in the *Bookman*, which I usually see; and noted you in particular as displaying a monstrous ingratitude about the *Footnote*.[3] Well, mankind is ungrateful; 'Man's ingratitude to man makes countless thousands mourn,' quo' Rab – or words to that effect.[4] By the way, an anecdote of a cautious sailor: 'Bill, Bill,' says I to him, '*or words to that effect*'.[5]

I shall never take that walk by the Fisher's Tryst and Glencorse;[6] I shall never see Auld Reekie; I shall never set my foot again upon the heather. Here I am until I die, and here will I be buried. The word is out and the doom written. Or, if I do come, it will be a voyage to a further goal, and in fact a suicide; which, however, if I could get my family all fixed up in the money way, I might perhaps perform, or attempt. But there is a plaguey risk of breaking down by the way; and I believe I shall stay here

---

[1] RLS appears to have written an untraced letter to Crockett in mid-February 1890 on board *S.S. Lübeck*, responding to his request for a contribution towards a relief fund for the families of sixty-three men killed in an accident at Mauricewood colliery, Penicuik, 5 September 1889.

[2] *The Stickit Minister and Some Common Men*, a collection of short stories, dedicated to RLS, was published on 20 March 1893. Crockett replied on 23 June explaining that he had sent a copy of the first edition at the same time as his letter, but the Post Office in London had failed to despatch it because of insufficient postage and it had been lost. He sent RLS a copy of the second edition that day. A 'stickit [stuck or failed] minister' is a probationer who has failed to become ordained (cf. Dominie Sampson in *Guy Mannering*, ch. 1).

[3] In the *Bookman* for March 1893, under the initials 'S.R.C.', Crockett had published what RLS told his mother was 'a very wild article' – 'The Apprenticeship of Robert Louis Stevenson'. In it he quoted letters from RLS but dealt mainly with his youthful *The Pentland Rising*. Crockett indignantly denied responsibility for an unfavourable review of the *Footnote*: 'I wrote a long article most gallantly defensive of it (in the *Standard* or *St James* I forget which). I rejoiced in every word of it.' The review of the *Footnote* in the *Bookman* for October 1892 was in fact by Edward Purcell (writing under the pseudonym 'Y.Y.').

[4] Burns, 'Man Was Made to Mourn'. RLS substitutes 'ingratitude' for 'inhumanity'.

[5] In his journal Balfour recorded the anecdote as having been told RLS by George Crawshaw, captain of the *S.S. Upolu* that plied between Auckland, Tonga and Apia.

[6] In his *Bookman* article Crockett quoted an earlier (untraced) letter from RLS saying that 'the dearest burn to me in the world is that which drums and pours in cunning wimples in that glen of yours behind Glencorse old kirk'. RLS had apparently expressed the hope of being able to walk there one day with Crockett.

until the end comes like a good boy, and a prolific milk cow, as I am. If I did it, I should put upon my trunks: Passenger to – Hades.

How strangely wrong your information is! In the first place, I should never carry a novel to Sydney; I should post it from here. In the second place, *Weir of Hermiston* is as yet scarce begun. It's going to be excellent, no doubt; but it consists of about 20 pp. I have a tale, a shortish tale in length, but it has proved long to do, *The Ebb-Tide*, some part of which goes home this mail. It is by me and Mr Osbourne, and is really a singular work. There are only four characters, and three of them are bandits – well, two of them are, and the third is their comrade and accomplice. It sounds cheering, doesn't it? Barratry, and drunkenness, and vitriol, and I cannot tell you all what, are the beams of the roof. And yet – I don't know – I sort of think there's something in it. You'll see (which is more than I ever can) whether Davis and Attwater come off or not.[7]

Weir of Hermiston is a much greater undertaking, and the plot is not good, I fear; but Lord Justice-Clerk Hermiston ought to be a plum. Of other schemes, more or less executed, it skills not to speak.

I am glad to hear so good an account of your activity and interest, and shall always hear from you with pleasure; though I am, and must continue, a mere sprite of the inkbottle, unseen in the flesh. Please remember me to your wife and to the four-year-old sweetheart,[8] if she be not too engrossed with higher matters. Do you know where the road crosses the burn under Glencorse Church? Go there, and say a prayer for me: *Moriturus salutat.*[9] See that it's a sunny day; I would like it to be a Sunday, but that's not possible in the premises; and stand on the right-hand bank just where the road goes down into the water, and shut your eyes, and if I don't appear to you! well, it can't be helped, and will be extremely funny.

I have no concern here but to work and to keep an eye on this distracted people. I live just now wholly alone in an upper room of my house; because the whole family are down with influenza, bar my wife and myself; I get my horse up sometimes in the afternoon and have a ride in the woods; and I sit here and smoke and write, and rewrite, and

---

[7] In February 1893, RLS (as he told Colvin) 'took up, pitched into, and about one half demolished another tale once intended to be called *The Pearl Fisher*, but now razeed and called *The Schooner Farallone*'. By 12 May the name had been changed to *The Ebb-Tide* and RLS was 'grinding singly' at it, writing and re-writing slowly: 'I break down at every paragraph . . . and lie here, and sweat, and curse over the blame thing, till I can get one sentence wrung out after another.' The first ten chapters were sent off on 23 May.

[8] Crockett married (1887) Ruth Mary Milner (1860–1932) of Manchester. Their eldest child was Ruth Mary Rutherford (Maisie) (1888–1957); she features in his *Sweetheart Travellers* (1895) and he called her 'Sweetheart' all his life.

[9] He who is about to die salutes you. RLS is remembering the story (by Suetonius) that gladiators in the arena saluted the Roman Emperor with the words: 'Hail Caesar: those who are about to die salute you.'

destroy, and rage at my own impotence, from six in the morning till eight at night with trifling and not always agreeable intervals for meals.

I am sure you chose wisely to keep your country charge. There a minister can be something, not in a town. In a town, the most of them are empty houses – and public speakers. Why should you suppose your book will be slated, because you have no friends? . . .[10] A new writer, if he is any good, will be acclaimed generally with more noise than he deserves. But by this time you will know for certain. I am yours sincerely

Robert Louis Stevenson

P.S. Be it known to this fluent generation that I, R.L.S., in the forty-third year of my age and the twentieth of my professional life, wrote twenty-four pages in twenty-one days: working from six to eleven, and again in the afternoon from two to four or so, without fail or interruption. Such are the gifts the gods have endowed us withal; such was the facility of this prolific writer! R.L.S.

⋆To Charles Baxter[1]

20 May 1893 [*Vailima*]

. . . But never mind, the business will all keep. We make haste and the water rises, we make haste and the tide ebbs. A great judicious coolness becomes us in the face of this obtrusive universe. . . . My dear fellow, you have my most earnest sympathy in your bereavement. I never really knew, but always heartily respected and admired your wife, as a handsome gallant honest woman of whom any one might be proud. As we go on into this pass in which we are already due, reminiscences, which I remember you of old a great maker of, must come to be ever more and more. Youth is now done, middle age begins to draw to an end, and soon we must look to be old men, the tellers of anecdotes under other men's mahogany. All that was beautiful in our past, becomes dear by just so much; and we must keep it and cling to it; and the beautiful legend of the bygone becomes ever more beautiful as the days go on. If Gracie can look back and behold us here, God knows! I do not. But at least we must try to be something that the dead need not be ashamed of. There are many now; my father, and Gracie, and such a lot of others. Well with all our deadly weaknesses, we must even try to be a little worthy.

---

[10] Six or seven words heavily deleted, apparently by RLS.

[1] Baxter's wife, Grace, died on 24 March 1893 from pneumonia following influenza. This copy is part of a longer letter which does not seem to have survived. Fanny also sent a warm letter of sympathy.

Dear fellow, I shake your hand. Come out here to us.[2] Yours ever

To Henry James

[Beginning dictated to Belle]
17 June 1893   *Vailima Plantation*

My dear Henry James, I believe I have neglected a mail in answering yours.[1] You will be very sorry to hear that my wife was exceedingly ill and very glad to hear that she is better. I cannot say that I feel any more anxiety about her. We shall send you a photograph of her taken in Sydney in her customary island habit as she walks and gardens and shrilly drills her brown assistants. She was very ill when she sat for it, which may a little explain the appearance of the photograph. It reminds me of a friend of my grandmother's who used to say when talking to younger women, 'Aweel, when I was young, I wasnae just exactly what ye wad call *bonny* but I was pale penetratin' and interestin'.' I would not venture to hint that Fanny is 'no bonny', but there is no doubt but that in this presentment she is 'pale penetratin' and interestin''.

As you are aware I have been wading deep waters and contending with the great ones of the earth, not wholly without success. It is, you may be interested to hear, a dreary and infuriating business. If you can get the fools to admit one thing, they will always save their face by denying another. If you can induce them to take a step to the right hand, they generally indemnify themselves by cutting a caper to the left. I always held (upon no evidence whatever, from a mere sentiment or intuition) that politics was the dirtiest, the most foolish and the most random of human employments. I always held, but now I know it![2] And the thought of Gladstone coopering away at his Home Rule and the whole lot of them tinkering daily at dishonest compromises makes me sad to the point of nausea. Fortunately you have nothing to do with anything of the kind and I may spare you the horror of further details. Suffice it to say that your friend Rosebery appears, from all point of view, human or divine, to be an exceptionally white man.[3]

---

[2] His wife's death was followed a year later by that of his father and Baxter suffered an emotional collapse. He gave way to heavy drinking and his continual drunkenness caused great anxiety, especially as RLS had made him responsible for handling all negotiations with publishers and editors. He was on his way to Samoa at the time of RLS's death.

[1] RLS is replying to James's letter of 17 February 1893. James replied to this one on 5 August 1893.

[2] James replied: '"Politics", dear politician – I rejoice that you're getting over them. When you say that you always "believed" them beastly I am tempted to become superior and say that I always knew them so. At least I don't see how one could have glanced, however cursorily, at the contemporary newspapers . . . and had any doubt of it.'

[3] See p. 566.

I received from you a book by a man by the name of Anatole France. Why should I disguise it? I have no use for Anatole.[4] He writes very prettily, and then afterwards? Baron Marbot was a different pair of shoes. So likewise is the Baron de Vitrolles whom I am now perusing with delight.[5] His escape in 1814 is one of the best pages I remember anywhere to have read. But de Marbot and Vitrolles are dead, and what has become of the living? It seems as if literature were coming to a stand. I am sure it is with me; and I am sure everybody will say so when they have the privilege of reading The Ebb-Tide. My dear man the grimness of that story is not to be depicted in words. There are only four characters to be sure, but they are such a troop of swine! And their behaviour is really so deeply beneath any possible standard, that on a retrospect I wonder I have been able to endure them myself until the yarn was finished. Well, there is always one thing: it will serve as a touchstone. If the admirers of Zola admire him for his pertinent ugliness and pessimism, I think they should admire this; but if, as I have long suspected, they neither admire nor understand the man's art, and only wallow in his rancidness like a hound in offal, then they will certainly be disappointed in The Ebb-Tide. Alas! Poor little tale, it is not even rancid.[6]

By way of an antidote or febrifuge, I am going on at a great rate with my history of the Stevensons,[7] which I hope may prove rather amusing in some parts at least. The excess of materials weighs upon me. My grandfather is a delightful comedy part; and I have to treat him besides as a serious and (in his way) a heroic figure; and at times I lose my way and I fear in the end will blur the effect. However, à la grâce de Dieu! I'll make a spoon or spoil a horn. You see, I have to do the Building of the Bell Rock by cutting down and packing my grandsire's book; which I rather hope I have done, but do not know. And it makes a huge chunk of a very different style and quality between Chapters II and IV. And it can't be helped! It is just a delightful and exasperating necessity. You know the stuff is really excellent narrative: only, perhaps there's too much of it! There is the rub. Well, well, it will be plain to you that my mind is affected; it might be with less. The Ebb-Tide and Northern Lights are a full meal for any plain man.[8]

[4] James had sent RLS 'the charming little Etui de Nacre of Anatole France – a real master'. This book of short stories appeared in 1892.

[5] Eugène François Auguste d'Arnaud, Baron de Vitrolles, French politician (1774–1854). Colvin had sent his Mémoires et Relations Politiques (Paris, 1884) in response to RLS's request for books about France in 1814.

[6] In early June RLS had been toiling over the last pages of The Ebb-Tide. It was finished on 5 June and he told Colvin that he had spent 'thirteen days about as nearly in Hell as a man could expect to live through'. Putting it in the post on 18 June he described it as 'the ever-to-be-execrated Ebb-Tide, or Stevenson's Blooming Error'.

[7] RLS takes over from Belle at this point.

[8] RLS told Colvin on 17 June that he had 'written a whole chapter of my Grandfather'. He listed the proposed eight chapters of the book (three of which had been completed), which he

I have written and ordered your last book *The Real Thing*, so be sure and don't send it.[9] What else are you doing or thinking of doing? News I have none, and don't want any. I have had to stop all strong drink and all tobacco; and am now in a transition state between the two which seems to be near madness. You never smoked, I think, so you can never taste the joys of stopping it. But at least you have drunk, and you can enter perhaps into my annoyance when I suddenly find a glass of claret or brandy and water give me a splitting headache the next morning. No mistake about it; drink anything, and there's your headache. Tobacco just as bad for me. If I live through this breach of habit I shall be a white-livered puppy indeed. Actually I am so made, or so twisted, that I do not like to think of a life without the red wine on the table and the tobacco with its lovely little coal of fire. It doesn't amuse me from a distance. I may find it the Garden of Eden when I go in, but I don't like the colour of the gateposts. Suppose somebody said to you, you are to leave your home, and your books, and your clubs, and go out and camp in mid-Africa, and command an expedition? You would howl, and kick, and flee. I think the same of a life without wine and tobacco; and if this goes on, I've got to go and do it, sir, in the living flesh!

I thought Bourget was a friend of yours? And I thought the French were a polite race? He has taken my dedication with a stately silence that has surprised me into apoplexy. Did I go and dedicate my book to the nasty alien, and the 'n'orrid Frenchman, and the Bloody Furrineer? Well, I wouldn't do it again; and unless his case is susceptible of Explanation, you might perhaps tell him so over the walnuts and the wine, by way of speeding the gay hours. Seriously, I thought my dedication worth a letter.[10] If anything be worth anything here below! Do you know the story of the man who found a button in his hash, and called the waiter? 'What do you call that?' says he. – 'Well,' said the waiter, 'what d'you expect? Expect to find a gold watch and chain?' Heavenly apologue, is it not? I expected (rather) to find a gold watch and chain; I expected to be able to smoke to excess and drink to comfort all the days of my life; and I am still

proposed to call *Northern Lights: Memoirs of a Family of Engineers*. These three chapters were sent to Colvin in September to be set up in proof. The name *Northern Lights* had to be abandoned because someone else had used it.

[9] James had said on 17 February that he was 'presently putting forth . . . two volumes of penny fiction' and that these would 'be (D.V.) deposited on your coral strand'. James despatched the two volumes – *The Real Thing and other Tales* and *The Private Life* – with another letter on 8 June.

[10] In December 1891 RLS had 'gone crazy' over *Sensations d'Italie* by the French novelist Paul Bourget (1852–1935), sent to him by his friend Henry James. In his enthusiasm RLS dedicated to Bourget his collection of reprinted essays, *Across the Plains with Other Memories and Essays* (1892). James met Bourget in London and in his reply on 5 August was able to enclose a letter from him to RLS dated 3 August, acknowledging RLS's dedication and apologising for the delay in writing.

indignantly staring on this button! It's not even a button; it's a teatotal badge! But we'll hope this cup may be taken away from me still. Ever yours   Robert Louis Stevenson

To Austin Strong[1]

[Beginning dictated to Belle]
Uncle Louis's Letter
18 June 1893   [Vailima]

Respected Hoskins,[2] This is to inform you that the Jersey cow had an elegant little cow-calf Sunday last. There was a great deal of rejoicing, for we were short of milk, but I don't know whether or not you remember the Jersey cow. Whatever else it is, it is *not* good-natured, and Dines,[3] who was up here on some other business, went down to the paddock to get a hood on and milk her. The hood is a little wooden board with two holes in it by which it is hung from her horns. I don't know how he got it on, and I don't believe *he* does. Anyway, in the middle of the operation, in came Bull Bazett with his head down and roaring like the last trumpet. Dines and all his merry men hid behind trees in the paddock, and skipped. Dines then got upon a horse – plied his spurs, and cleared for Apia. The next time he is asked to meddle with our cows he will probably want to know the reason why. Meanwhile there was the cow, with the board over her eyes, left tied by a pretty long rope to a small tree in the paddock – and who was to milk her? She roared, I was going to say like a bull, but it was Bazett who did that, walking up and down and switching his tail; and the noise of the pair of them was perfectly dreadful. Pelema[4] went up to the bush to call Lloyd, and Lloyd came down in one of his 'know-all-about-it' moods. 'It was perfectly simple,' he said. 'The cow was hooded; anybody could milk her. All you had to do was to draw her up close to the tree and get a hitch about it.' So he untied the cow and drew her up close to the tree and got a hitch about it right enough. And then the cow[5]

[1] An example of the letters RLS wrote to Austin while he was away at school in California.
[2] Austin was given a variety of nicknames. RLS called him General Hoskyns in their war games with toy soldiers and in a copy of The Wrecker addressed him as 'Hutchinson Hoskyns Hopkinson, Esq., better known as Austin Strong'. Belle says that Austin's name was pronounced 'Hoskyn' by Annie, the maid at Mrs Leaney's boarding house in Sydney in 1889.
[3] An Apia butcher.
[4] In a letter to Mrs Jenkin of 5 December 1892 Fanny explained that when they were expecting a visit from Rudyard Kipling and Graham Balfour, Austin asked: 'When is Wretched Kipling and Blame Balfour coming?' MIS recorded in her diary on 6 August 1892 that on arrival Graham had taken 'kindly to his name of Blame'. This was softened by the Samoans to 'Pelema' and the name was generally adopted.
[5] The rest of the letter is in the hand of RLS.

brought her intellect to bear on the subject, and proceeded to walk round the tree to get the hitch off. Now, this is Geometry which you'll have to learn some day. The Tree is the centre of two circles. The cow had a 'radius' of about two feet and went leisurely round a small circle; the man had a 'radius' of about thirty feet, and either he must let the cow get the hitch unwound or else he must take up his two feet to about the height of his eyes, and race for all he was worth, round a big circle.[6] There was racing and chasing on Cannobie Lee![7] The cow walked quietly round and round the tree to unwind herself; and first Lloyd, and then Pelema, and then Lloyd again, scampered round the big circle, and fell, and got up again, and bounded like deer, to keep her hitched. It was funny to see, but one couldn't laugh really good; for every now and then (when the man who was running tumbled down) the cow would get a bit ahead, and I promise you there was no word of any laughter, but we rather edged away towards the gate, looking to see the crazy beast loose and charging us. To add to her attractions, the board had fallen partly off and only covered one eye, giving her the look of a drunken old woman in a Sydney slum. And meanwhile the calf stood looking on, a little perplexed, and seemed to be saying: 'Well, now, is this life? It don't seem as if it was all it was cracked up to be. And is this my Mamma? What a very impulsive lady!' All the while, from the lower paddock, we could hear Bazett roaring like the deep seas, and if you cast your eye that way, could see him switching his tail, the way a very angry gentleman may sometimes switch his cane. And the Jersey would every now and then put up her head, and low like the pu[8] for dinner. And take it for all in all, it was a very striking scene. Poor Uncle Lloyd had plenty time to regret having been in such a hurry; so had poor Pelema, who was let into the business and ran till he was nearly dead. Afterwards he went and sat on a gate where your mother sketched him, and she is going to send you the sketch. And the end of it? Well, we got her tied again, I really don't know how; and came stringing back to the house with our tails between our legs. That night at dinner, Granny Fan bid us tell the boys to be very careful 'not to frighten the cow'. It was too much; the cow had frightened us in such fine style, that we all broke down and laughed like mad.

General Hoskyns, there is no further news, your Excellency, that I am aware of. But it may interest you to know that Mr Christian[9] held his

---

[6] The account is illustrated by two drawings. The first shows the cow's small circle round the tree; the second shows the cow's circle and the much larger man's circle.

[7] See Scott's ballad of 'Lochinvar' in *Marmion*, V. xii. MIS had taught Austin some of Scott's poems.

[8] 'The big conch-shell that was blown at certain hours every day' (Lloyd's note).

[9] Frederick William Christian (1868–1934), English traveller and author, who was interested in the study of Polynesian languages and wrote major works on *The Caroline Islands* (1899) and *Eastern Pacific Lands: Tahiti and the Marquesan Islands* (1910). After taking his BA at Oxford in

twenty-fifth birthday yesterday – quarter of a living century old, think of
it, drink of it, innocent youth! –[10] and asked down Lloyd and Daplyn[11] to
a feast at one o'clock, and Daplyn went at one, and got nothing to eat
until four, and Lloyd went at seven and got nothing to eat at all. Whether
they had anything to drink, I know not, no, not I; but it's to be hoped so.
Also, your Uncle Lloyd has stopped smoking, and your Uncle Louis has
stopped drinking; and they neither of them like it much. Also, that your
mother is most beautifully gotten up today, in a pink gown with a topaz
stud in front of it, and the most gaudy pink silk stockings; and is really
looking like an angel, only that she isn't like an angel at all – only like
your mother herself. Also that your Aunt Fanny has been waxing the floor
of the big room, so that it shines in the most ravishing manner; and then
we insisted on coming in, and she wouldn't let us, and we came anyway,
and have made the vilest mess of it – but still it shines. Also that I am, your
Excellency's obedient servant   Uncle Louis

To Sidney Colvin
(Abridged)

Saturday 24(?) June [1893]   [*Vailima*]

My dear Colvin, Yesterday morning, after a day of absolute temperance,
I awoke to the worst headache I had had yet. Accordingly temperance was
said farewell to; quinine instituted; and I believe my pains are soon to be
over. We wait, with a kind of sighing impatience, for war to be declared
or to blow finally off, living in the meanwhile in a kind of children's hour
of firelight and shadow and preposterous tales: the King seen at night
galloping up our road upon unknown errands and covering his face as he
passes our cook; Mataafa daily surrounded (when he awakes) with fresh
'white man's boxes' (query: ammunition?) and professing to be quite
ignorant of where they come from; marches of bodies of men across the
island; concealment of ditto in the bush; the coming on and off of
different chiefs; and such a mass of ravelment and rag-tag as the devil
himself could not unwind.[1]

1890 he went out to Samoa and was a neighbour of RLS for three years. In 1919 he was
   Headmaster of a native school in the Cook Islands; he later lived in New Zealand.
[10] Cf. Thomas Hood, 'The Bridge of Sighs': 'Picture it – think of it,/Dissolute man!/Lave in it,
   drink of it,/Then if you can!'
[11] Alfred James Daplyn (1844–1926), English painter, who went to Australia in 1885 and became
   the first art instructor at the Royal Art Society School in Sydney 1885–92. RLS knew him at
   Barbizon and met him again at Sydney in 1890. He stayed at Vailima in 1893.
[1] Over the previous few months, the political situation in Samoa had steadily deteriorated. From
   late January Cusack-Smith and his fellow-Consuls had recommended firm military action

Wednesday 28 June

Yesterday it rained with but little intermission, but I was jealous of news. Graham and I got into the saddle about one o'clock and off down to town. In town, there was nothing but rumours going; in the night, drums had been beat, the men had run to arms on Mulinuu from as far as Vaiala, and the alarm proved false. There were no signs of any gathering in Apia proper, and the Secretary of State[2] had no news to give. I believed him too, for we are Brither Scots. Then the temptation came upon me strong to go on to the west, and see the Mataafa villages, where we heard there was more afoot. Off we rode. When we came to Vaimoso, the houses were very full of men, but all seemingly unarmed. Immediately beyond is that river over which we passed in our scamper with Lady Jersey; it was all solitary. Three hundred yards beyond is a second ford: and there – I came face to face with war. Under the trees on the further bank, sat a picket of seven men with Winchesters; their faces bright, their eyes ardent. As we came up, they did not speak or move; only their eyes followed us. The horses drank, and we passed the ford. '*Talofa!*' I said, and the commandant of the picket said '*Talofa*'; and then, when we were almost by, remembered himself and asked where we were going. 'To Faamuinā,' I said and we rode on. Every house by the wayside was crowded with armed men. There was the European house of a Chinaman on the right hand side: a flag of truce flying over the gate – indeed we saw three of these in what little way we penetrated into Mataafa's lines – all the foreigners trying to protect their goods; and the Chinaman's verandah overflowed with men and girls and Winchesters. By the way we met a party of about ten or a dozen marching with their guns and cartridge belts, and the cheerful alacrity and brightness of their looks set my head turning with envy and sympathy. Arrived at Vaiusu, the houses about the *malae* (village green) were thronged with men, all armed. On the outside of the council house (which was all full within) there stood an orator; he had his back turned to his audience, and seemed to address the world at large; all

---

against Mataafa, but the three Powers had vacillated. Mataafa's own actions had become increasingly provocative and Malietoa Laupepa (whose own support among Samoan chiefs was by now greater than Mataafa's) was determined to overthrow the rebellion. Early in May, the three Consuls, still unaware of their Governments' intentions, could give him no promises of support and on 20 May he informed them of his Government's decision 'to take immediate steps to put down the Chief Mataafa and his followers'. As RLS himself put it in the opening sentence of his article 'War in Samoa' (*Pall Mall Gazette*, 4 September 1893): 'In June it became clear that the King's Government was weary of waiting upon Europe, as it had been clear long before that Europe would do nothing.' During June Laupepa's agents canvassed throughout Samoa for support, and what RLS called the 'cumbrous and dilatory' process of gathering a royal army began; in early July contingents of Laupepa's troops began to assemble.

[2] Thomas Maben, originally Surveyor General, was appointed Secretary of State and Surveyor General to the King in June 1892.

the time we were there his strong voice continued unabated, and I heard snatches of political wisdom rising and falling.

The house of Faamuinā stands on a knoll in the *malae*. Thither we mounted, a boy ran out and took our horses, and we went in. Faamuinā was there himself, his wife Lelepa, three other chiefs and some attendants; and here again was this exulting spectacle of people on their marriage day. Faamuinā (when I last saw him) was an elderly, limping gentleman, with much of the debility of age; it was a bright-eyed boy that greeted me; the lady was no less excited; all had cartridge belts. We stayed but a little while to smoke a *selui*; I would not have *kava* made, as I thought my escapade was already dangerous (perhaps even blameworthy) enough. On the way back, we were much greeted; and on coming to the ford, the command-ant came and asked me if there were many on the other side. Very many, said I – not that I knew, but I would not lead them on the ice. 'That is well!' said he, and the little picket laughed aloud as we splashed into the river. We returned to Apia, through Apia, and out to windward as far as Vaiala, where the word went that the men of the Vaimauga had assem-bled. . . . So home, a little before six, in a dashing squall of rain, to a bowl of *kava* and dinner. But the impression on our minds was extraordinary; the sight of that picket at the ford and those ardent, happy faces, whirls in my head; the old aboriginal awoke in both of us and knickered[3] like a stallion; and I believe I expressed the sentiment that was in the air when I turned to Graham and said 'after all there are only two things worth while – to have women and to kill men'.

It is dreadful to think that I must sit apart here and do nothing; I do not know if I can stand it out. But you see, I may be of use to these poor people, if I keep quiet; and if I threw myself in, I should have a bad job of it to save myself. There: I have written this to you; and it is still but 7.30 in the day, and the sun only about an hour up; can I go back to my old grandpapa – and men sitting with Winchesters in my mind's eye? No: war is a huge *entraînement*; there is no other temptation to be compared to it, not one. We were all wet, we had been about five hours in the saddle, mostly riding hard; and we came home like schoolboys, with such a lightness of spirit, and I am sure such a brightness of eye, as you could have lit a candle at![4]

Do you appreciate the height and depth of my temptation? that I have about nine miles to ride, and I can become a general officer? and tonight I might seize Mulinuu and have the C.J. under arrest? And yet I stay here!

---

[3] Neighed (Scots): usually spelled 'nickered'.

[4] Fanny (who resumed her diary on 3 July after a long interval) reported this visit by RLS and Balfour to the rebel outposts and commented: 'They came back quite wild with excitement, burning to join in the fray. It is going, I see, to be a difficult task to keep Louis from losing his head altogether.'

It seems incredible; so huge is the empire of prudence and the second thought! . . .

Friday [30 June]

Down with Fanny and Belle, to lunch at the International. . . . Luncheon over, we rode out on the Malie road. All was quiet in Vaiusu, and when we got to the second ford, alas! there was no picket – which was just what Belle had come to sketch. On, through quite empty roads, the houses deserted, never a gun to be seen; and at last a drum and a penny whistle playing in Vaiusu, and a cricket match on the *malae*! Went up to Faamuinā's; he is a trifle uneasy, though he gives us *kava*; I cannot see what ails him; then, it appears that he has an engagement with the Chief Justice at half-past two to sell a piece of land. Is this the reason why war has disappeared? We ride back, stopping to sketch here and there, the fords, a flag of truce, etc. Just before the Gase-Gase, we pass His Honour with a huge and grim salutation. 'He really does that very well,' I cried, in irresistible admiration. 'You did it very well yourself, Mr Stevens,' said Belle. Doubtless we were a pretty pair. Strange rudeness of a native while sketching at the second ford, who said Fanny was *Matapuaa* (pig face), a most unheard-of affair.[5] . . . To the hotel to dinner, then to the ball, and home by eleven, very tired. At the ball, I heard some curst news, of how the chief of Letogo said that I was the source of all this trouble and should be punished, and my family as well. . . . One good job, these threats to my house and family take away all my childish temptation to go out and fight. Our fun must be here, to protect ourselves. I see panic rising among the whites; I hear the shrill note of it in their voices, and they talk already about a refuge on the warships. There are two here, both German; and the *Orlando* is expected presently.

Sunday 9 July

Well, the war has at last begun. For four or five days, Apia has been filled by these poor children with their faces blacked, and the red handkerchief about their brows, that makes the Malietoa uniform; and the boats have been coming in from the windward, some of them fifty strong, with a drum and a bugle on board – the bugle always ill-played – and a sort of jester leaping and capering on the sparred nose of the boat, and the whole crew uttering from time to time a kind of menacing ululation. Friday they marched out to the bush; and yesterday morning we heard that some had returned to their homes for the night, as they found it 'so

---

[5] Fanny, in her own long account of this expedition, explains that 'The word pig-face is the most insulting epithet possible in the Samoan language.'

uncomfortable'. After dinner a messenger came up to me with a note, that the wounded were arriving at the Mission House. Fanny, Lloyd and I saddled and rode off with a lantern; it was a fine starry night, though pretty cold. . . . I found Apia, and myself, in a strange state of flusteration; my own excitement was gloomy and (I may say) truculent; others appeared imbecile; some sullen. The best place in the whole town was the hospital: A largish frame-house it was, with a big table in the middle for operations, and ten Samoans, each with an average of four sympathisers, stretched along the walls. Clarke was there, steady as a die; Miss Large, ugly little spectacled angel,[6] showed herself a real trump; the nice clean German orderlies in their white uniforms looked and meant business. (I hear a fine story of Miss Large a cast-iron teetotaller going to the public-house for a bottle of brandy.)

The doctors were not there, when I arrived; but presently it was observed that one of the men was growing cold. He was a magnificent Samoan, very dark, with a noble aquiline countenance, like an Arab I suppose; and was surrounded by seven people fondling his limbs as he lay: he was shot through both lungs. And an orderly was sent to the Firm for the (German naval) doctors, who were dining there. . . . Back to the hospital about 11.30; found the German doctor there, a little after-dinnerish, but not too much I hope. Two men were going now; one that was shot in the bowels – he was dying rather hard, in a gloomy stupor of pain and laudanum, silent, with contorted face. The chief, shot through the lungs, was lying on one side, awaiting the last angel; his family held his hands and legs; they were all speechless; only one woman suddenly clasped his knee, and 'keened' for the inside of five seconds, and fell silent again. Went home, and to bed about two A.M. What actually passed seems undiscoverable; but the Mataafas were surely driven back out of Vaitele; that is a blow to them; and the resistance was far greater than had been anticipated – which is a blow to the Laupepas. All seems to indicate a long and bloody war – and German annexation. Funk's house[7] in Mulinuu was likewise filled with wounded; many dead bodies were brought in, I hear with certainty of five, wrapped in mats; and a pastor goes tomorrow to the field to bury others. . . .

Evening

Can I write or not? I played lawn tennis in the morning, and after lunch down with Graham to Apia. Ulu, he that was shot in the lungs, still

---

[6] Agnes Eunice Large (1854–1917), L.M.S. missionary who arrived in Apia in April 1892 to work at the School for the Children of Foreigners. In January 1895 she went to Rarotonga and left the Society in 1902.

[7] Dr Bernard Funk. See p. 610 n.4.

lives; he that was shot in the bowels is gone to the fathers, poor, fierce child! I was able to be of some very small help, and in the way of helping myself to information, to prove myself – a mere gazer at meteors. But there seems no doubt the Mataafas for the time are scattered; the most of our friends are involved in this disaster, and Mataafa himself – who might have swept the islands a few months ago – for him to fall so poorly, doubles my regret. . . . I go down tomorrow at twelve to stay the afternoon, and help Miss Large. In the hospital today, when I first entered it, there were no attendants; only the wounded and their friends, all equally sleeping and their heads poised upon the wooden pillows. . . . I am so stiff I can scarce move without a howl.

Monday 10th

Some news that Mataafa is gone to Savaii by way of Manono; this may mean a great deal more warfaring, and no great issue. (When Sosimo came in this morning with my breakfast he had to lift me up. It is no joke to play lawn tennis after carrying your right arm in a sling so many years.) What a hard unjust business this is! On the 28th, if Mataafa had moved, he could have still swept Mulinuu. He waited, and I fear he is now only the stick of a rocket.

Wednesday 12th

No more probative news: but many rumours. The Government troops are off to Manono; no word of Mataafa. . . .

A man brought in a head to Mulinuu in great glory; they washed the black paint off, and behold! it was his brother. When I last heard he was sitting in his house, with the head upon his lap, and weeping. Barbarous war is an ugly business; but I believe the civilised is fully uglier; but Lord! what fun! . . .

Thursday 13th

Mataafa driven away from Savaii. I cannot write about this, and do not know what should be the end of it.

Monday 17th

Haggard and Ahrens (a German clerk) to lunch yesterday. I hear from Ahrens that the C.J. has all my letters to Mataafa, and was weeping over them! over the grammar, I suppose. But they were not complimentary, it's a fact, and no doubt could be held libellous, if he had only enough law to know it. There is no real certain news, yet: I must say, no man could *swear* to any result; but the sky looks horribly black for Mataafa and so many of our friends along with him. The thing has an abominable, a beastly, nightmare interest. But it's wonderful generally how little one cares about the wounded, hospital sights, etc.: things that used to murder me. I was far more struck with the excellent way in which things were managed, as if it had been a peep-show; I held some of the things as an operation, and did not care a dump.

Tuesday 18th

Sunday came the *Katoomba*, Captain Bickford C.M.G.[8] Yesterday, Graham and I went down to call, and find he has orders to suppress Mataafa at once, and has to go down today before daybreak to Manono. He is a very capable, energetic man, and entirely on the Mataafa side; said it was simply a disgrace to the three Powers that the thing had gone so far. If he had only come ten days ago, all this would have gone by; but now the questions are thick and difficult (1) Will Mataafa surrender? (2) Will his people allow themselves to be disarmed? (3) What will happen to them if they do? (4) What will any of them believe after former deceptions? The three Consuls are escaping on horseback to Leulumoega to the King; no Cusack-Smith, without whose accession I could not send a letter to Mataafa. I rode up here, wrote my letter in the sweat of the concordance and with the able-bodied help of Lloyd; and we were d—d proud of it – and dined. Then down in continual showers and pitchy darkness, and to Cusack-Smith's; not returned. Back to the inn in a howling squall, and got wet and wretchedly angry. On board, and a long talk with Captain Bickford. Back to the inn for my horse, and to T.B.C.S.'s when I find him just returned and he accepts my letter. Thence home by 12.30, jolly tired and wet. And today have been in a crispation of energy and ill-temper, raking my wretched mail together. It is a hateful business, waiting for the news; it may come to a fearful massacre yet. Yours ever

R.L.S.

---

[8] The British Government had been reluctant to send a warship and the commanders of the two German warships already at Apia had been unwilling to act until joined by vessels from the other two Powers. It was not until Laupepa informed the three Consuls on 14 July that he intended to pursue Mataafa to Manono that they, on behalf of their Governments, agreed to help. Two days later the *Katoomba* reached Apia and on 18 July the three warships (with the Consuls aboard) escorted Laupepa's forces in canoes to Manono. Mataafa was presented with an ultimatum and surrendered to the captain of the *Katoomba*.

Andrew Kennedy Bickford (1844–1927) joined the Navy in 1858 and had a distinguished career, ending up as an Admiral. His report on the operations against Mataafa shows him to have been a compassionate man; he made a special plea that the chiefs should be allowed to take their wives into exile with them.

⋆To Mataafa[1]
(Translation)

[17 July 1893]   [Vailima]

To His Highness Mataafa.

Your Highness: Heavy is the tale that I have heard. The Captain of the British warship has just spoken to me thus: 'If Mataafa and his Chiefs and wounded men will come on board my ship I will look after them faithfully. But if Mataafa will not, there is here an order from the three Powers to make war upon him at once.'

Your Highness – it is impossible for you to make war upon the three Great Powers.

For which reason I beseech you for the love of the Lord that you should obey the Captain of the ship. He will be answerable for your life. There is no other way in which your life can be secured.

My heart is sore because of my very great love for you. My family has been weeping because of the Chiefs who are dead.

Great is our love to you and great also our distress. Your true and distressed friend   Tusitala

To Henry James

[c. 15 August 1893]   [Vailima]

My dear Henry James, Yes. *Les Trophées*[1] is, on the whole, a Book. It is excellent; but is it a life's work? I always suspect *you* of a volume of sonnets up your sleeve; when is it coming down? I am in one of my moods of wholesale impatience with all fiction and all verging on it, reading instead, with rapture, Fountainhall's *Decisions*.[2] You never read it;

---

[1] This translation of RLS's letter was enclosed in Cusack-Smith's despatch to the Foreign Office dated 12 August 1893. In it he explained that when he returned at 10.45 p.m. on 17 July from a meeting with the King and Samoan Government, he found RLS had been waiting at the Consulate all the afternoon 'much distressed at the action against Mataafa'. Cusack-Smith had agreed to give the letter to Mataafa but the other Consuls objected to the letter being given to Mataafa with the ultimatum; it was therefore handed to him on board the *Katoomba* after he had surrendered. Fanny records that when the *Katoomba* returned to Apia on the morning of 19 July, RLS and Lloyd were 'the first aboard, and the only friendly faces the prisoners had seen'. Mataafa and ten of his chiefs were deported, first to Fakaofu atoll in the Tokelau Group, and then in November 1893 to Jaluit in the Marshall Islands under German control.

[1] A volume of sonnets by José Maria de Hérédia sent by James, who wrote to RLS on 8 June: 'In Paris was nothing nutritive save the sonnets of Hérédia, which decidedly I must send you: they are to me of a beauty so noble and a perfection so rare. They make the English muse (of the hour) seem (strange combination) both illiterate and dumb.'

[2] *The Decisions of the Lords of Council and Session from June 6th, 1678 to July 30th, 1712*, collected by the Honourable Sir John Lauder of Fountainhall. . . . (Edinburgh 1759–61). When asking

well, it hasn't much form, and is inexpressibly dreary, I should suppose, to others − and even to me for pages. It's like walking in a mine underground, and with a damned bad lantern, and picking out pieces of ore. This, and war, will be my excuse for not having read your (doubtless) charming work of fiction. The revolving year[3] will bring me round to it; and I know, when fiction shall begin to feel a little *solid* to me again, that I shall love it, because it's James. Do you know, when I am in this mood I would rather try to read a bad book? it's not so disappointing, anyway. And Fountainhall is prime, two big folio volumes, and all dreary, and all true, and all as terse as an obituary; and about one interesting fact on an average in twenty pages, and ten of them unintelligible from technicalities. There's literature, if you like! It feeds; it falls about you genuine like rain. Rain: nobody has done justice to rain in literature yet: surely a subject for a Scot. But then you can't do rain in that ledger-book style that I am trying for − or between a ledger-book and an old ballad. How to get over, how to escape from, the besotting *particularity* of fiction. 'Roland approached the house; it had green doors and window blinds; and there was a scraper on the upper step.' To hell with Roland and the scraper!

Yours ever affectionately

R.L.S.

The Bewildered, Ambitious Romancer,

engaged in cherishing

A Chimaera

Which will prove to be

A Bottle (in Italian).[4]

To S.R. Crockett

[*c. 15 August 1893*]   [*Vailima*]

Dear Mr Crockett, Thank you from my heart, and see, with what dull pedantry I have been tempted to extend your beautiful phrase of prose into three indifferent stanzas.[1] It may amuse you to know that *Weir of*

Baxter, on 16 April, to send him this book, RLS commented: 'I remember as a boy that there was some good reading there.'

[3] Cf. Shelley, 'Adonais' XVIII.

[4] A 'fiasco', derived from the Italian phrase *far fiasco* (literally to make a bottle), originally in the sense to break down or fail in a dramatic performance but later of general application.

[1] Crockett had dedicated the first edition of *The Stickit Minister and Some Common Men*: 'To/ Robert Louis Stevenson/of Scotland and Samoa,/I dedicate these stories/of that grey Galloway land,/where, about the graves of the martyrs,/the whaups are crying −/his heart has not forgotten how.' In the second edition (which he sent to RLS on 23 June) he added a long dedicatory letter reminding RLS of his promise in an earlier letter that if Crockett wrote something in the future, 'I'll read it every word.' Crockett later altered the last line of his dedication to accord with RLS's phrase − 'his heart remembers how'.

Hermiston (or *The Hanging Judge*, or whatever the mischief the name of it is going to be) actually centres about the gravestone of the *Praying Weaver of Balweary*. And when *Heathercat* is written, if ever it is, – O, well, there's another chance for the Societies.[2]

I have carried out my promise and read every word, and while some of your tales are a trifle light and one at least seems too slender and fantastic – qualities that rarely mingle well, the fantastic demanding considerable solidity of texture – the whole book breathes admirably of the soil. 'The Stickit Minister', 'The Heather Lintie', are two that recur to me particularly; they are *drowned* in Scotland, they have refreshed me like a visit home. Cleg is a delightful fellow; I enjoyed his acquaintance particularly, likewise that of the Junior Partner. By all accounts, you have described at least a possible descent for me in your fickle maiden; daft Elliot blood I have – And now it appears I may also have some of the tide of the Red Macgregors in my veins. So you see I am, by many directions, sib to your volume.[3]

I have to speak of Gavin Ogilvy, however; he and you are complementary. When I read your first page, the Stickit Minister ploughing, I knew I was in Scotland – and I knew I was not with Gavin Ogilvy. You are out-of-doors; he is within doors. You could die (and I think all the rest of us might be hanged) ere we could write the inimitable tragedy called 'The Glove' in the *Window*. That is great literature. But ask Barrie to do the scenery and atmosphere of your Stickit one, and where is he? Look at his flood in *The Little Minister*; it is pitiful. Do you believe in that island? No. No more do I. By different ways, ye shall attain. Might I just breathe in your lug, that Angus is raither a dreary pairt of the country? Yours very sincerely   Robert Louis Stevenson[4]

> Blows the wind today, and the sun and the rain are flying –
> Blows the wind on the moors today and now,
> Where about the graves of the martyrs the whaups are crying,
> *My* heart remembers how!

---

[2] I.e. the United Societies, generally known as the Cameronians, followers of Richard Cameron, an extreme group of Covenanters.

[3] RLS is commenting on some of the short stories making up the volume. Cleg Kelly is the hero of 'A Knight-Errant of the Streets' and 'The Progress of Cleg Kelly, Mission Worker'. Meg MacGregor, the heroine of 'A Midsummer Idyll', is said to combine the 'wild blood' of the MacGregors with that of the Border Elliots – 'So what could you expect of a lassie that had the daftness in her from both sides of the house.'

[4] RLS was later indignant that a substantial extract from this letter was published in the *Scotsman* on 8 November 1893, and a different extract was quoted in the *Bookman* for December 1893. The publisher T. Fisher Unwin printed the *Scotsman* extract from the letter in an advertisement for *The Stickit Minister* opposite the title page of Crockett's new novel *The Raiders*, published in March 1894.

Gray, recumbent tombs of the dead in desert places,
Standing Stones on the vacant, wine-red moor,
Hills of sheep, and the howes of the silent vanished races,
And winds, austere and pure!

Be it granted me to behold you again in dying,
Hills of home! and to hear again the call —
Hear about the graves of the martyrs the pee-wees crying,
And hear no more at all.[5]

To George Meredith

5 September 1893   *Vailima Plantation*

My dear Meredith, I have again and again taken up the pen to write to
you, and many beginnings have gone into the wastepaper basket. (I have
one now — for the second time in my life — and feel a big man on the
strength of it.) And no doubt it requires some decision to break so long a
silence. My health is vastly restored, and I am now living patriarchally in
this place six hundred feet above the sea on the shoulder of a mountain of
1500. Behind me, the unbroken bush slopes up to the backbone of the
island (3 to 4000) without a house, with no inhabitants save a few
runaway black boys, wild pigs and cattle, and wild doves and flying-foxes,
and many particoloured birds, and many black, and many white: a very
eerie, dim, strange place and hard to travel. I am the head of a household
of five whites, and of twelve Samoans, to all of whom I am the chief and
father; my cook comes to me and asks leave to marry — and his mother a
fine old chief woman, who has never lived here, does the same. You may
be sure I granted the petition. It is a life of great interest, complicated by
the Tower of Babel, that old enemy. And I have all the time on my hands
for literary work. My house is a great place; we have a hall fifty feet long
with a great redwood stair ascending from it, where we dine in state —
myself usually dressed in a singlet and a pair of trousers — and attended on
by servants in a single garment, a kind of kilt — also flowers and leaves —
and their hair often powdered with lime. The European who came upon
it suddenly would think it was a dream. We have prayers on Sunday night
— I am a perfect pariah in the island not to have them oftener, but the

---

[5] Crockett acknowledged RLS's letter on 13 September: 'Dear Master of Mine, Your beautiful
verses are heady like wine to me. That my phrase should have suggested them to you is beyond
my thought or hope.' The poem was later published in the *Pall Mall Gazette* of 12 December
1894 as 'Home Thoughts from Samoa' and in *Songs of Travel* XLV as 'To S. R. Crockett (On
receiving a Dedication)'. In verse 2, l. 3 of that and many subsequent editions 'howes' was
misread as 'homes'.

spirit is unwilling and the flesh proud, and I cannot go it more. It is strange to see the long line of the brown folk crouched along the wall with lanterns at intervals before them in the big shadowy hall, with an oak cabinet at one end of it and a group of Rodin's (which native taste regards as *prodigieusement leste*) presiding over all from the top – and to hear the long rambling Samoan hymn rolling up. God bless me, what style! But I am off business today, and this is not meant to be literature.

I have asked Colvin to send you a copy of *Catriona*, which I am sometimes tempted to think is about my best work.[1] I hear word occasionally of *The Amazing Marriage*. It will be a brave day for me when I get hold of it. Gower Woodseer is now an ancient, lean, grim, exiled Scot, living and labouring as for a wager in the tropics; still active, still with lots of fire in him, but the youth – ah, the youth where is it?[2] For years after I came here, the critics (those genial gentlemen) used to deplore the relaxation of my fibre and the idleness to which I had succumbed. I hear less of this now; the next thing is they will tell me I am writing myself out! and that my unconscientious conduct is bringing their gray hairs with sorrow to the dust.[3] I do not know – I mean I do know one thing. For fourteen years I have not had a day's real health; I have wakened sick and gone to bed weary; and I have done my work unflinchingly. I have written in bed, and written out of it, written in hemorrhages, written in sickness, written torn by coughing, written when my head swam for weakness; and for so long, it seems to me I have won my wager and recovered my glove. I am better now, have been rightly speaking since first I came to the Pacific; and still, few are the days when I am not in some physical distress. And the battle goes on – ill or well, is a trifle; so as it goes. I was made for a contest, and the Powers have so willed that my battlefield should be this dingy, inglorious one of the bed and the physic bottle. At least I have not failed, but I could have preferred a place of trumpetings and the open air over my head.

This is a devilish egotistical yarn. Will you try to imitate me in that if the spirit ever moves you to reply? And meantime be sure that away in the midst of the Pacific there is a house on a wooded island where the name of George Meredith is very dear, and his memory (since it must be no more) is continually honoured. Ever your friend

Robert Louis Stevenson

---

[1] Cassell's had been worried that the title *David Balfour* might lead to confusion with *Kidnapped* hence the decision that it be called *Catriona* in Britain; the original title was retained in the USA. The book was published in both countries on 1 September. RLS wrote to Mrs Sitwell in April 1894: 'I shall never do a better book than *Catriona*, that is my high-water mark.'

[2] Meredith had told RLS as early as 1879 that he was working on *The Amazing Marriage*; it was not completed and published until 1895. In the early chapters the character of Gower Woodseer is modelled on the youthful RLS.

[3] Cf. Genesis 42:38.

Remember me to Mariette,[4] if you please; and my wife sends her most kind remembrances to yourself. By the bye, I met Miss Shaw; but alas! her head seemed to be half-turned with adulation, and she would do nothing but discuss trenchantly social and intellectual problems.[5] So I had no use of her, nor even any trait of yourself to add to what I have.   R.L.S.

To W.F. Reynolds[1]

[*October 1893*]   *Sans Souci, Waikiki*[2]
W.F. Reynolds Esq.

Dear Sir, As I am still abominably out of sorts, I have taken the desperate step of chucking my Samoan Cook-boy⋆ at the head of total strangers! Can you find nobody who would be a guide to him. A boy of ten or so would be best; and I want him to see Punch Bowl, and the railway, and Pearl Lochs, and all the Raree Show. I am perfectly willing to pay for him in reason.

If you cannot help him to this, somebody that would take him out and bring him back sober; well, talk a little to him, an you love me! – and talk slow. Yours truly   Robert Louis Stevenson

⋆He is the bearer.

---

[4] Meredith's daughter.

[5] Flora Louise Shaw (1852–1929) began as an author of children's books but made her name as a special correspondent for *The Times* and as an acknowledged authority on colonial matters. She married (1902) Sir Frederick (later Lord) Lugard, the famous colonial administrator. As a young woman she was a neighbour and friend of George Meredith and through him met RLS at Bournemouth and again at Box Hill in August 1886. She recorded her meeting with RLS on board the *Mariposa* on the journey from Auckland to Apia in March 1893: 'One quarter hour, in which I saw gleams of his old self, was all I had. The worst to me was that when we met he showed little or no interest in the old topics. He seemed able or willing to talk only of Samoa. I could hardly escape from the reflection that he – so cosmopolitan – had after all become a bourgeois, and what is worse, a Samoan bourgeois' (E. Moberly Bell, *Flora Shaw*, 1947). Fanny had a different memory of the meeting. In her Prefatory Note to *St Ives* she bitterly recalled the 'lady journalist' who 'waylaid [RLS] for an interview in a draughty part of the ship, holding him with a monologue until he caught a heavy cold that kept him confined to his cabin until we reached the tropics'.

[1] A Honolulu businessman (died 1909), founder of the Golden Rule Bazaar.

[2] RLS accompanied Graham Balfour (who was returning to England) on the *S.S. Mariposa* to Honolulu and took Talolo with him. They reached Honolulu on 20 September and RLS went to stay at the Sans Souci hotel, a rambling beach hostelry about three miles outside the town. Talolo went down with measles as soon as they arrived; when he began to recover RLS himself was taken ill with fever. Fanny, alarmed by reports of his illness came to Honolulu to look after him and they went back together, reaching Samoa in early November.

To Sidney Colvin

[Late November 1893]   *[Vailima]*

My dear Colvin, This is disgraceful. I have done nothing; neither work
nor letters. I may say, I thought the reviews of *Catriona* beastly, and then
go to some news. First of all on the *Me* (May) day, we had a great
triumph; our Protestant boys, instead of going with their own villages and
families, went of their own accord in the Vailima uniform;[1] Belle made
coats for them on purpose to complete the uniform, they having bought
the stuff; and they were hailed as they marched in as the *Tama-ona* – the
rich man's children. This is really a score; it means that Vailima is publicly
taken as a family. Then we had my birthday feast a week late,[2] owing to
diarrhoea on the proper occasion. The Feast was laid in the Hall, and was
a singular mass of food; 15 pigs, 100lb beef, 100lb pork, and the fruit and
filigree in a proportion.[3] We had sixty horse posts driven in the gate
paddock; how many guests, I cannot guess, perhaps 150. They came
between three and four and left about seven. Seumanu gave me one of his
names;[4] and when my name was called at the *ava* drinking, behold it was
Au mai taua ma manu-vao! You would scarce recognise me, if you heard
me thus referred to!

   Two days after, we hired a carriage in Apia, Fanny, Belle, Lloyd and I
and drove in great style, with a native outrider, to the prison: a huge gift
of *ava* and tobacco under the seats. The prison is now under the *pule*[5] of
an Austrian, Captain Wurmbrand,[6] a soldier of fortune in Servia and

---

[1] The Apia 'May-meeting' when the inhabitants of eighteen neighbouring villages came together
to pay in their subscriptions to the Mission funds.

[2] MIS noted that the birthday feast was on 21 November.

[3] RLS gave more details to the journalist, W.H. Triggs:

> The feast was laid on the floor of the hall; fifty feet by about eight, of solid provisions, fifteen
> pigs cooked whole underground, two hundred pounds of beef, ditto of pork, two hundred
> pineapples, over four hundred head of *taro*, together with fish, chickens, Samoan prepared
> dishes, shrimps, oranges, sugar cane, bananas, biscuit and tinned salmon in a proportion. The
> biscuit and tinned salmon, though not exactly to our taste, are a favourite luxury of the
> Samoan. By night, and we sat down at four P.M., there was nothing left beyond a few
> oranges and a single bunch of bananas.

[4] RLS explained to Triggs that every Samoan chief had to have a *Tulafale* (speaking man) whose
main function was to call out the names at the *ava* drinking in a 'peculiar howl'. An important
chief was never 'called' under his own name but had another *ava* name for this purpose: 'I had
not only no *Tulafale*, I had no *ava* name. I was 'called' plain bald '*Tusitala*' or '*Ona*' which is only
a soubriquet at the best. Lloyd, after a competition picked a Vailima 'boy' as *Tulafale*. Then
Seumanu gave RLS one of his own names.

[5] Control or authority.

[6] Count Robert von Wurmbrand-Stuppach (1851–1911) appears to have been the black sheep of
an old Austrian noble family. Several of his brothers held distinguished positions at court or in
the Austrian army. He later stayed at Vailima for several months. In January 1894 RLS described

Turkey, a charming, clever, kindly creature, who is adored by '*his* chiefs'
(as he calls them) meaning *our* political prisoners. And we came in to the
yard, walled about with tinned iron, and drank *ava* with the prisoners and
the Captain. It may amuse you to hear how it is proper to drink *ava*.
When the cup is handed you, you reach your arm out somewhat behind
you, and slowly pour a libation, saying with somewhat the manner of
prayer, '*Ia taumafa e le Atua. Ua matagofie le fesilafa'iga ne'i.*' 'Be it (high
chief) partaken of by the God. How (high chief) beautiful to view is this
(high chief) gathering.' This pagan practice is very queer. I should say that
the prison *ava* was of that not very welcome form that we elegantly call
spit-*ava*; but of course there was no escape, and it had to be drunk. Fanny
and I rode home, and I moralised by the way. Could we ever stand
Europe again? did she appreciate that if we were in London, we should be
actually jostled on the street? and there was nobody in the whole of Britain
who knew how to take *ava* like a gentleman? 'Tis funny to be thus of two
civilisations – or, if you like, of one civilisation and one barbarism. And as
usual the barbarism is the more engaging. Colvin, you have to come here
and see us in our $\left.{{\text{mortal} \atop \text{native}}}\right\}$ spot. I just don't seem to be able to make up
my mind to your not coming. By this time, you will have seen Graham,
I hope, and he will be able to tell you something about us, and something
reliable. I shall feel for the first time as if you knew a little about Samoa
after that.

Fanny seems to be in the right way now; the doctor in Honolulu was
quite sure her whole history was Bright's disease, and treated her for
it with seemingly good results; he declares it explains every fact and
symptom; that though she can never recover, she may live long; and, to
her joy, that exercise, gardening, etc. are excellent for her. I must say she
is very, very well for her, and complains scarce at all.[7] Yesterday, she went
down *sola* (at least accompanied by a groom) to pay a visit. Belle, Lloyd
and I went a walk up the mountain road – the great public highway of the
island, where you have to go single file. The object was to show Belle that
gaudy valley of the Vaisingano which the road follows. If the road is to be
made and opened,[8] as our new Chief Justice promises, it will be one of the
most beautiful roads in the world. But the point·is this: I forgot I had been
three months in civilisation, wearing shoes and stockings, and I tell you I

the Count to his mother: 'He is a man of about my age, but looks rather older from exposure;
has been a rough rider and shepherd in Australia; and is an intensely excitable little man, with
the appearance of a bandit and the manners of a French Jack-in-the-box.'

[7] RLS told his mother in October that Fanny was 'in great form': 'But I *must* add she has to be
a great deal humoured these days; and is (at least not yet) not quite herself. I have no fear now
for the future, but I think it was a near touch.'

[8] RLS later added above this the comment: '(if you had seen these roads before they were made
etc.).'.

suffered on my soft feet: coming home, down hill, on that stairway of loose stones, I could have cried.

O yes, another story I knew I had. The house boys had not been behaving well, so the other night I announced a *fono*, and Lloyd and I went into the boys' quarters, and I talked to them I suppose for half an hour, and Talolo translated; Lloyd was there principally to keep another ear on the interpreter, else there may be dreadful misconceptions. I rubbed all their ears, except two whom I particularly praised; and one man's wages I announced I had cut down by one half. Imagine his taking this smiling! Ever since, he has been specially attentive and greets me with a face of really heavenly brightness. This is another good sign of their really and fairly accepting me as a chief. When I first came here, if I had fined a man a sixpence, he would have quit work that hour; and now I remove half his income, and he is glad to stay on – nay, does not seem to entertain the possibility of leaving. And this in the face of our particular difficulty – I mean our house in the bush, and no society, and no women society, within decent reach.

I think I must give your our staff in a tabular form.

	HOUSE:		KITCHEN:		OUTSIDE:
x°	Sosimo, Provost and butler, and my valet!	x°	Talolo, Provost and chief cook.	x°	Henry Simelē, Provost and overseer of
°	Misifolo, who is Fanny and Belle's chamberlain.	x°	Iopú, second cook. Tali, his wife, no wages. Ti'a, Samoan cook. Feiloa'i, his child, no wages, likewise no work, Belle's pet.		4 outside boys:– Lú Tasi Sele Maiele Púlú, who is also our talking man and cries the ava.
		x°	Leúelo, Fanny's boy, gardener, odd-jobs.		

IN APIA:
x Eliga, the daily errand man.

The crosses mark out the really excellent boys. Ti'a is the man who has just been fined half his wages; he is a beautiful old man, the living image of Fighting Gladiator, my favourite statue[9] – but a dreadful humbug. I

[9] The marble statue, now usually called the Borghese Warrior, by the Ephesian artist Agasias (of the late second or early first century B.C.) was discovered in Anzio, Italy, at the beginning of the seventeenth century and is now in the Louvre; many casts and copies have been made. It depicts a nude figure striding forward with his left arm outstretched to parry an attack from above, and his right hand clutching his sword.

think we keep him on a little on account of his looks. This sign ° marks those who have been two years or upwards in the family. I note all my old boys have the cross of honour, except Misifolo: well, well, poor dog, he does his best, I suppose. You should see him scour. It is a remark that has been often made by visitors: you never see a Samoan run, except at Vailima. Do you not suppose that makes me proud?

I say I thought the reviews beastly, but I must exclude two: the *Saturday* and Quiller-Couch.[10] The rest filled me with a sense of personal insult as no reviews ever did before: almost every one of them had a cut or a sneer, or an insinuation somewhere. And I comminated the band. But if the book sells, what matters it? I shall know in a day now. I am pleased to see what a success *The Wrecker* was, having already in little more than a year outstripped *The Master of Ballantrae.*

About *David Balfour* in two volumes: do see that they make it a decent looking book,[11] and tell me, do you think a little historical appendix would be of service? Lang bleats for one, and I thought I might address it to him as a kind of open letter.[12]

4 December

No time after all. Good-bye   R.L.S.

To Henry James

[c. *5 December 1893*]   [*Vailima*]

My dear Henry James, The mail has come upon me like an armed man three days earlier than was expected; and the Lord help me! it is impossible I should answer anybody the way they should be. Your jubilation over *Catriona* did me good, and still more the subtlety and truth of your remark on the starving of the visual sense in that book.[1] 'Tis true, and unless I

---

[10] The reviewer in the *Saturday Review* of 16 September 1893 of 'this very delightful book' picked out for special praise the portrayal of Barbara Grant. Arthur Quiller-Couch in 'First Thoughts on *Catriona*', in the *Speaker*, 9 September 1893 (reprinted in his *Adventures in Criticism*, 1896) praised Catriona: 'Everyone knew that Mr Stevenson would draw a woman beautifully as soon as he was minded', and looking at both *Kidnapped* and *Catriona* together as one story concluded that it was 'a very big feat – a gay and gallant tale'.

[11] When agreeing that Cassell's should publish *David Balfour* under the name *Catriona*, RLS also agreed that there should later be a two-volume edition of *Kidnapped* and *Catriona* under the general title of *The Adventures of David Balfour*. RLS sent back a revised copy of *Kidnapped* for this purpose. The edition was finally published in 1895.

[12] Lang's plea was made in the *Illustrated London News* of 16 September 1893.

[1] James wrote to RLS on 21 October 1893 a long letter in praise of *Catriona* – 'If it hadn't been for *Catriona* we couldn't, this year, have held up our head. It had been long, before that, since any decent sentence was turned in English.' In the course of it he wrote:

make the greater effort – and am, as a step to that, convinced of its necessity – it will be more true I fear in the future. I *hear* people talking, and I *feel* them acting, and that seems to me to be fiction. My two aims may be described as –

1st War to the adjective.

2nd Death to the optic nerve.

Admitted we live in an age of the optic nerve in literature. For how many centuries did literature get along without a sign of it? However I'll consider your letter.

How exquisite is your character of the critic in *Essays in London!*[2] I doubt if you have done any single thing so satisfying as a piece of style and of insight. Yours ever   R.L.S.

To Lord Rosebery[1]

5 November [actually December] 1893   *Vailima*

Dear Lord Rosebery, The book returns to you herewith with a *dédicace*, 'as effeirs'.[2] For your kind note, I can but thank you.[3] And what you say of the Lothians has pleased me beyond measure. I had always designed to make a book that should travel over and illustrate that beloved piece of country: beloved – and yet to me, except in the retrospect, almost hateful also. I have been vigorously unhappy there in old days – more unhappy than the death of all my friends, and a dose of leprosy to myself, could make me now; my father is dead; many of my friends are 'lapped in lead';[4]

> The one thing I miss in the book is the note of *visibility* – it subjects my visual sense, my *seeing* imagination, to an almost painful underfeeding. The *hearing* imagination, as it were, is nourished like an alderman, . . . so that I seem to myself . . . in the presence of voices in the darkness – voices the more distinct and vivid, the more brave and sonorous, as voices always are (but also the more tormenting and confounding) by reason of these bandaged eyes.

[2] James sent RLS on 5 August 1893 what he called 'a volume of thin trifles lately put forth by me and entitled *Essays in London and Elsewhere*'. RLS is referring to the essay, 'Criticism'.

[1] Archibald Philip Primrose, fifth Earl of Rosebery (1847–1929), Liberal statesman and author. He became Secretary of State for Foreign Affairs in August 1892 in Gladstone's administration and succeeded Gladstone as Prime Minister 1894–5. He was later disillusioned with political life and is now better remembered as a biographer and as a successful racehorse owner whose horses won the Derby three times. A warm admirer of RLS and his work, he took the chair at the meeting in Edinburgh in December 1896 to consider the question of a public memorial to RLS. RLS wrote several letters to Rosebery as Foreign Secretary about the political situation in Samoa and his relations with Cusack-Smith.

[2] In the proper way, in due form (a Scots legal phrase).

[3] Rosebery had written on 4 September asking RLS to inscribe a copy of *Catriona* for his children.

[4] A favourite quotation from Richard Barnfield, 'The Address to the Nightingale': 'King Pandion he is dead,/All thy friends are lapp'd in lead.' RLS quoted it in ch. 21 of *The Wrecker*; in his Valedictory Address to the Speculative Society in 1873 and in an article 'San Carlos Day' in the *Monterey Californian*, 11 November 1879.

and to return would be to me superlatively painful. Only I wish I could be buried there – among the hills, say on the head of Allermuir – with a table tombstone like a Cameronian.

Will you present my compliments to your youngsters, who I fear must have been sadly disappointed in the singularly grown up David? and believe me to be, Dear Lord Rosebery, Yours sincerely

Robert Louis Stevenson

The Earl of Rosebery
    K.G.

To Alison Cunningham

5 December 1893   *Vailima*

My dearest Cummy, This goes to you with a Merry Christmas and a Happy New Year. The Happy New Year anyway, for I think it should reach you about *Noor's Day*. I daresay it may be cold and frosty. Do you remember when you used to take me out of bed in the early morning, carry me to the back windows, show me the hills of Fife: and quote to me

> 'A' the hills are covered wi' snaw
> An' winter's noo come fairly?'[1]

There is not much chance of that here! I wonder how my mother is going to stand the winter. If she can it will be a very good thing for her. We are in that part of the year which I like the best: the Rainy or Hurricane Season. 'When it is good it is very, very good, And when it is bad it is horrid.' And our fair days are certainly fair like heaven; such a blue of the sea, such green of the trees, and such crimson of the hibiscus flowers, you never saw; and the air as mild and gentle as a baby's breath, and yet not hot!

The mail is on the move, and I must let up. With much love, I am, Your laddie   R.L.S.

To J.M. Barrie

[*Dictated to Belle*]
7 December 1893   *Vailima*

My dear Barrie, I have received duly the *magnum opus* and it really is a *magnum opus*. It is a beautiful specimen of Clark's printing, paper sufficient,

---

[1] Slightly misquoted from Burns, 'Up in the Morning Early', the chorus of which he says he took from an 'old song'.

and the illustrations all my fancy painted.[1] But the particular flower of the flock to whom I have hopelessly lost my heart is Tibby Birse. I must have known Tibby Birse when she was a servant's mantua maker in Edinburgh and answered to the name of Miss Broddie. She used to come and sew with my nurse, sitting with her leg crossed in a masculine manner; and swinging her foot emphatically, she used to pour forth a perfectly unbroken stream of gossip. I didn't hear it, I was immersed in far more important business with a box of bricks, but the recollection of that thin perpetual shrill sound of a voice has echoed in my ears sinsyne. I am bound to say she was younger than Tibby, but there is no mistaking that subtle indescribable and eminently Scottish expression.

I have been very much prevented of late, having carried out thoroughly to my own satisfaction two considerable illnesses, had a birthday, visited Honolulu, where politics are (if possible) a shade more exasperating than they are with us, and generally employed myself upon what I suppose must be my Father's business,[2] for at least it's not mine. I am told that it was just when I was on the point of leaving that I received your superlative epistle about the cricket eleven.[3] In that case it is impossible I should have answered it which is inconsistent with my own recollection of the fact. What *I* remember is that I sat down under your immediate inspiration and wrote an answer in every way worthy. If I didn't as it seems proved that I couldn't, it will never be done now. However I did the next best thing. I equipped my cousin Graham Balfour with a letter of introduction and from him, if you know how – for he is rather of the Scottish character – you may elicit all the information you can possibly wish to have as to us and ours. I believe you were also made a member of our great Temperance Society for the Consumption of Whiskey Punch,[4] and Balfour, who is perfectly qualified, will doubtless proceed to initiate you if he can find the chance and the punch. Do not be bluffed off by the somewhat stern and monumental first impression that he may make upon you. He is one of the best fellows in the world, and the same sort of fool that we are, only better looking, with all the faults of Vailimans and some of his own – I say nothing about virtues.

---

[1] A de-luxe, limited edition of *A Window in Thrums*, illustrated by W.B. Hole, 1892. RLS's copy with a long inscription by Barrie is at Yale.

[2] Cf. Luke 2:49.

[3] In his letter of 23 July 1893 (written in response to RLS's letter at p. 535), Barrie had given a humorous description of the Allahakbarries, the cricket club of which he was captain, formed from fellow-writers and other friends.

[4] On the journey to Honolulu on board the *S.S. Mariposa* in September 1893 RLS concocted a joke document setting up the *Mariposa Sanitary Association* extolling Temperance Principles and the virtues of Whiskey Punch and having as its motto, 'It's a long time between drinks', the phrase used by the Governor of North Carolina in the story. RLS was elected President, Balfour Vice-President and the 'Ordinary Members' included Barrie and Baxter.

I have lately been returning to my wallowing in the mire. When I was a child and indeed until I was nearly a man I consistently read Covenanting books. Now that I am a graybeard – or would be if I could raise the beard – I have returned and for weeks back have read little else but Wodrow, Walker, Shields,[5] etc. Of course this is with an idea of a novel; but in the course of it I made a very curious discovery. I have been accustomed to hear refined and intelligent critics – those who know so much better what we are than we do ourselves – those who tell us it is time to stop working in l and to work in b.c.[6] – trace down my literary descent from all sorts of people, including Addison, of whom I could never read a word.[7] Well, laigh i' your lug sir – the clue was found. My style is from the Covenanting writers. Take a particular case – the fondness for rhymes. I don't know of any English prose writer who rhymes except by accident, and then a stone had better be tied around his neck and himself cast into the sea.[8] But my Covenanting buckies rhyme all the time – a beautiful example of the unconscious rhyme above referred to.

Do you know, and have you really tasted, these delightful works? If not, it should be remedied. There is enough of the Auld Licht in you to be ravished.

I suppose you know that success has so far attended my banners – my political banners I mean – and not my literary. In conjunction with the three Great Powers I have succeeded in getting rid of My President and My Chief Justice. They're gone home, the one to Germany, the other to Souwegia. I hear little echoes of footfalls of their departing footsteps through the medium of the newspapers. Here is a flower: 'Is Robert Louis Stevenson in Apia, you ask? The reply given with a shrug of the shoulders is that he has been away to Honolulu. He went to Honolulu for a change. He is writing, I understand, writing novels. He also writes a great deal about me. I don't know why it is – what purpose he has. It may be something personal against me. I do not know. I know he has written against me in strong terms.' O Barrie! What an overflowing sneaking love I have for a rogue! And how little humour there is in the world that I should be prevented from taking this lovely villain to my bosom now when trouble is over and the battle won.

<hr />

[5] Robert Wodrow (1679–1734), the historian of the Covenanters; Patrick Walker wrote lives of the leading Covenanters first collected in *Biographia Presbyteriana*, 1827; Alexander Shields or Sheilds (1660–1700), a Covenanter, wrote, among other treatises, *A Hind Let Loose* (1687).

[6] The closing words of Barrie's rather patronising essay on RLS in *An Edinburgh Eleven* (1888) are: 'The great thing is that he should now give to one ambitious book the time in which he has hitherto written half a dozen small ones. He will have to take existence a little more seriously – to weave broadcloth instead of lace.'

[7] Lionel Johnson, reviewing *Island Nights' Entertainments* in the *Academy*, 3 June 1893, called RLS 'a modern Addison, with the old graces and the old humours'.

[8] Mark 9:42 and Luke 17:2

Whereupon I make you my salute with the firm remark that it is time to be done with trifling and give us a great book, and my ladies fall into line with me and pay you a most respectful courtesy, and we all join in the cry of 'Come to Vailima!'

My dear sir, your soul's health is in it. You will never do the great book, you will never cease to work in L. etc. till you come to Vailima

Robert Louis Stevenson

⋆*To Richard Le Gallienne*[1]

28 December 1893   *Vailima*

Dear Mr Le Gallienne, I have received some time ago, through our friend Miss Taylor, a book of yours.[2] But that was by no means my first introduction to your name. The same book had stood already on my shelves; I had read articles of yours in the *Academy*; and by a piece of constructive criticism (which I trust was sound) had arrived at the conclusion that you were 'Logroller'.[3] Since then I have seen your beautiful verses to your wife.[4] You are to conceive me, then, as only too ready to make the acquaintance of a man who loved good literature and could make it. I had to thank you, besides, for a triumphant exposure of a paradox of my own: the literary-prostitute disappeared from view at a phrase of yours – 'The essence is not in the pleasure but the sale'.[5] True: you are right, I was wrong; the author is not the whore, but the libertine; and yet I shall let the passage stand. It is an error, but it illustrated the truth for which I was contending, that literature – painting – all art, are no other than pleasures, which we turn into trades.

---

[1] Richard Thomas Le Gallienne (1866–1947), poet, journalist and *littérateur*. A friend of Wilde's and a contributor to *The Yellow Book*, Le Gallienne was a well-known literary figure of the Nineties. A great admirer of RLS, he wrote a much-quoted elegy on his death.

[2] *The Book-Bills of Narcissus* (1891).

[3] Le Gallienne wrote a literary column for the London evening paper the *Star* under the pseudonym 'Logroller'.

[4] 'To My Wife, Mildred' in *English Poems* (1892).

[5] In his signed review of *Across the Plains* in the *Academy* of 14 May 1892 (reprinted in the first volume of his *Retrospective Reviews*, 1896), Le Gallienne quoted RLS's comment in 'Letter to a Young Gentleman' that the artist worked mainly to please himself: 'To live by a pleasure is not a high calling: . . . it numbers the artist . . . along with dancing girls and billiard markers. The French have a romantic evasion for one employment, and call its practitioners the Daughters of Joy. The artist is of the same family, he is of the Sons of Joy, chose his trade to please himself, gains his livelihood by pleasing others, and has parted with something of the sterner dignity of man.' Le Gallienne pointed out that to call the artist, in effect, a spiritual prostitute was 'hardly true at all': 'For the essence of prostitution is not in the pleasure, but in the sale; and Mr Stevenson admits that the artist (when he does his real things . . .) works first to please himself . . . The idea of sale is but a second thought. . . . If either is of the Children of Joy, the writer or the reader, it is surely the reader; his is the barren pleasure . . .' As 'Logroller', Le Gallienne made the same point in almost the same words in the *Star* of 19 April 1892.

And more than all this, I had, and I have to thank you for the intimate loyalty you have shown to myself; for the eager welcome you give to what is good – for the courtly tenderness with which you touch on my defects. I begin to grow old; I have given my top note, I fancy; – and I have written too many books. The world begins to be weary of the old booth; and if not weary, familiar with the familiarity that breeds contempt. I do not know that I am sensitive to criticism, if it be hostile; I am sensitive indeed, when it is friendly; and when I read such criticism as yours, I am emboldened to go on and praise God.

You are still young, and you may live to do much. The little, artificial popularity of style in England tends, I think, to die out; the British pig returns to his vomit – to his true love, the love of the style-less, of the shapeless, of the slapdash and the disorderly. Kipling with all his genius, with all his Morrowbie Jukeses, and At-the-End-of-the-Passages, is still a move in that direction, and it is the wrong one.[6] There is trouble coming, I think; and you may have to hold the fort for us in evil days.

Lastly, let me apologise for the crucifixion that I am inflicting on you (*bien à contre-coeur*) by my bad writing. I was once the best of writers; landladies, puzzled as to my 'trade,' used to have their honest bosoms set at rest by a sight of a page of manuscript. – 'Ah,' they would say, 'no wonder they pay you for that'; – and when I sent it to the printers, it was given to the boys! I was about thirty-nine, I think, when I had a turn of scrivener's palsy; my hand got worse; and for the first time, I received clean proofs. But it has gone beyond that now. I know I am like my old friend James Payn, a terror to correspondents; and you would not believe the care with which this has been written. Believe me to be, very sincerely yours   Robert Louis Stevenson

Richard Le Gallienne, Esq.

To Sidney Colvin

[c. *28 December 1893*]   [*Vailima*]

My dear Colvin, One page out of my picture book, I must give you. Fine burning day: half past two P.M. We four begin to rouse up from reparatory slumbers, yawn, and groan, get a cup of tea, and miserably dress: we have had a party the day before, Xmas Day, with all the boys absent but one, and latterly two; we had cooked all day long, a cold dinner; and lo! at two our guests began to arrive, though dinner was not till six; they were

---

[6] The reference is to two short stories by Kipling: 'The Strange Ride of Morrowbie Jukes' in *Wee Willie Winkie* (1889) and 'At the End of the Passage' in *Life's Handicap* (1891).

sixteen, and fifteen slept the night and breakfasted; Haggard I regret to say
drank too much and kept the six men in Lloyd's house awake till 3 A.M.
Conceive then, how unwillingly we climb on our horses and start off in
the hottest part of the afternoon to ride $4^1/_2$ miles, attend a native feast in
the gaol, and ride four and a half miles back. But there is no help for it.
I am a sort of father of the political prisoners, and have *charge d'âmes* in that
riotously absurd establishment, Apia gaol. The twenty-three (I think it is)
chiefs act as under gaolers. The other day they told the Captain of an
attempt to escape. One of the lesser political prisoners the other day
effected a swift capture, while the Captain was trailing about with the
warrant; the man came to see what was wanted; came, too, flanked by the
former jailor; my prisoner offers to show him the dark cell, shoves him in,
and locks the door. 'Why do you do that?' cries the former jailer. 'A
warrant,' says he. Finally, the chiefs actually feed the soldiery who watch
them! The jail is a wretched little building, containing a little room, and
three cells, on each side of a central passage; it is surrounded by a fence of
corrugated iron, and shows, over the top of that, only a gable end with the
inscription, *O le Fale Puipui*.[1] It is on the edge of the mangrove swamp,
and is reached by a sort of causeway of turf. When we drew near, we saw
the gates standing open and a prodigious crowd outside – I mean prodigious for Apia, perhaps a hundred and fifty people. The two sentries at
the gate stood to arms passively, and there seemed to be a continuous
circulation inside and out. The Captain came to meet us; our boy, who
had been sent ahead was there to take the horses; and we passed inside the
court which was full of food, and rang continuously to the voice of the
caller of gifts; I had to blush a little later when my own present came, and
I heard my one pig and eight miserable pineapples being counted out like
guineas. In the four corners of the yard and along one wall, there are
makeshift, dwarfish, Samoan houses or huts, which have been run up since
Captain Wurmbrand came, to accommodate the chiefs. Before that they
were all crammed into the six cells, and locked in for the night, some of
them with dysentery. They are wretched constructions enough; but sanctified by the presence of chiefs. We heard a man corrected loudly today
for saying '*Fale*' of one of them; '*Maota*,' roared the highest chief present
– 'palace'. About eighteen chiefs gorgeously arrayed stood up to greet us
and led us into one of these *maotas*, where you may be sure we had to
crouch, almost to kneel, to enter, and where a row of pretty girls occupied
one side to make the *ava (kava)*.[2] The highest chief present was a magnificent man, as high chiefs usually are; I find I cannot describe him; his face
is full of shrewdness and authority, his figure like Ajax; his name Auĭlŭa.

[1] Samoan for prison.
[2] Here and later RLS added the word '*kava*' above the original word '*ava*' perhaps as being the
more familiar word.

He took the head of the building and put Belle on his right hand. Fanny was called first for the *ava* (*kava*). Our names were called in English style, the high-chief wife of Mr St (an unpronounceable something); Mrs Straw, and the like. And when we went into the other house to eat, we found we were seated alternately with chiefs about the – table, I was about to say, but rather floor. Everything was to be done European style with a vengeance! We were the only whites present, except Wurmbrand, and still I had no suspicion of the truth. They began to take off their *ulas* (necklaces of scarlet seeds) and hang them about our necks; we politely resisted, and were told that the King (who had stopped off their *siva*) had sent down to the prison a message to the effect that he was to give a dinner tomorrow, and wished their second-hand *ulas* for it. Some of them were content; others not. There was a ring of anger in the boy's voice, as he told us we were to wear them past the King's house. Dinner over, I must say they are moderate eaters at a feast, we returned to the *ava* house; and then the curtain drew suddenly up upon the set scene. We took our seats, and Auiluᷓ began to give me a present, recapitulating each article as he gave it out, with some appropriate comment. He called me several times 'their only friend', said they were all in slavery, had no money, and these things were all made by the hands of their families – nothing bought; he had one phrase, in which I heard his voice rise up to a note of triumph: 'This is a present from the poor prisoners to the rich man.' Thirteen pieces of *tapa*, some of them surprisingly fine, one I think unique; thirty fans of every shape and colour; a *kava* cup etc., etc. At first Auiluᷓ conducted the business with weighty gravity; but before the end of the thirty fans, his comments began to be humorous. When it came to a little basket, he said: 'Here was a little basket for Tusitala to put sixpence in, when he could get hold of one' – with a delicious grimace. I answered as best I was able through a miserable interpreter; and all the while, as I went on, I heard the crier outside in the court calling my gift of food, which I perceived was to be Gargantuan. I had brought but three boys with me. It was plain that they were wholly overpowered. We proposed to send for our gifts on the morrow; but no, said the interpreter, that would never do, they must go away today, Mulinuu must see my porters taking away the gifts, – 'make em jella,' quoth the interpreter. And I began to see the reason of this really splendid gift; one half, gratitude to me – one half, a wipe at the King.

And now, to introduce darker colours, you must know this visit of mine to the jail was just a little bit risky; we had several causes for anxiety; it *might* have been put up, to connect with a Tamasese rising[3] – Tusitala

---

[3] Tupua Tamasese Lealofi (died 1915), son of the former German puppet-king, himself became a contender for the kingship. His followers, first in the Aana district and later in the Atua district raised rebellions in 1894.

and his family would be good hostages; on the other hand, there were the Mulinuu people all about. We could see the anxiety of Captain Wurmbrand, no less anxious to have us go, than he had been to see us come; he was deadly white and plainly had a bad headache, in the noisy scene. Presently, the noise grew uproarious; there was a rush at the gates (a rush *in*, not a rush *out*),[4] where the two sentries still stood passive; Aŭilŭa leaped from his place (it was then that I got the name of Ajax for him) and the next moment we heard his voice roaring and saw his mighty figure swaying to and fro in the hurly-burly. As the deuce would have it, we could not understand a word of what was going on. It might be nothing more than the ordinary 'grab racket' with which a feast commonly concludes; it might be something more. We made what arrangements we could for my *tapa*, fans, etc., as well as for my five pigs, my masses of fish, *palusamis*,[5] *taro*, etc.; and with great dignity and ourselves laden with *ulas* and other decorations, passed between the sentries among the howling mob to our horses. All's well that ends well. Owing to Fanny and Belle, we had to walk; and, as Lloyd said, 'he had at last ridden in a circus'. The whole length of Apia we paced our triumphal progress; past the King's palace, past the German Firm at Sogi – you can follow it on the map – amidst admiring exclamations of '*Manaia*' – beautiful – it may be rendered, 'O my! ain't they dandy' – until we turned up at last into our road as the dusk deepened into night. It was really exciting. And there is one thing sure: no such feast was ever made for a single family, and no such present ever given to a single white man. It is something to have been the hero of it. And whatever other ingredients there were, undoubtedly gratitude was present. As money value I have actually gained on the transaction!

[c. *1 January 1894*]

Your note arrived; little profit, I must say. Scott has already put his nose in, in *St Ives*, sir; but his appearance is not yet complete;[6] nothing is in that romance, except the story. I have to announce, that I am off work probably for six months. I must own that I have overworked bitterly – overworked – there, that's legible. My hand is a thing that was; and in the meanwhile so are my brains. And here in the very midst, comes a plausible scheme to make Vailima pay, which will perhaps let me into considerable expense just when I don't want it. You know the vast cynicism of my

---

[4] Added in the margin.
[5] A Samoan delicacy: coconut cream mixed with sea-water and wrapped in young *taro* leaves.
[6] In his letter of 1 December 1893 Colvin asked: 'Couldn't you let Scott walk across the stage in one or other of your 1812 novels?' In ch. 10 of the novel, St Ives and the two drovers are overtaken by a 'tall, stoutish, elderly gentleman' on a hill pony accompanied by his daughter on horseback. The drover Sim later identifies him as 'The Shirra, man! A' body kens the Shirra!'

view of affairs, and how readily (and as some people say) with how much gusto, I take the darker view? Well, I am going to ask you if you could make arrangements to pay your insurances[7] *next year*, or till I get my pen in hand again? If this be too inconvenient, let me know. And at any rate, the fear with which I view this year will likely prove chimerical.

Why do you not send me Jerome K. Jerome's paper, and let me see *The Ebb-Tide* as a serial?[8] It is always very important to see a thing in different presentments. I want every number. Politically we begin the new year with every expectation of a bust in two or three days: a bust which may spell destruction to Samoa. I have written to Baxter about his proposal.[9]

*To W.B. Yeats[1]

14 April 1894								*Vailima*

Dear Sir, Long since when I was a boy I remember the emotions with which I repeated Swinburne's poems and ballads. Some ten years ago, a

[7] RLS had been paying Colvin's annual insurance premium for several years (see p. 405, n. 9). On 29 November 1893 Baxter wrote: '... this morning arrives the notice of Colvin's insurance premium £137.15/–. Is this to go on for ever? It did not seem extraordinary at first when Colvin was in trouble but he seems to acquiesce now in leaving this as a fixed charge on you – Is it to be so? ... I suppose I must pay it this year but really –.' Lloyd wrote to Balfour, 14 October 1895: 'Louis was intensely annoyed to find that this loan had become a thing of permanency and that he had been paying Colvin a hundred a year until shortly before his death. It required my strongest efforts to prevent him breaking with Colvin forthwith. He called him all sorts of names, and covered him with reproaches. Really it was only my stand that prevented a rupture that would have alienated both for ever'. This story later became distorted into an allegation that Colvin had appropriated money from RLS's royalties.
[8] Jerome K. Jerome (1859–1927), author and journalist, who won great popular success with *Three Men in a Boat* (1889). In 1892 he was one of the founders of the *Idler* and a year later he founded the twopenny weekly magazine *To-day* which he edited until 1897. *The Ebb-Tide* was serialised in its first thirteen issues, 11 November 1893–3 February 1894. In his letter Colvin called him 'That little (not ill-meaning) cad of a cockney humourist and literary caterer for people with aspirations but not aspirates.'
[9] RLS wrote to Baxter on 1 January 1894, welcoming his proposal for a collected edition – the Edinburgh Edition – of his works. He put forward detailed comments on the contents and arrangement of the volumes. He wrote:

I am particularly pleased with this idea of yours because I am come to a dead stop. I never can remember how bad I have been before, but at any rate I am bad enough just now – I mean as to literature; in health I am well and strong. I take it I shall be six months before I'm heard of again, and this time I could put in to some advantage in revising the text and (if it were thought desirable) writing prefaces.

[1] William Butler Yeats (1865–1939) was a regular contributor to the *Scots Observer* and the *National Observer,* and 'The Lake Isle of Innisfree' first appeared in the latter on 13 December 1890. It was reprinted in *The Book of the Rhymers' Club* (1892) and *The Countess Kathleen* (1892). Yeats acknowledged this letter on 24 October 1894, expressing his 'great pleasure' at RLS's praise and promising to send him his next work, *The Shadowy Waters.*

similar spell was cast upon me by Meredith's 'Love in the Valley'; the
stanzas beginning 'When her mother tends her' haunted me and made me
drunk like wine; and I remember waking with them all the echoes of the
hills about Hyères. It may interest you to hear that I have a third time
fallen in slavery: this is to your poem called 'The Lake Isle of Innisfree'.
It is so quaint and airy, simple, artful and eloquent to the heart – but I seek
words in vain. Enough that 'always night and day I hear lake water lapping
with low sounds on the shore', and am, Yours gratefully

Robert Louis Stevenson

To Sidney Colvin

[24 or 25 April 1894]   *[Vailima]*

My dear Colvin, This is the very day the mail goes, and I have as yet
written you nothing. But it was just as well – as it was all about my 'blacks
and chocolates',[1] and what of it had relation to whites you will read some
of in *The Times*. It means as you will see that I have at one blow quarrelled
with *all* the officials of Samoa, the Foreign Office, and I suppose her
Majesty the Golden with milk and honey blest.[2] But you'll see in *The
Times*.[3] I am very well indeed but just about dead and mighty glad the
mail is near here, and I can just give up all hope of contending with my
letters, and lie down for the rest of the day. These *Times* letters are not
easy to write. And I dare say the Consuls say, 'Why, then, does he write
them?'

---

[1] Colvin wrote to RLS on 21 March 1894:

> Do these things interest you at all: or do any of our white affairs? I could remark in passing
> that for three letters or more you have not uttered a single word about anything but your
> beloved blacks – or chocolates – confound them; beloved no doubt to you; to us detested,
> as shutting out your thoughts, or so it often seems, from the main currents of human affairs,
> and oh so much less interesting than any dog, cat, mouse, house, or jenny-wren of our own
> known and hereditary associations, loves and latitudes. Forgive this 'expectoration', as your
> German friends would call it; it comes from the heart; and please let us have a letter or two
> with something besides native politics, prisons, *kava* feasts, and such things as our Cockney
> stomachs can ill assimilate.

[2] Cf. J.M. Neale's hymn 'Jerusalem the Golden' (1858) translated from the Latin of St Bernard of
Cluny.

[3] A long letter by RLS, dated 23 April, was published in *The Times* of 2 June 1894. He strongly
criticised the fact that, contrary to the provisions of the Berlin Treaty, the Consular Triumvirate
rather than the two Treaty officials, were effectively in control. He summarised the story of
Mataafa's defeat and deportation and pleaded for leniency towards the twenty-seven followers
still in jail, who were not even being fed by the Government. He contrasted all this with the
more lenient behaviour of the three Consuls towards the rebellion, early in 1894, by Tupua
Tamasese Lealofi and his followers, and the continued failure to take action against 'the bestial
practice of head-hunting'.

I had miserable luck with *St Ives*; being already half-way through it, a book I had ordered six months ago arrives at last, and I have to change the first half of it from top to bottom! How could I have dreamed the French prisoners were watched over like a female charity school, kept in a grotesque livery, and shaved twice a week?[4] And I had made all my points on the idea that they were unshaved and clothed anyhow. However this last is better business; if only the book had come when I ordered it! *À propos*, many of the books you announce don't come as a matter of fact. When they are of any value it is best to register them.

Your letter, alas! is not here; I sent it down to the cottage[5] with all my mail for Fanny; on Sunday night a boy comes up with a lantern and a note from Fanny, to say the woods are full of Atuas,[6] and I must bring a horse down that instant, as the posts are established beyond her on the road and she does not want to brave the fight going on between us. Impossible to get a horse, so I started in the dark on foot, with a revolver, and my spurs on my bare feet, leaving directions that the boy should mount after me with the horse. Try such an experience on Our Road once, and do it if you please after you have been down town from nine o'clock till six, on board the ship-of-war lunching, teaching Sunday School (I actually do) and making necessary visits, and the Saturday before, having sat all day from half past six to half past four scriving at my *Times* letter. About half way up, just in fact at 'point' of the outposts I met Fanny coming up. Then all night long, I was being wakened with scares that really should be looked into, though I *knew* there was nothing in them and no bottom to the whole story, and the drums and shouts and cries from Tanugamanono and the town keeping up an all night corybantic chorus in the moonlight – the moon rose late – and the searchlight of the warship in the harbour, making a jewel of brightness as it lit up the bay of Apia in the distance. And then next morning about eight o'clock, a drum coming out of the woods and a party of patrols who had been in the woods on our left front (which is our true rear) coming up to the house, and meeting there another party who had been in the woods on our right $\left\{ \begin{matrix} \text{front} \\ \text{rear} \end{matrix} \right\}$ which is Vaea Mountain, and forty-three of them being entertained to *ava* and biscuits on the verandah, and marching off at last in single file for Apia. Briefly, it is not much wonder if your letter and my whole mail was left

[4] RLS had received from Scribner's *Les Prisonniers de Cabrera: Mémoires d'un Conscrit de 1808* (Paris, 1892). In it Louis François Gille described the dress and routine of French prisoners of war at Portchester near Portsmouth.

[5] In August 1893 RLS had bought a piece of land from their neighbour, F.W. Christian, when he left Samoa. It was called Vanu Manutagi (the vale of crying birds); RLS and Fanny had a cottage there.

[6] Supporters of Tupua Tamasese in the district of Atua were on the verge of rebellion. Fighting broke out a few months later.

at the cottage, and I have no means of seeing or answering particulars. The whole thing was nothing but a bottomless scare; it was *obviously* so; you couldn't make a child believe it was anything else; but it has made the Consuls sit up, whereat I rejoice. My own private scares were really abominably annoying; as for instance after I had got to sleep for the ninth time perhaps – and that was no easy matter either, for I had a crick in my neck so agonising that I had to sleep sitting up – I heard noises as of a man being murdered in the boys' house. To be sure, said I, this is nothing again, but if a man's head were being taken, the noises would be the same! So I had to get up, stifle my cries of agony from the crick, get my revolver, and creep out stealthily to the boys' house. And there were two of them sitting up, keeping watch of their own accord like good boys, and whiling the time over a game of Sweepia (Casino[7] – the whist of our islanders) – and one of them was our champion idiot, Misifolo, and I suppose he was holding bad cards, and losing all the tens – and these noises were his humorous protests against Fortune!

Well, excuse this excursion into my 'blacks or chocolates'. It is the last. You will have heard from Lysaght how I failed to write last mail. The said Lysaght seems to me a very nice fellow, we were only sorry he could not stay with us longer.[8] Austin Strong came back from school last week, which made a great time for the Amanuensis, you may be sure.[9] He seems rather improved I think. Then on Saturday, the *Curaçoa* came in – same commission, with all our old friends; and on Sunday, as already mentioned, Austin and I went down to service and had lunch afterwards in the wardroom. The officers were awfully nice to Austin; they are the most amiable ship in the world; and after lunch we had a paper handed round on which we were to guess, and sign our guess, of the number of leaves on the pineapple; I never saw this game before but it seems it is much practised in the Queen's Navee. When all have betted, one of the party begins to strip the pineapple head, and the person whose guess is farthest out has to pay for the sherry. My equanimity was disturbed by shouts of the *American Commodore*, and I found that Austin had entered and lost about a bottle of sherry! He turned with great composure and addressed me: 'I am afraid I must look to you, Uncle Louis.' The Sunday School racket is only an experiment which I took up at the request of the late American Land Commissioner; I am trying it for a month, and if I do as ill as I believe, and the boys find it only half as tedious as I do, I think it

[7] A card game (played in *Sense and Sensibility*) in which the ten of diamonds counts as two points.

[8] The Irish poet and novelist Sidney Royse Lysaght (died 1941) paid a brief visit to Vailima in March 1894, bearing a letter of introduction from George Meredith.

[9] Austin Strong returned from San Francisco on 19 April. He later went to school in New Zealand and then trained there as a landscape architect. He eventually became a successful playwright with plays such as *Seventh Heaven* (1927). He died in 1952.

will end in a month. I have *carte blanche*, and say what I like; but does any single soul understand me? Ugh![10]

Fanny is on the whole very much better. Lloyd has been under the weather, and goes for a month to the South Island of New Zealand for some skating, save the mark! I get all the skating I want among officials. They are a bad lot, I say so boldly: By-ends is their family name;[11] I never more specifically despised the politician for what I believed to be his character, as I do now that I know him from actual, tactual handling – an oily, ugly, false reptile. About him, he commands an atmosphere of falsity, and his one eye is fixed on an appointment.

Dear Colvin, please remember that my life passes among my 'blacks or chocolates'. If I were to do as you propose, in a bit of a tiff, it would cut you entirely off from my life. You must try to exercise a trifle of imagination, and put yourself, perhaps with an effort, into some sort of sympathy with these people, or how am I to write to you? I think you are truly a little too Cockney with me.[12] Your letters are now brought up; I should like well enough to see some of the novels.[13] Please tell Mr Blumenthal[14] that for my part I consent with all my heart, but that part of my business has gone wholly into C.B.'s hands, and he'll have to apply to

---

[10] Henry Clay Ide had returned to Samoa as the new Chief Justice in November 1893, accompanied by his three daughters, Adelaide, Annie and Marjorie, who were great favourites at Vailima. RLS's experiences at Eunice Large's Sunday School were short-lived. Miss Large remembered that on the third Sunday he offered sixpence to any boy who would ask a question; not until half-a-crown was offered did he get one. According to Mrs Bourke Cockran (Annie Ide) the question was, 'Who made God?': 'He said it was worth the half-crown but effectively ended his career as a missionary.' In the complete edition (VII, 385), this anecdote is wrongly linked to an earlier occasion in October 1892 when RLS gave an address at the Sunday School.

[11] RLS was no doubt thinking of Mr By-ends (from the Town of Fair-speech) in *The Pilgrim's Progress*. 'By-end' is a subordinate end or aim, especially a secret selfish purpose.

[12] Colvin replied on 10 June:

> I want to say that I am very anxious of having been, and being, a beast, in much of what I write to you: and to ask you and Fanny to read between the lines and not let yourselves be hurt by any of my *boutades*. Writing across half the planet is a horrid difficult job, at best: the glance of the eye is wanting, and the tone of the voice, to make all right when the words are cutting . . . but please remember, both of you, always to put down anything that reads horribly to the mere clumsiness of an over-anxious affection . . . As to that particular *boutade* about the natives and your correspondence, please forgive: . . . I suppose I had been disappointed at there being nothing about yourself, or your work, or the books I had sent you, for two whole letters – not a word about anything except politics and prisoners: and I suppose I have a trick of biting phrases . . . And please write just whatever comes into your head – provided you do write – only giving a preference if you can manage it, to the answering of questions, especially when they are of a business or editorial nature.

[13] In his letter Colvin asked whether RLS would be interested in seeing 'the latest fashion of home fiction – the books written by women' such as George Egerton's *Keynotes*.

[14] Jacques Blumenthal (1829–1908), composer of songs, had presumably asked for permission to set one or more of RLS's poems to music. In forwarding his letter Colvin referred to him as 'a very kind old friend and experienced musician'.

him for the permission, and perhaps pay for it, I don't know; *je m'en suis lavé les mains*. By the bye, do you think you give me much news, whether of blacks or whites? Because, if so, you are deceived.

Adieu, I conceive your miserable embarrassments:[15] conceive some of mine. Ever yours   Robert Louis Stevenson

To Charles Baxter
(Slightly Abridged)

[*First part dictated to Belle*]
[*18 May 1894*]   [*Vailima*]

My dear Charles, I have received Melville's report and the very encouraging documents that he encloses.[1] It would really seem to be going ahead. I am sending Colvin some copy. And I have no doubt he will see to my having proofs in time. But the point is now that the Edinburgh Edition takes shape, that I should try to tell you what I really feel about it. In the first place, don't put in any trash. I would rather die than have *The Pentland Rising* foisted upon any reader as my idea of literature. See my letter this mail to Colvin.[2] In the second place, my dear fellow, I wish to assure you of the greatness of the pleasure that this Edinburgh Edition gives me. I suppose it was your idea to give it that name. No other would have affected me in the same manner. Do you remember, how many years ago I would be afraid to hazard a guess, one night when I was very drunk indeed and communicated to you certain 'intimations of early death' and aspirations after fame? I was particularly maudlin; and my remorse the next morning on a review of my folly has written the matter very deeply in my mind; from yours it may easily have fled. If anyone at that moment could have shown me the Edinburgh Edition, I suppose I should have died. It is with gratitude and wonder that I consider 'the way in which I have

---

[15] In his letter Colvin had referred obliquely to the death (on 27 January 1894) of the Revd Albert Sitwell. RLS wrote to Mrs Sitwell: 'To you, I have little to say about the Vicar's death; it was something late, is all my comment.' Colvin also mentioned the uncertainties over his possible appointment as Director of the National Gallery; he did not get the post.

[1] Andrew Patterson Melville (1867–1938) was apprenticed to Mitchell and Baxter; he became a W.S. in 1896. He had sent RLS a report (with copies of letters) of the arrangements being made with the various publishers of his books.

[2] RLS wrote to Colvin on the same day: 'I heartily abominate and reject the idea of reprinting *The Pentland Rising*. For God's sake let me get buried first.' Later in the letter, rejecting two other stories, he added: 'Think of having a new set of type cast, paper specially made etc. in order to set up rubbish that is not fit for the *Saturday Scotsman*. It would be the climax of shame.' A month later he wrote to Baxter giving him and Colvin 'a free hand': 'I even take back the restrictions announced in my last. It is to be your edition. Please yourselves. And this not only from humility, which I sincerely feel, but from a sense of what is possible and what is not at so great an interval of posts.' *The Pentland Rising* duly appeared in the *Juvenilia* volume of the Edinburgh Edition.

been led'. Could a more preposterous idea have occurred to us in those days when we used to search our pockets for coppers, too often in vain, and combine forces to produce the threepence necessary for two glasses of beer, or wander down the Lothian Road without any, than that I should be well and strong at the age of forty-three in the island of Upolu, and that you should be at home bringing out the Edinburgh Edition? If it had been possible, I should have almost preferred the Lothian Road Edition, say, with a picture of the old Dutch smuggler on the covers.

I have now something heavy on my mind. I had always a great sense of kinship with poor Robert Fergusson – so clever a boy, so wild, of such a mixed strain, so unfortunate, born in the same town with me, and, as I always felt rather by express intimation than from evidence, so like myself. Now the injustice with which the one Robert is rewarded and the other left out in the cold sits heavy on me, and I wish you could think of some way in which I could do honour to my unfortunate namesake. Do you think it would look like affectation to dedicate the whole edition to his memory? I think it would. The sentiment which would dictate it to me is too abstruse; and besides I think my wife is the proper person to receive the dedication of my life's work. At the same time – it is very odd, it really looks like transmigration of souls – I feel that I must do something for Fergusson; Burns has been before me with 'The Gravestone'. It occurs to me you might take a walk down the Canongate and see in what condition the stone is.[3] If it be at all uncared for, we might repair it and perhaps add a few words of inscription.

I must tell you, what I just remembered in a flash as I was walking about dictating this letter – there was in the original plan of *The Master of Ballantrae* a sort of introduction describing my arrival in Edinburgh on a visit to yourself and your placing in my hands the papers of the story. I actually wrote it and then condemned the idea as being a little too like Scott, I suppose. Now I must really find the MS and try to finish it for the E.E. It will give you, what I should so much like you to have, another corner of your own in that lofty monument.[4]

Suppose we do what I have proposed about Fergusson's monument. I wonder if an inscription like this would look arrogant.

This stone originally erected by Robert Burns, has been repaired at the charges of Robert Louis Stevenson and is by him re-dedicated to the Memory of Robert Fergusson as the gift of one Edinburgh lad to another.

---

[3] Baxter replied on 11 July that he had been to the Canongate and found that Fergusson's tombstone was 'in perfect preservation and kept freshly painted'.

[4] Colvin later claimed that the MS of this Preface had been lost and he was therefore unable to include it in *The Master of Ballantrae*. He eventually published it (from RLS's draft) in the Appendix volume.

In spacing this inscription I would detach the names of Fergusson and Burns but leave mine in the text;[5] or would that look like sham modesty and is it better to bring out the three Roberts?

I shall send – no, come to think of it, I send now with some blanks which I may perhaps fill up ere the mail goes, a dedication to my wife. It was not intended for the E.E. but for *The Justice-Clerk* when it should be finished, which accounts for the blanks.

To my wife[6]
I dedicate
This Edinburgh Edition of my works.

I see rain falling and the rainbow drawn
On Lammermuir; hearkening, I hear again
In my precipitous city beaten bells.
Winnow the keen sea wind;[7] and looking back
Upon so much already endured and done
From then to now – reverent, I bow the head!

Take thou the writing; thine it is. For who
Burnished the sword, blew on the drowsy coal,
Held still the target higher, chary of praise
And prodigal of counsel[8] – who but thou?
So now, in the end, if this the least be good,
If any deed be done, if any fire
Burn in the imperfect page, the praise be thine!

[9]See, for business remarks, my letter to Melville. I am really concerned about the American affair. Do you suppose I could have six[10] copies of the E.E. for myself? I mean that I should like to give one to my wife, one to Lloyd, and one to the Amanuensis. With a small edition like that I think they will turn out to be – I was about to say portable property but the phrase is hardly descriptive of a twenty vol. edition – real estate will perhaps better express my idea. I should like to, and I suppose it could easily be done, to have six sets marked in every copy, say, on the false title: 'To my wife' on one; 'To Lloyd Osbourne. *Quorum pars magna fuit*'[11] on

---

[5] The rest of the sentence is in RLS's hand.

[6] The next two lines were added later by RLS.

[7] The rest of this line and the next two lines were evidently added later by RLS in the blank left by Belle.

[8] RLS added 'censure?' as an alternative reading in the margin.

[9] RLS deleted the following sentence: 'Well, I shall see about this before the mail goes. It don't seem the right thing for the purpose somehow.' Colvin advised against publishing the poem in the general dedication and in its final form it was published, with Fanny's approval, as the dedication to *Weir of Hermiston* (1896).

[10] RLS altered Belle's 'three' to 'six'.

[11] 'Of which he had a large share' – Virgil, *Aeneid*, II. 6.

the second; 'To Isobel Strong my Amanuensis. *Filiae amicae grataeque*'[12] on the third; 'To Sidney Colvin. *Te, Palinure!*'[13] or should it be '*Tibi, Palinure*'? on the fourth; 'To Robert Alan Mowbray Stevenson. *Olim Arcades ambo.*'[14] on the fifth; and for the sixth, which I mean to be your ain, sir, I would put 'To Charles Baxter. *Amicus amico.*'[15] These six sets may I suppose be thrown off in addition to the thousand copies; and they will form something of real value for the six of you to keep. And if I'm ever to spend money this is the occasion. . . .

[RLS takes over]

. . . *St Ives* still plods along; not at an alarming rate, but still so as probably to be in hand erelong. I had miscounted a little and we have no more than 70,000 words. Perhaps you had better consider an application to Scribner's about the American rights? To continue: 70,000 is only about half what a three volumineer should run to; and whether it will run out or not in the sequel, is an anxious thought to me. I had miscalculated by counting Belle's page 250 words, and I find it only 200; strange that so little a difference should make up so much in the total! I have been delayed in *St Ives* by native bothers, and a certain preliminary clearing of decks involved in the E.E.; but it will go on. . . .   R.L. Stevenson

To Bob Stevenson
(Abridged)

[17 June 1894]   *[Vailima]*

My dear Bob, I must make out a letter this mail or perish in the attempt. All the same I am deeply stupid, in bed with a cold, deprived of my amanuensis, and conscious of the wish but not the furnished will. You may be interested to hear how the family inquiries go. It is now quite certain that we are a second-rate lot, and came out of Cunningham or Clydesdale, therefore *British* folk; so that you are Cymry on both sides – and I Cymry and Pict. We may have fought with King Arthur and known Merlin. . . .[1]

So much, though all inchoate, I trouble you with: knowing that you, at least, must take an interest in it. So much is certain of that strange Celtic

---

[12] 'To my dear and charming daughter'.

[13] 'To thee, Palinurus' – *Aeneid*, VI. 341. Palinurus was Aeneas's pilot.

[14] 'Once we were Arcadians together': RLS significantly added *Olim* to Virgil's phrase from *Eclogues*, VII. 4.

[15] 'A friend to a friend'.

[1] I have omitted a summary by RLS of his attempts to trace their Stevenson ancestry and, in the following paragraph, a family tree.

descent, that the past has an interest from it apparently gratuitous, but fiercely strong. I wish to trace my ancestors a thousand years, if I trace them by gallowses. It is not love, not pride, not admiration; it is an expansion of the identity, intimately pleasing, and wholly uncritical; I can expend myself in the person of an inglorious ancestor with perfect comfort; or a disgraced, if I could find one. I suppose, perhaps, it is more to me who am childless, and refrain with a certain shock from looking forwards. But I am sure, in the solid grounds of race, that you have it also in some degree. . . .

Enough genealogy. I do not know if you will be able to read my hand. Unhappily Belle, who is my amanuensis, is out of the way on other affairs and I have to make the unwelcome effort. (O, this is beautiful, I am quite pleased with myself.) Graham has just arrived last night[2] (my mother is coming by the other steamer in three days) and has told me of your meeting. The same report, the best talker that God ever made! But he said you looked a little older than I did; so that I suppose we keep step fairly on the downward side of the hill. He thought you looked harassed; and I could imagine that too. I sometimes feel harassed. I have a great family here about me: a great anxiety. The loss (to use my grandfather's expression), the 'loss' of our family is that we are disbelievers in the morrow – perhaps I should say, rather, in next year. The future is *always* black to us; it was to Robert Stevenson; to Thomas; I suspect, to Alan; to R.A.M.S., it was so almost to his ruin in youth; to R.L.S., who had a hard hopeful strain in him from his mother, it was not so much so once, but becomes daily more so. Daily so much more so that I have a painful difficulty in believing I can ever finish another book or that the public will ever read it.

I have so huge a desire to know exactly what you are doing, that I suppose I should tell you what I am doing by way of an example. I have a room now, a part of the twelve-foot verandah sparred in, at the most inaccessible end of the house. Daily, I see the sunrise out of my bed, which I still value as a tonic, a perpetual tuning fork, a look of God's face once in the day. At six my breakfast comes up to me here, and I work till eleven. If I am quite well, I sometimes go out and bathe in the river before lunch, twelve. In the afternoon I generally work again, now alone drafting, now with Belle dictating. Dinner is at six, and I am often in bed by eight. This is supposing me to stay at home. But I must often be away, sometimes all day long, sometimes till twelve, one or two at night; when you might see me coming home to the sleeping house – sometimes in a trackless darkness, sometimes with a glorious tropic moon, everything

---

[2] Graham Balfour (who had travelled from England with MIS) arrived from New Zealand on 16 June. He left in October on a visit to Fiji and a long cruise in the Islands.

drenched with dew – unsaddling and creeping to bed; and you would no longer be surprised that I live out in this country, and not in Bournemouth – in bed.

My great recent interruptions have (as you know) come from politics. Not much in my line, you will say. But it is impossible to live here and not feel very sorely the consequences of the horrid white mismanagement. I tried standing by and looking on, and it became too much for me. They are such *illogical* fools; a logical fool, in an office, with a lot of red tape, is conceivable. Furthermore, he is as much as we have any reason to expect of officials, a thoroughly commonplace, unintellectual lot. But these people are wholly on wires; laying their ears down, skimming away, pausing as though shot, and presto! full spread on the other tack. I observe in the official class mostly an insane jealousy of the smallest kind as compared to which the artist's is a grave, modest character – the actor's, even; a desire to extend his little authority and to relish it like a glass of wine, that is *impayable*. Sometimes, when I see one of these little kings strutting over one of his victories – wholly illegal, perhaps, and certain to be reversed to his shame if his superiors ever heard of it – I could weep. The strange thing is that they *have nothing else*. I auscultate them in vain; no real sense of duty, no real comprehension – no real attempt to comprehend, no wish for information – you cannot offend one of them more bitterly than by offering information, though it is certain that you have *more*, and obvious that you have *other*, information than they have; and talking of policy! they could not play a better stroke than by listening to you, and it need by no means influence their action.[3] *Tenez*, you know what a French post office or railway official is? That is the diplomatic card to the life. Dickens is not in it; caricature fails.

All this keeps me from my work and gives me the unpleasant side of the world. When your letters are disbelieved it makes you angry, and that is rot; and I wish I could keep out of it with all my soul. But I have just got into it again, and farewell, peace!

My work goes along but slowly. I have got to a crossing place, I suppose; the present book *Saint Ives*, is nothing – it is in no style, in particular, a tissue of adventures, the central character not very well done, no philosophic pith under the yarn, and in short, if people will read it, that's all I ask – and if they won't, damn them! I like doing it, though; and if you asked me why! After that I am on *Weir of Hermiston* and *Heathercat*, two Scotch stories, which will either be something different or I shall have failed. The first is generally designed, and is a private story of two or three characters in a very grim vein. The second, alas the thought! is an attempt

---

[3] RLS deleted the continuation of this sentence and the next: 'by that. I did not know how stupid men were.'

at a real historical novel to present a whole field of time; the race – our own race – the west land and Clydesdale blue bonnets – under the influence of their last trial, when they got to a pitch of organisation in madness that no other peasantry has ever made an offer at. I was going to call it *The Killing Time*, but this man Crockett has forestalled me in that.[4] Well, it'll be a big smash if I fail in it; but a gallant attempt. All my weary reading as a boy, which you remember well enough, will come to bear on it, and if my mind will keep up to the point it was in a while back, perhaps I can pull it through.

For two months past, Fanny, Belle, Austin (her child), and I, have been alone; but yesterday, as I mentioned, Graham Balfour arrived, and on Wednesday my mother and Lloyd will make up the party to its full strength.[5] I wish you could drop in for a month or a week – or two hours. That is my chief want. On the whole it is an unexpectedly pleasant corner I have dropped into for an end of it, which I would scarcely have foreseen from Wilson's shop[6] or the Princes Street Gardens or the Portobello Road. Still I would like to hear what my *alter ego* thought of it; and I would sometimes like to have my old *maitre ès arts* express an opinion on what I do. I put this very tamely, being on the whole a quiet elderly man; but it is a strong passion with me, though intermittent. I believe in the Chrono-thairmal[7] Theory of All Diseases – and all Eases, also. Now, try to follow my example and tell me something about yourself, Louisa, the Bab,[8] and your work – and kindly send me some specimens of what you're about. I have only seen one thing by you – about Notre Dame in the *Westminster* or *St Jingo*[9] since I left England – now I suppose six years ago.

I have looked this trash over, and it is not at all the letter I want to write you – not truck about officials, ancestors, and the like rancidness – but you have to let your pen go in its own broken-down gait, like an old butcher's pony, stop when it pleases, and go on again as it will. Ever, my dear Bob, your affectionate cousin   R.L. Stevenson

---

[4] The *Bookman* for May 1894 reported that Crockett was to contribute to *Good Words* a serial story called *The Killing Time*. Crockett later changed the title to *The Men of the Moss Hags*.

[5] MIS left Sydney on 11 June on the *S.S. Monowai*; Lloyd joined the ship at Auckland on 16 June and they arrived in Apia on Thursday 21 June. MIS recorded that RLS could not meet her in Apia because of his cold.

[6] The tobacconist's shop in Edinburgh which RLS made his headquarters.

[7] Presumably a joke adaptation of the word 'chronothermal' (relating to time and temperature); 'thairm' is a Scots word (used by Burns) meaning belly or intestines.

[8] Bob's son, Thomas Alan Humphrey, born 21 April 1893 (he died in 1971). MIS had seen him as soon as she arrived in London in April 1893.

[9] 'The Devils of Notre Dame', a descriptive article by Bob to accompany drawings by Joseph Pennell, appeared in the *Pall Mall Budget*, 14, 21, 28 December 1893; collected in a limited de-luxe edition in February 1894.

To J.M. Barrie

[*Beginning dictated to Belle*]
13 July 1894   *Vailima*

My dear Barrie, This is the last effort of an ulcerated conscience. I have been so long owing you a letter, I have heard so much of you, fresh from the press, from my mother and Graham Balfour, that I have to write a letter no later than today or perish in my shame. But the deuce of it is, my dear fellow, that you write such a very good letter that I am ashamed to exhibit myself before my junior (which you are after all) in the light of the dreary idiot I feel. Understand that there will be nothing funny in the following pages. If I can manage to be rationally coherent, I shall be more than satisfied.

In the first place I have had the extreme satisfaction to be shown that photograph of your mother.[1] It bears evident traces of the hand of an amateur. How is it that amateurs invariably take better photographs than professionals? I must qualify invariably. My own negatives have always represented a province of chaos and old night in which you might dimly perceive fleecy spots of twilight, representing nothing; so that, if I am right in supposing the portrait of your mother to be yours, I must salute you as my superior. Is that your mother's breakfast? Or is it only afternoon tea? If the first, do let me recommend to Mrs Barrie to add an egg to her ordinary. Which, if you please, I will ask her to eat to the honour of her son, and I am sure she will live much longer for it, to enjoy his fresh successes. I never in my life saw anything more deliciously characteristic. I declare I can hear her speak. I wonder my mother could resist the temptation of your proposed visit to Kirriemuir, which it was like your kindness to propose. By the way, I was twice in Kirriemuir, I believe in the year '77, when I was going on a visit to Glenogil.[2] It was Kirriemuir, was it not? I have a distinct recollection of an inn at the end – I think the upper end – of an irregular open place or square, in which I always see your characters evolve. But, indeed, I did not pay much attention; being all bent upon my visit to a shooting-box, where I should fish a real trout-stream, and I believe preserved. I did too, and it was a charming stream, clear as crystal, without a trace of peat – a strange thing in Scotland – and alive with trout; the name of it I cannot remember, it was something like the Queen's River, and in some hazy way connected with memories of

---

[1] Evidently the basis of the engraving forming the frontispiece of Barrie's *Margaret Ogilvy* (1896).
[2] MIS recorded in her 1871 diary that RLS visited Glenogil (ten miles north-east of Barrie's birthplace of Kirriemuir) to stay with the Leveson Stewarts 1–11 September. This was John Leveson Douglas Stewart (1842–87). The year '77 given in the letter may well be Belle's mistake.

Mary Queen of Scots.[3] It formed an epoch in my life, being the end of all my trout-fishing; I had always been accustomed to pause and very laboriously to kill every fish as I took it. But in the Queen's River I took so good a basket that I forgot these niceties; and when I sat down, in a hard rain shower, under a bank, to take my sandwiches and sherry, lo and behold, there was the basketful of trouts still kicking in their agony.

I had a very unpleasant conversation with my conscience. All that afternoon I persevered in fishing, brought home my basket in triumph, and sometime that night, 'in the wee sma' hours ayont the twal',[4] I finally forswore the gentle craft of fishing. I daresay your local knowledge may identify this historic river; I wish it could go farther and identify also that particular Free Kirk in which I sat and groaned on Sunday.[5] While my hand is in I must tell you a story. At that antique epoch you must not fall into the vulgar error that I was myself ancient. I was, on the contrary, very young, very green, and (what you will appreciate, Mr Barrie) very shy. There came one day to lunch at the house two very formidable old ladies – or one very formidable, and the other what you please – answering to the honoured and historic name of the Miss Carnegie Arbuthnotts of Balnamoon.[6] At table I was exceedingly funny, and entertained the company with tales of geese and bubbly-jocks. I was great in the expression of my terror for these bipeds, and suddenly this horrid, severe, and eminently matronly old lady put up a pair of gold eyeglasses, looked at me awhile in silence, and pronounced in a clangorous voice her verdict. 'You give me very much the effect of a coward, Mr Stevenson!' I had very nearly left two vices behind me at Glenogil: fishing and jesting at table. And of one thing you may be very sure, my lips were no more opened at that meal.

[*RLS takes over*]
29 July

No, Barrie, 'tis in vain they try to alarm me with their bulletins. No doubt you're ill and unco ill[7] I believe; but I have been so often in the same case that I know pleurisy and pneumonia are in vain against Scotsmen who can write. (I once could.) You cannot imagine probably how near me this common calamity brings you. *Ce que j'ai toussé dans ma vie!* How often and how long have I been on the rack at night and learned

---

[3] This must have been Noran Water, which flows through the estate. A local historian recorded a tradition that one of Scotland's queens washed her linen cap in the Noran and pronounced it the clearest stream in Scotland.

[4] 'Some wee, short hour ayont the *twal*' (i.e. twelve, midnight), in the last verse of Burns, 'Death and Doctor Hornbook'.

[5] Barrie identified the Free Kirk as being at Memus, five miles north-east of Kirriemuir.

[6] Anne Carnegy-Arbuthnott (1817–72) and her sister Helen (1819–92), daughters of James Carnegy-Arbuthnott, 8th Laird of Balnamoon.

[7] Barrie's serious illness in May and June 1894 was the subject of daily reports in the newspapers.

to appreciate that noble passage in the Psalms when somebody or other is said to be more set on something than they 'who dig for hid treasure – yea, than those who long for the morning'[8] – for all the world, as you have been racked and you have longed. Keep your heart up, and you'll do. Tell that to your mother, if you are still in any danger or suffering. And by the way, if you are at all like me – and I tell myself you are very like me – be sure there is only one thing good for you, and that is the sea in hot climates. Mount, sir, into 'a little frigot'[9] of 5000 tons or so, and steer peremptorily for the tropics; and what if the ancient mariner, who guides your frigot, should startle the silence of the ocean with the cry of land ho! – say when the day is dawning – and you should see the turquoise mountain tops of Upolu coming hand over fist above the horizon? Mr Barrie, sir, 'tis then there would be larks! The fatted bottle should be immediately slain in the halls of Vailima. And though I cannot be certain that our climate would suit you (for it does not suit some), I am sure as death the voyage would do you good – would do you *Best* – and if Samoa didn't do, you needn't stay beyond the month, and I should have had another pleasure in my life, which is a serious consideration for me. I take this as the hand of the Lord preparing your way to Vailima – in the desert, certainly – in the desert of Cough and by the ghoul-haunted woodland[10] of Fever – but whither that way points there can be no question – and there will be a meeting of the twa Hoasting Scots Makers in spite of fate, fortune and the Devil. *Absit omen.*

My dear Barrie, I am a little in the dark about this new work of yours:[11] what is to become of me afterwards? You say carefully – methought anxiously – that I was no longer me when I grew up? I cannot bear this suspense: what is it? It's no forgery? And AM I HANGIT? These are the elements of a very pretty lawsuit which you had better come to Samoa to compromise. I am enjoying a great pleasure that I had long looked forward to, reading Orme's *History of Indostan;*[12] I had been looking out for it everywhere; but at last, in four volumes, large quarto, beautiful type and page, and with a delectable set of maps and plans, and all the names of the places wrongly spelled – it came to Samoa like Barrie. I tell you frankly you had better come soon. I am sair failed a'ready; and what I may be if you continue to dally, I dread to conceive. I may be speechless; already, or at least for a month or so, I'm little better than a teatoller – I beg

---

[8] Cf. Psalm 130:6 and Job 3:21.
[9] Spenser, *The Faerie Queen*, II.vi.7, l. 9.
[10] Poe, 'Ulalume', l. 9 (and elsewhere). Cf. p. 345.
[11] *Sentimental Tommy* (1896). Barrie had written on 4 February 1894 about his ideas for basing his boy hero on RLS; in the event, the character owed more to Barrie's own childhood.
[12] [Robert Orme], *A History of the Military Transactions of the British Nation in Indostan, from the Year MDCCXLV* (2 vols, 1763, 1768).

pardon a tea-totaller. It is not exactly physical, for I am in good health, working four or five hours a day in my plantation, and intending to ride a paper-chase next Sunday – ay, man, that's a fact and I havena had the hert to break it to my mother yet – the obligation's poleetical, for I am trying every means to live well with my German neighbours – and, O! Barrie, but it's no easy! I think they are going to annex; and that's another reason to hurry up your visit, for if the Herrs come I'll have to leave. They are such a stiff-backed and sour-natured people: people with permanent hot coppers,[13] scouring to find offence, exulting to take it. To be sure there are many exceptions. And the whole of the above must be regarded as private – strickly private. Breathe it not in Kirriemuir, tell it not to the daughters of Dundee! What a nice extract this would make for the daily papers! and how it would facilitate my position here! An idea: suppose you printed it on the fly-leaf of your next book?[14] It might conciliate or at least distract the critics; me, it would distract with a vengeance; and it is quite in the practice of contemporary Scots Letters. 'The Professional Etiquette of Scottish Authors; being a handbook of the Courtesy and Chivalry practised by Scottish Authors among themselves: with an Appendix (315 pp.) on the Art of Advertisement by ——' ay, by whom? He went up like a crocket and came down like a stick. Not but what I thought his first book decidedly good, and was well pleased with the dedication, and was fool enough to tell him so in verses – which he is good enough to publish for me,[15] and his publisher (at least) to describe in a manner hardly to be reconciled with fact. Well, well, *Tantae ne irae?*[16] (is that right?).

5 August

To recover myself from these waters of bitterness. This is Sunday, the Lord's Day. 'The hour of attack approaches'.[17] And it is a singular consideration what I risk; I may yet be the subject of a tract, and a good tract too – such as one which I remember reading with recreant awe and rising hair in my youth, of a boy who was a very good boy, and went to Sunday Schule, and one day kipped[18] from it, and went and actually bathed, and was dashed over a waterfall, and he was the only son of his

---

[13] A slang phrase meaning a mouth or throat parched by excessive drinking. It is used by Huish in ch. 11 of *The Ebb-Tide*.

[14] A reference to the publication of part of his letter to Crockett opposite the title page of *The Raiders* (see p. 558, n. 4).

[15] The *Bookman* for December 1893 and April 1894 had reported that RLS's poem to Crockett was to be published in a new illustrated edition of *The Stickit Minister*. Crockett had informed his publisher (T. Fisher Unwin) that RLS had sent the poem for publication in the next edition.

[16] Cf. Virgil, *Aeneid*, I. 11: *Tantaene animis caelestibus irae?* Why such great anger in those heavenly minds?

[17] Matt's song in John Gay, *The Beggar's Opera*, II. 2.

[18] Played truant (Scots).

mother, and she was a widow.[19] A dangerous trade, that, and one that I have to practise. I'll put in a word when I get home again, to tell you whether I'm killed or not. 'Accident in the (Paper) Hunting Field: death of a notorious author. We deeply regret to announce the death of the most unpopular man in Samoa, who broke his neck at the descent of Magiagi, from the misconduct of his little raving lunatic of an old beast of a pony. It is proposed to commemorate the incident by the erection of a suitable pile. The design (by our local architect, Mr Walker) is highly artificial, with a rich and voluminous Crockett at each corner, a small but impervious Barrie'er at the entrance, an arch at the top, an Archer of a pleasing but solid character at the bottom; the colour will be genuine William-Black; and Lang, lang may the ladies sit wi' their fans in their hands!'[20] Well, well, they may sit as they sat for me, and little they'll reck, the ungrateful jauds! Muckle they cared about Tusitala when they had him! But now ye can see the difference; now, leddies, ye can repent, when ower late, o' your former cauldness and what ye'll perhaps allow me to ca' your *tepeedity*! He was beautiful as the day, but he's by wi' it! And perhaps, as he was maybe gettin' a wee thing fly-blawn, its nane too shune.

Monday 6 August

Well, sir, I have escaped the dangerous conjunction of the widow's eldest son and the Sabbath Day. We had a most enjoyable time and Lloyd and I were 3 and 4 to arrive; I will not tell here what interval had elapsed between our arrival and the arrival of 1 and 2; the question, sir, is otiose and malign; it deserves, it shall have no answer.[21] And now without further delay to the main purpose of this hasty note. We received and we have already in part distributed the gorgeous fahbrics of Kirriemuir. Whether from the splendour of the robes themselves, or from the direct nature of the compliments with which you had directed us to accompany the presentation, one young lady blushed as she received the proofs of your munificence. Her position however was delicate. Her father, an ambitious, loud, hearty, dull, man, comparable to a second-class Yorkshire Squire, desired her to be united with Lloyd – and still desires.[22] Gifts of all kinds literally besiege our portals; the last one was an (entire) Bull; some

[19] Luke 7:12.

[20] The ballad 'Sir Patrick Spens'.

[21] RLS told Colvin that the distance was about fifteen miles and that he felt himself 'about seventeen again, a pleasant experience'. Because it was held on a Sunday the exploit upset the missionaries: 'I am now a pariah among the English . . . Mrs Clarke, the missionary's wife, gave me it hot; far from disagreeably, but therefore the more effective. I must not go again . . .'

[22] RLS told Balfour in January 1893 about Lloyd's involvement with a Samoan girl, Sosifina, the daughter of Fono at the nearby village of Tanugamanono. He refused to marry her but a new 'chief's house' had been built for her in the village.

say however, it is an ox; opinions halt. Strange that there should be dubiety on a point so vital and conspicuous! It is white, anyway; that you may take on the authority of Tusitala; whether or not it is really *faalavelave* (delicious Samoan expression: lit, *hindered*) will require a closer inspection. In the course of these negotiations, the young lady herself was sent to call; she found it very embarrassing, and we found her very pretty, and the (ahem!) towel was presented with becoming words, and she blushed. Bad ink, and the dregs of it at that, but the heart in the right place, still very cordially interested in my Barrie, and wishing him well through his sickness, which is of the body, and long defended from mine, which is of the head and by the impolite might be described as idiocy. The whole head is useless, and the whole bottom painful: reason, the recent Paper Chase.

> There was racing and chasing in Vailele plantation,[23]
> And vastly we enjoyed it,
> But alas! for the state of my foundation,
> For it wholly has destroyed it.

Come, my mind is looking up. The above is wholly impromptu. On oath.   Tusitala

I le susuga
   a le alii Pali★   (★Barrie)
      i lona maota i Tilimula★   (★Kirriemuir)
         i Secotia
            Ua latalata ani i Lonetona[24]

12 August 1894

And here, Mr Barrie, is news with a vengeance. Mother Hubbard's dog is well again – what did I tell you? Pleurisy, pneumonia, and all that kind of truck is quite unavailing against a Scotchman who can write – and not only that, but it appears the perfidious dog is married.[25] This incident, so far as I remember, is omitted from the original epic –

> She went to the graveyard
> To see him get him buried,
> And when she came back
> The Deil had got married.

---

[23] Cf. 'There was racing and chasing on Cannobie Lee'. See p. 548, n. 7.

[24] To Mr Barrie, in his estate at Kirriemuir, in Scotland, near London.

[25] Barrie married Mary Ansell (1862–1950), the actress who had appeared in his play *Walker, London*, on 9 July 1894. She had helped to nurse him through his illness. They were divorced in 1909.

It now remains to inform you that I have taken what we call here 'German offence' at not receiving cards, and that the only reparation I will accept is that Mrs Barrie shall incontinently upon the receipt of this Take and Bring you to Vailima in order to apologise and be pardoned for this offence. The commentary of Tamaitai upon the event was brief but pregnant: 'Well, it's a comfort our guest-room is furnished for two.'

This letter, about nothing, has already endured too long. I shall just present the family to Mrs Barrie – Tamaitai, Tamaitai Matua, Teuila, Pelema, Loia, and with an extra low bow, Yours   Tusitala

★*To W.E. Henley*[1]

15 July 1894   *Vailima*

My dear lad, Man is born to trouble as the sparks fly upward,[2] and truly you have your share. It is strange, but I don't seem to have mine, or not yet: there is a good time coming, I suppose. My only serious annoyance is that, with the cards on my side, I have failed to die at the happy moment, and I begin to look forward with alarm to old age and the time when I shall be writing later Wilkie Collins, not to say *Knights of Malta*.[3] But you get it thick and hard, like a December rain with a gale behind it. I am sure you have more verses in you, and I am sure they will be fine when they come. You and Meredith and Yeats are the only people I would have singing, and not the present Meredith, but the singer of 'Love in a Valley'. Yeats I mention, though I may say I do not know his work; but all the snatches that have come my way are very tuneful and genuine; and one piece, 'The Lake Isle of Innisfree', has simply refused to leave my memory: 'And always, day and night, I hear lake water lapping with low sounds on the shore.' How good that spondee is! It is almost a discovery of modern prosody what a good effect is to be got of the English spondee.

About the *Pilgrim's Progress*, I would gladly do it. And I will tell you what my trouble is.[4] I have many engagements, every day I work more slowly, and I am easily appalled and panicked when I think on what I have before me. Please can you manage to let it lie in the meanwhile. When I have *St Ives*, and the *Justice-Clerk*, and my *Grandfather* off my mind, I may be able to attend to Bunyan, but not now – now I could not bear to think of any other burden.

---

[1] Henley wrote a long, friendly letter to RLS on 22 May telling him that he had lost the editorship of the *National Observer* and gossiping about literary matters and his own activities.
[2] Job 5:7.
[3] *The Siege of Malta*, Scott's unfinished novel.
[4] Henley asked whether RLS would be prepared to edit *The Pilgrim's Progress* for a new edition of 'English Classics', published by Methuen, of which he was general editor.

Marcel Schwob has been something of my correspondent, but he does not come out in correspondence, and remains for me a very shadowy figure; very clever though. Did you see his *Mimes*? One piece there, 'Hermes psychagôgos', is a nailer.[5] You would have liked to do it in verse. The young men keep coming and coming; for the most part, they are no great matter; but since you and I began, Barrie and Kipling and Bourget have arisen, and G.M. gets £1200 for a novel,[6] and Stevenson's complete works are advertised, so there are changes too that deserve mention and remembrance. What ails you at poor Crockett? He seems to me not without parts from what I have seen of him.[7] But you know I was always inclined to be a merciful and hopeful critic, except to poor George Eliot. Well, she died, and was none the worse for my opinion, nor aware of it, for she put her feet in hot water and did not read reviews, in both of which I daresay she was very right, but she lost a lot of fun, and would have made a poor customer to Romeike.[8] Soon, soon must we also follow where there is no more scribbling, and the plaudits and the hisses and the chiefs-of-works and the failures are all one.

For this is the end of all things, of all things under the sky,
To love a little, to work a little, and then to arise and die.

Impromptu – or remembered. A commonplace at least, and the pun a work of genius. Ever sincerely yours   Robert Louis Stevenson

To Charles Baxter
(Slightly Abridged)

[c. 15 July 1894]   [Vailima]

My dear Baxter, I have received the balloon books from your bookseller, and I must say he is a daisy. I could not have chosen better myself. I desire you to communicate to him this certificate of merit. I would write it to him but cannot for my soul recollect his name.[1]

Your great success over the Edition leaves me gaping. Hip, hip, hurray![2]

[5] Marcel Schwob (1867–1905), French essayist and critic and author of a number of imaginative tales; he also wrote scholarly studies on Villon and the language of his time.
[6] Henley told RLS that Meredith was being paid £1200 for the serialisation of *Lord Ormont and his Aminta* in the *Pall Mall Magazine*.
[7] Henley's generally unfavourable review of Crockett's *The Raiders* in the *National Observer* of 17 March 1894 was mainly devoted to criticism of the way in which his publishers had used RLS's praise of *The Stickit Minister* in a private letter as a means of promoting sales of the new book.
[8] Henry Romeike established his press-cutting agency in London in 1881.
[1] Baxter was ordering books from George P. Johnston, an Edinburgh bookseller, The hero of *St Ives* escapes from Edinburgh by balloon.
[2] Baxter wrote to RLS on 15 June announcing that the Edinburgh Edition (comprising 1000 sets of 20 volumes sold to subscribers at 12/6 per volume) had been sold, save for 100 sets reserved for the Colonies.

[*Belle takes over*]

Allow me to congratulate you on the return to duty of the Amanuensis. 'Tis a damned good thing for you and me. I do not quite understand what you mean by the Astor bargain. Does it mean £22.10 for a thousand words? If it does, it means a big deal.[3]

I have still to expect explanations about my American publisher, but I hope to hear next mail and to be satisfied. The eight sets will do me admirably – you must have already received my disposition of (I think) six of them. The exact number I do not remember. But if I am right, the seventh must go to my mother with the dedication: To My Mother.

Well, I don't know what I want in the way of this dedication. Colvin might help. I want something to express (in Latin) that I am her only son and that these are her grandchildren. I know it can be well said in Latin, but not by me, who have not so much as a Latin grammar to aid my stumbling steps.

I have had a letter from Henley, which I thought in very good taste and rather touching. My wife, with that appalling instinct of the injured female to see mischief, thought it was a letter preparatory to the asking of money; and truly, when I read it again, it will bear this construction. This leads us direct to the consideration of what is to be done if H. does ask for money. I may say at once that I give it with a great deal of distaste. He has had bad luck of course; but he has had good luck too and has never known how to behave under it. On the other hand I feel as if I were near the end of my production. If it were nothing else, the growing effort and time that it takes me to produce anything forms a very broad hint. Now I want all the money that I can make for my family, and alas, for my possible old age, which is on the cards and will never be a lively affair for me, money or no money; but which would be a hideous humiliation to me if I had squandered all this money in the meanwhile and had to come forward as a beggar at the last. All which premised, I hereby authorise you to pay (when necessary) five pounds a month to Henley. He can't starve at that; it's enough – more than he had when I first knew him; and if I gave him more, it would only lead to his starting a gig and a Pomeranian dog.[4] I

[3] Baxter wrote: 'Tomorrow I hope to get from Astor £22.10/– per ⅞ for *St Ives*.' William Waldorf Astor (1848–1919), later Viscount Astor, founded the *Pall Mall Magazine* in 1893. *St Ives* (completed by Quiller-Couch) was serialised in it November 1896–November 1897.

[4] Balfour quoted this in his biography, omitting Henley's name and the amount, as an example of RLS's generosity. Furnas in his biography *Voyage to Windward* shrewdly guessed that Henley recognised the allusion and that this was the reason for the bitterness of his posthumous attack in the *Pall Mall Magazine* (December 1901). Henley dragged the phrase into his article and denounced it furiously at great length: "Tis wittily put, of course; but it scarce becomes the lips of a man who had several kennels of Pomeranians, [and] kept gigs innumerable.' Baxter had, in fact, already pointed this out in letters to Lord Guthrie in 1914, describing it as an intentional slight on the part of Fanny – 'I have no doubt its quotation by a blazing indiscretion (but Fanny Stevenson was much too clever not to know how it would wound) . . . was the match that set fire to Henley's explosion' (letter of 4 April 1914).

hope you won't think me hard about this. If you think the sum insufficient, you can communicate with me by return on the subject. And by the bye, don't forget to let me know exactly how I stand. It is possible that I forge myself fears that need not exist. The sheet of questions was not returned in my last letter, owing to some hurry to the day of making up the mail. I believe, however, all the questions were answered in the body of my letter, but send it on anyway.

The dummy has never come to hand.[5] Was it registered? It is no use sending anything connected with business unless you register it. Now I must end my letter with the same subject that it began with, your excellent if nameless bookseller. He is to choose at his own peril the very nicest illustrated edition of *Robinson Crusoe* in existence and despatch it to Master Louis Sanchez, Monterey, Monterey Co., California. Understand, I mean the nicest edition from the point of view of a young schoolboy of ten, not at all from the point of view of the Bibliophile. Your admirable man will certainly be able to fill the bill. There is another thing in his way. We want an old school-book, in use I imagine twenty years ago, if not now, called *The Child's Guide to Knowledge*. The child in question is guided by a sort of catechism inculcating as far as I can find out every species of wisdom, from How to Take Care of a Cold, the Remedies of Different Poisons, down to How to Grease your Boots. If Mr Johnston — there's his name — finds this book not very expensive, he might even send two copies or even three. This is for the deserving native.

I have been and am in communication with Mr Edmund Baxter, Jr. I trust I am giving satisfaction as his agent in these distant parts.[6] Should he have to complain of any neglect, I'm of opinion that the civility with which the correspondence has been throughout conducted gives me a decided claim to receive a statement and to be allowed to answer it with an explanation. Ever affectionately yours   R.L. Stevenson[7]

To Bob Stevenson

[c. *9 September 1894*]   [*Vailima*]

Dear Bob, You are in error about the Picts. They were a Gaelic race, spoke a Celtic tongue, and we have no evidence that I know of that they were blacker than other Celts. The Balfours, I take it, were plainly Celts;

[5] Of the Edinburgh Edition. RLS wrote to Colvin on 10 September: 'I forgot to tell Baxter that the dummy had turned up and is a fine, personable-looking volume and very good reading.'

[6] Edmund Baxter, Baxter's elder son, then a sixteen-year-old schoolboy. RLS was providing him with Samoan stamps.

[7] I have omitted two postscripts on financial matters and a sheet of queries by Baxter, mainly dealing with the Edinburgh Edition, which RLS answered briefly.

their name shows it – the 'cold croft', it means; so does their country. Where the *black* Scotch came from nobody knows; but I recognise with you the fact that the whole of Britain is rapidly and progressively becoming more pigmented; already in one man's life, I can decidedly trace a difference in the children about a school door. But colour is not an essential part of a man or a race. Take my Polynesians, an Asiatic People probably from the neighbourhood of the Persian Gulf. They range through any amount of shades, from the burnt hue of the Low Archipelago islander which seems half negro, to the 'bleached' pretty women of the Marquesas (close by on the map) who come out for a festival no darker than an Italian; their colour seems to vary directly with the degree of exposure to the sun. And as with negroes the babes are born white; only it should seem a *little sack* of pigment at the lower part of the spine which presently spreads over the whole field. Very puzzling. But to return – the Picts furnish today perhaps a third of the population of Scotland, say another third for Scots and Britons, and the third for Norse and Angles is a bad third. Edinburgh was a Pictish place. But the fact is, we don't know their frontiers. Tell some of your journalist friends with a good style to popularise old Skene; or say your prayers, and read him for yourself; he was a Great Historian – and I was his blessed clerk and did not know it;[1] and you will not be in a state of grace about the Picts till you have studied him. J. Horne Stevenson (do you know him?) is working this up with me,[2] and the fact is – it's not interesting to the public – but it's interesting, and very interesting, in itself, and just now very embarrassing – this rural parish supplied Glasgow with such a quantity of Stevensons in the beginning of last century! There is just a link wanting; and we might be able to go back to the eleventh century, always undistinguished but clearly traceable. When I say just a link, I guess I may be taken to mean a dozen. What a singular thing is this undistinguished perpetuation of a family throughout the centuries, and the sudden bursting forth of character and capacity that began with our grandfather! But as I go on in life, day by day, I become more of a bewildered child: I cannot get used to this world, to procreation, to heredity, to sight, to hearing; the commonest things are a burthen; the sight of Belle and her twelve-year-old boy, already taller than herself, is enough to turn my hair grey; as for Fanny and her brood, it is insane to think of. The prim obliterated polite face of life, and the

---

[1] William Forbes Skene (1809–92), Scottish lawyer, historian and Celtic scholar, author of *Celtic Scotland* (1876–80) and other works. RLS had briefly worked as a copyist for Skene's law firm in 1872.

[2] John Horne Stevenson (1855–1939) was at Edinburgh University and a member of the Speculative Society 1873–7; he became an advocate, 1884. He was a specialist on genealogy and heraldry and wrote or edited many books on the subject; Unicorn Pursuivant 1902–5; Marchmont Herald 1925; K.C. 1919. RLS was corresponding with him about his Stevenson ancestry.

broad, bawdy, and orgiastic – or maenadic – foundations, form a spectacle to which no habit reconciles me; and 'I could wish my days to be bound to each'[3] by the same open-mouthed wonder. They *are* anyway, and whether I wish it or not.

I remember very well your attitude to life, this conventional surface of it. You had none of that curiosity for the social stage-directions, the trivial *ficelles* of the business; it is simian, but that is how the wild youth of man is captured; you wouldn't imitate, hence you kept free – a wild dog, outside the kennel – and came dam' near starving for your pains. The key to the business is of course the belly; difficult as it is to keep that in view in the zone of three miraculous meals a day in which we were brought up. Civilisation has become reflex with us; you might think that hunger was the name of the best sauce; and hunger to the cold solitary under a bush of a rainy night is the name of something quite different. I defend civilisation for the thing it is, for the thing it has *come* to be; the standpoint of a real old Tory. My ideal would be the Female Clan. But how can you turn these crowding dumb multitudes *back*? They don't do anything *because*; they do things, write able articles, stitch shoes, dig, from the purely simian impulse. Go and reason with monkeys!

No, I am right about Jean Lillie. Jean Lillie, our double great-grandmother, the daughter of David Lillie sometime Deacon of the Wrights, married (first) Alan Stevenson, who died May 26th 1774, 'at Santt Kittes of a fiver', by whom she had Robert Stevenson, born 8th June 1772; and second, in May or June 1787, Thomas Smith, a widower and already the father of our grandmother.[4] This improbably double connexion always tends to confuse a student of the family, Thomas Smith being doubly our great-grandfather.

Your idea about the cup is probably correct. O, get Stevenson the architect[5] to put his back to the wheel, it is highly possible he may clear up some of the ambiguities: we have this whole group in Glasgow about 200 years ago, and we know they are related but not how.

I looked on the perpetuation of our honoured name with veneration. My mother collared one of the photos of course. The other is stuck up on my wall as the chief of our sept. Do you know any of the Gaelic-Celtic sharps? You might ask what the name means. It puzzles me. I find a *McStein* and a *MacStephane*; and our own great-grandfather always called himself Steenson, though he wrote it Stevenson. There are at least three *places* called Stevenson, *Stevenson* in Cunningham, *Stevenson* in Peebles, and *Stevenson* in Haddington. And it was not the Celtic trick I understand, to

---

[3] Cf. Wordsworth, 'My heart leaps up', ll. 8–9.

[4] RLS did not know that Jean Lillie (Robert Stevenson's mother) had made a mysterious second marriage to James Hogg, before she married Thomas Smith in 1792 (not 1787 as RLS has it).

[5] Presumably John James Stevenson (1831–1908), the Glasgow-born architect.

call places after people. I am going to write to Sir Herbert Maxwell[6] about the name, but you might find someone.

'Imagine Graham Balfour a Celt?' say you. But that is just what he is; his name bewrays him. Balfour = cold croft. Get the Anglo-Saxon heresy out of your head; they superimposed their language, they scarce modified the race; only in Berwickshire and Roxburgh, have they very largely affected the place names. The Scandinavians did much more to Scotland, than the Angles. The Saxons didn't come.

Enough of this sham antiquarianism. Yes, it is in the matter of the book, of course, that collaboration shows; as for the manner, it is superficially all mine, in the sense that the last copy is all in my hand. Lloyd did not even put pen to paper in the Paris scenes or the Barbizon scene; it was no good; he wrote and often rewrote, all the rest; I had the best service from him on the character of Nares. You see we had been just meeting the man, and his memory was full of the man's words and ways. And Lloyd is an impressionist, pure and simple; the great difficulty of collaboration is that you can't *tell* what you mean. I know what kind of effect I mean a character to give – what kind of *tache* he is to make; but how am I to tell my collaborator in words? Hence it was necessary to say, 'Make him so-and-so'; and this was all right for Nares and Pinkerton and Loudon Dodd, whom we both knew,[7] but for Bellairs, for instance – a man with whom I passed ten minutes fifteen years ago – what was I to say? and what could Lloyd do? I, as a personal artist, can begin a character with only a haze in my head, but how if I have to translate the haze into words before I begin? In our manner of collaboration (which I think the only possible – I mean that of one person being responsible, and giving the *coup de pouce* to every part of the work) I was spared the obviously hopeless business of trying to explain to my collaborator what *style* I wished a passage to be treated in. These are the times that illustrate to a man the inadequacy of spoken language. Now – to be just to written language – I can (or could) find a language for my every mood, but how could I *tell* anyone beforehand, what this effect was to be, which it would take every art that I possessed, and hours and hours of deliberate labour and selection and rejection, to produce? There are the impossibilities of collaboration. Its immediate advantage is to focus two minds together on the stuff, and to produce in consequence an extraordinary greater richness of purview,

---

[6] Sir Herbert Maxwell (1845–1937), seventh Baronet of Monreith, country gentleman and author of many books ranging from history and biography to archaeology, topography, natural history and sport. Maxwell, a man of great charm and versatility, was Rhind Lecturer in Archaeology at Edinburgh in 1893 and 1911. RLS, who had read his 1893 lectures published as *Scottish Land-Names. Their Origin and Meaning* (1894), wrote to Maxwell on 10 September.

[7] In *The Wrecker* Nares was based on Captain Albert Otis of the *Casco*, Pinkerton on S.S. McClure and Loudon Dodd on Will H. Low.

consideration and invention. The hardest chapter of all was 'Cross Questions and Crooked Answers.' You would not believe what that cost us before it assumed the least unity and colour. Lloyd wrote it at least thrice, and I at least five times – this is from memory. And was that chapter worth the trouble it cost? Alas, that I should ask the question! Two classes of men, the artist and the educationalist, are sworn, on soul and conscience, not to ask it. You get an ordinary, grinning, red-headed boy, and you have to educate him. Faith supports you; you give your valuable hours, the boy does not seem to profit; but that way your duty lies, for which you are paid, and you must persevere. Education has always seemed to me one of the few possible and dignified ways of life. A sailor, a shepherd, a schoolmaster – to a less degree, a soldier – and (I don't know why, upon my soul, except as a sort of schoolmaster's unofficial assistant, and a kind of acrobat in tights) an artist, almost exhausts the category.

If I had to begin again – I know not – *si jeunesse savait, si vieillesse pouvait.*[8] – I know not at all – I believe I should do as I have done – except that I believe I should try to be more chaste in early youth, and honour Sex more religiously. The damned thing of our education is that Christianity does not recognize and hallow Sex. It looks askance at it, over its shoulder, oppressed as it is by reminiscences of hermits and Asiatic self-torturers. When I came to myself fairly about twenty-five I recognized once for all the Lingam and the Yoni[9] as the true religious symbols. An eye also might do. It is a terrible hiatus in our modern religions that they cannot see and make venerable that which they ought to see first and hallow most. Well, it is so; I cannot be wiser than my generation.

But no doubt there is something great in the half-success that has attended the effort of turning into an emotional religion, Bald Conduct, without any appeal, or almost none, to the figurative, mysterious and constitutive facts of life. Not that conduct is not constitutive, but dear! it's dreary! On the whole, conduct is better dealt with on the cast-iron, 'gentleman' and duty formula, with as little fervour and poetry as possible; stoical and short. And behold! the introduction of conduct into religion, their prolonged liaison looks as if it were going to be fruitful. There is a new something or other in the wind, which exercises me hugely: anarchy – I mean, anarchism. People who (for pity's sake) commit dastardly murders very basely, die like saints, and leave beautiful letters behind 'em; (did you see Vaillant[10] to his daughter? it was the New Testament over again) people whose conduct is inexplicable to me, and yet their spiritual

---

[8] Henri Estienne (1531–98), *Les Prémices*, Épigramme cxci.

[9] RLS first wrote 'Linga' then wrote '? Lingam' above it. Lingam and Yoni are the symbols of the male and female sexual organs venerated by Hindus.

[10] Auguste Vaillant, an anarchist, threw a bomb into the French Chamber of Deputies on 9 December 1893. He was sentenced to death on 10 January 1894 and executed on 4 February.

life higher than that of most. This is just what the early Christians must have seemed to the Romans. Is this then a new *Drive* among the monkeys? Mind you, Bob, if they go on being martyred a few years more, the gross, dull most unkindly Bourgeois may get tired or ashamed or afraid of going on martyring; and the anarchists come out at the top just like the early Christians. That is of course they will step into power as a *personnel*, but God knows what they may believe when they come to do so: it can't be funnier or more improbable than what Christianity had come to be by the same time.

Your letter was easily read, the pagination presented no difficulty, and I read it with much edification and gusto. To look back, and to stereotype one bygone humour – what a hopeless thing! The mind runs ever in a thousand eddies like a river between cliffs. You (the ego) are always spinning round in it, east, west, north and south. You are twenty, and forty, and five, and the next moment you are freezing at an imaginary eighty; you are never the plain forty-four that you should be by dates. (The most philosophical language is the Gaelic which has *no present tense* – and the most useless). How then to choose some former age, and stick there?   R.L.S.

To Sidney Colvin

[*Beginning dictated to Belle*]
6 October 1894   *Vailima*

My dear Colvin, I think your cure must have done wonders for you.[1] I do not remember when I have received a letter so interesting and personal. Silly fellow! I can conceive that Mrs Jay, whom I have heard so much of, though never seen, is a part of your surroundings, and is interesting to me therefore. I know it means a bigger stretch of the imagination and yet I sometimes wonder you should not be able to conceive that Mataafa and Tui and Po'e[2] are of my surroundings and flow naturally into what I write. But this is not at all meant to be a complaint, rather a thanksgiving.

We have had quite an interesting month and mostly in consideration of that road which I think I told you was about to be made.[3] It was made without a hitch, though I confess I was considerably surprised. When they

[1] Colvin had been taking a 'nerve-cure' in Schlangenbad, a small German spa town near Wiesbaden.

[2] Tui is the high chief Tui-ma-le-alii-fano with whom RLS discussed political problems. Po'e was one of the chiefs who supported Mataafa; he was the husband of Tauilo (mother of Talolo, RLS's cook).

[3] Po'e and his fellow chiefs, whom RLS had visited in prison and helped secure their release, had volunteered to build a road to show their gratitude.

got through I wrote a speech to them, sent it down to a missionary to be translated and invited the lot to a feast.[4] I thought a good deal of this feast. The occasion was really interesting. I wanted to pitch it in hot. And I wished to have as many influential witnesses present as possible. Well, as it drew towards the day I had nothing but refusals. Everybody supposed it was to be a political occasion, that I had made a hive of rebels up here and was going to push for new hostilities.

[*RLS takes over*]

The Amanuensis has been ill, and after the above trial petered out. I must return to my own, lone *Waverley*.[5] The Captain refused, telling me why; and at last I had to beat up for people almost with prayers. However, I got a good lot as you will see by the accompanying newspaper report, whose jaunty vulgarity I leave you to appreciate. The board contained this inscription, drawn up by the chiefs themselves:

The Road of Gratitude.

'Considering the great love of Tusitala in his loving care of us in our distress in the prison, we have therefore prepared a splendid gift. It shall never be muddy, it shall endure forever, this road that we have dug.'

This he could not give, not knowing any Samoan. The same reason explains his sneering references to Seumanutafa's speech, which was not long and *was* important, for it was a speech of courtesy and forgiveness to his former enemies. It was very much applauded. Secondly it was not Po'e; it was Mataafā (don't confuse with Mataafa) who spoke for the prisoners. Otherwise it is extremely correct.

I beg your pardon for so much upon my aboriginals. Even you must sympathise with me in this unheard-of compliment, and my having been able to deliver so severe a sermon with acceptance. It remains a nice point of conscience what I should wish done in the matter. I think this meeting, its immediate results, and the terms of what I said to them, desirable to be known. It will do a little justice to me, who have not had too much justice done me. At the same time, to send this report to the papers is truly an act of self-advertisement, and I dislike the thought. Query, in a man who has been so much calumniated, is that not justifiable? I do not know;

[4] In his speech RLS warned the Samoans that unless they did something themselves, their land would be taken over by foreigners, and he cited the examples of the Highlands of Scotland where 'other people's sheep' now grazed and Hawaii where 'white men's sugar fields' had taken the place of native villages: 'You Samoans may fight, you may conquer twenty times, and thirty times, and all will be in vain. There is but one way to defend Samoa . . . It is to make roads, and gardens, and care for your trees, and sell their produce wisely, and, in one word, to occupy and use your country. If you do not, others will.'

[5] To preserve his anonymity, Scott's MS was copied for the press by John Ballantyne; RLS may also be remembering that he himself had reached the age at which Scott published *Waverley*.

be my judge. Mankind is too complicated for me; even myself. Do I wish to advertise? I think I do, God help me! I have had hard times here, as every man must have who mixes up with public business; and I bemoan myself, knowing that all I have done has been in the interest of peace and good government; and having once delivered my mind, I would like it, I think, to be made public. But the other part of me *regimbs*.[6] . . . Cusack-Smith is going home at last, having done his best to dismember Samoa and to spoil my influence, *telle quelle*. I shall send you some paragraphs from the other paper, which will show you what the attitude *there* is. I know not, I can only guess, whence the wind blows. As Captain Gibson[7] said, about a previous article: 'I prefer *not* to know who it is.' My beloved *Curaçoas*, as you justly call 'em, are on the move themselves,[8] and from an earlier date, alas! I wish they could take Smith along with them.

I know I am at a climacteric for all men who live by their wits, so I do not despair. But the truth is I am pretty nearly useless at literature, and I will ask you to spare *St Ives* when it goes to you; it is a sort of *Count Robert of Paris*.[9] But I hope rather a *Dombey and Son*, to be succeeded by *Our Mutual Friend* and *Great Expectations* and *A Tale of Two Cities*. No toil has been spared over the ungrateful canvas; and it *will not* come together, and I must live, and my family. Were it not for my health, which made it impossible, I could not find it in my heart to forgive myself that I did not stick to an honest, commonplace trade, when I was young, which might have now supported me during these ill years.[10] But do not suppose me to be down in anything else; only, for the nonce, my skill deserts me, such as it is, or was. It was a very little dose of inspiration, and a pretty little trick of style, long lost, improved by the most heroic industry. So far, I have managed to please the people I have least sympathy with – the journalists. But I am a fictitious article and have long known it. I am read by journalists, by my fellow novelists, and by boys: with these, *incipit et explicit* my vogue. Beastly good thing anyway! for it seems to have sold the Edition. And I look forward confidently to an aftermath; I do not think my health can be so hugely improved, without some subsequent improvement in my brains. Though, of course, there is the possibility that literature is a morbid secretion, and abhors health! I do not think it is possible

---

[6] Cf. the French *regimber*, to kick at, jib. Colvin obliterated the next two or three words, evidently an uncomplimentary reference to Cusack-Smith.

[7] Herbert William Sumner Gibson (1846–1923), Captain of the *Curaçoa*, joined the Navy in 1859 and retired in 1901.

[8] The *Curaçoa* was being relieved by another British warship.

[9] Scott's novel, published a year before his death, showed the decline of his powers.

[10] In a similar mood RLS had written to Will H. Low in January 1894: 'I think *David Balfour* a nice little book, and very artistic, and just the thing to occupy the leisure of a busy man; but for the top flower of a man's life it seems to me inadequate. . . . I ought to have been able to build lighthouses and write *David Balfours* too.'

to have fewer illusions than I. I sometimes wish I had more. They are amusing. But I cannot take myself seriously as an artist; the limitations are so obvious. I did take myself seriously as a workman of old, but my practice has fallen off. I am now an idler and cumberer of the ground, it may be excused to me perhaps by twenty years of industry and ill-health, which have taken the cream off the milk. As I was writing this last sentence, I heard the strident rain drawing near across the forest, and by the time I was come to the word 'cream', it burst upon my roof, and has since redoubled, and roared upon it. A very welcome change. All smells of the good wet earth, sweetly, with a kind of Highland touch; the crystal rods of the shower, as I look up, have drawn their criss-cross over everything; and a gentle and very welcome coolness comes up around me in little draughts, blessed draughts, not chilling, only equalising the temperature. Now the rain is off in this spot, but I hear it roaring still in the nigh neighbourhood – and that moment I was driven from the verandah by random raindrops, spitting at me through the Japanese blinds. These are not tears with which the page is spotted! Now the windows stream, the roof reverberates. It is good; it answers something which is in my heart; I know not what; old memories of the wet moorland belike. Well, it has blown by again, and I am in my place on the verandah once more, with an accompaniment of perpetual dripping on the verandah. And very much inclined for a chat. The exact subject, I do not know! It will be bitter at least; and that is strange for my attitude is essentially *not* bitter, but I have come into these days when a man sees above all the seamy side, and I have dwelt some time in a small place where he has an opportunity of reading little motives that he would miss in the great world, and indeed, today, I am almost ready to call the world an error. Because? Because I have not drugged myself with successful work, and there are all kinds of trifles buzzing in my ear, unfriendly trifles, from the least to the – well, to the pretty big. All these that touch me are Pretty Big; and yet none touch me in the least, if rightly looked at, except the one eternal burthen to go on making an income for my family. That is rightly the root and ground of my ill. The jingling tingling damned mint sauce[11] is the trouble always; and if I could find a place where I could lie down and give up for (say) two years, and allow the sainted public to support me, if it were a lunatic asylum, wouldn't I go there, just! But we can't have both extremes at once, worse luck! I should like to put my savings into a proprietarian investment, and retire in the meanwhile into a communistic retreat: which is double dealing. But you men with salaries don't know how a family weighs on a fellow's mind.

[11] A slang term for money.

I hear the article in next week's *Herald* is to be a great affair, and all the officials who came to me the other day are to be attacked! This is the unpleasant side of being (without a salary) in public life. I will leave anyone to judge if my speech was well intended, and calculated to do good. It was even daring. I assure you one of the chiefs looked like a fiend at my description of Samoan warfare.[12] And here is this fat little vulgarian, our 'Society Cobbler', as we call him, finding all sorts of purposes of rebellion in the meeting and the speech, and proposing to attack the officials who consented to be present! Sickening, is it not? And we have to endure him, and smile, and hold our peace. Your warning was not needed; we are all determined to *keep the peace* and to *hold our peace*. I know, my dear fellow, how remote all this sounds! Kindly pardon your friend. I have my life to live here; these interests are for me immediate; and if I do not write of them, I might as soon not write at all. There is the difficulty in a distant correspondence. It is perhaps easy for me to enter into and understand your interests; I own it is difficult for you; but you must just wade through them, for friendship's sake, and try to find tolerable what is vital for your friend. I cannot forbear challenging you to it, as to intellectual lists. It is the proof of intelligence, the proof of not being a barbarian, to be able to enter into something outside of oneself, something that does not touch one's next neighbour in the city omnibus.

Good-bye my lord. May your cure[13] continue and you flourish. Yours ever   Tusitala

To Edmund Gosse[1]

1 December 1894   *Vailima*

I am afraid, my dear Weg, that this must be the result of bribery and corruption! The volume to which the dedication stands as preface seems to me to stand alone in your work;[2] it is so natural, so personal, so sincere, so articulate, in substance, and what you always were sure of – so rich in adornment.

---

[12] 'And who is the true champion of Samoa? It is not the man who blackens his face, and cuts down trees, and kills pigs and wounded men. It is the man who makes roads, who plants food trees, who gathers harvests . . .'

[13] Colvin altered the word to 'race'. This was the last of the letters to be published as *Vailima Letters* and the amended phrase made an appropriate conclusion.

[1] This is one of the last letters written by RLS. Five more are known to have been written on 1 December; there were probably others.

[2] Gosse's book of poems *In Russet and Silver* (1894) has a long dedication in verse 'To Tusitala in Vailima'. MIS records that RLS read it to them 'with so much pleasure' on 30 November, the day after it had arrived. The other poems mentioned by RLS are in the volume.

Let me speak first of the dedication. I thank you for it from the heart. It is beautifully said, beautifully and kindly felt; and I should be a churl indeed if I were not grateful, and an ass if I were not proud. I remember, when Symonds dedicated a book to me, I wrote and told him of 'the pang of gratified vanity' with which I had read it. The pang was present again, but how much more sober and autumnal! like your volume. Let me tell you a story, or remind you of a story. In the year of grace something or other, anything between '76 and '78, I mentioned to you in my usual autobiographical and inconsiderate manner that I was hard up. You said promptly that you had a balance at your banker's and could make it convenient to let me have a cheque, and I accepted and got the money – how much was it? – twenty, or perhaps thirty pounds? I know not – but it was a great convenience. The same evening or the next day, I fell in conversation (in my usual autobiographical and etc., see above) with a denizen of the Savile Club, name now gone from me, only his figure and a dim three-quarter view of his face remaining. By George, wasn't it *Roberts*?[3] It might have been. At any rate to him I mentioned that you had given me a loan, remarking easily that of course it didn't matter to you. Whereupon he read me a lecture, corrected the legends on your wife's enormous fortune,[4] and told me how it stood with you financially. He was pretty serious, fearing as I could not help perceiving, that I would take too light a view of the responsibility and the service. (I was always thought too light – the irresponsible jester – you remember. Oh, *quantum mutatus ab illo!*)[5] If I remember rightly, the money was repaid before the end of the week – or, to be more exact and a trifle pedantic the se'nnight, but the service has never been forgotten; and I send you back this piece of ancient history, *Consule Planco*,[6] as a salute for your dedication, and propose that we should both drink the health of the nameless one, Roberts or another, who opened my eyes as to the true nature of what you did for me on that occasion.

[*Remainder dictated to Belle*]

But here comes my Amanuensis, so will get on more swimmingly now. You will understand perhaps that what so particularly pleased me in the new volume, what seems to me to have so personal and original a note, are the middle-aged pieces in the beginning. The whole of them, I may say, though, I must own an especial liking to

---

[3] The only Roberts who was a member of the Savile at this time was Charles Roberts, F.R.C.S. (died 1901) who was a consulting surgeon in Mayfair and later in Eastbourne.

[4] Nellie Gosse was the niece of the extremely rich James Epps of Epps Cocoa fame, and RLS evidently thought that she too was wealthy. She did in fact inherit a share in her uncle's estate when he died in 1907.

[5] How much changed from what he was. *Aeneid*, II. 274.

[6] When Plancus was Consul (i.e. in his youth). Horace, *Odes*, III.xxiv.28.

> I yearn not for the fighting fate,
> That holds and hath achieved,
> I live to watch and meditate,
> And dream – and be deceived.[7]

You take the change gallantly. Not I, I must confess. It is all very well to talk of renunciation, and of course it has to be done. But for my part give me a roaring toothache! I do like to be deceived and to dream, but I have very little use for either watching or meditation. I was not born for age. And curiously enough I seem to see a contrary drift in my work from that which is so remarkable in yours. You are going on sedately travelling through your ages, decently changing with the years to the proper tune. And here am I, quite out of my true course, and with nothing in my foolish elderly head but love-stories. This must repose upon some curious distinction of temperaments. I gather from a phrase, boldly autobiographical that you are – well, not precisely growing thin?[8] Can that be the difference?

It is rather funny that this matter should come up just now, as I am at present engaged in treating a severe case of middle age in one of my stories – *The Justice-Clerk*.[9] The case is that of a woman and I think that I am doing her justice. You will be interested, I believe, to see the difference in our treatments. 'Secreta Vitae' comes nearer to the case of my poor Kirstie. Come to think of it Gosse, I believe the main distinction is that you have a family growing up around you, and I am a childless, rather bitter, very clear-eyed, blighted youth. I have in fact lost the path that makes it easy and natural for you to descend the hill. I am going at it straight. And where I have to go down it is a precipice.

I must not forget to give you a word of thanks for 'An English Village'. It reminds me strongly of Keats, which is enough to say; and I was particularly pleased with the petulant sincerity of the concluding sentiment.

Well, my dear Gosse, here's wishing you all health and prosperity as well as to the Mistress and the bairns. May you live long, since it seems as if you would continue to enjoy life. May you write many more books as good as this one – only there's one thing impossible, you can never

---

[7] The opening lines of Gosse's poem, 'Clasping the Cloud'.

[8] Gosse's poem 'In Russet and Silver', which gives its name to the volume, is about growing old. It includes the lines thanking God

> That tho' the crescent flesh be wound
> In soft unseemly folds around,
> The heart may, all the days we live,
> Grow more alert and sensitive.

[9] In September 1894, unable to make progress on *St Ives*, RLS resumed working with enthusiasm on *Weir of Hermiston*.

write another dedication that can give the same pleasure to the vanished Tusitala. Here's Merry Christmas and Happy New Year and the health of the person whose name may have been Roberts or may not, but who was rather tall, and possessed a weedy kind of good looks, and authentic whiskers, which were not at all the rule in Savile in our days.

[*RLS concludes*] (Matter petered out). Yours ever   R.L. Stevenson

EPILOGUE: THE DEATH OF STEVENSON

The standard account of Stevenson's death and burial is that prepared by Lloyd Osbourne and privately printed in Apia with other material in a pamphlet called *A Letter to Mr Stevenson's Friends*. It was reprinted in Colvin's editions of the *Letters* and in Balfour's *Life*. I have preferred to print the more personal account written by Belle Strong in her journal, supplemented by an account of the funeral written by Lloyd in a private letter to Colvin published in *The Times* on 7 January 1895.

From Belle Strong's Journal

[4 or 5 December 1894]

He had been very well for a long time, and every morning I hurried through my household work to write for him in *Hermiston*. The last day – and we little thought it was to be his last – we worked steadily till nearly twelve, and then he walked up and down the room talking to me of his work, of future chapters, of bits of his past life that bore on what he had been writing – as he only could talk. In the afternoon as I was writing my letters, I heard him and Austin on the verandah by his study making a great noise over their French lesson, learning a little French dialogue to recite at Christmas. I was still writing when I heard my mother's voice calling for hot water. I was not much alarmed, though I went downstairs to see what was the matter. Louis was lying back in the big green leather chair in the hall breathing heavily and seemed unconscious.[1] Talolo was bringing hot water for his feet and his mother and Mamma were both chafing his hands, and I ran at once for Lloyd. He was coming over from his cottage, quite cheerfully swinging a wreath he had had made for the Consul-General. He rushed off at once, Sosimo after him for the fastest horses to go for the doctor, and when I went back Louis was still the same. It seems he had been looking on watching my mother making a salad, and was dropping the oil for her with a perfectly steady hand. He suddenly said, 'What's that?' or 'What a pain!' and put both hands to his

---

[1] In a letter to Mrs Jenkin on 5 December Fanny wrote: 'For several days I had been crushed by a sense of impending disaster, but more particularly that day; he had been trying to cheer me up, and one of the last things he did was to play a game of solitaire [i.e. patience] with cards for me to watch, thinking it would amuse me and take my mind off the terror that oppressed me.'

head. 'Do I look strange?' he asked, and then he reeled and fell backwards.
His favourite boy Sosimo caught him and carried him into the big room,
and he never was conscious after.[2] We saw that he was dying though each
said to the other 'he is surely better' or 'his pulse is stronger'. Talolo and
I knelt before him chafing his feet and putting them into hot water, and
as the room darkened one by one all the Samoans on the place crept in
silently and sat on the floor in a wide semi-circle around him. Some
fanned him, others waited on one knee for a message and others ran down
the road with lanterns to light the doctor. When the big lamps were lit the
first doctor arrived – he was the surgeon from *H.M.S. Wallaroo*.[3] Lloyd
had met him at the Tivoli Hotel and jumped off his horse, and the doctor
took it and rode back he said as though the animal knew what it was for.
And it was Louis's own Jack. The doctor looked at Louis's eyes, and felt
his pulse, one heavy and strong, one very faint, and we read no hope in
his face. He said we had done right to keep his head cool and his feet hot,
and ordered all the windows open, and the night air came in scented with
gardenias. Then, when they were still anxiously trying different remedies
I looked out and saw a twinkling of lanterns and knew that Lloyd had
come back. Dr Funk[4] with his lame foot could only get up here as far as
Skeens,[5] and had to walk the rest of the way. When he arrived he ordered
the little brass bedstead from the guest room and it was placed in the
middle of the great hall. Four boys carefully carried Louis and laid him
upon it, and then the missionary Mr Clarke came. We were all about the
bed then, and Mr Clarke knelt beside Aunt Maggie and prayed. Lloyd
supported Louis with his arm, he was still unconscious and only breathed
fainter and at longer intervals until at last he died at ten minutes past
eight.[6]

No stranger's hand touched Louis at the last. Lloyd and I and Sosimo
and Talolo dressed him and laid him out;[7] the two brown boys that he
loved kissed his hands and clasped them together upon his breast, interlac-
ing the fingers with tender care. He did not look at all ill, but lay with his

[2] In *A Letter to Mr Stevenson's Friends* Lloyd wrote: 'He was helped into the great hall, between
his wife and his body-servant Sosimo'. In his copy of his biography (formerly owned by his son
Michael) Graham Balfour noted that he was told by Austin Strong on 17 June 1910 that while
being helped into the hall RLS said, 'All right Fanny, I can walk.'

[3] Robert W. Anderson. The warship arrived in Apia on 10 November to relieve the *Curaçoa*.

[4] Dr Bernard Funk, who came out from Germany in 1880, was medical officer for the German
Firm as well as being in private practice in Apia. He was RLS and Fanny's usual doctor. Fanny
calls him in her diary 'a boisterous surgeon' with a strident voice.

[5] Robert Skeen was an Apia solicitor who lived near Vailima.

[6] In a letter to Mrs Sitwell later in the month Fanny said that the doctors gave the cause of death
as 'apoplexy combined with paralysis of the lungs': in modern medical terms, a cerebral
hemorrhage.

[7] MIS records that RLS was dressed 'in his dress trousers and a white shirt and gold studs, he had
the silver ring on his finger that Fanny gave him long ago'.

eyes closed and his hair slightly curling on his forehead as though he were asleep. Lloyd sent for the English flag, the one he flew on the *Casco* and laid it over the bed.[8] He looked so tall and slender lying there, and very handsome, the light shining on his clear profile. It was very quiet. There were no terrible outbursts of grief – we seemed dazed and numbed hardly drawing breath as we sat and looked at him lying so still and peaceful. . . .

The swinging door opened and the chief of Tanugamanono came in with his wife; they had come stumbling up the dark track over the stones to bring a last present to the chief. He came forward to Louis, leaned over and kissed him, and laid the fine mat at his feet, saying only '*Tofa Tusitala*'. Siuta, whose face was distorted with crying made only a deep bow and said '*Alofa Tusitala*', and backed away. Then Fono came bringing another mat and like the other spoke to Louis by his native name, reverently, and then stepped back and sat upon the floor. The Samoans all sat cross-legged in a wide semi-circle; they made no demonstrations of grief, but sat silent, bowed and reverent. Sosimo came and knelt by Lloyd and asked permission to 'do popey church' as he called it in Samoan. Only a few of them were Catholics, but when Sosimo in a soft voice that trembled in the big hushed room, read and chanted what I suppose were the Catholic prayers for the dead, those few chanted the responses; the others sat quietly.

*Lloyd Osbourne to Sidney Colvin (Extract)

5 December [1984]   *Vailima*

[*After an account of RLS's death Lloyd continued*]

It was always his wish to be buried on top of the mountain that bounds Vailima, *o le tia a Soalu* it is called – the grave of a famous chief of ancient times – he even had a window cut in his study so that he should always see the place. I was determined that his wishes should be carried out, so I sent that night to our best friends to bring in their men. Forty of them came with their chiefs; several of the Mataafa chiefs came, the few that are left in the countryside. . . .

The forty men went to work with their knives and axes and cut a straight road up the steep face of the mountain. I went up and chose the spot and prepared it. Nothing more bold or picturesque could be

---

[8] Other accounts make it clear that the flag placed over the body was in fact the large Union Jack that flew over the house.

imagined. It is a narrow ledge no wider than a room and flat as a table, the mountain descending precipitously on both sides; the vast ocean in front and the white beaches on which the surf is breaking everlastingly; mountains on either side adrift with mist. A year ago he was full of the project of making a road there, to prepare and plant the spot that would ultimately receive him; yet we shrank from it, not a little to his displeasure. I assure you, if we had thought a moment of the difficulties involved it could never have been done. But I did not think; I knew it had to be done, and in that spirit I did it. All the morning the Samoans were coming up with their flowers. There was no display of affection, no keening; yet they went and cried in corners. There was no pretence, thank God. We would have no strangers on that day; I had invited only the people I knew loved him, and none others.[1] There was none of the professionalism that makes death so horrible. Even the coffin was made by one of our oldest friends here,[2] and was a work of love. The tawdry plush and velvet that encased it I covered with the tattered flag we had flown over the yacht and buried it in the grave so. No hands touched his body save those of his own people; his own folk dug his grave, and when we covered it in they seized the spades from the strangers and would let them take no part. It was a terrible matter to get the whites up there; Haggard nearly fainted at the outset, and had to return. I sent the body up before we went with relief parties, knowing that it would be a terrible matter to get accomplished. I wanted no one to see this harassing work, the resting on the road and such things. When we got up the flag-covered coffin was lying decently beside the grave. Clarke, one of his oldest friends here (a missionary), read the Church of England service. I cut out many things in it and made it short and incorporated one of Louis's own prayers [in it] that he had written and said the Sunday night before his death. Another old friend who had risen from a sick bed to come, and who had to travel from another part of the island to arrive in time, made a Samoan speech.[3] As I said, there was no one there who was a mere acquaintance. There was no constrained sorrow, no empty faces, no one to stare at the weeping people. Friends all, every one, real friends. . . .

★   ★   ★

---

[1] MIS says: 'We only invited real friends to the funeral but a good many came without invitation, especially women.' In *A Letter* Lloyd says that 'nineteen Europeans and some sixty Samoans reached the summit'. Belle was the only one of the Vailima womenfolk who made what she called the 'terrible climb up the mountain'.

[2] Alex Willis, the Canadian carpenter.

[3] James Edward Newell (1852–1910), L.M.S. missionary, was ordained in 1880 and spent the rest of his life working in Samoa. From 1887 he was Senior Tutor at the Malua Training Institution and became a great authority on Samoan law and custom. He is credited with being responsible for giving RLS his Samoan name of 'Tusitala'.

By 1897 Stevenson's tomb had been built in Samoan fashion from large blocks of cement and bearing two bronze panels designed by Fanny's San Francisco friend, Gelett Burgess. One panel, decorated with a thistle and a hibiscus flower, is inscribed in Samoan 'The Tomb of Tusitala' and contains Ruth's speech to Naomi, taken from the Samoan Bible: 'Whither thou goest, I will go . . . thy people shall be my people . . . where thou diest, will I die, and there will I be buried.' The other, in English, carries Stevenson's name and the dates of his birth and death, followed by his own 'Requiem'.

In June 1915, over a year after her mother's death, Belle brought Fanny's ashes to Samoa for burial. A new bronze tablet was added to the tomb bearing a verse from RLS's poem to her, 'Teacher, tender comrade, wife . . .'[1]

---

[1] After her son's death MIS returned to Edinburgh and lived with her sister Jane; she died on 14 May 1897. As the widow of RLS, Fanny was a formidable figure (Henry James called her 'an old grizzled lioness'). She finally left Vailima in 1897 and settled first in San Francisco and then in a house called Stonehedge, near Santa Barbara, California. She died there on 18 February 1914. Six months after her mother's death, the fifty-six-year-old Belle married the thirty-four-year-old Edward (Ned) Salisbury Field, successful author of lightweight plays and film scripts, who had been Fanny's companion and secretary in her last years. Field died in 1936 and the following year Belle published her gossipy and attractive memoirs, *This Life I've Loved*. She lived to a great age, long enough to see the celebration of the centenary of her stepfather's birth and to correspond with Graham Greene. She died in 1953. Lloyd went on to write more than a dozen, now forgotten, novels and collections of short stories and was the rather careless editor of the Vailima Edition (1922–3); his affectionate memoirs of his stepfather were published as *An Intimate Portrait of RLS* (1924). After his mother's death he lived comfortably off the royalties from the Stevenson estate. He died in 1947.

INDEX OF CORRESPONDENTS

* from Lloyd Osbourne   ** jointly from RLS and Fanny   †from Fanny

GENERAL INDEX